A HISTORY OF WELSH MUSIC

From early medieval bards to the bands of the 'Cool Cymru' era, this book looks at Welsh musical practices and traditions, the forces that have influenced and directed them and the ways in which the idea of Wales as a 'musical nation' has been formed and embedded in popular consciousness in Wales and beyond. Beginning with early medieval descriptions of musical life in Wales, the book provides both an overarching study of Welsh music history and detailed consideration of the ideas, beliefs, practices and institutions that shaped it. Topics include the eisteddfod, the church and the chapel, the influence of the Welsh language and Welsh cultural traditions, the scholarship of the Celtic revival and the folk-song movement, the impacts of industrialisation and digitisation, and exposure to broader trends in popular culture, including commercial popular music and sport.

TREVOR HERBERT has written extensively on the cultural history of instrumental music, especially brass instruments in various periods and social contexts, and co-edited the award-winning *Cambridge Encyclopedia of Brass Instruments* (2018). He has also written on the cultural history of music in Wales. He was co-editor of the seven-volume Welsh History and Its Sources series.

MARTIN V. CLARKE has published widely on the relationships between music, theology and religious practice, including the monograph *British Methodist Hymnody: Theology, Heritage, and Experience* (2018) and the edited collection *Music and Theology in Nineteenth-Century Britain* (2012). He was a co-investigator on the AHRC-funded Listening Experience Database project.

HELEN BARLOW researches the intersections between history, music, literature and visual art. As a member of the Listening Experience Database project, she investigated the history of ordinary people's experiences of music. Her publications include *Music and the British Military in the Long Nineteenth Century* (2013), co-written with Trevor Herbert.

A HISTORY OF WELSH MUSIC

EDITED BY

TREVOR HERBERT
Royal College of Music London

MARTIN V. CLARKE
The Open University

HELEN BARLOW
The Open University

Shaftesbury Road, Cambridge CB2 8EA, United Kingdom

One Liberty Plaza, 20th Floor, New York, NY 10006, USA

477 Williamstown Road, Port Melbourne, VIC 3207, Australia

314–321, 3rd Floor, Plot 3, Splendor Forum, Jasola District Centre, New Delhi – 110025, India

103 Penang Road, #05–06/07, Visioncrest Commercial, Singapore 238467

Cambridge University Press is part of Cambridge University Press & Assessment, a department of the University of Cambridge.

We share the University's mission to contribute to society through the pursuit of education, learning and research at the highest international levels of excellence.

www.cambridge.org
Information on this title: www.cambridge.org/9781009005265

DOI: 10.1017/9781009036511

© Cambridge University Press & Assessment 2023

This publication is in copyright. Subject to statutory exception and to the provisions of relevant collective licensing agreements, no reproduction of any part may take place without the written permission of Cambridge University Press & Assessment.

First published 2023
First paperback edition 2023

A catalogue record for this publication is available from the British Library

Library of Congress Cataloging-in-Publication data
NAMES: Herbert, Trevor, editor. | Clarke, Martin (Martin V.), editor. | Barlow, Helen, editor.
TITLE: A history of Welsh music / edited by Trevor Herbert, Martin V. Clarke, Helen Barlow.
DESCRIPTION: [1.] | Cambridge, United Kingdom ; New York : Cambridge University Press, 2022. | Includes bibliographical references and index.
IDENTIFIERS: LCCN 2022012037 (print) | LCCN 2022012038 (ebook) | ISBN 9781316511060 (hardback) | ISBN 9781009005265 (paperback) | ISBN 9781009036511 (ebook)
SUBJECTS: LCSH: Music – Wales – History and criticism.
CLASSIFICATION: LCC ML289 .H57 2022 (print) | LCC ML289 (ebook) | DDC 780.9429–dc23 /eng/20220310
LC record available at https://lccn.loc.gov/2022012037
LC ebook record available at https://lccn.loc.gov/2022012038

ISBN 978-1-316-51106-0 Hardback
ISBN 978-1-009-00526-5 Paperback

Cambridge University Press & Assessment has no responsibility for the persistence or accuracy of URLs for external or third-party internet websites referred to in this publication and does not guarantee that any content on such websites is, or will remain, accurate or appropriate.

Contents

List of Figures	*page* vii
List of Maps	x
List of Music Examples	xi
List of Contributors	xii
Preface	xvii
Acknowledgements	xxvi
Glossary	xxvii
Maps	xxxi

1. Music in Welsh History   1
   Trevor Herbert

2. Words for Music: Describing Musical Practices in Medieval Welsh Literature   25
   Helen Fulton

3. Music in Worship before 1650   53
   John Harper

4. Secular Music before 1650   78
   Sally Harper

5. The Eisteddfod Tradition   100
   Rhidian Griffiths

6. Women and Welsh Folk Song   121
   Wyn Thomas

7. Instrumental Traditions after 1650   144
   Rhidian Griffiths, Trevor Herbert and Stephen P. Rees

8. The Celtic Revival   171
   Helen Barlow

9	Musical Communications in the Long Nineteenth Century *Rhidian Griffiths*	195
10	Nonconformists and Their Music *Martin V. Clarke*	218
11	Professionalisation in the Twentieth Century *Lyn Davies*	243
12	Composing Cymru: Art Music since 1940 *Nicholas Jones*	264
13	Traditions and Interventions: Popular Music 1840–1940 *Trevor Herbert*	291
14	New Traditions: Welsh Popular Music into the Twenty-First Century *Sarah Hill*	315
15	Singing Welshness: Sport, Music and the Crowd *Helen Barlow and Martin V. Clarke*	332
16	Postscript: Contemporary Wales, Devolution and Digitisation *Trevor Herbert, Sally Harper and Sarah Hill*	355

Appendix 1 Selective, Chronological List of Traditional Music Published up to 1920 — 366

Appendix 2 Selective, Chronological List of Hymn Collections Published in Wales or for Use by Welsh Congregations from 1621 to 1900 — 383

Appendix 3 Selective List of Major Published and Manuscript Sources Available in Open-Access Digitised Form — 397

Bibliography — 404

Index — 437

Figures

1.1	The National Library of Wales in Aberystwyth, 1941. Llyfrgell Genedlaethol Cymru – National Library of Wales	*page* 5
3.1	Edmwnd Prys, *Llyfr y Psalmau* (1621), fo. 1r. Psalm 1, with the melody known as 'Song 67', attributed to Orlando Gibbons (Withers, 1623), and part of Psalm 2, with the melody later known as 'Hackney' or 'St Mary's Tune' (Playford, 1674, 1677). Llyfrgell Genedlaethol Cymru – The National Library of Wales	76
4.1	Carved panel on a cupboard originally from Wales but now at Cotehele House, Cornwall, showing players of a crwth and a harp. © National Trust	85
5.1	An engraved image of the 'Rhuddlan Royal Eisteddvod' of 1850. *Illustrated London News*, 28 September 1850	107
6.1	Dr Mary Davies (seated) and Ruth Herbert Lewis in 'Gorsedd y Beirdd' robes. By kind permission of Mrs Nest Price, Caerwys, Flintshire	124
6.2	A phonograph cylinder from Ruth Herbert Lewis's collection. 'Cân Llwynog, L. Roberts, Smithy, Rhydyrarian' is written in her hand on the cover. The photograph was taken in Ruth Herbert Lewis's home at Penucha, Caerwys in 2009, with the permission of her granddaughter Nest Price. © Wyn Thomas	128
7.1	The harpist Nansi Richards (1888–1979) playing a triple harp, which rests on her left shoulder. Amgueddfa Cymru – National Museum Wales	146
7.2	Drawing of instruments owned by the Hon. Daines Barrington and included in his article 'Some Account of Two Musical Instruments Used in Wales'. *Archaeologia*, III (1775), 30–34	153

7.3 Itinerant Welsh Romani musicians (from the left), Cornelius, David (harp) and Adolphus Wood. The fiddles are home-made, and the mechanism of the pedal harp may have been removed to aid portability. Picture taken before 1914; the photographer is unidentified. Amgueddfa Cymru – National Museum Wales ... 158

8.1 The visit of Chandra Mohan Chatterjee to the 1842 Abergavenny Eisteddfod. The loyalty of the Cymreigyddion to the Crown is prominently displayed in the letters 'VR' (Victoria Regina); a banner bearing the name 'Victoria' hangs at the back of the marquee. *Illustrated London News*, 22 October 1842 ... 190

9.1 A page from *Cyfaill mewn Llogell* by John Williams and printed by John Daniel of Carmarthen: the first book printed in Wales to contain musical notation. The stave lines are printed, but the notes are added by hand. Photographic copy at Llyfrgell Genedlaethol Cymru – National Library of Wales ... 196

10.1 Tonic sol-fa score of the hymn 'Cwm Rhondda' (1907) in the hand of, and signed by, the composer John Hughes. By kind permission of the descendants of the composer's friend Mr Oliver Bown ... 237

11.1 First page of Joseph Parry's 'Myfanwy' (1875). This version, published by Snell of Swansea in 1931, used the plates of the original printing of 1875 by Isaac Jones of Treherbert ... 244

12.1 Daniel Jones, Fourth Symphony, first movement, bars 127–131, in the composer's hand. By kind permission of the composer's daughter Cathrin Roberts ... 273

13.1 A poster widely circulated in Neath by the local council following the success of Y Côr Mawr, which included some of the townspeople. By kind permission of Peter Stevens ... 299

13.2 Clara Novello Davies with her ten-year-old son Ivor. Taken in 1903 by an unidentified photographer ... 312

14.1 Datblygu performing at the Pesda Roc music festival in Bethesda, north Wales (1985). A young Gruff Rhys (later of the Super Furry Animals) is seated in the front row. The decidedly sparse audience is photographic proof of the disconnect between 'popular' and 'influential': fifteen years later, Super Furry Animals' version of the Datblygu song 'Y Teimlad' was included on their critically acclaimed album *Mwng* (2001). Unknown photographer. Creative Commons Licence CCBY 2.0 https://creativecommons.org/licenses/by/2.0/legalcode ... 326

15.1 A cartoon from a Cardiff newspaper satirising the enthusiasm 338
of the Welsh for rugby (at a time when the term 'football' was
used interchangeably for the different codes of the game).
Evening Express, 11 November 1893
16.1 The Wales Millennium Centre, Cardiff Bay; completed 2009. 359
By kind permission of the Wales Millennium Centre, Cardiff

Maps

P.1	The Shires of Wales after the Acts of Union, *c.*1550. © Helen Fulton	*page* xxxi
P.2	Counties of Wales before 1974. © Helen Fulton	xxxii
P.3	Counties of Wales, 1974–96. © Helen Fulton	xxxiii
P.4	Local authority areas of modern Wales. © Helen Fulton	xxxiv
2.1	The lands of the Welsh princes, *c.*1200. © Helen Fulton	26
2.2	The Principality and the Marcher Lordships, *c.*1400. © Helen Fulton	27

Music Examples

P.1	Helmholtz notation system	*page* xxiv
6.1	'Dacw 'Nghariad i Lawr yn y Berllan' ('There's My Sweetheart Down in the Orchard'). *Journal of the Welsh Folk-Song Society*, I/77	126
6.2	'Roedd yn y Wlad Honno' ('There Was in That Land'). *Journal of the Welsh Folk-Song Society*, II/128	130
6.3	'Titrwm Tatrwm'. *Journal of the Welsh Folk-Song Society*, II/29	132
6.4	'Lliw'r Heulwen' ('The Colour of Sunshine'). *Journal of the Welsh Folk-Song Society*, I/172	142
10.1	John Ellis, 'Claddedigaeth', *Mawl yr Arglwydd* (Trefriw: I. Davies, 1816), bars 1–13	231
12.1	Grace Williams, *Hiraeth* (1951), opening bars. © Cwmni Cyhoeddi Gwynn, reproduced with permission	266
12.2	William Mathias, Harp Concerto (1970), first movement, opening. © Oxford University Press, reproduced with permission of Oxford Publishing Limited (Music) through PLSclear	277
12.3	Alun Hoddinott, *Landscapes* (1975), second movement, conclusion. © Oxford University Press, reproduced with permission of Oxford Publishing Limited (Music) through PLSclear	280
15.1	'Mae Hen Wlad fy Nhadau', standard and modified endings	348

Contributors

HELEN BARLOW (editor) is a cultural historian and Senior Research Fellow in the Music Department of The Open University. Her research is interdisciplinary, exploring the intersections between history, music, literature and the visual arts. She was a member of the AHRC-funded Listening Experience Database project team. Her publications include *Music and the British Military in the Long Nineteenth Century* (2013), co-written with Trevor Herbert, and *Listening to Music: People, Practices and Experiences* (2017) and *The Experience of Listening to Music: Methodologies, Identities, Histories* (2019), both co-edited with David Rowland. She has a particular research interest in the relationship between music and Welsh identity.

MARTIN V. CLARKE (editor) is a Senior Lecturer in Music at The Open University. He has published widely on the intersections of music and religion in Britain, including his monograph *British Methodist Hymnody: Theology, Heritage and Experience* (2018) and an edited collection, *Music and Theology in Nineteenth-Century Britain* (2012). He is co-editor with Alexander Lingas of volume 3 of *The Oxford Handbook of Music and Christian Theology* (in press). He was a co-investigator on the AHRC-funded Listening Experience Database project and has held visiting fellowships at Southern Methodist University, Dallas. He is a Fellow of the Royal College of Organists and a Senior Fellow of the Higher Education Academy.

LYN DAVIES is a writer, composer, broadcaster and performer. He has been a lecturer at the University of Wales, Senior Officer in the Arts Council of Wales and Head of Vocal Studies at the Royal Welsh College of Music and Drama. He is currently a home and overseas examiner for Trinity College, London. He has also been a frequent broadcaster on radio and television, has published widely in journals and dictionaries and has written monographs on various Welsh composers. He was

Chair of the Executive Committee of the 1996 National Eisteddfod and of Tŷ Cerdd, an expert group member for the EU and a member of the British Council Music Advisory Committee and of the British Committee for Music in Higher Education.

HELEN FULTON is Chair of Medieval Literature at the University of Bristol. She is a specialist in medieval Welsh literature and has published widely on the literature, politics and geography of medieval Wales and England, with a particular interest in the geocultural dynamics of the medieval March of Wales. Her recent publications include the *Cambridge History of Welsh Literature* (co-editor, 2019), *Chaucer and Italian Culture* (editor, 2021) and the Historic Towns Trust map, *Bristol in 1480* (co-editor, 2020). She held a Leverhulme Major Research Fellowship in 2020–2 to work on medieval Welsh political poetry and has held Visiting Research Fellowships at Corpus Christi College, Cambridge, St John's College, Oxford and Magdalen College, Oxford. She is a Fellow of the Society of Antiquaries and Fellow and Vice-President for Humanities, Arts and Social Sciences at the Learned Society of Wales.

RHIDIAN GRIFFITHS was Keeper of Printed Books and Director of Public Services at the National Library of Wales. He has published on various aspects of Welsh music, including studies of the choral and congregational traditions, and has also written on folk music and publishing. His doctoral research was concerned with the development of music publishing in nineteenth-century Wales.

JOHN HARPER is the author of the widely used guide *The Forms and Orders of Western Liturgy from the Tenth to the Eighteenth Century* and continues to work on the medieval Use of Salisbury. He led the research project 'The Experience of Worship in Late Medieval Cathedral and Parish Church' and the Sacred Music Studies research group. These exemplify his career as a liturgical musician, scholar, teacher and administrator. As a church musician, he directed the music at St Chad's Cathedral, Birmingham and Magdalen College, Oxford and was director general of The Royal School of Church Music (now emeritus director). He has been a lecturer at the universities of Birmingham (now honorary professor) and Oxford, and professor of music at Bangor University (now emeritus), where he established the Centre for Advanced Welsh Music Studies and the bilingual journal *Welsh Music History/Hanes Cerddoriaeth Cymru*. He is a Fellow of the Learned Society of Wales.

SALLY HARPER has published widely on various aspects of music in medieval and early modern Wales as well as on medieval liturgy. She is author of the monograph *Music in Welsh Culture before 1650: A Study of the Principal Sources* (2007) and was co-investigator on the ESRC/AHRC-funded major research project 'The Experience of Worship in Late Medieval Cathedral and Parish Church' (2009–19). She was appointed Senior Lecturer in Music at Bangor University in 2006 and was for a period Director of the Centre for Advanced Welsh Music Studies at Bangor and co-editor of the bilingual journal *Welsh Music History/Hanes Cerddoriaeth Cymru*. She took early retirement from the University in 2018 to train as a priest in the Church in Wales and is now Director of Spirituality for the Diocese of St Asaph but continues her association with Bangor as an Honorary Research Fellow. She is a Fellow of the Royal Historical Society and a Fellow of the Learned Society of Wales.

TREVOR HERBERT (lead editor) is Emeritus Professor of Music at The Open University, Professor of Music Research at the Royal College of Music and Honorary Professor of Music at Cardiff University. He has written extensively on brass instruments and on the cultural history of Welsh music. He was also co-editor with Gareth Elwyn Jones of the seven-volume Welsh History and Its Sources series and editorial consultant for the *Welsh Academy Encyclopaedia of Wales* and the BBC television series *The Story of Wales* (2012). He is a Fellow of the Learned Society of Wales.

SARAH HILL is Associate Professor of Popular Music and a Fellow of St Peter's College, University of Oxford. She is Co-ordinating Editor of *Popular Music* and has published widely on issues of popular music historiography, popular music and politics, progressive rock, and popular music and cultural identity, particularly as it relates to the Welsh language. Her most recent book was *San Francisco and the Long 60s* (2016).

NICHOLAS JONES is Reader in Musicology at Cardiff University's School of Music. His research interests lie primarily in British music since 1900. He has co-edited books for Cambridge University Press on Peter Maxwell Davies (2009), Michael Tippett (2013) and Harrison Birtwistle (2015). Other publications include *Peter Maxwell Davies, Selected Writings* (2017) and *The Music of Peter Maxwell Davies* (2020, co-authored with Richard McGregor). He is Co-Director of the Cardiff

University British Music Research Centre (CUBRIT), Co-Curator of the Peter Maxwell Davies Research Network, a member of the Editorial Advisory Board for the music journal *Tempo* and Senior Fellow of the Higher Education Academy.

STEPHEN P. REES is Lecturer in Music at Bangor University. Alongside his classical music training, he has performed the traditional music of Wales in the UK, Europe, and North and South America and was instrumental in setting up two organisations for the promotion of Welsh traditional music. His current research centres on nineteenth-century harp-making in Wales.

WYN THOMAS is Honorary Research Fellow in Music at Bangor University, having previously served as Senior Lecturer in Music and Pro Vice-Chancellor. With financial support from the Arts Council of Wales, he established the Archive of Welsh Traditional Music at Bangor and was joint editor of *Welsh Music History/Hanes Cerddoriaeth Cymru* and *Cydymaith i Gerddoriaeth Cymru* (Companion to Welsh Music) (2018).

Preface

Scope and Structure

This is the first book to be devoted to the history of Welsh music. Others have been written on specific and more restricted topics and are properly regarded as seminal texts, but none have previously been devoted to the entire span of Welsh music or place it in the wider history of the country. We have settled on an approach which is both thematic and chronological. Following a mapping chapter, some chapters focus on topics that cover most of the period to which the book is devoted (such as the chapter on eisteddfodau), while most others, such as that on the Celtic revival, deal with a topic within a specific period. The earliest known sources for the history of Welsh music are found in poetry and other early narratives that describe how people of different stations in Welsh life engaged with music and the purposes it served for them. Most chapters address both this idea and the repertoires and practices that occurred in the various phases of Welsh music history. Instrumental and vocal music and the secular, sacred, popular and more elevated forms have similar prominence in the book, but all contributors have written of the context in which music was made and in which it was heard. It is inevitable that matters relevant to any one chapter have equal, or near-equal, relevance to another, because some themes are recurrent. We have envisaged the book as a collection of overlapping chapters rather than a single linear account, so we have taken care to ensure that the integrity of each one is protected even if some topics appear in more than one place.

We have been especially mindful of how we can best deliver the story of Welsh music to a global readership. The ideas, events and movements that unfolded in this history achieve full meaning only when understood in the context of a wider set of features and sources than can properly be examined in a single volume. The challenge is that very little is understood about Welsh music outside Wales, except among those who have had a specific reason for finding out about it. Furthermore, the place of music in the wider space of Welsh history cannot be navigated using the indicators routinely deployed to mark out the major developments in European and British music history. For example, the circumstances that defined the great style periods of western art music have limited utility, because while Welsh music has never been isolated from cultural trends that occurred elsewhere, there are genres and practices that are unique and that are explained neither helpfully nor accurately as variants of other better-known species. Added to this are the musicians who have shaped Welsh music history; most are invisible to musical worlds outside Wales but are shown here to be major figures. Such features may well be found to different degrees in most music cultures, but here they have unusual substance because of the extent to which musical and extra-musical factors are intermingled. Welsh music history presented in isolation from the wider history of the country is seriously impoverished. We hope that our organisation of the book, which at one end touches the earliest known literary sources that refer to Welsh music and at the other the place of Welsh music in the age of digitisation, conveys a fitting sense of these ideas.

Sources

This book is concerned with music history. It is not a reference work, but it contains material that will be helpful to those without an extensive knowledge of Wales and its history; this includes the prefatory notes given below, a glossary of Welsh words and phrases that frequently occur in the book and summary bibliographical appendices. An important enhancement is the ability to provide links to much of the most important primary source material cited in the book. The National Library of Wales's digitisation programme gives open access to a vast quantity of its materials and reference facilities. They include the *Dictionary of Welsh Biography/Y Bywgraffiadur Cymreig*,[1] which gives information (in both Welsh and English) about thousands of Welsh subjects, most of whom are not memorialised in other standard biographical sources. *Welsh Newspapers*[2] provides free and searchable access to most newspapers published in Wales, in English or Welsh, before 1919, and *Welsh Journals*[3] offers free access to many periodicals relating

---

[1] *Y Bywgraffiadur Cymreig/Dictionary of Welsh Biography*. Website. https://biography.wales (accessed 21 June 2021).
[2] Llyfrgell Genedlaethol Cymru/The National Library of Wales. *Welsh Newspapers*. Website. https://newspapers.library.wales (accessed 21 June 2021).
[3] Llyfrgell Genedlaethol Cymru/The National Library of Wales. *Welsh Journals*. Website. https://journals.library.wales (accessed 29 July 2021).

to Wales between 1735 and 2007, including academic and scientific publications as well as literary and popular magazines. Additionally, the National Library has digitised many early manuscripts and published works that are key primary sources for Welsh music history. These include early hymn and hymn-tune books, manuscript commonplace books and printed collections of traditional vocal and instrumental music. Staff at the National Library have helped us and given us privileged access to lists of digitised material which have enabled us to provide links to many primary source materials cited in the book. The links are given in footnotes, in almost all cases as permalinks (links that are intended to be permanent and unlikely to change). More information about these permalinks is given below.

Other important texts relating to Welsh social and cultural history are also included in the Library's online catalogue, which includes summary pages on music such as its Archives of Welsh Composers.[4] A wider selection of sources than those cited in footnotes in the chapters is summarily listed, described and aligned to the relevant permalinks in Appendix 3.

While we are confident in our claim that this is the first book to be devoted to the entire expanse of Welsh music history, it would be wrong not to acknowledge the value of existing literature that covers a wide range of topics and from which we have benefited. The first significant contributions to a scholarly literature of Welsh music date from the eighteenth century and the 'historical essays' which appeared in prefaces to collections such as *Antient British Music* (1742) by John Parry (Ruabon) and *Musical and Poetical Relicks of the Welsh Bards* (1784) by Edward Jones (Bardd y Brenin). It became common for song and hymn collections to contain prefatory texts, and while the accuracy of such writings is often suspect, at the time of their publication they were influential on contemporary knowledge. From the nineteenth century onwards, there has been a wealth of periodical literature devoted to, or containing articles about, Welsh music. These include titles such as *Y Cerddor Cymreig* (The Welsh Musician; 1861–73); *Y Cerddor* (The Musician; 1889–1921); *Cylchgrawn Cymdeithas Alawon Gwerin Cymru* (*Journal of the Welsh Folk-Song Society*), which has run continuously since 1909, renamed *Canu Gwerin* (Folk Song) in 1978; and *Welsh Music/Cerddoriaeth Cymru*, published by the Guild for the Promotion of Welsh Music between 1959 and 2009 (latterly called the Welsh Music Guild). The most important and

---

[4] Llyfrgell Genedlaethol Cymru/The National Library of Wales. *Archives of Welsh Composers*. Website. www.library.wales/collections/learn-more/archives/archives-of-welsh-composers (accessed 28 July 2021).

influential modern journal dedicated to Welsh music is *Welsh Music History/Hanes Cerddoriaeth Cymru*; edited at Bangor University and published by the University of Wales Press, it had seven issues between 1996 and 2007.

Monographs and other books devoted to topics about Welsh music have made a significant contribution to knowledge of the subjects they address. For instance, Sally Harper's *Music in Welsh Culture before 1650* (2007) elucidated the early history of Welsh music with an unprecedented level of detail and intelligence. Phyllis Kinney's *Welsh Traditional Music* (2011) offered the most lucid and richly illustrated overview of traditional song in Wales, while Wyn Thomas's *Cerddoriaeth Draddodiadol Yng Nghymru: Llyfryddiaeth/Traditional Music in Wales: Bibliography* (3rd ed., 2006) provided the most comprehensive bibliography of Welsh traditional music. The writings on music of the Welsh historian Gareth Williams include two important monographs on Welsh choralism, *Valleys of Song: Music and Society in Wales 1840–1914* (1998) and *Do You Hear the People Sing? The Male Voice Choirs of Wales* (2015). David Ian Allsobrook's *Music for Wales* (1992) provides a valuable overview of the era in twentieth-century Welsh music that was dominated by the Council of Music in Wales and its dynamic chairman Sir Henry Walford Davies. Sarah Hill's *'Blerwytirhwng?' The Place of Welsh Pop Music* (2007) was the first major monograph on the development of pop music in both languages in Wales. The Welsh-language *Cydymaith i Gerddoriaeth Cymru* (Companion to Welsh Music; 2018), edited by Pwyll ap Siôn and Wyn Thomas, is an ambitious reference work which sets out to encompass the spectrum of Welsh music. The partially bilingual *'Canu at Iws' ac Ysgrifau Eraill* (*'Song for Use' and Other Articles*; 2013) is a compilation of twenty-eight articles, many of them seminal, by Roy Saer, who between 1963 and 1995 was curator at what is now called the National Museum of History at St Fagans near Cardiff. The multi-authored festschrift volume *Cynheiliaid y Gân/ Bearers of Song* (2007), edited by Sally Harper and Wyn Thomas, is dedicated to Phyllis Kinney and Meredydd Evans, who jointly and individually have had a formidable influence on modern understandings of Welsh traditional song.

Some significant contributions to the understanding of Welsh music are less obvious, either by their location in large-scale projects in which music is but a part, or by their residence in a range of journals or other media. Rhidian Griffiths, who spent the greatest part of his career at the National Library of Wales, has been a prolific contributor to many journals and multi-authored books. The same can be said of Daniel Huws; best known

Preface xxi

as a seminal authority on early manuscripts, he has also published extensively on Welsh song, including the folk-song collecting of Maria Jane Williams and Edward Williams (Iolo Morganwg). This latter work was part of the research project 'Iolo Morganwg and the Romantic Tradition in Wales' at the University of Wales Centre for Advanced Welsh and Celtic Studies.[5]

Recordings of Welsh music are the most obviously illustrative sources on repertoire and style, and this is as true for light and popular music as for classical repertoire. Numerous recordings are available commercially, but the National Screen and Sound Archive of Wales at the National Library provides many that are not otherwise accessible.[6] The work of Meredydd Evans is especially important to the history of traditional song. He published many valuable learned articles, but through his exceptional gifts as a singer, his recordings serve as exemplars of the repertoire. His performances are captured in commercial recordings and also in interviews and song recordings made by the Smithsonian Institution as part of its Folkways project.[7]

Numerous journals on Welsh history have been published since the nineteenth century, including those of antiquarian and local history societies. A selective list is given in the bibliographical section of this book, but a more comprehensive catalogue of open-access content can be found by browsing the National Library of Wales's *Welsh Journals* website. Relatively few articles on Welsh music history are published in academic journals outside Wales; most of these are cited in this book.

The Welsh Language

Modern Wales is a bilingual country, and for a large part of its history, Welsh was the language of the majority.[8] As is to be expected, the Welsh language is present throughout the book. It is a complex language

---

[5] University of Wales/Prifysgol Cymru. Iolo Morganwg and the Romantic Tradition in Wales. Website. www.wales.ac.uk/en/CentreforAdvancedWelshCelticStudies/ResearchProjects/CompletedProjects/IoloMorganwgandtheRomanticTraditioninWales/IntroductiontotheProject.aspx (accessed 21 June 2021).

[6] Llyfrgell Genedlaethol Cymru/The National Library of Wales. Sound. Website. www.library.wales/collections/learn-more/screen-sound-archive/audio-visual-collections/sound (accessed 21 June 2021).

[7] Smithsonian Folkways Recordings. Meredydd Evans Interview. Website. https://folkways.si.edu/meredydd-evans/spoken-word-world/music/video/smithsonian (accessed 20 June 2021).

[8] Aspects of the history of the Welsh language as it has impacted and continues to impact on music are explained later in this book. The equality of Welsh and English in Wales is defined by law.

belonging to the Indo-European group of languages and does not consistently resemble Romance languages. All quoted texts in the book are given in the original language with English translations. Though this is an English-language book, passages in the Welsh language are not italicised because in Britain it is not a foreign language. In footnote and bibliography citations, where a publication is solely in the Welsh language we have used Welsh bibliographical abbreviated terms (for instance, gol. for ed., t./tt. for p./pp., rhif for no.).

Readers might find it helpful to have details of some of the more distinctive features of the language. The Welsh alphabet is different from the English. In its modern form, it does not include k, q, v, x or z (although some of these letters – k, for instance – sometimes appear in earlier Welsh orthography). The letters w and y are vowels (though 'w' can also function as a consonant before another vowel). Some pairs of letters form alphabetical characters in their own right: ch, dd, ff, ll, rh and th. Readers unfamiliar with the language may be confused by an apparent inconsistency in the way some words appear. This is a consequence of the mutations that are a feature of Welsh: the initial letters of a word may change according to its grammatical context. For example, Caerdydd, the Welsh word for Cardiff, the Welsh capital, can also appear as Gaerdydd, Chaerdydd or Nghaerdydd. It follows that even the best Welsh/English dictionaries are not always easy to use.

Welsh Personal Names and Pseudonyms

Welsh musicians and poets have often been known by a pseudonym as well as their proper name. This may be a consequence of the fact that so many people share a relatively small number of family names (Jones, Owen, Thomas, Davies and so on), but there were also other reasons. For example, the poet and musician John Owen (1821–83) was usually referred to by his bardic name 'Owain Alaw' ('alaw' meaning 'melody'). There was no consistency in the way these names were acquired: some were awarded by the eisteddfod gorsedd, others were just assumed. Sometimes they were indicative of status – for example, Edward Jones (1752–1824) was known as 'Bardd y Brenin', literally 'the King's bard'. Griffith Rhys Jones (1834–97), a renowned nineteenth-century choral conductor, acquired the nickname 'Caradog' in his youth and was most often referred to by that name. The singer and song collector Maria Jane Williams (1795–1873) was referred to as 'Llinos' (the linnet) because of the beauty of her voice. We have usually given both the proper name and the pseudonym on its first occurrence in a chapter, but thereafter used the name by which the subject was most frequently known. Subjects' proper names and pseudonyms are cross-referenced in the index.

Boundaries and Place Names

The present division of Wales into administrative regions is but the latest of several methods that have been used for administrating the country. Maps P.1–P.4 show the shire or county divisions used at various times between the sixteenth century and the present day. Maps showing Wales in earlier periods are given at the start of Chapter 2.

Many place names in Wales are markedly different in their Welsh and English forms (for example, the city of Swansea is Abertawe in Welsh), and other variances in spellings in both languages reflect orthographical transitions that occurred in the nineteenth and twentieth centuries. We have used the modern English spellings throughout the book, unless a different version occurs in quotation or (as is the case with chapters dealing with early periods) where common sense requires something different. The boundaries, names and organisation of Welsh administrative counties have changed several times. We have used the names relevant to the period and context in which each place name is used.

'The March', or more specifically the March of Wales or Welsh Marches – terms used frequently in earlier periods of Welsh history – refers to the border region between England and Wales. The word 'march' derives from an ancient Anglo-Saxon word meaning boundary. The Scottish Marches is similarly used to describe the border region that separates England from Scotland.

Dates and Eras

Unless indicated otherwise, the Gregorian calendar is used throughout the book. Citations of Welsh-language periodical publications are given only in Welsh. This is because the Welsh version is the correct formal citation. However, for good measure the translation of months of the year is as follows.

Ionawr	January
Chwefror	February
Mawrth	March
Ebrill	April
Mai	May
Mehefin	June

Gorffennaf	July
Awst	August
Medi	September
Hydref	October
Tachwedd	November
Rhagfyr	December

Hypertext Links and Permalinks

Internet sources are cited in footnotes, with the most recent date of access in parenthesis. Where possible, permalinks are given for referenced sources that we have discovered to be digitised, the vast majority of which are at the National Library of Wales. Permalinks, as the name suggests, are intended to be permanent and unchanging; for that reason and by convention, dates of access are unnecessary. It is important to stress that the permalinks included in footnotes and the larger collection included in Appendix 3 are not comprehensive for two reasons. Firstly, the project at the National Library of Wales is ongoing and the list of available sources is continuously expanding; and secondly, certain sources, particularly printed works dating from the eighteenth century, may have had several different editions, some or all of which have been digitised. We have cited only those that are directly relevant to the matter at hand in any given chapter; in some instances, other editions with attendant variances may be available in digitised form.

Note on Pitch Names

Pitch names for musical notes use the Helmholtz abbreviation system shown below in Example P.1, except for Chapter 3, where, to denote

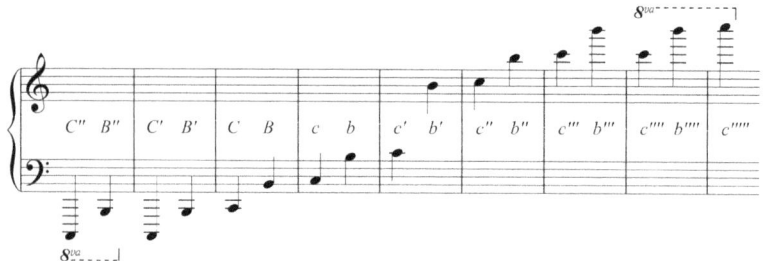

Example P.1 Helmholtz notation system

relative rather than absolute pitches, octaves are indicated by the use of superscript Arabic numerals.

References to Unpublished Materials

Throughout the book we have used the sigla reference system devised by RISM (*Répertoire International des Sources Musicales*). In this system a country code is followed by other abbreviations that define the holding institution precisely. The institution's catalogue identifier is then added for the relevant manuscript. The institutional identifiers used in this book are given below.

GB-AB	National Library of Wales, Aberystwyth
GB-BGul	University Library, Bangor
GB-CDf	St Fagans National Museum of History, Cardiff
GB-CDp	Cardiff Central Library
GB-Dru	University Library, Durham
GB-Lbl	British Library, London
GB-Lcm	Royal College of Music, London
GB-LF	Cathedral Library, Lichfield
GB-Lna	National Archives, London
GB-Ob	Bodleian Library, Oxford
GB-Och	Christ Church Library and Archives, Oxford
GB-Omc	Magdalen College Library, Oxford
GB-SHR	Shropshire Archives, Shrewsbury
US-NYp	New York Public Library for the Performing Arts, Music Division, New York

Acknowledgements

Our major debt of gratitude is to our contributors, both for the content they have provided and for helping in many other ways. We are particularly grateful to Rhidian Griffiths, who, in addition to providing his own chapters, acted as the Welsh-language proof editor, the compiler of the index and an invaluable source for advice.

The owners of rights to images and musical examples included in the book are acknowledged at the points of appearance, but we are grateful to each for their willingness to allow us to use this material. We are especially grateful to the Bown family, who allowed us to use a previously unpublished autograph copy of the hymn 'Cwm Rhondda' in Chapter 10. The cover picture *Chapel Lights* is a painting by the Cardiff artist Chris Griffin, who retains the copyright.

Others helped in a variety of ways. These include Prof. Gareth Williams, Roy Saer and staff at the National Museum of Wales, Tŷ Cerdd, the BBC and offices of the Welsh Government.

The book was written and assembled in the unusual circumstances of the Covid-19 pandemic, requiring us to elicit help from agencies to which we are especially grateful: staff at the National Library of Wales, particularly Iwan ap Dafydd, Nia Daniel, Maredudd ap Huw and Menna Morgan, were extremely helpful in enabling us to link the content of the book with its digitised resources. The London Library and the Library of the Royal College of Music provided access to published works that would otherwise have been unavailable to us. The Open University supported the book in several ways, not least by providing subventions that mitigated some of the difficulties we faced. At Cambridge University Press we were supported by Kate Brett, Nigel Graves, Felinda Sharmal and Frances Tye. Notwithstanding the assistance and advice we have had from so many people, we are keen, personally, to accept responsibility for any shortcomings that remain.

Glossary

The Glossary is limited to words and phrases that appear recurrently in the book or which have other importance. Words appear in their singular or plural form according to the way they are usually encountered.

alaw	Melody. Used in various pseudonyms (Owain Alaw, Llewelyn Alaw and so on).
anterliwt	Interlude. A metrical play for popular entertainment, often poking fun at the establishment.
awdl	Long poem written in traditional strict metre.
bardd teulu	Lit. 'family bard'; bard of the king's household or retinue; an office of a Welsh royal court.
Blue Books	Name given (because of the colour of the volumes' covers) to the 1847 *Report of the Commissioners of Inquiry into the State of Education in Wales*, which caused great offence to Welsh people.
boneddigion	Gentlemen, the landed gentry.
cerdd dafod	Lit. 'tongue craft'; poetry.
cerdd dant	Lit. 'string craft'; the singing of verse in counterpoint to harp accompaniment.
clerwr	Minstrel – the lowest order of poet, an itinerant popular entertainer. (Pl. clêr.)
crwth	A stringed instrument played with a bow. Used in other European countries but especially associated with Wales. A Middle English borrowing from the Welsh gives it as 'crowd'.
Cŵl Cymru/ Cool Cymru	Lit. 'Cool Wales'. The collective name given to progressive young Welsh pop musicians and

	their music, and to film-makers and others around the millennium. BBC Wales referred to 1999 as 'the year of Cool Cymru'.
cymanfa ganu	Hymn-singing festival, held primarily by nonconformist chapels since the 1860s. (Pl. cymanfaoedd canu.)
Cymmrodorion, Honourable Society of	'Cymmrodorion' does not translate literally, but broadly means 'the earliest natives'. A London-Welsh cultural society founded in 1751.
Cymreigyddion y Fenni	The Abergavenny Welsh Society, a literary and cultural society founded in 1833.
cynghanedd	The system of internal rhyme and repetition of consonants normally used in all traditional strict-metre poetry.
cywydd	Strict-metre poem written in rhyming couplets.
datgeiniad	Reciter – delivering poetry, usually to musical accompaniment.
eisteddfod	Lit. 'session' or 'assembly', but the modern meaning is a multifaceted, competitive cultural festival. Eisteddfodau (pl.) are held locally and nationally.
englyn	Traditional strict-metre poetic form, usually a verse of four lines.
Established Church	In England and Wales from 1534, the Church of England, with the sovereign as its head. The Church in Wales became disestablished through an Act of Parliament in 1914 (not enacted until 1920 because of World War I) and is a member of the worldwide Anglican Communion.
gorsedd	Lit. 'throne' but used to describe an assembly of bards, musicians, and other practitioners of Welsh culture. The gorsedd plays a major ceremonial role in the National Eisteddfod.
gwerin	The common people – essentially, everyone who was not one of the boneddigion (see above).

Gwyneddigion	Lit. 'Men of Gwynedd'. A London-Welsh society founded in 1770.
Independent	The name given in Wales to the denomination otherwise known as Congregationalists.
maes	Lit. 'field' – used to signify the site of an eisteddfod.
Marches, the March	The border lands between Wales and England.
Mari Lwyd	A folk ritual: a form of wassailing common in Wales in the nineteenth and early twentieth centuries.
nonconformist	The word used to collectively describe Protestant religious denominations other than the Church of England and the Church in Wales. The label 'Dissenters' was also used to describe some nonconformist groups, especially in the seventeenth and eighteenth centuries, while the term 'free churches' has been used more recently.
noson lawen	Lit. 'merry evening'. Term used since the early nineteenth century to signify a local informal musical entertainment, usually in rural districts. In modern times it survives as a popular television programme. (Pl. nosweithiau llawen.)
pencerdd	Master craftsman, chief poet, chief of the bardic craft – the highest level of the bardic hierarchy. In the medieval period, twelve years' apprenticeship were required to reach this level. In the nineteenth century, the word was used more loosely and romantically in bardic names such as Pencerdd Gwalia.
penillion	An alternative term for cerdd dant (spelt 'pennillion' in some sources). It has been used inconsistently and latterly has been largely abandoned in favour of cerdd dant.
pibgorn or pibcorn	Capped-reed musical instrument associated with Wales.
S4C	Abbreviation of Sianel Pedwar Cymru (Channel Four Wales), the Welsh-language television channel.

Senedd	The Welsh Parliament. The word is used to signify both the collective of members of the Parliament and the building at which it meets in Cardiff.
triple harp	Harp with three ranks of strings which produce a chromatic compass. It was used so frequently by Welsh harpers that it was referred to as the Welsh harp.
uchelwr	Nobleman, especially of the new elite who held offices of the English crown after the conquest of Wales in the thirteenth century and the demise of the courts of the Welsh princes. (Pl. uchelwyr.)
Urdd Gobaith Cymru	Lit. 'The Wales Guild of Hope', but usually in English referred to as the 'Welsh League of Youth'. Its mission is to promote Welsh culture among the young. Its annual eisteddfodau are major events. In 1922 when the organisation was formed, the postwar nation saw 'hope' for the future resting with the young.

Maps

Map P.1 The Shires of Wales after the Acts of Union, c.1550. © Helen Fulton

Map P.2 Counties of Wales before 1974. © Helen Fulton

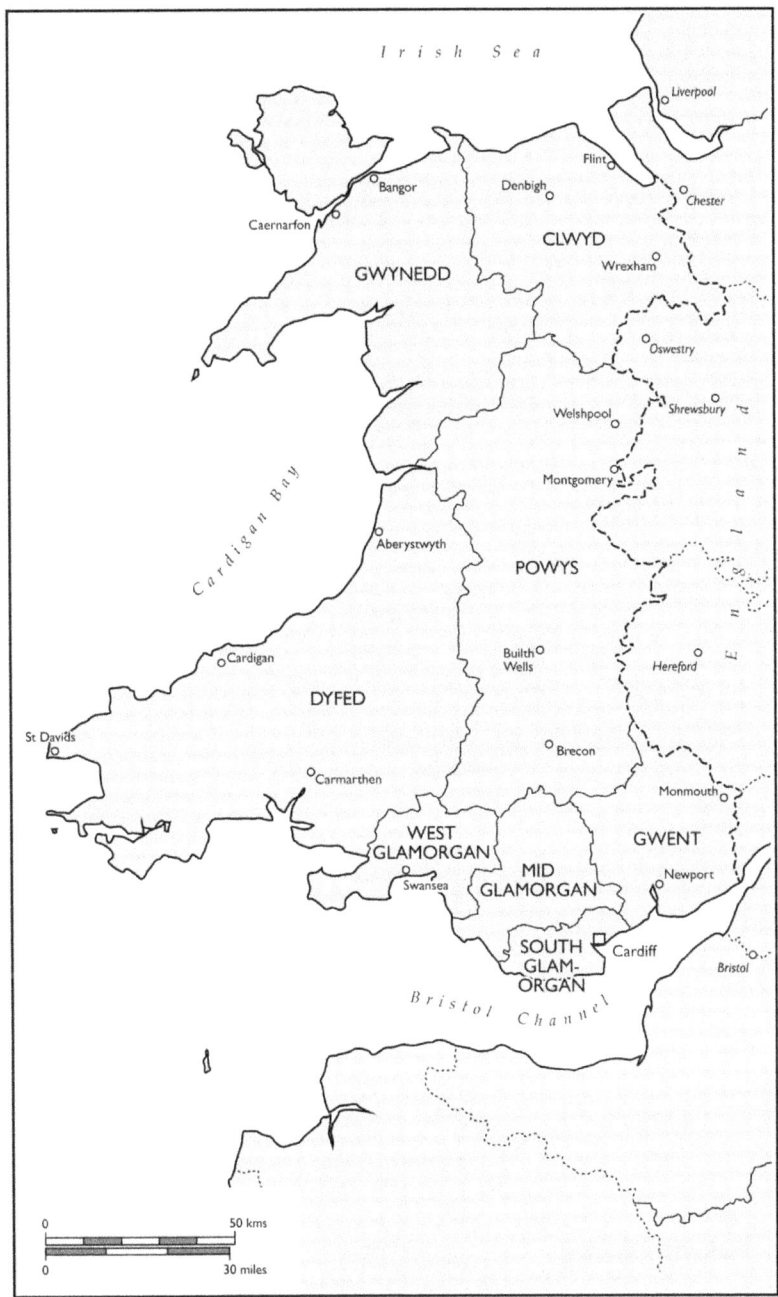

Map P.3 Counties of Wales, 1974–96. © Helen Fulton

Map P.4 Local authority areas of modern Wales. © Helen Fulton

CHAPTER I

Music in Welsh History

Trevor Herbert

All histories of music need contexts, but some more than others. The relevant contexts, at least in western music, have been patronage (whether benevolent or commercial), cultural production and distribution, the audiences for which music has been written and performed, the needs and purposes it has served, and how continuities have been interrupted by musical or extra-musical interventions. It would not be an enormous step to think of Welsh music history in similar terms were it not for the sizeable adjustment needed because Welsh music has not consistently followed the path of the mainstream European tradition. There is no body of secular works in the art music category from before the mid-twentieth century that has gained sustained public interest or deserved serious analytical attention, so no claim can be made for Welsh music to have a composer-led history. It can therefore reasonably be asked why Wales should famously be regarded as a 'musical nation' and a 'land of song'. These could be dismissed as stock phrases of the type routinely tagged to national stereotypes, which gain currency by repetition, but it would be a mistake to pass over them too lightly. They deserve unpicking because they contain historical substance and, to an extent, have configured the way the Welsh have regarded themselves and how others have often described them.

Traditional song of the type found in aural, oral and mainly rural practices has provided the main strand of continuity in Welsh music. From the nineteenth century, a new tradition emerged, as choralism became so widely and popularly practised that it too became one of the country's most quoted features. Welsh music has a coherent history, but taken as a whole it needs special attention, because, like other music cultures that reside fully or partly outside the European mainstream, its values must be understood in terms of its dynamic in the lives of the mass of the people and their communities rather than in those of just a social elite. In this respect, it is helpful to draw on methods used to investigate fields such as popular and non-western music, which show, with a good degree of consistency, that musical creativity and practice is the product of social processes and not just evolving repertoires.

A further complication is that Welsh music has been both an outsider and an intimate of the mainstream traditions in both art and popular music. The major style periods of European art music seldom map neatly onto the Welsh experience: for example, there is no major manifestation of the baroque or classical periods in Welsh music, and romanticism is revealed only in its broad intellectual and cultural sense rather than in a body of exemplar musical works. On the other hand, there is plenty of evidence of alignments to, and borrowings from, dominant external cultural trends. Secular and sacred music from the earliest periods of which we have knowledge were sophisticated and often show connections to wider European practices. The performance of sacred music in Welsh cathedrals and religious settlements before the sixteenth century always matched wider practices of the Latin Church and later of the Reformation; Lutheran congregational homophony can easily be identified as one of the models used by later Welsh hymnists; and oratorio, or derivatives of it, played an important part in nineteenth-century Welsh choralism. From the twentieth century, three categories of musical activity overlapped: one formed or preserved in the eisteddfod and chapel traditions, another mirroring global developments on both sides of the Atlantic and given pace by new media, and a third deliberately aimed at strengthening the alignment between Welsh music and the mainstream European art tradition. It was this latter strand that led, in the mid-twentieth century, to the professionalisation of a music culture that had previously been dominated by amateurs. Another conspicuous feature of Welsh music, perhaps offering mitigation for the general absence of 'great works', has been its massive emphasis on performance. The engagement of the Welsh with musical performance is discussed elsewhere in this book, but the many great Welsh opera soloists, singers such as Tom Jones and Shirley Bassey and pop groups such as The Manic Street Preachers are each, in different ways, beneficiaries of a tradition of singing and the distinctive structural processes that nurtured it from the early years of the nineteenth century.

There are also species of Welsh music that are unique. They include the oldest forms of which we have knowledge, such as cerdd dant (literally 'string craft'),[1] in which a voice improvises melodic declamations as

---

[1] 'Penillion' has also been used as the name for later versions of this form, but the genre from which it originated is cerdd dant. For an illustrated description of cerdd dant and penillion see Phyllis Kinney, *Welsh Traditional Music* (Cardiff: University of Wales Press, 2011), pp. 241–246.

a counterpoint to a predetermined instrumental (harp or crwth) melody. Knowledge of the origins of cerdd dant is opaque, mainly because it relied on oral rather than written transmission. It is described in early writings, but the musical sources date from much later than the time when it flourished. The most important is the Robert ap Huw manuscript, containing harp tablatures with extensive annotations.[2] The distinction between cerdd dant and vernacular song is beyond dispute. Sally Harper makes the point that despite all its 'elusive aspects . . . there is no doubt that this was an elevated music with a courtly function'.[3] It was a sophisticated practice, intimately connected to the bardic art cerdd dafod (tongue craft); many songs were settings of declamatory praise poems directed at noble patrons.

Wales, Britain and the Centres of Cultural Production

Leaving aside vernacular forms, the musical life of Britain before the eighteenth century was centred on the court, the larger churches and a relatively thin network of aristocratic and gentry residences. From the eighteenth century, this changed. London became a major centre for a greatly expanded musical life and a destination for leading Continental musicians. Musical commerce flourished, and theatres, concerts, music publishing houses, musical retail and the general paraphernalia of associated requisites took root. By the early nineteenth century, major and lasting institutions such as the Royal Philharmonic Society (1813) and the Royal Academy of Music (1822) had been established. For elite society at this time, subscription concerts had become a feature of 'the season', and while there is scope to question whether the interest of audiences was universally focused on music rather than the social interactions it generated, these congregations prompted the development of an infrastructure within which the music profession flourished, repertoires circulated and an increasingly widening music business functioned efficiently. The same can be said of Dublin and Edinburgh, even if on a smaller scale. Both were metropolitan centres: Edinburgh thrived as a capital city, and Dublin, if only briefly, was the second-largest city in the British Empire. Both had a social elite and institutions that mirrored developments in the British capital; for example, both cities had established national academies before

---

[2] The Robert ap Huw manuscript (GB-Lbl Add. MS 14905) is given close scrutiny in a special issue of the journal *Welsh Music History/Hanes Cerddoriaeth Cymru* – see Vol. l/Cyf. 3 (1999).
[3] Sally Harper, *Music in Welsh Culture before 1650: A Study of the Principal Sources* (Aldershot: Ashgate, 2007), p. 7.

the end of the eighteenth century.[4] At the start of the nineteenth century, London, Edinburgh and Dublin, with populations respectively of 1,088,000, 83,000 and c.182,000, were major centres of cultural production,[5] and it was not just material production that was generated: a shared aesthetic developed which led to the formation of yet more agencies and infrastructures that defined and stabilised musical taste and continuities of practice.[6]

Wales had no comparable centre of cultural production in this period and there was no place that could be meaningfully termed 'metropolitan'. Between the death in 1282 of Llywelyn ap Gruffudd, the only formally acknowledged native Prince of Wales, and the institution of a devolved Welsh Assembly in 1999, Wales was effectively assimilated with England. The Acts of Union of 1536 and 1543 consolidated the legal status for this arrangement. The Council of Wales and the Marches met at Ludlow between 1471 and 1689,[7] primarily to manage the estates and finances of the Prince of Wales. Provision was also made in Wales for the implementation of English laws and taxes.[8] Until the middle of the nineteenth century, Wales was a rural country with few towns of any size. In 1801, the most populated settlement was Merthyr Tydfil with 7,705 people. The largest towns in the north were Caernarfon in the west (3,626) and Wrexham in the east (2,575).[9] At this time Cardiff, which was not formally the Welsh capital until 1955, had a population of less than 2,000.

Merthyr Tydfil, on the northern rim of the south Wales valleys, owed its development to its iron industry. It was to remain the largest town in Wales until the 1870s, when it was overtaken by Cardiff, which grew as a seaport to serve the massive industrial expansion in the southern valleys that made Wales the world's most important centre for the production of steam coal. This phase caused a commensurate demographic shift in which internal migration from the rural areas to the industrial valleys, and immigration from England and Ireland, caused cultural adjustments for the entire

---

[4] The Royal Society of Edinburgh was founded in 1783, the Royal Irish Academy in 1785.
[5] The populations of London (county of) and Edinburgh are taken from the 1801 census; that for Dublin is from James Whitelaw's *An Essay on the Population of Dublin* (Dublin: Graisberry and Campbell, 1805), p. 15, which is widely cited and based on Whitelaw's 1798 house-to-house survey.
[6] For an outline of concert life in London at this time, see Simon McVeigh, *Concert Life in London from Mozart to Haydn* (Cambridge: Cambridge University Press, 1993).
[7] The Council was abolished by Parliament in 1641, revived in 1660 and finally abolished in 1689.
[8] For an overview of the various legal systems that have operated in Wales, see Thomas Glyn Watkin, *The Legal History of Wales*, 2nd ed. (Cardiff: University of Wales Press, 2012).
[9] Unless otherwise stated, data in this chapter is from L. J. Williams, *Digest of Welsh Historical Statistics* (Cardiff: The Welsh Office, 1998). Relevant pages for this passage are pp. 62–64.

country. For the greater part of the nineteenth century, a period which saw formidable advances in most developed countries, there was in Wales neither a place nor formal secular agencies that provided an official administrative or cultural focus. There was no university until 1872, when the first University College of Wales opened in Aberystwyth.[10] Following a popular petition, the National Library of Wales was established in 1907, also in Aberystwyth (see Figure 1.1). The placing of both institutions in the largest settlement geographically central to the country is indicative of the best logic that could have been applied at a time when neither the north nor the south held undisputed sway as the dominant centre of cultural influence. The Established Church, under the control of Canterbury, was the sole official British agency other than those concerned with the law or taxation.

Figure 1.1 The National Library of Wales in Aberystwyth, 1941. Llyfrgell Genedlaethol Cymru – National Library of Wales

---

[10] St David's College, Lampeter, which was to become a constituent college of the University of Wales in 1971, originated in 1822 as a training college for the clergy.

Present throughout Wales, it had a mixed reputation among the laity: while many held it in affection for much of the seventeenth and eighteenth centuries, it became largely unloved and perceived as 'English'. In the nineteenth century, realities such as these were primary causes for two unprescribed agencies to fill the void and provide a surrogate structure for the future development of musical life and, to an extent, the cultural coherence of Welsh society more generally: the revived and reconstructed form of the ancient Welsh eisteddfod, and the rapid consolidation of religious nonconformity.

History, Identity and Language

For much of its history, Wales has had a distinct and widely acknowledged cultural identity, but no administrative autonomy. Musical life has often been perceived as an agent in the formation of that identity. Whether this idea is realistic or sentimental can be considered from different but connected perspectives. One is that indigenous music and its associated practices transmit signals of identity by association; another (similar and obviously connected) is the reverse: that music makers consciously or subconsciously act out imitations of ethnic characteristics shaped over time that eventually find resolution through consensus.[11] Yet another, but also connected, is that by the twentieth century, cultural identities owed much to 'the invention of traditions', a common process in the nineteenth century when so many national identities were forming or selectively revising their tone and shape.[12] Each of these ideas has purchase in the story of Wales, but it would be wrong to underestimate the depth of history from which the Welsh can legitimately summon evidence of their distinctive ethnicity: many sources seem to testify to it. For example, Bernard, the first Norman bishop in Wales, writing to the Pope around 1140 to argue a case for the establishment of a discrete archbishopric for Wales (that by implication would be distinct from that of England), described it as 'entirely ... a nation (*natione*), in language, laws, habits, modes of judgement and customs'.[13] The musical life of the country has

---

[11] See, for example, Simon Frith, 'Music and Identity', in *Questions of Cultural Identity*, ed. by Stuart Hall and Paul du Gay (London: Sage Publications Ltd, 1996), an exploration of such ideas in respect of modern popular music.
[12] Eric Hobsbawm and Terence Ranger, eds., *The Invention of Tradition* (Cambridge: Cambridge University Press, 1983).
[13] R. R. Davies, 'The Peoples of Britain', *Transactions of the Royal Historical Society*, 4 (December 1994), 10. Davies makes the point that Bernard's prospective candidature for such a post, if it were created, may have caused him to emphasise the distinctiveness of Wales.

played an important part in those 'customs' in the sense that the social rituals of music making have contributed to the formation of collective memories that strengthen feelings of ethnicity.[14] Ultimately, three clearly discernible factors can be cited in support of the claim that Welsh music is distinctive. First, it contains genres, practices, agencies and even instruments that are absent, in the same form, from music cultures elsewhere. Second, to an unusual extent, ideas about the Welsh as a 'musical nation' have been inspired by, and even constructed from, interpretations of the country's cultural past, and irrespective of the veracity of those interpretations it remains the case that cultural inheritance has been a recurrent topic in historical narratives about Welsh music. And third, in almost every era, but especially before the twentieth century, the Welsh musical aesthetic has been shaped by the country's cultural, political, social, demographic and religious developments. To these factors can also be added a more provocative suggestion. In contrast to the experience of many other nations, particularly those of the British Isles, from at least the late eighteenth century the relationship between the mass of the people and music has been relatively uninhibited by gender or social class. The Welsh music tradition is the product of an unusual level of democratic engagement.

The population of Wales in 1600, calculated from an average of baptisms, burials and marriages, was a little over 350,000.[15] In 1801, by which time the first phase of industrialisation had occurred, it had grown to 587,245; by 1901 it was more than 2 million, and by 1970 it had risen to a little over 2,700,000.[16] Before the mid-nineteenth century, the country had a relatively small aristocracy, most of whom were absentee, and a larger gentry and mercantile class. The gentry included those who occupied the estates that covered large parts of the country. Many had country residences that maintained musicians, and from the later eighteenth century, the gentry was also responsible for funding the 'bands of music' attached to county militia but also serving the social needs of the gentry class. By this time, and to an unusual extent, many of the gentry families were joined through marriage to English or Scottish dynasties.[17] The massive majority

---

[14] See, for example, David Connerton, *How Societies Remember* (Cambridge: Cambridge University Press, 1989).
[15] Williams, *Digest*, vol. 1, p. 6.   [16] Ibid., p. 7.
[17] The unusual factor is the extent to which the men of these families remained unmarried or produced no male heirs. On this point see Philip Jenkins, *The Making of a Ruling Class: The Glamorgan Gentry 1640–1790* (Cambridge: Cambridge University Press, 1983), chapter 2. For a list and map of the estates of Wales in the eighteenth century, see Peter D. G. Thomas, *Politics in Eighteenth-Century Wales* (Cardiff: University of Wales Press, 1998), pp. x–xi.

of the population was proletarian: working on the land or in other modes of craft or labour. The conspicuous difference between the English and the Welsh among this class was that they spoke a different language. Welsh was the language of most of the population until the second half of the nineteenth century, when the most emphatic phase of industrialisation occurred. It was always both a vernacular language and the language of poets and learning: the richest and most ethnic strands of the Welsh music tradition are bound intimately to the language – most obviously cerdd dant, traditional song and nonconformist hymn singing. From the nineteenth century onwards, Wales began to become a more bilingual country because of immigration and educational legislation, but while the proportion of Welsh speakers decreased in Wales as a whole, it continued to be the dominant language in some industrial areas as well as the rural counties.

As is the case with most languages, among its speakers Welsh has always been more than a mode of communication: it has cultural weight. Those raised in the language regard it as a natural part of their being. A decline in its use was apparent in 1891 when the census (the first to measure language preference) recorded just 54 per cent of its population as Welsh speakers, but while the number had decreased further in percentage terms because of a rise in the population of the country, the actual number of Welsh speakers increased until 1911 when the census recorded a total of 977,366 Welsh speakers.[18] The trend was downwards in the twentieth century, and in 1981 Welsh was spoken by just 19 per cent of the population, but subsequent measures, including legislation and the provision of Welsh-medium education, have stimulated a dramatic reversal.[19]

Historicism, Romanticism and Eisteddfodau

From at least the fifteenth century onwards, the roads between Wales and the British capital were well-trod by those who sought intellectual, pecuniary or other advancements. One estimate suggests that even by the late sixteenth century more than 5 per cent of London households might have been of Welsh descent.[20] In the eighteenth century, the London Welsh

---

[18] Williams, *Digest*, Vol. 1, p. 78.
[19] In 2017 the Welsh government published its ambitious Cymraeg 2050 strategy, aiming to create a million Welsh speakers by 2050. Demographic signs suggest it could exceed that target. The Welsh Government Annual Population Survey (September 2020) showed that 28.8 per cent of the population spoke Welsh.
[20] W. P. Griffith, 'Tudor Prelude', in *The Welsh in London 1500–2000*, ed. by Emrys Jones (Cardiff: University of Wales Press, 2001), pp. 10–11.

started to organise themselves into coherent societies. There was a Welsh school in London from 1717, and in 1751 the Honourable Society of Cymmrodorion (broadly, 'the Earliest Natives') was founded to promote learning and philanthropy among the London Welsh. Other Welsh societies were established in London over the following two centuries, but the Cymmrodorion Society was the most significant and enduring. The importance of these organisations should not be underestimated, for in their midst, at various times, were some of the most influential Welsh musicians, including Edward Jones (Bardd y Brenin; 1752–1824), the harpist and antiquary, whose *Musical and Poetical Relicks of the Welsh Bards* (1784) is one of the most important early published sources for Welsh traditional music; the harpist John Thomas (Pencerdd Gwalia; 1826–1913), a writer, teacher at the Royal Academy of Music and harpist to Queen Victoria; and the pianist and composer Brinley Richards (Cerddor Towy; 1817–85), one of the most prominent motivators of the Cymmrodorion Society and a major wheeler-dealer in musical life between Wales and London. The importance of these organisations was twofold: they created an influential and articulate lobby for Wales and Welsh culture in the British capital, and from the late eighteenth century onwards, they provided a conspicuous focus for interest in the ancient origins of a distinctively Welsh cultural and musical aesthetic. Special attention was directed at the idea that poetic and musical culture had been nurtured in Wales from the twelfth century onwards in the bardic assemblies that became known as eisteddfodau (literally 'sittings' in the sense of 'sessions').[21] Many protagonists of a revival of this culture were speculators rather than conscientious scholars, but they were to have a profound influence on the way the Welsh and their music were understood or imagined, both within and outside Wales.

The instigation of a new version of the eisteddfod from the late eighteenth century had a major impact on the course of Welsh music. Original eisteddfodau were competitive events, and while they included instrumentalists even in their earliest manifestation, their primary focus was on poetry. One of the more significant temporary figures of the eighteenth-century London-Welsh fraternity was Edward Williams (Iolo Morganwg; 1747–1826), a Glamorganshire stonemason and intellectual polymath. Iolo has been the subject of prolonged and rigorous scholarly attention that has revealed him to be a vastly talented, many-sided individual who played

---

[21] Though these events had a much older ancestry, there is no evidence of the word 'eisteddfod' being used to describe them prior to the 1520s.

a critical part in shaping the romantic tradition of Wales. In 1792, as part of his druidic-bardic obsession, he assembled the first meeting of a gorsedd (an assembly of bards) at Primrose Hill, London. He introduced the gorsedd into the eisteddfod at Carmarthen in 1819, and from then on it was a permanent and central component of eisteddfod ritual. However, Iolo is most famous for his claim that he had discovered authentic early Welsh literary works, particularly those of the fourteenth-century poet Dafydd ap Gwilym (c.1320–70). Doubts were voiced in the nineteenth century by Sir John Morris-Jones of the University of North Wales, Bangor, but it was not until the Cardiff University academic G. J. Williams concluded a prolonged forensic examination that some of Iolo's 'discoveries' were revealed to be no more than brilliant forgeries.[22] By this time, the deceptions had been enthusiastically digested and had thereby made a significant contribution to both a Celtic revival and a lasting reconstitution of the eisteddfod. In this one sense, the eisteddfod that took shape in the Victorian era benefited from invention, but it would be entirely wrong to disregard its genuine origins or its positive effect on Welsh cultural life. It is also important to stress that Iolo lacked neither brilliance, knowledge nor veracity in most of his endeavours. He was not alone in taking an imaginative approach to Welsh history: many espoused its literary and musical richness while knowing much less about it than Iolo.

Such idealisation of the past is a shared feature of romantic movements more generally. In Wales, however, and irrespective of any truths, half-truths or forgeries that contributed directly or indirectly to its re-establishment, the eisteddfod took on enormous significance. Within two or three decades, eisteddfodau were being arranged across the country, and what had originated as primarily poetic events took on a more musical character. Furthermore, the competitive element engendered a level of popular enthusiasm that was unprecedented. Local eisteddfodau stimulated tribal loyalties as towns, villages and even hamlets pinned their hopes on local heroes and heroines. Criticism of the competitive ethos came from some of the distinguished English musicians who saw no inconsistency in accepting remuneration for adjudicating them. The English composer Frederic Hymen Cowen (1852–1935), having adjudicated at the Cardiff Eisteddfod in 1910, concluded that 'the Eisteddfod rather retards the progress of the music in Wales than advances it ... the purely competitive side seems to loom so largely as

---

[22] For an overview of these and other assessments, see Geraint H. Jenkins, 'On the Trail of a "Rattleskull Genius": Introduction', in *A Rattleskull Genius: The Many Faces of Iolo Morganwg*, ed. by Geraint H. Jenkins (Cardiff: University of Wales Press, 2009), pp. 1–28.

completely to overshadow everything else'.[23] Some probably shared this view, but Cowen was emphatically missing the point: his judgement was uttered from the temperate cultural position he usually inhabited.[24] Eisteddfod contesting was not temperate – it was hot and musically exciting. Irrespective of the partisanship it usually promoted among audiences, it caused them to listen intently and focus discerningly on what they heard: ultimately, it nurtured discriminating musical tastes. In nineteenth-century Wales, it was the thrill of contest that stimulated communities to musical engagement, and it followed that eisteddfodau at local and national levels formed a structure that compensated for the national cultural apparatus that Wales otherwise lacked.

Somewhat paradoxically, given the imaginative impetus that had contributed so markedly to the rebirth of eisteddfodau, one of its first and most valuable products was the instigation of measures for capturing and curating authentic Welsh musical traditions. At the Abergavenny eisteddfod in 1837, a prize was awarded 'for the best collection of original unpublished Welsh airs, with the words as sung by the peasantry of Wales'.[25] The winner was Maria Jane Williams of Aberpergwm (Llinos; 1795–1873), who later published much of that collection in her *Ancient National Airs of Gwent and Morganwg* (1844), one of the first collections based entirely on ethnographical research of Welsh vernacular song. Though the musical manifestation of eisteddfodau was to take various turns, the preservation of repertoires and practices that were indigenously Welsh comes primarily from such initiatives. There were earlier publications of song, described later in this book, but the attention paid to the traditions of Welsh music in eisteddfodau and the subsequent establishment of the Welsh Folk-Song Society (Cymdeithas Alawon Gwerin Cymru) in 1906 are undoubtedly the foundation of its lasting status in the musical life of the country.

Religion

While eisteddfodau operated at national and local levels, they were not entirely uniform. Local eisteddfodau were a law unto themselves, and the

---

[23] Quoted in Percy Scholes, *The Mirror of Music 1844–1944*, Vol. 2 (London: Novello & Co. with Oxford University Press, 1947), p. 643.
[24] For an English overview of the eisteddfod and of Welsh music more generally, see John Graham, *A Century of Welsh Music* (London: J. Curwen & Sons, 1923).
[25] Meredydd Evans, 'Pwy Oedd "Orpheus" Eisteddfod Llangollen 1858?/Who Was "Orpheus" of the 1858 Llangollen Eisteddfod?', *Welsh Music History/Hanes Cerddoriaeth Cymru*, 5 (2002), 65. The manuscript source for 'Orpheus' is GB-AB Minor Deposits 150B.

intense competitive spirit they stirred is illustrative of how the absence of metropolitan centres elevated the importance of locality. Community coherence was also enhanced by religious life, especially from the time that nonconformity took root. Both eisteddfodau and the choral societies formed in chapels and through other agencies (such as the temperance movement) played an important part in the formation of vibrant communities.

The Church in Britain was the Church of Rome until the first Act of Supremacy (1534), which ended the authority of the Pope in the kingdom and created the Church of England with the sovereign at its head. Wales was then organised into four dioceses under the Province of Canterbury. In 1914, after decades of pressure, some of it from the London-based Liberation Society that had been formed in 1844, the Welsh Church Act (1914) disestablished the Welsh Church from the Church of England; it took the title 'The Church in Wales' but remained part of the Anglican Communion.[26] Disestablishment was the result of several sometimes-related factors. There had been unconnected popular protest movements from the start of the nineteenth century but a more organised form of political radicalism emerged from the 1860s with the appearance of the radical wing of the Liberal Party. The Representation of the People Act of 1867 enfranchised new categories of voters, with the result that the Welsh electorate more than doubled. The 1868 General Election increased the number of Liberal Members of Parliament for the Welsh constituencies. There were many causes for discontent with the Established Church. The obligatory tithe levies that sustained the churches and their clergy provided no discernible benefits for the people and were regarded as an unwarranted privilege by the dissenters. There was also a widely shared sense that the Church, especially its leadership, was a persistent force for cultural anglicisation. Attitudes to England had taken a sharply negative turn from 1847 when British government commissioners produced a derisory *Report on the State of Education in Wales* (popularly referred to as 'the Blue Books') that characterised the Welsh population as backward, uncivilised and prone to moral turpitude. Furthermore, it proposed that the primary cause of such backwardness was the persistent use of the Welsh rather than the English

---

[26] The Act became law in 1914, but because of the intervention of World War I it was not enacted until 1920. As well as the Act of Disestablishment, there was an Act of Disendowment, which saw the endowments of the old Established Church distributed to the colleges of the University of Wales, the National Library and the County Councils. See Norman Doe, ed., *A New History of the Church in Wales: Governance and Ministry, Theology and Society* (Cambridge: Cambridge University Press, 2020), and Watkin, *Legal History*.

language. It was a remarkable condemnation, deeply and lastingly felt by the population, more so because of the brutal and imperialistic terms in which it was expressed.[27] The sense of resentment, especially at the idea that English was the language of education and advancement, lingered for decades. Thirty years later, in an address on 'Social life in rural Wales', the politician T. E. Ellis cited the dogmatic views of 'the English' whose 'estimate of Wales and Welshmen [is] ... still very largely coloured by the infamous report of three young barristers who formed the Welsh Education Commission of 1847'.[28] But the force that encouraged disestablishment most influentially was the relentless growth of religious nonconformity.

It is difficult to overstate the impact of nonconformity on Welsh life and its music culture. Though there were Independent movements somewhat earlier, large-scale religious dissent originated in Wales as a Calvinistic Methodist movement within the Established Church in the eighteenth century. It grew massively from 1811 when the Welsh Methodists separated from the Church of England, but there were other dissenting denominations as well as Methodism. Nonconformist chapels became a defining feature of the Welsh landscape: in the first fifty years of the century, an average of one new chapel was opened in Wales every eight days.[29] This prompted an impressive and probably well-meaning response from the Established Church: new churches were opened, those that had been left to languish were restored, and an 'army of assistant clergy' was deployed. Between 1832 and 1879 the number of resident incumbents had risen from 450 to 785, but even all this was both too late and insufficiently effective.[30] The religious census administered by the government official Horace Mann in 1851 revealed that only 19.31 per cent of those who attended a place of worship on the day of the census attended churches. The remaining majority went to nonconformist chapels. Independents and Welsh Methodists alone accounted for 60 per cent. Wales had rapidly become a nonconformist nation.[31]

Nonconformity brought with it strict and often stifling moral codes that frequently left congregations confused and fearful. Sermonising became at

---

[27] The episode became known as 'The Treason of the Blue Books', taking the title from the colour of the cover of the report itself and the title of an 1854 play by R. J. Derfel, which satirised the report. For a discussion of the language of the report, see Gwyneth Tyson Roberts, *The Language of the Blue Books: Wales and Colonial Prejudice* (Cardiff: University of Wales Press, 2011).
[28] Thomas E. Ellis, *Speeches and Addresses by the Late T. E. Ellis* (Wrexham: Hughes & Son, 1912), p. 119.
[29] Jeffrey Gainer, 'The Road to Disestablishment', in Doe, *A New History*, p. 31.
[30] Roger L. Brown, 'The Age of Saints to the Victorian Church', in Doe, *A New History*, p. 23.
[31] Ibid., p. 23.

once an inspiration, an art, a fetish and a device for social as well as moral control. Some saw nonconformity as an infringement that acted negatively on the country's traditions, including its traditional music, and there is evidence of individuals destroying or burying musical instruments in the heat of religious revivals.[32] Edward Jones (Bardd y Brenin), based in London but an ardent advocate of Welsh music, identified such dangers as early as 1802:

> The sudden decline of the national Minstrelsy, and Customs of Wales, is in a great degree to be attributed to the fanatick impostors, or illiterate plebeian preachers, who have too often been suffered to over-run the country, misleading the greater part of the common people from their lawful Church; and dissuading them from their innocent amusements, such as Singing, Dancing, and other rural Sports, and Games, which heretofore they had been accustomed to delight in, from the earliest time.[33]

However, there is scope to doubt whether Jones's pessimism was fully justified. Leaving aside the benefits that nonconformity provided for choralism, there were other offshoots of Christian evangelism, some originating in the radical wing of the eighteenth-century Established Church, that had a permanent and beneficial influence on the intellectual and aesthetic life of the nation.

Fundamental to most forms of evangelism was a belief in the urgent requirement for the mass of the people to engage with the scriptures. Schemes initiated by reformers, particularly the clergyman Griffith Jones of Llanddowror (1683–1761), were put in place to teach children and adults to read.[34] Griffith Jones had a didactic bent and advocated comprehensibility over the type of sermonising that was replete with 'lofty phrases' that were beyond the common understanding.[35] He devised and enacted one of the most successful educational experiments in Wales before the twentieth century. His 'circulating schools' system saw groups of itinerant teachers moving from village to village, teaching literacy intensively over a few weeks before moving to a new location. The new converts would then take the cause yet further in their communities to create a legacy of reading, implicitly stabilising the Welsh language yet further. During his lifetime

---

[32] Several such instances are cited in Roy Saer, *'Canu at Iws' ac Ysgrifau Eraill/'Song for Use' and Other Articles* (Talybont: Cymdeithas Alawon Gwerin Cymru, 2013), pp. 298–304.

[33] Edward Jones, *The Bardic Museum* (London: A. Strahan, 1802), p. xvi. Digitised by the National Library of Wales http://hdl.handle.net/10107/4675439.

[34] It is possible that in a later age Griffith Jones would have been a nonconformist. He was frequently brought before his superiors for departing from church laws and customs. People came from considerable distances to hear his sermons, which were often delivered on mountainsides.

[35] Geraint H. Jenkins, *The Foundations of Modern Wales 1642–1780* (Oxford: Oxford University Press, 1993), p. 181.

Jones and his followers taught an estimated quarter of a million people to read.[36] As a result, by the mid-nineteenth century this scheme and similar initiatives had made Wales one of the most literate countries in the world.[37]

Literacy had a critical impact on musical life. A capacity to engage with written verbal texts was but a step away from an ability to engage with notated music, and this, if the sale of hymn books is a reliable indicator, appears to be what happened in nineteenth-century Wales. Musical literacy circulated among the working class in two phases: 'yr hen nodiant' ('old notation' – or staff notation), and the more popular tonic sol-fa, which was introduced in the 1860s. The sales figures for *Llyfr Tonau Cynulleidfaol* (Congregational Tune Book) by John Roberts (Ieuan Gwyllt; 1822–77), which was put out in staff notation in 1859 (17,000 copies) and sol-fa in 1863 (25,000 copies), are usually deployed to illustrate the popularity of the sol-fa system, especially because of the speed at which stocks were exhausted.[38] But it is worth noting that the book contained almost no verbal text beyond its preface: it was a *tune* book organised into metric forms to which words might be applied. Yet even in 1859, 17,000 people, the equivalent of a third of the total population of Wales's largest town at that time, were able to engage meaningfully with staff and stave notation.

Nonconformist chapels quickly became centres of communal life in which congregational singing functioned both as an act of devotion and a mode of social leisure: most of the choral societies so formed also competed at eisteddfodau. Other agents for social reform, such as the temperance movement, used musical practice as a form of 'rational recreation'. But the term had a different nuance in Wales than in England, where it was used by more elevated classes to define self-improving pastimes among the working class that were worthy of their benevolence. In Wales, the engagement with choralism was more instinctive, spontaneous, organic and in all senses popular.

Genders and Diasporas

From at least the mid-nineteenth century discrimination against female musicians was less apparent in Wales than elsewhere. This might, at least in

---

[36] John Davies, Nigel Jenkins, Menna Baines and Peredur I. Lynch, eds., *The Welsh Academy Encyclopaedia of Wales* (Cardiff: University of Wales Press, 2008), p. 424.
[37] For an overview of the history of publishing in Wales, see Philip Henry Jones and Eiluned Rees, eds., *A Nation and Its Books: A History of the Book in Wales* (Aberystwyth: National Library of Wales, 1998).
[38] The 1859 edition has been digitised by the National Library of Wales: http://hdl.handle.net/10107/4814268.

part, be due to the prominence of vocal and especially mixed-voice choral music, which is democratised by necessity. When the Welsh Choral Union famously won the choral contest at the Crystal Palace in 1872 and 1873, a moment of vast importance in Welsh music history, national heroines were lauded in equal proportion to heroes, and this had a lasting effect. The historian John Rosselli, writing of the development of music in nineteenth-century Italy, noted the myriad inhibitions that women musicians endured, even in a country with such a buoyant tradition of vocal music, because of the weighty authority of the Catholic Church and the imposition of the values of a social elite.[39] There were fewer such impediments in Wales, and nonconformity had the opposite effect: it was the church of the common people in which the laity were able to organise themselves culturally rather than having their spirituality and modes of operation imposed from above.[40] Ministers were often itinerant, so their individual influence was not sustained, and there was consequently a strong tradition of lay leadership. Choralism was a product of this cultural process and it probably also contributed to a tradition in which women became more broadly prominent in the country's musical life. There are examples of communities supporting women musicians: for instance, a committee was formed at Dowlais in 1863 for the sole purpose of supporting the musical training of Megan Watts Hughes (1847–1907), the local soloist of the Gwent and Morganwg Choral Association, and this included her studentship at the Royal Academy of Music.[41]

Even when male choirs became extremely popular in the second half of the nineteenth century, it was in parallel with other formulations in which women were either constituents or the leading proponents. One of the first and best to rise through the ranks of choralism was Sarah Edith Wynne (Eos Cymru; 1842–97). She was raised in Flintshire, joined the Holywell Choral Society when only nine years old, took to singing Welsh airs as a soloist while in her teens and by the 1860s was one of the stars of London's musical life. There were many other famous female mentors. The writings of the hymn poet Ann Griffiths (1776–1805) were an inspiration for many

---

[39] John Rosselli, *The Opera Industry in Italy from Cimarosa to Verdi: The Role of the Impresario* (Cambridge: Cambridge University Press, 1984) and John Rosselli, *Music and Musicians in Nineteenth-Century Italy* (Portland, OR: Amadeus Press, 1991).

[40] R. Tudur Jones, *Faith and the Crisis of a Nation: Wales 1890–1914*, ed. by Robert Pope and trans. by Sylvia Prys Jones (Cardiff: University of Wales Press, 2004), pp. 38–39.

[41] David Morgans, *Music and Musicians of Merthyr and District* (Merthyr Tydfil: H. W. Southey, 1922), p. 118. Morgans gives her birth date as 1842, and other subsequent sources follow him. However, census records state that she was four years old in 1851. She was born Megan Watts; Watts Hughes was her married name, and her first name sometimes appears in anglicised form as Margaret.

later texts that were set to hymn tunes. Maria Jane Williams was among the most important of the traditional song collectors, and her legacy was taken up by women such as Ruth Herbert Lewis (1871–1946), Mary Davies (1855–1930), Grace Gwyneddon Davies (1878–1944) and Dora Herbert Jones (1890–1974), who were leading figures in the Welsh Folk-Song Society. Maria Jane Williams's friend and patron Lady Llanover was a major figure in the Celtic revival, not merely as a benefactor but as a strategist who acted as a catalyst for others. The teacher and conductor Clara Novello Davies (Pencerddes Morgannwg; 1861–1943) had a significant influence on singing in the late Victorian and Edwardian period and was one of the first musicians to forge a career as a professional musician with the future Welsh capital as her base. Many, possibly most, of the greatest harpists and singers have been women, including Nansi Richards (Telynores Maldwyn; 1888–1979), who was acknowledged by the great twentieth-century virtuoso harpist Osian Ellis as 'Queen of the Harp'. Composers such as Morfydd Llwyn Owen (1891–1918) and Grace Williams (1906–77) rose significantly above the mediocrity that characterised the work of most of their male counterparts.

From its foundation, the University of Wales admitted women as students and teachers – Dora Herbert Jones was one such. A review of the University in 1916 noted that 'absolute equality of the sexes has always been a fundamental principle of its charter' and even at the time, the review could note that 'women [formed a] ... large proportion of its students'.[42] And there has been a parallel tradition that has prevailed to modern times in which women have often played a leading part in radical political movements.[43] It is easy to speculate that this feature of Welsh musical life owes much to the absence in Wales of those Georgian and Victorian metropolitan agencies discussed earlier in this chapter that elsewhere implicitly nurtured male domination, but an important reason for the ease with which women navigated musical life was their place in what was primarily a working-class society. Women's engagement with singing in the home and locality was natural. Eisteddfod contests were organised into categories, some, but not all, by gender, but contestants almost always assumed a role representative of the place from which they came. It

---

[42] *Final Report of the Royal Commission on University Education in Wales* (London: HMSO, 1918), p. 68. These points were being made to encourage the University to move yet further in recruiting women to its teaching staff and to have them routinely represented in its senate.

[43] See Angela V. John, ed., *Our Mothers' Land: Chapters in Welsh Women's History 1830–1939* (Cardiff: University of Wales Press, 1991).

followed that all competitors of genuine talent were eagerly sought, encouraged and celebrated, and gender was seldom used as a barrier.

Clara Novello Davies and her Welsh Ladies' Choir were victors at the famous Welsh eisteddfod held as part of the Chicago World's Fair in 1893. The fact that an eisteddfod was held as a component of such an event is illustrative of the remarkable reputation that Wales was gaining as a 'land of song'. There were Welsh colonies in Patagonia, Oceania and North America, and in each place, the visible indicator of the Welsh presence was a nonconformist chapel that hosted the hymn-singing festivals known as cymanfaoedd canu, and eisteddfodau.[44] Welsh choirs toured the world, performing to packed houses in what had developed into a formulaic 'Welsh' idiom, and money was to be made. Individual musicians made a good living by travelling the world singing, adjudicating eisteddfodau or conducting. Remarkably, this brand of Welsh music, which developed into a commercial stereotype, was to continue for most of the century, but it ran in parallel with other important developments set in motion early in the new century, when such stereotypes were challenged.

Traditions and Disruptions

By the second decade of the twentieth century it was possible to view Welsh music with equivocation: to see amid the buoyancy of its popular traditions the possibility that it was less a beneficiary of them than a casualty. The repetitive cycle of eisteddfodau and cymanfaoedd canu had stimulated a remarkable level of popular musical participation, created a choral repertoire and ensured the survival of traditional song. Furthermore, the eisteddfod system had provided a structure that assured continuities. The concern focused on whether all this was at the expense of 'progress'. Cyril Jenkins (1885–1978), a Swansea-born composer who spent most of his life travelling the globe as an adjudicator, organist, choral conductor and composer, was one of the most intrepid critics of what he identified as the insular and self-absorbed Welsh music establishment, by which he meant the National Eisteddfod committee and the small coterie of academic musicians attached to the University of Wales. In 1913 he delivered the first of many pronouncements aimed at this group. 'Wales', he said, 'has no composer of the first, or even the second rank'.[45] It has to be

---

[44] See Ronald Rees, *A Nation of Singing Birds: Sermon and Song in Wales and among the Welsh in North America* (Talybont: Y Lolfa, 2021).

[45] Quoted in David Ian Allsobrook, *Music for Wales* (Cardiff: University of Wales Press, 1992), p. 42.

said that Jenkins was himself no stranger to mediocrity if his own compositions are anything to go by, but otherwise, he had an important point. There was no body of art music repertoire of any discernible worth and no prospect of it emerging; and if it had, there would have been neither a resident body of educated professional musicians to perform it nor dedicated edifices in which it could be heard.

It was against this background that a Royal Commission on University Education in Wales was assembled in 1916, the year that the Welsh Liberal politician David Lloyd George (1863–1945) became prime minister. The Commission's purpose was straightforward: 'to inquire into the organisation and work of the University of Wales and its three constituent Colleges', and consider improvements in its organisation, constitution, functions and powers.[46] Its conclusions had direct and transformative implications for the musical life of Wales. The Commission was chaired by Richard Burton Haldane (Viscount Haldane; 1856–1928) and among its eight other members was William Henry Hadow (1859–1937), a former Oxford University music academic and a talented musician and scholar, but also a rounded intellectual destined to hold senior positions in English universities. The wisdom contained in the report, certainly as far as music is concerned, owes much to Hadow's interventions and Haldane's accommodation of them. Both were men of considerable enlightenment and organisational flair who have been treated with undue lightness by historians.

Two things are especially striking in the final report delivered in 1918: the extent to which music was considered as rigorously and conscientiously as any other subject in the University's curriculum, including technology, the sciences, agriculture and Celtic studies; and the obvious intent on the part of the Commission that the University of Wales should become a national agency charged with the maintenance and elevation of the nation's musical standards. The idea of the University having a national role was prominent in the British government's thinking. By this time the three Welsh colleges (Bangor, Aberystwyth and Cardiff) were components of a federal University of Wales, but there was concern that they were overly focused on 'local interests' at the expense of 'the whole principality'. This concern had particular importance by 1914 when the idea of a National (Welsh) School of Medicine was under consideration. It was felt that for the developing university to fulfil a national role and engage public interest

---

[46] *Final Report*, p. 9.

in this development, there needed to be revisions to its constitution and its operational practices.⁴⁷

Among the Commission's final recommendations were the strengthening of the music departments in each of the three constituent colleges, advocacy for a closer liaison between the university and Welsh primary and secondary schools, the extension of the remit of the University of Wales Press to publish Welsh music and, most radically, the immediate implementation of a structure that would see the University engage with bodies such as national and local eisteddfodau, to raise standards and create a greater understanding of the music of the European classical tradition.

The Commission was aware that its interventions might be interpreted as an imposition, especially by eisteddfod organisers: 'It is obvious that here great care would have to be exercised in order to avoid any appearance of patronage or interference.' But equally, it did not hold back from trenchant criticism, most based on the evidence of Welsh witnesses. Due deference was paid to the richness of Welsh musical life and its traditions, but it was noted that at the 1916 Eisteddfod only one string quartet had entered, and the prize for a work of chamber music had attracted no competitors at all. It concluded that 'to a large number of the Welsh people the whole literature of symphonic and concerted music is virtually a sealed book'. Even cymanfaoedd canu did not escape castigation: it was noted that the cymanfa held at the National Eisteddfod in 1917 'was marred by the inclusion of some modern sentimental tunes which had no right to any place in such a gathering'. The general conclusion was that: 'Although there is much singing in the country, it must be confessed that there is no corresponding progress in musical taste and knowledge.'⁴⁸

The commissioners were clearly aware that their judgements could be at odds with those of the people to whom they were directed, and sensitive to the reality that their recommendations would be understood in cultural as well as practical terms:

> Closely connected to the above [criticisms] is the curious fact that a high proportion of the conductors of the smaller choirs, and precentors and the teachers of music classes are untrained; frequently they are artisans who have

---

⁴⁷ The quoted passages are from a Treasury Minute dated 30 January 1915 (GB-Lna T 1/11948). This and other documents that provide a background to the Commission and the relationship between the government and the University of Wales are included in Treasury files primarily concerned with the funding of a Welsh School of Medicine and of the University of Wales more generally. The files include a letter dated 29 November 1915 from the governing body of the University of Wales, which requests a Royal Commission.

⁴⁸ *Final Report*, p. 85.

enjoyed no educational advantages beyond elementary school. In most cases they refuse to give way to the professional musicians, and often for good reason. Their musical instinct, their unselfish though unrequited labours, and their tact in the management of men enable them to maintain an influence over their fellow singers which many trained musicians entirely fail to secure. One would be sorry to see this unique democratic factor disappear.[49]

The strategy recommended by the Commission, which was subsequently put in place, involved a twofold arrangement. The University of Wales would 'establish an office of Musical Director' who would have primacy in the organisation of music across all three colleges, and that same person would also be chair of a 'Council of Music in Wales', the membership of which would include the professors from the other two colleges and representatives from other interested bodies such as the Association of Headmasters and Headmistresses, the Welsh Folk-Song Society and the National Eisteddfod Association. Various suggestions were made as to how this Council should conduct its business, but it was made abundantly clear that it should act as 'the supreme consultative body on all matters with which the musical education of Wales is concerned'.[50] It was equally obvious that 'musical education' was to be understood in its widest sense and not just as it applied to formal, institutional curricula. The Council was to encourage 'an embodiment and expression of Welsh nationality in music [but] not by excluding or discouraging the practice of the great masterpieces of other countries'.[51]

Perhaps mindful of how ill-advised it would be to imply that such measures were fashioned on English tastes, it cited a surprisingly different model:

> Such a Council might do for music in Wales what, rather more than half a century ago, a group of enthusiasts did for that of Russia. The material on which Moussorgsky [sic] and his friends set to work was certainly not richer than that which is at the disposal of Welsh musicians to-day: the great fabric of Russian music which they have built up is a standing example of the value of a national movement widely conceived and skilfully treated.[52]

It was clear that the success of these proposals would depend on the principal executant: the new 'Director of Music'. The University looked beyond Wales and appointed Henry Walford Davies (1869–1941) to the vacant chair at Aberystwyth, which would be combined with the wider responsibilities.[53] A former Royal College of Music scholar, a composition

---

[49] Ibid.   [50] Ibid., p. 87.   [51] Ibid.   [52] Ibid., p. 88.
[53] Davies was of Welsh parentage and had been born in Oswestry on the Welsh border.

pupil of both C. H. H. Parry and Stanford, at the time of his appointment he was organist and choirmaster of the Temple Church. Davies held the post from 1919 to 1926, but he continued to chair the Council until his death in 1941, by which time he had succeeded Elgar as Master of the King's Music. He was a skilled composer, but above all a masterful communicator on music, especially through the new medium of the wireless. He also guided the Council of Music to set up music appreciation classes in rural and urban areas for working people. In all his work he had the desired effect of instilling a greater attachment to the mainstream of European music without obliterating the traditions that already flourished.

The composer David Wynne (1900–83) claimed half a century after the Council of Music was formed that it had 'played a greater part in changing the musical attitude of Welshmen than probably any other single factor'.[54] He was probably right in that the major consequence of the Haldane Report was that it altered the course of Welsh music. Traditional song, including cerdd dant, along with the multiplicity of musical practices that were embraced by eisteddfodau and chapel culture, had been the products of essentially organic processes. The Council of Music in Wales was prescriptive: the first official body instituted in the country with the intention of steering music in a unified direction. Walford Davies should probably be judged as popular and successful, but neither he nor his acolytes were devoid of elitist cultural baggage. He had little good to say about another influence that was active in Wales as strongly as it was elsewhere by the 1920s: the rise of new forms of commercial popular music.

Davies had little interest in commercial popular music, which he often referred to as 'jazz bands'. Others were capable of greater discrimination. Ross McKibbin has referred to a middlebrow canon that emerged at this time: a form of 'respectable' light music that captured the attention of a vast sector of the public between the wars.[55] This music, characterised by heavily programmatic, usually romantic content, eclipsed even the favourites of the Victorian music hall in popularity. It came to Wales in live performances, through the bands of silent movie houses, and later the talkies, the gramophone and BBC radio. It also ushered in romanticised performance conventions, including highly sentimental presentation formats of traditional Welsh song. Surprisingly, these developments

---

[54] Quoted in Meic Stephens, ed., *The Arts in Wales 1950–75* (Cardiff: The Welsh Arts Council, 1979), p. 9.

[55] Ross McKibbin, *Classes and Cultures, England 1918–51* (Oxford: Oxford University Press, 1998), chapter 10.

caused neither the eisteddfod nor the musical life of chapels to slip into terminal decline. Rather, different music cultures ran in parallel: the musical practices that had emerged in the nineteenth century; an increasing awareness of the European classical tradition; and the multifaceted forms of popular music. It would be a serious mistake, however, to assume that individuals or any social segments aligned themselves to just one of those options.

The first Welsh musician to attain truly global celebrity was Ivor Novello (1893–1951). Born in Cardiff, he spent little time in Wales after his childhood, but took advantage of the changing age in which he lived to create a metropolitan and transatlantic musical life. Novello, like so many others, benefited from new media that were developing exponentially. The BBC's output from Wales from the time it started in 1923 included eisteddfodau and hymn-singing programmes based on the cymanfa ganu format, but its most popular radio programme in the middle of the century was *Welsh Rarebit*, which was broadcast throughout the UK on Saturday evenings. The producer from 1941 was Mai Jones (1899–1960), one of the most brilliant Welsh musicians of her generation, and the composer of the perennial hit 'We'll Keep a Welcome in the Hillside'. The success of *Welsh Rarebit* was founded on her understanding of how popular music and its reception had changed. She had spent years playing and travelling with London dance bands and had a rounded outlook. She based her productions on the clever, multifaceted formatting of nationwide US radio shows.

Postwar Wales benefited from a new level of professionalisation in the music industry. The BBC Welsh Orchestra, originally formed as a small light-music orchestra, was eventually expanded to a symphony orchestra with a new name: the BBC National Orchestra of Wales. The Welsh National Opera, which had originated as a part-time company using a largely amateur chorus, became full-time and professional in the 1970s. By 2009 both organisations had purpose-built venues in the Welsh capital. In the same period the first recognisable school of Welsh art music composers emerged, including Grace Williams, William Mathias and Alun Hoddinott.

Equally important were developments in popular music. A new breed of popular music stars emerged in the 1960s, including Tom Jones and Shirley Bassey, who exceeded the level of celebrity enjoyed by Ivor Novello. It could be argued that the most interesting and original developments came in the late 1980s and 1990s with pop groups such as Catatonia, Stereophonics, The Manic Street Preachers, Super Furry

Animals and Gorky's Zygotic Mynci; some using the English language, some Welsh, some bilingual. Each band was commercially successful – some in the Anglo-American market – but they were all distinctive, Welsh and original, so much so that their collective endeavour made theirs the first 'school' of Welsh music to be given a name: 'Cŵl Cymru'. The question of whether the label is meaningful or just convenient could hardly be more interesting. Here, too, the answer lies in both musical content and wider contextual factors.

CHAPTER 2

Words for Music
Describing Musical Practices in Medieval Welsh Literature

Helen Fulton

In the early medieval Welsh prose tale, *Culhwch ac Olwen*, the young hero Culhwch comes to Arthur's court seeking help from the great king in his quest to find Olwen, the woman he is destined to marry. Arriving at the court, Culhwch is barred at the gate by an energetic porter who says that the meal has begun ('kyllell a edyw ymwyt', 'knife has gone into meat') and Culhwch and his men will have to be entertained overnight in the hostel outside the feast-hall, where the hospitality for them will include 'gwreic y gyscu gennyt, a didan gerdeu rac dy deulin' ('a woman to sleep with you and pleasant songs performed for you').[1] Music and singing were staple entertainments of noble courts in Wales, as elsewhere in medieval Europe, and references to the performance and practice of music, to musical instruments, and to the reception of musical events by audiences abound in the literature of medieval Wales.

The court poetry surviving from the eleventh to thirteenth centuries was sung at the courts of the independent princes of Wales, men such as Owain Gwynedd and Llywelyn ap Iorwerth, who ruled their territories in defiance of the Norman lordships encroaching to the east and south.[2] The collection of prose tales known as the *Mabinogion* was also composed during these centuries, providing intriguing images, mediated through folktale imaginings, of court life in the regions of *pura Wallia* (that is, independent Wales outside the Norman lordships). When Llywelyn ap Gruffudd, the last independent prince of Wales, was killed by the armies of Edward I in 1282, the age of the princes came to an end, and with it the end of princely patronage for the

---

[1] Rachel Bromwich and D. Simon Evans, eds., *Culhwch ac Olwen: An Edition and Study of the Oldest Arthurian Tale* (Cardiff: University of Wales Press, 1992), lines 98–99. The editors date the tale to about 1100. For a translation of the whole tale, see Sioned Davies, ed. and trans., *The Mabinogion* (Oxford: Oxford University Press, 2007), pp. 179–213. All translations given in this chapter are mine, unless otherwise credited.

[2] For the history of the Norman settlements in Wales and their social and political consequences, see R. R. Davies, *The Age of Conquest: Wales 1063–1415* (Oxford: Oxford University Press, 2000).

Map 2.1 The lands of the Welsh princes, *c.*1200. © Helen Fulton

2 Words for Music in Medieval Welsh Literature

Map 2.2 The Principality and the Marcher Lordships, c.1400. © Helen Fulton

poetry, storytelling and music that filled the courts. In time, a new elite class emerged in Wales, the uchelwyr (noblemen), who took on the role of patrons of Welsh culture and supported the poets, musicians and entertainers who performed at their gentry houses, at abbeys and priories, and – increasingly from the late fourteenth century – in the burgeoning market towns of the March, the borderlands between Wales and England where multiple languages and cultural practices co-existed.

In this large body of surviving poetry and prose from medieval Wales we find many references to making music and its impact on noble and urban audiences. What comes across clearly is the dependence of both poetry and storytelling on music; court poetry was recited or sung to the accompaniment of music, while stories such as those from the *Mabinogion*, intended to be recited aloud, are punctuated by short verses and dramatic set pieces that may signify a musical intervention. The musical instruments named in the literature are similar to those used in other European countries in the Middle Ages, though made locally and thus distinctive to Wales. The main stringed instruments were the crwth (crowd), a small and easily portable instrument, and the telyn (harp), a high-status instrument signifying nobility.[3] We also find references to pipes (pibau) and drum (tabwrdd), the latter borrowed from Middle English or French *tabour*, which suggests that the instrument was similar to ones used in France and England. An instrument called the timpan, borrowed ultimately from Latin *tympanum*, probably through Middle English or French, is recorded in Wales from the thirteenth century and is a type of stringed instrument similar to a lyre.[4] While a few literary references to music evoke a religious context of sung masses, others conjure up secular entertainment that includes dancing as well as singing in the halls of noble lords.

The Combined Arts of Music and Poetry

The medieval Welsh word for music, cerdd, documented from the thirteenth century, also signifies a number of other things, particularly 'craft', 'song', 'poetry' or 'musical instrument', which indicates the close links

---

[3] On the origins of these terms and their links with similar instruments in Ireland, see A. O. H. Jarman, 'Telyn a Chrwth', *Llên Cymru*, 6 (1960–61), 154–175. See also Sally Harper, 'Instrumental Music in Medieval Wales', *North American Journal of Welsh Studies*, 4 (2004), 20–42.

[4] *Geiriadur Prifysgol Cymru/A Dictionary of the Welsh Language* (*GPC*) gives the meanings 'drum, kettledrum, tambourine; unknown (?stringed) musical instrument'. *GPC* is accessible online www.welsh-dictionary.ac.uk/ (accessed 20 July 2021). The instrument was also used in Ireland (Ir. *tiompán*).

between music, poetry, and the craft of making instruments.[5] It also confirms that both music and poetry were regarded as types of professional craft, moderated by their own particular standards and hierarchies. The related form cerddor, signifying the performer, is also recorded from the thirteenth century and carries a similar range of meanings, including 'singer', 'musician', 'storyteller' and 'craftsman'. This semantic flexibility can sometimes create ambiguity in literary texts. In the scene with the porter in *Culhwch ac Olwen* cited above, the porter tells Culhwch that the only people who would be allowed to interrupt the feast would be 'mab brenhin gvlat teithiawc, neu y gerdawr a dycco y gerd' ('the son of a rightful territorial king, or a craftsman bringing his craft').[6] This may indicate a musician, but it might just as easily signify another type of useful artisan, one who makes shoes or polishes swords, as we see when Cei pretends that he is 'yslipanwr cledyueu goreu yn y byt' ('the best sword-polisher in the world') in order to get past another obstructive porter and gain entrance to the court of Wrnach the Giant.[7] The modern Welsh word for music, cerddoriaeth, does not seem to have been in circulation before the late fifteenth century and was perhaps coined to make a decisive break from the ambiguity of cerdd. However, the Welsh term miwsig (also musig) was borrowed either from English 'music' or directly from French *musique* at quite an early stage, at least the thirteenth century, which suggests there was a perceived need for such a term. Already by the fourteenth century (and certainly earlier in oral tradition), writers were making a distinction between cerdd dafod (literally 'tongue craft') signifying 'poetic art, poetry' (particularly strict-metre poetry), and cerdd dant ('string craft'), where tant is an old word (documented from the ninth century) meaning 'string of an instrument'. Sally Harper describes cerdd dant as 'high-status "bardic" music for harp and *crwth*, conceived within the context of the noble household and functioning as an essential adjunct to sophisticated vernacular poetry'.[8]

References to poets in the Welsh Laws imply that they were regarded as musicians who accompanied their poems with a harp (a smaller instrument

---

[5] The same semantic range also applies to the cognate Old Irish word, *cerd*, which suggests a musical tradition that was common to the Celtic-speaking peoples of Britain and Ireland and thus predates the Middle Ages. While *GPC* gives the earliest recorded example of cerdd from the thirteenth century (in the Black Book of Carmarthen), the word was in circulation considerably earlier than this. This caveat applies to most of the Welsh musical terms cited in this chapter: we can be sure that music was played in Wales well before the thirteenth century.
[6] Bromwich and Evans, eds., *Culhwch ac Olwen*, ll. 91–92.   [7] Ibid., ll. 775–776.
[8] Sally Harper, *Music in Welsh Culture before 1650: A Study of the Principal Sources* (Aldershot: Ashgate, 2007), p. 2.

than the modern concert harp).⁹ The Laws, an unstable set of texts in Latin and Welsh emerging from the twelfth century but surviving in copies only from the mid-thirteenth century, describe two kinds of poets who were officers in the king's household, supported by the cerddorion, or musicians, who worked for the poets.¹⁰ The pencerdd, or 'chief poet', and the bardd teulu, 'bard of the household', were ranked among the officers of the court and had specific privileges as well as specific duties:

> The bard of the household (*bardd teulu*)... is entitled to sit next to the captain of the household (*penteulu*) at the three special feasts, so as to have the harp put into his hand...
>
> When a song is required to be sung, the chaired bard (*pencerdd*) starts, [singing] first of God, [and secondly] of the king to whom the court belongs, and if he has nothing to sing of him, let him sing of another king. After the chaired bard, the bard of the household is to sing three songs of some other kind ... Every harp *pencerdd* is entitled to twenty-four pence from the young *cerddorion* who want to give up the horsehair harp and be competent *cerddorion*.¹¹

In other words, the master harpist would receive a fee of twenty-four pence from each apprentice harpist who exchanged his inferior horsehair harp for a more professional one.

The fourteenth-century grammatical tracts known as the Bardic Grammar, a sort of handbook of grammar, phonics and metrics for poets, describes three grades of poet, the pencerdd, the bardd teulu and the clerwr, the latter regarded as a popular entertainer performing his own and others' songs at informal gatherings.¹² Unlike the beirdd cadeiriog ('chaired bards') – that is, poets awarded their own chair at a king's court as a mark of status – and the household poets, all of whom had been formally trained in the appropriate style, language and metres of court poetry, the clêr¹³ were untrained, or rather self-trained, and thus objects of disdain to the higher grades of poet. The Bardic Grammar clearly distinguishes

---

⁹ On early Welsh musical instruments, see Chapter 7 in this volume, and Harper, *Music in Welsh Culture*, pp. 18–20.
¹⁰ On the manuscript context of the Welsh Laws (often referred to as the 'Laws of Hywel Dda'), see Dafydd Jenkins, ed. and trans., *The Law of Hywel Dda: Law Texts from Medieval Wales*, The Welsh Classics Vol. 2 (Llandysul: Gwasg Gomer, 1986), pp. xxi–xxiii. The Laws have been transcribed from the major sources as part of the online project *Rhyddiaith Gymraeg/Welsh Prose 1300–1425*, available at www.rhyddiaithganoloesol.caerdydd.ac.uk/cy/texts.php?genre=law (accessed 30 July 2021).
¹¹ Jenkins, *Law of Hywel Dda*, p. 20 and pp. 38–39. The Law states, regarding the captain of the household: 'It is right for him to put the harp into the hand of the bard of the household at the three special feasts' (p. 9), which are Christmas, Easter and Whitsun.
¹² On the Bardic Grammar, see Harper, *Music in Welsh Culture*, pp. 25–27.   ¹³ Plural of clerwr.

between the prydydd, that is, any trained bard, and the lowest kind of clerwr:

> Ny pherthyn ar brydyd ymyrru ar glerwryaeth, yr aruer ohonei, kanys gwrthwyneb yw eu kreffteu. Kanys krefft prydyd yw kanmawl, a chlotuori, a digrifhau, a gwneuthur molyant a gogonyant a didanwch, a dosparthus yw y gerd, a barnu a ellir arnei; a chrefft y klerwr kroessan yw anghanmawl, ac anglotuori, a goganu, a gwneuthur kywilyd a mefyl ac anglot, a chroessangerd anossparthus yw heb allel barnu arnei, kanys ymboergerd vvdyr yw.[14]

> (The prydydd should have nothing to do with clerwriaeth [popular song], its style, since their crafts are directly opposed to each other. For the craft of the prydydd is to praise, and to celebrate, and to entertain, and to create eulogy and diversion, and their poetry is classifiable and can be assessed [i.e. by judges who maintain the bardic order]; but the craft of the clerwr croessan [ribald minstrel] is to dispraise and to disparage and to satirise, and to create disgrace and shame and dishonour, and minstrel-song is unclassifiable and ineligible to be assessed, since it is foul drivel-song.)

In other contexts, the clêr are included among the general range of entertainers who might perform at the courts of the nobility and gentry, as well as at less exalted venues (see below, 'Court Poetry and Music after 1282', for examples).

The Bardic Grammar includes a taxonomy, using the traditional method of triads, which confirms the overlap between poetry and music, and which indicates that poets sang or recited their work, at least on some occasions, to their own accompaniment on the harp. Describing the art of prydyddiaeth, that is, the art of poetry practised by licensed bards, the compiler says:

> Tri ryw brifgerd ysyd, nyt amgen: kerd dant, kerd vegin, a cherd dauawt.
> Teir prifgerd tant ysyd, nyt amgen: kerd grwth, kerd delyn, a cherd timpan.
> Teir prifgerd megin ysyd, nyt amgen: organ, a phibeu, a cherd y got.
> Teir prifgerd tauawt ysyd: prydu, a dachanu, a chanu gan delyn.[15]

> (There are three main types of poetic/musical art, namely: cerdd dant [string music], cerdd fegin [wind music], and cerdd dafod [poetry or song].

---

[14] G. J. Williams and E. J. Jones, goln, *Gramadegau'r Penceirddiaid* (Caerdydd: Gwasg Prifysgol Cymru, 1934), tt. 56–57. The Bardic Grammar has been transcribed from the major sources as part of the project *Rhyddiaith Gymraeg/Welsh Prose 1300–1425* www.rhyddiaithganoloesol.caerdydd.ac.uk/en/texts.php?genre=grammar (accessed 13 August 2021).

[15] *Gramadegau'r Penceirddiaid*, t. 57.

There are three main types of string music, namely: the music of the crwth, the music of the harp, and the music of the timpan.

There are three main types of wind instrument, namely: organ, and pipes, and bagpipe.[16]

There are three main types of cerdd dafod: [praise] poetry, and satire, and singing with a harp.)

The hierarchy of poets, and their professional status compared to untrained minstrels and entertainers, were maintained by a process of training and apprenticeship which became increasingly formalised during the later Middle Ages. The earliest recorded eisteddfod, during which poets displayed their skills in order to be assessed by bardic judges and granted a licence, took place at Carmarthen in about 1452, but earlier competitions must also have taken place throughout Wales, as is suggested by the Bardic Grammar. Large meetings were held at Caerwys (Flintshire) in 1523 and again in 1567, and it was at the 1523 eisteddfod that the document known as the Statute of Gruffudd ap Cynan was produced, with a revised version appearing at the 1567 meeting.[17] Purporting to codify bardic practice from the time of the great twelfth-century ruler of southern Gwynedd (north Wales), the Statute sets out the regulations governing both cerdd dant and cerdd dafod, including the system of apprenticeship, the classification of poets and musicians, metrical requirements and the appropriate conduct for members of the bardic order. According to David Klausner, at the 1567 eisteddfod 'approximately fifty-three poets, harpers, and crwth players were awarded degrees according to the regulations of the statute'.[18]

While it is clear that poets often sang or recited their own material, there was also, within the bardic order, a class of professional reciter known as the datgeiniad. This person seems to have acted as a kind of stand-in for a licensed poet, reciting the poet's work from memory either in the presence of the poet or when the poet was unable to be present in person.[19] The more

---

[16] Welsh cod, 'bag, pouch', is borrowed directly from Middle English and is first attested in the fourteenth century.

[17] The statutes of 1523 and 1567 have been edited and translated by David Klausner in *Records of Early Drama: Wales*, Records of Early English Drama (Toronto: University of Toronto Press, 2005), pp. 159–165 (translation on pp. 349–356) and pp. 172–181 (translation on pp. 360–368). Caerwys was a Welsh borough and important commercial centre. David Klausner speculates that it may have been chosen as the site of the two sixteenth-century eisteddfodau because of its proximity to Mostyn Hall, home of the Mostyn family of patrons. See Klausner, *Records of Early Drama: Wales*, p. xlvii.

[18] Klausner, *Records of Early Drama: Wales*, p. lxxi.

[19] Bleddyn Owen Huws assumes that poems were sometimes sent to patrons to be recited, in the form of a message from the poet, especially when the poet was asking for gifts or sending thanks for gifts.

humble datgeiniad acted as a kind of servant to the master poet, according to the Statute of Gruffudd ap Cynan: 'And for a master poet or a teacher in poetry it is fitting that a declaimer (*atgeiniad*, a later spelling) perform the poem that he composes ... and it is not fitting that a declaimer should travel a circuit, except by following a master craftsman of poetry or of music'.[20] The more skilled datgeiniaid were also musicians who could perform on the harp or crwth and were required to know the principal melodies, or ceinciau, which accompanied the poems.[21] Despite the long-standing practice of poetry being accompanied by music, the Statute, perhaps describing sixteenth-century notions of professionalism, makes a clear distinction between the two crafts of cerdd dant and cerdd dafod and insists that no man could be a master of both:

> Hevyd na bo i neb arwain dwy gelvyddyd megis Telynior nev grythor a ffrydyddiaeth nev a chrefft arall nev brydydd yn of ac yn brydydd.[22]
>
> (Also let no one practise two arts, such as a harpist or crwth player practising poetry or another craft, or a poet being both a blacksmith and a poet.)

It seems likely, then, that poets and reciters could perform poetry accompanied either by themselves on a harp or crwth or by professional musicians, who could also play instrumental music, resulting in a certain rivalry between the two crafts. The early fourteenth-century poet Iorwerth Beli recounts an evidently popular anecdote about Maelgwn Gwynedd, the sixth-century king of north Wales who was denounced as a tyrant by the historian Gildas in his *De Excidio Britanniae* ('The Ruin of Britain'), in which he deplores Maelgwn's demonic preference for the praise-songs of his poets, 'the rascally crew yelling forth, like Bacchanalian revellers, full of lies and foaming phlegm', over the religious music of the church.[23] On his way to Môn (Anglesey), Maelgwn reached the Menai strait and ordered his poets and harpists to swim across to the island. The poets, to Iorwerth's satisfaction, came out of it the best:

> Pan ddoethant i'r tir, terfyn Môn,—ar drai,
> Dimai nis talai i'r telynorion!
> Tyst yw Duw ar hyn, tystion—a'i gwybydd:
> Herwydd hardd gynnydd, gynneddf doethion,

See Huws, *Y Canu Gofyn a Diolch, c. 1350–c. 1630* (Caerdydd: Gwasg Prifysgol Cymru, 1998), tt. 128–129.

[20] Klausner, *Records of Early Drama: Wales*, p. 354. For the Welsh, see p. 163, lines 38–39 and p. 164, lines 12–13.
[21] Harper, *Music in Welsh Culture*, p. 16.
[22] Klausner, *Records of Early Drama: Wales*, p. 164, lines 21–22.
[23] Hugh Williams, ed. and trans., *Gildas: De Excidio Britanniae, or the Ruin of Britain* (Gloucester: Dodo Press, 2010) (Originally published in London by The Honourable Society of Cymmrodorion, 1899), p. 28.

Cystal y prydai'r prydyddion—â chynt
Er a nofiesynt, helynt haelion.[24]

(When they came to land on the edge of Môn, on the ebb tide,
You wouldn't give a halfpenny for the harpists!
God is a witness to it, and witnesses know it:
On account of a fine superiority, the natural quality of the wise,
The poets could versify as well as before,
Despite all their swimming, the conduct of noblemen.)

But at other times, poets and musicians respected each other's talents. One of the most moving descriptions of a gifted professional telynor or harpist at work is in the elegy for Siôn Eos ('the nightingale'), composed for him by Dafydd ab Edmwnd (*fl.* c.1450–97) in the mid-fifteenth century. Siôn was hung for the murder of another man in a brawl, and Dafydd laments the waste of such a talent, noting that Siôn would not have been executed under Welsh law but made to pay compensation instead, making the death doubly wasteful. The poet describes Siôn as 'eos y gerdd' ('music's nightingale') and laments the death of this gifted musician whose fingers created music of all kinds, formal and informal, playing treble and bass, mean and descant: 'Nid oes nag angel na dyn/Nad wyl pen gano delyn' ('there is no angel or person who would not weep when he played the harp').[25]

References to Music in Early Court Poetry

From the earliest surviving copies of Welsh court poetry, it is clear that the main function of this ancient art was to heap praise on the regional princes and their families in order to shore up their power in their own territories and to advertise their status to rivals elsewhere. Poetry and music melded together into an art form that was partly celebratory, partly propaganda and partly sheer entertainment for the men and women of the court. The sixth-century poet Taliesin said of his patron Owain ab Urien ruler of Rheged in the 'old north' of Britain, 'iscell kerdglyt clotuawr/escyll gawr gwaywawr llifeit' ('renowned in song, of great fame, like the wing of dawn

---

[24] R. Iestyn Daniel, gol., 'Iorwerth Beli', in *Gwaith Gruffudd ap Dafydd ap Tudur, Gwilym Ddu o Arfon, Trahaearn Brydydd Mawr ac Iorwerth Beli*, gol. N. G. Costigan et al. (Aberystwyth: Canolfan Uwchefrydiau Cymreig a Cheltaidd Prifysgol Cymru, 1995), rhif 15, ll. 35–40. For further discussion of the poem see Patrick K. Ford, 'Performance and Literacy in Medieval Welsh Poetry', *Modern Language Review*, 100 (2005), xxx–xlviii (on p. xli).

[25] Thomas Roberts, gol., *Gwaith Dafydd ab Edmwnd* (Bangor: Bangor Welsh Manuscripts Society, 1914), rhif 42, ll. 67–68, with the editor's note on Siôn Eos on t. 155. For a translation of the whole poem, see Gwyn Williams, trans., *Welsh Poems: Sixth Century to 1600* (London: Faber, 1973), no. 31.

his sharpened spear').²⁶ Following the Norman conquest and settlements along the eastern border and southern coastline of Wales, the court poets of the independent princes of *pura Wallia*, poets known to modern critics as gogynfeirdd (literally 'quite early poets'), continued to practise their craft at public events. Hywel ab Owain Gwynedd (d. 1170) was both a poet and a prince – given the lordship of southern Ceredigion by his father Owain, prince of Gwynedd – and a vigorous military campaigner against the Normans of west Wales.²⁷ In one of his most famous poems, known as 'Gorhoffedd' or 'Celebration', he dedicates his song to a list of women, real or imaginary, whom he has loved. Attributing his poetic gift to God, he moves swiftly from the religious to the secular:

> Cyfarchaf i'r Dewin gwerthefin,—gwyrthfawr,
>   Gwrth ei fod yn Frenin,
> Cysylltu canu cysefin,
> Cerdd foliant, fal y cant Myrddin,
> I'r gwragedd a'i medd fy marddrin
> (Mor hir hwyrweddawg ŷnt am rin!)²⁸

> (I petition the supreme and miraculous Enchanter,
> Because he is King,
> For [the power to] compose song in the traditional manner,
> Praise song, such as Myrddin sang,
> To the women who are worthy of my poetic gift –
> How slow and reluctant they are to meet me in secret!)

It is easy to imagine the entertainment value of this song when delivered in a court setting to a mixed audience of men and women; in it, Hywel compares himself to the legendary Myrddin (Geoffrey of Monmouth's Merlin) who was more famous as a prophet than as a praise-poet. The irreverent tenor of the words – 'am Enerys wyry . . . ni orpo hi deweirdawd' ('for chaste Generys . . . may she not keep her chastity', ll. 71–72) – makes an amusing contrast to the formal rhetoric and metre of the poem, which display Hywel's knowledge of the bardic craft. Though the poem refers to singing (canu), it is not clear whether Hywel is accompanying himself on

---

²⁶ Ifor Williams, ed., *The Poems of Taliesin* (Dublin: Dublin Institute for Advanced Studies, 1968), no. X, 'Marwnat Owein' ('Elegy for Owain'), lines 5–6.
²⁷ For a detailed study of Hywel and his poetry, see Nerys Ann Jones, *Hywel ab Owain Gwynedd: Bardd-Dywysog* (Caerdydd: Gwasg Prifysgol Cymru, 2009).
²⁸ Kathleen A. Bramley, gol., 'Gwaith Hywel ab Owain Gwynedd', in *Gwaith Llywelyn Fardd I ac Eraill o Feirdd y Ddeuddegfed Ganrif*, gol. Kathleen A. Bramley et al. (Caerdydd: Gwasg Prifysgol Cymru, 1994), tt. 103–188, rhif 6, ll. 43–48. For a translation of the whole poem see Joseph P. Clancy, *Medieval Welsh Poems* (Dublin: Four Courts Press, 2003), pp. 136–138. Clancy translates these lines as the opening of a separate poem, while Bramley edits the lines as part of a single poem.

an instrument or whether a musician is supplying the accompaniment, but it is certain that music was involved in the performance of the poem.

For most of the gogynfeirdd, the patronage of a prince was their main source of income and of resources such as clothes, weapons and horses, while the presence of poets and musicians in their courts, singing the praises of the lord and his family, was essential to the status of the princes of Wales before 1282. One of the greatest court poets of the twelfth century was Cynddelw (*fl.* 1155–1200), whose epithet, 'Prydydd Mawr', or 'great poet', indicates the high reputation he held among his contemporaries and later generations. Cynddelw sang the praises of many of the independent princes, including Owain Gwynedd (d. 1170), the son of Gruffudd ap Cynan, saying to Owain: 'Cyrdd ydd awn am ddawn, am ddadwyrain glyw,/Cerddorion amryw am rodd Owain' ('Songs we bring for a blessing, for the elevation of a lord, all kinds of musicians for a gift from Owain').[29] To the Lord Rhys of Deheubarth (Rhys ap Gruffudd, *c.*1132–97), Cynddelw acknowledges his patronage as câr cerddawr ('poet's friend'), and asks to be reconciled to his lord and protected from his anger:

> Wyf cerddawr i'm rhwyf, rhwysg môr-gymlawdd—gwyrdd,
>   Rhwysg ffyrdd cyrdd, cerdd wahawdd,
> Aswyn aserw herw hirflawdd,
> Aswynaf ar udd naf nawdd.[30]

> (I am a singer to my lord, the force of a green sea-tide,
> The rush of song-roads, an invited song,
> Sheltering protection on a tumultuous raid,
> I entreat a noble lord for refuge.)

Despite this co-dependence between poets and their patrons, the court poets did not hesitate to turn their praise into satire – another of the functions of the court poet, according to the Bardic Grammar – if the lord was not generous enough with his gifts. Llywarch ap Llywelyn (*fl.* 1173–1220), who rejoiced in the enigmatic epithet of 'Prydydd y Moch' ('Poet of the Pigs'), sang to the princes of Gwynedd, lords of Aberffraw, whose line culminated in the rule of Llywarch's great hero, Llywelyn Fawr, or Llywelyn ap Iorwerth (d. 1240). Earlier in his career, Llywarch sang a satire to Gruffudd ap Cynan (d. 1200), grandson of Owain Gwynedd

---

[29] Cynddelw, 'Arwyrain Owain Gwynedd' ('Exaltation of Owain Gwynedd'), in *Welsh Court Poems*, ed. by Rhian M. Andrews (Cardiff: University of Wales Press, 2007), no. 2, lines 31–32.

[30] Cynddelw, 'Dadolwch Rhys ap Gruffudd' ('Seeking Reconciliation with Rhys ap Gruffudd'), in *Welsh Court Poems*, ed. by Andrews, no. 16, lines 37–40.

and prince of southern Gwynedd, complaining about Gruffudd's meanness with gifts and his failure to appreciate Llywarch's poetry:

> A thithau, arf cadau cydlid,
> Athrugar, cerddgar, cyfrdelid,
> It hëu fy ngherdd nac ef fid
> Mal hëu rhag moch merierid.[31]

> (And you, weapon of wrathful battles,
> Merciless, music-loving, majestic,
> May casting my song before you not be
> Like pearls being cast before swine.)

The reference to casting pearls before swine (from Matthew 7:6) is suggestive, given Llywarch's nickname, and it may even be the origin of the epithet.[32]

Another of Llywarch's poems was sung to Dafydd ab Owain, composed when this prince was ruler of Gwynedd in 1174–75. Described in the manuscript as awdl fygwth, that is, a poem that threatens the patron with satire if he does not amply reward the poet, the poem is actually closer to an awdl ddyhuddiant, or a poem seeking reconciliation after a falling-out with the patron. If Dafydd will only accept him once more into his court, says Llywarch, he will be rewarded with the finest poetry:

> Gwynygawd dy glod hynod honni
> O angerdd a'm cerdd a'm cymelri.
> Gwelais feirdd yn gryg, nid egrygi,
> Gâl flawdd, yn adrawdd dy wrhydri:
> Cenais dy foliant mal nas ryganant,
>   Milwr pedrydant, pedrydawg ri.[33]

> (Your praise will shine out from being clearly proclaimed
> Through the strength of my song and my passion.
> I saw poets grow hoarse – there's no vanity [in saying this],
> Or fearful hostility – recounting your valour:
> I sang your praise as they never sang it,
> Mighty soldier, powerful king.)

---

[31] Llywarch ap Llywelyn, 'Bygwth Gruffudd ap Cynan' ('Threatening Gruffudd ap Cynan'), in *Welsh Court Poems*, ed. by Andrews, no. 15, lines 11–14. On the historical context, see Andrews, *Welsh Court Poems*, p. 97.

[32] This is Rhian Andrews's suggestion, in her note on these lines. *Welsh Court Poems*, p. 98.

[33] Llywarch ap Llywelyn, 'Bygwth Dafydd, Prydydd y Moch a'i Cant', in *Gwaith Llywarch ap Llywelyn 'Prydydd y Moch'*, gol. Elin M. Jones with Nerys Ann Jones (Caerdydd: Gwasg Prifysgol Cymru, 1991), rhif 2, ll. 39–44.

Court Poetry and Music after 1282

With the death in 1282 of Llywelyn ap Gruffudd, the last independent prince of the regions of Wales outside the Norman Marcher lordships, the days of praise poetry and musical entertainment at princely courts came to an end. Instead, new forms of poetry and song evolved to support a new kind of nobility emerging from the upper ranks of the class of uchelwyr, or freemen. Holding large estates and with influential standing in their own localities, the uchelwyr were the obvious people to hold office in the English crown lordships. These lordships replaced the former territories of the Welsh princes in north and west Wales and became known as the 'Principality'. By virtue of their high office and relative wealth, these uchelwyr became the new nobility of Wales and assumed the role – or perhaps expanded their existing practices – of supporting the prestige arts of poetry and music. The cultural break before and after 1282 was not absolute, with many of the later poets continuing to use the metres (particularly the awdl) and ornate style of the gogynfeirdd. One of the most significant innovations of the post-1282 poets was the adaptation of a less formal metre – the cywydd, rarely used by the gogynfeirdd – to the function of formal court poetry, praise poetry and love poetry, as well as its use for more popular themes such as satire and humour.[34] Performed at the courts and abbeys of the wealthier uchelwyr, these cywyddau (poems in the cywydd metre) gave a name to the new generation of court poets, who are referred to by modern critics as cywyddwyr (that is, poets who regularly use the cywydd metre). With its seven-syllable lines, light-touch syntax and complex system of internal rhyme and alliteration known as cynghanedd, the cywydd was ideally adapted to musical performance and interpretation compared to the more sonorous and linguistically encrusted awdl, a metre that was retained by the cywyddwyr for particularly solemn occasions.

One of the earliest and most famous of the cywyddwyr is Dafydd ap Gwilym (*c*.1320–*c*.1370), who came from the region of Ceredigion, near Aberystwyth, and travelled around west Wales to sing at the houses of patrons. In some of his praise poetry, Dafydd consciously follows some of the style of the gogynfeirdd, as a way of implicitly associating his patrons with the great princes of old. To Ieuan Llwyd of Genau'r Glyn, in Ceredigion, Dafydd composed an awdl praising Ieuan's lineage, his

---

[34] It is more correct to think of the awdl, the cywydd and the third main type of strict metre, the englyn, as umbrella terms for a set of metrical variants within each type. For a very useful description of the Welsh 'strict metres' used by the medieval poets, see Tony Conran, *Welsh Verse* (Bridgend: Seren, 1992), pp. 310–339.

generosity at feasts, and his love of music, all themes that occur frequently in the earlier court poetry: 'Gwaredfeirdd ydiw, gwirodfaeth—cerddawr, / Gwawr a garodd awr y gerddwriaeth' ('He is the redemption of poets, provider of drink to a musician, a lord who loved the minstrel hour').[35] But in his cywyddau, Dafydd dedicates his music and poetry to the service of the two main preoccupations of his poetic art, namely love and nature. The women he pursues in his poetry, whether Dyddgu, Morfudd or unnamed women, have their praises sung far and wide at noble feasts so that their beauty and virtue are known to all:

> Rhoais iddi, rhyw swyddau,
> Rhugl foliant o'r meddiant mau,
> Gwrle telyn ac orloes,
> Gormodd rhodd; gŵr meddw a'i rhoes.
> Heais mal oraihian
> Ei chlod yng Ngwynedd achlân.
> Hydwf y mae'n ehedeg
> Had tew, llyna head teg.
> Pybyr fu pawb ar fy ôl,
> Ai 'Pwy?' oedd ym mhob heol.
> Pater noster annistaw
> Pawb o'r a gant llorfdant llaw
> Ym mhob cyfedd, ryfedd ri,
> Yw ei cherdd yn wych erddi.[36]

> (I gave to her, a few services,
> Fluent praise from my stock,
> The voice of a harp and clock,
> Too great a gift; a drunk man gave it.
> Like a shouting boaster I sowed
> Her praise through the whole of Gwynedd.
> Sturdily it flies,
> A fat seed, that's a fine sowing.
> Staunchly was everyone behind me,
> And their 'Who?' was on every street.
> The sonorous paternoster
> Of all those who play a bass string by hand
> In every feast, a wondrous number,
> Is her song, an excellent one just for her.)

---

[35] Dafydd Johnston et al., goln, *Cerddi Dafydd ap Gwilym* (Caerdydd: Gwasg Prifysgol Cymru, 2010), rhif 7, ll. 27–28.
[36] Johnston et al., goln, *Cerddi Dafydd ap Gwilym*, rhif 99, ll. 9–22.

These lines to Morfudd, offering the poet's love without expectation of reward, confirm the close relationship between poetry, the music needed to perform it and the audience at feasts who listen to the songs. Here as elsewhere Dafydd makes a bold comparison between his secular love songs to women and religious verse, like the 'paternoster', which was also performed to music in church. When a stern friar warns Dafydd against spreading his immoral love songs around the country, Dafydd has his answer ready:

> Cerdd a bair yn llawenach
> Hen ac ieuanc, claf ac iach.
> Cyn rheitied i mi brydu
> Ag i tithau bregethu,
> A chyn iawned ym glera
> Ag i tithau gardota.
> Pand englynion ac odlau
> Yw'r hymnau a'r segwensiau,
> A chywyddau i Dduw lwyd
> Yw llaswyr Dafydd Broffwyd?[37]

> (Music causes happiness
> For young and old, sick and well.
> It is as fitting for me to perform songs
> As for you to preach,
> And it is as right for me to be a minstrel
> As for you to beg.
> What are hymns and sequences
> If not englynion and odes,
> And what are the psalms of the Prophet David
> If not cywyddau to holy God?)

To Dafydd, the songs sung at feasts to please young women are as valid as the prayers sung in church for a higher purpose. As he says, echoing the Bible, 'amser i bregethu/ac amser i gyfanheddu' ('there is a time for preaching and a time for entertaining').[38]

The importance of the harp as a high-status musical instrument, and one played by women as well as men, is suggested by one of Dafydd's love poems to an unnamed woman, in which he describes her as 'hudoles yr hoyw delyn' ('enchantress of the lively harp').[39] Imagining his beloved playing the harp, the poet makes the harp a metaphor for the girl herself, an

---

[37] Johnston et al., goln, *Cerddi Dafydd ap Gwilym*, rhif 148, ll. 51–60.
[38] Ibid., rhif 148, ll. 65–66.
[39] Ibid., rhif 135, l. 48. A poem once attributed to the fifteenth-century female poet Gwerful Mechain, but now thought to be by Gwerful ferch Gutun, a female poet of the mid-sixteenth century, is composed in the form of a request for a harp to liven up the evenings in Gwerful's tavern, implying

instrument built on deceit and betrayal, and yet one which produces an enchanting beauty:

> Da dlyy, wen gymhenbwyll,
> Delyn ariant, tant y twyll.
> Henw yt fydd, tra fo dydd dyn:
> Hudoles yr Hoyw Delyn;
> Enwog y'th wnair, gair gyrddbwyll,
> Armes, telynores twyll.
> Y delyn a adeilwyd
> O radd nwyf, aur o ddyn wyd;
> Mae erni nadd o radd rus
> Ac ysgwthr celg ac esgus;
> Ei chwr y sydd, nid gwŷdd gwyll,
> O ffyrf gelfyddyd Fferyll;
> Ei llorf a'm pair yn llwyrfarw
> O hud gwir ac o hoed garw;
> Twyll yw ebillion honno
> A thruth a gweniaith a thro.
> Deulafn o aur a dalant
> Y dwylo tau yn daly tant;
> Wi o'r wengerdd, wawr wingoeth,
> A fedry di o fydr doeth!⁴⁰
>
> (Well you deserve, clever smart girl,
> A silver harp, the string of deception.
> Your name will be, as long as man may live,
> Enchantress of the Lively Harp.
> You will be made famous, in the words of wise songs,
> In a prophecy, as a harpist of deceit.
> The harp was crafted
> From the dignity of passion (you are a golden girl);
> On it is a carving signifying discouragement
> And an engraving of guile and pretence;
> Its border – not dark is the wood –
> Is made from the shapes of Virgil's art;
> Its pillar causes me sudden death
> From true magic and bitter longing;
> Its pegs are betrayal
> And falsehood and flattery and trickery.
> Your two hands plucking the string

---

that Gwerful herself will play it. See Katie Gramich, ed. and trans., *The Works of Gwerful Mechain* (Peterborough, Canada: Broadview Press, 2018), no. 24.

⁴⁰ Johnston et al, goln, *Cerddi Dafydd ap Gwilym*, rhif 135, ll. 45–64.

>   Are worth two bars of gold.
>   Ah, what a fine song, with your bloom like fine wine,
>   You can make from a well-chosen metre!)

This description of the harp as a physical object, with its wooden frame and pillar and pegs, placed in the context of courtship and the playing of music on feast days, emphasises the role of music in the courts of the nobility and the familiarity of the poets with the musical instruments that accompanied their song.

Dafydd's evident skill with the harp is suggested by one of his poems, in which he describes composing a song on the harp, inspired by his love of Dyddgu. The poet speculates that the young women who hear his song will think it is a poor effort, while the young men will want to sing it themselves to impress their girlfriends. He wants Dyddgu to hear his song in the clear voice of the nightingale: 'Llef eurloyw fygr llafurlais,/Lleddf ddatbing llwybr sawtring Sais' ('a golden bright call of beautiful voice-work, plangent reverberation in the tenor of an Englishman's psaltery').[41] The poet concludes by asserting his confidence in his musical skill: 'Ni wnaeth pibydd ffraeth o Ffrainc/Na phencerdd ryw siffancainc' ('no fluent piper from France nor any master poet has ever composed such a melody for strings').[42] These lines indicate a wide general knowledge of music and musical instruments of the kind used by both English and French musicians. The Welsh word *sawtring* is borrowed either from French or Middle English and refers to a psaltery, a type of stringed instrument played by plucking the strings with the fingers (and Dafydd refers to his *deg ewin*, or 'ten nails' which pluck the strings). The word *siffan*, compounded here with *cainc*, 'tune, melody', is probably a form of the word *sinffan*, borrowed from Middle English *synphan*, another kind of stringed instrument.[43]

In many of his nature poems, Dafydd projects his awareness of music on to those great choristers of the sky, the birds. The skylark is figured as a cleric who sings God's praises:

>   Modd awdur serch, mae'dd ydwyd?
>   Mwyn groyw yw'r llais mewn grae llwyd.

---

[41] Ibid., rhif 91, ll. 27–28. [42] Ibid., rhif 91, ll. 29–30.
[43] For a discussion of this poem and the wider significance of Dafydd's music, see Sally Harper, 'Dafydd ap Gwilym, Poet and Musician', in *Dafydd ap Gwilym.net* (Swansea University, n.d.), http://dafyddapgwilym.net/essays/sally_harper/index_eng.php (accessed 5 July 2021).

> Cathlef lân diddan yw'r dau,
> Cethlydd, awenydd winau.
> Cantor o gapel Celi,
> Coel fydd teg, celfydd wyd di.⁴⁴
>
> (Like an author of love, where are you?
> Gentle and clear is the voice in brown-grey cloth.
> Yours is a pure delightful singing voice,
> An inspired song-bird, olive-coloured.
> A cantor in the chapel of heaven,
> The omen will be fair, you are highly skilled.)

Similarly, the song thrush (ceiliog bronfraith) is 'cantor hydr' ('a sturdy singer'), who is compared to a preacher, a sheriff, a linguist: 'saith ugeiniaith a ganai' ('he can sing in seven-score tongues').⁴⁵ Because of the bird's skills as a singer, the poet chooses him as a llatai or love messenger to take a message to his beloved, and although the message does not achieve the desired aim of winning over his beloved, the poet cannot help delighting in the bird: 'Ceiniad yw goreuryw gân/A gynnull pwyll ac anian' ('he is a singer of the best kind of song, bringing together wisdom and instinct').⁴⁶

While Dafydd's enjoyment of music is often metaphorical, dedicated mainly to love and nature, the later cywyddwyr are more inclined to describe the reality of music and other entertainments as they were performed at the courts of their patrons. The atmosphere conjured up in such poems is altogether more festive than that of the courts of the princes before 1282; the poetry of the gogynfeirdd suggests that it had been performed in an atmosphere of sober formality, despite the traditional large amounts of wine and mead on offer to the poets. In the courts of the uchelwyr, by contrast, music, dancing and song are hallmarks not only of the patron's generosity but also of his hospitality to guests and entertainers. Writing towards the end of the fourteenth century, Iolo Goch composed praise poems to some of the great noblemen of his day, including Sir Hywel ap Gruffudd (d. c.1381), also known as Syr Hywel y Fwyall ('Sir Hywel of the Axe') because of his legendary exploits during the Hundred Years' War. Sir Hywel was also constable of Criccieth Castle, which Iolo describes as a magnificent

---

⁴⁴ Johnston et al., goln., *Cerddi Dafydd ap Gwilym*, rhif 44, ll. 31–36.
⁴⁵ Ibid., rhif 49, ll. 3 and 10.   ⁴⁶ Ibid., rhif 49, ll. 17–18.

fortress right on the seashore, where men sit at tables to eat by candlelight:

> A cherdd chwibenygl a chod
> Gorhoenus, a gwŷr hynod
> Yn chwarae dawns a charawl,
> Yn cymryd mynwyd a mawl.[47]
>
> (And cheerful music of flutes and bagpipe
> And distinguished men
> Enjoying dancing and carols,
> Accepting pleasure and praise.)

Even the Bishop of St Asaph, another patron of Iolo's verse, is not averse to the power of music, which can be enjoyed in both religious and secular settings. Here is the music that Iolo hears in church:

> Offeren fawr hoff eirian
> A gawn, a hynny ar gân,
> Trebl, chwatrebl, awch atreg,
> A byrdwn cyson, tôn teg.[48]
>
> (A large delightful radiant mass
> Would I get, and that in song,
> Treble, quatreble, bringing sharpness of repentance,
> And a constant refrain, a fine tune.)

And this is what Iolo enjoys later on in the Bishop's hall:

> Cerdd dafod ffraeth hiraethlawn,
> Cerdd dant, gogoniant a gawn;
> Cytgerdd ddiddan lân lonydd,
> Pibau, dawns, a gawn pob dydd.[49]
>
> (Poetry fluent and full of longing,
> String music, I would have glory;
> Delightful harmony, pure and peaceful,
> I would have pipes and dancing every day.)

---

[47] Dafydd Johnston, gol., *Gwaith Iolo Goch* (Caerdydd: Gwasg Prifysgol Cymru, 1988), rhif 2, ll. 11–14. The Welsh chwibenygl is the plural of chwibanogl, from chwiban, 'whistling'. The term carol, borrowed directly from Middle English, was originally a type of dance.

[48] Ibid., rhif 16, ll. 39–42. The quatreble (borrowed straight from English into Welsh) is a type of medieval descant sung above the treble. Byrdwn, borrowed from English 'burden', refers to a song's chorus or refrain but it can also signify the bass string on an instrument.

[49] Ibid., rhif 16, ll. 53–56.

2 Words for Music in Medieval Welsh Literature

In these lines, Iolo uses the technical terms that describe the two types of craft, poetry (cerdd dafod) and music (cerdd dant), indicating that the two work together to create gogoniant, 'glory'.

Iolo's elegy to a fellow poet, Llywelyn Goch ap Meurig Hen, who died in about 1390, provides two particular insights about musical performance. The first is that requests for songs were made by the audience:

> Pan ofynner, arfer oedd
> Y lleisiau yn y llysoedd,
> Cyntaf gofynnir, wir waith,
> I'r purorion, pêr araith,
> Rhieingerdd y gŵr hengoch.[50]

> (When there are requests, as was the custom
> Of the voices in the courts,
> The first request, true work,
> To the minstrels, sweet their singing,
> Is a love-song composed by the old red man [i.e., Llywelyn Goch].)

This implies that part of the function of minstrels was to perform the songs composed by the poets. But the elegy also suggests that a poet or singer with a particularly fine voice, like Llywelyn, could sing unaccompanied:

> Ni bydd digrif ar ddifys
> Nac un acen ara ben bys
> Ond cywydd cethlydd coethlef,
> Ni myn neb gywydd namyn ef.[51]

> (Nothing is pleasant without any accompaniment
> Or sound at the fingertip
> Except a cywydd by a fine-voiced singer:
> No one wants any cywydd but his.)

Appreciation of music and poetry marked a nobleman out as being particularly well educated and accomplished. At the other end of the spectrum, noisy entertainments provided by a host for his guests could create a far rowdier atmosphere. In a poem from the early fifteenth century by Rhys Goch Eryri, a speaker describes an unnamed patron who loves all kinds of games and entertainments. The poet creates a lively scene full of noise and movement that captures the mood in the patron's hall:

> Derbyn bob ddau i'r neuadd,
> Llwyth grym, ar y lleithig radd,

[50] Ibid., rhif 22, ll. 21–25. [51] Ibid., rhif 22, ll. 29–32.

Pob amryw ofer glerwr,
Angerdd mawr gerdd, y mae'r gŵr.
Bid wir air, Bedwyr wryd,
Beirdd a phrydyddion y byd;
Pob crythor, ddihepgor ddyn,
Dilys a phob cerdd delyn;
Pob trwmpls propr hirgorn copr cau,
Pob sôn pobl, pob swn pibau;
Pob hudol, anfoddol fydd,
Llwm hadl, a phob llamhidydd;
Pob ffidler law draw y dring,
Pob swtr tabwrdd, pob sawtring.[52]

(The man receives them in twos into the hall,
Strength of numbers, stepping up to the stage,
Every variety of ordinary minstrel,
Great is the skill of their craft;
May it be a true word, by the might of Bedivere,
The bards and poets of the world;
Every crwth player, indispensable reliable man,
And every tune of the harp;
Every suitable trumpet with its long hollow copper horn,
Every noise from people, every sound of pipes;
Every conjuror who's unwilling,
Threadbare and addled, and every acrobat;
Every fiddler whose hand climbs up,
Every hammerer on a drum, every psaltery.)

Such an excess of people, noise and music creates a party mood suggestive of lavish hospitality among the local gentry. The addition of entertainers such as acrobats and conjurors, ranked among the lowest grades of performers, perhaps indicates a desire to emulate the great feasts of the English and French nobility on a somewhat smaller scale. The expense involved in such an event would be enough to affirm the wealth and status of the host.

The homes of the Welsh gentry and higher clergy were not the only venues where music was performed, mainly for private entertainments. Travelling minstrels and other kinds of entertainers also performed in public at local fairs and in the growing towns of both the Marcher and crown lordships throughout Wales. The post-1282 anxiety about the relative status of poets, from the highest (pencerdd) to the lowest (clerwr), as evidenced by the Bardic Grammar and the competitions where the

---

[52] Dylan Foster Evans, gol., *Gwaith Rhys Goch Eryri* (Aberystwyth: Canolfan Uwchefrydiau Cymreig a Cheltaidd Prifsgol Cymru, 2007), rhif 12, ll. 41–54.

distinction between licensed and unlicensed poets was constantly reinforced, rested not only on the quality and training of the poets but also on the places where they performed. Certainly before 1282, and for some time afterwards, the higher grades of licensed poets, with their accompanying musicians, performed almost exclusively at the courts of the princes or uchelwyr; there is very little evidence about what must have been a thriving culture of popular entertainment in taverns and marketplaces. From the fourteenth century, when the term clêr begins to appear as a generic word for travelling poets who performed for all kinds of audiences in a variety of venues, urban culture begins to become more visible.[53] Already by the mid-fourteenth century the clêr were singing at the courts of the nobility – Dafydd ap Gwilym praises the generosity of Ieuan ap Gruffudd ap Llywelyn towards the clêr at his court, 'dy fedd glas difaddau i glêr' ('your unlimited fresh mead for poets')[54] – as well as in taverns: 'Treiglais, gweais yn gywir,/Defyrn gwin, Duw a farn gwir' ('I haunted wine taverns, I wove poetry in good faith, as God is my judge').[55]

A glimpse of urban life appears in a poem by Tudur Penllyn (c.1420–90), in which he describes his visit to the town of Flint, one of the earliest English towns planted in north Wales in 1277 as part of Edward I's campaigns against the princes of Gwynedd.[56] The poet arrives in Flint to sing at an 'English feast' ('Seisnigwledd') but is booed off by the English audience:

> Dechreuais, ffrostiais yn ffraeth,
> Ganu awdl i'r genhedlaeth;
> Gwatwaru, llysu fy llais,
> Gan y Saeson a gefais.
> Hawdd gan borthmyn haidd ac ŷd
> Faddau fy holl gelfyddyd.[57]
>
> (I began, I projected eloquently,
> By singing an awdl to the townspeople;

---

[53] The term clêr (singular clerwr) is not attested before the fourteenth century, though it was almost certainly used before then. The meanings provided in *Geiriadur Prifysgol Cymru* are: 'a wandering bard of the lowest grade permitted to satirize as well as to present eulogies for payment, itinerant minstrel; entertainer or actor; bard or musician (in a general sense)'. For a useful note on the word, see Thomas Parry, gol., *Gwaith Dafydd ap Gwilym* (Caerdydd: Gwasg Prifysgol Cymru, 1952), t. 439, note on rhif 7, ll. 14.
[54] Johnston et al., goln, *Cerddi Dafydd ap Gwilym*, rhif 86, l. 11.   [55] Ibid., rhif 107, ll. 17–18.
[56] See Maurice Beresford, *The New Towns of the Middle Ages: Town Plantation in England, Wales and Gascony* (London: Phillimore, 1966), p. 165.
[57] Thomas Roberts, gol., *Gwaith Tudur Penllyn ac Ieuan ap Tudur Penllyn* (Caerdydd: Gwasg Prifysgol Cymru, 1958), rhif 30, ll. 9–14.

> Ridicule, objection to my voice,
> Did I get from the English.
> Easy for barley and corn traders
> To dismiss my whole craft.)

To the poet's fury, the crowd then call on Wiliam Beisir ('William Long-Coat') to play the bagpipes, the sight and sound of which are roundly mocked by the poet:

> Rhygnu, syndremu, swn drwg,
> Rhwth gaul, a rhythu golwg,
> A throi ei gorff yma a thraw,
> A chwyddo'r dwyfoch eiddaw;
> Chwerw foes, chware â'i fysedd,
> A chroen glwth, chwerw yn eu gwledd;
> Ymsgrwtian, ymysg rhowter,
> Tan ei glog fal tin y glêr.[58]

> (Grating, staring, an evil noise,
> Gaping maw and staring eyes,
> Turning his body this way and that,
> And blowing out his two cheeks;
> Rough behaviour, playing with his fingers,
> With a gluttonous bag, painful at their feast,
> Jolting among the crowd
> Under his cloak like the backside of a minstrel.)

To add insult to injury, William 'Bean-Soup', as the poet mockingly calls him, is given money by the crowd, whereas the poet himself has to leave empty-handed. He ends by renouncing the whole of Flint, 'a'i phobl Seisnig a'i phibydd' ('and its English people and its piper').[59]

Music in the *Mabinogion*

The cultural practices of music, poetry and entertainment in the halls of the nobility, articulated most notably in the poetry of the gogynfeirdd and cywyddwyr, can also be observed in the collection of medieval Welsh prose tales known as the *Mabinogion*. Although these tales are found together in two fourteenth-century manuscript compilations known as Llyfr Gwyn Rhydderch (the White Book of Rhydderch, *c*.1350) and Llyfr Coch Hergest (the Red Book of Hergest, *c*.1400), the tales are largely unconnected and of different dates, apart from the group known as the Four Branches of the

---

[58] Ibid., rhif 30, ll. 25–32. [59] Ibid., rhif 30, ll. 52.

Mabinogi, which are explicitly linked together.⁶⁰ The earliest of the eleven tales is *Culhwch ac Olwen*, mentioned at the beginning of this chapter, an original Arthurian story that has been dated to about 1100; while later tales include three Arthurian romances, largely adapted from French narrative poems composed by the twelfth-century poet Chrétien de Troyes. Taken together, the prose tales were composed during the same period that the gogynfeirdd were singing in the courts of the Welsh princes, roughly 1100 to 1282, and it is not surprising, then, that beneath a generic veneer of the supernatural, the marvellous and the folkloric, the prose tales evoke similar audiences of princely families, whose experiences are shaped by the ongoing presence of the Normans in Wales.

References to music and singing, in the context of courtly entertainment during feasts, provide a stylistic similarity across all eleven tales which overrides their different histories and binds them into a single genre of native Welsh prose narrative. In the story of 'Branwen uerch Lyr' ('Branwen daughter of Llŷr'), the Second Branch of the *Mabinogi*, the Irish king Matholwch sails over to Wales and is given Branwen, sister of the British king Bendigeidfran, in marriage. After Matholwch has told the court a tale one evening, the narrator says:

> Dilit ymdidan a wnaethant y nos honno, tra uu da ganthunt, a cherd a chyuedach. A phan welsant uot yn llessach udunt uynet y gyscu noc eisted a wei hwy, y gyscu yd aethant. Ac yuelly y treulyssant y wled honno drwy digriuwch.⁶¹

> (They continued to converse that night, as long as they pleased, along with music and carousal. And when they saw that it was better for them to go and sleep than to sit up any longer, they went to sleep. And thus they spent that feast by means of entertainment.)

These are almost formulaic sentences, found repeated in most of the tales, and not just in the Four Branches. In the romance of Geraint and Enid, adapted from Chrétien's *Erec et Enide*, when Arthur is relaxing at night with his men the narrator says: 'A threulaw y nos a orugant drwy gymydrolder o gerdeu a didanwch ac ymdidaneu a didlawt wasanaeth' ('and they spent that night by means of a moderate amount of songs and entertainment and conversations and unstinting service [of food and

---

⁶⁰ For a brief description of the eleven tales that comprise the *Mabinogion*, see Davies, trans., *The Mabinogion*, pp. ix–xiii.
⁶¹ Derick S. Thomson, ed., *Branwen Uerch Lyr* (Dublin: Dublin Institute for Advanced Studies, 1976), lines 197–200.

drink]').⁶² Music and singing, provided by professional musicians and poets, were clearly a key part of princely feasts, whose function was to prove the generosity of the lord through his hospitality and to bind hosts and guests, lords and men, together through the shared experience of entertainment.

It follows that when the nature of the entertainment differs in some way from what is typically expected, this creates moments of drama or suspense in the narrative, often in a supernatural context. In the Fourth Branch of the *Mabinogi*, *Math uab Mathonwy* ('Math son of Mathonwy'), the narrator describes the faithless wife, the magical Blodeuwedd, preparing to betray her husband: 'Treulaw y dyd a wnaethant drwy ymdidan, a cherd, a chyuedach' ('they spent the day in conversation, and music, and carousal'), so that a normally innocuous phrase becomes imbued with a baleful significance.⁶³ In *Breuddwyd Maxen Wledic* ('The Dream of Maxen the Emperor'), Maxen (Maximus) the emperor of Rome falls desperately in love with a girl he has only dreamed about. His lovesickness means that he cannot participate in the normal rituals of courtly life:

> Ac ena e doeth e gaer Ruvein ac e velly e bu er wythnos honno ar e hyt. Pan elhei y deulu y yvet o eurlestri ac e gemryt eu llewenyd nyt aei ef y gyt a nep onadunt wy. Pan elynt e warandaw kerdeu a didanuch nyt aei ef y gyt a neb.⁶⁴

> (And then he came to the city of Rome and he was there for the length of that week. When his retinue went to drink from golden vessels and to take their pleasure, he would not go with any one of them. When they went to listen to songs and entertainment, he would not go with anyone.)

In disrupting the syntax of the usual courtly entertainments – music, conversation, entertainment – the narrator indicates the extent of Maxen's suffering, which has arisen from a strange and supernatural situation.

As well as these kinds of intradiegetic references to music within the texts, we have to assume that extradiegetic music was played from time to time to accompany events in the tales, particularly at moments of drama

---

⁶² Robert L. Thomson, ed., *Ystorya Gereint uab Erbin* (Dublin: Dublin Institute for Advanced Studies, 1997), lines 60–61.
⁶³ Ian Hughes, ed., *Math Uab Mathonwy: The Fourth Branch of the Mabinogi* (Dublin: Dublin Institute for Advanced Studies, 2013), lines 436–437.
⁶⁴ Brynley F. Roberts, ed., *Breuddwyt Maxen Wledic* (Dublin: Dublin Institute for Advanced Studies, 2005), lines 98–100.

or pathos. Towards the end of the story of Branwen, when seven men are the only survivors of a terrible war with Ireland, they return to Harlech, the court of their dead king Bendigeidfran, and sit down at a feast. Then they hear the music of the 'birds of Rhiannon', supernatural birds (mentioned also in *Culhwch ac Olwen*) that have the power to wake the dead and to send the living to sleep: 'Ac y gyt ac y dechreuyssant wynteu uwyta ac yuet, dyuot tri ederyn, a dechreu canu udunt ryw gerd, ac oc a glywssynt o gerd, diuwyn oed pob un iwrthi hi' ('and as soon as they began to eat and drink, three birds came and began to sing a song to them, and whatever songs they had heard, they were all unpleasant compared to that one').[65] In the Fourth Branch, the wounded hero Lleu, transformed into an eagle, is enticed down from his tree by a series of three englynion sung by his uncle Gwydion, who uses his magic to turn Lleu back into his own shape.[66] Both these events may have prompted attendant musicians to support the cyfarwydd, or storyteller, in the delivery of the tale and to add to the entertainment for the listening audience.

Conclusion

Medieval Welsh prose and poetry are full of references to music, especially that of the crwth and harp, creating a context in which poetry, song and story were performed to listening audiences, either in the courts of the nobility or in the streets of the towns. As well as literal references to singing poets and professional musicians, we find music used metaphorically to signify wealth, status, beauty and religious faith. While the poetry of the gogynfeirdd was sung in the courts of the princes before the Edwardian conquest of 1282, the later poetry of the fourteenth and fifteenth centuries was more diverse in metre, subject and audience, with professional poets competing with minstrels and other entertainers who flourished in the new towns of Wales. The influence of the English language and English cultural forms, which became increasingly pervasive from the late fourteenth century, changed the way that music was composed and performed. Where noble and gentry audiences had once controlled the livelihoods of poets and musicians, the rise of urban audiences, including English

---

[65] Thomson, ed., *Branwen Uerch Lyr*, lines 426–429. Compare Bromwich and Evans, eds, *Culhwch ac Olwen*, line 632 and note on pp. 126–127.
[66] Hughes, ed., *Math Uab Mathonwy*, lines 513–539. For a translation of this section, see Davies, trans., *The Mabinogion*, pp. 62–63.

townspeople, provided new sources of income for entertainers of all kinds, leading to a convergence of the types of entertainment enjoyed in gentry houses and in the taverns and streets of the towns. New patrons among the Marcher gentry, including many English families, marked their status by commissioning praise poems and supporting poets and musicians. But as Tudur Penllyn's satire on the piper of Flint shows, there was also a market for the kinds of popular entertainment that were characteristic of urban culture, and which gentry audiences could also enjoy.

CHAPTER 3

Music in Worship before 1650
John Harper

Contexts

Before the Reformation, the usual way of voicing text in church was in song. Formulaic tones served for the recitation of prayers, prefaces and readings by a single cleric, and of psalms and canticles sung by the gathered body of clergy present, whether monastic, religious or secular;[1] more elaborate melodies enriched the texts of antiphons, responsories, tracts, hymns and proses. Even in small churches this was the norm; and much of this repertory was committed to memory, since books were few. That was true of the whole Latin church in the West; yet the extant evidence from Wales is exceptionally scarce. There is much better evidence of the built environment of the medieval church in Wales than there is of its written sources, and above all of its music. For the liturgy and its music, both before and after the Reformation, much is reliant on fragments of information or documentation; and there is much that is entirely lost and unknown.

Sally Harper has undertaken a comprehensive review of what survives and placed it in its historical context in her authoritative study of *Music in Welsh Culture before 1650*.[2] This chapter cannot include reference to all that material. Instead, it explores some of the principal survivals – musical, liturgical, archival, physical and topographical – in order to draw out some of the key themes of pre- and post-Reformation music in worship in Wales. There is no attempt to construct a historical continuity; rather it is

---

[1] In secular foundations these might include boys and, from the fifteenth century onwards, lay singers.
[2] Sally Harper, *Music in Welsh Culture before 1650: A Study of the Principal Sources* (Aldershot: Ashgate, 2007), especially pp. 163–293, and 331–370. To this may be added Thomas William Reynolds, 'A Study of Music and Liturgy: Choirs and Organs in Monastic and Secular Foundations in Wales and the Borderlands, 1485–1645' (PhD thesis, Bangor University, 2002), available online: https://research.bangor.ac.uk/portal/en/theses/a-study-of-music-and-liturgy--choirs-and-organs-in-monastic-and-secular-foundations-in-wales-and-the-borderlands-14851645(7d84e8de-005e-49e2-a6a4-2d64b028c137).html (accessed 30 June 2021).

a question of examining particular times, places, people and artefacts across a millennium, and showing how they may be typical or distinct within both the Welsh and wider context of their time.[3]

Defining Wales in the late Middle Ages is not straightforward. The creation of Edward, son of King Edward I, as Prince of Wales at Caernarfon Castle in 1301 is a marker of an imposed English sovereignty both political and ecclesial. As such, it defined Wales as a single principality, rather than a series of regional princedoms, though political turbulence, sometimes erupting into war and destruction, continued until the fifteenth century. By at least the mid-twelfth century, the Welsh dioceses fell within the province of Canterbury, overseen by the archbishop of Canterbury. In his *Life* of St David, Rhygyfarch (1056/7–99), eldest son of Sulien, bishop of St Davids, twice named David as archbishop;[4] and a century later, Gerald of Wales (*c*.1146–1220×23), not without self-interest, argued that the Welsh dioceses should form their own province.[5] Yet, from Norman times until 1920, the Welsh dioceses remained within the province of Canterbury.

The extent of the four medieval Welsh dioceses did not always coincide with the county boundaries drawn up in the sixteenth century: the church at Montgomery, a Welsh county town, was within the diocese of Hereford, not St Asaph; Oswestry (Shropshire) was constitutionally part of England, yet culturally strongly Welsh. From 1472 to 1689, Wales and the bordering English counties were overseen by the Council of Wales and the Marches, based in Ludlow (Shropshire). Long before that, Anglo-Norman nobility gained lands and exercised patronage and influence over the church in Wales. With the accession of the Welsh family of the Tudors to the English throne in 1485, aspiring Welsh families took the opportunity to establish a London base and activity alongside their lands in Wales. The sixteenth-century foundations of Jesus College, Oxford, and St John's College, Cambridge, both had strong Welsh associations. Musicians of Welsh origin made their careers in England, among them the composers John Lloyd (*c*.1475–1523) and John Gwynneth (d. 1560x63). Thomas Tomkins

---

[3] For the broader history of the church in Wales, see Glanmor Williams, *The Welsh Church from Conquest to Reformation*, 2nd ed. (Cardiff: University of Wales Press, 1976); Glanmor Williams, *Wales and the Reformation* (Cardiff: University of Wales Press, 1997).

[4] Richard Sharpe and John Reuben Davies, eds. and trans., 'Rhygyfarch's *Life* of St David', in *St David of Wales: Cult, Church and Nation*, ed. by J. Wyn Evans and Jonathan M. Wooding (Woodbridge: The Boydell Press, 2007), pp. 107–155, specifically sections 46 (pp. 140–141) and 53 (pp. 146–147). The manuscript containing the *Life*, GB-Lbl Cotton MS Vespasian A XIV, ff. 61r–70v has been digitised by the British Library www.bl.uk/manuscripts/FullDisplay.aspx?ref=Cotton_MS_Vespasian_A_XIV

[5] Robert Bartlett, 'Gerald of Wales', *Oxford Dictionary of National Biography*, online revised text (2006) (accessed 30 June 2021).

senior (*c*.1545–1627) came to St Davids Cathedral as vicar choral from Cornwall by 1565 before moving on to Gloucester Cathedral by 1594; his son, Thomas Tomkins junior (1572–1656), organist and composer, was born and spent his early years in St Davids, and then made his career at Worcester Cathedral (from 1596) and in the Chapel Royal (by 1621).[6] Such fluidity and ambivalence are part of the story of church music in Wales, and essential to its understanding.

From Roman Times to the English Conquest

Christianity, at least in the far west of Wales, may have persisted since late Roman times. The parish church of St Peblig, Caernarfon, some two miles inland of the late medieval castle town, was built in the centre of what had been a Roman cemetery next to the fort of Segontium. The church of St Cybi, Holyhead (Anglesey), is situated within the Roman fort. Both may imply continuity of Christian observance from the time of the Roman occupation, a claim also made at Llandaff Cathedral in the south-east. Many of the medieval parish churches have dedications to local saints of the sixth to the tenth centuries, with no fewer than seventy on Anglesey, for instance.[7] The cathedrals of Bangor, Llandaff and St Davids trace their establishment to the middle of the sixth century, half a century before the mission of Augustine to south-east England in 597. Their dedications are also to early local saints: Deiniol, Dyfrig and Teilo, and David. The cathedral at St Asaph was not formally established until 1143, but this was already the holy site of Llanelwy (the sacred place by the River Elwy). Each of the four cathedrals was built on comparatively low ground near the sea but a little inland; hidden from sea-borne invaders, but still readily accessible to the principal artery of early medieval travel on the waters of the Irish Sea.[8]

The church in Wales was always part of the western Latin church; it was firmly established by the mid-sixth century; it was less likely affected by the reforming influences on liturgy and chant in the eighth century

---

[6] Anthony Boden, ed., *Thomas Tomkins, the Last Elizabethan* (Aldershot: Ashgate, 2005).
[7] Emrys Bowen, 'Yr Eglwys Geltaidd – Oes y Seintiau', in *Atlas Môn*, ed. by Melville Richards (Llangefni: Cyngor Gwlad Môn, 1972), pp. 24–27. For more comprehensive information, see E. G. Bowen, *The Settlements of the Celtic Saints in Wales*, 2nd ed. (Cardiff: University of Wales Press, 1956). On church dedications, see Owen Chadwick, 'The Evidence of Welsh Dedications in the Early History of the Welsh Church', in *Studies in Early British History*, ed. by Nora K. Chadwick (Cambridge: Cambridge University Press, 1959), pp. 173–188.
[8] Emrys Bowen, *Saints, Seaways and Settlements in the Celtic Lands* (Cardiff: University of Wales Press, 1969).

that Bede recounted and championed in his ecclesiastical history, or the monastic revival of the tenth century in southern England; the lives of saints that include Welsh dimensions like Patrick, patron of Ireland, Samson, bishop of Dol in Brittany and Kentigern (Mungo), bishop of Glasgow, imply stronger links with the Celtic regions of north-west Europe than with Norse or Saxon cultures. That said, any attempt to construct a 'Celtic' scenario for the Welsh church's worship and sacred song has to remain largely speculative.[9] Nonetheless, the eighth-century Gospel book now at Lichfield Cathedral (GB-LF, MS 1) was used at the high altar in the important religious centre of Llandeilo Fawr (Carmarthenshire) in the ninth century, a mark of high culture in that church.[10] Rhygyfarch's *Life* of St David confirms a rule of conventual life and prayer in the monastic community (in Welsh, 'clas') before the influx of Benedictine monasticism. It may, perhaps, record the specific practice that Rhygyfarch himself experienced in the clas at Llanbadarn Fawr (Cardiganshire), a major centre of learning in the tenth and eleventh centuries. The pattern of work and communal prayer is set out, with the claim that David 'imitated the monks of Egypt and lived a life like theirs' ('*Sed Egyptios monachos imitatus similem eis duxit uitam*').[11] However, neither the Lichfield Gospel book nor the *Life* of St David can bear witness to the sonic experience of worship, rich as the descriptions suggest that it will have been.

The growing influence of Anglo-Norman nobility after the Norman Conquest, the foundation of Benedictine monasteries, the rise of the reformed Benedictine, strictly ascetic order of Cistercians, and of the order of Augustinian regular canons, all had an impact on religious life in Wales in the twelfth century. Benedictine monasteries were each independent; they followed Benedict's Rule but had distinctions in their customs and repertories of chant. No liturgical sources survive from the Welsh Benedictine priories (none was large enough to merit the status of an abbey), but there is evidence from their parent abbeys, among them Abergavenny (originally founded from St Vincent Abbey, Le Mans), Brecon (Battle Abbey), Ewenny (Gloucester Abbey) and Pembroke

---

[9] On the early church in Wales, see Wendy Davies, *Wales in the Early Middle Ages* (Leicester: Leicester University Press, 1982), pp. 141–168. On Celtic dimensions, Oliver Davies, *Celtic Christianity in Early Medieval Wales* (Cardiff: University of Wales Press, 1996).

[10] Michelle P. Brown, 'The Lichfield/Llandeilo Gospels Reinterpreted', in *Authority and Subjugation in Writing of Medieval Wales*, ed. by Ruth Kennedy and Simon Meecham-Jones, New Middle Ages series, ed. by Bonnie Wheeler (New York: Palgrave Macmillan, 2008), pp. 57–70.

[11] Sharpe and Davies, eds. and trans., 'Rhygyfarch's *Life* of St David', pp. 107–155, especially sections 21–31, pp. 124–129.

(St Albans Abbey). The Cistercian order was more centralised. In principle, their Welsh abbeys therefore followed the liturgical practice and reformed chant of the mother houses, notably Cîteaux (Côte-d'Or) and Savigny (Manche), though the majestic abbey at Tintern (Monmouthshire) was founded from L'Aumone Abbey (Loir et Cher).

Llanthony Prima (Monmouthshire) was the first of the Augustinian priories, but a number of former clas communities adopted the Augustinian rule, including those at Penmon (Anglesey), Bardsey Island and Beddgelert (both Gwynedd). Other clasau adopted the reformed Benedictine order of the abbey of Tiron (Eure et Loire), including those at St Dogmaels and Caldey Island (both Pembrokeshire). In the thirteenth century, the new mendicant orders established a small number of friaries, mostly in urban centres: Dominicans in Bangor, Brecon, Cardiff, Haverfordwest; Franciscans in Cardiff, Carmarthen and Llanfaes (outside Beaumaris, Anglesey). They followed a reformed form of liturgy and chant set down centrally by their orders. Thus, by the end of the thirteenth century the monastic and religious houses in Wales were assimilated within a larger European network of Benedictine, Cistercian, Augustinian, Tironensian, Dominican and Franciscan orders, each with distinctive liturgical repertoires and customs, often coloured by local variants.[12]

The formalisation of churches with a body of secular (that is, non-monastic) clergy also occurred in the twelfth and thirteenth centuries. Again, this was part of a wider European movement of ecclesial regulation and codification, in this case based on a statutory instrument rather than a monastic rule. Each institution was independent and governed by the clergy who were members of the foundation (canons) headed by a dean, master or warden. Each usually had a precentor, suitably skilled to oversee the liturgy and its music. Inevitably such institutions looked for a model, and in the thirteenth century the most comprehensive and fully formed insular model was that of Salisbury Cathedral (Wiltshire).

Apart from the four cathedrals, collegiate churches in Wales were not numerous. At the time of the sixteenth-century Reformation they included foundations at Abergwili (Carmarthenshire), Clynnog Fawr (Gwynedd), Holyhead (Anglesey) and Llanddewibrefi (Ceredigion). Two of these colleges were founded by Thomas Bek (d. 1293), bishop of St Davids (1280–93): Abergwili and Llanddewibrefi. Bek came from an established

---

[12] The website *Monastic Wales*, overseen by Janet Burton, has details of all monastic and religious foundations, including a bibliography: www.monasticwales.org/index.php (accessed 30 June 2021). There were few monastic communities of women: Usk (Monmouthshire) was Benedictine; Llanllugan (Powys) and Llanllyr (Ceredigion) were Cistercian.

Lincolnshire family and held significant posts at court as the keeper of the king's wardrobe (from 1274), as archdeacon of Dorset in the diocese of Salisbury (1275–80), and as chancellor of Oxford University (1279–81). That accumulated experience will have served him well in shaping these collegiate foundations.

Bek's first foundation was his most ambitious. Initially founded at Llangadog (Carmarthenshire) in 1283, it was moved twenty miles west to Abergwili, near Carmarthen, in 1287, the year in which he also instituted his second collegiate foundation at Llanddewibrefi.[13] The foundation charter for Llangadog specifies twenty-one canons (equally divided between priests, deacons and subdeacons), with prebends funded by income from other churches in the diocese.[14] There was an expectation that seven canons would be in residence at any one time (a comparable arrangement to that at Salisbury and other English cathedrals by this time). The precentor, with oversight of the liturgy, was to be in residence permanently (and to enjoy one third of the prebendal income). Each canon was to appoint a vicar, permanently in residence, who was to act as his substitute in order to sustain the full round of daily mass and office according to the liturgical Use of St Davids Cathedral, and there were five junior clerks and an unspecified number of boys. By 1535, the canons were non-resident, and the daily office and mass were sustained by a small group of four priests, four choristers and two clerks.[15] The college at Abergwili was subsequently transferred to Brecon (see p. 67), while the buildings became the bishop's palace.

Bek's episcopate coincided with the years of Edward I's conquest of Wales, and the visitations of John Pecham (c.1230–92), archbishop of Canterbury (1279–92), in 1284 to instigate reform in the Welsh dioceses, further strengthening English authority in affairs of state and church in Wales. By this time, the Welsh dioceses were firmly embedded within the province of Canterbury, and Welsh bishops frequently acted as suffragans to the English diocesans, men who were often occupied with matters of state or church that took them out of their dioceses, and on occasion abroad, for considerable periods. It is from this period that the exemplars

---

[13] Glanmor Williams, 'The Collegiate Church of Llanddewibrefi', *Ceredigion: Journal of the Cardiganshire Antiquarian Society* 4 (1960–3), 336–352.

[14] William Dugdale, *Monasticon Anglicanum*, ed. by John Caley, Henry Ellis and Bulkeley Bandinel, 6 vols. in 8 books (London, 1849), VI, iii, pp. 1332–1333. There was no dean, since the bishop headed the college.

[15] *Valor Ecclesiasticus Temp. Henr. VIII*, ed. by John Caley and Joseph Hunter; 6 vols. (London: Record Commission, 1810–34), IV, p. 410.

for two important liturgical manuscripts probably originate. The pontifical of Bishop Anian of Bangor and the so-called Penpont antiphonal, both made in the fourteenth century, are the only substantial, extant late medieval sources containing chant with Welsh association or provenance.

Two Fourteenth-Century Sources

The Pontifical of Anian, Bishop of Bangor (Deposited at GB-BGul, s.n.)

Anian's pontifical was decorated by the Subsidiary Queen Mary Artist in East Anglia (perhaps Ely) in the period 1315–20, an indication of its high status as a manuscript.[16] Behind its liturgical contents is a complex narrative deriving from the activities of Welsh bishops in England as well as Wales.[17] The pontifical was written and decorated as a coherent whole for Anian II, bishop of Bangor (1309–28), but it represents a fair copy of a compilation made over a period of time, most likely during the episcopate of Anian I, bishop of Bangor (1267–1305/6). Both of these bishops undertook duties in England, acting on behalf of English bishops at times when they were unable to fulfil all their diocesan duties. During the conflict between Edward I and the Welsh princes, Anian I spent much of 1277–80 and 1282–4 out of his diocese, based in south-east and eastern England. The king granted him a house in Holborn in 1280, providing a London base for him and subsequent bishops of Bangor. On his return, he saw through the reform of the church in north Wales, following the visitation made by Archbishop John Pecham in 1284.

One specific event is reflected in the musical contents of the pontifical. Anian I consecrated the cemetery at the Augustinian friary in Clare (Suffolk) in 1279. There he also issued two indulgences, found in both the pontifical and the Clare cartulary. The Augustinian friars at Clare followed the newly reformed liturgy and chant prepared by the Franciscan friars, and subsequently adopted by the Roman church. The pontifical contains two rites of the sick and dead; one follows the normal liturgy and chant of the Use of Salisbury, the other follows the Franciscan liturgy with the Romano-Franciscan forms of twelve chant melodies. The

---

[16] Deposited at GB-BGul, s. n. Digital images of the complete pontifical are available: www.diamm.ac.uk/sources/3785/#/ (log in required, accessed 30 June 2021).

[17] The most recent review of the pontifical, which includes new findings, is John Harper, 'Contexts for the Late Medieval Pontifical of Anian, Bishop of Bangor: Issues of the "Local" and the "More-than-local"', in *Music and Liturgy in Medieval Britain and Ireland*, ed. by Ann Buckley and Lisa Colton (Cambridge: Cambridge University Press, 2022), pp. 17–49.

Franciscan rites and chants may be associated with a specific event at Clare, but they serve as a reminder of the different forms of ritual practice and chant repertories present in late medieval Wales, as elsewhere, which bishops both in their own Welsh dioceses and as suffragans elsewhere would encounter in the course of their episcopal duties.

One of the agenda of nineteenth-century scholars examining the pontifical was to search out the elusive liturgical Use of Bangor, mentioned in the preface of The Book of Common Prayer. Anian's pontifical was the sole (and vain) quarry for such evidence.[18] In practice this was a book belonging to the bishop, and it was not until 1485 that Bishop Richard Ednam (bishop 1465–94) presented the book to Bangor Cathedral, by which time he presumably had a new pontifical of his own. (Ednam himself had associations with Clare (Suffolk). Given the inadequacy of his income as bishop of Bangor to maintain an episcopal household, he was appointed warden of the college in Clare.)

The great majority of chant in Anian's pontifical belongs to the Salisbury tradition; but there are distinctive features and variants. A particularly beautiful chant in the rite of the blessing of a bell stands outside the Salisbury (and Continental) mainstream. This melody of *In civitate Domini* (fo. 77v) has so far been found in only two other sources: a gradual made at the Benedictine cathedral priory in Canterbury, *c*.1100, and sent to the new Benedictine cathedral priory at Durham (the Cosin Gradual, GB-DRu, MS Cosin V.v.6, fo. 99r); and a mid-twelfth-century pontifical, for which some have suggested a Hereford provenance (the Magdalen Pontifical, GB-Omc, MS 226, fo. 166v). One chant for the election of a bishop has not as yet been traced elsewhere (*Unguentum in capite quid descendit*, fo. 115r), and there are significant variants in some other chants, including the Maundy Thursday hymn, *O redemptor sume carmen* (fo. 126r). However, apart from the twelve Romano-Franciscan chants, the remaining fifty-three chants are predominantly concordant with those found in other late medieval English pontificals and the Use of Salisbury.

That is not the case with the tones for the prefaces in the canon of the mass and at other points in the episcopal rites. Those for the episcopal rites follow the usual pattern, with an opening inflection of a rising minor third

---

[18] That the Use of Bangor did exist is confirmed by a record at Royston Priory, 1517, where the Augustinian canons sought to replace their worn-out Bangor books with those of the Use of Salisbury. Doris Jones-Baker, 'Mediaeval and Tudor Music and Musicians in Hertfordshire: The Graffiti Evidence', *Hertfordshire in History: Essays Presented to Lionel Munby*, ed. by Doris Jones-Baker, 2nd ed. (Hatfield: Hertfordshire Publications, 2004), p. 29.

(nominally *a-c′* or *d-f*, with eleven instances spread throughout the book); but those for the regular mass prefaces are distinctive, with a rising tone (nominally *a-b* or *d-e*, with twelve occurrences found as a group in the canon of the mass, fos. 65r–69v). Evidently this second group belongs to a different tradition, for which no contemporary parallel has yet been traced. Whether this was local to Bangor cannot yet be ascertained.

Penpont Antiphonal (GB-AB MS 20541E)

By contrast with Anian's pontifical, the fourteenth-century Penpont antiphonal (named after its post-Reformation resting place at Penpont House, near Brecon) is a source made for use in the diocese of St Davids.[19] What survives of the antiphonal represents a repertory of chants for the office for the whole liturgical year according to the Use of Salisbury. Over 300 folios are extant, but there are some substantial losses: Advent from the Temporal, the first half of the psalter and much of the Common of Saints. Three elements set this antiphonal apart from the usual Sarum antiphonal of the time. Of these, the most significant is the group of texts and chants for a unique rhymed office of St David, underlining its local, diocesan provenance (fos. 205r–208v). Another unique rhymed office of St Leonard has text but blank staves (fos. 283r–286v). This is also the case with additional items for the rhymed office of St Thomas of Canterbury (fos. 20r–24v). These offices are not interpolated additions: they appear in the main sequence of the Sanctoral, and supplement what is normative in books of the Use of Salisbury. No provision was made at this time for the feast, let alone the octave, of St David in books of the Use of Salisbury; and though St Leonard had proper prayers and readings provided, the chants were to be taken from the general repertory of the Common of Saints.

In a wider context, it was normative for each cathedral to have its own liturgical Use, and for that to be adopted in the other churches within the diocese. Such was the case, for instance, in France. In England and Wales, only Hereford maintained a diocesan Use up to the Reformation. Otherwise, non-monastic churches in northern England, within the province of York, followed the liturgical Use of York. That could not be the case in southern England and in Wales, where the principal cathedral of the province of Canterbury was a Benedictine monastery, following the

---

[19] GB-AB MS 20541E. Facsimile edition, with introduction and indices by Owain Tudor Edwards, *National Library of Wales MS 20541E: The Penpont Antiphonal* (Ottawa: The Institute of Mediaeval Music, 1997).

Benedictine forms of the liturgy. By 1200, and perhaps earlier, the Use of Salisbury offered an exceptionally comprehensive and stable order of the non-monastic form of the liturgy. It was therefore a ready resource to be introduced and locally adapted in other non-monastic cathedrals and dioceses, and in the parish churches of dioceses with a Benedictine cathedral priory. In rebuilding the non-monastic St Patrick's Cathedral, Dublin, the architectural layout of the first Salisbury Cathedral (at what is now known as Old Sarum) was adopted, as well its ritual customs and chant from the 1220s.[20] Similarly, at least some elements of the Use of Salisbury were adopted at St Davids Cathedral from 1224 onwards. Not that Canterbury exercised no liturgical influence: the office for the new feast of St Thomas of Canterbury was compiled, and the proper chants written and composed, by Benedict of Peterborough, prior of Christ Church, Canterbury, 1175–7.[21]

The cult of Thomas Becket had spread rapidly through Britain and Europe, and the texts and melodies of the proper chants offered a source for adaptation to local saints. Such was the case with the office of St David as found in the Penpont antiphonal. Some of the chants drew on the melodies of the Becket office; others adapted melodies from the office of St Nicholas, St Michael, St Vincent and the Common of Confessors.[22] There is no evidence to establish when this process of textual composition and melodic adaptation was undertaken. Gerald of Wales (*c.*1146–1220x23) selected passages from Rhygyfarch's *Life* of St David (*c.*1090) for liturgical reading, but the rest of the office may not have been compiled and composed until the late thirteenth century when the new shrine of St David was made at the cathedral.[23]

From the Later Fourteenth to the Early Sixteenth Century

While the Penpont antiphonal was intended for the diocese of St Davids, its exact provenance remains uncertain. Daniel Huws has suggested that it may originally have been made for the household of a bishop of St Davids, and perhaps copied in a London or Oxford scriptorium, given its quality.[24]

---

[20] John Harper, 'Contexts for the Late Medieval Pontifical of Anian, Bishop of Bangor', pp. 24–25.
[21] Kay B. Slocum, *Liturgies in Honour of Thomas Becket* (Toronto: University of Toronto Press, 2004), part 2.
[22] For a detailed study of the chant of the office of St David and its context, see Owain Tudor Edwards, *Matins, Lauds and Vespers for St David's Day: The Medieval Office of the Welsh Patron Saint in National Library of Wales MS 20541E* (Cambridge: D. S. Brewer, 1990).
[23] Sally Harper, *Music in Welsh Culture before 1650*, pp. 227–229.
[24] Daniel Huws, 'St David in the Liturgy', in *St David of Wales: Cult, Church and Nation*, ed. by J. Wyn Evans and Jonathan M. Wooding (Woodbridge: The Boydell Press, 2007), pp. 220–232, here pp. 228–229.

If so, Henry Gower (1277/8–1347) might be a possible patron, whether for his own household or even for the collegiate church at Abergwili, where new provision for a chancellor and treasurer was made at his instigation in 1331. Gower also enhanced St Davids Cathedral, including the building of the eastern Lady chapel and the rebuilding of the chapel of St Thomas of Canterbury. Each indicate the enrichment of worship in the cathedral. This was further enhanced in 1365 by the foundation of the college of St Mary adjacent to the cathedral by Bishop Adam Houghton (bishop 1361–93), together with John of Gaunt (1340–99) and his wife Blanche (d. 1368). It was regulated by statutes issued in 1372.[25] Although the college maintained its own pattern of worship in its chapel, with particular emphasis on the singing of the office and mass of the Blessed Virgin Mary, the master, seven fellows and two choristers joined with the cathedral clergy and choristers on Sundays and great feasts. By 1504, the college had effectively merged with the cathedral to form a single but sizeable choral force, including an organist from at least 1490. At the Reformation, with the dissolution of the college foundation, the cathedral surrendered those endowments to the crown.

The musical enrichment of the liturgy evident in St Davids from the later fourteenth century onwards, including the use of organs from at least the later fifteenth century, is typical of the pattern throughout the British Isles. Chantries founded for priests to pray for the souls of their patrons and their families after death also expanded the overall provision of clergy in a cathedral or church, enabling more elaborate ritual and musical provision, including polyphony. In some cases, as at St John's parish church, Cardiff, in the sixteenth century, funds for the chantry of St Catherine were used to pay a layman as organist.[26] In other places, such additional priests could take on a series of roles. By 1549 at the parish church of St Nicholas, Montgomery (Powys), the fraternity of Our Lady of Montgomery funded three stipendiary priests (one of whom was schoolmaster), a choirmaster, organist, two choristers and a holy-water bearer.[27]

Such small choral bodies had as much need of books with chant as larger institutions. This may perhaps account for the later locations of the Penpont antiphonal. Names of owners and others in the margins of the antiphonal suggest that it was in Brecon by the early sixteenth century and

---

[25] Dugdale, *Monasticon Anglicanum*, VI, iii, pp. 1388–1390; Edward Yardley, *Menevia Sacra*, ed. by Francis Green (London: Bedford Press, 1927), pp. 372–376.
[26] Sally Harper, *Music in Welsh Culture before 1650*, p. 276.
[27] Williams, *The Welsh Church from Conquest to Reformation*, p. 296.

in nearby Talgarth in the mid-sixteenth century, perhaps to meet the needs of the revived Latin rite during the reign of Mary.[28] One of these marginalia names John Wylyam as organ player in Talgarth, suggesting the liturgical use of the organ at that church. An earlier indenture made in 1516 by the bailiff and the twenty-four elected members of the commonalty of Brecon with Sir Thomas ap Howell, chaplain of Brecon, granted him the income from St Catherine's chapel (part of the leper hospital just outside the town) and a stipend.[29] In return he was to sustain sung services in St Mary's chapel in the centre of the town: matins, mass and vespers on Sundays and holy days, and daily Lady mass. Where practical, these services were to be sung in polyphony. He was also to maintain the organ and teach two children to sing polyphony as well as plainsong. Here is evidence of civic support for music typical of the time, in this case undertaken by the bailiff and commonalty, rather than a guild or fraternity.

The parish church in the nave of Brecon priory church, St Mary's chapel in the town, and Talgarth parish church were all held by Brecon Priory. Both Brecon and Talgarth had their own vicars funded by the priory, but the priory retained responsibility for mass in Brecon Castle chapel.[30] While the monastic community will have followed the Benedictine form of liturgy, their dependent churches and chapels will have followed the Use of Salisbury, with local inflections. Another book of the Use of Salisbury, a fifteenth-century ordinal, listing the contents of all the services throughout the year, was in the possession of Brecon Priory.[31] In it the feast of St David is listed in the calendar as a double feast (that is, high ranking). Perhaps there may have been occasion for Thomas ap Howell to use the Penpont antiphonal at St Mary's chapel for the feast of St David?

The Organ in the Liturgy

Records of organs, organists and organ books – both before and after the Reformation – may be found throughout the British Isles, but there is very

---

[28] Daniel Huws, 'St David in the Liturgy', pp. 227–228 and 231–232.
[29] Indenture printed as Appendix II in Theophilus Jones, *A History of the County of Brecknock*, 2 vols in 3 books (Brecon: George North, 1805–9), II, ii, pp. 788–790. Digitised by the National Library of Wales http://hdl.handle.net/10107/4806924.
[30] Confirmed in an agreement of 1527 between the prior and convent and Thomas ap Jenkin, vicar of Brecon, printed in John Stevens, *The History of the Antient Abbeys, Monasteries, Hospitals, Cathedrals and Collegiate Churches: Being Two Additional Volumes to Sir W. Dugdale's Monasticon Anglicanum*, 2 vols (London, 1722–3), I, pp. 400–402.
[31] GB-Ob, MS Laud 667.

little extant evidence of either the instruments or their repertory. That is what makes the surviving pre-Reformation case of the organ at Old Radnor (Powys) so significant.

The substantial late medieval church of St Stephen, Old Radnor, complements other greater churches in the Marches, in its size and provision.[32] The stalls in the chancel, and the surviving wooden screens, suggest that this was a place where there were resources to celebrate the Latin liturgy with music in the fifteenth and earlier sixteenth centuries. Though there is no surviving evidence of either a college or a less formal group of chantries, this church must have been served by a group of clergy, no doubt assisted by lay persons.[33] Visiting Old Radnor in c.1538, Leland observed that 'There is yet a very fair church, and well served',[34] and in 1545 the schoolmaster was paid 48s for his stipend, suggesting the availability of choristers.[35]

The richly carved and decorated oak organ case is the only surviving evidence of music making. It stands to the east of the stalls on the north side of the chancel, probably in the location for which it was originally made in the first half of the sixteenth century. It is not only the oldest but also the sole pre-Reformation organ case to survive in the British Isles. It was substantially but sensitively restored in 1872, under the direction of Frederick Sutton, and a new instrument by J. W. Walker was installed. The evidence of the case is sufficient to establish the layout of the front principal pipes, the placing of the stop levers at the right-hand end of the case and the likely number of ranks. In the wider context of Wales (and of Britain), these archaeological and organological remains complement the documentary evidence elsewhere.

This was an organ intended for liturgical use. From the archaeological remains it is possible to deduce that it had at least five ranks and a compass of forty-five notes, typical of British organs of the time: keyboard C to $a2$ (probably without $C\,sharp$), nominally sounding F to $d3$ on a 5-ft principal.[36] An instrument made in 2010–11 by Goetze and Gwynn for a Bangor University research project endeavoured to emulate some of its characteristics, with six ranks: diapason (stopped rank), two principals, two octaves and

---

[32] As with Montgomery, the church was in the diocese of Hereford.
[33] There is a record of a chantry priest in 1541, Sir Walter Willat, who became vicar in 1554 (d. 1579). R. W. D. Fenn and J. B. Sinclair, 'Old Radnor Church', *The Radnorshire Society Transactions*, 58 (1988), 78–91; here, 84.
[34] Lucy Toulmin Smith, ed., *The Itinerary of John Leland in Wales in or about the Years 1536–1539* (London: George Bell & Sons, 1906), p. 42.
[35] Fenn and Sinclair, 'Old Radnor Parish Church', 84.
[36] Details confirmed by Dominic Gwynn, private communication, June 2021.

fifteenth.[37] Such an instrument may have been available to the organist and composer John Bull (1559x63–1628) in his youth: he is reputed to have been born in Old Radnor. More importantly in this context, it was the kind of instrument for which the surviving liturgical music for the Latin rite was written, the most substantial source of which is GB-Lbl Add MS 29996.[38] This source contains all the extant organ music of Philip ap Rhys.[39]

Philip ap Rhys (d. 1566) was a vicar choral of St Paul's Cathedral, London. He was paid for playing the organ at St Mary-at-Hill, Billingsgate, in 1547. He may have played there earlier, but there is a gap in the otherwise extensive parish accounts between 1540 and 1547. He may have moved to St Paul's following the death of John Redford (d. 1547), organist and almoner. There is no record of him being born or living in Wales, but he used the Welsh form of his name in his will and in his assent to the Acts of Supremacy and Uniformity of 1559. Seven of his organ works appear in the first layer of Add MS 29996, and this may suggest that they date from the 1540s, when he was playing at St Mary-at-Hill.[40] A short setting of the Compline psalm antiphon *Miserere* is the first piece in the whole collection, and there is a setting of the Offertory *Felix namque* for mass of the Blessed Virgin Mary as celebrated from after Epiphany up to Advent. By far the most significant of the compositions are the five pieces that form the sole example in Britain of a complete organ mass. There are four movements of the ordinary of the mass: Kyrie, Gloria, Sanctus and Agnus Dei. (An opening was left blank for a setting of Credo to be entered.) The fifth movement is an offertory, *Beatus sit Deus Pater* for mass on Trinity Sunday. The psalm antiphon and the two offertories are through-composed organ pieces; the four movements of the ordinary of the mass were intended for alternatim performance. Alternatim – the alternation of voices and organ – was the norm: there is no evidence that organs accompanied voices before the Reformation. In these movements, the organ played the alternate strains, paraphrasing the chant, to which one

---

[37] John Harper, 'An Organ for St Teilo: A Welsh Instrument in the Pre-Reformation Tradition', *Journal of the British Institute of Organ Studies*, 35 (2011), 134–153.
[38] Digitised images of the MS at www.bl.uk/manuscripts/Viewer.aspx?ref=add_ms_29996_fs001r (accessed 30 June 2021).
[39] John Harper, 'Philip ap Rhys and his Liturgical Organ Music Revisited/Ailolwg ar Philip ap Rhys a'i Gerddoriaeth Organ Litwrgïaidd', *Welsh Music History/Hanes Cerddoriaeth Cymru*, 2 (1997), 126–172.
[40] John Caldwell, ed., *Early Tudor Organ Music I: Music for the Office*, Early English Church Music, 6 (London: Stainer and Bell for The British Academy, [1966]), p. 42; Denis Stevens, ed., *Early Tudor Organ Music II: Music for the Mass*, Early English Church Music, 10 (London: Stainer and Bell for The British Academy, [1969]), pp. 1–15, 92–93.

or more singers responded by singing the next strain of the chant, or improvising polyphony upon the chant in faburden or in composed polyphony.

This body of music could well have been performed at Old Radnor as much as at St Mary-at-Hill or St Paul's. It would have been particularly useful during the reign of Mary Tudor. The Latin rite may have been reinstated in 1554, but many of the additional clergy and the income from chantries, fraternities and guilds, which supported them and other singers and organ players in churches, had been lost.

The Consequences of the Reformation

In the space of less than two decades between 1534 and 1552, the infrastructure and funding of the church in England and Wales were significantly reduced and substantially weakened. Monasteries, friaries, non-educational colleges, chantries, guilds and fraternities were all dissolved. In Brecon, that involved the suppression of the priory with its Benedictine liturgy, the friary with its Dominican pattern, and several craft guilds (including cordwainers) which generated funds to support the parish church and St Mary's chapel. The cathedrals and parish churches survived; but they lost the income from chantries, guilds and fraternities that had so often enabled them to enrich their liturgy both ritually and musically.

That transition can be observed at an early stage of the Reformation at Abergwili and Brecon, where a reforming bishop not only instigated the transfer of the collegiate foundation from rural Abergwili to urban Brecon, forty miles west, but used the funds for sung liturgy to provide instead for education. In 1541, on the recommendation of William Barlow (d. 1568), bishop of St Davids (1536–48), Henry VIII ordered the refoundation of the college of Abergwili to the buildings of the former Dominican friary in Brecon.[41] Furthermore, the king directed that the income of £53 per annum used at Abergwili to maintain a choir should be put to better use (*in meliores usus potest disponi*) in meeting educational needs. The new Christ College included master, usher, lecturer, chaplain and twenty scholars. It can be compared with other new foundations of Henry VIII and Edward VI, where ecclesiastical buildings and funds were redirected to education, as at the new king's schools at the former monasteries of Coventry, Gloucester, Peterborough, Rochester and Worcester.

---

[41] William Dugdale, *Monasticon Anglicanum*, VI, iii, pp. 1496–1500.

With the introduction of The Book of Common Prayer in 1549, all the books of chant, Latin polyphony and liturgical organ music were redundant. The reformed theology that underpinned the second Book of Common Prayer (1552), only temporarily suspended during the reign of Mary, further diminished the role of music in worship. Queen Elizabeth I did her best to resist the pressures of the radical reformers, and her Royal Injunctions (1559) protected those choral foundations that still remained, and defended singing in church, both by choirs and congregation.[42] However, in the 1560s and 1570s, organs which had for the most part remained silent for some years were removed from the great majority of churches for the scrap value of their metal pipes and for the avoidance of superstitious practices, which church music represented for some Protestants.

There were exceptions, including St Mary's parish church in Swansea (Glamorgan). Before the Reformation this church had come under the aegis of St David's Hospital. From 1549 the town corporation evidently assumed this role, supplying some two thirds of the church's funds. Except for gaps in the church records, there are payments for an organist, an organ blower, and maintenance and repair of the organ from 1549 until 1627, when the organist was William Curtis. A final payment to John Hayward, organ maker of Bath, in 1631 for finishing, fitting and tuning what must have been a new organ, and the occurrence of Curtis's name in other corporation records, suggest the continuation of the organist's post and role through the 1630s.[43]

Chirk Castle Chapel

One of the best funded of the post-Reformation parish churches was St Giles, Wrexham. That wealth is still visually proclaimed by the fifteenth-century tower, but by the early seventeenth century it was famed for its wonderful organ.[44] There are no records of the choral establishment or practice at the church, and the organ was one of a number lost during the Civil War in this part of Wales. Nevertheless, evidence from Chirk Castle, south of Wrexham, may be an indicator of the musical competences and repertory at St Giles. From Chirk comes the richest source of information

---

[42] W. H. Frere, ed., *Visitation Articles and Injunctions of the Period of the Reformation*, 3 vols., Alcuin Club Collections, 14–16 (London: Longmans, Green, 1910), III, pp. 8–29; injunction 49, which deals with music, on pp. 22–23.
[43] Reynolds, 'A Study of Music and Liturgy', pp. 208–212.
[44] Reynolds, 'A Study of Music and Liturgy', pp. 213–215.

about church music in Wales in the earlier seventeenth century: four vocal partbooks and a related organ book, and the indenture for a new organ installed in the castle chapel in 1632.[45]

Chirk was one of the last of the ring of great castles built by Edward I and his nobles after the conquest of Wales. Begun in the early fourteenth century, it was (like Beaumaris Castle) never finished. In subsequent centuries it was adapted and modified for domestic rather than defensive use (though it suffered siege in the Civil War). Ownership passed through several noble families, but in 1595 it was purchased for £5,000 by Thomas Myddelton (1550–1631), a younger son of an established Denbighshire family, who made his fortune in trade in London as a founder shareholder of the East India Company, was created baronet (1603) and served as Lord Mayor of London (1613). From 1615 Sir Thomas Myddelton made his home at Stansted Hall, Essex (another acquisition), and oversight of Chirk Castle passed to his son, also Thomas (1586–1666). Following the death of his father, the younger Thomas inherited the castle and large Welsh estate. Educated at Oxford and Gray's Inn, knighted in 1617 and elected Member of Parliament in 1624, Sir Thomas was typical of the Welsh gentry whose lives were divided between their Welsh estates and London. His own life was transformed by new wealth acquired through his father's commercial success.[46]

One of the younger Thomas Myddelton's early acts as inheritor of the castle was to work on the chapel. This space had been subjected to change before, during and after the Myddeltons. What may in the fourteenth and fifteenth centuries have been a single-storey space had become double height by the seventeenth century. It is almost 15 metres (48 feet) long and 6 metres (20 feet) wide. Here Myddelton established modest choral provision, by commissioning a new organ from John Burward, organ maker to the king, and engaging a local organist, William Deane, at that time organist of Wrexham parish church, with its renowned instrument.

The organ, though relatively modest in size and in a single case, was typical of its time: a 'double' organ with two manuals consisting of seven stops on the upper manual (equivalent to the Great organ) and three stops

---

[45] Partbooks, US-NYp, Mus. Res. *MNZ (Chirk) [2]; organ book, GB-Och, Mus 6; indenture, GB-AB, Chirk collection, group F, MS 5526. Peter Le Huray, 'The Chirk Castle Partbooks', *Early Music History*, 2 (1982), 17–42.

[46] Charles Welch, rev. Trevor Dickie, 'Sir Thomas Myddelton [I]', *Oxford Dictionary of National Biography*, online version rev. 2008 (accessed 30 June 2021); J. Gwynn Williams, 'Sir Thomas Myddelton [II]', *Oxford Dictionary of National Biography*, print and online version, 2004 (accessed 30 June 2021).

on the lower manual (effectively a Chair organ, though in the same case). The indenture gives details of its dimensions and decoration: 12 ft 6 ins high, 9 ft wide and 6 ft 6 ins deep (3.8 × 2.7 × 2 metres) with five 'towers' of pipes and four 'flat towers' between them, an arrangement comparable with the much larger Great case of the contemporary organ made for Magdalen College, Oxford, c.1631, and now in Tewkesbury Abbey. It may have stood on a gallery at the western end of the chapel: the stud wall shows signs of this, and in 1663 carpenters did remedial work on the 'loft above the chapel'.[47]

The details of the organ are important, for they provide the context for the directions in the organ book regarding the pitch and registration to be used in some of the accompaniments.[48] As at Old Radnor, and as was typical of church organs in Britain up to the later seventeenth century, the organ was pitched in F; that is to say, tenor c on the keys sounded F below on the 10-ft diapason or f above on the 5-ft principal. This information has a significance far beyond Chirk, extending more generally to performance practice in church music in Britain.

The organ book provides accompaniments to thirty-six of the sixty-five choral works found in the four vocal partbooks, including two quite different organ parts for Thomas Morley's anthem, 'Out of the deep'. It must be assumed that a second organ book with the remaining accompaniments is lost. The overall repertory gives an indication of the likely liturgical practice in the chapel, and indeed of Wrexham parish church where William Deane must have composed and compiled some of the music: there are works dated 1620 naming Deane as organist of Wrexham, some twelve years before the castle chapel was provided with an organ. A listing gives the impression that fifty-one anthems dominate the collection; but that disguises the extent of the service music grouped in sets or suites of 'whole services', totalling sixty items. These include two settings of the Litany, ten sets of canticles for Morning Prayer (twenty-two items), seven sets for Evening Prayer (fourteen items), seven sets for Holy Communion (thirteen items) and five Burial Sentences. The extent of music for Holy Communion is significant at a time when the sacrament was celebrated very rarely in parish churches, perhaps no more than four

---

[47] 'February 2018 – The South Wing Laid Bare!' *National Trust*. www.nationaltrust.org.uk/chirk-castle/news/february-2018-the-south-wing-laid-bare (accessed 30 June 2021). W. M. Myddelton, *Chirk Castle Accounts, AD 1605–66* (St Albans: privately printed, 1908), p. 112.

[48] William Reynolds, 'Chirk Castle Organ and Organbook: An Insight into Performance Practice involving a Seventeenth-Century "Transposing" Organ', *Journal of the British Institute of Organ Studies*, 21 (1997), 28–55; indenture transcribed, 48–51.

times in the year. Though in due course Thomas Myddelton supported Parliament in the Civil War, this suggests that his religious outlook accorded with the 'high church' practices of the Chapel Royal and cathedrals like Durham.

The partbooks are each divided into two sections: works for four voices, and works for five or six voices. Some of the works for five or six voices lack one or more voice parts: at least one partbook is lost. Three vocal scorings are identified: for men (two contratenors, tenor and bass), for means (mean, contratenor, tenor and bass), and for trebles (treble, mean, contratenor, tenor and bass). There are works in both the full and verse styles. Thirty composers are represented, including twenty-one works (thirty-nine items) unique to the Chirk manuscripts; some are by composers not known elsewhere, while others are widely known. It is the only source of seven works (fourteen items) by William Deane.

The composers fall into two broad geographical groups: those with London appointments and associations, and those from Somerset and Devon, especially Exeter. The London group includes Edwardian and earlier Elizabethan composers (Causton, Richard Farrant, William Mundy, Morley, Robert Parsons I, Sheppard, Strogers, Tallis and Tye), and those active in the later sixteenth and earlier seventeenth century (Batten, Byrd, East, Gibbons, Hooper, John Mundy, Tomkins, Ward, Weelkes). The West Country composers range similarly from early Elizabethan to Caroline: William Parsons (Wells), Elway Bevin (Wells and Bristol) and those with Exeter connections – Hugh Facy, John Lugge, Robert Parsons II, William Randall and Solomon Tozer. John Amner (Ely) stands out as an East Anglian exception, but he enjoyed the patronage of William Bourchier, third Earl of Bath (1557–1623), who resided at Tawstock Court, south of Barnstaple, Devon, and that may possibly account for the inclusion of four anthems (three of them unique to the Chirk books). The strong West Country representation suggests that William Deane had associations there. He may perhaps be identified with the chorister at Salisbury Cathedral who was a witness in the case against John Farrant in 1591–2.[49] The origins and dates of John Alcock (five Burial Sentences) and John Boyce (a setting of 'If ye love me') are unknown, though it may be noted that William Mundy's wife was Mary Alcock.

---

[49] Dora H. Robertson, *Sarum Close*, 2nd ed. (Bath: Firecrest Publishing, 1969), pp. 151–153.

The relatively large number of works by the earlier London composers may suggest a repertory already in Wrexham before William Deane's arrival; this would be comparable with the fragmentary partbooks from Ludlow parish church, perhaps dating from no later than 1580.[50] The more contemporary London representation may in part reflect the Myddelton family's influence or London connections. The inclusion of works as vocally demanding as Gibbons's verse anthem 'Glorious and powerful God' or as extensive as William Mundy's Te Deum and Benedictus in the 'great' full style with trebles is indicative of the capabilities of the singers, not least the children, whom Deane directed, as well as of the musical richness of festal services at Chirk. Deane's own skill and sensitivity as a composer can be observed in the substantial full anthem 'O Lord, thou hast dealt graciously', and the delightful setting of The Grace.[51] How often the choir was active is unclear: Thomas Myddelton installed three family pews in the chancel of Chirk parish church to hear divine service, suggesting his attendance there. (He was also lay rector of the church.)[52] The inclusion of music for men only, for means and for trebles suggests different choral groupings at services, and perhaps ritual distinctions between liturgical feasts, Sundays and ordinary days (as also, for instance, at the Chapel Royal).

To what extent was the provision of Chirk Castle chapel (and implicitly in St Giles, Wrexham) in the 1630s indicative of the practice of church music in Welsh cathedrals and other urban parish churches in the first half of the seventeenth century? Or does it represent an isolated instance of a wealthy member of the local gentry who, on acquiring a substantial inheritance, indulged his tastes in his household chapel as well as in the courtly masque performed in 1634 (the year of Milton's *Comus* at Ludlow Castle) and the antimasque after a wedding in 1641? As ever, the paucity of documentary evidence makes a judgement difficult. Nonetheless, in 1631 it was recorded that Thomas Bulkeley of the long-established family of south-east Anglesey 'kept good hospitality, a handsome attendance, a great household, an organist and music, and had prayers and anthems every ten a clock in the morning in his house'.[53]

---

[50] GB-SHR, LB/15/1/226, 227, 229. Alan Smith, 'Elizabethan Church Music at Ludlow', *Music and Letters*, 49 (1968), 108–121.

[51] An anthology of sixteen items from the MSS has been recorded: *Music from the Chirk Castle Part-Books*, The Brabant Ensemble, dir. Stephen Rice (Hyperion, CDA67695, 2009).

[52] Myddelton, *Chirk Castle Accounts, AD 1605–66*, p. 14.

[53] David N. Klausner, *Records of Early Drama: Wales* (Toronto: University of Toronto Press, 2005), pp. 46–47 (Bulkeley), pp. 141–150 (Chirk).

Worship in Welsh

The Chirk Castle chapel manuscripts confirm the performance of church music matching that of English cathedrals and even of the Chapel Royal in quality and technical demands, if not overall extent. None of that repertory takes account of the Welsh vernacular. For a monoglot Welsh parishioner, the Reformation simply replaced one alien language (Latin) with another (English). The initiatives to address the need for prayers and Scripture in Welsh involved men based in Wales collaborating with London printers, often with the support of Welshmen who had moved to London.

The publication of the first Book of Common Prayer in 1549 stimulated William Salesbury (before 1520–*c.*1580) to undertake the first of a series of publications of liturgical and Scriptural texts into Welsh. *Kynniver Llith a Ban* (London, 1551) is a Welsh translation of the Epistles and Gospels at Holy Communion on Sundays and holy days.[54] Responding to the Act of Parliament (1563) which ordered the bishops of Wales and Hereford to commission a Welsh translation of the whole Bible and Book of Common Prayer and administration of the sacraments by March 1567, Salesbury was the principal compiler of the Welsh Book of Common Prayer, *Lliver Gweddi Gyffredin* (London, 1567).[55] A Welsh version of the New Testament followed, *Testament Newydd ein Arglwydd Iesv Christ* (London, 1567).[56] This was a collaboration between Salesbury, Richard Davies, bishop of St Davids, and Thomas Huet, precentor of St Davids Cathedral. The complete Bible took longer. *Y Beibl Cyssegr-lan* (London, 1588)[57] was principally the work of William Morgan (1544/5–1604), by then vicar of Llanrhaeadr-ym-Mochnant (Powys), but subsequently bishop of Llandaff and then St Asaph. It took a year for Morgan to oversee the setting and printing of the Welsh Bible in London, during which time he stayed with the dean of Westminster Abbey, Gabriel Goodman, founder of Ruthin School (Denbighshire). In the following decade, Morgan, assisted by John Davies and others, prepared a revised translation of The Book of Common Prayer, *Llyfr Gweddi Gyffredin* (London, 1599).[58]

---

[54] Digitised by the National Library of Wales http://hdl.handle.net/10107/5413188.
[55] Digitised by the National Library of Wales http://hdl.handle.net/10107/4856515.
[56] Digitised by the National Library of Wales http://hdl.handle.net/10107/4755114.
[57] Digitised by the National Library of Wales http://hdl.handle.net/10107/4701320.
[58] Though published under this title and catalogued as such by the National Library of Wales, other catalogues, including the Short-Title Catalogue, list it as *Llyfer Gweddi Gyffredin*.

The Metrical Psalter in Welsh

There are no surviving choral settings of texts from *Llyfr Gweddi Gyffredin*, although, as in English, the old Latin plainsong tones could be employed to sing the prose texts of versicles and responses, psalms and canticles, either in unison or with improvised faburden. Such prose texts were the domain of clerk and minister, or perhaps of a small parish choir. Texts for congregational singing needed to be metrical, but still Scriptural – especially psalms and canticles in metre. English metrical psalms originated in a domestic context, and migrated to church, to be sung not during the service itself (which had to follow the authorised texts of the prayer book) but before and after both the service and the sermon. By stages, Thomas Sternhold's selection of *Certayne Psalmes* (London, 1549) was expanded to the complete psalter in John Day's *The Whole Booke of Psalmes Collected into Englysh Metre* (London, 1562) with additional contributions by John Hopkins and others.

Early attempts to create Welsh translations of the psalms in metre date from the 1570s. However, there was a tension between the use of strict Welsh metres of the high poetic tradition and the need for settings that were simple and singable, comparable with the dominant use of Poulter's measure ('fourteeners') in the English metrical psalms, or those found in comparable continental collections. Strict metre was used for ten psalms in Welsh by the poet Siôn Tudor in the 1570s, and Captain William Middelton employed forty-three metres in a complete metrical psalter published posthumously (London, 1603), with funding from the elder Sir Thomas Myddelton, his kinsman. None of these strict-metre versions offered a ready resource for congregational song.

Edward Kyffin (c.1558–1603) wrote a sample of psalms in a singable regular metre, 'mesur salm', with a syllable pattern 8787 (*Rhann o Psalmae Dafydd Brophwyd*, London, 1603), 'i'w canu ar ôl y dôn arferedig yn Eglwys Loegr' ('to be sung in accordance with the usual tune of the English church'). Though originally from Oswestry (Shropshire), Kyffin was then curate of St Martin Outwich, London. His death from plague may have prevented the completion of the project, and it was nearly two decades later that a complete metrical psalter was published: *Llyfr y Psalmau* (London, 1621),[59] written by the aged Edmwnd Prys (1542/3–1623), who since 1576 had been archdeacon of Merioneth. Like Kyffin, Prys opted for mesur salm for all but five of his metrical psalms, a metre closely

---

[59] Digitised by the National Library of Wales http://hdl.handle.net/10107/5191521.

related to the popular carol metre. In his preface, Prys stated that 'pob plant, gweinidogion, a phobl annyscedic a ddyscant benill o garol' ('all children, servants and uneducated people can learn a verse of a carol') which 'can be sung together in a holy congregation of many praising God with one voice, one mind, one heart'.

Prys's psalter was the first Welsh book in which music was printed. There are twelve psalm tunes.[60] Nine tunes serve all but the five texts not written in mesur salm. Though mesur salm follows the syllable pattern 8787, the melodies are presented in the dominant English metre (now identified in hymnals as Common Metre), 8686. Where there is a seventh syllable in the text, it is simply sung to the same pitch as the sixth syllable. Five of these tunes had appeared in earlier collections published in London (1579, 1591, 1592) and Edinburgh (1564, 1615). The three melodies in other metres were also well established.

Psalms 51 and 67 are the only texts in a short metre (text, 6786; melody 6686), and use a melody presented as 'the church tune' in William Daman's posthumous collection (London, 1591). Prys's only use of Long Metre (8888) is Psalm 100, with the melody popularly known as 'The Old 100th', first published in a French psalter for Psalm 134 (Geneva, 1551). The third melody (set for Psalm 113) is the longest, with the unusual metre 888.888.888.888; it first appeared in a German collection, *Psalmen Gebett und Kirchenübung* (Strasbourg, 1526) with Psalm 119. It was William Kethe (d. 1594) who first linked these continental melodies to Psalm 100 and Psalm 113 in the new translations which he made for exiled English and Scottish Protestants in Geneva, and they were printed in the enlarged Anglo-Genevan psalter (Geneva, 1560).[61] From there they migrated to both English and Scottish metrical psalters, including some of Day's collections.[62]

All eight of these melodies appeared in *The Whole Books of Psalmes* published by Thomas Ravenscroft in 1621, confirming their currency in the same year as Prys's collection. Four melodies were, however, new to *Llyfr y Psalmau*, all in Common Metre. Pride of place was given to a melody by Orlando Gibbons (1583–1625) for Psalm 1, suggesting perhaps that this tune was written for this collection (see Figure 3.1). Now known as 'Song 67', it appeared as the setting of Song 67 in the second part of George

---

[60] Sally Harper, 'Tunes for a Welsh Psalter: Edmwnd Prys's *Llyfr y Psalmau*', *Studia Celtica*, 37 (2003), 221–267. This includes transcriptions of all twelve tunes.

[61] Beth Quitsland, *The Reformation in Rhyme: Sternhold, Hopkins and the English Metrical Psalter, 1547–1603* (Aldershot: Ashgate, 2008), pp. 169–176.

[62] Beth Quitsland sets out the complex narrative of different contents in Day's psalm collections printed between 1559 and 1562. Only two included Kethe's version of Psalms 100 and its associated melody, whereas his Psalm 113 and its melody were more firmly established. Beth Quitsland, *The Reformation in Rhyme*, pp. 193–238.

Beatus vir. Pſal. 1.

Dyma wynebni y pſalmau: yn dangos tycciant y duwiol ac aflwydd y rhai anuwiol.

ni ſaif ar ffoꝛdd troſeddwyr ffol,
nid eiſte 'n ſtol y gwatwoꝛ.

2 Ond ei holl ſerch ef ſydd yn rhwydd,
ar ddeddf yr Arglwydd vchod:
Ac ar ei ddeddf, rhydd ddydd a nos,
yn ddidaos ei fyfyꝛdod.

3 Ef ſydd fel pꝛen plan ar lan dol,
dwg ffrwyth amſerol arno:
Ni chrina 'i ddalen, a'i holl waith,
a lwydda 'n berffaith iddo.
4 Pid felly bydd y dꝛwg di-rus,
ond fel ʒ us ar goꝛwynt:
Yr hwn o'ꝛ tir â'i chwyth a'i chwal,
anwadal ſydd ei helynt.

5 Am hyn y dꝛwg ni ſaif mewn barn,
o flaen y cadarn dniawn:
Na'r pechaduriaid mawꝛ eu bar,
ynghynulleidfa'r cyſtawn.
6 Canys yr Arglwydd Donw, ſel hyn,
a edwyn ffyꝛdd gwirionaid:
Ac ef ni ad byth i barhau,
'mo lwybꝛau pechaduriaid.

Pſalm. II.

Quare fremuerunt. Pſal. II.

Mae'r prophwyd Dafydd yn yr yſpryd glan yn rhagweled gwrthwyneb mawr i eglwys Chriſt. Lle y mae efe yn newid perſonau yn yr ymadrodd, mae'r yſpryd yn gryfach na rheſwm dyn.

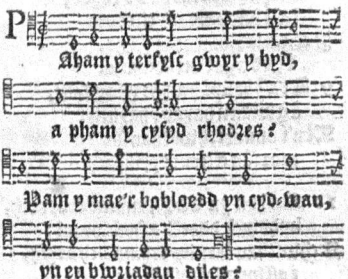

yn eu bwꝛiadau diles?

2 Cody mae bꝛenhinoedd byd,
a'i bꝛyd yn gyd-gynghoꝛal:
Yn erbyn Duw a'i Ghꝛiſt (ein plaid)
y mae pennaethiaid bydol.
3 Dꝛylliwn eu rhwymau, meddan hwy,
ni wnawn ni mwy ofydd-dod:
Ac ymaith taflwn eu trom iau,
ni chant yn frau 'mo'n goꝛfod.

4 Ond Duw 'r hwn ſydd vwch wybꝛol
a chwardd am ben eu geiriau: (len
Yr Arglwydd nef a wel en bar,
efe a'i gwatwaꝛ hwythau.
5 Yna y dywaid yn ei lid,
a hyn ſydd rhybꝛid iddyn:
D'i eiriau ef y cyſyd bꝛaw,
a'i ddig a ddaw yn ddychꝛyn.

6 Goſod ais innau (meddai ef)
â llaw gref yn dꝛagywydd:
B Fy mrenin

Figure 3.1 Edmwnd Prys, *Llyfr y Psalmau* (1621), fo. 1r. Psalm 1, with the melody known as 'Song 67', attributed to Orlando Gibbons (Withers, 1623), and part of Psalm 2, with the melody later known as 'Hackney' or 'St Mary's Tune' (Playford, 1674, 1677). Llyfrgell Genedlaethol Cymru – The National Library of Wales

Withers' *Hymnes and Songs of the Church* (London, 1623), but with one note different from Prys. The melodies printed with Psalms 2, 5 and 8 were also new to the psalm-tune repertory; their composers are unknown. That for Psalm 2 was later used by John Playford for Psalm 61 (named 'Hackney' in *An Introduction to the Skill of Musick*, 4th ed., London, 1674) and Psalm 91 (now named 'St Mary's Tune' in *The Whole Book of Psalms*, London, 1677). There are no recorded concordances for the other two melodies either before or after Prys.[63]

The provision of specific music for parish worship in Welsh was tiny, consisting of no more than the twelve tunes in *Llyfr y Psalmau*; but they provide an important indicator. As with the choral repertory at Chirk Castle, there was no thought of being distinctly Welsh. Rather, the selection of psalm tunes demonstrates a pragmatic balance. The dominant metre, mesur salm, related to a familiar Welsh tradition of carolling, and it was accessible to all regardless of social standing or intellect; it was also compatible with the dominant metre of English metrical psalms, Common Metre, itself related to the popular ballad. Furthermore, eight of the twelve psalm tunes were current in England; those who lived or worked in both Welsh and English, including those who spent time in both cultures, could find common musical ground in worship. This represents a melding of regional cultures and languages, rather than mere borrowing by Wales from England.

---

[63] All the tunes are found in Maurice Frost, *English and Scottish Psalm and Hymn Tunes c. 1543–1677* (London: SPCK and Oxford University Press, 1953).

CHAPTER 4

Secular Music before 1650

Sally Harper

A wickedly humorous mid-sixteenth-century travelogue offers a fascinating vignette of some of the characteristics that shaped Welsh secular music throughout the late medieval and early modern periods.[1] In 1542, the English itinerant physician Andrew Boorde (*c*.1490–1549) published his *Fyrst Bok of the Introduction of Knowledge*,[2] intended to help the reader 'know the usage and fashion of all manner of countries' from Norway to Jerusalem. Wales and its people are the subject of chapter two. Having characterised the Welsh as light-fingered, work-shy, prone to catch coughs because they choose to go bare-legged and addicted to both 'cawse boby' ('rosted cheese') and 'swyshe swashe metheglyn' (spiced mead), Boorde notes their all-consuming obsession with ancestry. Likely to be called ap Ryce, ap Davy or ap Flood, and related to ap Hoby, ap Ienkin and ap Goffe, the average Welshman can trace his lineage back to Brutus, great-grandson of Aeneas of Troy, and will even claim direct kinship with Our Lady, whom he loves devoutly. But above all, Boorde notes the Welsh passion for the harp:

> And yf I haue my harpe, I care for no more;
> It is my treasure, I do kepe it in store,
> For my harpe is made, of a good mares skyn,
> The stringes be of horse heare, it maketh a good din
> My songe, and my voyce, and my harpe doth agree,
> Muche lyke the hussyng of a homble be;
> Yet in my countrey I do make good pastyme,
> In tellyng of prophyces whyche be not in ryme.[3]

---

[1] Most of the themes addressed in this chapter are explored more fully in Sally Harper, *Music in Welsh Culture before 1650: A Study of the Principal Sources* (Aldershot: Ashgate, 2007).

[2] Andrew Boorde, *The Fyrst Bok of the Introduction of Knowledge*, ed. by Frederick James Furnivall (London: published for the Early English Text Society, Extra Series, 10, by N. T. Trübner & Co., 1870).

[3] Ibid., p. 126.

For all its playful satire, Boorde's caricature is invaluable in identifying three predominant features of Welsh secular music before 1650: the use of a distinctive form of harp; the partnership of voice and instrument; and the celebration of ancestry and the prophetic. The last characteristic, recorded from at least the twelfth century, is also signalled in more sober terms in an undated document headed 'The state of North Wales towchinge religion', returned to the Council in the Marches towards the end of the sixteenth century.[4] This expresses concern about the superstitious custom of summoning 'all sortes of men woomen and Childerne of everie parishe' to large outdoor assemblies on Sundays and holidays, where 'harpers and Crowthers' would 'singe them songes of the doeinges of their Auncestors namelie of their warrs againste the kinges of this realme and the English nacion'. Pedigrees would also be recited, showing 'howe eche of them is discended from those theire ould princes', as well as 'some parte of the lives of Thalaassyn Marlin Beno Kybbye Iernin, and suche other the intended Prophettes and Sainctes of the cuntrie'.[5] The gatherings were overseen by the 'Pencars or heade minstrelles' of the bardic community, apparently operating at the behest of the nobility. Events of this nature were also known to take place in much more exalted surroundings. In 1507, for instance, the anniversary of the admission of Rhys ap Thomas to the Order of the Garter two years earlier was marked by a five-day tournament at Carew Castle, allegedly attended by a thousand people. Dinner, 'Seasoned with diversity of musicke', was taken in the great hall, where 'Bardes and pryduides [poets] Sung many a Song in commeration of the vertues and famous Achieuements of those Gentlemen's Ancestors there present', apparently in the manner of the ancient Greeks, who would sing the deeds of mighty men to the lyre at banquets.[6]

---

[4] GB-Lbl Add MS Lansdowne 111, fol. 10rv, transcribed David Klausner, ed., *Records of Early Drama: Wales*, Records of Early English Drama (Toronto: University of Toronto Press, 2005), pp. 29, 401. Klausner suggests that the report may have been commissioned by William Cecil, Lord Burghley while serving as lord treasurer (1572–1598). See also Sally Harper, '"Songes of the Doeinges of Their Auncestors": Aspects of Welsh and English Musical Traditions', in *Authority and Subjugation in Writing of Medieval Wales*, ed. by Ruth Kennedy and Simon Meecham-Jones, New Middle Ages Series, ed. by Bonnie Wheeler (New York: Palgrave Macmillan, 2008), pp. 231–250.

[5] Taliesin is the sixth-century bard, and Merlin the mythological character of Arthurian legend. Beuno and Cybi are both North Walian saints, while 'Iernin' may be St Germanus, said to have led the native Britons to victory at a mountainous site near a river, traditionally identified with Mold, north-east Wales.

[6] The account is part of the Life of Sir Rhys ap Thomas (c.1449–1525), written by his direct descendant Henry Rice (c.1590–c.1651). Transcription in Klausner, ed., *Records: Wales*, pp. 256–267; see also Ralph A. Griffiths, *Sir Rhys ap Thomas and His Family: A Study in the Wars of the Roses and Early Tudor Politics* (Cardiff: University of Wales Press, 1993), pp. 273–282 (p. 277).

This tradition of celebrating ancestry and the nation's history with string accompaniment has an auspicious pedigree. Welsh bards had long been regarded as champions of their native culture and the keepers of genealogy. Giraldus Cambrensis observed in his *Descriptio Kambriae* (1193/4),[7] based on a tour of Wales made in 1188, that Welsh poets recited pedigrees from memory and added the genealogies of contemporary princes to their ancient books, while the Denbighshire historian David Powel (1552?–98) noted almost four centuries later that the bards were still greatly esteemed for their keeping of 'records of Gentlemens armes and petegrees', supported by 'plaiers vpon instruments, cheefelie the Harpe and the Crowthe'.[8] This partnership of voice and instrument in the context of national celebration signals the close cooperation of poets and musicians in Wales. They were collectively referred to as gwŷr wrth gerdd ('men at their craft') and belonged to a hierarchical bardic order that shared some parallels with the craft guilds of the medieval trades. These parallels included a lengthy apprenticeship: a harper or crythor typically took twelve years to rise to the level of pencerdd (master craftsman). Poetry was referred to as cerdd dafod ('the craft of the tongue') and music as cerdd dant ('the craft of the string'); terms first appearing together in the set of mnemonic triads that concludes the earliest known copy of the bardic 'grammar' used by apprentices and their instructors (*c*.1330):

> Tri ryw brifgerd ysyd, nyt amgen: kerd dant, kerd vegin, a cherd dauawt.
> Teir prifgerd tant ysyd, nyt amgen: kerd grwth, kerd delyn, a cherd timpan.
> Teir prifgerd megin ysyd, nyt amgen: organ, a phibeu, a cherd y got [god].
> Teir prifgerd tauawt ysyd: prydu, a dachanu, a chanu gan delyn.[9]

> (There are three main crafts, namely: the craft of the string, the craft of wind, and the craft of the tongue.

> There are three main types of string music, namely: crwth music, harp music, and tiompán music.

> There are three main types of wind music, namely: organ, and pipes, and bagpipe music.

---

[7] *Descriptio Kambriae, Giraldi Cambrensis Opera*, ed. by J. F. Dimock (London: Rolls Series, 8 vols., 1861–1891), VI (1868), p. 167; *The Description of Wales*, translated by L. Thorpe (London: Penguin, 1978), p. 223.

[8] David Powel, *The Historie of Cambria* (London, 1584). Facs. ed. in the series The English Experience, its record in early printed books published in facsimile, no. 163 (Amsterdam and New York: Theatrum Orbis Terrarum and Da Capo Press, 1969), pp. 191–192. Digitised by the National Library of Wales: http://hdl.handle.net/10107/4787807.

[9] GB-AB NLW MS Peniarth 20, p. 346, transcribed in *Gramadegau'r Penceirddiaid*, ed. by G. J. Williams and E. J. Jones (Cardiff: Gwasg Prifysgol Cymru, 1934), p. 57. MS Peniarth 20 has been digitised by the National Library of Wales: http://hdl.handle.net/10107/4754463.

There are three main crafts of the tongue: making poetry, and reciting, and singing it with the harp.)

Of the instruments listed here, the harp dominated Welsh music throughout the period in question and is still an obvious signifier of national musical identity. The crwth was also an instrument of status, and though it fell from favour in the eighteenth century, it is now enjoying a revival.[10] The tiompán (long since obsolete, but probably a relative of the lyre)[11] was perhaps little used in Wales but known in Ireland and Scotland. Pipes (and occasionally bagpipes) are mentioned in several earlier Welsh sources (as described later in this chapter), and there are fourteenth-century poetic references to fine organs at the cathedrals of Bangor and St Davids. Most striking, however, is the emphasis in the triads on poetic declamation with harp accompaniment ('canu gan delyn'). Strict-metre poetry in Welsh was (and in many cases still is) designed for performance before an audience rather than for private reading. Many poets would declaim their own work while accompanying themselves on the harp, though by the fifteenth century there are references to poets travelling in company with independent harp and crwth players, and in some cases with professional reciters.[12]

The Roots of the Welsh Bardic Tradition

Prior to Edward I's invasion of Wales at the end of the thirteenth century, bardic craftsmen earned their living under the patronage of the Welsh princes. These early 'beirdd y tywysogion' ('bards of the princes') were generally attached to a single court, where their main role was to sustain the honour of the prince and his family through praise poetry. The earliest known reference to this 'praise of both tongue and string' ('can folawd â thafod a thant') appears in a poetic awdl of c.1213 addressed to one of the great rulers of the House of Gwynedd, Llywelyn ap Iorwerth. A fuller picture of this bardic role emerges from the native Law of Hywel Dda

---

[10] For a useful short account of the crwth, see Bethan Miles and Robert Evans, 'Crwth', *The New Grove Dictionary of Music and Musicians*, 2nd ed. (London: Macmillan, 2001), VI, pp. 747–753. For recent recordings, see Cass Meurig, *Crwth* (Fflach, 2004) and Bragod, *Kaingk* (Robert Evans and Mary-Anne Roberts, privately produced, 2004).
[11] A. Buckley, 'What Was the Timpán? A Problem in Ethnohistorical Organology: Evidence in Irish Literature', *Jahrbuch für musikalische Volks- und Volkerkunde*, 9 (1978), 53–88.
[12] For a fuller exploration of poetic performance, see Sally Harper, 'Dafydd ap Gwilym, Poet and Musician', in *Gwaith Dafydd ap Gwilym*, ed. by Dafydd Johnston (published online, University of Wales, Swansea, www.dafyddapgwilym.net, accessed 25 June 2021). The site also features video recordings of experimental declamations.

(d. 949/950), a much-copied document surviving in various redactions from c.1250, though reflecting elements of much earlier legal practice.[13] Book 1, the Laws of Court, refers to three types of poet-musician. The bardd teulu ('bard of the retinue') was the eighth of twenty-four court officers who travelled into battle with the king's war-band (teulu) when such a body existed (perhaps only up to the twelfth century). He inspired the warriors from the front by singing a text identified in many copies of the Law as 'Unbeiniaeth Prydain' ('The Sovereignty of Britain'), perhaps synonymous with the great vaticinatory poem of c.930 found in the Book of Taliesin, 'Armes Prydain' ('The Great Prophecy of Britain').[14] The bardd teulu also offered songs in the princely hall and sang for the queen at her request. The second category of musician was the pencerdd (in this context 'chief of craft'), who was a respected visitor to the court rather than an integral member of it. When in residence he lodged with the heir and entertained the company with two types of song: one of God, the other of kingship. Beyond the environs of the court he could solicit for business, earning his living by instructing a lowlier third category of musician, the cerddor (minstrel). One redaction of the Law preserved in the mid-thirteenth-century 'Llyfr Colan' notes that a competent cerddor would eventually exchange his horsehair-strung harp (telyn raun) for another unspecified harp and become an independent eirchiad (supplicant) for his own work.[15]

The harp was an instrument of great status within this princely context. In addition to the telyn raun (or rawn) used by the cerddor, the law books refer to three 'legal harps' (telyn kyfreithawl): those of the king, the pencerdd and the gwrda or nobleman,[16] each with its own cyweirgorn or 'tuning horn'. References to other instruments are rarer,

---

[13] Relevant extracts from several different redactions of the Law are given in Klausner, ed., *Records: Wales*, pp. 4–7 and pp. 11–28 (trans. pp. 310–311 and pp. 314–326). See also Dafydd Jenkins, ed. and trans., *The Law of Hywel Dda: Law Texts from Medieval Wales*, The Welsh Classics 2 (Llandysul: Gomer Press, 1986) and T. M. Charles-Edwards, *The Welsh Laws* (Cardiff: University of Wales Press, 1989) for discussion of the various versions and their dating. Several redactions have been digitised by the National Library of Wales, including the early Latin text Peniarth MS 28, probably copied and illuminated in the middle of the 13th century: http://hdl.handle.net/10107/4400109.

[14] Dafydd Jenkins, 'Bardd Teulu and *Pencerdd*', in *The Welsh King and His Court*, ed. by T. M. Charles-Edwards, Morfydd E. Owen and Paul Russell (Cardiff: University of Wales Press, 2000), pp. 142–166.

[15] 'Pob penkerd telyn a dyly e'r kerdoryon yeueyng a uynno emadau a telyn raun a mynnu [bot] en kerdaur keweythas a bot en eyrchat.' Dafydd Jenkins, gol., *Damweiniau Colan: Llyfr y Damweiniau yn ôl Llawysgrif Peniarth 30* (Aberystwyth: Cymdeithas Lyfrau Ceredigion, 1973), t. 75.

[16] 'Teyr telyn kyureythyaul esyd: telyn e brenhyn a thelyn penkerd a thelyn gurda. Guerth e due gyntaf chue ugeynt, a pedeyr ar ugeynt ar eu keweyrgorn; telyn gurda try ugeynt, a deudec keynnyauc ar e kyweyrgorn.' Aled Rhys Wiliam, ed., *Llyfr Iorwerth: a Critical Text of the Venedotian Code of*

though one mid-thirteenth-century version of the Law indicates that the king could reward a pencerdd with the gift of a crwth or pipes rather than a harp, presumably in accordance with musical ability. These three instruments are also mentioned together by Giraldus Cambrensis in two documents: the *Descriptio Kambriae* (1193/4), mentioned above, and the slightly earlier *Topographia Hibernica* (1188), recording his travels in Ireland.[17] Giraldus implies that the harp (*cithara*) was popular in Wales, Scotland and Ireland, while the crwth (*choro*) held sway in Wales and Scotland, and the tiompán (*tympano*) in Scotland and Ireland, though the pipes (*tibias*) are apparently known only in Wales.[18]

Harps were evidently ubiquitous and used by both professionals and amateurs in Wales. 'Guests who arrive early in the day are entertained until nightfall by girls who play to them on the harp. In every house there are young women just waiting to play for you, and there is certainly no lack of harps. . . . in every Welsh court or family the menfolk consider playing on the harp to be the greatest of all accomplishments'.[19] Gerald was also impressed by Welsh dexterity: 'When they play their instruments they charm and delight the ear with the sweetness of their music. They play quickly and in subtle harmony. Their fingering is so rapid that they produce this harmony out of discord'.[20]

The death of Llywelyn ap Gruffudd, 'ein llyw olaf' ('our last leader'), in 1282 signalled the demise of the princely courts, and bardic patronage now passed to the next layer of society – Welsh landowners of good stock, referred to as uchelwyr ('high men'). The bards who served them were largely itinerant, and their genealogical knowledge was

---

Medieval Welsh Law; Mainly from BM. Cotton Ms Titus Dii (Cardiff: University of Wales Press, 1960), pp. 22–23.

[17] Giraldus Cambrensis, *Topographia Hibernica*, *Giraldi Cambrensis Opera*, ed. by J. F. Dimock, V (London: Rolls Series, 1867), pp. 3–204, translated by John J. O'Meara as Giraldus Cambrensis (Gerald of Wales), *The History and Topography of Ireland*, rev. ed. (Portlaoise: North America Humanities Press; Dolmen Press, 1982). See also Philip Weller, 'Gerald of Wales's View of Music/ Golwg Gerallt Gymro ar Gerddoriaeth', *Welsh Music History/Hanes Cerddoriaeth Cymru*, 2 (1997), 1–32.

[18] 'Hibernia quidem tantum duobus utitur et delectatur instrumentis; cithara scilicet, et tympano. Scotia tribus; cithara, tympano, et choro. Wallia vero cithara, tibiis, et choro', *Topographia Hibernica*, V, p. 154; translated in *The History and Topography of Ireland*, p. 104.

[19] 'Qui matutinis autem horis adveniunt, puellarum affatibus et citharisque modulis usque ad vesperam delectantur. Domus enim hic quaelibet puellas habet, et citharas, ad hoc deputatas. . . omnes quoque de curia seu familia viri, citra doctrinam omnem, citharizandi per se peritiam tenet.' Giraldus, *Descriptio Kambriae*, VI, p. 183; translated in *The Description of Wales*, p. 236.

[20] 'In musicis instrumentis, tanta sonoritatis dulcedine aures deliniunt et demulcent; tanta modulorum celeritate pariter et subtilitate feruntur; tantamque discrepantium sub tam praecipiti digitorum rapacitate consonantiam praestant.' Giraldus, *Descriptio Kambriae*, VI, p. 186; translated in *The Description of Wales*, p. 239.

increasingly valued: verse crafted by the beirdd yr uchelwyr from the fourteenth to the seventeenth century often affirms not only a patron's lineage, but also his status and generosity, praising everything from his house and his horse to his harp. The poetry of this era is dominated by a lively new form known as the cywydd deuair hirion: the 'long-lined couplet', characterised by assonance and a form of internal alliteration termed cynghanedd ('sound-chiming'). The cywydd first flourished during the era of the great Welsh poet Dafydd ap Gwilym (*fl.* 1330–50), whose cywydd 'Y Gainc' ('The melody') describes him crafting verse at the harp while simultaneously creating an accompaniment.[21]

A self-accompanying poet like Dafydd ap Gwilym would have used a small, portable harp, perhaps a form of the telyn raun (or rawn) first mentioned in the 'Llyfr Colan'. This horsehair-strung instrument remained prevalent in the Welsh bardic context until at least the seventeenth century, and evidently made an impact on Andrew Boorde in 1542. Other types of harp were nevertheless known in Wales, including the metal-strung harp used by the Irish (and there is evidence for significant cultural and musical interchange between Wales and Ireland until at least the twelfth century, explored further below). Gut strings were the norm elsewhere in Europe and England, but apparently despised in Wales, at least by some: a cywydd by Iolo Goch (*c.*1325–*c.*1398) berates a new type of gut-strung 'leather harp' (telyn ledr), regarded as far inferior to the telyn rawn.[22] Iolo condemns both its studded soundboard and 'hoarse voice', reminiscent of the 'wild neighing of a yellow mare', perhaps recalling the mare's-skin covering noted by Boorde. Siôn Phylip of Ardudwy similarly describes a harp with skin-covered sound box and bone tuning pins in a cywydd of *c.*1580.

From the fifteenth century larger bray harps were probably common in Wales for more ambitious solo repertory, such as that preserved in the harp tablature of Robert ap Huw (see the section 'The Robert ap Huw Manuscript', later in this chapter). This 'telyn gwrachod' featured small wooden L-shaped pegs or 'brays' (gwrachïod), fitted to the bottom of each string, which result in a distinctive braying or buzzing sound, akin to Boorde's 'hussyng of a homble bee'. The extant repertory suggests a harp of approximately twenty-five strings, while the poet Huw Machno (*c.*1560–

---

[21] 'Y Gainc', in *Gwaith Dafydd ap Gwilym*, no. 91, ed. by Dafydd Johnston (www.dafyddapgwilym.net, accessed 25 June 2021).

[22] Dafydd Johnston, ed., *Iolo Goch: Poems* (Llandysul: Gomer, 1993), pp. 130–132.

1637) refers to a harp with twenty-two 'purposeful curved brays' ('cimion wrachïod cymwys'). Bray harps like these (albeit with gut strings) were by no means exclusive to Wales: they were common across Renaissance Europe and are often styled 'Gothic harps', characterised by their tall, slender shape and elegant bowed front.

The idiosyncratic pairing of bray harp and crwth is depicted in a much-anthologised mid-sixteenth-century Welsh carved wooden panel now at Cotehele House, Cornwall,[23] in which the players are dressed in courtly attire (see Figure 4.1). The crwth is rectangular and has five strings, though eighteenth-century diagrams confirm that six were the norm. The crythor's bow is lost from this panel, probably due to damage, but the instrument

Figure 4.1 Carved panel on a cupboard originally from Wales but now at Cotehele House, Cornwall, showing players of a crwth and a harp. © National Trust

---

[23] For recent work on the dating of the Cotehele panel see Nicholas Riall, 'A Tudor Cupboard at Cotehele and Associated Carpentry Work from the Welsh Marches', *Journal of the Regional Furniture Society*, 26 (2012): https://regionalfurnituresociety.files.wordpress.com/2013/02/a02-riall.pdf (accessed 22 Sept. 2021), and Tina O'Connor, 'The Cotehele Cupboard: An Elegy in Oak': https://regionalfurnituresociety.files.wordpress.com/2013/02/01-oconnor.pdf (accessed 22 Sept. 2021) and Adam Bowett, 'The Cotehele Cupboard Revisited: One Cupboard or Two?', both ibid., 28 (2014): https://regionalfurnituresociety.files.wordpress.com/2013/02/02-bowett-cotehele.pdf (accessed 22 Sept. 2021).

could be played with a bow or by plucking the strings: four were set across the fingerboard in octave pairs, with the other two (more often plucked) at an oblique: a cywydd by Dafydd ab Hywel (*fl.* 1480–1520) describing a sycamore-framed crwth calls them the 'two strings for the thumb' (daudant i'r fawd).[24]

Bardic Progression and the Eisteddfod

From at least the mid-fifteenth century, progression within the Welsh bardic hierarchy was dependent on the well-regulated acquisition of carefully defined techniques and repertory. Accomplishments were typically celebrated and examined at an eisteddfod (see Chapter 5) or other public event, such as a wedding feast, where progression was confirmed. The great Christmas feast hosted in Cardigan Castle in 1176 by the Lord Rhys ap Gruffudd, described in the chronicle *Brut y Tywysogion* (c.1330),[25] is sometimes regarded as the first eisteddfod, though that term does not occur in written sources until the early 1520s. Advertised a year in advance throughout Wales, England, Scotland, Ireland and the other islands, the feast included separate contests for poets and musicians, here defined as harpers, crwth players, pipers and 'various classes of music-craft' ('telynoryon a chrythoryon a phibydyon ac amrauaelyon genedloed gerd music'). A chair was awarded to the winner in both overall categories, and a young man from Rhys's own court was pronounced as the victorious harpist.

Whatever the authenticity of this early description, an event held at Carmarthen Castle in the early 1450s had certain impact on the Welsh bardic community as a whole and was mentioned by several contemporary poets who attended. The chaired bard on this occasion was the gentleman-poet Dafydd ab Edmwnd, and some sources name Cynwrig Bencerdd as the best harpist and eventual winner of the 'ariandlws' (silver trophy). Carmarthen was probably instrumental in enforcing rigorous graduation requirements: Dafydd allegedly revised the twenty-four metres of cerdd dafod specially for it, declaring some obsolete, and making others more demanding. This was a likely spur for bardic musicians to begin codifying

---

[24] GB-AB NLW MS 37B. Text and translation may be found in the liner notes to *Kaingk*, a CD by Bragod (voice and crwth duo).

[25] Thomas Jones, trans., *Brut y Tywysogyon or the Chronicle of the Princes. Peniarth Ms. 20 Version* (Cardiff: University of Wales Press, 1952), pp. 127–128. See also Klausner, ed., *Records: Wales*, pp. 81–82 and p. 333. It has been digitised by the National Library of Wales: http://hdl.handle.net/10107/4754463.

their own repertory, for it was in the later years of the fifteenth century that cerdd dant apparently began to flourish as a solo craft.

The two eisteddfodau held at the small town of Caerwys, Flintshire, in 1523 and 1567 had an even greater impact on bardic musicians. Both events required mastery of a demanding repertory so that 'degrees' could be awarded: trained craftsmen were constantly in danger of being undermined by unlicensed strolling entertainers, and stringent attempts were needed to safeguard their livelihood. Patrons remained a vital part of this process, and three prominent noblemen presided as commissioners in 1523 along with two poets (one of whom, Tudur Aled, was allegedly an accomplished harper too). The senior commissioner, Richard ap Howel ab Ieuan Fychan, squire of the great house of Mostyn, was singled out as the main patron, and the silver trophy (ariandlws) that was donated as a prize for the best harper at this and subsequent contests still exists among the Mostyn family treasures.

The 1567 eisteddfod was overseen by an even larger team of auspicious patrons than its 1523 predecessor, its authority further enhanced by an official royal commission signed by Elizabeth I, which emphasises the continual need to cull the ever-increasing numbers of 'vagraunt and idle persons naming themselves mystrelles Rithmers and Barthes'.[26] Among its overseers were Richard ap Howel's grandson William Mostyn MP, who had inherited responsibility for 'the gyfte and bestowing of the sylver harper appertaining to the Cheff of that facultie': a telling reminder that the Welsh gentry, supported by 'such expert men in the said facultie of the welshe musick', still played a vital role in the regulation of poets and musicians and the awarding of degrees.

The Caerwys eisteddfodau are especially significant in our understanding of cerdd dant, since they engendered a comprehensive set of bardic regulations known as the Statute of Gruffudd ap Cynan.[27] Devised shortly before 1523 by an anonymous compiler (perhaps Tudur Aled himself), the Statute purported to reproduce parts of a document associated with a much earlier eisteddfod at Caerwys, presided over by the half-Irish prince Gruffudd ap Cynan (1054/5–1137), which had also sought to 'legislate and rule on all compositions' and root out 'worthless weeds' ('gorweigion chwynn').

---

[26] Transcribed Klausner, ed., *Records: Wales*, pp. 170–171.
[27] Two versions of the Statute, together with various other associated documents, are given in Klausner, ed., *Records: Wales*, pp. 159–183 (trans. pp. 349–370), with notes on sources at pp. cxvii–cxix.

The Statute spells out complex requirements for both poets and musicians, who were examined in broadly comparable tasks, and graded identically up to the level of pencerdd;[28] the text also decrees that instructors were to carry a copy of the Statute to prove their worth to apprentices. Harp and crwth players were to master a range of set musical forms to advance their position within the bardic hierarchy, rising through three levels of apprenticeship to attain the status of pencerdd. An outstanding harper (though apparently not a crwth player) might also proceed to the exalted category of master instructor (athro). Some versions of the Statute also contain instructions for the datgeiniad, the declaimer or reciter required to develop various musical skills as well as knowing the poetic metres.

The Statute initially envisaged that an eisteddfod would be held every three years, although in practice it was more than four decades before an event of comparable scale took place. Efforts to organise a third eisteddfod in 1594 proved abortive, although the objectives of the planned gathering remained identical: to nurture 'skillful honest and sober men exercised and brought up to play on the instruments called the harp and crwth' and '... to trie & examine who be worthie to weare & beare awaye the same silver prices ... & to represse suche as be vnskillfull & leade a roguishe life'.[29]

Recording the History of Cerdd Dant

The Statute of Gruffudd ap Cynan confirms the extent to which bardic musicians were acutely aware of the ancient roots of their craft. The eponymous Gruffudd himself was the Dublin-born king of Gwynedd, related both to Scandinavian kings and to several Irish dynasties on his mother's side. He sailed between Ireland and Wales several times in a series of turbulent attempts to establish his authority in his patrimonial kingdom, sometimes seeking help from his great Irish ally Muirchertach Ua Briain (d.1119) king of Munster and ultimately high king of Ireland. Though there is no evidence to confirm David Powel's claim that Gruffudd himself imported 'divers cunning musicians' from Ireland,[30]

---

[28] Fuller discussion in Sally Harper, 'The Robert ap Huw Manuscript and the Canon of Sixteenth-Century Harp Music/Llawysgrif Robert ap Huw a Chanon Cerddoriaeth Gymreig i'r Delyn yn yr Unfed Ganrif ar Bymtheg', *Welsh Music History/Hanes Cerddoriaeth Cymru*, 3 (1999), 130–161.

[29] The 1594 petition is reproduced in Royal Commission on Historical Manuscripts, *Report on Manuscripts in the Welsh Language*, 2 vols (London, HMSO, 1898–1910) I, 293–295 and Klausner, ed., *Records: Wales*, pp. 31–33.

[30] Powel, *The Historie of Cambria*, pp. 191–192.

the idea of a partnership between Welsh and Irish musicians is a long-standing one. The collections of bardic 'lore' that began to be copied from c.1560 often contain an important item entitled 'Cadwedigaeth Cerdd Dannau' ('The Conservation of Cerdd Dant'), which opens with a pseudo-history describing a council of named musicians meeting at 'Glyn Achlach' (Glendalough) in the time of 'Mwrthan Wyddel', a pseudonym for Muirchertach Ua Briain himself.[31] Though Gruffudd ap Cynan is not mentioned, the council shares some of the features of the Caerwys eisteddfodau: its purpose was to establish a set of rules to assist the composition, memorisation, performance and classification of cerdd dant and to create twenty-four musical measures 'in the Irish language',[32] with Mwrthan presiding over a gathering of four penceirddiaid and two named witnesses and commanding that the musical regulations be kept secure and correctly classified to prevent mistakes. These rules are created 'through the unity and counsel of those wise teachers' ('thrwy yndeb gyd gyngor yr athrawon doethion hynny') and through his 'whole ability and authority' ('drwy i holl allv ai swddav'), Mwrthan also commands everyone 'to secure and correctly classify the twenty-four measures and to keep them authentically, unmuddled, and to classify the gamut each one together' ('I swkyrio ac yn wir dosbarth y iiij messvr ar xx o bydd ai gwypo yn ddilys ddidramgwydd a dosbarth y gamwth pob vn at i gilydd').

The twenty-four measures ('mesurau') emphasised in the 'Cadwedigaeth' (discussed further later in this chapter) were a vital element of cerdd dant and surely confirm some earlier association with Irish music. Though at least some of them must have been in use for many years, their first known appearance as a canonical set of twenty-four is as an addition of c.1480 to a collection of cywyddau copied into GB-AB NLW MS Peniarth 54. Irish elements are very clearly discernible in some of the titles. The prefix 'cor' (Irish for 'tune' or 'melody') occurs in six, and 'mak' in another four: 'mak y mwn' translating as 'son of Munster', and 'mak y delgi' as 'son of Dalkey'. The measure 'Karsi' recalls the supposed twelfth-century Council even more explicitly: 'Carsi Delynior' ('the harper') is listed as one of the named witnesses at Glendalough, and Karsi is identified as the Irish father of St Kevin of Glendalough in one late medieval Welsh genealogy. Other measures among the twenty-four, however, suggest Middle Welsh titles (such as 'brut odidog', 'excellent feat'), while 'alban' suggests a Scots association and 'hatyr' is probable 'háttr', Old Norse for

---

[31] For transcription, translation and fuller discussion of sources in this section, see Harper, *Music in Welsh Culture before 1650*, pp. 110–121.

[32] Fuller discussion in Sally Harper, 'So How Many Irishmen Went to Glyn Achlach? Early Accounts of the Formation of *Cerdd Dant*', *Cambrian Medieval Celtic Studies*, 42 (2001), 1–25.

metre. This mix of languages, and the choice of an Irish rather than a Welsh authority figure to sanction the measures at Glendalough, all lend weight to the claim that Welsh music could indeed trace some influence from Ireland.

In practice, cerdd dant probably drew on many musical measures of this kind by the later sixteenth century, but the 'canonic' set of twenty-four seems to have taken precedence and was copied out many times by both bardic and antiquarian scribes. Often they appear in combination with other texts, and sometimes follow a short theoretical essay entitled 'Dosbarth Cerdd Dannau' ('the classification of cerdd dant'), a rather garbled piece discussing use of the chord types cyweirdant and tyniad and various playing techniques, with more focus on the crwth than the harp. Like the 'Cadwedigaeth' this was part of 'bardic lore', expanded in some collections to include short discussions of the foundation and origin of the crwth (citing Mercury and Pythagoras) and of the discovery of harmony itself (citing the biblical figures Tubal, Tubalcain and King David).

These anonymous quasi-historical and theoretical writings were almost certainly authored by bards (or perhaps their patrons) during the mid-sixteenth century to bolster the status of the craft and emphasise its longevity. However, a slightly later Welsh essay on music took a far more ambitious approach. Its author was the learned bardic harper Robert Peilin, known to have graduated as a pencerdd by 1605.[33] Intended as a didactic tool for young people in Wales, Peilin's 'Josseffus' runs to 9,000 words, and follows the pupil–master dialogue format adopted by several English and European theorists. Peilin looked beyond Wales for his sources: his primary model was John Dowland's English translation of *Andreas Ornithoparcus His Micrologus or Introduction, Containing the Art of Singing* (London, 1609),[34] parts of which he translated into rather impenetrable Welsh, making numerous digressions to include material from other writers. 'Josseffus' ends with a theoretical attempt to reconcile cerdd dant with both the modal system described by Ornithoparcus and with more recent hexachord theory from Thomas Morley's *Plaine and Easie Introduction to Practicall Musick* (1597). Though far from easy to understand, Peilin's approach represents a genuinely sophisticated attempt to engage with the wider European musical tradition.

---

[33] Text in GB-CDp MS 2.617 (Hafod 3), ff. 99v–122r, with complete transcription by Irwen Cockman, 'Traethawd ar Gerddoriaeth gan y Telynor Robert Peilin (*c*.1613)' (MPhil thesis, University of Wales, Aberystwyth, 1999). See also Harper, *Music in Welsh Culture before 1650*, pp. 121–130.

[34] A facsimile edition exists in The English Experience series (1969).

4 Secular Music before 1650

The Robert ap Huw Manuscript

Cerdd dant was in essence an oral craft: for centuries it had relied on oral and aural transmission. The complex tablature notation eventually devised for it (probably no earlier than 1560) therefore comes as something of a surprise, for its period of use was remarkably short: its purpose may have been primarily pedagogical, or even to preserve a declining repertory for posterity. It is known to survive in only one contemporary source: a modest anthology of pieces written out c.1613 by the Anglesey harper, Robert ap Huw (c.1580–1665),[35] who indicates in the back of the manuscript (pages 102–105) that he also had copied many other items elsewhere. These pieces (now lost) included several of the genres mentioned in the Statute of Gruffudd ap Cynan as eisteddfod requirements: the four cadeiriau, four colofnau, the tri mwchl odidog and tri mwchl newydd and many clymau.[36]

The body of the surviving anthology comprises thirty-three items, including three further genres mentioned in the Statute: the caniad (fifteen of which survive, in two separate groups), four gostegion (one incomplete), and four sets of 'exercises' entitled cwlwm cytgerdd. An eighteenth-century hand notes that these clymau cytgerdd were copied from a book (also lost) belonging to the harper Wiliam Penllyn (c.1560–80),[37] who graduated pencerdd at the 1567 Caerwys eisteddfod (and may be a candidate for invention of the notation, for it was surely the work of a skilled craftsman). The book also contains some additional genres outside the official eisteddfod requirements: seven profiadau (a genre mentioned just once in the Statute in a peripheral reference associated with the datgeiniad) and some smaller-scale pieces termed erddigan, pwnc and cainc. None of this later group is based on the twenty-four measures, although the short ceinciau may have been repeated over and over as a simple accompanying pattern for poetic recitation.

---

[35] GB-Lbl MS Additional 14905. Two facsimiles are available: *Musica neu Beroriaeth: B.M. Additional MS 14905*, with preface by Henry Lewis (Cardiff: University of Wales Press, 1936), and *Musica: Llawysgrif Robert ap Huw/Musica: The Robert ap Huw Manuscript*, with preface by Wyn Thomas (Godstone: Scolar Press, 1982). An attempt to transcribe the manuscript complete appears in Paul D. Whittaker, 'British Museum Additional MS 14905: An Interpretation and Re-examination of the Music and Text', 2 vols. (MA dissertation, University of Wales, 1974) www.bangor.ac.uk/music-and-media/CAWMS/roberta phuw.php.en (accessed 25 June 2021). See also Osian Ellis, *The Story of the Harp in Wales* (Cardiff: University of Wales Press, 1991), pp. 11–43, for a concise discussion, and *Welsh Music History/Hanes Cerddoriaeth Cymru*, 3 (1999) for essays on various aspects of the manuscript.
[36] Brief notes on all of these musical genres and those mentioned below are given in the glossary to *Welsh Music History/Hanes Cerddoriaeth Cymru*, 3 (1999), 299–307.
[37] Page 22 includes a note in an eighteenth-century hand: 'Yma canlyn y pedwar kwlwm cydgerdd ar hugain; wedi ei prikio allan Lyfr Wiliam Penllyn' ('here follow the twenty-four clymau cytgerdd, copied from Wiliam Penllyn's book').

The tablature is highly concise and bears no close resemblance to any other form of notation known elsewhere in Europe.[38] It uses graphic icons to represent the many different types of idiosyncratic figuration required of the player (who used both fingertips and fingernails), and often resorts to abbreviated verbal instructions rather than giving the notation in full.

Pitches are represented by letter symbols running from a to g (representing the harp strings), though there are no key signatures, accidentals or stave lines. Sometimes the player has no more than a brief verbal instruction specifying how to proceed, with a system of spiral and cross signs indicating various points of return and repetition, though there are some signs that Robert ap Huw made several blunders in copying and sometimes added his own layer of modern rhythmic notation, apparently to elucidate.

Some features are clarified by material elsewhere in the manuscript. A table on page 35 headed 'gogwyddor i ddysgu y prikiad' ('an alphabet to learn the pricking') depicts seventeen types of melodic figuration, involving different ways of plucking and damping the harp strings: most of these are executed by the upper hand and some require the use of fingernails. There are also various patterns of notes labelled 'kower' (pages 108–109), which may bear some relation to *scordatura* tunings, and a list of the twenty-four measures with their symbols (page 107).

Analysis of the repertory reveals something of the function of the measures, essentially comprising simple binary patterns based on the alternation of two contrasting chord types known as 'cyweirdant' and 'tyniad'. (In earlier manuscript lists they are sometimes recorded as 'c' and 't', though more often '1' and '0': 'mak y mwn byr', for example, is notated as 1100.1111. and its longer relative 'mak y mwn hir' as 1111.0000.1010.1111.0000.1011.) Each pattern is based on interlocking groups of notes situated a major-second apart. Sometimes this is used in a straightforward regular manner, as a later composer might use a repeated 'ground'; sometimes in a much more sophisticated way to generate different harmonies. In practice, the recurring notes of each element of the measure may be heard clearly in the lower notes of the harp while the upper hand develops a series of variations over it, drawing on the different types of figuration mentioned above. The measure seems also to have controlled

---

[38] See Paul D. Whittaker, 'The Role of Robert ap Huw in the Creation of *Lbl* Ms Add. 14905/ Swyddogaeth Robert ap Huw yng Nghreadigaeth *Lbl* Ms Add. 14905', *Welsh Music History/Hanes Cerddoriaeth Cymru*, 6 (2004), 62–103.

the overall metrical pattern of a piece, with each digital element of equal duration.³⁹

Despite the late copying date, most of the repertory in Robert ap Huw's anthology seems to date from the later fifteenth century, and one or two items may even come from the era of Dafydd ap Gwilym himself (including 'Cainc Ruffudd ab Adda ap Dafydd', associated with Dafydd's contemporary and friend). Other items may be loosely dated by their association with a named musician or poet-musician, including Caniad Cynwrig Bencerdd (the winning harper at the Carmarthen eisteddfod), Caniad Y Brido (mentioned by the poet Guto'r Glyn, *fl. c.*1435–93), and the fragmentary Gosteg Y Llwyteg (Y Llwyteg was a harper known to have been active in the later fifteenth century). Other titles gleaned from extant bardic repertory lists suggest that many items were conceived as eulogies or praise-pieces for named individuals, and with the exception of mythological figures and saints, most of those who lent their names to cerdd dant compositions belong to the fifteenth century, with a much smaller number from the fourteenth.⁴⁰

The Gradual Decline of Medieval Bardic Culture

By the time that Andrew Boorde published his *Fyrst Bok of the Introduction of Knowledge* in 1542, the slow decline of professional bardic poets and musicians in Wales was already beginning. The continuous threat of popular entertainers was constantly increasing, and the scale of informal music-making is hinted at by the numerous indictments of travelling entertainers in the records of the assize courts, particularly during the first half of the seventeenth century. Many of these name crythors or fiddlers as a persistent nuisance.

But the attractions of English-style culture were also becoming far stronger for the Welsh nobility. The very fabric of Welsh society was changing: the Acts of Union passed in 1536 and 1543 now required English to become the language of justice and administration, ensuring that only a minority within Wales were qualified to hold legal office, and the need to acquire an education became vital. The sons of even moderately endowed families were sent to England for their schooling, with a period at

---

[39] See Peter Greenhill, 'The Robert ap Huw Manuscript: An Exploration of Its Possible Solutions' (private dissertation, 1995–), www.cl.cam.ac.uk/~rja14/musicfiles/manuscripts/aphuw/ (accessed 25 June 2021).
[40] For further discussion, see Sally Harper, 'Issues in Dating the Repertory of *Cerdd Dant*', *Studia Celtica*, 35 (2001), 325–340.

Oxford or Cambridge or one of the Inns of Court often following. Many gentlemen returned to Wales with a new-found taste for more varied musical styles and genres, with affluent households increasingly investing in instruments, instrumentalists, books and even tutors imported from across the border.

This wave of anglicisation nevertheless did little to weaken pride in Welsh ancestry, for pedigree was an important denoter of gentility at a time of social flux. To some extent this enabled bardic patronage to survive in more modest form right up to the end of the period covered in this chapter. The records of some affluent households suggest a fascinating musical duality, where an indigenous traditional culture was maintained alongside musical entertainment of a very different style. The great house of Lleweni, near Denbigh, is a particularly good example of this. During the Elizabethan period, it was home to the Welsh-speaking courtier John Salusbury (1566/7–1612), elected Esquire of the Body to Elizabeth I in 1595 and knighted in 1601.[41] The family accounts indicate that gwŷr wrth gerdd had long been welcomed here in significant numbers, and the names of a mixed group of thirteen poets, crwth players and harpers (including the learned Robert Peilin) who visited the house one Christmas in the 1590s (probably 1595) were carefully recorded. A variety of praise poetry by the distinguished poets Siôn Tudur, Simwnt Fychan and Wiliam Cynwal was similarly copied into a Lleweni family anthology between 1570 and 1606, though here it rubs shoulders with English verse (discussed later in the chapter). Some of the bards welcomed at Lleweni evidently developed other skills – and indeed cultivated other patrons – beyond Wales too. The 'Thomas ap Richard' named in the Christmas list was also known as Thomas Richards of Coety, later eulogised in a Latin epitaph by Sir John Stradling of St Donats, Glamorgan as 'prince of Welsh lyre players'.[42] Richards was also proficient on an unnamed 'instrument stringed with wires' – presumably an Irish harp – which during the 1580s took him into the English houses of some of the great Elizabethans, Sir Philip Sidney included.[43] Such harps were becoming something of a status symbol in

---

[41] For fuller exploration of music at Lleweni, see Sally Harper, 'An Elizabethan Tune List from Lleweni Hall, North Wales', *Royal Musical Association Research Chronicle*, 39 (2005), 45–98.

[42] John Stradling, *J. Stradlingi Epigrammatum Libri Qvatvor* (London: Impensis Georgii Bishop & Ioannis Norton, 1607), Bk. 4, p. 148. Digitised by the National Library of Wales http://hdl.handle.net/10107/5346980.

[43] Richards and his harp are commended in a letter of 1584 written to Sir John Stradling by Sir Arthur Bassett, a Devonshire landowner. See J. M. Traherne, ed., *Stradling Correspondence: A Series of Letters Written in the Reign of Queen Elizabeth* (London: Longmans, 1840), pp. 238–240.

Wales, and the will of Sir Robert Salusbury of Bachymbyd, not far from Lleweni, lists 'one Irishe harpe', kept in the parlour (15 June 1601).

The accounts of Sir William Aubrey of Llantrithyd in the Vale of Glamorgan also contain numerous payments to musicians, minstrels, dancers and players, particularly at the traditional 'circuiting' season of Christmas, New Year and the associated 'twelve days'. Annual payments were made to Sir William's own harper, 'George', up to 1633; on two occasions he was joined by another harper. Aubrey's son, Anthony Gwyn of Llansannor Court, and his nephew, John Games of Aberbrân, outside Brecon, both maintained harpers, as did Sir Henry Williams, the lawyer and judge of Gwernyfed, Brecknock, Sir Thomas Morgan of Rhiwperra Castle (steward to the third Earl of Pembroke) and a number of other eminent figures. Elsewhere arrangements may have been more informal: the Oxford-educated gentleman farmer Robert Bulkeley of Dronwy near Llanfachreth, for instance, a member of the Bulkeley family of Anglesey and Justice of the Peace, regularly paid local harpers, crwth players and fiddlers during the 1630s.[44] His detailed journal of 1630–6 indicates that most of these musicians received about 2d for an individual visit, although a larger sum of 14d was given to 'strange harpers & a Bard' at the house of Robert's friend Hugh Powell (21 January 1634/5).

The latest known evidence for old-style bardic patronage conveniently ends only a little beyond 1650. The poet Siôn Cain (c.1575–c.1650), whose remit covered families within Maelor, Montgomeryshire, the Vale of Clwyd, Arfon and Merioneth, was still composing genealogical tributes to patrons up to 1648, while the prolific Gruffydd Philip (d. 1666), whose father graduated at Caerwys in 1567, regarded himself as the last of the professional bards. As late as 1654 Gruffydd (known also as Griffith Phillip) was one of three bards, together with Harry Howell and the harper John Morgan, receiving a collective payment of 25s at Chirk Castle: Gruffydd and Harry both provided cywyddau, presumably in honour of the patron, the London Welshman Sir Thomas Myddelton (1550–1631). Chirk, situated just inside the Welsh border between Oswestry and Wrexham, was acquired by the Middleton family only in 1595, and is discussed later in this chapter.[45]

---

[44] GB-AB NLW MS 3150B, transcr. Hugh Owen, 'The Diary of Bulkeley of Dronwy, Anglesey, 1630–1636', *Transactions of the Anglesey Antiquarian Society and Field Club* (1937), 26–172; relevant extracts also in Klausner, ed., *Records: Wales*, pp. 48–52. It has been digitised by the National Library of Wales http://hdl.handle.net/10107/4703116.

[45] '[P]aid Iohn Morgan the harper v s. paid harry howell the bard for his cowydd x s. and to Griffith Phillip for his cowydd x s. in all' (13–16 June 1654). Accounts of Sir Thomas Myddelton, GB-AB NLW Chirk Castle F12572, f. [74], transcribed Klausner, ed., *Records: Wales*, p. 151.

All of this suggests at least lip service to earlier indigenous tradition, but there are also strong signs that English-style entertainment or education was taking precedence. Though Sir John Wynn (1553–1627), head of the great Welsh house of Gwydir, near Llanrwst in the Conwy Valley, was one of the twelve 'men of worship, gentility and power' to sign the petition for the abortive third eisteddfod in Caerwys in 1594,[46] he took great pains to ensure that all four of his sons had the benefits of a sound English schooling.[47] In 1597, Wynn's attorney, Thomas Martyn, wrote to say that the younger John was learning not only classical and modern languages (Greek, Hebrew, Latin grammar, French and Italian) and 'preceptes of religion' at Bedford School, but also 'musicke bye voice and Instrument'.[48] The younger John subsequently took pains in 1606/7 to arrange accommodation in London for his siblings where they might be taught to sing and play upon instruments,[49] and in 1611 he sent a viol to his brother Robert, who was then training for holy orders at St John's Cambridge.[50] Another letter of 1621 was sent to Sir John Wynn by Humffrey Jones of Craflwyn, near Beddgelert, confirming that his own household had hired a young man from Salisbury, 'a very good musician on the base violl and virginals' who was not only able to teach young gentlewomen to play these and other instruments (including the virginals) but also to 'trayne them up in their prick songes'.[51] Other households similarly invested in virginals, lutes and viols: the accounts of Sir William Aubrey of Llantrithyd in the Vale of Glamorgan reveal particular interest in musical activity during the 1620s and 1630s, including purchase of a bass viol for Aubrey's secretary, Challis, and a payment to one Panner for showing Challis the 'true fingering thereof'.[52]

The most interesting picture of cultural duality comes from Lleweni, where the family promoted English entertainments which

---

[46] The 1594 petition is reproduced in Royal Commission, *Report on Manuscripts in the Welsh Language*, I, pp. 293–295.
[47] See John Gwynfor Jones, *The Wynn Family of Guydir: Origins, Growth and Development c.1490–1674* (Aberystwyth: Centre for Educational Services, 1995). See also John Gwynfor Jones, 'Cerdd a Bonedd Yng Nghymru 1540–1640: Rhai Argraffiadau', *Welsh Music*, 6 (1981), 22–33; 7 (1982), 25–40; 8 (1983), 30–47.
[48] The letter survives as GB-AB NLW MS 9052E, f. [1], transcribed in Klausner, ed., *Records: Wales*, pp. 67–68. See also John Ballinger, ed., *Calendar of Wynn (of Gwydir) Papers, 1515–1690, in the National Library of Wales and Elsewhere* (Aberystwyth: National Library of Wales, 1926), p. 24, no. 180.
[49] Ibid., pp. 72–73, no. 438.   [50] Ibid., p. 91, no. 572.
[51] Ballinger, ed., *Calendar of Wynn*, 151–152, no. 967 from GB-AB NLW MS 9057E.
[52] GB-Lna C 106/99, 100/101, pt. 2. Lloyd Bowen, ed., *Family and Society in Early Stuart Glamorgan: the Household Accounts of Sir Thomas Aubrey of Llantrithyd, c.1565–1641* (Cardiff: South Wales Record Society, 2006).

were probably modelled on those they had witnessed in London. The Elizabethan John Salusbury matriculated at Jesus College, Oxford, in 1581, and in March 1594/5 was admitted to the Middle Temple (a typical pattern for a number of other landed gentlemen).[53] The family correspondence suggests that he spent at least as much time in London as at Lleweni, and when his younger brother Thomas was executed for complicity in the Babington Plot in 1586, social reinstatement was facilitated both by Robert Dudley, Lord Leicester and by John's own brother-in-law Ferdinando, Lord Strange.[54]

The same anthology that contains bardic tributes to the family also includes some of Sir John's own poetry, together with two poems from an English masque devised to celebrate his wedding in 1586 to Ursula Stanley, daughter of the Earl of Derby, and an undated poem for a 'merriment of christmas' by Robert Chester (*fl. c.*1586–1604), probably a secretary or household chaplain.[55] Though no music survives for either of these entertainments, some of the associated repertory may be suggested by an inventory of some eighty tunes known as the 'Lleweni tune-list', copied in the 1590s.[56] This includes many well-known English ballad and dance tunes (including 'fourtune', 'grine slifes', 'donne right [downright] squier' and 'loth to depart'), many of them known from amateur lute books, consort arrangements or as country dance tunes. One of the listed titles, 'mistres wite his choyse', is evidently the solo lute piece written for an unknown Mrs White by John Dowland in the 1580s, while some nine or ten of the titles suggest close association with the Elizabethan stage jigg, an improvised song-and-dance form popularised by the renowned comic actor Richard Tarlton (d. 1588). Tarlton's characteristic clowning habit is suggested by the Lleweni tunes 'tarlton trunke hose' and 'tarlton is buten cape', while others derive from jiggs whose plots were published posthumously in the early seventeenth century, including 'Goe to bed sweet hart & I will com to thee' and 'shifling the knave of klobes'. Tarlton was also popular in south Wales, and the subject of another of Sir John Stradling's Latin epitaphs in *c.*1607. Two further tunes in the list, 'Alen his flapes' and 'Alen his marche', also suggest contemporary theatrical influence: Edward Alleyn (1566–1626) was the actor and theatre manager who later founded

---

[53] C. H. Hopwood, ed., *A Calendar of the Middle Temple Records* (London, 1903), I, p. 351.
[54] W. J. Smith, ed., *Calendar of Salusbury Correspondence 1553–c.1700* (Cardiff: University of Wales Press, 1954), p. 30, no. 25.
[55] Carleton Brown, ed., *Poems by Sir John Salusbury and Robert Chester*, EETS, Extra Series, 113 (London: Kegan Paul Trench Truebner, 1914).
[56] Harper, 'An Elizabethan Tune List'.

Dulwich College.[57] He was a partner of Philip Henslowe, with whom he not only built the Fortune Theatre in London but also subsequently headed the Lord Admiral's Company. Though there is no documented evidence of English players visiting Lleweni, Sir William Aubrey of Llantrithyd paid 20s in 1622 to the 'Kings Players', apparently members of the company associated with the Lord Chamberlain (the Earl of Pembroke), who owned lands in Glamorgan. It may have been this same group that received 30s the following October, while lesser payments of 5s went to the players of one 'Perry' at nearby St Nicholas on 14 and 15 March 1623.

The changing pattern of Welsh musical patronage is perhaps seen most clearly at Chirk Castle. Thomas Myddelton (1586–1666) spent very considerable sums on this property in the 1630s, refurbishing the chapel, installing a new organ imported from London and commissioning a set of partbooks containing English anthems and services (see Chapter 3).[58] Two masques were also devised for the household during the 1630s, almost certainly by Sir Thomas Salusbury (1612–43), grandson of John Salusbury of Lleweni.[59] The earlier of the two, an 'entertainment' that survives in GB-Lbl MS Egerton 2623, was to be played as a series of interludes between the courses of a banquet, and concluded with communal dancing once the tables had been cleared. The masque may well have been devised to celebrate the visit to Chirk in 1634 of the Earl of Bridgewater, recently appointed Lord President of Wales and the Council of the Marches; Bridgewater was similarly greeted at Ludlow Castle on 29 September of that same year with a performance of Milton's masque *Comus*, for which five songs by Henry Lawes (1602–45) survive.[60] The banqueting framework of the Chirk masque is distinct: though its music is lost, the text of four songs for Orpheus survives, and the work concludes with a cycle of four dances led by seasonal characters. 'Christmas Gamboles' dances 'a single Anticke with a forme'; Autumn leads an 'Anticke of drunkards';

---

[57] J. P. Collier, ed., *Memoirs of Edward Alleyn, Founder of Dulwich College* (London: Shakespeare Society, 1841).

[58] See William Reynolds, 'Middleton's Household Chapel: Church Music on the Welsh Border in the Seventeenth Century/Capel Teuluol Middleton: Cerddoriaeth Eglwysig ar y Gororau yn yr Ail Ganrif ar Bymtheg', *Welsh Music History/Hanes Cerddoriaeth Cymru*, 4 (2000), 111–137.

[59] The complete texts for the masques are given in Klausner, ed., *Records: Wales*, pp. 141–146; see also David Klausner, 'Family Entertainments among the Salusburys of Lleweni and Their Circle, 1595–1641/Diddanwch Teuluaidd ymysg Salsbriaid Lleweni a'u Cylch, 1595–1641', *Welsh Music History/Hanes Cerddoriaeth Cymru*, 6 (2006), 129–154.

[60] Cedric Brown, 'The Chirk Castle Entertainment of 1634', *Milton Quarterly*, 11 (1977), 76–86.

Summer, 'a country dance of haymaker or reapers'; and Spring, a morris dance. These 'anticks' or 'antemasques' were no doubt conventional comic burlesques, using popular dance and ballad tunes, with the morris and country dances drawing on a more specific repertory.

To all intents and purposes, landed Welsh families were now looking beyond Wales for their musical and poetic inspiration, and the Civil War (1642–51) and Commonwealth (1649–60) effectively coincide with a natural watershed in indigenous Welsh music. The following century would see the dominance of the so-called 'Welch tunes' of the collection *Aria di Camera* (1726?),[61] and the harp airs of *Antient British Music* (1742),[62] published by John Parry of Ruabon: they go hand in hand with the new popularity of the triple harp, which probably reached Wales during the 1660s.

---

[61] Digitised by the National Library of Wales: http://hdl.handle.net/10107/5470148.
[62] Digitised by the National Library of Wales: http://hdl.handle.net/10107/4675582.

CHAPTER 5

The Eisteddfod Tradition
Rhidian Griffiths

Eisteddfod is a word which does not translate. Its historic meaning is an assembly or a gathering; its broader meaning is a competitive festival. Yet to Welsh minds it embraces more than these definitions would suggest. A modern eisteddfod will include competitions in music, literature and verse-speaking; larger eisteddfodau will embrace drama, arts and crafts and much else besides. But it is the atmosphere of an eisteddfod which is hard to encapsulate, with its mixture of competition, rivalry, warmth and good humour. It is a phenomenon which can amaze and frustrate outsiders. In terms of cultural development, eisteddfodau have contributed immensely to Welsh music and the arts and have lent support to the cherished concept of 'the musical nation'. Eisteddfodau are held in all parts of Wales at local, regional and national level: they vary from a straightforward sequence of stage competitions in music and recitation, with some literary competitions, to the multifaceted festival of literature and the arts that is the modern National Eisteddfod. Wherever Welsh people have settled in their diaspora – be it in England, Ireland, North America, South Africa, Australia or Patagonia – they have founded chapels, choirs and eisteddfodau. The eisteddfod in all its many shapes or sizes is in essence an expression of Welsh identity; and it is striking that both in the *Oxford Companion to Music* and the *New Oxford Companion to Music* the heading 'Eisteddfod' has 'see Wales', as if the word itself is key to understanding the country and its culture.

Origins

It is customary to trace the origins of the eisteddfod to the great Christmas feast held at Cardigan Castle in 1176, when Rhys ap Gruffudd, the Lord Rhys of Deheubarth, organised two competitions, one for poets and another 'between harpists and crowders [players of the crwth] and pipers and various classes of music-craft';[1] this Celtic event, with its echoes of the continental *puy*, offered an opportunity for musicians from all parts of Wales and the Celtic countries to compete against each other. Another element in common with the modern eisteddfod was that the event was proclaimed a whole year in advance throughout Wales, England, Scotland and Ireland. While it did not, as far as is known, instigate a tradition of such events in the Middle Ages, it no doubt had some precedent in its own time, and provides in retrospect a useful starting point for a characteristically Welsh tradition. It also gives an appearance of antiquity, albeit illusory, to the cultural pastime that is the modern eisteddfod.

Eisteddfodau in succeeding centuries for which evidence has survived appear to have focused on literary rather than musical accomplishments and can be seen as attempts by the bardic order in Wales to safeguard the purity of their craft against interlopers. Yet at the eisteddfod held at Carmarthen around 1452, under the patronage of Gruffudd ap Nicolas, it is recorded that Cynwrig of Holywell won a silver harp for cerdd dant, the traditional Welsh style of musical declamation to harp accompaniment. Likewise, the eisteddfod at Caerwys in 1523 appears to have its origins in a concern for the maintenance of proper standards in the traditional poetic craft; but the proclamation of the eisteddfod invited craftsmen in poetry *and music* to attend an eisteddfod on 2 July. A silver harp for the best musician was won by Dafydd Nantglyn, and other musicians were confirmed in their craft. A subsequent eisteddfod at Caerwys in 1567 saw 'judgement ... passed on poets and musicians'.[2] The importance of the Caerwys eisteddfodau of 1523 and 1567 was underlined by Thomas Pennant in his *A Tour in Wales* (1778);[3] they were referred to by Edward Jones (Bardd y Brenin; 1752–1824) in his *Musical and Poetical Relicks of the Welsh Bards* (1784)[4] and Charles Burney in his *A General History of Music* (1776–89). But their principal function was to protect the status of professional poets in society, and to get rid of itinerants and beggars who feigned that craft. The scarcity of references to such events in the Middle Ages and the sixteenth and seventeenth centuries suggests that they were not common occurrences: they depended on the patronage of wealthy and influential people, and from the seventeenth century onwards the Welsh gentry (with

---

[1] Thomas Jones, trans., *Brut y Tywysogyon or the Chronicle of the Princes: Peniarth Ms 20 Version* (Cardiff: University of Wales Press, 1952), p. 71.
[2] Gwyn Thomas, *Eisteddfodau Caerwys: The Caerwys Eisteddfodau* (Caerdydd: Gwasg Prifysgol Cymru, 1968), p. 97.
[3] Digitised by the National Library of Wales: http://hdl.handle.net/10107/4692237 (1784 edition).
[4] Digitised by the National Library of Wales: http://hdl.handle.net/10107/4675108.

some exceptions) became preoccupied with other interests at the expense of their role as patrons of the arts in Wales. If there were eisteddfodau in the late seventeenth and early eighteenth centuries, they were poetic gatherings with apparently little musical content.

The modern eisteddfod originated in the late eighteenth century under the patronage of the London-based Gwyneddigion Society (the Society of the Men of Gwynedd), a group of Welshmen strongly influenced by the so-called 'Welsh renaissance' of the time, which showed renewed interest in antiquities: one of its expressions was the publication by Welsh musicians of collections of Welsh melodies such as Bardd y Brenin's *Relicks*. In similar vein, the wayward genius Edward Williams (Iolo Morganwg; 1747–1826) devised his gorsedd (assembly of bards) in 1792 as an expression of the perceived antiquity of Welsh poetic tradition. It was to become an essential component of eisteddfod life. Eisteddfodau of this period were small-scale affairs enjoyed by a coterie of poets who competed against each other in a reasonably amicable way, as for instance at Bala and Corwen in 1789. Even so, there was singing of penillion at Corwen, and a day-long competition won by Lewis Roberts (Eos Twrog; 1756–1844).[5] Writing to Edward Jones on 2 August 1789, Thomas Jones, an exciseman and penillion singer from Corwen who had a prominent role in establishing these eisteddfodau, said:

> The Eisteddfod is now become the topic of discourse in most company here: I can sit no where without having a continual ring in my Ears, of their Poetry and Singing.[6]

But if these early forays did not divorce poetry and song, it was the movement led by an enthusiastic group of clergymen with scholarly and antiquarian interests, known as 'yr hen bersoniaid llengar' (the old literature-loving parsons), which reinstated music as an integral part of eisteddfod activity. These were clergymen of the Established Church who were strongly interested in Welsh traditional poetry and music: one of them, John Jenkins (Ifor Ceri; 1770–1829), was an important collector of Welsh traditional melodies. Between 1819 and 1834 a series of regional eisteddfodau offered opportunities for musicians, with a focus on the traditional, in line with the

---

[5] Tecwyn Ellis, 'Welsh Music in Georgian Times', *Welsh Music/Cerddoriaeth Cymru*, 3/10 (1971), 11–19, on p. 15.

[6] Quoted by Geraint Phillips, *'Dyn Heb ei Gyffelyb yn y Byd': Owain Myfyr a'i Gysylltiadau Llenyddol* (Caerdydd: Gwasg Prifysgol Cymru, 2010), t. 117. I am grateful to Dr Phillips for discussion of this point.

interests of their sponsors. The Cambrian Society, which first met at the White Lion in Carmarthen on 28 October 1818, had as its aim 'the preservation of the remains of Ancient British Literatures, Poetical, Historical, Antiquarian, Sacred and Moral; and ... the Encouragement of the National Music', and agreed that 'the annual Meetings be appropriated to the recitation of the Prize Verses and Essays; and to the performances on the Harp'.[7] Competition as well as performance was a part of these meetings: at an eisteddfod in Wrexham in September 1820, Bardd y Brenin adjudicated performances by harpists. A Cambrian Society was established in Gwent in 1821, with the same ambition of encouraging 'native Poetry and Music in the Principality'. At its eisteddfod held at Brecon in 1822 there was, in addition to competitions, an evening concert organised by the impresario and collector of Welsh traditional melodies, John Parry (Bardd Alaw; 1776–1851). Parry popularised and promoted Welsh music in London, and it was London artists who performed at the concert. These early eisteddfodau thus sowed the seeds of a certain tension between responsibility for the maintenance of tradition on the one hand, and on the other a desire to use events as a vehicle for the promotion of professional performance, a tension that would continue in the eisteddfod world well into the twentieth century. A literary society, Cymreigyddion a Phrydyddion Merthyr (Welsh Scholars and Poets of Merthyr), formed at Merthyr Tydfil on St David's Day 1821, made no bones about its role as defender and promoter of Welsh literature and tradition, and held its first eisteddfod in 1822. The first Eisteddfod Cadair Merthyr (Merthyr Chair Eisteddfod, so called because it offered a chair as its major prize) was held at New Year in 1824, and in succeeding years there were competitions for harpists and singers as well as poets. Other societies held eisteddfodau in Merthyr, many in public houses, reflecting the pattern of the early eisteddfodau of the Gwyneddigion. The critic and composer D. Emlyn Evans (1843–1913) suggested that the Merthyr Chair Eisteddfod was the first in Wales to invite vocal soloists to compete for a prize of a silver medal.[8] Less significant than the medals is the fact that music was gradually creeping into eisteddfod programmes and taking a more prominent position.

---

[7] GB-AB NLW MS 11116E.
[8] David Morgans (Cerddwyson), *Music and Musicians of Merthyr and District* (Merthyr Tydfil: H. W. Southey, 1922), p. 70.

From Local to National

Welsh music was very much to the fore in the next wave of eisteddfod activity, held under the patronage of Cymreigyddion y Fenni (The Abergavenny Welsh Society), a Welsh-language association established in south-east Wales in 1833. Its *éminence grise* was the formidable, eccentric and determined Augusta Hall (Lady Llanover; 1802–96). An enthusiastic proponent of all things Welsh, from costume to the language itself, she galvanised her followers in support of a notable series of eisteddfodau held between 1834 and 1853.[9] Given her interests, it was inevitable that music at these eisteddfodau should give prominence to the triple harp and traditional music: at the 1834 eisteddfod the seventeen-year-old Brinley Richards (1817–85), a Carmarthen-born pianist and composer who became a professor at the Royal Academy of Music and a champion of Welsh music in London, was awarded a prize for a set of variations on the traditional tune 'Llwyn Onn' ('The Ash Grove').[10] These eisteddfodau were also to spawn two notable collections of Welsh traditional music, namely *Ancient National Airs of Gwent and Morganwg* by Maria Jane Williams (Llinos; 1795–1873), published in 1844,[11] and *Y Caniedydd Cymreig/The Cambrian Minstrel* by John Thomas (Ieuan Ddu; 1795–1871), issued in the following year,[12] which had been awarded first and second prize respectively at the Abergavenny eisteddfod of 1837. Lady Llanover would, however, live to see very different musical influences dominate eisteddfodau, with both the triple harp and traditional music being eclipsed.

These eisteddfodau were organised and held under patronage, but at about the same time social movements were beginning to recognise the potential of the eisteddfod as a force for good. During the 1830s the temperance movement took hold in Wales, with temperance societies being founded in order 'to reclaim drunkards to sobriety by restoring their self-respect'.[13] One way of achieving this reclamation was to encourage healthy eisteddfod activity, and again Merthyr was to the fore: a temperance association, the Cymmrodorion

---

[9] These eisteddfodau, which were held at various locations, are discussed by Mair Elvet Thomas, *Afiaith yng Ngwent: Hanes Cymdeithas Cymreigyddion y Fenni 1833–1854* (Caerdydd: Gwasg Prifysgol Cymru, 1978).

[10] A. J. Heward Rees, 'Henry Brinley Richards (1817–1885): A Nineteenth-Century Propagandist for Welsh Music/Henry Brinley Richards (1817–1885): Propagandydd dros Gerddoriaeth Gymreig o'r Bedwaredd Ganrif ar Bymtheg', *Hanes Cerddoriaeth Cymru/Welsh Music History* 2 (1998), 173–192, on p. 174.

[11] Digitised by the National Library of Wales: http://hdl.handle.net/10107/5726885.

[12] Digitised by the National Library of Wales: http://hdl.handle.net/10107/5727212.

[13] W. R. Lambert, *Drink and Sobriety in Victorian Wales c.1820–c.1895* (Cardiff: University of Wales Press, 1983), p. 87.

Dirwestol (Temperance Brotherhood) of Merthyr Tydfil, held a series of Christmas Day eisteddfodau annually from 1848 to 1879, with choral singing featuring from 1849; and the association of temperance and choralism was to persist. It went beyond eisteddfodau to embrace the activities of regional choral unions such as that of Gwent and Glamorgan, which was active from the 1850s, and Ardudwy and Eryri, from the 1860s onwards.

One of the distinctive features of eisteddfod development in the nineteenth century was local particularism. An eisteddfod became a hallmark of local identity, and the size of a local festival could be a topic of rivalry between neighbouring communities. As a mid-twentieth-century commentator remarked:

> We must think of Wales during the nineteenth century as a country in which there was a nation-wide application to this kind of cultural entertainment, remembering always that the standards of achievement varied considerably, but were nowhere very high. It would be wrong to call them extra-mural education, but only because there was no intra-mural form of it until towards the end of the century. The competitive element in them added greatly to their popularity, of course, without doing any harm worth mentioning. Much of their value, and their vigour, arose from the fact that they were in no way federated or centrally organized: they were a local responsibility, and they reflected local tastes and standards.[14]

Local eisteddfodau, often on a very limited scale, were held if not regularly, at least frequently in the period up to the mid-century. It was, however, towards the end of the period of the eisteddfodau organised by Cymreigyddion y Fenni that the beginnings of a widespread eisteddfod movement emerged. In part this was a response to the notorious 'Blue Books' controversy. The 'Blue Books', published in 1847, which contained the report of the Commissioners on Education in Wales, were scathing about all things relating to the Welsh language and extreme in their accusations concerning the supposed moral turpitude of the Welsh people. In many respects much of what followed in Welsh culture and religion during the remainder of the nineteenth century was a reaction against this wholesale damnation. A renewed interest in eisteddfodau was at least in part an attempt to reassert the value of that unique Welsh culture which the Commissioners had dismissed as of little worth, and it is no accident that the eisteddfod movement developed markedly in the second half of the nineteenth century as an assertion of Welshness. This coincided with an exponential growth of interest in choral singing and the spread of

---

[14] Wyn Griffith, *The Welsh* (Harmondsworth: Penguin, 1950), p. 138.

community music making, and eisteddfodau everywhere became major musical as well as literary events. It was in 1850 that the musician and lexicographer Thomas Edwards (Caerfallwch; 1779–1858) coined the term 'carofydd' as a Welsh word for 'amateur': though his Welsh term did not catch on, the fact that it was found necessary to coin it suggests that amateur music was becoming a force on the social scene in Wales, and was recognised as being different from professional, metropolitan-based music making.

By the late 1850s local eisteddfodau in Wales had gathered momentum and were becoming significant events. The eisteddfod held at Merthyr on 21 and 22 September 1859 included choral as well as vocal and instrumental solo competitions.[15] Gatherings such as these, which offered medals and money prizes, acquired a unique atmosphere and helped to foster a sense of achievement among working people. Choirs came into being for the express purpose of competing at eisteddfodau, and musical development could easily be lost sight of in the scramble for badges of victory, a tendency which became more marked as time went on. Between 1882 and 1898 the tempestuous Dan Davies conducted his Merthyr choir to a string of choral victories which scooped a total of £3,185 in prize money, as well as medals and batons galore, which the conductor loved to display. Implicit in this desire to win at all costs was the practice adopted by many choirs of going straight from one eisteddfod to the next and subsisting on a few well-worn test pieces. In 1874 the *Western Mail* cautioned against

> the habit of hawking from eisteddfod to eisteddfod ... Some measure ought to be adopted to prevent the same choir from competing in the same kind of thing consecutively, so that all choirs may eventually have a chance, or there will be some who will be discouraged.[16]

In this rather fetid world of competition, it was also inevitable that petty jealousies and rivalries should emerge. Musicians liked to claim that poets had the best of it and that prizes for poetry were more generous than those for music, whereas poets railed against musicians for taking over their eisteddfodau – a fair point, given that eisteddfodau originated as literary gatherings. The Llanrwst eisteddfod of 1878 was criticised for offering a prize of £25 for one poem as opposed to £1 11s 6d for the composition of three anthems.[17] Such jealousies could become the stuff of litigation. The periodical *Y Gerddorfa* (The Music Place) reported that Justice

---

[15] Morgans, *Music and Musicians of Merthyr*, pp. 219–221.
[16] 'Abergavenny Eisteddfod', *Western Mail*, 15 April 1874, 4.   [17] *Y Gerddorfa*, 6 (1878), 21.

5 The Eisteddfod Tradition

Homersham Cox had heard a dispute at Dolgellau Small Claims Court between brass bands from Aberystwyth and Corris over a competition at Eisteddfod Meirion in Dolgellau on New Year's Day 1881. The dispute centred on the fact that the Corris band, deemed winners by the adjudicator, David Jenkins, had played a different arrangement of the music from that specified in the regulations. Exhibiting the wisdom of Solomon, the judge persuaded the two bands to share the £10 prize equally.[18] Disputes of this kind had induced the sober-minded and humourless critic and journalist John Roberts (Ieuan Gwyllt; 1822–77) to give up on eisteddfodau as early as 1870 because of

> y ffolineb, y llygredigaeth, a'r gwastraff ar arian, ar amser, ac ar alluoedd a fyddai mewn cysylltiad a hwynt ...
>
> (the stupidity, the corruption, and the waste of money, and time, and abilities in connexion with them).[19]

This severe judgement, however, while characteristic of Ieuan's moral tone, hardly takes into account the fact that by the latter half of the nineteenth century local and regional eisteddfodau were successful events which attracted large numbers of competitors and significant audiences (see Figure 5.1). Some local events began to transcend their locality: it was

Figure 5.1 An engraved image of the 'Rhuddlan Royal Eisteddvod' of 1850. *Illustrated London News*, 28 September 1850

---

[18] *Y Gerddorfa*, 9 [recte 8] (1881), 141–142.   [19] *Y Cerddor Cymreig*, 8 (1870), 52.

said of the eisteddfod held at Abergavenny in March 1874 that it had 'assumed a truly national and representative character'.[20]

A National Institution

The move to 'national' eisteddfodau had, however, begun well before 1874. The grand Merthyr eisteddfod of 1859 had been advertised as a 'National Eisteddfod',[21] and at an eisteddfod held in Denbigh in 1860, a Council and Executive Committee were formed to run 'The Eisteddfod' as a national movement.[22] Beginning at Aberdare in 1861, a series of eisteddfodau inaugurated, albeit haltingly, the tradition of a national event held alternately at a location in north or south Wales, drawing together people from all over the country. This movement was facilitated by the growth of the railway network: 2,300 kilometres or 1,500 miles of railway were laid in Wales between 1840 and 1870, a factor widely recognised as central to the development of Welsh culture in the nineteenth century.[23] These national events recorded milestones in the history of Welsh music: the compositional talent of Joseph Parry (1841–1903), born in Merthyr Tydfil and nurtured in Pennsylvania, came to the fore when he scooped prizes at the National Eisteddfodau in Swansea (1863) and Llandudno (1864), culminating in his admission to the Gorsedd of Bards at Aberystwyth in 1865. The singer Megan Watts Hughes (1847–1907), born in Dowlais, was awarded a £50 scholarship at the Swansea National Eisteddfod in 1863 which enabled her to study with Manuel Garcia at the Royal Academy of Music in London; she was probably one of the earliest students from Wales to follow that particular career path. It was these early National Eisteddfodau which confirmed the practice – already established in some localities, and harking back to the days of Bardd Alaw – of evening concerts to follow the competitions. At Merthyr in 1859 a 'grand concert' ended the two-day eisteddfod: an audience of two to three thousand heard contralto Charlotte Sainton-Dolby, violinist Adolf Pollitzer, violist Schreurs and cellist Guillaume Paque, 'who reportedly "astonished the audience with their artistic skill", even though Sainton-Dolby felt slighted at being

---

[20] *Western Mail*, 28 March 1874, 4.
[21] *Y Gwladgarwr*, 13 August 1859, 1, advertised the event as 'Eisteddfod Genedlaethol Merthyr Tydfil' ('Merthyr Tydfil National Eisteddfod').
[22] The development of the National Eisteddfod in the 1860s is vividly discussed by Hywel Teifi Edwards, *Gŵyl Gwalia: Yr Eisteddfod Genedlaethol yn Oes Aur Victoria 1858–1868* (Llandysul: Gomer, 1980).
[23] John Davies, *Hanes Cymru: A History of Wales in Welsh* (London: Allen Lane, 1990), p. 395.

eclipsed by Edith Wynne (1842–97) in Welsh dress singing the plaintive "Mae Robin yn swil".[24] The quartet apparently moved on to a tour of more 'refined' venues where there was less danger of being upstaged by a Welsh folk song. But the fact that the audience expressed such enthusiasm for Holywell-born Edith Wynne highlighted the tension between popular native art and metropolitan concert culture. When Brinley Richards attempted to raise the tone of the Carmarthen National Eisteddfod of 1867 by showing off the talents of luminaries of the London stage, his efforts descended to farce when the contralto, Janet Patey-Whytock, singing under the shelter of an umbrella to shield her from the rain dripping through a leaking roof, was drowned out by calls from the audience for their idol, Llew Llwyfo (Lewis William Lewis; 1831–1901), a popular balladeer and no mean singer, who knew exactly how to handle a Welsh crowd. The question of whether the eisteddfod should be a celebration of indigenous Welsh music and poetry or a showcase for the high art of the concert stage was to remain unresolved.

Also important in this formative decade was the role of the National Eisteddfod in encouraging musical composition through competition: Joseph Parry was the most talented Welsh composer of his generation, but the works of others who won prizes at National Eisteddfodau, such as John Ambrose Lloyd (1815–74), John Thomas (1839–1921) and David Lewis (1828–1908), also enjoyed a vogue as test pieces for competition, even though their popularity did not endure. A pioneering competition at the Aberdare National Eisteddfod in 1885 was for the composition of a string quartet, a medium scarcely known in Wales at the time. It was won by J. T. Rees (1857–1949), who sadly did not pursue string-writing skills, despite his long career. Competitions in composition persisted as a feature of the National Eisteddfod, though comparatively few lasting works emerged, and it was not until more than a century later, in 1990, that the National Eisteddfod began to honour composers with the award of a special medal, 'Tlws y Cerddor' (The Musician's Medal), for a new composition.

During the last quarter of the nineteenth century, the National Eisteddfod emerged as a major venue for Welsh musical activity. Local eisteddfodau continued to flourish, with some acquiring regional and 'semi-national' status; opportunities for competition and performance abounded, and local success could be a springboard to national eminence. Following a chequered series of events during the 1870s, the National

---

[24] Gareth Williams, *Valleys of Song: Music and Society in Wales 1840–1914* (Cardiff: University of Wales Press, 1998), p. 67.

Eisteddfod was reformed under a new National Eisteddfod Association in 1880 and began a series of annual events which were to continue and become a focus for Welsh cultural life: for generations the appellation 'National winner' could be counted a badge of honour in Welsh society. And it was in the late nineteenth century that the dominance of music at the National Eisteddfod, and indeed at smaller eisteddfodau, was confirmed. Writing of the National Eisteddfod held at Dolgellau in 1949, Wyn Griffith suggested that

> the impression gained by the uninformed visitor would be that the Eisteddfod is a musical festival interrupted by two ceremonies, chairing the bard and crowning the bard, especially as there are eleven choral competitions and thirteen competitions for solo voices.[25]

From the humble beginnings of the 1830s, when there were few, if any, choirs at eisteddfodau, their number steadily grew. There was not one at Beaumaris in 1832; at Carmarthen in 1867 the choirs were all comparatively small, none having more than forty members, and singing madrigals and simple part-songs.[26] The National Eisteddfod held at Mold in 1873 boasted six choirs in the chief choral competition, and in 1897, when the National Eisteddfod was held at Newport, there were fifteen mixed and ten male choirs competing. By the time of the Carmarthen National Eisteddfod in 1911, there were as many as sixty-nine choirs taking part in the various choral competitions.[27] It was this growth in the popularity of choral singing in all parts of Wales that helped to make the National Eisteddfod a significant crowd-puller. Marquees and temporary pavilions erected to house it were built to hold thousands rather than hundreds. Fired by the success of the South Wales Choral Union at the Crystal Palace in 1873 – the victory of a Welsh choir over a London choir was mightily symbolic – choral Wales set about confirming the enduring perception of itself as a land of song.

Cross-Currents and Stimuli

As they competed, the more ambitious choirs – and those with the best conductors – acquired new repertoire, learning classical works which might not otherwise have been attempted. From the 1860s, the availability of cheaper sheet music enabled choirs to broaden their horizons. Whereas

---

[25] Griffith, *The Welsh*, p. 145.
[26] John Graham, *A Century of Welsh Music* (London: Kegan Paul, Trench, Trubner, 1923), p. 47.
[27] Williams, *Valleys of Song*, p. 13.

local eisteddfodau and early National Eisteddfodau had set simple part-songs and even hymn tunes as test pieces for competition, the choirs of later generations could set their sights higher and sing more complex choruses. By the time of the Cardiff National Eisteddfod of 1938, it was possible to ask competing choirs in the chief choral competition to prepare the whole of Brahms's Requiem, from which they would be asked to sing a chorus or two on the day of the competition. Nevertheless, eisteddfodau in general were often strongly criticised for limitations of repertoire. Controversy over this became more marked by the early years of the twentieth century, with the emergence of musicians who had gained professional qualifications and had become dissatisfied with the excessive amateurism which characterised eisteddfod activity. Dowlais-born Harry Evans (1873–1914), whose untimely death robbed Wales of one of its brightest musical talents, was a first-rate organist; but it was as a conductor and critic that he made his mark. As conductor of the Liverpool Welsh Choral Society he championed the complex and challenging music of his friend Granville Bantock and was highly regarded by Edward Elgar. At the Liverpool National Eisteddfod in 1900 he scored a notable success with his male voice choir from Dowlais, the only choir from Wales to win one of the major choral prizes; but he was severe in his criticism of the lack of ambition shown by eisteddfodau and competitors alike in their choice of test pieces.[28] Granville Bantock resigned as a choral adjudicator at the Abergavenny National Eisteddfod of 1913 because he felt that the choice of choral test pieces was not sufficiently challenging, and indeed represented a regression from the progress made in Welsh choral music in the years before then. His stance was supported by the *Musical Times*, which thought it 'lamentable that gifted Wales should voluntarily cut itself away from the stream of progress that has distinguished the competition movement in England'; the local committee, which was responsible for the choice of test pieces, justified its actions on the grounds that attempts to raise standards had tended to alienate competitors. It was the old tension between standards and populism.[29]

There was also an ugly side to the competitive spirit, evident from early days. More than one adjudicator had tales to tell of being hounded out of a place because of an unpopular decision. Samuel Coleridge-Taylor (1875–1912), who as a black composer had run the gauntlet of racism and

---

[28] Graham, *Century of Welsh Music*, pp. 49–50.
[29] *Musical Times*, 53 (1912, December) extra supplement, 'Competition Festival Record'.

prejudice, was quite content to come to Wales to adjudicate, as he told an American agent:

> Please don't make any arrangements to wrap me in cotton wool ... I do a great deal of adjudicating in Wales among a very rough class of people, [where] most adjudicators have had eggs and boots thrown at them[.][30]

Public disputes were not uncommon. At a Whit Monday eisteddfod at Cadoxton in 1892, adjudicator Dyfed Lewys (1852–1927) exploded with fury when the conductor of a male voice choir objected to having to share the first prize in the competition with another choir, and Lewys harangued the meeting at length. This streak in eisteddfod life was still in evidence in the twentieth century; witness the nervousness of the scholar-musician Edmund H. Fellowes (1870–1951) when people tried to dissuade him from accepting an invitation to adjudicate at the Llanelli National Eisteddfod in 1930, an experience which he nevertheless enjoyed.[31] Disputes about competition outcomes could spill over into newspaper correspondence columns, and even into literature. With time, negative feelings were kept under better control, and exhibitions of ill-feeling became scarcer.

Another serious criticism was Englishness. While local eisteddfodau retained to a great extent the primacy of the Welsh language, the National Eisteddfod came under fire in the late nineteenth century for its anglicised character and excessive use of English, especially in music competitions. In 1886 a correspondent in the periodical *Y Cerddor Sol-ffa* (The Sol-fa Musician) lamented this tendency, which undermined the true character of the eisteddfod, a movement claimed for the common people and intended first and foremost for the promotion of Welsh music and literature. Yet the National Eisteddfod from the 1880s on, perhaps reflecting class divisions in Welsh society, was heavily influenced by Victorian ideas of self-advancement and an imperialistic belief in the supremacy of the English language. Such tensions were to continue well into the twentieth century. At Caernarfon in 1886, Bangor in 1902 and even into the 1930s feelings were expressed that the National Eisteddfod was too English in character, and at Machynlleth in 1937 some adjudicators resigned in opposition to the selection of presidents who were unable to speak Welsh. Poets and prose writers who upheld the Welsh-language character of the festival blamed the musicians: not only did music competitions take up most of the time in the programme, but the test pieces were often sung

---

[30] Quoted in Williams, *Valleys of Song*, p. 174.
[31] Edmund H. Fellowes, *Memoirs of an Amateur Musician* (London: Methuen, 1946), pp. 195–199.

in English, irrespective of their original language, and too few works by Welsh composers were performed. Choirs from England often gained prizes at National Eisteddfodau in the years up to World War II. Moreover, many of the adjudicators appointed to music competitions were not Welsh speakers, and of necessity had to deliver their adjudications in English: they were nevertheless musicians of the highest calibre, such as Walter Parratt, Frederick Bridge, Henry Coward and Edward Bairstow. There could also be conflicts of taste among adjudicators, as Edmund Fellowes found at Llanelli in 1930, when the panel of three English and four Welsh adjudicators was divided over the style of singing of the competing choirs, the English adjudicators favouring a controlled approach and the Welsh preferring passionate singing.[32] The Ystalyfera mixed choir, under their conductor W. D. Clee (1884–1946), enjoyed a run of successes in the chief choral competition at the National Eisteddfod between 1926 and their last appearance in 1938, winning the competition on four occasions; but their fondness for overtly dramatic performance, with surging crescendi and thrilling climaxes, though it tended to appeal to audiences, did not find favour with all adjudicators. At Fishguard in 1936 they were heavily criticised by R. R. Terry for 'vocal stunting', and never again achieved the success of previous years. Such conflicts underline a marked difference in traditions. Many of the English adjudicators came from a background in cathedral music; the Welsh preference was for rousing and full-throated declamation, the heritage of the legendary Crystal Palace victory of 1873.

The National Eisteddfodau of the 1860s had introduced Welsh audiences to classical works: Handel's *Messiah* was given an early outing at Chester in 1866 and again at Ruthin in 1868, though these were not the first occasions on which the work was heard in Wales. This formative decade in eisteddfod history also saw the beginning of the role of the eisteddfod as a platform for Wales's own composers. John Thomas (Pencerdd Gwalia; 1826–1913) not only caused controversy in traditional circles with his promotion of the pedal harp: the National Eisteddfod staged performances of his cantatas *Llewelyn* in 1863 and *The Bride of Neath Valley* in 1866, works more significant in what they represented – an emergent Welsh musical voice – than for any intrinsic musical merit. In the twentieth century the National Eisteddfod stage became a platform for the introduction to Welsh audiences of new repertoire, not always with the best results. The musical evangelist Henry Walford Davies (1869–1941), who regarded his

---

[32] Fellowes, *Memoirs*, pp. 197–198.

appointment as Director of the National Council of Music in 1919 as an opportunity to educate the Welsh people and refine their musical taste, found to his cost in 1923 that the National Eisteddfod was not the best place to perform Bach's St. Matthew Passion – the rather bored audience, unused to such music, were poor listeners, and many walked out. Even so, more modern works did find favour, including Elgar's *Dream of Gerontius* in 1918, Delius's *Mass of Life* in 1933 and Walton's *Belshazzar's Feast* in 1934, all performed by the Eisteddfod choir, made up of local choristers assembled for the occasion, and singing in English. The implementation of the Welsh-language rule in 1950 meant that the libretti of such works would from then on be translated into Welsh for performance, but this hardly limited the scope of repertoire, with works ranging from Haydn's Masses and Verdi's Requiem to Vaughan Williams's *Sea Symphony* and Carl Orff's *Carmina Burana* being given successfully in Welsh guise, emphasising that the promotion and support of the Welsh language was ultimately the primary purpose of the National Eisteddfod.

The availability of eisteddfodau as a platform for performance encouraged Welsh composers, who would not shrink from sending their compositions to local eisteddfod committees, and publishers like Snell of Swansea invited committees to choose test pieces from their catalogues, providing financial incentives for doing so. It was not unknown, so claimed *Y Cerddor* (The Musician) in 1914, for publishers to receive letters from eisteddfod organisers offering to use some of their publications as test pieces in return for payment.[33] The following year, organist and composer John Owen Jones (1876–1962) deplored the tendency of eisteddfod committees to select music by non-Welsh composers at the expense of native talent.[34] On the other hand, the composer W. Albert Williams (1909–46) cautioned against the belief that new music should be performed, regardless of its quality, only because it was Welsh:

> Y mae i gerddoriaeth ei safonau, ac ynfydrwydd yw canmol gwaith o gelfyddyd wrth safonau iaith a chenedl.[35]
>
> (Music has its standards, and it is madness to praise a work of art according to standards of language and nation.)

During the twentieth century regular competitions for new compositions were held, but few of the prizewinning works were published, and fewer

---

[33] *Y Cerddor*, 26 (1914), 52.   [34] Quoted in *Y Cerddor*, 27 (1915), 39.
[35] *Y Cymro*, 22 Awst 1942, 4; quoted in Alan Llwyd, *Y Gaer Fechan Olaf: Hanes Eisteddfod Genedlaethol Cymru 1937–1950* (Felindre: Cyhoeddiadau Barddas, 2006), t. 97.

still became widely known or were regularly performed. As in other countries, there is a distinct disparity between the production of acceptable musical works for competition and their acceptance in the repertoire. The National Eisteddfod, however, continued to fulfil the role it had established for itself in the nineteenth century by performing works by contemporary Welsh composers at its evening concerts: for example, Llandybïe in 1944 premiered *Gweddi* by Arwel Hughes (1909–88); Ystradgynlais in 1954 the Fourth Symphony of Daniel Jones (1912–93), composed in memory of his friend Dylan Thomas; and Aberystwyth in 1992 an orchestral piece by Ian Parrott (1916–2012), *Arfordir Ceredigion*. The Eisteddfod also commissioned and staged lighter choral works and stage shows by contemporary Welsh composers.

The eisteddfod movement has provided a fillip to many a performer. Gifted vocalists honed their skills on the eisteddfod platform before embarking on a professional career; equally, there were those who, although they exhibited great talent, were prevented by lack of means from progressing to formal study. Nevertheless, there were many who followed the trail blazed by Edith Wynne, one of the earliest Welsh singers to find fame outside her native land. Dyfed Lewys, the adjudicator at the Cadoxton eisteddfod, was raised in the Swansea Valley and scored numerous successes at local eisteddfodau before winning the tenor solo competition at three successive National Eisteddfodau. His community raised money to enable him to study at the Royal Academy of Music, and he enjoyed success as a concert singer in late Victorian and Edwardian London. David Lloyd (1912–69) from Trelogan in Flintshire won hundreds of prizes at local and regional eisteddfodau before gaining a scholarship to the Guildhall School of Music and Drama and embarking on a career as a tenor which embraced Glyndebourne, Sadler's Wells and the recording studio. Another tenor, Stuart Burrows, inaugurated his own distinguished career by winning the Blue Riband as champion soloist at the Caernarfon National Eisteddfod in 1959, and bass-baritone Bryn Terfel gained experience on the eisteddfod platform before beginning on a path that brought him international acclaim. The W. Towyn Roberts scholarship, first awarded at the National Eisteddfod in 1982, is aimed specifically at young singers who wish to develop their careers, and recipients are encouraged to use the prize money to pay for further study.

The modern National Eisteddfod continues to award a range of trophies for choirs and brass bands, in addition to money prizes: but it is not the financial incentive that attracts competitors as much as the wish to support the festival for what it represents. Choral competition has continued: though the age of massed choirs has passed, and veterans such as

Treorchy Male Voice Choir and Morriston Orpheus Choir have decided to concentrate on activities other than competition,[36] the late twentieth century saw the emergence of younger Welsh-speaking choirs, notably Côr Eifionydd, Cantorion Teifi, Côrdydd and CF1, who have competed at the National Eisteddfod not only for the love of music but because they value its Welshness.

Dissemination and Development

The eisteddfod as a badge of Welshness became exportable early in its history, as Welsh people who went far afield created expatriate communities which sought to preserve their identity in a new environment. William Griffiths (Ivander; 1830–1910) left the scene of his triumphs in south Wales, where he had founded and conducted the Dyffryn Tawe Temperance Choral Society and given performances of oratorio in the 1860s, for Workington in Cumbria. Here he established an eisteddfod which spawned a tradition of competitive music festivals in the area. In a study of music in North Staffordshire, Reginald Nettel suggested that local singing competitions in the English Potteries of the 1870s were 'largely encouraged by the Welsh residents in the Potteries towns, who had immigrated during times of distress in the Welsh towns'.[37] The eisteddfod run by the Welsh community in Middlesbrough was large enough in 1889 to fill the new town hall, and in the following year took the grand title of Cleveland and Durham Eisteddfod.[38] In Australia, Ballarat was the home of regular eisteddfodau during the late nineteenth century and into the twentieth,[39] while many Welsh settlements in the United States formed their own eisteddfod tradition: Scranton in Pennsylvania, which had many Welsh immigrants, hosted the first American National Eisteddfod in 1875, and a lavish eisteddfod formed part of the World's Fair at Chicago in 1893.[40]

---

[36] The achievements of these and other male choirs are discussed by Gareth Williams in *Do You Hear the People Sing? The Male Voice Choirs of Wales* (Llandysul: Gomer, 2015).

[37] Reginald Nettel, *North Staffordshire Music: A Social Experiment* (Rickmansworth: Triad, 1977), p. 29.

[38] Richard Lewis and David Wood, 'Culture, Politics and Assimilation: The Welsh on Teesside, c. 1850–1940', *Welsh History Review*, 17 (1994–5), 550–570, on p. 559.

[39] Bill Jones, 'Welsh Identities in Ballarat, Australia, During the Late Nineteenth Century', *Welsh History Review*, 20 (2000–1), 283–307.

[40] W. D. Jones, *Wales in America: Scranton and the Welsh 1860–1920* (Cardiff: University of Wales Press, 1993), especially pp. 101–105. The World's Fair Eisteddfod is discussed by Hywel Teifi Edwards, *Eisteddfod Ffair y Byd Chicago, 1893* (Llandysul: Gomer, 1990).

In essence, the eisteddfod as created in the nineteenth century formed the basis of the modern eisteddfod, at every level, but there have been changes. Two world wars took their toll on communities, and economic depression in the 1920s and 1930s made cultural life difficult. From the early twentieth century there was increasing room for instrumental competitions, and solo and choral contests became more diverse. A major step forward had come as early as 1923 with the creation of a central music committee to give guidance to local committees on the selection of test pieces for competition and to ensure greater consistency. Brass bands had become an established part of the National Eisteddfod programme by the 1930s and would come to occupy a cherished place. Although the National Eisteddfod planned to be held at Bangor in 1914 was postponed for a year because of the outbreak of war, the festival continued annually thereafter, circumstances notwithstanding. During World War II it was held without interruption, albeit on a much smaller scale, with the 1940 National being a purely radio eisteddfod, an experiment echoed under different circumstances in 2020 and 2021 when an 'alternative' eisteddfod (Eisteddfod AmGen) was organised over the World Wide Web, as the Covid-19 pandemic made holding the normal National Eisteddfod impossible. It was during World War II that the National Eisteddfod established the concept of a champion soloist from among the winners of the different vocal categories: in 1943 an annual award in memory of the tenor David Ellis (1873–1941), the 'Blue Riband', was instituted. Similar Blue Riband awards were created for champion solo singers under twenty-five years of age (in memory of the Welsh composer T. Osborne Roberts, 1879–1948) and for instrumental soloists.

During the 1930s there was concerted action by those who wished to improve the quality of the ceremonial side of the National Eisteddfod, as shown in the ceremonies of the Gorsedd of Bards, and reaffirm the status of the National Eisteddfod as a Welsh-language festival, reflecting the growth in Welsh national consciousness which had seen the formation of the Welsh National Party, Plaid Cymru, in 1925. Until 1937 the National Eisteddfod had been organised jointly by the National Eisteddfod Association and the Gorsedd of Bards, in what was not always a harmonious partnership. In that year, the two bodies came together to form a National Eisteddfod Council, which introduced an all-Welsh rule to ensure that Welsh would be the language of the Eisteddfod. With the interruption caused by World War II, the rule was not fully implemented until the National Eisteddfod at Caerphilly in 1950. As might be expected, it was not universally welcomed. In advance of its implementation, the

Western Mail condemned this 'latest eisteddfodic trend' in terms which became familiar in many subsequent discussions:

> Many seem to believe that by these restrictive measures the Eisteddfod will strengthen the hold upon the Welsh people of their native culture and the native tongue. By eliminating, or at least strongly discouraging, the English-speaking Welshman, some eisteddfodwyr think they are doing a service to the nation.[41]

And a year later, when local Member of Parliament Ness Edwards insisted on giving his address at the Caerphilly National entirely in English as a protest against the all-Welsh rule, the paper was equally vitriolic:

> Caerphilly warns us that [i]f the all Welsh rule, strongly reminiscent as it is of the iron curtain and of the most extreme propaganda of the republicans and extreme nationalists, were to become permanent the whole character of the Eisteddfod would be radically changed very much for the worse.[42]

The Welsh-American choral conductor Charles Dawe (1886–1958), who had brought his Cleveland Orpheus male choir to the National Eisteddfod and had won first prize at Mold in 1923 and Swansea in 1926, strongly disapproved of an all-Welsh rule, which he felt would inhibit competitors and alienate outsiders, although he was a Welsh speaker. The rule, however, gradually gained acceptance as the public profile of the Welsh language grew from the 1960s, and in spite of warnings to the contrary, those areas of Wales in which the Welsh language was not frequently used were not precluded from hosting the National Eisteddfod successfully; indeed, the event's presence was often a stimulus to many to learn Welsh. One incidental benefit in musical terms was that song texts and libretti of major works were translated into Welsh for competition and performance. In the late twentieth century the National Eisteddfod became ever larger and more diverse, with competitions in different formats and in a variety of venues outside the main pavilion, and its very size and cost presented money-raising challenges to local committees. A degree of government subvention to supplement local fundraising became inevitable.

Despite its pre-eminence, the National is not the only eisteddfod to have Wales-wide impact. In 1922, Ifan ab Owen Edwards founded Urdd Gobaith Cymru (the Welsh League of Youth).[43] Established in the

---

[41] *Western Mail*, 30 July 1949, 2; quoted in Llwyd, *Y Gaer Fechan Olaf*, tt. 141–142.
[42] *Western Mail*, 14 August 1950, 2; quoted in Llwyd, *Y Gaer Fechan Olaf*, t. 147.
[43] Its literal (and suggestive) meaning is 'the League of Hope for Wales': the name reflects a sense of postwar optimism.

aftermath of World War I, its aim was to develop a feeling of national identity among young people. As a part of its work, the Urdd (as it is commonly known) founded its own national eisteddfod, first held at Corwen in 1929. This annual festival, acknowledged as the largest young people's festival in Europe, and held entirely through the medium of Welsh, has been proactive in developing the eisteddfod idea to embrace new competitions for rock and pop music and hip-hop/street/disco-dancing, as well as preserving more traditional aspects. The Urdd Eisteddfod has also benefited from the tiered structure of the movement, which has its basis in local and area groups. Eisteddfod heats are held at local and county level, and the winners go forward to the National Eisteddfod, so ensuring that national-level competitions are often of a high standard. Many singers and instrumentalists in Wales have perfected their artistic skills in Urdd competitions. From 1999, winners of certain Urdd competitions were able to compete for a special Bryn Terfel scholarship which aims to nurture the talents of some of Wales's best young performers and offers a prize towards further training in performing arts; while the winner of the main competition in composition receives a medal in memory of one of Wales's foremost classical composers, one-time schoolteacher Grace Williams (1906–77).

That the eisteddfod tradition is characteristically Welsh was emphasised in the immediate aftermath of World War II with the foundation in 1947 of another special contribution to the musical world: the Llangollen International Musical Eisteddfod. Harold Tudor (1907–86), an official of the British Council, saw the potential of the eisteddfod and its music as a vehicle for international reconciliation during his visits to the scaled-down National Eisteddfodau in 1943 and 1944 (the latter hosted an international concert), and with the co-operation of the Welsh musician W. S. Gwynn Williams (1896–1978), he established the international eisteddfod in Gwynn Williams's home town of Llangollen. The Llangollen eisteddfod has made a valuable contribution to international friendship: it is a thoroughly musical event, without the literary side of the 'standard' eisteddfod, but it has advertised the best of the eisteddfod tradition to a wider world and has given the lie to accusations that the eisteddfod movement is by definition inward-looking.

The modern eisteddfod has many 'levels', ranging from the very local to the national and international. Many schools in Wales hold their own eisteddfodau, usually in celebration of St David's Day on 1 March. Informal eisteddfodau may be held at pubs, very often to raise money for a charitable cause. Local eisteddfodau are held all over Wales: they may be one-day events, or in some cases, such as Gŵyl Fawr Aberteifi in Cardigan or the Pantyfedwen eisteddfodau at Lampeter and Pontrhydfendigaid, spread over two or three days. The website of Cymdeithas Eisteddfodau Cymru (the Wales Eisteddfod Society), an association of local eisteddfodau established in 1998, estimated that there were over 120 local eisteddfodau in Wales in 2020, some with a considerable continuous history: the eisteddfod at the village of Pandy Tudur near Llanrwst dates back to 1857; that at Swyddffynnon in mid-Ceredigion to 1875.[44] Others are of more recent creation – Eisteddfod y Cymoedd in the Rhymni Valley was founded in 2006. In some areas of Wales where Welsh is not strong as a community language, local eisteddfodau have been held largely through the medium of English, for instance at Upper Chapel and Kerry, both in Powys, but they remain Welsh in character. Virtually all these events will have the usual range of musical, elocution and literary competitions and will embrace competitors of all ages. While they do not always reach great heights of excellence in performance, their strength could be said to lie in their encouragement of local talent and in giving competitors the opportunity from an early age to learn the discipline of performing on stage before an audience. They may be rooted in amateurism, but they have fostered music making for generations. Above all, at national, subnational and local levels, eisteddfodau remain a potent symbol and affirmation of Welshness, or as the writer Emyr Humphreys claimed, the 'flagship' of Welsh nationhood.[45]

---

[44] See Cymdeithas Eisteddfodau Cymru: http://smala.net/steddfota (accessed 9 June 2021).
[45] A comment made in an interview with Beti George in her programme *Beti a'i Phobol*, broadcast on BBC Radio Cymru on 30 November 2020, and originally broadcast in August 1985.

CHAPTER 6

Women and Welsh Folk Song

Wyn Thomas

The Welsh musical tradition in the nineteenth century rarely gave women the opportunity to contribute to its growth and development. After all, was Wales not 'The Land of My Fathers' and a breeding ground for male voice choirs, brass bands and Welsh rugby? It was home to the great poets of the medieval period and their descendants – mostly men – including Dafydd ap Gwilym, Iolo Goch, Tudur Aled – and the country that provided a platform for eminent musicians such as Griffith Rhys Jones (Caradog), Joseph Parry (Pencerdd America) and John Parry (Bardd Alaw). The role of women in nineteenth-century Welsh literature has been well established – examples include Lady Charlotte Guest and her translation of the *Mabinogion* into English, Angharad Llwyd and her topographical study of the Isle of Anglesey and Amy Dillwyn, whose writing encapsulates issues of class and gender and places her at the forefront of Welsh women's writing. The female musician, however (whether performer, composer or collector) was a relatively unknown phenomenon. Women were rarely associated with Welsh music during the eighteenth century and though evidence of female involvement exists during the nineteenth century (for instance, Maria Jane Williams and her *Ancient National Airs of Gwent and Morganwg*, published in 1844, and Clara Novello Davies as conductor and musical director of the Royal Welsh Ladies' Choir), their names have often gone unnoticed and their contribution overlooked, primarily because men dominated the field. Men also compiled the dictionaries, articles, books, reviews and collections that outline the main musical activities of the age.

During the early years of the twentieth century and the events surrounding the establishing of the Welsh Folk-Song Society (Cymdeithas Alawon Gwerin Cymru), it was the extraordinary efforts of several pioneering women in Wales that heralded the dawn of a new age and an opportunity for female musicians. When J. Lloyd Williams (a botany lecturer at the University College of North Wales, Bangor) summarised the main events related to the history of the Welsh Folk-Song Society in the mid-1930s, he commented that:

> Much of the success has been due to the enthusiasm and vision of a number of lady workers, collecting and publishing the songs, singing them in public and organising the activities of the Society.[1]

Later in the same article, he continued,

> In view of the splendid services rendered to the Society . . . by the ladies, it is difficult to understand why the men monopolised the membership of the Committee![2]

J. Lloyd Williams, part-time musical director at the University College of North Wales, Bangor, was undoubtedly 'the grand old man of the [folk-song] movement'[3] in Wales. Yet, documentary evidence proves unequivocally that several influential women played a significant role in the activities of the newly founded Welsh Folk-Song Society; that they drew on their experience and political associations and influenced the nature and direction of the revival in traditional music activities in Wales at the time. These women infused a considerable degree of professionalism into the field in Wales – a professionalism that had already been seen in the English and Irish folk-song-revival movements.[4] Indeed, were it not for their involvement during the early years, the rise and development of folk-song collecting, scholarship and traditional performances in Wales and further afield would have been rather different.

Mary Davies

As a mezzo-soprano, Mary Davies (Mair Mynorydd; 1855–1930) gained considerable recognition during the late nineteenth century in her oratorio and ballad concerts throughout the United Kingdom. Her early performances had been held in music halls, music clubs and at festivals and her professional interests were primarily in western art music (works by Berlioz, Gounod, Sterndale Bennett, Arthur Sullivan and so on). She occasionally visited Wales to perform in the National Eisteddfod and the Harlech Music Festival, but as a Londoner, her experience and understanding of Welsh folk song and traditional melodies from Wales was

---

[1] J. Lloyd Williams, 'The History of the Welsh Folk-Song Society', *Journal of the Welsh Folk-Song Society*, III/2 (1934), 89.
[2] Ibid., 93.   [3] GB-CDf, MS 1459/260. Radio script by Dora Herbert Jones (*c.* September 1958).
[4] The English Folk-Song Society was established in 1898 and the Irish Folk Song Society in 1904.

somewhat limited. She was, however, consciously and ardently Welsh and despite never having lived in Wales during her youth, her appreciation of indigenous Welsh music would have come via vocal arrangements by Brinley Richards (Cerddor Towy; 1817–85)[5] and John Thomas (Pencerdd Gwalia; 1826–1913),[6] both of whom were active in the capital.

It was her marriage to William Cadwaladr Davies (1849–1905), the first Secretary and Registrar of the University College of North Wales, that brought her to Bangor. It was here that she heard Welsh folk songs – not as contemporary Victorian drawing-room arrangements but rather in their wild and original state. It was here also that she contributed to the early attempts to gather such material from oral sources, which continued for the rest of her days. Mary Davies's role in the newly formed Welsh Folk-Song Society was to gain the interest and support of politicians (for example, David Lloyd George, MP for Caernarfon and later Chancellor and Prime Minister, and John Herbert Lewis, MP for Flintshire) and musicians (including Anne Gilchrist and Lucy Broadwood), and to ensure that the folk-song movement in Wales was established on a sure foundation. Her aim also was to bring international recognition to the field and to proclaim that Wales had a wealth of indigenous musical traditions that were worthy of note. In so doing, her vision for the development of Welsh folk music was far greater than that of Lloyd Williams. Despite his specialism and considerable musical experience, it was Mary Davies who gained the support of other folk-song specialists from England including Frank Kidson, Cecil Sharp and Ralph Vaughan Williams. Without the allegiance of these well-established outsiders, the folk-song society in Wales would have struggled – limited in its resources, workers and understanding of what was, at the time, a relatively new area of scholarship. Davies also deserves recognition as one of the earliest Welsh folk-song collectors and an influence on others including Ruth Herbert Lewis (1871–1946) of Penucha, Caerwys (see Figure 6.1).[7] The fascination of discovering a hitherto undocumented melody fuelled both women's participation in the movement for many years.

Thomas Edison's invention of the phonograph and his association with Welsh electrical engineer Sir William Preece of Caernarfon gave rise to a revolution in what was to become the field of ethnomusicology, not only in Wales but also in England, Hungary and beyond. Preece presented his

---

[5] His *The Songs of Wales* (London: Boosey & Hawkes, 1873) had a very wide circulation.
[6] John Thomas was professor of harp at the Royal Academy of Music, Royal College of Music and the Guildhall School of Music.
[7] Lady Ruth Herbert Lewis was a pioneer collector of Welsh folk songs. Her husband was Sir John Herbert Lewis (1858–1933), MP for Flintshire.

Figure 6.1 Dr Mary Davies (seated) and Ruth Herbert Lewis in 'Gorsedd y Beirdd' robes. By kind permission of Mrs Nest Price, Caerwys, Flintshire

Edison Gem phonograph (which he had received as a gift from its inventor) to the Welsh Folk-Song Society in 1908, and the growing interest in recording, transcribing and studying different melodic variants and 'tune families', together with the introduction of comparative techniques, led to the widespread use of the technology among its members in

Wales.[8] In summarising Edison's pioneering achievements on the pages of *The Etude*, James Francis Cooke commented: 'What the printing press did for the composer, you [Edison] have done for the instrumentalist and singer.'[9] Despite its initial limitations and its inability to record more than two minutes of music on a single wax cylinder, the phonograph became an essential tool in folk-song collecting and in the Society's nationwide activities.

Wherever Mary Davies was invited to lecture or adjudicate, she took the opportunity to record and collect traditional Welsh songs from oral and manuscript sources, and though she never kept a field diary, her numerous letters to Lloyd Williams highlight her most memorable and ambitious experiences.[10]

> I have left Megan Evans my phonograph to use at Barmouth. We have also set another phonograph working at Llanfair, near Harlech. It belongs to Ben Rowlands the blacksmith there. We went under Mrs Davison's guidance to see him and found that he possesses one – he was too shy to sing, but has promised to get others to sing into it and I am to send him some blank cylinders for this purpose.[11]

Gradually, the principles of ethnomusicology in general – and folk-song collecting in particular – became more evident in the study of Welsh traditional music. Mary Davies realised that there was a pressing need to organise the methodology behind folk-song collection and steer the Society and its limited number of amateur collectors located throughout Wales towards good fieldwork practices. Nevertheless, she encountered some major difficulties during many of her collecting expeditions. Because women travelling alone in rural communities were not a familiar sight in Wales at the time, it is hardly surprising that her motives in carrying out such work were questioned and often ridiculed. Likewise, the social chasm separating her as a collector from many of her informants often proved to be an unsurmountable problem given that she belonged to the higher echelons of the London Welsh community and was regarded as a celebrity performer of

---

[8] During his visits to several Celtic countries in 1907–9, Rudolf Trebitsch (1876–1918) used the phonograph to record Welsh language dialects and Welsh harp music. His collection is housed in the Austrian Academy of Sciences, Vienna.
[9] James Francis Cooke, 'A Momentous Musical Meeting: Thomas A. Edison and Lt. Comm. John Philip Sousa Meet for the First Time and Talk Upon Music', *The Etude*, 41/10, October (1923), 663.
[10] Mary Davies's extensive correspondence is available in the National Library of Wales, Aberystwyth. See GB-AB Dr Mary Davies and W. Cadwaladr Davies Papers, NLW ex 2306, and Dr J. Lloyd Williams Music MSS and Papers (1908–27), AL 1/4.
[11] GB-AB Dr J. Lloyd Williams Music MSS and Papers (2), Box 112, GB 0210 JLLW. Correspondence from Mary Davies to J. Lloyd Williams, dated 25 April 1911.

considerable standing and experience, even in Wales. To many of her informants, the use of a phonograph was also far removed from the reality of traditional life in the remote corners of the Principality. Above all else, however, she wrestled continually with her lack of fluency in the Welsh language, and difficulties arose during conversations as well as during the process of transcribing song texts in preparation for publication in the *Journal of the Welsh Folk-Song Society*.[12] However, she possessed a considerable degree of tenacity and perseverance. Her involvement in the Welsh folk-song movement was no fleeting experience either; she had the energy and drive to venture, and in view of the fact that she had no family responsibilities (nor, in later life, a concern with pursuing a professional career) she was free to devote her time to the promotion and propagation of the field. During a visit to Whitchurch, Cardiff in September 1908, she recorded her most familiar folk song – 'Dacw 'Nghariad i Lawr yn y Berllan'[13] ('There's My Sweetheart Down in the Orchard'; see Example 6.1), and while visiting family in the Barmouth district of Merioneth, she collected 'Wrth Fynd efo Deio i Dywyn' ('Travelling with Deio to Tywyn').[14] While she might be working in Aberystwyth one week, she could be researching in Oxford the next, or at home in her native London, before setting off for Anglesey. Indeed, there was

Example 6.1 'Dacw 'Nghariad i Lawr yn y Berllan' ('There's My Sweetheart Down in the Orchard'). *Journal of the Welsh Folk-Song Society*, I/77

---

[12] The *Journal* was relaunched under a new title, *Canu Gwerin/Folk Song* in 1978 and has appeared annually since.
[13] *Journal of the Welsh Folk-Song Society*, I/2 (1910), 77–78.   [14] Ibid., 132–133.

no end to her enthusiasm, and every two or three days she would correspond with Lloyd Williams, outlining her latest discoveries.

Ruth Herbert Lewis

Ruth Herbert Lewis joined the Welsh Folk-Song Society in October 1908, which marked the commencement of her thirty-five-year involvement in traditional music activities. Born in Liverpool of Manx descent, Lewis's interest in the field was kindled by the vibrant Welsh cultural life at Charing Cross Chapel, London, where her husband, John Herbert Lewis, was a member. It was during their visits to the capital that she heard Mary Davies's lectures on Welsh music and attended performances of *Aelwyd Angharad* (an operetta based on traditional melodies and customs by J. Lloyd Williams), and that her determination to gather Welsh folk songs became a lifetime calling. Following Mary Davies's instigation, Ruth Lewis purchased an Edison Gem Model D phonograph in order to support the work of collecting tunes in the vicinity of her home in Caerwys, Flintshire (see Figure 6.2). 'If only more people would use the phonograph in folk song collecting', she wrote:

> The whole outfit does not cost more than £3 and the amount of pleasure that one gets out of it is very great indeed. . . . Folk song collecting is superior to all other sorts of collecting for your finds are alive. Stamps, pictures or china are all dead things, but the folk song is alive.[15]

Due to her lack of musical training and her limited ability to converse in Welsh, she realised that in order to contribute to the understanding of folk song in Wales, she would be totally dependent on the latest recording technology and the support of local informants or 'guides', as well as the expertise of competent musicians to transcribe her newly discovered melodies. As she admitted:

> collecting was not the easy matter which to some it may appear; it is difficult to find the singers and after they have been discovered, it is equally difficult to get them to yield up their treasure. . . . Much tact and patience is required and worthless productions of modern date must be suffered before the real old song appears.[16]

With the exception of a brief field excursion to Llandysul and Newcastle Emlyn during June 1913, Ruth Herbert Lewis, accompanied

---

[15] Welsh Folk-Song Society, *Third Annual Report, 30 June 1911* (Bangor: Jarvis & Foster, 1911), 10–11.
[16] GB-CDf, MS 1459/248. Dora Herbert Jones Collection, 'They found the songs', Radio script #5 (Lady Ruth Herbert Lewis).

Figure 6.2 A phonograph cylinder from Ruth Herbert Lewis's collection. 'Cân Llwynog, L. Roberts, Smithy, Rhydyrarian' is written in her hand on the cover. The photograph was taken in Ruth Herbert Lewis's home at Penucha, Caerwys in 2009, with the permission of her granddaughter Nest Price. © Wyn Thomas

by Annie Ellis,[17] focused her attention primarily on collecting folk songs in the north-east region of Flintshire, Denbighshire and the Vale of Clwyd. Her visits to Buckley, Hawarden, Flint, Ruthin and Mold were carried out despite the demanding family and household responsibilities she also had to fulfil. In return, however, she befriended many local inhabitants, familiarised herself with indigenous traditions and produced the most extensive and varied Welsh folk-song collection on phonograph cylinders that has survived to the present day.[18] Her particular interests included narrative ballad tunes, traditional carols, work songs, May-Day song and dance tunes (Cadi-ha) as well as north and south Wales variants of traditional Welsh melodies. In fact, though she was musically illiterate, her systematic approach to describing folk-song features was more

[17] Annie Jane Ellis (née Davies; 1873–1942), of Cwrt Mawr farm, Llangeitho, was married to Tom Ellis (1859–99), Liberal MP for Merionethshire and leader of Cymru Fydd, a movement that aimed to gain political independence for Wales.
[18] Ruth Herbert Lewis's recordings are kept in the St Fagans National Museum of History, Cardiff, and in the British Library.

detailed and far in advance of those of many of the Society's other members.

> Many of these original songs show traces of older scales which cannot be written in *sol-fa*. ... When it came to writing them down, there was no method to indicate the quarter notes and I doubt, if any modern singer could do them. Some of you may remember the happy days before every country chapel had its harmonium and when the old modal hymn tunes were sung traditionally (with all their trills and ornaments) – but of course, to modern ears, wrong. I believe the old people were right and sang as their forefathers taught them – by ear.[19]

It was her contact with Jane Williams, an elderly resident at the Union Workhouse, Holywell that proved to be her most fruitful discovery. From August 1911 until January 1915, Ruth Herbert Lewis visited Jane on several occasions, during which she recorded her singing over two-dozen folk songs in both Welsh and English. Learned from Williams's mother and other local inhabitants during her childhood in the 1830s, many of her songs appear in Lady Lewis's first published collection, *Folk Songs: Collected in Flintshire and the Vale of Clwyd*[20] – a volume dedicated to Lewis's friend and colleague, Mary Davies, and to Jane Williams in recognition of her invaluable contribution. Ruth Herbert Lewis was undoubtedly a born collector; she was a skilled negotiator with a marked sense of humour, undimmed energy and a complete disregard of all obstacles. During her frequent visits to Holywell, she recorded Jane 'Sheeptrotters' singing 'Mynwent Eglwys' ('The Church Graveyard'), 'Ffarwel i Dre Caernarfon Lon' ('Farewell to Fair Caernarfon Town') and 'Lliw Gwyn Rhosyn yr Haf' ('The White Coloured Summer Rose'). However, it was from Henry Williams, an old weaver at Rhydyrarian factory, near Llansannan, Denbighshire that she collected one of her most familiar traditional Welsh carols, 'Roedd yn y Wlad Honno' ('There Was in That Land'; see Example 6.2).

Throughout her professional life, Ruth Herbert Lewis campaigned to raise the standards of primary and secondary education and regarded music as a foundational aspect of the school curriculum in Wales – a key to an individual's well-being and to the nation's cultural life. She acknowledged that Welsh music lay in the hands of its teachers and, consequently, visited every training college and university to lecture to its students and promote

---

[19] GB-CDf MS 2505/06, Ruth Herbert Lewis lecture notes (n.d.).
[20] Ruth Herbert Lewis, *Folk Songs Collected in Flintshire and the Vale of Clwyd* (Wrexham: Hughes & Son, 1914).

Example 6.2 'Roedd yn y Wlad Honno' ('There Was in That Land'). *Journal of the Welsh Folk-Song Society*, II/128

the use of Wales's traditional music among those who would be directly responsible for educating future generations. In collaboration with the National Council of Music in Wales,[21] her aim was to publish folk-song collections that would serve as textbooks for children (with emphasis on the songs' historical and cultural importance) and as performing material for term-time concerts and events. She also campaigned fervently on the sensitive issue of copyright in folk-song collecting and served as Secretary and later, President of the Welsh Folk-Song Society; she was one of its prime instigators and leaders.

Grace Gwyneddon Davies

The involvement of Grace Gwyneddon Davies (1878–1944) in the Welsh folk-song movement began in 1906 when she was invited to perform

---

[21] The Council was established in 1919 following the recommendations of the Haldane Commission on University Education in Wales. Henry Walford Davies was its first chairman.

a selection of traditional Welsh melodies during a Cymmrodorion Society meeting held at the National Eisteddfod of Wales, Caernarfon.[22] As an experienced singer and accompanist, she had travelled widely in Europe and established a successful career in the field of oratorio. Her husband, Robert Gwyneddon Davies (1870–1928), was actively involved in the local community (as a Justice of the Peace, local councillor and mayor) and an enthusiastic collector of ancient Welsh manuscripts. Together they combined their musical and literary interests for the benefit of the newly established Folk-Song Society.

Prior to the publication of the *Journal of the Welsh Folk-Song Society* (1909), the editor, J. Lloyd Williams, appealed for support from other collectors in Wales and for a greater variety of musical items to engender interest:

> As yet, there are few who do any systematic collection themselves, but there are many who take an interest in the subject and who indicate localities where songs may be obtained or persons who happen to know some of the old songs.[23]

Grace Gwyneddon Davies responded to the request for new traditional repertoire by visiting members of her family at Tyddyn-y-gwynt farm, Dwyran, Anglesey, where Owen Parry was a tenant. She records that he had a magnificent store of songs and though he spoke deprecatingly of his own singing, he was intelligently interested in the songs' preservation and took great pains in recording them. He was not shy of singing into the phonograph either, and appeared to be pleased to hear his own quivering voice being reproduced with such clarity.[24] During her time at Dwyran, Grace Davies recorded her most interesting songs, including 'Cob Malltraeth' ('Malltraeth's Dyke'), 'Y Gelynen' ('The Holly'), 'Cwyn Mam-yng-nghyfraith' ('Mother-in-Law's Complaint') and 'Titrwm Tatrwm', and in 1914, vocal arrangements with simple piano accompaniments appeared in her first published collection of Anglesey folk songs, entitled *Alawon Gwerin Môn* (see Example 6.3).[25]

This was an age marked by political unrest in north-west Wales and the establishing of the Anglesey Workers' Union under Liberal leadership,

---

[22] Following lectures by Harry Reichel (Principal of University College of North Wales, Bangor) and Alfred Perceval Graves, it was agreed that a Welsh Folk-Song Society should be established.
[23] GB-AB Minor Lists A1, Welsh Folk-Song Society, Minute Book, 1908–34.
[24] Robert Gwyneddon Davies, 'The Collecting of Anglesey Folk Songs', *Anglesey Antiquarian and Field Club Transactions*, 23 (1923), 95.
[25] Grace Gwyneddon Davies, *Alawon Gwerin Môn/Folk Songs from Anglesey* (Caernarfon: The Welsh Publishing Company, 1914).

Example 6.3 'Titrwm Tatrwm'. *Journal of the Welsh Folk-Song Society*, II/29

Tit - rwm, tat - rwm, Gwen lliw'r ŵyn, Lliw'r meil - lion mwyn, 'rwy'n cu - ro; Mae'r

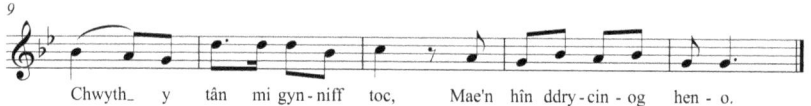

gwynt yn oer oddi - ar y llyn, O flo - dyn y dyff - ryn deff - ro!

Chwyth_ y tân mi gyn - niff toc, Mae'n hîn ddry - cin - og hen - o.

which aimed to secure employment rights and a fair salary for farm labourers living on the island. Workers in Newborough, Dwyran and Brynsiencyn sought justice and were eager to spread their propaganda by way of poetry and song. During her field trips in the locality, Grace Gwyneddon Davies discovered several call-and-response (or 'question-and-answer') melodies, communal tunes, calendar and agricultural work songs – all of which would have been performed by farm workers during nosweithiau llawen (merry evenings) in the stable loft.

> The explanation of the prevalence of songs of this nature may be in the fact that Anglesey was always a county where large farms abounded ... and that the proverbial hospitality of its folk conduced to frequent convivial gatherings in the *gegin fawr* [the large kitchen] and in the *neuadd* [hall] of its mansions.[26]

Further fieldwork in south-west Anglesey during the early 1920s resulted in the discovery of 'Y Gog Lwydlas' ('The Grey Cuckoo'), 'Y Ddau Farch' ('The Two Horses') and a Welsh-language equivalent to 'The Twelve Days of Christmas' ('Y Cyntaf Dydd o'r Gwyliau') which were published in her fourth collection of folk-song arrangements, entitled *Chwech o Alawon Gwerin Cymreig/Six Welsh Songs* (1933).[27] Grace Gwyneddon Davies's main contribution to the musical revival, however, was in her sterling

---

[26] Robert Gwyneddon Davies, 'The Collecting of Anglesey Folk Songs', 95.
[27] Grace Gwyneddon Davies, *Chwech o Alawon Gwerin Cymreig/Six Welsh Folk Songs* (Wrexham: Hughes & Son, 1933), 16 pp.

efforts in performing and promoting the use of traditional melodies in Wales and further afield. Visits to local history societies in Bethesda, Caernarfon, Harlech and Porthmadog were regular occurrences. During such events, she would outline her collecting experiences, sing several examples and explain their musical characteristics and origin. While visiting the USA and Canada she notated versions of indigenous songs[28] performed by exiled Welshmen and women that were eventually presented to the annual meeting of the Welsh Folk-Song Society, together with her advice to future collectors:

> Care should be taken not to correct an apparent 'mistake', whether a word, note or method ... [for] it may be no mistake at all – the suspected word may be an obsolete or archaic form preserved in the song; the singer may be, indeed, almost surely is, singing in a mode with which we are not familiar in modern music, and it must always be remembered that the vocal method of the folk singer is not that of the cultured or trained singer.[29]

Visits to Ireland, Norway, Belgium, Switzerland, Palestine, Egypt and Algeria gave rise to a broadening of her understanding of foreign musical cultures and in turn, provided an opportunity to introduce comparative methodologies to her study of Welsh folk-song repertoire. Following the establishing of the Women's Institute in the United Kingdom and its first public meeting in Llanfairpwllgwyngyll, Anglesey in 1915,[30] Grace Gwyneddon Davies dedicated her time to visiting branches of the movement throughout north Wales to educate its members in traditional Welsh songs. She single-handedly choreographed the Institute's involvement in music (local, regional and national) in order that the homemakers of Wales could, in time, be the means of transmitting the melodies and popularising their use among the younger generation, thus developing a long-term interest in the field. Her influence in the Welsh Folk-Song Society as well as in other closely related organisations (including the University College of North Wales, Bangor, the Early Welsh Music Society, the National Eisteddfod of Wales and National Council of Music in Wales) provided a lasting legacy and represented significant progress in the nationwide performance and understanding of traditional music.

---

[28] GB-AB, Kitty Idwal Jones Papers, *Seventeenth Annual Report and Financial Statement of the Welsh Folk-Song Society, 1924–26* (1926), 6.
[29] Robert Gwyneddon Davies, 'The Collecting of Anglesey Folk Songs', 96.
[30] The Women's Institute aimed to revitalise rural communities and encourage women to become more involved in producing food during World War I.

Lucie Barbier

The French singer and pianist, Lucie Barbier (1875–1963)[31] arrived in Aberystwyth in 1909 following her six-year tenure as voice tutor at the University College of North Wales, Bangor. At the time, she was the Secretary of La Société des Concerts Français, which had been established to promote French music in Britain and which flourished from 1907 to 1916, arranging professional performances in Manchester, Sheffield and London. After settling in mid-Wales, she founded the University College of Wales Musical Club in Aberystwyth and corresponded with French and British composers (including Debussy, Saint-Saëns, Ethel Smyth and Arthur Somervell), primarily to promote their music and to invite them to give lectures to local enthusiasts. Following several appearances as an accompanist during Welsh Folk-Song Society meetings held in Newtown, Aberystwyth and Swansea,[32] and after interactions with Mary Davies, Amy Preece[33] and Grace Gwyneddon Davies, she became a keen supporter of traditional Welsh song and an ardent devotee of using the Welsh language in her voice lessons. During March 1911, four undergraduate students from Aberystwyth[34] (pupils of Mme Barbier) visited Paris to present a series of six Welsh folk-song concerts organised by various clubs and societies, including Le Lied en Tous Pays, Audition d'Élèves and L'Association des Professeurs de Langues Vivantes de l'Enseignement Public, which met at the Richelieu Amphitheatre, University of Paris-Sorbonne. The appearance of the Welsh vocal ensemble in France was the direct result of various musical activities initiated by Lucie Barbier in Aberystwyth. It was the first time that performances of Welsh folk songs had been given in France and probably in mainland Europe. Politically, it was the most tangible expression of the *entente cordiale* signed by the British and French governments in 1904, when the two nations made a concerted effort to attain better mutual understanding. It was a natural outcome that the vocal quartet's public performance in Paris was celebrated by

---

[31] Madame Lucie Barbier (née Hirsch) was the wife of André Barbier, French lecturer at the University College of North Wales, Bangor (1903–9) and later at the University College of Wales, Aberystwyth.
[32] Lucie Barbier would regularly accompany Dora Rowlands, an undergraduate student in the Department of Welsh at Aberystwyth University.
[33] Amy Preece, daughter of Sir William Preece, was present at the Cymmrodorion Society meeting in Caernarfon (1906) and later served as Secretary of the Welsh Folk-Song Society (1908–22) and President (1959–60).
[34] Dora Rowlands, Gwen Taylor, Tudor Williams and Stanley Knight were known as 'The Welsh Quartet'. Their visit to Paris was supervised by Ruth Herbert Lewis and Annie Ellis.

the press as a real manifestation of the musical *entente cordiale* – a term which had been used to describe the appearance of French musicians in England and Wales during that period.

The idea that Welsh folk songs were good enough to be presented before the Parisian public was novel to one member of the ensemble, Dora Rowlands (later Dora Herbert Jones), who claimed that the Welsh 'despised their own music ... always measuring it against, and competing with, England'.[35] At the time, indigenous music in Wales was regarded 'as dirt'[36] – a sentiment often expressed by many Welsh people at the turn of the century. Consequently, membership of the Welsh Quartet for the four young singers who visited Paris was an extraordinary experience. As Rowlands later commented:

> Madame Barbier gave the same preparation and thought, and demanded the same high standards, from Welsh folk songs as from all the music we sang – Franck, Schubert or whatever.[37]

To place folk music at this level was a complete reversal of everything the singers had known in Wales, for apart from at Madame Barbier's Musical Club, students rarely heard Welsh performers, much less Welsh music, in Aberystwyth at the time – the concert repertoire heard in the town came mostly from beyond Wales.

Preparation for the six Parisian concerts involved a significant amount of work by the students, Lucie Barbier (as musical director) and J. Lloyd Williams, who had arranged several of the songs sung by the group; but it also required a considerable amount of practical groundwork to be carried out, such as booking venues and preparing promotional literature, press releases and tickets. Mme Barbier also drew on the support of several French journalists and music critics whom she had known during her time in France, including Henry Dupré, René Lenormand, Jules Écorcheville and Théodore Lyndenberger.[38] The highlight of the Welsh Quartet's appearance was undoubtedly the Sorbonne concert, which was to arouse the greatest interest among the public and press. Théodore Lyndenberger of *Le Temps* commented in his newspaper:

> *Un quatuor vocal d'étudiants de l'université d'Aberystwyth (Pays de Galle) donnera une audition de chants gallois originaux ... précédée d'une courte causerie sur le 'Folk-Lore' gallois par le professeur J. H. Davies, de l'University College d'Aberystwyth.*

---

[35] GB-CDf, recorded interview (AWC 1460–1462), Dora Herbert Jones and D. Roy Saer.
[36] Ibid.   [37] Ibid.   [38] GB-AB GB 0210 MSLBARB, Lucie Barbier Papers.

> *Ce sera, croyons-nous, la première audition à Paris de cette intéressante musique populaire des Celtes d'Angleterre.*
>
> (A vocal quartet of students from the University of Aberystwyth (Wales) will give a concert of original Welsh songs ... preceded by a short talk on Welsh 'Folk-Lore' by Professor J. H. Davies, of the University College of Aberystwyth.
> We believe that this will be the first concert in Paris of this interesting folk music of the Celts of Britain.)[39]

None of the members of the Welsh Quartet had travelled on the continent before. Timothy Lewis, a member of staff at Aberystwyth's Department of Welsh, was called upon to replace John Humphreys Davies as speaker prior to the Sorbonne concert, and in the Aberystwyth college magazine, *The Dragon*, he wrote a detailed overview of the trip to Paris.[40] The enthusiasm and excitement felt by Dora Rowlands was captured many years later, when she spoke about her experience:

> You can't imagine four more innocent young things than we were ... Paris was utterly the city of sin to us, we were thrilled to death and scared witless. The Quartet was the most naïve bunch you could imagine. One of the concerts didn't start till 10.00 p.m. – imagine! At the Sorbonne, we had a superb audience, we swept them! They stood up, waved their programmes, cheered – they wouldn't let us stop! The folk-songs were like a glass of cold water to the Paris public – totally and utterly new to them![41]

Solo performances, sung by Dora Rowlands and Lewis Knight, interspersed with quartet arrangements of 'Gwcw Fach' ('Little Cuckoo'), 'Tra Bo Dau' ('While There Are Two'), 'Yr Hen Erddygan' ('The Old Tune') and 'Mentra Gwen' ('Venture, Gwen') appealed to the Sorbonne audience and contributed to the evening's success.

The *Cambrian News* and the *Aberystwyth Observer* wrote articles on the vocal quartet's visit to Paris, giving as much attention to its national as its musical significance. J. Lloyd Williams also wrote a letter of appreciation to Lucie Barbier following her return to Wales:

> From several independent sources, I have heard unstinted praise of the singing of your quartet. To win such unanimous praise you must have

---

[39] *Le Temps*, 20 March 1911, 3. See also GB-AB MSS 22692-3E, Letters to Lucie Barbier, 1900–21. Editorial note: 'Angleterre' is translated as 'Britain' rather than 'England' in this context, this being a common usage in French of the period and what is intended here.

[40] Timothy Lewis, 'The Paris Hexameron', *The Dragon* (Magazine of the University College of Wales, Aberystwyth), XXXVI (1910–11), 219–222.

[41] Ibid.

trained them well. .... The success of your party is due entirely to the melodies themselves – to the pleasant voices that sang them, and to their having been instructed by one who had an artistic sympathy with the music.[42]

The Welsh Quartet's concerts in France were unique: musically, historically and politically. Perhaps the finest tribute to them and the best summary of what the visit achieved was the account published in *Le Matin* on 2 April 1911:

> *Ce ne sont pas des professionnels; ce sont des étudiants. Leur voix est juste; leur style est pur. Ils ont chanté avec un admirable ensemble des mélodies populaires galloises, tantôt graves ou héroïques, tantôt joyeuses ou tendres, dont le couleur et l'accent ont une force singulièrement grande et dont M. le professeur Lewis a parlé d'éloquent manière. Ces jeunes gens, MM. Williams et Knight, Mlles Rowlands et Taylor, que l'on n'a cessé d'acclamer et de fêter, etaient accompagnés et dirigés par Mme Barbier, une Française, à qui notre musique doit d'avoir remporté en Angleterre de belles victoires. Dans un très charmant petit discours, elle a exprimé le voeu que nos compositeurs aillent s'inspirer là-bas de l'art rude et sain qu'elle nous faisait connaître, et elle a indiqué ainsi une des plus jolie formes que puisse prendre 'l'entente cordiale'.*

> (They are not professionals: they are students. Their voices are true; their style is pure. Their ensemble was excellent in singing Welsh folk melodies, now serious or heroic, now joyful or tender, the colour and accent of which was singularly powerful, and of which Professor Lewis spoke eloquently. These young people, Mr Williams and Mr Knight, Miss Rowlands and Miss Taylor, who were endlessly acclaimed and celebrated, were accompanied and directed by Mme Barbier, a Frenchwoman, who has achieved great success with our music in Britain. In a charming little address, she expressed the wish that our composers might go there to be inspired by the unpolished and healthy art which she has made known to us, and she thus pointed out one of the best ways to achieve the *entente cordiale*.)[43]

Unlike Mary Davies, Ruth Herbert Lewis and Grace Gwyneddon Davies, Lucie Barbier never collected Welsh folk songs during her career at Bangor and Aberystwyth universities; nevertheless she became a passionate supporter of the tradition and established its international reputation both in 1911 and again in 1913, during a return visit to Paris and Berck-Plage (Pas-de-Calais).

---

[42] GB-AB MSS 22692-3E, Letters to Lucie Barbier, 1900–21.
[43] Editorial note: As with the quotation from *Le Temps* above, 'Angleterre' is translated here as 'Britain' rather than 'England', this being a common usage in French of the period and what is intended in this context.

Annie Ellis

Following the Welsh Quartet's success in France, Annie Ellis's close association with the University College of Wales, Aberystwyth continued.[44] She had chaperoned the vocal ensemble throughout its tour of Paris and now felt qualified to encourage and support several student performances at Aberystwyth of J. Lloyd Williams's *Aelwyd Angharad* which, according to its author:

> offered a peep into some of the agreeable and worthwhile old customs of Wales as it used to be, and the homely, simple style of spending the leisure hours during the long winter evenings. If it were possible to restore some of these old customs to the hearths of present-day Wales, we should not fear that.[45]

By 1914, Lloyd Williams had left north Wales and had been appointed Professor of Botany at Aberystwyth, establishing his famous Angharad Choir, which came to play a prominent role in the cultural life of the college and locality. In the meantime, however, Annie Ellis's work on behalf of the folk-song movement in Wales and her dedication to the cause in mid-Wales led her to venture into the field of collecting in the Llandysul and Newcastle Emlyn district. At first, such musical activities had little if no impact on college life – they merely served as extracurricular entertainment for students and the occasional member of staff. However, as members of the Aberystwyth Canorion choir became increasingly confident in their understanding and handling of traditional Welsh song, the impact on the town's cultural activities (as well as official university events and ceremonies) became increasingly apparent – in the same way that the discovery of Welsh folk music at Bangor had a transforming effect on music making in the north.[46]

Annie Ellis was central to such developments. Despite the fact that folk-song collecting and the study of music in its cultural context was not a priority for the Canorion, the increased involvement in traditional singing among the students would undoubtedly have been the cause of much celebration for her. Vocal quartets and trios were soon established in the College with the sole purpose of performing newly discovered melodies

---

[44] From 1892, Annie Ellis studied Welsh, History and English at the University College of Wales, Aberystwyth. Her brother, John Humphreys Davies (1871–1926) was appointed Registrar of the University in 1905 and was later promoted to Principal in 1919.

[45] J. Lloyd Williams and L. D. Jones, *Aelwyd Angharad* (Bangor: Evan Thomas, 1910).

[46] The Canorion Society at Bangor and Aberystwyth universities enabled students to sing and perform folk-song arrangements and encouraged fieldwork activity during vacation time.

arranged by Lloyd Williams which had been published in his *Ceinion y Canorion*.[47] Dora Rowlands became the embodiment of the resurgence of interest in Welsh traditional music, and her renditions of 'Doli' and 'Gwcw Fach' during her undergraduate days were the means of drawing considerable interest and enthusiasm in the field. As the editor of *The Dragon* commented, 'We have been led confidently to expect artistic and sympathetic excellence in performance from her.'[48] During the Celtic Society Eisteddfod in February 1910,[49] Annie Ellis was seen encouraging student involvement even further, by announcing a competition to produce an original collection of unpublished Welsh folk songs by the following year. In line with the Society's policy, such a competition had already been widely accepted as part of the National Eisteddfod of Wales, to encourage local interest in indigenous Welsh song and the production of small-scale, regional collections to serve the needs of the *Journal of the Welsh Folk-Song Society*.

Meanwhile, Mary Davies's frequent visits and lectures on Welsh folk song had undoubtedly convinced many of the Aberystwyth students that engaging with Welsh music was both vital for the continuation of the tradition and a wholesome and worthwhile activity worthy of academic and scholarly study. During her early visits to mid-Wales, Annie Ellis had gained some limited experience of fieldwork methods, though nothing would compare with the three days of scouring the countryside with Ruth Herbert Lewis in June 1913. As the editor of the *Journal of the Welsh Folk-Song Society* indicated: 'The centre of interest ... has shifted from Caernarfon and Merioneth to Cardiganshire and Montgomery where Mrs Mary Davies, assisted by Mrs Annie Ellis and others have secured some interesting finds and several new workers.'[50]

Prior to their adventure, Annie Ellis and Ruth Herbert Lewis had enlisted the help of Mary Hughes, an Aberystwyth graduate, Canorion Society member and drama enthusiast, to tease out singers of genuine Welsh traditional song in the locality.[51] She was well acquainted with the

---

[47] J. Lloyd Williams, *Ceinion y Canorion* (Bangor: Evan Thomas, c.1909).
[48] *The Dragon*, XXXVII (1912–13), 248.
[49] Y Gymdeithas Geltaidd is Aberystwyth University's main Welsh Society. It was established in the late nineteenth century and continues to serve the cultural and recreational needs of the students and the local community.
[50] J. Lloyd Williams, 'The History of the Welsh Folk-Song Society', *Journal of the Welsh Folk-Song Society/Cylchgrawn Cymdeithas Alawon Gwerin Cymru*, III/2 (1934), 100.
[51] Mary Hughes, Llanllwni was a teacher at Llandysul Grammar School and later, a lecturer in Swansea Teacher Training College. It was her brother, John, who won the prize for the best collection of unpublished Welsh folk songs in the Celtic Society Eisteddfod (1912).

tradition and would have understood that classical performances of Victorian drawing-room songs or sentimental Welsh ballads would not have been acceptable. In her correspondence, Ruth Herbert Lewis recorded the highlights of her folk-song adventures in south Ceredigion and north Carmarthenshire[52] and referred to the significant contribution made by Annie Ellis to the overall success of the trip – in particular, her innate ability to convince her informants to sing their songs and to be recorded by the phonograph. Annie Ellis's thoroughbred nonconformist background and her close associations in the field in Wales were determining factors among many of her informants that influenced whether they would sing or not. As J. Lloyd Williams later commented:

> A great deal of tact and diplomacy had to be used in dealing with the old singers, and the arguments employed varied according to the temperament of the persons. In spite of every effort, they failed to induce one old lady of 96 to sing any of her songs.[53]

It was during this visit that songs such as 'Cân Dei Cantwr' ('The Song of Dei the Singer'), 'Cân yr Asyn' ('The Donkey'), 'Cŵn Hela' ('Hunting Dogs') and a macaronic song, 'Merch o Bedlam' ('A Girl from Bedlam') were discovered. In due course, these were transcribed and published in the *Journal of the Welsh Folk-Song Society* and became particularly popular within the academic community in mid-Wales.

Jennie Williams

Between 1903 and 1906, Jennie Williams (1884–1971), from Aberystwyth, was a student at London's Royal Academy of Music. As a singer and accompanist, her interest was piqued by the works of Cécile Chaminade and Camille Saint-Saëns – contributors to the nationalist movement in France at that time. In order to develop her career as a *répétiteur* and vocal coach, she endeavoured to learn Russian, French and Spanish, and her interest in languages, as well as her musical talent, led her to Paris before the end of the decade, into a musical climate completely removed from her London experience some months earlier. She had ventured to France to receive lessons from two of the most eminent operatic soloists of the time, Jean and Édouard de Reszke. Jennie Williams had a talented sister, Mary, who had already settled at the University of Paris-Sorbonne researching

---

[52] See Kitty Idwal Jones, 'Adventures in Folk-Song Collecting', *Welsh Music/Cerddoriaeth Cymru*, 5/5 (Spring 1977), 33–52.
[53] Lloyd Williams, 'The History of the Welsh Folk-Song Society', 101.

aspects of the Arthurian legend in medieval French literature. On the banks of the Seine and through the activities of the 'Celtic Club', Jennie and Mary came to appreciate the beauty and style of Welsh folk melodies and hymn tunes. There, in the company of Gwladys Williams (J. Lloyd Williams's niece), some of the gems notated by members of the Bangor Canorion and other precursors of the Welsh Folk-Song Society at the beginning of the century were performed. Here too, Jennie Williams was reacquainted with the work of presenting Welsh melodies to foreign audiences, as Gwladys recorded in correspondence with her uncle:

> At the Celtic Club, we are going to learn all the 'Canorion' songs and at the end we shall give a concert. We have harp, violin and pianoforte players amongst us – so we have a little orchestra as well. Jennie Williams's lecture takes place Saturday week. I am singing 'Tra bo dau', 'Cyfri'r Geifr' and 'Yr hen ŵr mwyn'. Dr Mary Williams is singing 'Dacw nghariad i lawr yn y berllan' and 'Yr Hufen Melyn' and we are singing 'Y Pren ar y bryn' together – and possibly, the duet 'Y Fwyalchen'.[54]

During her stay in Paris, Jennie Williams heard performances of Debussy's most recent orchestral works as well as recitals given by some of the leaders of the music world, including Charles-Marie Widor and Jan Paderewski. It is likely that her time away from home, coupled with the encouragement of Maurice Duhamel,[55] a specialist in French and Breton folk song, also led her to realise the importance of safeguarding the product of the Welsh music tradition, and urged her to begin work on a collection of unpublished folk songs from Cardiganshire, Carmarthenshire and Pembrokeshire for the National Eisteddfod of Wales at Carmarthen in 1911. As she later admitted: 'The main activity in collecting melodies occurred in Aberystwyth. I collected every time I went on holiday there ... I was always collecting in a rush.'[56] Despite her limited practical experience in the field, she ventured alone, without direct guidance from more experienced collectors in Wales. She recorded the songs by ear (without the aid of a phonograph) and used sol-fa rather than conventional staff notation. Though the outcome of her work was the music recorded in Cardiganshire, meeting people from Pembrokeshire and Carmarthenshire in London served to fulfil the needs of the competition. Some of her singers were Welsh people visiting the city and staying at the Gwalia Hotel in Upper Woburn Place, which had also

---

[54] GB-AB Dr. J. Lloyd Williams Music MSS and Papers, MS 110. Letter dated 4 March 1912 from Gwladys Williams to J. Lloyd Williams.
[55] Maurice Duhamel (alias Maurice Bourgeaux; 1884–1940).
[56] GB-CDf, recorded interview (AWC Audio tape 618).

served as a popular source for her aunt, Mary Davies, when collecting folk tunes. Others, however, were maids and servants from south Wales working in stately homes and private residences in the capital. Jennie Williams's main informant was undoubtedly Evan Rowlands, an eighty-year-old butcher from Aberystwyth. He sang thirteen songs, based on his recollection of the singing of his father, Daniel Rowland, in the area of Mynydd Bach (near Ysbyty Ystwyth, Cardiganshire). He was a dependable source, but difficult to record, mainly because he was well advanced in years by the time that Jennie Williams began collecting, and his voice was imbued with a natural tremor that produced notes of ambiguous pitch. Rowlands sang songs such as 'Y Folantein' ('The Valentine'), 'Cariad Cywir' ('True Love') and 'Lliw'r Heulwen' ('The Colour of Sunshine'; see Example 6.4).

However valuable and timely her recording activities, Jennie Williams was struck by the lack of real interest shown by the inhabitants of south-west Wales in their native songs. 'There were enough of them [folk songs] about and there must be hundreds of songs that have gone forever as a result

Example 6.4 'Lliw'r Heulwen' ('The Colour of Sunshine'). *Journal of the Welsh Folk-Song Society,* I/172

of their indifference'.⁵⁷ Years later, she commented on the unusual features that characterised her informants' singing, in particular their use of quartertones as a remnant of the old modal singing once common in Wales – 'it was as though they were singing "out of tune". Over time, I came to feel that that was how the songs ought to be sung'.⁵⁸ In her National Eisteddfod collection (1911), she included a series of emendations to denote the use of 'quartertones' between the intervals of a third, fourth and seventh, and thus highlighted the importance of modality in indigenous Welsh singing. Throughout her career, the appeal of these traditional modes and the memory of such unusual singing among the inhabitants of Cardiganshire, Pembrokeshire and Carmarthenshire were the subject of several of her lectures and conference addresses, having formed the basis of her early experience of collecting folk melodies. As one of the Folk-Song Society's Vice-Presidents, and later its President, she prepared the way for a comparative approach to the study of Welsh folk song, and in time, her unpublished collection of traditional melodies became a model for others in the late twentieth century to emulate.

It seems reasonable to conclude that during the decade 1906–16, collecting and performing traditional songs for the majority of the Welsh Folk-Song Society's women began as little more than a hobby but gradually became a vocation. Except for a few months here and there, fieldwork, lecturing and performing were not their primary occupation, and yet they were at least as committed to their amateur careers as to their involvement in the wider cultural movement. Looking back over the decade, such pioneers may well have been a little surprised at how much they had accomplished; their role in the development of the folk-song revival in Wales was a major one.

---

⁵⁷ Ibid.   ⁵⁸ Ibid.

CHAPTER 7

Instrumental Traditions after 1650

Rhidian Griffiths, Trevor Herbert and Stephen P. Rees

The word 'traditions' is important in this chapter title because it signals both the limits and the emphasis of the chapter: it is almost entirely restricted to the instruments and practices that have had an important role in those parts of the musical life of Wales that can be confidently claimed to be distinctive. So, the emphasis is on three categories: harps, other string instruments (the crwth and fiddle) and wind instruments. To this is added a section on the way Welsh instrumental traditions have been projected in modern popular practices. The chapter does not give attention to orchestral and other instruments such as those used in amateur brass bands. They have been ubiquitous in Wales since the nineteenth century, but they have been ubiquitous in the same way elsewhere too, and there is little to suggest that their use in Wales was especially distinctive. This is also true, for example, of the harmonium. The widespread use of harmoniums coincided with, and was caused by, the growth of nonconformity in Wales in the nineteenth century. The increase in the number of chapels in the period was so remarkable that within a few decades at least one harmonium was present in every settlement in the country. Wales must have been a paradise for harmonium salesmen. But these instruments were utilities rather than modes of expression in their own right: didactic aids and devices that settled a common sense of pitch in congregational choralism. They did not prompt the creation of idiomatic repertoires, nor did they substantially impact on the way hymns were sung. With the instruments mentioned in this chapter, the story is different.

Fiddles and wind instruments were integral to vernacular musical practices. We cannot tell surely and comprehensively what was played and how, because as is the case with so much Welsh music from before the nineteenth century, traditions were conveyed and perpetuated in oral and aural cultures. However, sources that emerged in the nineteenth century probably evidence much older traditions, and there are sufficient accounts of practices to facilitate tenable conjectures. The crwth and the harp are different because both had origins in more elevated practices. The harp was associated with distinctive vocal forms, and from the eighteenth century the musical sources are sufficiently numerous for us to understand them with confidence. It is important to emphasise that these instruments did not originate in Wales: their Welshness comes from the idioms that were formed by their repertoires and especially the roles they played in the routines of ordinary life.

Harps and Harpists

That the harp became an emblem of Wales is evidence of its importance in Welsh musical tradition, while the giving of a silver harp as a prize at the Caerwys eisteddfodau in 1523 and 1567 (see Chapter 5) suggests that the instrument itself had prestige in medieval and Renaissance poetic and musical practice. But from the seventeenth century, as the old bardic order declined and sources of patronage became scarce, while retaining its importance, it began to occupy a different place in the social order.[1]

According to Edward Williams (Iolo Morganwg; 1747–1826), the single harp, with one row of strings tuned to the diatonic scale, was 'yr hen delyn Gymreig' (the old Welsh harp), and it appears to have been widely used in the eighteenth century and into the nineteenth in some places.[2] Writing in 1794, Edward Jones (Bardd y Brenin; 1752–1824) notes the use of 'gwrachod' or angular pegs to vary the tone produced, a point supported by the antiquarian Thomas Price (Carnhuanawc), referring to his old teacher:

> As old David Watkins played a good deal for dancing, his harp was not furnished with pegs of the usual make, but the strings were fastened in the sounding board with *Gwrachod* or angular pegs ... the nose of each being close to the string which it fastened, giving it a jarring sound, which produced a good effect in a dancing tune.[3]

Harps were widely used for dancing both indoors and outside, and dancing to harp accompaniment was a regular feature of local events such as the gwylmabsant (local patronal festival) and the gwylnos (wake). In 1828,

---

[1] Ann Rosser, *Telyn a Thelynor: Hanes y Delyn yng Nghymru 1700–1900* ([Caerdydd]: Amgueddfa Werin Cymru, 1981) offers an overview of the history of the harp in Wales, as does Osian Ellis, *The Story of the Harp in Wales* (Cardiff: University of Wales Press, 1991). See also D. Roy Saer, *Y Delyn yng Nghymru mewn Lluniau/The Harp in Wales in Pictures* (Llandysul and Caerdydd: Gwasg Gomer/ Amgueddfa Genedlaethol Cymru, 1991).

[2] Rosser, *Telyn a Thelynor*, t. 3.

[3] Quoted in Jane Williams (Ysgafell), *The Literary Remains of the Rev. Thomas Price, Carnhuanawc* (Llandovery and London: William Rees/Longman & Co., 1855), vol. II, p. 22.

Rhys Cox described how in Glamorgan the Easter festival began on Saturday afternoon to the accompaniment of crwth and harp, with dancing again on Easter Monday, and whole areas would come together for spirited dancing and singing to the harp.[4] The harp was also frequently heard at the fairground, alongside the fiddle and the ballad singer, well into the nineteenth century: Robert Griffith (1845–1909) recalled hearing the single and the triple harp at many fairs in the Llanrwst of his boyhood.[5]

Yet while the single harp continued to be played, it was overtaken in popularity during the eighteenth century by the triple harp, to the extent that the latter came to be generally recognised as a characteristically Welsh instrument. As its name suggests, the triple harp has three rows of strings arranged in parallel, the outer two tuned to the diatonic scale and the inner row providing the chromatic notes (see Figure 7.1). In spite of its strong association with Wales, it was an Italian invention, created around 1600. How it reached Wales is a matter of debate, with some suggesting that it arrived before the end of the seventeenth century;[6] but it appears to have

Figure 7.1 The harpist Nansi Richards (1888–1979) playing a triple harp, which rests on her left shoulder. Amgueddfa Cymru – National Museum Wales

---

[4] Quoted in Rosser, *Telyn a Thelynor*, t. 38.
[5] Robert Griffith, *Llyfr Cerdd Dannau* (Caernarfon: Cwmni y Cyhoeddwyr Cymreig, [1913]), t. vii.
[6] Roy Saer provides a summary of the evidence in 'Welsh Gipsies and the Triple Harp' in his *'Canu at Iws' ac Ysgrifau Eraill* (Talybont: Cymdeithas Alawon Gwerin Cymru, 2013), pp. 251–267.

become popular in the early eighteenth, and by 1758 was said to be widespread, particularly in north Wales, when Margaret Davies of Coetgae-du, Trawsfynydd, wrote to Dafydd Jones of Trefriw, 'wele yn awr Delynau Tri phâr Danau gan bob math agos: i gael haner y llais' ('behold now triple-strung harps in the possession of almost all sorts: to obtain the semi-tone').[7] Evidently the greater tonal variety provided by the triple harp compared with its single-strung counterpart was a welcome development. Wales became a manufacturing base for the triple harp, with Llanrwst being a major centre.[8] The most distinguished harp maker, though not the earliest, was John Richard (1711–89), who worked there from 1744 to 1759; according to Edward Jones, he had learned his craft from David Evans, an instrument maker of Rose Court in London. It was during 1755 that Richard built a triple harp for John Parry (c.1710–82). 'Blind Parry', as he was known, was regarded as the finest Welsh harpist of the eighteenth century. Born in Penmorfa, Nefyn on the Llŷn Peninsula, Parry was harpist to Sir Watkin Williams Wynn at his homes at Wynnstay and London, where his playing impressed the poet Thomas Gray. Though the continental practice was to rest the triple harp on the right shoulder when playing, Welsh harpists like Parry appear always to have played on the left shoulder.[9] Parry was responsible, with Evan Williams (Ifan Wiliam) for publishing Welsh airs in his collection *Antient British Music* in 1742, which was followed by later collections in 1761 and 1781 in which the content is less Welsh but the arrangements for harp more complex.[10] He more than anyone made the triple harp known outside Wales, establishing it in people's minds as the Welsh harp. His successor in many respects was Edward Jones (Bardd y Brenin; 1752–1824) who, in addition to his important work on the collection published as *Musical and Poetical Relicks of the Welsh Bards* (1784, enlarged edition 1794) and its successor volumes *The Bardic Museum* (1802) and *Hên Ganiadau Cymru* (1825),[11] was

---

[7] Quoted ibid., p. 254.
[8] R. M. Williams, *Seiri Cerdd Nanconwy* (Llanrwst: Gwasg Carreg Gwalch, 1982).
[9] A painting by Domenico Zampieri (1581–1641) depicts King David playing the triple harp on his right shoulder (reproduced in Rosser, *Telyn a Thelynor*, t. 10). Portraits of John Parry always show the harp on his left shoulder.
[10] These have been digitised by the National Library of Wales: *Antient British Music* (1742) http://hdl.handle.net/10107/4675582; *A Collection of Welsh, English and Scotch Airs* (1761) http://hdl.handle.net/10107/4675850; and *British Harmony* (1781) http://hdl.handle.net/10107/4675640
[11] These have been digitised by the National Library of Wales: *Musical and Poetical Relicks of the Welsh Bards* (1784), http://hdl.handle.net/10107/4675108; the enlarged edition of 1794, http://hdl.handle.net/10107/4674868; *The Bardic Museum* (1802), http://hdl.handle.net/10107/4675439; *Hên Ganiadau Cymru* (1825), http://hdl.handle.net/10107/4675268.

a fine performer who played both the single and triple harp. He particularly liked the triple harp:

> I am rather an advocate for the Triple Harp, because I admire its venerable and stately appearance; and particularly the sweet re-echoing effect of its unisons, which are played with both hands, and are peculiar to that instrument.[12]

Both Parry and Jones made the most of their opportunities in the London salons, and some London gentry with no obvious Welsh connection subscribed to their publications.

It was not only in London that the Welsh harp was admired. In the late eighteenth century, travellers from the upper social class discovered Wales, especially the mountainous north, and on such travels encountered Welsh musicians. On a tour of north Wales in 1784 Sir John Byng was much taken by a harpist he heard at Dolgellau:

> A messenger was detach'd ... for a Welsh harper; who had play'd to us, during supper, and the two following hours, many delightful tunes; our landlord also ... favor'd us with his accompanying voice; and I don't recollect when I was more gratified; and exhilerated [sic]. Were I a man of great fortune I wou'd retain one of these musicians in my family.[13]

At Caernarfon he was even more impressed:

> our evening was spent in reading, and list'ning to the best harper we have yet met with; (by name Erasmus, a sound bespeaking great learning, and antiquity). This is an instrument which I allways admir'd, but, now, on its native ground, (connected with the ideas of former hospitality and antient minstrelsy) it becomes quite enthusiastic.[14]

Interestingly, Byng lamented that his grandchildren would not hear such playing, 'but only its merits, and fame', as the craft was dying out.

Not all visitors were taken with the sound of the harp, however. During his stay with the Taylor family at Rhyd-y-mwyn in north-east Wales in

---

[12] Edward Jones, *Musical and Poetical Relicks of the Welsh Bards* (London: printed for the author, 1794), p. 105.

[13] C. Bruyn Andrews, ed., *The Torrington Diaries: Containing the Tours through England and Wales of the Hon. John Byng* (London: Eyre & Spottiswoode, 1934), vol. 1, pp. 142–143. In a footnote Byng adds the names of some of the tunes: 'Sr. Watkin's Delight. Conceits of Lady Owen. Sweet Richard. Morvar-Rhudlan. The Dimples. Davy of Garry-Gwyn, &c.&c.&c.'

[14] Ibid., p. 161.

1829, Felix Mendelssohn, though delighted with the scenery, was less than impressed by the music:

> *Zehntausend Teufel sollen doch alles Volksthum holen! Da bin ich hier in Welschland, und, o wie schön, ein Harfenist sitzt auf dem Flur jedes Wirthshauses von Ruf und spielt in einem fort sogenannte Volksmelodieen, d. h. infames, gemeines, falsches Zeug, zu gleicher Zeit dudelt eben ein Leierkasten auch Melodieen ab, zum Tollwerden ist es, Zahnschmerzen habe ich leider davon[.]*
>
> (Ten thousand devils take all nationalism! So here I am in Wales, and, O how lovely, a harpist sits in the lobby of every inn of repute and incessantly plays so-called folk melodies, viz. infamous, low, bogus rubbish, and at just the same time a hurdy-gurdy drones out tunes, it's driving me mad, and I'm sorry to say I have toothache because of it.)[15]

His remarks do, however, confirm the ubiquity of the harper in the hall of every reputable tavern. Players made their living by the harp well into the nineteenth century, and some 'tavern harpists', such as Thomas David Llewelyn (Llewelyn Alaw; 1828–79) were associated with a particular inn, in his case the 'Welsh Harp' at Abercynon.

The ascendancy of the triple harp continued well into the nineteenth century. It was portable, which was important for those who took their craft to eisteddfodau: a drawing depicts the ballad singer Richard Williams (Dic Dywyll) and Huw Puw of Dolgellau returning from the Cardiff eisteddfod in 1834, with Dic riding his mount and the harp strapped to his back.[16] But harp playing and fairground revelry were undermined from the late eighteenth century by the opposition of religious leaders who railed against the profanity of much popular entertainment. It did not help that, perhaps because of the association with taverns, harpers in general were regarded as coarse drunkards. Edward Jones wrote of the 'fanatick impostors, or illiterate plebeian preachers' who dissuaded the people from 'their innocent amusements', with the result that 'Wales, which was formerly one of the merriest, and happiest countries in the World, is now become one of the dullest'.[17] And many stories were told of individuals who, under the influence of religious conversion, 'gave up the harp, and threw it under the bed'.[18]

---

[15] Author's translation. The original German from Sebastian Hensel, *Die Familie Mendelssohn 1729–1847: Nach Briefen und Tagebüchern*, vol. 1 (Berlin: B. Behr's Verlag, 1904), p. 242.
[16] Reproduced in Griffith, *Llyfr Cerdd Dannau*, t. 304.
[17] Edward Jones, *The Bardic Museum* (London: A. Strahan, 1802), p. xvi.
[18] *Bye-gones*, 16 May 1894, 344; quoted by Phyllis Kinney, *Welsh Traditional Music* (Cardiff: University of Wales Press in association with Cymdeithas Alawon Gwerin Cymru, 2011), p. 177.

Yet there was also a weakening of oral tradition from the mid-eighteenth century, and Jones himself records that music was not being passed from one generation to the next. It was partly in response to this decline that Lady Llanover supported the triple harp. From its stronghold in north Wales, the triple harp moved south when the harp builder John Richard was established in 1759 at Glanbrân near Llandovery, the home of Sackville Gwynn, himself an enthusiastic performer and advocate of the instrument. Lady Llanover established a workshop at Llanofer where the harp maker Bassett Jones (1809–69) of Cardiff produced triple harps, some of which were given as prizes at the eisteddfodau sponsored by Cymreigyddion y Fenni between 1834 and 1853. Even after Lady Llanover's death in 1896, her daughter Augusta Herbert continued to invite prospective players to Llanofer to be instructed on the triple harp by Susan Barrington Griffith Richards, daughter of Thomas Griffith, who had been one of Llanofer's harpists in residence. Some of the credit for the continued use of the triple harp and other folk instruments in nineteenth-century Wales must go to Romani players. The triple harp was kept alive by Romani-born John Roberts (Telynor Cymru), who with his several sons, gave masterful performances as a 'côr telynau' (harp choir).[19] When in 1899 a questionnaire went out from Llanofer to determine how many triple harpists remained in Wales, Roberts's son, J. L. Roberts, replied that he and his brother still played, as did three brothers (not Romani) at the Britannia Inn in Llannerch-y-medd on Anglesey.[20]

The nineteenth century saw a gradual eclipse of the triple harp in favour of the pedal instrument as patented by Sébastien Érard in London in 1810. John Parry (Bardd Alaw; 1776–1851) produced publications of Welsh music suitable for both instruments, and his son, John Orlando Parry (1810–79), played the pedal harp. The transition from the traditional instrument to the concert harp is well illustrated in the career of John Thomas (Pencerdd Gwalia; 1826–1913), a native of Bridgend, who learned the triple harp as a boy but moved to the pedal harp when he studied with J. B. Chatterton at the Royal Academy of Music. Following a concert career which took him to many European cities,[21] Thomas settled in London and became

---

[19] E. Ernest Roberts, *John Roberts, Telynor Cymru* (Dinbych: Gwasg Gee, 1978); Wyn Thomas, 'John Roberts, "Telynor Cymru" (1816–1894)', *Welsh Music History/ Hanes Cerddoriaeth Cymru*, 1 (1996), 164–179.

[20] Huw Roberts and Llio Rhydderch, *Telynorion Llannerch-y-medd: Teulu'r Britannia ac Eraill/The Harpers of Llannerch-y-medd: The Britannia Family and Others* (Cyngor Sir Ynys Môn, 2000), p. 47.

[21] Carys Ann Roberts, 'Agwedd Gosmopolitanaidd John Thomas, "Pencerdd Gwalia" (1826–1913)'/ 'The Cosmopolitan Aspect of John Thomas, "Pencerdd Gwalia" (1826–1913)', *Welsh Music History Hanes/Cerddoriaeth Cymru*, 4 (2000), 88–110.

professor of harp at the Royal Academy. He promoted Welsh music in London, formed the London Welsh Choral Union and published choral arrangements of Welsh melodies. A frequent visitor to Wales to adjudicate at eisteddfodau, he never failed to vaunt the superiority of the pedal harp over the old triple harp because of its sonority and potential for musical expression. In the age of vast eisteddfod pavilions, sonority was an important consideration: the gentle tone of the triple harp was far better suited to intimate settings. Even John Roberts's family were converted to some extent: a picture published in the *Illustrated London News* of the performance by nine members of the family before Queen Victoria at Palé Hall near Llandderfel in 1889 shows a majority of pedal harps.[22] By World War I the dominance of the pedal harp was complete, and not until the later twentieth century would the triple harp regain popularity.

The eclipse of the triple harp did not eliminate 'Welshness' from the harp tradition. The pedal harp grew in popularity in Wales throughout the twentieth century and took on a national character as a Welsh icon, a solo instrument and one suited to the accompaniment of folk singing, folk dancing and cerdd dant. Wales has bred harpists of international renown such as Osian Ellis (1928–2021), and its popularity is attested by its presence in homes in every part of the country. Cymdeithas Cerdd Dant Cymru (the national cerdd dant society) regularly assists students of the instrument by lending out harps.

A Note on Cerdd Dant

From medieval times there has been a close association of harp and voice. The origins of cerdd dant are not entirely clear, but the modern craft has a strong affinity with that practised in earlier centuries. The declamation of strict metre poetry to harp accompaniment had developed by the eighteenth century into a style generally called penillion, the singing of free verse in counterpoint to harp accompaniment. John Parry gives examples of the practice in *Antient British Music*. It appears to have been an improvisatory style in which the harp elaborated the melody while the singer sang an unadorned line. 'Canu penillion' (penillion singing) continued in eisteddfodau throughout the nineteenth century and into the twentieth, and produced notable exponents such as Daniel Evans (Eos Dâr; 1846–1915),[23] but fell into decline. When Robert Griffith's *Llyfr Cerdd Dannau* was published in 1913 it was intended to be the chronicle of a dying art. The

---

[22] 'The Royal Visit to Wales', *Illustrated London News*, 7 September 1889, 331.
[23] Roy Saer, 'Eos Dâr: "Y Canwr Penillion Digyffelyb"' in *Canu at Iws*, pp. 123–137.

art was revived, however, by the work of people such as Dafydd Roberts (Telynor Mawddwy; 1873–1956), who produced his collection of penillion settings, *Y Tant Aur* (The Golden String) in 1911, followed by *Cainc y Delyn* (The Harp Tune) in 1916. This renewal of interest led in 1934 to the formation of Cymdeithas Cerdd Dant Cymru, which, by adopting the old term cerdd dant, elevated the craft to new heights. This 'form of social entertainment' appears to be unique to Wales.[24] It is a craft in which the harp has an essential role, but in modern cerdd dant it is the singer or singers who provide the melodic elaboration of words. By the late twentieth century, cerdd dant as practised in Wales had become a sophisticated genre where intricate musical settings of complex poetry could be sung by choirs and ensembles as much as by individuals.

Crwth, Fiddles and Fiddlers

In his *Musical and Poetical Relicks of the Welsh Bards* Edward Jones included a section on 'The Musical Instruments of the Welsh'. He placed the harp foremost among these, and the crwth next:

> The *Crŵth* is the second in rank of the Welsh musical instruments. I believe it to be the parent of the violin. It has a most agreeable melody, and was frequently used as a tenor accompaniment to the Harp. It is now become extremely rare in *Wales*.[25]

The crwth, a five- or six-stringed instrument which was widely played in medieval and early modern Wales, was evidently going out of fashion by the eighteenth century. The crwth of Huw Gruffudd of Penrhosllugwy, who died around 1723, passed as a relic into the hands of the scholar and writer Lewis Morris (1701–65), one of a gifted family of Anglesey brothers who preserved many elements of folk culture in eighteenth-century Wales. When Lewis moved to Cardiganshire in the 1740s, he left the crwth behind, and in July 1763 his brother William said that it was 'yn awr yn sprotus yn y garet fau' ('now in splinters in my garret').[26] The antiquarian Daines Barrington, who published a description and illustration of the crwth in the journal *Archaeologia* in 1775[27] (see Figure 7.2) believed that John Morgan of

---

[24] Kinney, *Welsh Traditional Music*, p. 241. On pp. 241–246 there is a lucid explanation of the basics of cerdd dant.
[25] Jones, *Musical and Poetical Relicks* (1784), p. 42.
[26] Dafydd Wyn Wiliam, *Cofiant William Morris (1705–63)* (D. W. Wiliam, 1995), t. 182.
[27] Daines Barrington, 'Some Account of Two Musical Instruments Used in Wales', *Archaeologia*, III (1775), 30–34.

7 Instrumental Traditions after 1650

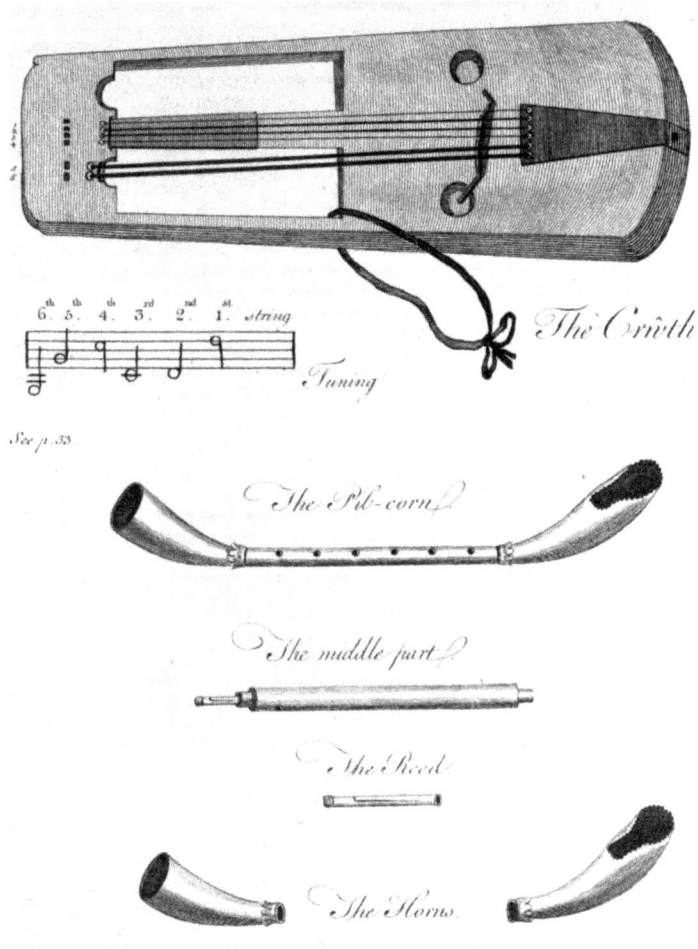

Figure 7.2 Drawing of instruments owned by the Hon. Daines Barrington and included in his article 'Some Account of Two Musical Instruments Used in Wales'. *Archaeologia*, III (1775), 30–34

Newborough on Anglesey was the last remaining crwth player in Wales. This was probably an exaggeration, since it appears, as Edward Jones indicated, that the crwth was in use until the beginning of the nineteenth century, if only rarely by that time.

The fate of Huw Gruffudd's crwth, left to rot in a garret, is symbolic of the death of a tradition of crwth making and crwth playing which was revived only in the late twentieth century. As the old bardic order had declined and gentry patronage diminished, so the crwth went out of regular use. Perhaps it was the inability of the crwth to compete with the stronger and brighter tone of the violin that was responsible for its disappearance.[28] Some crwth players may have adapted their instruments to violin tuning, and others would have adopted the violin while still calling it the crwth. This is consistent with the practice of nineteenth-century authors writing in Welsh, from Iolo Morganwg onwards, who often used the word 'crwth' for violin or fiddle, and 'crythor' for the player.

The fiddle was established in Wales well before the end of the eighteenth century. Some have claimed that it was introduced by the Romani musician Abram Wood (c.1699–1799), but although he was a noted performer on the instrument, and his numerous descendants were to become celebrated exponents of the triple harp, the violin had probably been in Wales since the seventeenth century. It is difficult to identify precisely which instrument is referred to during the period of transition from the crwth and viol to the violin. Richard Morris of Anglesey, brother of Lewis and William, recorded in 1717 'The names of the tunes that I can sing [play] on the viol', and the viol appears to have continued in use in Wales until the end of the eighteenth century.[29] In another part of the same manuscript, he notes: 'yr un flwyddyn y dechreuais Ganu ffidil, ar Wul Fair' ('in the same year I began to play the fiddle, at Candlemas'); the year is not given, but is thought to be 1713.[30]

Gentry families, while they may not have retained fiddlers on a permanent basis, frequently hired them for special occasions. At Baron Hill, the home of the Bulkeley family on Anglesey, three fiddlers were paid 10s each for their services at Christmas 1711, and at Christmas during the years 1762 to 1767, the Meyrick family of Bodorgan, Anglesey, retained John Morgan the fiddler and Howel the harper.[31] Thomas Lewis (d. 1763), who was said to be the best fiddler

---

[28] Bethan Miles, 'Crwth' and 'Crythorion', *Cydymaith i Gerddoriaeth Cymru* (Talybont: Y Lolfa, 2018), 107–109, 109–112.

[29] T. H. Parry-Williams, ed., *Llawysgrif Richard Morris o Gerddi [B.M. Add. Ms. 14, 992]* (Caerdydd: Gwasg Prifysgol Cymru, 1931), tt. 80–81; Meredydd Evans, 'Cipdrem ar Rai o Alawon Richard Morris', *Welsh Music/Cerddoriaeth Cymru*, 4/6 (Spring/Gwanwyn 1974), 20–26.

[30] *Llawysgrif Richard Morris*, t. 214; Dafydd Wyn Wiliam, *Cofiant Richard Morris (1702/3–79)* (D. W. Wiliam, 1999), t. 36.

[31] Ibid., 24. Cass Meurig believes that this John Morgan may be the last crwth player identified by Daines Barrington (see earlier in this section).

in Glamorgan, made around five pounds every summer when he accompanied dancing at St Fagans Castle.[32] A few years later, surgeon, botanist and antiquarian Sir Thomas Gery Cullum (1741–1831) visited Llandrindod Wells to take the waters, and expressed a belief that music aided recovery:

> after supper a small company danced to a fiddler and Harp. The Fiddle and the Harp are plaid upon every meal; and make very agreeable Harmony: and no doubt but the cheerfulness they inspire must assist the efficacy of the waters.[33]

The fiddle was also used outdoors. The anterliwt (interlude) was a popular form of open-air dramatic entertainment in the late eighteenth and early nineteenth centuries; its most noted exponent was the Denbighshire poet and actor Thomas Edwards (Twm o'r Nant; 1739–1810). Anterliwtiau, performed in farmyards and market squares with improvised staging, contained stock characters and poked fun at the establishment. They included songs and dances with fiddle. John Thomas, whose manuscript of fiddle music is a particularly valuable source for the identification of repertoire in the eighteenth century, evidently followed the anterliwt.[34] Various folk customs are also known to have depended on the support of fiddle players. They played at gwyliau mabsant and accompanied morris dancing. John Hughes of Dolhiryd, Llangollen, who was born in 1802, had a childhood memory of seeing such dancing, accompanied by fiddles, at the Llangollen gwylmabsant on the first Sunday in June:

> Mae genyf gof tywyll o weled Dynion yn llewis eu crysau mainion, a rhaini wedi ei haddurno a ribbanau o wahanol liwiau, ac yn rhosynau o bennau ei gliniau i fyny i'w hetiau; Yr oeddynt yn eu slippers, a chanddynt ddau neu dri o ffidlers. Byddai y rhai hyn (y Morris dance[r]s,) yn mynd o dy i dy, lle y caent dderbyniad; i ganu ac i ddawnsio, ac i feggio arian cwrw.

> (I do have a hazy recollection of seeing Men in their linen shirt-sleeves, and those decorated with ribbons of different colours, and covered with roses from their knees up to their hats. They were in their slippers, and had two or three fiddlers with them. These (the Morris dance[r]s,) went from house to house, where they might get a welcome, to sing and dance, and to beg beer-money.)[35]

---

[32] Ibid., 26. [33] Quoted ibid., 28. [34] Kinney, *Welsh Traditional Music*, p. 126.
[35] Quoted with translation in Roy Saer, 'Traditional Dance in Wales during the Eighteenth Century', in his *Canu at Iws*, pp. 287–304, at p. 289.

Morgan Rhys of Ystradowen in Glamorgan, writing in 1842 but recollecting the customs of a previous generation, likewise described fiddle playing at Easter:

> At daybreak on Easter Saturday the mistresses and their maids arose in order to finish their work by two o'clock in the afternoon, the time fixed for meeting in the pavilion or church-yard, to commence dancing, which was continued until sunset, when all departed for their respective homes. Musicians were hired for this dance, that is, a harper and a fiddler; and great was the desire of both old and young to witness the periodical return of this festive season.[36]

Fiddle and harp are often mentioned together, particularly in relation to folk customs. At a much later date, between 1880 and 1920, they were part of the Mari Lwyd wassailing ritual at Nantgarw, Glamorgan:

> There was great merriment, the singing of ballads and love songs, such as *The Maid of Cefn Ydfa* and *The Maid of Sker*, dancing to the fiddle and harp and after some hours the Feri [i.e., the Mari Lwyd] would sing her farewell at the door.[37]

W. Meredith Morris (1867–1921) claimed that the folk fiddle survived in Pembrokeshire until the late nineteenth century, though his recollections may be tinged with romance:

> At Haverfordwest, during my Grammar School days, my youthful imagination was fired by the sweet strains of the old strolling fiddler, Dick of Dale, who visited all the principal fairs held in the town, and who used to delight the lads and lasses from the country that were assembled on St. Thomas's Green, or in Barn Street, for a dance. At these Terpsichorean revelries, Dick's bow was at a gallop the live long day, and many an hour did I spend sitting on a wall or on the top spar of a hurdle listening to melodies that never wearied.[38]

Of Aby Biddle of Jeffreyston (d. 1852), he records: 'At wakes he played weird, frenzied music to scare the ghouls who lurked near the chamber of the dead. At weddings he played in the light, fantastic vein'; and of Swansea Bill, who attended the important fairs of Carmarthenshire and neighbouring counties: 'He attracted large crowds of rustic dancers and never lacked patronage. At all villages where convenient he hired a barn or granary for his dances, charging a penny for admission.'[39]

An indication of the repertoire of the folk fiddler is given in three sources. The first is Richard Morris's 1717 listing of 379 tune names, three-quarters of

---

[36] Quoted ibid., p. 295. [37] Kinney, *Welsh Traditional Music*, p. 73.
[38] W. Meredith Morris, *Famous Fiddlers*, ed. by D. Roy Saer ([Cardiff]: Welsh Folk Museum, 1983), p. 3.
[39] Ibid., p. 12.

which appear to originate outside Wales. The other two are collections of fiddle tunes in notation: that of John Thomas, a fiddler probably from northeast Wales, bears the date 1752 on its cover, but its owner appears to have been active from the 1720s to the mid-century.[40] As is the case with Richard Morris's list, many of Thomas's 526 items, representing 393 different tunes, are found in English and Scottish country-dance books; dance tunes predominate in the collection, and were no doubt used to accompany dancing both indoors and outside, showing a practice that was flexible and eclectic. His repertoire has much in common with similar collections from other parts of the British Isles, and his choice of melodies is 'consistent with the fact that the main job of the professional fiddler was to play for dancing'.[41] There are also tunes for accompanying singing, dance tunes used for anterliwtiau, and tunes such as 'Mwynen Mai', evidently used for Mayday celebrations. Present also are instrumental tunes which 'may have been used as background music for functions in the houses of the local gentry'.[42] In contrast, the third source, the manuscript collection dated 1778 to 1779 of Morris Edward(s), who came probably from Anglesey, is much smaller than Thomas's, containing 158 tunes, and has a more Welsh orientation.[43] It has none of the English and classical-music tunes found in Thomas's collection, nor any indication that its owner played for the anterliwt; but his tunes bear indications of having been taken down from performers and not copied from a book. This probably reflects his personal interest in Welsh tunes rather than any substantial divergence of the Anglesey repertoire from that of other parts of Wales. Tune names often changed, as they were miscopied from written sources or misinterpreted when heard: in Richard Morris's list 'Country Bumpkin' is 'Contraboncin' and 'Bonny Dundee' becomes 'Boni Dawn Di', while other tunes acquired completely new names: 'About the Banks of Helicon' is for John Thomas 'Y Fedle Fawr' (The Great Medley).

As with the harp, there are instances of people giving up their fiddles under the influence of Methodist preaching: the biographer of the great Welsh preacher John Jones of Tal-y-sarn (1797–1857) made great play of the effect of Jones's preaching at a fair on Greenhill in Swansea in 1827, oratory which gradually sucked in the fairground dancers until in the end the fiddler himself stopped playing and came forward to listen to the

---

[40] GB-AB J. Lloyd Williams Music MSS, AH1/36; Cass Meurig, ed., *Alawon John Thomas: A Fiddler's Tune Book from Eighteenth-Century Wales* (Aberystwyth: Llyfrgell Genedlaethol Cymru/The National Library of Wales, 2004).
[41] Meurig, *Alawon John Thomas*, p. v.   [42] Ibid.
[43] GB-BGul MS 2294; Phyllis Kinney, 'John Thomas's Fiddle Manuscript', *Canu Gwerin*, 22 (1999), 43–51; Meurig, *Alawon John Thomas*, p. iii.

sermon.[44] But there was some use of instruments in churches and even in chapels in the nineteenth century: writing in 1839, 'O. T.' from Holyhead claimed that he had introduced the 'bass violin' to a chapel in Llanddeiniolen, near Caernarfon, and later to chapels on Anglesey.[45] If Meredith Morris is correct that the itinerant tradition continued well into the nineteenth century, it is possible that the effect of the religious revivals was more limited than is sometimes claimed: even in the early years of the twentieth century descendants of Abram Wood could still be seen playing at street corners, their home-made fiddles carved out of chocolate boxes (see Figure 7.3). By that time the

Figure 7.3 Itinerant Welsh Romani musicians (from the left), Cornelius, David (harp) and Adolphus Wood. The fiddles are home-made, and the mechanism of the pedal harp may have been removed to aid portability. Picture taken before 1914; the photographer is unidentified. Amgueddfa Cymru – National Museum Wales

[44] Owen Thomas, *Cofiant y Parchedig John Jones, Talsarn* (Wrexham: Hughes a'i Fab, [1874]), tt. 181–183.
[45] O. T., Holyhead in a letter to *Yr Eurgrawn Wesleyaidd* 31 (1839), 283.

tradition was on the wane, and it would not be revived until the later twentieth century.

Wind Instruments

The history of wind instruments in Wales has received less attention than has the history of string instruments – probably with good reason. The major provider for training and performance on wind instruments in Wales from the late eighteenth century was the military, especially the militia bands formed in each Welsh county under the patronage of local gentry. This was in response to the Militia Acts of the 1870s and the subsequent development of military drill as public spectacle in support of British propaganda.[46] All the bands so formed had developed into sophisticated and musically literate ensembles by the early nineteenth century; their players included one or two – usually German – professionals, and a few local amateurs, but otherwise they were made up of *ab initio* recruits, taught by the professionals who had been appointed partly for that purpose. The extent to which alumni of militia bands made an impact on wider spheres of musical practice is difficult to gauge, but it is likely to have been significant. There are signs that clarinets and flageolets were in circulation early in the century, as were people of local prominence who were skilled performers on them. For example, John Parry (1776–1851), was a flageolet player in the Denbigh militia prior to becoming its leader and it was as a teacher of that instrument that he sustained himself in London from 1805. There is also evidence in south Wales, which includes a carefully posed photographic portrait of David Llewelyn of Aberdare, the father of Thomas David Llewelyn (Llewelyn Alaw; 1828–79), taken in the mid-nineteenth century, by which time he was a very old man; it shows him reclining in a chair holding a clarinet.[47]

Brass instruments were rarer than woodwind before the militia band era. Such was the case elsewhere in Britain, other than among professionals. In his *Musical and Poetical Relicks* Edward Jones illustrated what he called the '*Corn Buelin*, Cornet, or Bugle Horn' as one of the five instruments

---

[46] The propaganda was aimed at promoting a popular sense of Britishness at a time of war and increasing recruitment to the regular army, but militia units were also intended to be a home defence force. See Trevor Herbert and Helen Barlow, *Music and the British Military in the Long Nineteenth Century* (New York: Oxford University Press, 2013), chapter 5.

[47] GB-AB MS Minor Deposit 150. The photograph is pasted in a handwritten book containing writings on various subjects.

'anciently used in Wales' and which are 'as different from those of other nations, as their Music and Poetry'.[48] He goes on to describe it as a military or hunting horn. The instrument shown is, in fact, identical to what was known in Germany and elsewhere from the eighteenth century as the *Halbmond* (half-moon) bugle, which had the exact same function and ancestry that Jones described.[49] The brief but important phase in virtuoso brass playing by the Cyfarthfa Band at Merthyr Tydfil in the middle of the nineteenth century is discussed in Chapter 13 of this book. It was an extraordinary phenomenon – an isolated case of British provincial musical patronage occurring in what was, at that time, the most populous town in Wales – and there is no evidence of a comparable ensemble, contemporary or earlier, anywhere in the world; but there was nothing especially Welsh about it apart from its location.

The bagpipe is mentioned in several Welsh sources from the fourteenth century, and words used to describe pipes in earlier sources may have referred to the same instrument. There is also iconographical evidence: the instrument is shown in the hands of its player in a detailed drawing contained in the papers of the Pembrokeshire antiquary George Owen (1552–1613).[50] Edward Jones does not mention it in the first edition of his *Relicks*, but includes it in the extended 1794 edition, though he appears to have had little personal knowledge of it.[51] It is described consistently in several Welsh sources from the eighteenth and nineteenth centuries as an instrument used in wedding rituals in which bagpipers led wedding processions, particularly in south Wales.[52]

The wind instrument associated most closely and ethnically with Wales, and which is also listed and illustrated by Jones, is the pibgorn or pibcorn. The name derives from two etymological elements of equal weight, 'pib' (pipe) and 'corn' or 'gorn' (horn): literally a hornpipe. Almost certainly the name derives from the materials of its fabrication.[53] Both 'pipe' and words meaning 'horn' were deployed to describe a range of wind instruments in Europe from at least the medieval

---

[48] Jones, *Musical and Poetical Relicks* (1784), p. 41.
[49] See Trevor Herbert, Arnold Myers and John Wallace, eds., *The Cambridge Encyclopedia of Brass Instruments* (Cambridge: Cambridge University Press, 2019), p. 90. This instrument was so ubiquitous as a signal instrument in the military that it became one of the most utilised emblems for both cavalry and foot regiments.
[50] Sally Harper, *Music in Welsh Culture before 1650: A Study of the Principal Sources* (Aldershot: Ashgate, 2007), p. 314.
[51] Jones, *Musical and Poetical Relicks* (1794), pp. 116–117.
[52] Saer, *Canu at Iws*, chapters 22 and 23.
[53] Jones also gives this reason for the name in *Musical and Poetical Relicks* (1784), p. 43.

7 Instrumental Traditions after 1650

period (crumhorn, cornamuse and so on). Indeed, instruments using the same method of sound generation are described by Agricola in his *Musica Getutscht* (1511), the first European book devoted to musical instruments.[54] Agricola and subsequent writers describe an array of capped and uncapped reed instruments that developed from the fifteenth century, some of which owe their origins to Moorish influences.[55] The pibgorn is one of the simplest and probably oldest of the species, with versions of it being found in several countries. Archaeological sites in northern Europe have revealed instruments very similar to the pibgorn from the medieval period.[56] A Welsh word taken to resemble 'pibgorn' (given as 'bybeu') and optimistically claimed to be a synonym for the same instrument is found in transcriptions of the tenth-century Laws of Hywel Dda, where it is mentioned along with the crwth and the harp as instruments necessary for musicians aspiring to the rank of pencerdd. This source may be accurate, but as is generally the case when considering early precedents of musical instruments, in the absence of documentary description and iconographical evidence, instrument names should not be taken at face value.

However, from the turn of the fourteenth and fifteenth centuries, sources increase in both frequency and quality. Iconographical images show the instrument or cognate versions of it. For example, the 'Beauchamp window' (1417) at St Mary's Church, Warwick shows a realistic representation. Eighteenth-century sources include extant specimens from that period. Three are in the possession of the St Fagans National Museum of History.[57] They reveal it to be a wooden pipe (some other specimens have bone pipes) with six front finger holes and one back thumb-hole. At one end of the pipe is a single wooden reed, covered with an animal-horn mouthpiece (referred to by some as a 'mouth horn'); at the other end is a horn 'bell' that radiates the sound. The length of two of the St Fagans instruments is 48 cm, and this approximates to the 18¼ inches mentioned by Galpin and other organologists, and the 19 inches

---

[54] See, for example, Beth Bullard, ed., *Musica Getutscht: A Treatise on Musical Instruments by Sebastian Virdung* (Cambridge: Cambridge University Press, 1993), pp. 105–108.
[55] See David Munrow, *Instruments of the Middle Ages and Renaissance* (Oxford: Oxford University Press, 1976), chapters 1 and 6.
[56] See Annemies Tamboer and Raino Ritta, 'A Singing Bone from the Convent Quarter of Medieval Turku, Finland: Swedish or German Import, Baltic Influence or Variation on a Finnish Theme?', *Publications of the ICTM Study Group for Musicology*, 2 (2020), 109–131.
[57] GB-CDf Item Number 57.110, https://museum.wales/collections/online/object/fcea6c2f-755c-3f52-9601-c9a92a273b978/Pibgorn/ (accessed 20 July 2021). All three instruments share the same item number.

given by Jones in 1784.⁵⁸ Modern reproductions are made with a nominal pitch of d' with a natural range of one diatonic octave. The reproductions use d' as the pitch because of its utility when performing melodies drawn from traditional song, a pragmatism that might well have firm roots in historic practice. The sound is generated by a mechanism like that used for the chanter of a bagpipe. As with other capped-reed instruments, it is capable of a relatively narrow dynamic range.

The pibgorn was mentioned briefly by Hawkins in his *History of Music*,⁵⁹ and from the eighteenth century it attracted the scrutiny of antiquarians. Though he owned an instrument obtained from a 'Mr Wynn of Penhescedd' (who sponsored an annual prize for performance on it), Daines Barrington's article says little of the pibgorn, but his illustration of the instrument is extremely accurate.⁶⁰ A more extensive article on 'The Old British "Pibcorn" or "Hornpipe" and its Affinities', by the Victorian antiquarian Henry Balfour, was published in 1891.⁶¹ Balfour believed the instrument had been widely distributed across 'Wales, Cornwall, Lancashire, South Scotland, Ireland, and ... Brittany'.⁶² The presence of the instrument in so many places, albeit in slightly different forms, and the broad acknowledgement that many reed-capped instruments owe their origins to Moorish influence, invite questions about how 'Welsh' the pibgorn is or was, because since at least the eighteenth century it has been widely regarded as a *Welsh* instrument, a belief that endures in modern times. *The Grove Dictionary of Musical Instruments* (2014) describes it as a 'Single hornpipe with mouth horn, of Wales', and the *Oxford English Dictionary* labels it in similar terms.

The disclaimers can, of course, be applied with equal propriety to the harp. The reality, however, is that Welsh sources for the pibgorn are sufficiently abundant to suggest that it occupied an important place in the country's musical life and that it acquired what may have been a distinctive idiom. It was also clearly a rural instrument when Wales was almost entirely a rural country. Daines Barrington praised it in terms that

---

⁵⁸ Francis Galpin, *Old English Instruments of Music* (London: Methuen, 1910), p.128. Jones, *Musical and Poetical Relicks* (1784), p. 43. Galpin's measurements were of an instrument in the possession of the Society of Antiquaries, and which was probably the instrument previously owned by Daines Barrington.
⁵⁹ John Hawkins, *A General History of the Science and Practice of Music* (London: T. Payne and Son, 1776).
⁶⁰ Barrington, 'Some Account', 33–34 and Plate VII.
⁶¹ Henry Balfour, 'The Old British "Pibcorn" or "Hornpipe" and Its Affinities', *Journal of the Anthropological Institute of Great Britain and Ireland*, 20 (1891), 142–154.
⁶² Ibid., 145.

to him were probably free of irony. He had heard it played by a winner of Mr Wynn's annual prize and pronounced that 'Its tone ... considering the materials of which [it] is composed, is really very tolerable and resembles an indifferent hautbois'.[63] Edward Jones believed that it was used mainly or even exclusively in Anglesey in the closing decades of the eighteenth century, and described its idiom more helpfully: 'Its tone is medium between the flute and the clarinet, and is remarkable for its melody ... it is played by shepherds and tends greatly to enhance the innocent delight of pastoral life'.[64]

Jones was not alone in referring to the pibgorn as a pastoral instrument. If we can take this as legitimate, with a meaning close to what is understood of 'pastoral' in the modern sense, it is possible that softer reeds were sometimes used, and this might align it with the pastoral 'topics' that are associated with reed instruments in art music. However, it is easy to make too much of such alignments and to associate the instrument too closely with the substantial written repertoire that has the word 'hornpipe' in the title. Several such tunes are included in Llewelyn Alaw's manuscript collections[65] which were assembled in the mid-nineteenth century and devoted to dances that, by that time, had acquired fixed forms. There is no reliable evidence that links the instrument to the dance that carries that name. Indeed, even the first issue of Grove's *Dictionary of Music and Musicians* (1879) described the hornpipe as an 'English dance'.[66] The likely repertoire of the pibgorn is either lost in a tradition of orality and memory, or buried in adaptations of Welsh song, and it is from the lyricism of such traditions that the pastoral associations were probably drawn. As the instrument had a range of no more than an octave it would have been restricted to songs that did not exceed that range or were adapted. There are several such songs that would have been appropriate.

Twentieth-Century Revivals

There was a revival of Welsh instrument traditions in the last quarter of the twentieth century,[67] but the absence of living exemplars of the tradition

---

[63] Barrington, 'Some Account', pp. 33–34. [64] Jones, *Musical and Poetical Relicks* (1784), p. 43.
[65] GB-AB MS337D. [66] The entry was written by Grove himself.
[67] The presence of 'revival informants and/or original sources' is the second of six 'basic ingredients' of music revivals as proposed by Tamara Livingston in her article 'Music Revivals: Towards a General Theory', *Ethnomusicology*, 43 (1999), 66–85, on p. 69. All six may be observed in the revival of instrumental music in Wales, from 'core revivalists' to 'non-profit and/or commercial enterprises catering to the revivalist market'.

presented challenges. Harpists were the exception. Foremost among these was Nansi Richards (Telynores Maldwyn; 1888–1979), who taught many players in mid- and north Wales. Though her fame came as a performer of the triple harp, she also played the modern double-action pedal instrument – both on the left shoulder. She studied formally at the Guildhall School of Music and Drama in London,[68] but claimed two other formidable influences: her primary harp teacher in Wales, Tom Lloyd (Telynor Ceiriog), and the repertoire learned from the Romani who had such an important influence on the Welsh harp tradition.

The revival from the mid-1970s can be traced, at least in part, through the increasing number of commercially produced recordings of folk groups and soloists. Many Welsh groups of this period were formed under the influence of a wider 'Celtic' revival, made up primarily of professional folk ensembles from Ireland and Scotland, and later Breton musicians such as Alan Stivell. The influence of these professional groups influenced choices of instrumentation and performance styles more widely. The Welsh group Ar Log (On Hire) was one of the first to combine a balance of instrumental items alongside Welsh folk songs. Formed in 1976, it was unique in that two of the four original members were harpists: Gwyndaf and Dafydd Roberts were both taught the triple harp by Nansi Richards in the oral tradition. Ar Log was one of the first Welsh folk groups to turn professional; the original formation used two harps, a fiddle and guitar/mandolin.[69]

There was no certain knowledge of distinctively Welsh instrumental idioms, but repertoire was a simpler matter: revival musicians plundered manuscripts and printed collections of Welsh tunes from the eighteenth and nineteenth centuries. In the absence of firm evidence as to original performance conventions they developed highly individual styles, some taking the ornamentations used in Irish and Scottish traditions as a starting point. Instruments closely associated with Irish and Scottish folk music, such as the tenor banjo; the accordion and the lower-pitched instruments of the mandolin family, particularly the mandola; and the bouzouki – which had been introduced into Irish music from the late 1960s – were used freely in performances of Welsh repertoire. The ambition to rediscover (or invent) an authentically Welsh instrumental idiom and sound

---

[68] See Nia Gwyn Evans, *Bywyd a Gwaith Dr Nansi Richards Jones 'Telynores Maldwyn' (1888–1979)* (Llanrwst: Gwasg Carreg Gwalch, 2015); and Joan Rimmer, 'Telynores Maldwyn: Nansi Richards, a Welsh Harpist, 1888–1979', *Studia Instrumentorum Musicae Popularis*, 7 (1981) 127–133.

[69] See Lyn Ebenezer, *Ar Log ers Ugain Mlynedd* (Llanrwst: Gwasg Carreg Gwalch, 1996).

was frequently expressed in the pages of the folk magazine *Taplas* during the 1980s.[70]

The 1990s saw a reinvigoration of traditional instrumental music on several fronts. The first was an increase in the number and diversity of commercial folk music recordings, several featuring purely instrumental repertoire. Sain, the record label founded in 1969 and located at this time near Caernarfon, had featured folk music since its early years, but had primarily concentrated on vocal repertoire. The triple harpist Robin Huw Bowen (b. 1957) recorded several solo instrumental albums for Sain as well as other labels. His repertoire featured reinterpretations of canonical aspects of the triple harp repertoire such as that included in the collections published by John Parry and Edward Jones, along with dance tunes from the manuscript collections of Llewelyn Alaw, as well as original compositions. A notable contribution was his reintroduction of Welsh Romani harp repertoire, learned aurally from Eldra Jarman (1913–2001).[71]

Sain's Cardigan-based competitor Fflach was established in 1981, and in 1997 initiated a sub-label specifically devoted to traditional music, fflach:tradd. Among Fflach's instrumental releases were albums devoted to fiddle players, accordionists, the crwth and a solo recording of a Welsh bagpipe.[72] It was on this label that Llio Rhydderch (b. 1937) released a series of increasingly innovative solo recordings on triple harp, taking traditional melodies as the basis for explorations both in variation sets and in more extensive contemporary compositions.[73] Her own links to living harp traditions came through her lessons with Nansi Richards and contacts with descendants of Anglesey harpists, particularly those associated with the village of Llannerch-y-medd.[74]

---

[70] Stephen P. Rees, 'A New Celtic Tradition? Group Instrumental Performance in the Welsh Folk Revival, *c*.1975–*c*.1989/Traddodiad Celtaidd Newydd? Perfformiad Offerynnol gan Grwpiau yn yr Adfywiad Gwerin yng Nghymru, *c*.1975–*c*.1989', *Welsh Music History/Hanes Cerddoriaeth Cymru*, 7 (2007), 304–343.

[71] Robin Huw Bowen, *Hela'r Draenog: Telyn Sipsi Cymru/Hunting the Hedgehog: The Gypsy Harp of Wales* (Recordiau Teires, CDRHB002, 1994). Eldra Jarman was the great-granddaughter of John Roberts, 'Telynor Cymru'.

[72] Ceri Rhys Mathews, *Pibddawns* (fflach:tradd, CD 293H, 2006). The bagpipe used by Ceri Rhys Mathews for this recording has a single drone, with a chanter with a single reed based on that of the pibgorn.

[73] For example, *Sir Fôn Bach* (fflach:tradd CD 270H, 2019).

[74] See Huw Roberts and Llio Rhydderch, *Telynorion Llannerch-y-medd: Teulu'r Britannia ac Eraill/The Harpers of Llannerch-y-medd: The Britannia Family and Others* (Llangefni: Cyngor Sir Ynys Môn, 2000), p. 137.

Repertoire

Many of the Welsh tunes found in the eighteenth- and nineteenth-century printed collections were cast in the generic musical language of popular music of that period: in standard major or minor keys, and measures which did not readily agree with the conventions used by Celtic revival bands of the 1970s.[75] This had three consequences. First, tunes were often selected because of their resemblance to those in other Celtic traditions, either in genre or modality, and melodies that were more idiosyncratic in structure tended to be ignored. Second, traditional musicians began to compose 'new' traditional tunes, some of which circulated with the composer's name attached; others found their way anonymously into informal sessions and recordings.[76] Third, musicians began to recast extant traditional melodies, taking them from diatonic keys into modal versions. This might involve, for example, raising the sixth degree and/or flattening the seventh degree of a harmonic-minor scale to move the melody into the Dorian mode, a common mode in Welsh folk song; or flattening the seventh degree of a major melody, taking it into the Mixolydian mode – far less commonly found in the recorded song repertoire.[77] This practice of 'modalising' melodies became increasingly common among Welsh folk instrumentalists from the 1990s, as did the composition of new tunes exploiting both familiar and less-familiar modal features.[78]

As well as reviving specifically Welsh or Welsh-sourced repertoire, instrumentalists adopted aspects of other traditions and historical performance practice. For example, no historic Welsh bagpipe survives and though some putative reconstructions of instruments have been made, many modern pipers have adopted continental instruments, such as the *veuze* of Upper Brittany, or the Galician *gaita*. From the 1980s, the groups Cromlech and Aberjaber integrated the *gaita* with Celtic harp and various

---

[75] See Joan Rimmer, 'Edward Jones's *Musical and Poetical Relicks of the Welsh Bards*, 1784: A Reassessment', *The Galpin Society Journal*, 39 (1986), 77–96 for an analysis of the relationship of some of Jones's music to more widely known dance measures. In *Welsh Traditional Music* (pp. 57–69), Phyllis Kinney gives a more recent perspective on how his collection related to oral tradition and how the tunes were extensively republished during the following century.

[76] Cass Meurig, 'Composing Traditional Music', in *Cynheiliaid y Gân/Bearers of Song: Essays in Honour of Phyllis Kinney and Meredydd Evans*, ed. by Sally Harper and Wyn Thomas (Cardiff: University of Wales Press, 2007), pp. 240–250.

[77] Peter Crossley-Holland, 'The Tonal Limits of Welsh Folk Song', *Journal of the Welsh Folk-Song Society/Cylchgrawn Cymdeithas Alawon Gwerin Cymru*, 5 (1964), 46–73. Crossley-Holland explicitly omitted instrumental music from his survey.

[78] See Stephen P. Rees, 'Adnewyddiad Creadigol yn y Traddodiad Offerynnol yng Nghymru', *Canu Gwerin/Folk Song*, 42 (2019), 27–46, for examples of modal adaptation, and a notable instrumental transformation of modal song melody 'Trip i Aberystwyth' involving microtonal inflection.

instruments familiar from the contemporary early music revival, such as the crumhorn, the medieval fiddle and the hurdy-gurdy.[79] Both Aberjaber and Yr Hwntws ('The South Walians') recorded versions of music from the bardic tradition as found in the seventeenth-century harp manuscript of Robert ap Huw, thereby affording some historical legitimacy for a Welsh instrumental tradition that did not possess an equivalent contemporary currency to those of other Celtic nations.

Instruments

The revival of an instrumental tradition is difficult without access to the original instruments on which the revival is intended to be based. By the late twentieth century, few triple harps of the eighteenth and nineteenth centuries were in playing condition. The combined tension of a hundred or so strings attached to one side of the neck of a harp frequently caused structural problems: the forepillar could warp to one side, both the neck and shoulder might crack and the soundboard could distort and fracture. The harp maker Bassett Jones addressed these issues both in his own harps and in earlier instruments which he repaired. However, it was not until John Weston Thomas (1921–92) designed his 'perpendicular' triple harp in the 1970s that a robust modern triple harp became more widely available. His solution was to fix the outer rows of strings to both sides of the harp neck, and the central row to its underside; instruments built to this design by Thomas and his apprentices are still the most encountered triple harps in Wales.[80]

Since the 1970s, several makers have produced modern copies of the surviving examples of the crwth and pibgorn. As with the modern triple harp, these instruments have not been immune to modern interventions, with players substituting gut strings for metal, and makers using synthetic materials for both pibgorn reeds and the sections of the instrument traditionally made from animal horn.

---

[79] Mendelssohn's well-known 1829 letter from Wales complaining about national music, quoted earlier in this chapter, also takes the instruments to task: his ire is aroused by a harp and a hurdy-gurdy playing simultaneously. While the term he used for hurdy-gurdy – '*Leierkasten*' – is widely known, no equivalent Welsh term seems to have had modern currency. A fifteenth-century term for an undefined musical instrument – 'perwg' – was defined by 1803 as 'probably, a hurdy-gurdy' by the lexicographer William Owen Pughe (*Geiriadur Prifysgol Cymru*). The term was recently reintroduced on an eponymous CD recording, featuring Sille Ilves playing music from Wales and Estonia on the hurdy-gurdy: *Perwg* (Libahundix CD0113, 2013).

[80] The discovery and restoration of triple harps by Bassett Jones has led to a growing appreciation of the lighter, more penetrating tone of earlier instruments. Makers such as Tim Hampson are now building instruments based on eighteenth- and nineteenth-century models.

Transmissions

Welsh instrumentalists of the past would have typically learned their craft partly or entirely in an oral tradition.[81] With increasing musical literacy came a commensurate decline in oral transmission; but paradoxically, the oral tradition experienced a revival in the 1990s, through the personal initiatives of individuals, group teaching (through aural methods) at workshops and folk festivals, and at events held by newly formed organisations to promote traditional music. Notable among these were two organisations with a stated national remit for Wales: Clera and trac.[82]

The first wave of revivalists was active from the 1970s, with some acting as tutors in the new spate of workshops from the 1990s. Younger musicians attending these workshops perceived the music and techniques they learned as part of an ongoing tradition – though it had not existed in its current form for much more than a generation. Alongside residential courses, informal 'musicking'[83] of Welsh traditional repertoire increased around Wales, sometimes supported by local tune clubs, which might devote events to specific local or regional repertoire, or even to the repertoire of an individual musician. Although informal music making in sessions in Wales has not been studied extensively, the repertoire performed in them can be seen as having various origins: Welsh, Scottish, English, Irish, Breton, Galician and so on[84] – and the mixture may change

---

[81] The two extant Welsh manuscripts of fiddle music display both of these traits to different extents: GB-AB J. Lloyd Williams Music MSS, AH1/36 (edited by Cass Meurig as *Alawon John Thomas: A Fiddler's Tune Book from Eighteenth-Century Wales* (Aberystwyth: Llyfrgell Genedlaethol Cymru/National Library of Wales, 2004)); and GB-BGul MS 2294: Morris Edward's manuscript (1779). See Kinney, *Welsh Traditional Music*, pp. 64–65.

[82] Clera ('to go on circuit as bard or minstrel', *Geiriadur Prifysgol Cymru*) was founded as Cymdeithas Offerynnau Traddodiadol Cymru (The Society for the Traditional Instruments of Wales) in 1996 and holds workshops concentrating on traditional instrumental music. From 2006 Clera also organised a 'folk orchestra', the 'Clerorfa', featuring fiddles, flutes and harps in an ensemble which at times included as many as fifty-five instrumentalists; see http://clera.org (accessed 29 July 2021). Trac (Traddodiadau Cerdd Cymru/Music Traditions Wales) was formed in 1997, and from 2008 has held residential weekends dedicated to teaching Welsh-music-based folk arts, including instrumental music alongside song, cerdd dant, plygain carols and step dance. Trac also organises a National Youth Folk Ensemble. See https://trac.cymru (accessed 29 July 2021). New organisations dedicated to promoting traditional music sprang up across the UK during the 1980s, many with the support of centrally funded arts councils. See Simon Keegan-Phipps, 'Déjà Vu? Folk Music, Education, and Institutionalization in Contemporary England', *Yearbook for Traditional Music*, 39 (2007), 84–107; and Simon McKerrell, 'Traditional Arts and the State: The Scottish Case', *Cultural Trends*, 23 (2014), 159–168 for discussions of this phenomenon in England and Scotland.

[83] The concept of studying music as an activity rather than an object is elaborated in Christopher Small, *Musicking: The Meanings of Performing and Listening* (Hanover, NH and London: Wesleyan University Press, 1998).

[84] The trac website lists a regular session of Galician music in Cardiff: https://trac.cymru/en/directory/cardiff-galician-session (accessed 29 July 2021).

according to the context of any given session. For example, one session may be specifically based on Irish tunes, another – in a different pub on a different evening – may feature more distinctively Welsh repertoire.

In revivals of instrumental tradition in other parts of Europe – especially where there are a greater number of living informants – regional repertoires and styles have been even more strongly emphasised. In Ireland, characteristics of the fiddle style and repertoire of County Donegal in the north-west are recognisably distinct from the style and repertoire of County Kerry in the south-west, for example. These styles and those of other regions have been promoted as distinctive, and codified as such in workshops and tutorial publications. Likewise, the fiddle traditions of Sweden have long been characterised as distinctively regional. It has been a matter of debate whether emphasis on regional style has obscured appropriate consideration of the style of the individual musician; but in the absence of regional instrumental performance styles in Wales, there may turn out to be greater emphasis on the playing of individual musicians as the revival proceeds.

Revival or Invention?

Despite the allegiance that performers have had to the ideal of preservation, most would agree that there have been various mutations and reformations of 'tradition' since the eighteenth century.[85] That said, musical traditions are based on what musicians actually do in a given time and context. That context could be informal music making at sessions or dances, teaching or participating in institutionalised workshops, listening or performing in concerts and competitive eisteddfodau or producing commercial recordings. As with other folk revivals, an important facet of the revival in Wales was a growing concern to recycle instrumental music into an ongoing oral/aural tradition. Historical sources reveal a complex mutual interaction between oral and print culture, and the eighteenth- and nineteenth-century collectors effectively shifted music from the former to the latter: however, transformations of the musical material along the way were inevitable. The situation in modern Wales is yet more complex: current traditions may be mediated through personal contact, printed notation and recordings, but also through audio and video platforms on the internet. While the expansion of media channels increases the potential

---

[85] Prys Morgan, 'From a Death to a View: The Hunt for the Welsh Past in the Romantic Period', *The Invention of Tradition*, ed. by Eric Hobsbawm and Terence Ranger (Cambridge: Cambridge University Press, 1983), pp. 43–100, especially pp. 73–79. See also Livingston, 'Music Revivals', 69.

for external influence on repertoire and instrumentation, it also shifts the focus on transmission to individual performers and their own version of a tune – which, of course, may change over time. And these different versions are immediately accessible to a wider audience than previously. The period since the 1970s has seen several changes, of which these seem most significant: an increasing awareness of a previously disregarded instrumental repertoire; a resurgence of interest in instruments that were recognised as distinctively Welsh (if effectively moribund) by the late eighteenth century; and a contemporary revitalisation of instrumental performance in a range of different contexts, embracing a wide variety of instrumentations and modes of transmission. Whether revived or invented, traditional instrumental music has become something that musicians in Wales *perform* – in other words, a living tradition.

CHAPTER 8

The Celtic Revival

Helen Barlow

Revivals have been a frequent occurrence in Welsh history, but they are usually revivals of the religious kind. The 'Celtic revival' of the eighteenth and early nineteenth centuries was different – it was a cultural revival: a revival (sometimes referred to by historians as a 'renaissance') of interest and scholarship among the Welsh in their language, literature, history and culture. The decline that lay behind and prompted such a renewal is well documented.¹ In brief, the Tudor period had seen the assimilation of Wales into England as a single state, governed by common political, legal and administrative systems, under the Acts of Union of 1536 and 1543. There were many Welshmen – principally the boneddigion, the landed gentry – who benefited substantially from the Union and who quickly came to regard the English language, English education and English culture as indicators of modernity and advancement. Their native language and traditions began to seem embarrassingly backward, and the professional bardic culture began to decline for want of patronage. However, there were many others who were alarmed at the effect on the Welsh language and Welsh culture, and who recognised that the assimilation of Wales effectively deprived the Welsh of 'a distinct history', leaving 'only traditions which were either discredited or merely contributory to English traditions'.² These were the people whose scholarship, combined with a passionate sense of Welsh identity, drove the revival.

There were also other factors at work. The Celtic revival more broadly was a part of a pan-European phenomenon, a quickening of interest in the idea of the common people (in Welsh, the gwerin) and the 'authentic' culture of those people, and Welsh scholars and antiquarians were closely in touch with their colleagues in other parts of Europe. One strand of this

---

¹ For example, Geraint H. Jenkins, *The Foundations of Modern Wales 1642–1780* (Oxford: Oxford University Press, 1987/1993); Prys Morgan, *The Eighteenth Century Renaissance*, A New History of Wales (Llandybie: Christopher Davies, 1981).
² Morgan, *The Eighteenth Century Renaissance*, p. 17.

scholarship was the attempt to collect and preserve the traditional 'national airs' of the people, and in musical terms, Wales's Celtic revival might be said to be framed by two significant publications – John Parry's *Antient British Music* (1742), 'the first book claiming to consist entirely of traditional Welsh melodies', and Maria Jane Williams's *Ancient National Airs of Gwent and Morganwg* (1844), 'the first book of traditional Welsh airs to be published with Welsh words to all the melodies'.[3]

One constant feature in the story of Wales's Celtic revival is the influence of London. Wales at this time lacked a cultural and political centre – or rather, the Union had confirmed London as the centre. The industrial towns of Wales grew rapidly during the second half of the eighteenth century, but by 1801 when the first official census was taken, Wales had no town larger than Merthyr Tydfil, with a population of just over 7,700,[4] and there were none of the cultural institutions of the sort that were to be found in London, Edinburgh or Dublin. Before 1804, Wales lacked even a domestic newspaper press.[5] One important consequence of the dominance of London was that from the Tudor period onwards the flow of Welsh people who went to settle there or to conduct trade was considerable. The antiquarian and lexicographer William Owen Pughe (1759–1835), who headed for London aged seventeen, described it as seeming to a Welsh boy to be 'the primary point in the geography of the world',[6] as indeed it was for so many of his compatriots. The nature of London's influence changed over the hundred or so years that elapsed between *Antient British Music* and *Ancient National Airs of Gwent and Morganwg*, as Wales became less inclined to look to London and the London Welsh for cultural leadership and established its own cultural societies and institutions. Nonetheless London remained a constant, in particular for the boneddigion, who continued to move in a world where it was usual to maintain both a house in Wales and one in London, and to go 'up' to London for the social events and entertainments of 'the season'; to represent their Welsh constituencies in Parliament, and for their sons to be educated at English public schools and universities; and to subscribe to many of the values of an

---

[3] Phyllis Kinney, *Welsh Traditional Music* (Cardiff: University of Wales Press in association with Cymdeithas Alawon Gwerin Cymru, 2011), p. 41 and p. 166.
[4] Jenkins, *The Foundations of Modern Wales*, p. 286; L. J. Williams, *Digest of Welsh Historical Statistics*, vol. 1 (Cardiff: The Welsh Office, 1985), pp. 62–63.
[5] Paul O'Leary, 'Revolution, Culture, and Industry, c. 1700–1850', in *The Cambridge History of Welsh Literature*, ed. by Geraint Evans and Helen Fulton (Cambridge: Cambridge University Press, 2019), p. 257.
[6] Glenda Carr, *William Owen Pughe* (Caerdydd: Gwasg Prifysgol Cymru, 1983), t. 6.

English ruling class. The function of music in positioning Wales and the Welsh in this context is more important than might be thought.

There were several key underpinning texts on which the revival of interest in Welsh music was founded. Chief among these was Edward Lhuyd's *Archaeologia Britannica* (1707). Lhuyd (1660–1709) was born near Oswestry and spent his career at Oxford, where he was a brilliant and versatile scholar and Keeper of the Ashmolean Museum. In a pioneering piece of comparative philology, he established the relationship of Welsh to the other Celtic languages, and their common origin. His influence on the thinking of his compatriots was to come to fruition less in his own short lifetime than later in the eighteenth century; he was 'one of the great minds of the age', who 'sowed the seeds of ideological concepts which would grow and blossom luxuriantly in the future'.[7] Blossom they did, but often among less erudite and agile minds than Lhuyd's – typically, among the Welsh clergy of the Established Church, many of whom were antiquarians[8] of varying degrees of methodological reliability.

The key lesson that many took from *Archaeologia Britannica* was that the language had 'an impeccable ancient pedigree'.[9] This idea resonated with a long-held belief in the ancient lineage of the Welsh language and people, which had been fundamental to the thinking of the Welsh about their history. It was thought that they had been the aboriginal inhabitants of Britain and the founders of British Christianity, and that the native princes of Wales had been the rightful rulers of Britain. This claim to be the original inhabitants of the island explains certain peculiarities of the vocabulary used by the Welsh to describe themselves and their culture in this period – the word 'ancient/antient' is prominent in the titles of both John Parry and Maria Jane Williams's books, and it reverberates throughout the literary, historical and musical products of the period. Furthermore, Parry's volume was a collection of 'antient *British* music' because the Welsh were the original Britons, and their culture the original British culture. ('British' was often elaborated, with a latinised flourish, to 'Cambro-British', in acknowledgement of the latinised derivative of Cymru, 'Cambria'.) Ironically for a work of such scholarly rigour,

---

[7] Jenkins, *The Foundations of Modern Wales*, pp. 217–218.
[8] On the complicated distinctions between the antiquarian and the historian, see Rosemary Sweet, *Antiquaries: The Discovery of the Past in Eighteenth-Century Britain* (London and New York: Hambledon and London, 2004), chapter 1. As Sweet explains (pp. 49–56), clergymen were the dominant group not only among Welsh but among British antiquarians in this period
[9] Morgan, *The Eighteenth Century Renaissance*, p. 69.

Archaeologia Britannica seemed to give this way of thinking academic credibility.

Significant among those who followed unsteadily in Lhuyd's footsteps was Rev. Theophilus Evans (1693–1767), whose *Drych y Prif Oesoedd* (Mirror of the First Ages; 1716, second enlarged edition 1740)[10] influenced many Welsh people's understanding of their history well into the nineteenth century, presenting readers with 'at least the gist of Lhuyd's arguments'.[11] The book traced the 'history' of the Welsh from their supposed origins, through the arrival of Christianity in Britain, and asserted that the Established Church was the legitimate successor to the early British church. As such, it points to the cultural schizophrenia of many Welsh people of the period, who maintained loyalty to English institutions while being passionately interested in their own Welsh history and culture. Rev. Henry Rowlands (1655–1723) published *Mona Antiqua Restaurata* (Ancient Anglesey Restored; 1723, second edition 1766), and in so doing contributed a particularly colourful and beguiling element to the romanticised potpourri by popularising the image of the druid-bard resisting Roman oppression in the druidic stronghold of Anglesey. This was 'a theme which offered an ideal breeding-ground for idealists, dreamers and charlatans',[12] and it was taken up enthusiastically later in the century by Edward Williams (Iolo Morganwg; 1747–1826), the greatest of all inventors of Welsh traditions. For a radical like Iolo, inspired by the contemporary context of revolution in America and France, the druid-bard was a figure of 'resistance, egalitarianism, freedom, and peace'.[13] It captured his imagination, leading him to claim that he was one of two surviving druidic bards and to 'revive' the Gorsedd Beirdd Ynys Prydain (Assembly of the Bards of the Island of Britain), which had its inaugural meeting on 21 June 1792 – not in Wales, but on Primrose Hill in London.

The London-Welsh Societies

A strong current running through this chapter – one of the consequences of the Union and the close ties between Wales and London – is the emphasis

---

[10] The National Library of Wales has digitised two of the many later editions of *Drych y Prif Oesoedd*; the 1794 edition http://hdl.handle.net/10107/5218245 and the 1795 edition http://hdl.handle.net/10107/5216223.

[11] Morgan, *The Eighteenth Century Renaissance*, p. 90.

[12] Gwyn Thomas, 'Two Prose Writers: Ellis Wynne and Theophilus Evans', in *A Guide to Welsh Literature c. 1700–1800*, ed. by Branwen Jarvis (Cardiff: University of Wales Press, 2000), p. 33.

[13] Elizabeth Edwards, 'Romantic Wales and the Eisteddfod', in *The Cambridge History of Welsh Literature*, ed. by Evans and Fulton, pp. 292–293.

of many of its principal characters on the loyalty of the Welsh people to the Crown. Theophilus Evans was far from unusual in finding it unproblematic to be simultaneously 'a fervent monarchist' and 'a cultural patriot'.[14] In 1715 the Honourable and Loyal Society of Antient Britons was formed, the first of the London-Welsh societies. Primarily a charitable institution (supporting a Welsh school in London), it met annually on St David's Day, and as its name conspicuously advertised, it was also founded to defend the Welsh against any suspicion of Jacobite sympathies (with the previous royal House of Stuart) or disloyalty to the new Hanoverian Crown.[15] The Honourable Society of Cymmrodorion was founded in 1751. It has had three manifestations in the course of its history: the first lasted until 1787, when it was dissolved; it was then revived in 1820, and in this incarnation lasted until 1843; and finally it was revived again in 1873 and continues in active existence.

The membership of the 'First Cymmrodorion' overlapped substantially with that of the Antient Britons, but the Cymmrodorion had wider ambitions which included the cultural leadership of the Welsh in Wales, and literary and historical scholarship which aspired to the collection of 'all the scarce and valuable antient British MSS' and their publication in critical editions (a massive undertaking that went unrealised).[16] Its founder was Richard Morris (1702/3–79), originally from Anglesey but a London Welshman by the early 1720s. Lewis Morris (Llewelyn Ddu o Fôn; 1701–65), his elder brother, remained largely based in Wales, but it was he, nonetheless, who was the driving force of the scholarly and intellectual aims of the Cymmrodorion and who coined the name of the society, originally conceiving of it as 'cyn-frodorion' (roughly translating as 'the old native inhabitants').[17]

The Cymmrodorion membership (an individual member is a 'Cymmrodor') covered a wide social spectrum – it was a society where tradesmen and professionals mixed with the boneddigion. Among its membership were, for example, both Sir Watkin Williams Wynn, 4th Baronet (1749–89), owner of huge estates in Denbighshire, Merioneth, Montgomeryshire and Shropshire, and John Parry (John Parry Ruabon/

---

[14] Geraint H. Jenkins, 'Historical Writing in the Eighteenth Century', in *A Guide to Welsh Literature c. 1700–1800*, ed. by Jarvis, p. 28.
[15] For a detailed discussion of the Antient Britons, see Sarah Prescott, *Eighteenth-Century Writing from Wales: Bards and Britons* (Cardiff: University of Wales Press, 2008), chapter 1.
[16] R. T. Jenkins and Helen M. Ramage, *A History of the Honourable Society of Cymmrodorion and of the Gwyneddigion and Cymreigyddion Societies (1751–1951)* (London: The Honourable Society of Cymmrodorion, 1951), p. 78.
[17] Jenkins and Ramage, *History of the Honourable Society of Cymmrodorion*, p. 51.

Blind Parry; c.1710–82), his domestic harper. Wynn was perhaps the most liberal (indeed, spendthrift) patron of the arts of his generation, and a leading figure in London society. He was both Vice-President of the Antient Britons and the second 'Chief President' of the Cymmrodorion. He was not among the boneddigion who had a knowledge of the Welsh language, and he was undoubtedly anglicised and metropolitan, but the fact that he retained a domestic harper is significant for the place of Welsh music in the Celtic revival given that the harper was John Parry, who, with the help of his amanuensis, fellow harper and fellow Cymmrodor, Evan Williams (1706–?), was the compiler of *Antient British Music*.

The social breadth of the Cymmrodorion gave rise to tensions. In April 1770 Richard Morris noted enthusiastically that 'llawer o wŷr mawr wedi dyfod yn aelodau ... ac os Duw a gynnal fy hoedl nid wy'n ammau gweled holl bendefigion yn ein plith' ('many great men have become members ... and if God gives me life, I don't doubt to see all the aristocrats among us.').[18] However, the society also listed in its membership many tradesmen and artisans, and not everyone was as comfortable as Richard Morris purported to be among '[g]wŷr mawr'. There was also a sense among some of the membership that some rather dry and dusty scholarly avenues took precedence over other perhaps more congenial and vital ones at the Cymmrodorion meetings, and a number of other London-Welsh societies were formed in the late eighteenth and early nineteenth centuries, whose social make-up and political and intellectual interests were somewhat different.[19]

The society of greatest interest in this respect is the Gwyneddigion (Men of Gwynedd), established in 1770. Its membership overlapped with the Cymmrodorion, but its make-up was largely, though not exclusively, north Walian (as its name implies), 'rather more plebeian' than the Cymmrodorion[20] and inclined towards radical politics. Against the backdrop of revolution in France and sympathetic radical circles in London, in 1789 one of its founders, Owen Jones (Owain Myfyr; 1741–1814), declared that 'Rhydddid [sic] mewn Gwlad ac Eglwys yw amcan y Gymdeithas' ('Freedom in State and Church is the aim of the Society').[21] Two publications of particular significance came out of the work of the Gwyneddigion,

---

[18] Hugh Owen, ed., *Additional Letters of the Morrises of Anglesey (1735–1786)*, Vol. XLIX, Part II (London: The Honourable Society of Cymmrodorion, 1949), p. 767.
[19] A summary of these is given by Prys Morgan on the Cymmrodorion website www.cymmrodorion.org/the-society/our-history/ (accessed 4 December 2020).
[20] Glenda Carr, 'William Owen Pughe and the London Societies', in *A Guide to Welsh Literature c. 1700–1800*, ed. by Jarvis, p. 171.
[21] Letter from Owain Myfyr to Gwallter Mechain, 31 October 1789, GB-AB 1806E, letter 665.

and specifically of William Owen Pughe and Iolo Morganwg under the patronage of Owain Myfyr: *Barddoniaeth Dafydd ap Gwilym* (1789), a 'collected works' of the great medieval poet; and a three-volume collection of old Welsh poetry and prose writing, *The Myvyrian Archaiology of Wales* (1801–7), so-named in honour of Owain Myfyr. Iolo's contribution went somewhat beyond what his colleagues had imagined – both collections were subsequently discovered to have been laced with his forgeries. However, Volume 3 of *The Myvyrian Archaiology* is notable musically for its inclusion of a transcription by Iolo of the Robert ap Huw manuscript of harp music (see Chapter 4).[22]

In keeping with their 'plebeian' and radical leanings, the Gwyneddigion were concerned not only with historical and literary scholarship of the past but also with living traditions that were still to be observed, in the present, in the culture of the gwerin – the common people – and one of their main complaints against the Cymmrodorion was an insufficient interest in the *music* of Wales:

> One of their most important objects was the encouragement of Cambria's ancient minstrelsy; they retained a harper, and such of the members who could '*canu efo'r Delyn*', [sing to the harp] assisted in endeavouring to perpetuate the custom of chanting pennillion after the manner of our forefathers.[23]

It was also under the auspices of the Gwyneddigion that the eisteddfod, also kept just about alive in the culture of the gwerin, began to be revived. It had survived in north Wales in the 'irregular, beery' form[24] of the 'almanack eisteddfodau' (so-called because they were advertised in the popular almanacks of the period), which might involve no more than 'half a dozen poets and all the signs of apathy and dejection'.[25] The Gwyneddigion agreed to support the Bala Eisteddfod of 1789, seeing their chance 'to turn the eisteddfod into an Academy that would act as a forcing house for Welsh culture'.[26] Under the patronage of the Gwyneddigion, penillion singing featured in eisteddfodic competition, but the real object

---

[22] The Robert ap Huw manuscript survives in the British Library, GB-Lbl Add MS 14905. It is the subject of a special issue of *Welsh Music History/Hanes Cerddoriaeth Cymru* (see Vol. 3, 1999). The National Library of Wales has digitised all three volumes of *The Myvyrian Archaiology*: Vol. 1, http://hdl.handle.net/10107/4791917; Vol. 2, http://hdl.handle.net/10107/4797084; Vol. 3, http://hdl.handle.net/10107/4805623.
[23] William Leathart, *The Origin and Progress of the Gwyneddigion Society of London, Instituted 1770* (London: Hugh Pierce Hughes, 1831), p. 14.
[24] Hywel Teifi Edwards, *The Eisteddfod* (Cardiff: University of Wales Press, 1990), p. 3.
[25] Ibid., p. 11.   [26] Ibid., p. 13.

of the eisteddfod was for them the revival of strict-metre poetry, and it was not directly through their agency that the eisteddfod was to take on a distinctively musical character but rather through the 'provincial' Welsh societies and their eisteddfodau of 1819 to 1834.

The First Publications of Welsh Traditional Music

Whatever the limitations of the London-Welsh societies with respect to music, they did claim among their membership the key figures behind the first published collections of 'traditional Welsh melodies', as well as many of the subscribers who helped finance these books (mostly published, almost inevitably, in London). 'Welsh' melodies had appeared in several published collections in the early eighteenth century, the most notable of which was *Aria di Camera* (c.1726),[27] but the first of the significant publications that advertised its contents as specifically Welsh was *Antient British Music* in 1742.[28] Published as Part I, a second volume was intended but never appeared, though the unfinished manuscript turned up in the 1970s in the library of the Royal College of Music in London.[29] John Parry Ruabon and Evan Williams were already, some years before the founding of the Cymmrodorion, well enough acquainted with the Morrises to appeal to them as fellow scholars of Welsh history and culture. In a letter dated 28 October 1741, William Morris (1705–63) mentioned to Richard that a letter had arrived for Lewis from Evan Williams:

> Dyma lythr gida'r post heddyw oddiwrth Evan Delynior yna at y brawd i erchi ei gymorth; mae ef a Mr. John Parry ar fedr gwneuthur gwrthiau [*sic*]. The letter is an elaborate piece; all Welch; bad orthography, ag englyn i'r gelfyddyd.[30]
>
> (There's a letter in the post today from that Evan the harpist to [our] brother demanding his help; he and Mr John Parry are on the point of working miracles. The letter is an elaborate piece; all Welch; bad orthography, with an englyn to the art [of music, presumably].)

---

[27] For these earlier publications, see Wyn Thomas, *Cerddoriaeth Draddodiadol yng Nghymru: Llyfryddiaeth/Traditional Music in Wales: Bibliography*, 3rd ed. (Llanrwst: Gwasg Carreg Gwalch, 2006), pp. 12–13. *Aria di Camera* has been digitised by the National Library of Wales, http://hdl.handle.net/10107/4796728.

[28] Digitised by the National Library of Wales, http://hdl.handle.net/10107/4675582.

[29] GB-Lcm MS 4861.

[30] J. H. Davies, ed., *The Letters of Lewis, Richard, William and John Morris, of Anglesey (Morrisiaid Mon), 1728–1765*, Vol. 1 (Aberystwyth: published privately by the Editor, 1907), p. 60.

This was to result the following year in the publication of *Antient British Music*, a collection of twenty-four untitled melodies without words (Parry called them 'Arias', a familiar term for an English readership used to Italian musical terminology);[31] and it seems that Lewis did indeed provide considerable assistance. According to Richard Morris's annotations on his own copy of *Antient British Music*,[32] the 'historical account' that prefaces the book is to be attributed to Lewis.[33]

Lewis Morris was a noted and widely consulted antiquarian, and Richard and William passionately shared his intellectual and cultural interests. The Morris brothers embodied the combination of cultural patriotism and loyalty to the Union that underpinned so much Welsh thinking and scholarship of the period. They were also musical. They sang penillion and pursued an interest in traditional Welsh music. Richard had compiled a list of the names of traditional melodies[34] of assorted origin, and the considerable overlap between the contents of the list and the melodies in *Antient British Music* suggests that Lewis was not the only Morris brother who had a hand in Parry and Williams's research. Furthermore, Lewis had in his possession the Robert ap Huw manuscript, which he seems to have acquired through his connection with Owen Meyrick (1682–1760) of Bodorgan, Anglesey,[35] his employer. Richard inherited the manuscript on Lewis's death and left it with the rest of his library to the London Welsh School – where Iolo Morganwg transcribed it for *The Myvyrian Archaiology*.

On 30 December 1738, Lewis sent 'A New Year's Gift' to Owen Meyrick – an essay 'On the Cambro British Musick'. In it, he described the metres of 'the most common kinds of Penills' (verses), and mentions one, the '*Englyn Milwr* i.e. soldier's verse', for which he cites Lhuyd, who considered that it was 'one of the most Ancient, if not the very oldest sort of Verse we ever had; and that 'twas in this sort of Meeter the Druids taught their Disciples'.[36] Morris concluded this to be 'one of ye plainest marks

---

[31] For a detailed discussion of the melodies, see Kinney, *Welsh Traditional Music*, pp. 42–52.
[32] GB-Lbl Add MS 14939.
[33] Daniel Huws, 'Iolo Morganwg and Traditional Music', in *A Rattleskull Genius: The Many Faces of Iolo Morganwg*, ed. by Geraint H. Jenkins (Cardiff: University of Wales Press, 2009), pp. 334–335 and n. 8.
[34] See T. H. Parry-Williams, gol., *Llawysgrif Richard Morris o Gerddi [B.M. Add. Ms. 14, 992]* (Caerdydd: Gwasg Prifysgol Cymru, 1931).
[35] Stephen P. Rees and Sally Harper, 'Aspects of the Palaeography and History of the Robert ap Huw Manuscript/Agweddau ar Balaeograffeg a Hanes Llawysgrif Robert ap Huw', *Welsh Music History/Hanes Cerddoriaeth Cymru*, 3 (1999), 54–55.
[36] Edward Lhuyd, *Archaeologia Britannica, Giving Some Account Additional to What Has Been Hitherto Publish'd, of the Languages, Histories and Customs of the Original Inhabitants of Great Britain: From*

I can see of ye remains of druidical Learning left among us perhaps not to be met with in any other nation'.[37] The themes of his essay are enlarged upon in the introduction to *Antient British Music*, which also cites Rowlands's *Mona Antiqua Restaurata* as Morris's authority for druidism:

> The most antient Account we find of our British Music, is in the Time of the *Druids*, it being a very considerable Branch of the Pagan Religion. ... Mr. *Rowlands* points out the very Spot to be *Anglesey*, where their chief Schools were. *Ammianus Marcellinus*, who flourished about Three hundred and eighty Years after *Christ*, tells us, that the Tribe of them, called the *Bards*, sung in well-made Compositions to the *Lyra*, the heroic Acts of their great Men.[38]

Lewis was convinced that in the penillion metres lay proof of a druidic system for 'the transmission of learning and wisdom in such verse-forms, and so, too, the accompanying harp music',[39] and that the Welsh bardic tradition had therefore been directly handed down from the druids.

By 1760 he was not so confident. Writing to Richard, he had clearly been shaken into greater circumspection by challenges to his understanding of the druidic roots of Welsh music:

> Will not the flash about the Druids' music hurt Parry? Supposed to be the music of the Druids would have been better with men of sense. Let Jack Parry write to me and I'll give him all the assistance in my power. Let him send his plan or scheme and possibly I may judge something of the matter.[40]

Parry's 'scheme or plan' at this time was probably for *A Collection of Welsh, English and Scotch Airs* (1752 or 1761 – there is some ambiguity about the publication date).[41] If so, Lewis need not have worried, as the book makes no controversial claims of druidical heritage. The fact that it contains named tunes (rather than the generic 'arias' of *Antient British Music*) is worth pausing over, since it suggests a greater readiness to signal connections with Celtic culture – perhaps because Parry was now confident that a more overtly Celtic flavour would be marketable. Parry's final publication

---

Collections and Observations in Travels through Wales, Cornwal, Bas-Bretagne, Ireland and Scotland (Oxford: Printed at the Theater for the Author, 1707), p. 250.

[37] Owen, *Additional Letters*, Volume XLIX, Part I, pp. 72–80.

[38] John Parry and Evan Williams, *Antient British Music* (London: Printed for and sold by the Compilers, 1742), pp. 1–2.

[39] Huws, 'Iolo Morganwg', p. 335.

[40] Letter dated 'Penbryn, June 13th, 1760', J. H. Davies, ed., *The Letters of Lewis, Richard, William and John Morris of Anglesey (Morrisiaid Môn) 1728–1765*, Vol. II (Aberystwyth: Published privately by the Editor, 1909), p. 212.

[41] Digitised by the National Library of Wales, http://hdl.handle.net/10107/4675850.

was to be *British Harmony* (1781).[42] Dedicated 'with all due Esteem and Gratitude' to his patron Sir Watkin Williams Wynn, it is thought to have been published after Parry left London to return home to Ruabon. Again, the melodies appear without words, but as with *A Collection of Welsh, English and Scotch Airs*, the tunes have specific titles, and some are clearly connected with Welsh customs. While druids are not mentioned, Parry did specify on the title page that the melodies were 'The traditional Remains of those Originally Sung By the Bards of Wales'.

The next major publication of Welsh music also advertised its bardic heritage. This was *Musical and Poetical Relicks of the Welsh Bards* (1784, enlarged edition 1794), by Edward Jones (1752–1824).[43] Jones was harper to the Prince of Wales (the Prince Regent), subsequently George IV, and on this basis he himself laid claim to a bardic title: Bardd y Brenin (the King's Bard). He was a well-educated man embedded in the antiquarian networks of the day, and he corresponded widely in the research for his book. Though Lewis was long gone, the Morrises' hand is still to be traced in this process. In 1779, Richard Morris supplied Jones with another of his lists. Entitled 'Henwau Mesurau Cerdd Dafod a Thant a arferir yn gyffredinol gan y Prydyddion a'r Telynorion yng Nghymru' ('The names of poetic and musical measures generally used by the poets and harpists in Wales'), it identified those melodies that he considered to be specifically Welsh.[44] However, this is questionable since the Welsh tradition was oral, the provenance of the melodies was uncertain and many 'had been popular over such a long period in Wales that they had acquired Welsh names and were considered to be Welsh'.[45]

Jones emphasised his scholarship on the title page of *Relicks*, stating that they were 'preserved, by tradition and authentic manuscripts, from very remote antiquity', and including a lengthy prefatory essay entitled 'A History of the Bards and Druids'. Extensive footnotes cite – among many others – Edward Lhuyd, Theophilus Evans, Henry Rowlands and Lewis Morris, and his claim to have consulted 'authentic manuscripts' is underlined by references to collections of Welsh manuscripts 'in the

---

[42] Two copies, apparently of the same (1781) edition, have been digitised by the National Library of Wales, http://hdl.handle.net/10107/4675640 and http://hdl.handle.net/10107/5586333.
[43] The National Library of Wales has digitised the first edition, http://hdl.handle.net/10107/4675108, the second edition, http://hdl.handle.net/10107/4674868, and the fourth edition, http://hdl.handle.net/10107/4675201.
[44] Kinney, *Welsh Traditional Music*, p. 38. The 1779 list also appears on the last page of Richard Morris's personal copy of *Antient British Music*, GB-Lbl Add MS 14939.
[45] Kinney, *Welsh Traditional Music*, p. 39. See Kinney, chapter 4, for a discussion of the music in all three of Jones's publications.

Harleian Library, and in many other private Libraries in Wales'.[46] His account of the descent of Welsh music from the druids goes into considerable detail about druids and bards, explaining that they parted company with the expulsion of the druids from Britain by the Romans, when the bards 'lost their sacred Druidical character', but 'began to appear in an honourable, though less dignified capacity at the courts of the British kings'.[47] Jones's account concludes with the bard composing 'poetical effusions' on the harp for the Welsh princes,[48] thus dovetailing neatly with his own effusions to the Prince of Wales, his patron, with which he prefaced the volume.

The introductory essay in his second volume, *The Bardic Museum* (1802),[49] further emphasises the figure of the bard over the figure of the druid. As Bardd y Brenin, and in a climate of reaction to the revolutionary politics across the English Channel, he had good reason to wish to do so. While the druid was all too easily co-opted to the radical cause as a symbol of resistance to oppression, the bard could be portrayed as a comfortable inhabitant of royal courts, rubbing shoulders with princes. He again emphasises on the title page that the volume is 'drawn from authentic documents of remote antiquity'; but he also signals that there was another strand in his methodology, and that it was not reliant solely on antiquarian correspondence and archival research:

> The greatest part of these melodies I have committed to writing from hearing them sung by the old people, and from their being played by the most venerable Harpers, in North Wales; and it is very fortunate that I did so, because most of them are since dead. Being a native of Meirionydd, where our national customs are best retained, and where I generally used to pass my summers; being also well acquainted with most of the popular Welsh airs from my infancy, from having been brought up in the musical profession, and having always had a predilection for native customs; I may perhaps, have the advantage of my contemporaries on this subject.[50]

Jones mostly presented the melodies as harp tunes without words, though *Relicks* contains a few tunes with words in English, and a few with Welsh words. The majority of these are penillion tunes, perhaps because he did not consider other forms of traditional song 'venerable enough to be

---

[46] Edward Jones, *Musical and Poetical Relicks of the Welsh Bards* (London: Printed for the author, 1784, revised 1794), p. 1, asterisked footnote.
[47] Jones, *Musical and Poetical Relicks*, p. 9.   [48] Ibid., p. 13.
[49] Digitised by the National Library of Wales, http://hdl.handle.net/10107/4675439.
[50] Edward Jones, *The Bardic Museum* (London: A. Strahan, 1802), p. xi.

considered "relicks"'.[51] The changes Jones made to the enlarged 1794 edition add up to a greater anglicisation of the volume, presumably in deference to his English subscribers.[52] The few melodies with words in *The Bardic Museum* are entirely in English. By the time he was preparing the third and final volume, *Hên Ganiadau Cymru* (Old Songs of Wales; 1820, 1825),[53] he was ageing, ill and impoverished, and the book seems to show the signs; it is slimmer than the previous volumes and contains no scholarly essays. It was published in two parts, and Jones did not live to see the publication of the second, which came out posthumously the year after his death. However, his collections were a work of great scholarship in which antiquarian research met lived experience of the musical traditions of north Wales.

Jones's publications focused attention on Welsh traditional music at a time when the romantic discovery of the 'national airs' of the common people was a matter of widespread European interest[54] and Welsh airs were collected, or included in more mixed collections, by compilers who were not Welsh.[55] The most significant of these 'non-Welsh' publications was a three-volume work entitled *A Select Collection of Original Welsh Airs* (1809, 1811 and 1817) compiled by the Scottish publisher and collector of traditional music George Thomson (1757–1851). The melodies were 'United to Characteristic English Poetry', and arrangements were made at Thomson's behest by composers including Haydn and Beethoven – clearly indicating the sophisticated English-speaking market at which they were aimed.

Edward Jones's three volumes were the foundation for the popular consumption of Welsh music by the English and the anglicised Welsh in the nineteenth century, in the form of arrangements by another John Parry (Bardd Alaw; 1776–1851). Bardd Alaw came from a quite different musical background to the harp tradition in which John Parry Ruabon and Edward Jones had been raised. He had been a wind-instrument player in the Denbighshire Militia Band where he quickly rose to the position of bandmaster, and from which he moved on to London, establishing himself

---

[51] Huws, 'Iolo Morganwg', p. 336. [52] Kinney, *Welsh Traditional Music*, p. 63.
[53] The National Library of Wales has digitised a composite volume which it has tentatively dated 1825, http://hdl.handle.net/10107/4675268.
[54] See Matthew Gelbart, *The Invention of 'Folk Music' and 'Art Music': Emerging Categories from Ossian to Wagner* (Cambridge: Cambridge University Press, 2011), and Karen McAulay, *Our Ancient National Airs: Scottish Song Collecting from the Enlightenment to the Romantic Era* (Farnham: Ashgate, 2013).
[55] William Bingley, *Sixty of the Most Admired Welsh Airs* (London: E. Williams, 1803); William Crotch, *Specimens of Various Styles of Music* ... (London: Robert Birchall, 1806–7).

as a conductor and composer at Vauxhall Gardens. He had an entrepreneurial eye for the promotion of Welsh music, and his publications did a great deal to popularise it and bring it to the attention of an English audience. A member of the Gwyneddigion and the 'Registrar of Music' of the Second Cymmrodorion on its reconstitution in 1820, he was another Welshman who succeeded in subscribing simultaneously to a proud cultural patriotism and deference to English institutions and values. In his approach to arranging Welsh music for an anglicised market, he 'mangl[ed] the tunes and chang[ed] the titles arbitrarily, but he also published them out of pride in his country and a desire to show its unique culture'.[56] In 1809 he published *A Selection of Welsh Melodies*, swiftly following it with two further volumes, *A Collection of Welch Airs* and *National Melodies* (both 1810), but his most important publication was *The Welsh Harper*, of which the first volume was published in 1839, the second in 1848.[57] The first volume was explicitly drawn from the work of Edward Jones and John Parry Ruabon – it was, as its subtitle explained, 'an extensive collection of Welsh music, including most of the contents of the three volumes published by the late Edward Jones ... also several airs from the publications of the late Mr Parry of Ruabon'. The second volume was to be largely a product of his association with John Jenkins (Ifor Ceri; 1770–1829), with whom he was closely involved in the development of the Provincial Eisteddfodau (Eisteddfodau Taleithiol) and especially the introduction of music into the eisteddfod, though Bardd Alaw's influence would quickly come to be regarded by some as a mixed blessing.

Welsh Societies in Wales and Their Eisteddfodau

If the London-Welsh societies can be said to have emerged (directly and indirectly) from the enthusiasm of the Morris brothers, Ifor Ceri fulfils a similar role in the move to establish 'provincial' Welsh societies and eisteddfodau in Wales after the Napoleonic wars. Ifor Ceri's great passion was Welsh traditional song. Born in Cardiganshire, he graduated from Oxford and was ordained into the Established Church. He became vicar of Kerry (Ceri) in Montgomeryshire, and here he extended an annual New Year invitation to 'poets, harpists and singers' and his fellow clergy to spend time 'in singing Welsh songs to the harp, and in composing and reciting

---

[56] Kinney, *Welsh Traditional Music*, p. 163.
[57] The National Library of Wales has digitised both volumes as a single item, http://hdl.handle.net/10107/4675974.

poetry'[58] – hence his pseudonym 'Ifor Ceri', after Ifor Hael (Ifor the Generous), the patron of Dafydd ap Gwilym. The idea for 'Cambrian Societies' in Wales which would support local eisteddfodau came out of these meetings – it was the creation of a small group of clerics including Ifor Ceri's close friend and colleague David Rowland, curate of St Peter's, Carmarthen and first Secretary of the Cambrian Society of Dyfed, and Thomas Burgess, the (English) bishop of St Davids. Burgess's involvement says much about the character and underlying values of the Cambrian Societies and the Provincial Eisteddfodau.

There were ten Provincial Eisteddfodau, the first (Carmarthen) in 1819, the last (Cardiff) in 1834, and their patronage was markedly different in character from the radical-leaning Gwyneddigion and their patronage of the eisteddfodau of the late 1780s and 1790s. The Carmarthen Eisteddfod of 1819, supported by the newly formed Cambrian Society of Dyfed, set the pattern. While it was notable on the one hand for the introduction by Iolo Morganwg of the gorsedd into the proceedings of the modern eisteddfod, on the other, any hint of Iolo's radicalism was more than counterbalanced by the weight of the official patrons of the event, Lord Dynevor and George III himself. The set subjects for the poetry competitions indicate the tone of the proceedings – where the Gwyneddigion at the St Asaph eisteddfod of 1791 had set 'Liberty' as the topic of their main competition, the subjects at Carmarthen included an 'Ode on the Death of our late Queen', and an 'Ode on the lamented Death of General Picton' at Waterloo[59] (though it must be said that the Gwyneddigion themselves were distinctly less radical by 1819).

It was at Carmarthen that the eisteddfod took on a conspicuously musical character – a change which seems to have been largely down to Ifor Ceri himself.[60] In addition to the usual competitions for poetry, prose and penillion, in the evenings there were 'Concerts of Instrumental and Vocal Music', the programmes for which included the 'masterly performances' of the Harmonic Society of Bath.[61] In a detailed letter to David Rowland, Ifor Ceri set out a programme for a 'Concert at Carmarthen July 9 1819 For the Benefit of the Harpers and the encouragement of the National Music', in which the participation of musicians from both the

---

[58] Jenkins and Ramage, *The Honourable Society of Cymmrodorion*, p. 142.
[59] Cathryn Charnell-White, *Welsh Poetry of the French Revolution, 1789–1805* (Cardiff: University of Wales Press), pp. 32–33.
[60] Leila Salisbury, 'Jenkins, John (Ifor Ceri: 1770–1829)', in *Cydymaith i Gerddoriaeth Cymru*, goln. Pwyll ap Siôn a Wyn Thomas (Talybont: Y Lolfa, 2018), t. 267.
[61] Letter to the Editor, *The Cambrian*, 24 July 1819, p. 3.

Carmarthenshire and the Cardiganshire Militia Bands was to be enlisted. The programme alternated traditional melodies performed by the entrants to the harp competition with pieces from European repertoire, including Johann Paul Aegidius Martini's 'Overture to Henry 4th' and a Sinfonia by Giovanni Battista Lampugnani. Ceri's intention was to highlight 'the National Instrument the Harp, as frequently as possible, and Welsh Airs: But the Other Music will assist the effect and afford Variety.'[62] However, he quickly came to regret the innovation, as a pattern was established that was to be typical of the Provincial Eisteddfodau whereby the musical competitions were followed by evening entertainments and concerts of sacred music, for which both local band musicians and (increasingly) more sophisticated performers from London and the spa towns of Bath or Cheltenham were brought in. From 1820 onwards Bardd Alaw directed the musical events, and Ifor Ceri watched with increasing disquiet as this aspect of the eisteddfodau turned into what he regarded as 'an Anglo-Italian farce'.[63] It is perhaps just as well that he did not live to witness the Cardiff Eisteddfod of 1834 (by now described as the Gwent and Dyfed 'Royal Eisteddfod'), for which some of the most celebrated musicians from London, well known on the English provincial music festival circuit, were engaged to perform.[64] The programmes included works by Mozart, Handel and Corelli:

> [A]t the evening concert ... Mr and Mrs Wm. Knyvet, Braham, Miss Stephens and Miss Bishop gave us many very pretty popular things, and Parry (Bardd Alaw) sang and played on the Harp as did his son. Welsh airs were introduced as much as possible and with good effect, and I was highly delighted by one of Handel's Trios, played by Cramer, Linley and Dragonetti – it was perfection[.]

The audience was reminded of the Welshness of the context primarily by Bardd Alaw bringing on to the stage

> the N[orth]. W[ales]. Harper blind Robert ... [to] play 'Sweet Richard' on the triple string'd harp; this he did with beautiful variations in the most light, delicate, and brilliant manner imaginable ... it was very striking, the modest, natural manner of the aged mild-looking, blind man, with his grey head and his grateful, rustic bows to the audience, and his plain, unadorned old Harp, contrasted with the scientific performers around him.[65]

---

[62] GB-AB Add. 587B (Celynog 61), pp. 24–27.   [63] Edwards, *The Eisteddfod*, p. 16.
[64] See, for example, 'Proceedings at the Gwent and Dyfed Royal Eisteddfod', *The Cambrian*, 30 August 1834, 4.
[65] Lady Greenly to Mrs. Hastings, 22 August 1834, transcribed in GB-AB Maxwell Fraser Papers, 1912–1980 CB/6, pp. 41–42.

This somewhat jarring juxtaposition of the 'scientific' London musicians and the 'grateful, rustic' Welsh harper suggests very clearly some of the reasons for Ifor Ceri's growing unease. Furthermore, the cost of putting on such concerts was substantial – the music at the Beaumaris Eisteddfod of 1832 accounted for £600, half the total costs of the eisteddfod, which was left in debt for £89 – and it became a significant factor in the demise of the Provincial Eisteddfodau.[66]

The Provincial Eisteddfodau are notable, however, for another musical innovation, again at Ifor Ceri's behest, one that would have a significant impact on the scholarship of Welsh traditional music. At the Powys Eisteddfod of 1824, he sponsored and judged a competition for 'the best collection of [previously unpublished] old Welsh Tunes' – 'the first competition of its kind in any eisteddfod'.[67] Two collections were put forward, both of melodies without words, but a precedent had been set that would fulfil its potential in the Abergavenny Eisteddfod of 1837, organised by the Cymreigyddion y Fenni (the Abergavenny Welsh Society).

The enthusiasm generated by the original Cambrian Societies and the Provincial Eisteddfodau prompted the foundation of further local societies (as well as the reconstitution of the Cymmrodorion in 1820). Of all of them, the Cymreigyddion y Fenni, founded in 1833, was perhaps the most significant in terms of the musical and literary scholarship that came out of it. It gave rise to the Welsh Manuscripts Society, founded in 1836, which continued until the 1860s and which was responsible for some significant publications including the manuscripts of Iolo Morganwg, published in 1848 and edited by Iolo's son, Taliesin Williams (Taliesin ab Iolo; 1787–1847) and Thomas Price (Carnhuanawc; 1787–1848), though the Society's editorial standards declined after their day.

Carnhuanawc was the intellectual force behind the Cymreigyddion y Fenni. An exceptional and inspirational figure, he was a noted antiquarian, a member of the Gwyneddigion, and a keen supporter of the Provincial Eisteddfodau. He was a close friend of Ifor Ceri and shared his love of Welsh traditional music. Born in a rural parish near Builth Wells in the historical county of Brecknockshire, he was the son of a Welsh-speaking clergyman and was himself ordained into the Established Church. Although his formal education was limited, he was a clever

---

[66] Hywel Teifi Edwards, *Yr Eisteddfod: Cyfrol Ddathlu Wythganmlwyddiant yr Eisteddfod, 1176–1976* (Llandysul: Llys yr Eisteddfod Genedlaethol gyda chymorth Cyngor Celfyddydau Cymru, 1976), t. 43.

[67] Meredydd Evans, 'Pwy Oedd "Orpheus" Eisteddfod Llangollen 1858?/Who Was "Orpheus" of the 1858 Llangollen Eisteddfod?', *Welsh Music History/Hanes Cerddoriaeth Cymru*, 5 (2002), 65.

child and a compulsive self-educator, and he spent a great deal of time at the home of the historian Theophilus Jones (1759–1812). His friendship with Jones was a significant one, drawing him into a line of Welsh scholarship that included not only Jones himself, who was then working on the second volume of his *History of the County of Brecknock* (for which Carnhuanawc drew illustrations), but also Jones's celebrated grandfather, Theophilus Evans.

Recounting childhood memories, Carnhuanawc remembered in some detail several players of the single-string harp: 'Old Sam' (Samuel Davies), a harper from Builth Wells, 'Old David Watkins' of Brecon, and 'Old Daniel' of Llanwrtyd Wells. The triple harp was, he said, a rarity in the area, although he remembered the visits of Thomas Blayney, a triple-harp player from North Wales. He blamed Methodism for a deleterious effect on Welsh musical culture:

> Dancing was altogether discouraged as profane. My father told me that he remembered an old man, I think about Llangammarch or Abergwessin; who played the harp, but who joined the Methodists or Dissenters and then gave up the harp, and threw it under the bed, where it lay till it got unglewed and worm-eaten, and fell to pieces.[68]

He learned to play the harp with David Watkins and recalled in particular learning the tune 'Pys a Menin' (known in English as 'Butter and Pease').[69] He remained fascinated by the Welsh harp tradition throughout his life, regarding both the single-string and the triple harp as native instruments. The historian Jane Williams (Ysgafell; 1806–85), who wrote a memoir of him, describes among his papers a 'large folio volume, bound in green cloth' in which he kept notes on 'Welsh Music', and which she surmised had been 'intended, perhaps, for some work of yet indefinite form'.[70] If it was intended for publication, this never came to fruition, but he corresponded widely on Welsh music with other scholars and was closely involved with the preparation of Bardd Alaw's *The Welsh Harper*.[71]

At the heart of the Cymreigyddion y Fenni was a group of women scholars and enthusiasts for Welsh culture. Several significant publications came out of this group – most notably the translation of the *Mabinogion* (1838–49) by Charlotte Guest (1812–95) for the Welsh Manuscripts Society, in which she drew on the help of her fellow Cymreigyddion Carnhuanawc and Rev. John Jones (Tegid/Ioan Tegid; 1792–1852); and *Ancient National*

---

[68] Jane Williams (Ysgafell), *The Literary Remains of The Rev. Thomas Price, Carnhuanawc*, Vol. 2 (Llandovery and London: William Rees/Longman & Co., 1855), pp. 42–43.
[69] Ibid., pp. 20–23 and pp. 42–43. [70] Ibid., pp. 393–394. [71] Ibid., pp. 398–399.

Airs of Gwent and Morganwg by Maria Jane Williams (Llinos; 1795–1873). The group also included Jane Williams Ysgafell and Lady Elizabeth Greenly (1771–1839), a patron of Iolo Morganwg. The most colourful character among them was undoubtedly Augusta Hall, later Lady Llanover (Gwenynen Gwent; 1802–96), an arch-inventor of Welsh traditions, of which she is best remembered for Welsh 'traditional' dress. Although she grew up in Monmouthshire, she was English, and while it is unclear quite what sparked her impassioned championship of Welsh culture, her interest gained focus and direction when she first met Carnhuanawc, probably at the second Brecon Eisteddfod in 1826. He became a central figure in her circle; it seems likely, for example, that her partisanship for the triple harp was based on Carnhuanawc's authority, and a domestic harper was always employed at Llanover Court under Augusta Hall and her husband Benjamin. The Halls acquired the greater part of Iolo Morganwg's manuscripts on the death of Taliesin ab Iolo, and these were ultimately deposited in the National Library of Wales.[72] The Halls' connections also brought European scholars into the Cymreigyddion's orbit – notably the Breton art historian and theologian Alexis-François Rio, and Augusta Hall's brother-in-law, the Prussian diplomat, philologist and historian, Charles (Christian Karl Josias) Bunsen. The Halls' influence attracted interest in the Cymreigyddion from yet further afield: the 1842 Abergavenny Eisteddfod was attended by Chandra Mohan Chatterjee (see Figure 8.1), representing his uncle Dwarkanath Tagore of the Tagore dynasty of immensely wealthy merchants and free-thinking writers, philosophers and artists, who was on a visit to Britain and taking London society by storm.[73]

The members of the Llanover circle were at the forefront of contemporary life in south Wales, embedded in industrial concerns, landownership and national and local politics. Augusta Hall's husband Benjamin Hall was a Member of Parliament (MP), landowner and industrialist; Charlotte Guest's husband Josiah John Guest was a major industrialist and an MP for Merthyr Tydfil; the Williamses were an old Welsh gentry family, recently enriched through the ownership of coal and iron ore mines, and William Williams, Maria Jane's brother, was briefly Sheriff of Glamorgan. And this was a period of significant industrial, political and social unrest, much of it very local indeed. The Scotch Cattle (1820s–30s) – a secret society

---

[72] GB-AB MSLLANOV Llanover Manuscripts.
[73] Maxwell Fraser, 'Sir Benjamin and Lady Hall in the 1840's: Part I: 1840–1845', *The National Library of Wales Journal/Cylchgrawn Llyfrgell Genedlaethol Cymru*, 14/1 (1965), 41. For Dwarkanath Tagore and the Tagore dynasty, see *Oxford Dictionary of National Biography* (Oxford: Oxford University Press, 2008).

Figure 8.1 The visit of Chandra Mohan Chatterjee to the 1842 Abergavenny Eisteddfod. The loyalty of the Cymreigyddion to the Crown is prominently displayed in the letters 'VR' (Victoria Regina); a banner bearing the name 'Victoria' hangs at the back of the marquee. *Illustrated London News*, 22 October 1842

of industrial workers who punished strike-breakers and attacked company property – were active in Monmouthshire, just down the road from Llanover Court and Abergavenny; William Williams had only just relinquished his office as Sheriff when the Merthyr Rising (1831) broke out; and the Chartist rising (1839) culminated violently in Newport a few miles south of Llanover Court. (John Frost, its leader, had worked for Benjamin Hall, and Hall was called to give evidence at his trial for treason.) No one was more aware of the contemporary context than the boneddigion of the Cymreigyddion y Fenni, but their interest in Welsh culture was no mere distraction from what was going on locally. They regarded the revival of Welsh traditions and the perpetuation of the language as a safeguard against the climate of protest and radicalism they saw building up around them, referring to their efforts as the promotion of 'nationality'. As Augusta Hall put it in a prize-winning essay submitted to the 1834 Cardiff Eisteddfod:

> Nationality is the soil in which all good feelings flourish ... The Welsh have long and faithfully served the ancestors of the King of Great Britain. ... They have been exemplary in their allegiance in times of trouble and discontent, and the continuance of their loyalty is *best promoted* by encouraging the preservation of that fine language ... [W]e must by no means overlook the firm and hitherto impenetrable barrier it has presented to the progress of sedition and infidelity[.][74]

The word 'nationality' resonates in the writings of the Cymreigyddion y Fenni, not quite in its modern sense but as a feeling of identity fed by language and tradition – and it functioned rather as 'ancient' and 'British' had in an earlier period, as a touchstone for loyalty to the Crown and the Union rooted in the original Britishness of the Welsh.

Collecting Welsh Folk Song

At the 1837 Abergavenny Eisteddfod, Lady Greenly offered a prize, and the terms in which she couched it were significant – it was to be awarded 'For the best collection of original unpublished Welsh airs, with the words as sung by the peasantry of Wales'.[75] That is, it asked not simply for traditional melodies but specifically for the *songs* of the common people, with their Welsh-language words. This marked a major shift of both emphasis and methodology, from the collection of instrumental airs grounded in antiquarian research to the collection of folk songs[76] largely by transcribing them directly from their singers. The winner was Maria Jane Williams, and in second place came John Thomas (Ieuan Ddu; 1795–1871). Both would go on to publish collections of Welsh traditional songs.[77]

---

[74] Gwenynen Gwent (Mrs. Hall of Llanover), *Gwent and Dyfed Royal Eisteddfod 1834. The Prize Essay on the Advantages Resulting from the Preservation of the Welsh Language and National Costumes of Wales* (London: Longman, Rees, Orme, Brown, Green and Longman; Cardiff: William Bird, 1836), pp. 7–8.

[75] Evans, 'Who Was "Orpheus"', 65.

[76] 'Folk song' has been a contested term – see, for example, Dave Harker, *Fakesong: The Manufacture of British Folk Song, 1700 to the Present Day* (Milton Keynes: Open University Press, 1985); but it is widely used in the context of the study and performance of Welsh traditional songs – from its foundation in 1906, the English-language name of Cymdeithas Alawon Gwerin Cymru has remained the Welsh Folk-Song Society.

[77] Both have been digitised by the National Library of Wales: Williams, *Ancient National Airs of Gwent and Morganwg*, http://hdl.handle.net/10107/5726885; Thomas, *The Cambrian Minstrel/Y Caniedydd Cymreig*, http://hdl.handle.net/10107/5727212.

Maria Jane Williams was not, however, the first Welsh person to collect folk songs directly from the people who still sung them. That title goes to Iolo Morganwg, among whose papers are over sixty songs and airs, probably collected between about 1795 and 1806, largely in Iolo's native Glamorgan. Though he has become notorious for his literary forgeries, the songs he notated are apparently more or less untainted by inventions. Yet more surprisingly, in spite of his captivation by the idea of the druid-bard, Iolo's (unpublished) collection was uncontaminated by the claims of druidic heritage that clothed so much of the published Welsh music of the day.[78] Daniel Huws points out that while his musical knowledge was basic, in some respects he was a better judge than, say, Edward Jones had been of the likely origins of Welsh folk songs: his knowledge of the rhythmic patterns of Welsh poetry gave him 'a surer feeling for what was primitive' (while the fact that he counted Lewis Morris among his many bêtes noires 'might alone have been sufficient to immunize Iolo against associating Welsh music with the Druids'[79]).

Also ahead of Maria Jane Williams was Ifor Ceri, who far outstripped Iolo in the sheer number and variety of songs he collected. He transcribed some as they were sung to him, others from memory, and still others were collected by friends, again sometimes from memory and sometimes directly transcribed from the singers.[80] Whether from ignorance of the modal tonalities in which folk songs were actually sung or a pragmatic desire to produce versions that would be widely used, he rendered the melodies diatonically. He left three manuscript volumes (with some overlap between them): 'Melus-geingciau Deheubarth Cymru' ([c.1815]; 'The Sweet Melodies of South Wales')[81], and two volumes of 'The Melodies of Wales' (both translate literally as 'Sweet Sounds of Wales'): 'Melus-seiniau Cymru' ([1817]–[1825]) and 'Per-seiniau Cymru' ([1824]–[1825]).[82] Motivated by his sense that, driven by the influence of Methodism, 'A rapid change was taking place in the habits and manners of our country people', he concluded that:

> unless a collection was made at present of the Hen Donau [Old Tunes], Marwnadau [Elegies], Carolau [Carols], &c. Cymru, it would be in vain to

---

[78] Huws, 'Iolo Morganwg', p. 333.   [79] Ibid., pp. 336–337.
[80] Kinney, *Welsh Traditional Music*, pp. 138–141.
[81] GB-AB JLLW, Dr J. Lloyd Williams Music MSS and Papers, AH1/34.
[82] Digitised by the National Library of Wales: 'Melus-seiniau Cymru', GB-AB MS 1940iA, http://hdl.handle.net/10107/4655107; 'Per-seiniau Cymru', GB-AB MS 1940iiA, http://hdl.handle.net/10107/4654909; 'Melus-geingciau Deheubarth Cymru', GB-AB J. Lloyd Williams AH1/34, http://hdl.handle.net/10107/4655492.

look for them in thirty years time; they would be superseded by strains of a very different description (and in my opinion of very inferior quality) under the name of hymns.[83]

His collection amounted to several hundred songs, none of which he ever published himself. Rather, with the generosity for which he was known, he sent 258 of them to Bardd Alaw,[84] and many later appeared in Volume 2 of *The Welsh Harper*.

An early hint of what would become *Ancient National Airs of Gwent and Morganwg* and of the work of collection that lay behind it is given by Lady Greenly, in a vivid description of first hearing Maria Jane Williams singing some of the songs, at Llanover Court a few days before the 1836 Abergavenny Eisteddfod:

> Tuesday to dinner came ... the Miss Williams of Aberpergwm. The youngest, Miss Jane, has a fine voice, and is very musical. She sang to us several beautiful airs which she had learned of an old woman in the Glamorganshire hills now 70 years old, but still having a good voice – she learned them of her mother, who lived to 95 and so traced them back for centuries transmitted orally, never written down. They are of a very different character to any Welsh music I ever heard before, are plaintive or devotional, with a touching wildness, Miss Jane Williams intends to have them written down, for she knows no one who sings them, besides this one old woman. But I remember Margaret Rickards used to tell me of them as being sung among the hills, and I have heard wild notes along the mountain sides from the Peasants, in my rambles with her. There are Welsh words to them all, and each has its separate title. One is called 'Aderyn pêr' (the pretty bird). Miss Jane W. said she believed she knew 100 of them.[85]

Though the publication took another seven years to appear, Maria Jane Williams set about preparing it within a year of winning Lady Greenly's prize. The book was to contain forty-three songs. Like other early folk-song collectors, she notated them using modern diatonic keys rather than the traditional modes. Whether she made other interventions to the melodies is uncertain, though Daniel Huws has drawn attention to the unusual amount of ornamentation they include.[86] There were certainly

---

[83] Daniel Huws, 'Melus-Seiniau Cymru: Atodiadau', *Canu Gwerin/Folk Song*, 9 (1986), 47. The letter is in the National Library of Wales, GB-AB MS 1882B.
[84] GB-AB JLLW, Dr J. Lloyd Williams Music MSS and Papers, AH4/3.
[85] Lady Greenly to Mrs Hastings, Llanover, 28 November 1836, transcribed in GB-AB Maxwell Fraser Papers CB/6, p. 65.
[86] Daniel Huws, 'Introduction', in *Ancient National Airs of Gwent and Morganwg*, ed. by Maria Jane Williams, facsimile edition (Aberystwyth: Cymdeithas Alawon Gwerin Cymru/The Welsh Folk-Song Society, 1988), p. xxxiv.

interventions to the words. Taliesin ab Iolo offered to 'look over and correct' them, and Maria Jane wrote to him gratefully accepting, and saying apologetically that '*Some of the poetry* is not of the *first class* and I wish you would substitute some better – indeed there are two by which I have put a cross are sad trash.'[87] In fact, she had initially not intended to publish the words at all, only the melodies; but if the words were to be included, she wanted them polished, and English rhyming translations printed alongside the music. Accordingly, Taliesin ab Iolo stripped out local Welsh dialect, replaced it with standardised Welsh and translated it into English rhyme. Seven of the songs were published with his alternative words in place of the originals.[88]

Her motivation is not hard to work out. Like others of their class, the Williamses moved comfortably in London-Welsh society, where Maria Jane was noted for her singing. Accordingly, the publication was to be financed by the common practice of signing up a list of subscribers, many of whom were London-based. Augusta Hall (whom she pressed to get royal permission for the book's dedication to Queen Victoria) certainly understood her thinking, and disapproved. Writing to Taliesin ab Iolo, she commented darkly, 'I know well the class Miss W. is most anxious to please in London.'[89] She was not happy about the idea of English rhyming translations, and it was probably she who called in Tegid as an ally. Tegid urged Maria Jane not to submit to the demands of an English market, but to print only free, unrhymed translations and to put them in the back of the volume as notes. In the end, Taliesin ab Iolo's tidied-up Welsh and rhyming translations remained, but Tegid did win a compromise in getting the translations relegated to the notes, so that the songs are presented on the page with only the Welsh texts (although the titles are translated, and the performance directions given in English).

Ancient National Airs of Gwent and Morganwg can be seen as the culmination of the Celtic revival's rehabilitation of Welsh traditional music: a progression from antiquarian research into the origins of that music to collecting it 'in the field', and a shift in focus from mythicised druids to the gwerin, the common people. It certainly laid the ground for the major work of folk-song collection that was to come with the foundation of the Welsh Folk-Song Society more than fifty years later. But there is also a constant in the story – the deployment of traditional culture, particularly in times when there might be reason to doubt the loyalty of the Welsh, as evidence of their literally and figuratively harmonious national character.

---

[87] Quoted in ibid., p. xxx.   [88] Ibid., p. xxxiii.   [89] Ibid., p. xxx.

CHAPTER 9

Musical Communications in the Long Nineteenth Century

Rhidian Griffiths

The long nineteenth century was a period of change in Welsh society, with growing industrialisation and improved means of communication. Religion, particularly nonconformity, dominated much of Welsh life and permeated culture at almost every level. In musical terms the period is remarkable for the growth in amateur music making and the emergence of writers on music and publishers, and though much of this activity was on a limited scale, it was underpinned by striking enthusiasm. Choral and congregational singing grew in popularity, and tonic sol-fa became a widespread musical currency which aided the dissemination of music in Wales.

Music Literature and Journalism

The story begins with the publication in 1797 of *Cyfaill mewn Llogell* (A Friend in the Pocket), a short music primer written by a Baptist minister, John Williams (c.1750–1807), who was known – because of his interest in singing – as 'Siôn Singer' (see Figure 9.1). Not only is it the first book on music to be printed in Wales, by John Daniel of Carmarthen; certain aspects of its history reflect something of the culture which gave it birth.[1] Only one copy is known to survive, and the likelihood is that very few copies were printed: it was reissued in 1810 as *Difyrwch i'r Pererinion* (Pilgrims' Delight).[2] It had been a long while in gestation, as it had been advertised as early as 1779.[3] Facilities for printing music were as yet

---

[1] John Parry's *British Harmony* of 1781 bears the imprint 'Printed for & Sold by John Parry, Ruabon, Denbighshire' but was printed in London. Digitised by the National Library of Wales http://hdl.handle.net/10107/4675640.
[2] Digitised by the National Library of Wales, http://hdl.handle.net/10107/5212315.
[3] William Rowlands ('Gwilym Lleyn'), *Llyfryddiaeth y Cymry/Cambrian Bibliography* (Llanidloes: John Pryse, 1869), p. 595; Eiluned Rees, *Libri Walliae* (Aberystwyth: Llyfrgell Genedlaethol Cymru/National Library of Wales, 1987), no. 5326.

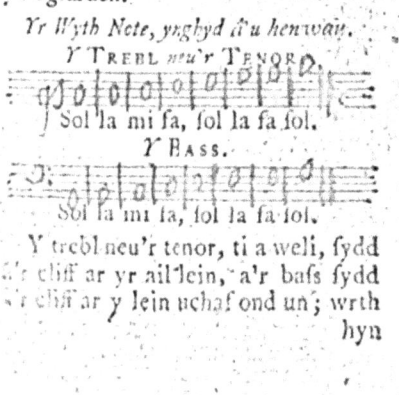

Figure 9.1 A page from *Cyfaill mewn Llogell* by John Williams and printed by John Daniel of Carmarthen: the first book printed in Wales to contain musical notation. The stave lines are printed, but the notes are added by hand. Photographic copy at Llyfrgell Genedlaethol Cymru – National Library of Wales

undeveloped in Wales, and in both the 1797 and 1810 editions, while music staves were printed, notes were entered by hand on individual copies, in the absence of suitable music type. The same was true of *The Rudiments of Thorough Bass* by 'An Amateur of Pembroke' (1810) and *Agoriad Byr ar y Gamut* (A Brief Introduction to the Gamut), published in a hymn collection in 1811.[4] Evidently the world in which these were created was

---

[4] *The Rudiments of Thorough Bass* is known only from a catalogue description of 1863; *Agoriad Byr ar y Gamut* is a version of John Williams's text contained within *Pigion o Hymnau* (Choice Hymns) by

fragile and limited. Nevertheless, the fact of their publication suggests that interest in music was emerging as a part of Welsh native culture, particularly in the context of the religious revivals of the eighteenth century which had made hymn singing popular as a musical activity.

Cyfaill mewn Llogell was followed by other works which attempted to provide instruction in music, among them *Y Caniedydd Crefyddol* (The Religious Singer), by William Owen (Gwilym Ddu Glan Hafren; 1788–1838) of Newtown in 1828, and *Egwyddorion Peroriaeth* (The Principles of Music), by Hugh Evans (1790–1853) of Cerrigydrudion, published in 1837. The printers of both had become adept at using music type. Some instruction in the rudiments also formed a preface to collections of tunes, such as *Mawl yr Arglwydd* (The Praise of the Lord) by John Ellis (1760–1839), published in 1816: this is the first music known to have been printed on Welsh soil (but from plates engraved in London), at Trefriw in the Conwy Valley. As late as 1852, the tune collection *Cydymaith yr Addolydd* (The Worshipper's Companion) by Robert Williams (1804–55), intended for the use of Welsh-speaking Wesleyan congregations, contained thirty-four pages of guidance on how to read music, written by the book's printer, John Mendus Jones of Llanidloes.

Llanidloes had become a significant centre of musical activity, and a new benchmark was set there in 1838 when John Mills (1812–73), one of a talented local family who had considerable influence on music making in mid-Wales, published his *Gramadeg Cerddoriaeth* (Grammar of Music), which ran to four editions between 1838 and 1862.[5] Another member of this family, Richard Mills (1809–44), published practical instruction books with tunes and simple anthems for singing. Issued in three parts between 1842 and 1845, *Yr Arweinydd Cerddorol* (The Music Guide), which like many others at that time used dialogue as a technique of instruction, had as its aim the support of musical societies and singing meetings:

> y rhai mewn amryw ranau o'r wlad ydynt yn arferol o gynal eu cyfarfodydd yn wythnosol, dros yspaid oddeutu tri mis, yn nhymor y gauaf.[6]

> (which in several parts of the country are used to holding their meetings weekly, for a period of three months, in the wintertime.)

John James (1777–1848): Rees, *Libri Walliae*, nos. 4531, 2669. *Cyfaill mewn Llogell* and *Difyrwch i'r Pererinion* also contained a selection of hymns.

[5] Richard Mills and N. Cynhafal Jones, *Buchdraeth y Parch. John Mills* (Aberdar: Mills a Lynch, 1881), tt. 51–52; digitised by the National Library of Wales, http://hdl.handle.net/10107/5578818.

[6] Richard Mills, *Yr Arweinydd Cerddorol*, y rhan gyntaf (Llanidloes: John Mendus Jones, ail arg. 1844), 'Rhagymadrodd'. The (posthumous) third edition of *Yr Arweinydd Cerddorol* may be viewed at http://hdl.handle.net/10107/5565456.

These local music societies had been established in several parts of Wales in the 1820s and 1830s, at Bethesda, Rhosllannerchrugog, Aberystwyth, Cerrigydrudion (the home of Hugh Evans) and elsewhere: they had strict rules and aimed to foster a knowledge of music and the raising of standards in singing, and took on the mantle of the peripatetic singing masters of a previous generation such as John Williams (Ioan Rhagfyr; 1740–1821) of Dolgellau and Dafydd Siencyn Morgan (1752–1844) of Llechryd, who had relied on oral instruction for the transmission of musical knowledge. The societies made use of existing handbooks and inspired new ones: it was for the society at Cerrigydrudion that Hugh Evans had developed his *Egwyddorion Peroriaeth*, and it was the society at Bethesda which sponsored the publication in 1848 of another textbook, *Gramadeg Cerddorol* (Musical Grammar) by David Roberts (Alawydd; 1820–72), which took a more functional approach than John Mills's rather philosophical *Gramadeg*.[7] Though the books remained mainly in the hands of instructors, it is evident that the response of pupils to their masters helped develop techniques of instruction and assisted the production of new works of a higher standard.

John Mills's work had included a discursive element defining different genres of music: religious, which he believed to be the highest form of the art; moral, or music to raise the mind and soul (what might loosely be called 'classical' music); and national (or secular) music, which had no place in the sanctuary. These distinctions, with their obvious favouring of the sacred, were to influence the thinking of many later authors, in particular the rigid differentiation of sacred and secular.[8] Discussion was to move forward with the emergence of Welsh-language music periodicals in the 1850s. While some earlier titles, such as the religious magazines *Seren Cymru* (The Star of Wales), *Y Drysorfa* (The Treasury) and *Y Dysgedydd* (The Instructor), had included a single page of music, usually a hymn tune, they did not devote much space to discussion on music except for observations and correspondence concerning its place in worship. Early attempts at dedicated music periodicals, such as *Blodau Cerdd* (Flowers of Music) in 1852 and *Yr Athraw Cerddorol* (The Music Teacher) in 1854, proved short-lived, neither title lasting for more than a year.

Much greater success attended *Y Cerddor Cymreig* (The Welsh Musician), launched in March 1861 by John Roberts (Ieuan Gwyllt;

---

[7] A second edition, with the modified title *Gramadeg Cerddoriaeth* (Grammar of Music), appeared in 1862.

[8] *Yr Arweinydd Cerddorol*, for instance, defines the same genres, and Ieuan Gwyllt's thinking followed similar lines.

1822–77) and modelled on Novello's *Musical Times*, which had been founded in 1844. During his years spent as a newspaper editor in Liverpool, Ieuan had been given ample opportunity to become acquainted with concert life; he had also frequently attended concerts in London, his musical horizons had been broadened by experience and he was aware of the revival of interest in the music of J. S. Bach and the work of the Sacred Harmonic Society in performing oratorios and other sacred music. All these things he brought to bear on his music journalism, aimed at the education of his compatriots and the raising of musical standards in Wales. *Y Cerddor Cymreig* breathed the same air of musical reformism that had shaped Ieuan's *Llyfr Tonau Cynulleidfaol* (Congregational Tune Book) of 1859. Moreover, he aped the *Musical Times* in another important respect: the provision of a monthly supplement of four to eight pages of music. In these supplements he put out works by Handel, Orlando Gibbons and Palestrina with Welsh words, alongside compositions by emergent Welsh composers like John Ambrose Lloyd (1815–74) and John Thomas of Llanwrtyd (1839–1921), whose part-songs and anthems reached choirs through this channel. Initially published by Ieuan from his home in Pant-tywyll, Merthyr Tydfil, and printed by Isaac Clarke of Ruthin, *Y Cerddor Cymreig* was taken over by Hughes and Son of Wrexham in 1865 and continued until 1873, after which its music supplements were incorporated in the Hughes catalogue. A mixture of biography, musical instruction, reviews of new publications and the reporting of musical events, it inspired many musicians who became prominent in Welsh music in succeeding decades. Because Ieuan drew freely on non-Welsh sources, *Y Cerddor Cymreig* also made the music-reading public aware of events in contemporary Europe, and it was in its pages that many Welsh readers first encountered the still-living Verdi and Wagner, as well as Haydn, Mozart and Beethoven.

Ieuan's example was followed with more limited success in the 1870s and 1880s. David Davies (Dewi Alaw; 1832–1914) founded *Y Gerddorfa* (The Music Place) at Pontypridd in 1872 and kept it going until 1881;[9] the Llanelli-based musician William Thomas Rees (Alaw Ddu; 1838–1904) edited two musical monthlies, *Yr Ysgol Gerddorol* (The Music School) from 1878 to 1880 and *Cerddor y Cymry* (The Welsh People's Musician) from 1883 to 1894. None of these reached the heights of *Y Cerddor Cymreig*, being rather more limited in scope and inward-looking in tone, but they

[9] In modern Welsh, 'Y Gerddorfa' would be translated as 'The Orchestra', but the periodical placed no great emphasis on instrumental music.

provide an insight into musical life with reports of concerts and reviews of new publications, and they followed the practice of providing monthly music supplements, so adding to the growing corpus of published Welsh music. The gauntlet thrown down by *Y Cerddor Cymreig* was properly taken up in January 1889 with the foundation of *Y Cerddor* (The Musician). Published by Hughes and Son at the instigation of their employee William Morgan Roberts (1853–1923), who did most of the work, *Y Cerddor* had as its nominal editors D. Emlyn Evans (1843–1913) and David Jenkins (1848–1915), both of whom provided regular editorials with trenchant and often caustic criticism of music in Wales.[10] At its best, it provided instruction and informed comment, along with much information about music and musicians; its high standards were maintained at least until World War I, and it eventually ceased publication in 1921. Although Hughes maintained two successor publications until 1939, the whole enterprise depended on generous subsidies from the publisher, and *Y Cerddor* was not immune from the problems of lack of support which had beset its predecessors in the field.

These periodicals were all published in the Welsh language, at a time when a significant proportion of the population were Welsh speakers. *Y Cerddor* did, however, include some English-language content in its columns, in acknowledgement of the growing number of English speakers in Wales. The greatest challenge they faced was securing effective means of distribution, since they depended on local distributors whose reliability was variable. Repeatedly Ieuan Gwyllt had to urge distributors of *Y Cerddor Cymreig* to remit moneys promptly to him, but some were reported as being two to three years behind with their payments.[11] Similar litanies of non-payment are encountered in the pages of other titles in the 1870s and 1880s. It was a problem which did not fade with time: in 1900, a generation later, *Y Cerddor* was appealing for 'energetic distributors' to promote the title locally.[12] The problem was common to other branches of the book trade in Wales, so much so that the writer and Inspector of Schools O. M. Edwards recommended in 1913 the establishment of a central warehouse for the distribution of all Welsh publications.[13]

---

[10] Delyth Morgans, '*Y Cerddor*: Cyfnodolyn y Werin'/'*Y Cerddor*: Periodical of the People', *Welsh Music History/Hanes Cerddoriaeth Cymru*, 5 (2002), 105–134.

[11] *Y Cerddor Cymreig*, 1 (1861–3), 176, 184, 19; 2 (1863–4), 104.

[12] *Y Cerddor*, 12 (1900), cover advertisement in the March issue.

[13] Philip Henry Jones, 'A Golden Age Reappraised: Welsh-Language Publishing in the Nineteenth Century', in *Images and Texts: Their Production and Distribution in the 18th and 19th Centuries*, ed. by Peter Isaac and Barry McKay (Winchester: St Paul's Bibliographies; Delaware: Oak Knoll Press, 1997), pp. 121–141, on p. 129.

Nevertheless, it is striking that despite endemic difficulties, Wales had at least one periodical devoted to music in publication for every year between 1861 and 1914.

Tonic Sol-fa

In April 1895 a reviewer observed that 'y mae Cymru *gorawl* wedi troi yn Sol-ffayddol yn mron yn llwyr' ('*choral* Wales has turned sol-faist almost entirely').[14] A little over twenty years later, the Haldane Commission reviewed university education in Wales and made important recommendations, not least concerning education in music. In his evidence to the Commission, David Evans (1874–1948), professor of music at Cardiff University and an influential teacher, defended the value of tonic sol-fa as:

> a system which has taught the Welsh democracy to sing, and has been the means of enlarging the musical knowledge of thousands, who would, without it, have depended entirely upon their memory of tune.[15]

Evans's view may appear a little speculative, but tonic sol-fa was undeniably an important means of musical communication in nineteenth-century Wales. As a formalised musical notation it was a creation of the 'age of improvement', when teachers, ministers and Sunday School leaders were concerned to find a simple method of teaching singing to the young, particularly in economically disadvantaged areas. The sol-fa which became widely used was developed from a method used by Sarah Glover of Norwich (1786–1867) for the teaching of sight-singing, and perfected by the Congregationalist minister John Curwen (1816–80), who published his *Grammar of Vocal Music* in 1843. It was in the 1850s that he began issuing a series of textbooks containing carefully graded lessons in sol-fa, notably *The Standard Course of Lessons on the Tonic Sol-fa Method of Teaching to Sing* (1858). He also established a journal, *The Tonic Sol-fa Reporter*, aimed primarily at sol-fa classes.

Although tonic sol-fa existed in one form or another in the Wales of the 1850s, the really dramatic burst of enthusiasm for 'the tonic' (as it came to be known) came in the early 1860s, thanks largely to a Liverpool Welshman, Eleazar Roberts (1825–1912). Much impressed by a lecture he heard Curwen give in Liverpool, Roberts took up the study of sol-fa before moving on to found classes in which he proved the success of the method by teaching children to sight-sing in several parts. He saw that tonic sol-fa could be highly beneficial in Wales, particularly in the context of Sunday

[14] *Y Cerddor*, 7 (1895), 37. [15] Quoted in *Y Cerddor*, 30 (1918), 64.

Schools and chapel singing: Curwen's ultimate purpose was as much moral as musical, and the sol-fa movement in Wales was to be very closely linked to chapel life. Roberts obtained Curwen's permission to translate his textbooks into Welsh, and began publishing *Llawlyfr Caniadaeth* (Handbook of Singing), the first part of which appeared in 1861. It was followed by others, notably *Y Gyfres Safonol*, Roberts's digest of Curwen's *Standard Course*. Also in 1861, Roberts issued the first of five parts of his collection of hymns and tunes, *Hymnau a Thonau* (Hymns and Tunes), the first Welsh book to appear in the sol-fa notation.

While Roberts himself actively promoted sol-fa, he was fortunate to find a useful and powerful ally in Ieuan Gwyllt: having convinced Ieuan of its potential, he was able to harness his crusading zeal and the resources he had at his disposal in *Y Cerddor Cymreig*. By 1865 some of the music supplements to the journal had begun to appear in sol-fa; as these were also issued and sold separately, Hughes and Son quickly accumulated their own catalogue of sol-fa music. This coming together of forces helped the sol-fa juggernaut to get moving, and in 1869 Hughes and Son embarked on a periodical, *Cerddor y Tonic Sol-ffa* (The Tonic Sol-fa Musician), edited by Ieuan Gwyllt, and, like Curwen's *Tonic Sol-fa Reporter* on which it was modelled, aimed specifically at sol-faists. Both it and *Y Cerddor Cymreig* gave significant attention to the growth of the movement in Wales in the late 1860s and early 1870s, and recorded the activities of sol-fa classes, showing how well and how rapidly the new notation caught on. In 1871 the choral conductor Silas Evans (1838–81) had classes within a radius of a few miles at Clydach, Craig-cefn-parc, Felindre and Llwynbrwydrau, numbering 320 in all.[16] These classes were not exclusively attached to places of worship: while W. T. Samuel (1852–1917), a leader of the movement in Wales, had a sol-fa class at Mount Pleasant chapel in Swansea, he also held one at Ben Evans's department store nearby.[17] Whether all of these songsters became proficient sol-faists or not, their number indicates enthusiasm.

This enthusiasm was supported by an escalation in the printing of music in sol-fa. As early as 1863 Ieuan Gwyllt was sufficiently confident of the potential of the new notation to issue a sol-fa edition of his *Llyfr Tonau Cynulleidfaol*, and virtually every subsequent hymnal and tune book published in Wales would appear in staff notation and sol-fa editions, including the interdenominational *Caneuon Ffydd* (Songs of Faith), published in 2001. Welsh music periodicals regularly issued music supplements in tonic sol-fa: these included

---

[16] *Cerddor y Tonic Sol-ffa*, 3 (1871), 32. [17] *Cronicl y Cerddor*, 1 (1880–1), 109.

not only *Cerddor y Tonic Sol-ffa*, its successor *Y Cerddor Sol-ffa* (The Sol-fa Musician, 1881–6) and *Y Solffaydd* (The Sol-faist, 1891–2) which were aimed directly at practitioners in the sol-fa movement, but others such as *Cerddor y Cymry* and *Y Cerddor*. Short pieces – songs, hymns and choruses often aimed at Sunday Schools and Band of Hope meetings – appeared in sol-fa in various popular religious and secular periodicals for children. Sol-fa was easier and cheaper to print than staff notation: the Tonic Sol-fa Agency, established by Curwen as the publishing arm of the sol-fa movement, and which was later renamed the Curwen Press, produced tonic sol-fa type, and because many Welsh printers could read sol-fa themselves, they became proficient at setting it. The Agency could depend on good sales in Wales:

> Wales, especially industrialized South Wales, made heavy demands on the Tonic Sol-fa Agency. Hundreds of thousands of song sheets were sold in Wales to meet the requirements of singers at choral festivals and in local chapels. It was unusual in most of this work to print the music in the old notation; there was usually no demand for staff as the singers were more than likely to read from Tonic Sol-fa.[18]

It was not only choral singers who benefited, as Welsh printers and publishers would sometimes venture on publications in other forms: Hughes and Son published *Ceinion y Gan* (Jewels of Song), a collection chiefly of solo songs and duets, in ten parts from 1873 onwards with the piano accompaniments as well as the vocal lines entirely in sol-fa. Benjamin Parry of Swansea was to do the same with a selection of arias by Balfe and Wallace, with Welsh translations.[19]

The popularity of tonic sol-fa was not confined to Wales: it was widely used in Scotland and parts of England, particularly in industrial areas where a strong choral tradition developed. Yet the Welsh love affair with sol-fa has persisted with greater intensity than elsewhere, and its influence can still be felt. It was closely linked to those religious forces which sustained so much musical activity in nineteenth- and early twentieth-century Wales, when the chapel doubled as a concert hall and many members of choral societies were experienced congregational singers. Sol-fa appeared at the right time, a period of significant growth in the popularity of choral and congregational singing, part of a musical reform

---

[18] Herbert Simon, *Song and Words: A History of the Curwen Press* (London: George Allen & Unwin, 1973), p. 81.

[19] J. Gray and J. Richards, *Eight Operatic Songs from the Bohemian Girl by M. W. Balfe and Maritana by W. V. Wallace*; the Welsh translations by J. Gray (Eurfryn); arranged and transcribed into the sol-fa notation by J. Richards (Isalaw) (Swansea: B. Parry, [1889]).

movement led by members of the Mills family of Llanidloes, Ieuan Gwyllt, Edward Stephen (Tanymarian; 1822–85) and others who were anxious to raise musical standards and promote education. One vehicle for this was the cymanfa ganu, which grew in popularity from around 1859 as a by-product of the growth in chapel attendance following the religious revival of the same year. The period from the 1860s until World War I saw considerable consolidation of chapel life – larger, more settled congregations, new and bigger buildings and a more formal organisational structure at local and national level. Musical activity fitted readily into this pattern of growth. It was also the period when the eisteddfod developed significantly as a competitive festival with a growing emphasis on music, particularly solo and choral singing, and not merely a festival of poetry. In all this, tonic sol-fa proved an important stimulus. The system was actively promoted by influential musicians such as Ieuan Gwyllt and later David Jenkins, lecturer and subsequently professor of music at the University College of Wales, Aberystwyth, which later became Aberystwyth University. They wrote extensively in support of it as a medium of instruction and so encouraged its dissemination and consolidation in Wales's musical life. Not all Welsh musicians were so supportive. Joseph Parry (1841–1903), who had acquired his musical education before sol-fa became common, saw little merit in Curwen's method, but despite Parry's legendary popularity, his opposition to the sol-fa system does not appear to have deterred its many adherents.

It can also be said, as David Evans claimed, that tonic sol-fa was a democratic method of teaching singing. It did not depend on the learning of notes as an expression of sound, nor on the availability of a musical instrument. The modulator, a chart on which the sequence of sounds (doh, ray, me, and so on) was set out in tabular form, could be hung on a wall or on the back of a door; all that was needed was an instructor who would use the modulator or standard hand signs to teach a group of singers. In poorer communities and remote rural areas, of which Wales had more than its share in the nineteenth century, this was an advantage. Another aspect that appealed was that qualifications in sol-fa were available, as the Tonic Sol-fa College established by Curwen in 1863 offered certificates and diplomas at all levels as an incentive to learning. In an age when educational opportunities were limited, obtaining certificates of this kind had a popular attraction. In 1884 it was reported that the pupils of Griffith Anthony in the industrial village of Cwmbwrla near Swansea had between them scooped 107 certificates at elementary, intermediate and advanced levels. Such qualifications might be decried by professionals, but the tonic sol-fa method had technical merit. People found it quick and straightforward to learn. It did not make fluent readers of everyone – a survey conducted in 1881 suggested that only a third of choral singers in Wales could read music at all, while most learnt everything, even the lengthiest choruses, by ear. But those who could read were almost all sol-faists, and good readers of tonic sol-fa proved highly accurate singers. Ieuan Gwyllt went so far as to say that it was difficult to sing wrong notes when singing from sol-fa.[20]

Nevertheless, sol-fa had its detractors. The principal substantive criticism was that it was limiting. The Welsh-American newspaper *Y Drych* (The Mirror) commented that it was to their loss that young people in Wales did not learn staff notation along with tonic sol-fa, because their ignorance of staff notation prevented them from getting employment as precentors and organists in American churches.[21] Created as a method of teaching sight-singing, sol-fa could not easily be extended to all branches of music. It was to counter this criticism that the young David de Lloyd (1883–1948), a sol-fa prodigy who in 1927 became professor of music at the University College of Wales, Aberystwyth, was taken on lecture tours by John Spencer Curwen, the son of John Curwen and his successor as the movement's chief apostle, to show that it was possible to play on the piano quite intricate music written in sol-fa. Nevertheless, being limited to sol-fa did tend to close musical doors. Initially, as was often emphasised by professionals, sol-fa was intended as a means of acquiring staff notation, and it was perhaps to its disadvantage in the long term that it became an alternative for many. Welsh musicians were deeply offended that the organisers of the Cardiff Triennial Festival in 1892 banned from the festival chorus any singers who could read only sol-fa and were inclined to attribute the decision to English snobbery;[22] but it is undeniable that some music, especially the more complex, does not easily translate to letter notation.

There was also a danger that because sol-fa was cheap and easy to print, it encouraged substandard publications. According to David Jenkins, composers themselves were largely to blame:

> Teimlwn er's blynyddau fod yna berygl i'n cerddorion ieuaingc gyhoeddi darnau anaddfed. Mae y ffaith y gellir argraffu mor rhâd yn nodiant y Sol-ffa yn brofedigaeth i lawer i ruthro i'r Wasg. Mae yn wir y llwyddir i gael rhyw fath o gylchrediad am flwyddyn neu ddwy trwy gymhorth cyfeillion caredig, ond i lawr yr ânt yn aml, ac ni fydd sôn amdanynt mwy[.][23]

---

[20] John Graham, *A Century of Welsh Music* (London: Kegan Paul, Trench, Trubner, 1923), p. 39; *Y Cerddor Cymreig*, 9 (1870), 62.
[21] Quoted in *Y Cerddor*, 9 (1897), 83.   [22] *Y Cerddor*, 4 (1892), 41.   [23] *Y Cerddor*, 1 (1889), 34.

(We have felt for years that there is a danger that young musicians will publish immature pieces. The fact that printing in the Sol-fa notation is so cheap is a misfortune for many who rush into print. It is true that some sort of circulation can be achieved for a year or two through the assistance of kind friends, but they [the pieces] often go down, and will not be heard of again[.])

The problem was that the authority conferred on a composer by having work published bred false confidence. The comparative ease and cheapness with which sol-fa could be printed locally could lead amateur musicians to assume an importance (and self-importance) they did not deserve, since they believed that having work in print was proof of its quality.

Nevertheless, many of those who became professional musicians in twentieth-century Wales began as sol-faists. And it is open to question whether the popular choral tradition which emerged in Wales in the later nineteenth century would have flourished to the same extent without sol-fa. In 1897 David Jenkins, who was the first person in Wales to gain the Advanced Certificate in sol-fa and was the author of a primer on how to learn staff notation through the medium of sol-fa,[24] wrote a spirited defence of 'the tonic' against the criticism of W. H. Cummings (1831–1915), newly appointed Principal of the Guildhall School of Music, that sol-fa had 'nearly killed music in Wales'. Referring to a choral festival held at the Crystal Palace in the previous year, Jenkins pointed out that of the 2,400 choristers who took part, 2,200 were sol-faists, and that but for them, such a festival could not be held at all.[25]

Publishing and the Music Trade

The largest publishing concern from the second half of the nineteenth century onwards, sometimes misleadingly dubbed 'the Welsh Novellos',[26] was Hughes and Son of Wrexham.[27] Founded as a printing firm in 1820 by Richard Hughes (1794–1871), it moved into music publishing when it acquired the stock and copyrights of the pioneer printer-publisher Isaac Clarke (1824–75) of Ruthin, who had produced the collection *Gems of Welsh Melody* (1860–4) and was the

---

[24] D. Jenkins, *Sut i Ddysgu yr Hen Nodiant drwy y Sol-ffa* (Wrexham: Hughes & Son, 1898).
[25] *Y Cerddor*, 9 (1897), [1].   [26] '[E]in *Novellos* Cymreig', *Y Gerddorfa*, 1 (1872), 28.
[27] Thomas Bassett, *Braslun o Hanes Hughes a'i Fab, Cyhoeddwyr, Wrecsam* (Croesoswallt: dros Gymdeithas Lyfryddol Cymru, 1946).

first Welsh publisher to issue solo songs. Hughes's acquisition in 1865 of the periodical *Y Cerddor Cymreig*, along with its music supplements, immediately expanded its catalogue, which by 1909 would run to 66 pages, representing more than 2,000 titles. Yet, unlike the successful London publisher Novello, Hughes and Son was primarily a book publisher, with printed music being only a subsidiary activity: authors of literary works tended to fare better than composers when selling their manuscripts for publication. Whereas a composer might receive 10s 6d or a guinea for the copyright of a song or part-song, the writer Daniel Owen (1836–95) was paid 100 guineas for the copyright of his novel *Enoc Huws* in 1891, and the same sum for his *Gwen Tomos* in 1894. Admittedly Owen's works were hugely popular and would be expected to sell well, but even the author of a manual on voice production fared better than most composers: Brynaman-based D. W. Lewis (1845–1920) got £25 for his *Llawlyfr y Llais* (Handbook of the Voice) in 1894.[28]

Whereas Hughes and Son was in Welsh terms a business of some size located in a populous town and, in 1899, employing over forty people,[29] music publishing was not purely an urban activity. Many of the firms involved were modest concerns, located in small towns and villages in every part of Wales. Llanidloes was the home of John Mendus Jones (1814–99), who published the music primers and tune collections of various members of the Mills family in the 1840s and 1850s,[30] in addition to such tune collections as *Telyn Seion* (The Harp of Zion) by Rosser Beynon (1811–76), which appeared in 1848 as a joint publication with the printer David Jones of Merthyr. In north Wales, Bethesda was also an active musical centre: there, Robert Jones (1811–77) printed sheet music as well as periodicals and books. His most notable venture at his ambitiously named Cambrian Music Office was the printing of *Ystorm Tiberias* (The Storm of Tiberias) by Tanymarian, the first Welsh oratorio to be published. It was issued in parts from 1855, and as a complete work in 1857. Carmarthen had been a well-established centre of printing since the eighteenth century: Mary Jones of Priory Street took over the press of her husband Evan at his death in 1832 and printed the interesting collections of tunes compiled by

---

[28] Hughes and Son, Copyrights Book, 1 July, 1 November 1891; [no date] 1894, 5 March 1894. This item formed part of the Hughes and Son Deposit at the National Library of Wales but was withdrawn by the depositor. Its subsequent location has not been identified.

[29] Bassett, *Braslun o Hanes Hughes a'i Fab*, has a photograph of the staff (numbering forty-one) in the summer of 1899, opposite p. 41. At around the same time, Novello had 230 staff on its payroll: Michael Hurd, *Vincent Novello – and Company* (St Albans: Granada, 1981), p. 98.

[30] John Iorwerth Davies, *Argraffwyr Sir Drefaldwyn o 1789 Ymlaen* (Machynlleth: Eisteddfod Genedlaethol Maldwyn a'i Chyffiniau, 1981), tt. 12–13.

Griffith Harris (1811–92), *Halelwiah* (Hallelujah) (1849) and *Halelwiah Drachefn* (Hallelujah Again) (1855).[31] In the pre-sol-fa era, each of these printer-publishers set conventional music type.[32]

A boom in publishing saw the emergence of others. The village of Llannerch-y-medd on Anglesey might appear an unlikely place for a publisher, but Lewis Jones (1841–77), succeeded in business by his sisters Jane (1837–91) and Elisabeth (1848–1920), printed and published cantatas and songs, including a series of short pieces of popular appeal for a mass audience called 'Y Geiniogwerth Gerddorol' (The Musical Pennyworth).[33] Other publishers flourished in more obviously commercial locations. Isaac Jones (1835–99) moved from the Swansea Valley to Treherbert, Rhondda to take advantage of the opportunities offered by the dramatic growth in the south Wales coal industry. His business, established in 1872, would do its fair share of jobbing printing, without which it would not have survived: early advertisements offer a range of printing services as well as the supply of books, periodicals, newspapers, stationery, fancy goods and paper hangings.[34] But he also took on the printing of music. From his office came the periodical *Cronicl y Cerddor* (The Musician's Chronicle) (1880–3) as well as over a hundred solo songs, anthems and part-songs published under his own imprint, including the first edition of Joseph Parry's well-known part-song for male voices, 'Myfanwy' in 1875. He also printed music for composers to self-publish, in addition to programmes for cymanfaoedd canu in many parts of Wales. Though he made use of music type and employed the experienced music compositor Benjamin Morris Williams (1832–1903), who had served an apprenticeship with Robert Jones in Bethesda, Isaac Jones came to rely more in later years on the services of the London music engravers, who gave a more professional finish to his output. Swansea was already a well-established musical centre when Benjamin Parry (1835–1910) set up shop there in 1878, with active choirs, numerous private music teachers and a music hall which seated 2,500 and which housed concerts and eisteddfodau.[35] Parry had experience as

---

[31] The value of these two collections is that they contain many traditional tunes, otherwise unrecorded, which were popular in the religious revivals of the late eighteenth and early nineteenth centuries.

[32] Mair Dafydd, 'Argraffu, Cyhoeddi a Llyfrwerthu yng Nghaerfyrddin, 1840–1890', *Y Llyfr yng Nghymru/Welsh Book Studies*, 8 (2007), 54–76, at p. 66.

[33] Dafydd Wyn Wiliam, 'Ffarwel i Inc Llannerch-y-medd', *Y Casglwr*, 21 (Nadolig 1983), 13; 'Mwy am Inc Llannerch-y-medd', *Y Casglwr*, 23 (Awst 1984), 15.

[34] See for instance *Jones's Rhondda Valley Illustrated Almanack and Diary, for 1875*, published by Isaac Jones himself.

[35] John Hugh Thomas, 'Music', in *The City of Swansea: Challenges and Change*, ed. by R. A. Griffiths (Stroud: Alan Sutton, 1990), pp. 218–229.

a printer in Wales and the United States and had been a travelling representative for Hughes and Son; in Swansea, he was sufficiently ambitious to print a Welsh-language newspaper, *Y Deheuwr* (The Southerner), which ran for one quarter in 1886, and also local guidebooks and books of views; but his most original and significant contribution was his printing and publishing of around sixty music titles, chiefly songs and part-songs.[36]

Parry was, however, unusual in that he issued some instrumental items. The music which Welsh firms published was the work of native Welsh musicians, mainly songs, part-songs and anthems, which reflected the predominance of the vocal in musical life. For editions of oratorios, Welsh choristers could depend on Novello and others, and instrumentalists played music that was available from English and European publishers. There was in general no need to create Welsh editions of such music. Moreover, the number of original instrumental works produced by Welsh composers and published in Wales was very small before 1914. There were, however, a few exceptions. Instrumental works can be found among the monthly supplements to periodicals, but only very occasionally: of the 112 supplements issued with *Cerddor y Cymry* between 1883 and 1894, three alone are instrumental pieces, and another has a string quartet accompaniment to a vocal line. Hugh Humphreys (1817–96) of Caernarfon, an enterprising publisher who included books, periodicals, ballad sheets, lithographs and photographic prints in his output, published collections of Welsh airs for instruments. Benjamin Parry issued at least three collections of Welsh airs for drum and fife bands, but it was only towards the end of his career that he published two short pieces for piano, the 'Abertawe Barn Dance' and 'The Welsh Brigade March' by Swansea composer G. M. Butt (1867–1952).

Newspapers frequently advertised music publications. The front page of Aberdare-based *Y Gwladgarwr* on 25 August 1882 had numerous notices of publishers and composers jostling for attention: advertisements for Joseph Parry's works published by Hughes and Son, new works by Hugh Davies ('Pencerdd Maelor'; 1844–1907), W. Jarrett Roberts (1846–86) and David Jenkins, alongside an advertisement for Parry's Musical College of Wales in Swansea and a notice of the forthcoming National Eisteddfod at Denbigh, with performances of *Elijah* and *Messiah* by a choir of around 400 scheduled in the evening concerts. Such advertisements reflect the somewhat introverted nature of the Welsh musical world, while at the same time illustrating

---

[36] Rhidian Griffiths, 'Benjamin Parry, Cyhoeddwr Cerddoriaeth'/'Benjamin Parry, Music Publisher', *Welsh Music History/Hanes Cerddoriaeth Cymru*, 6 (2004), 193–216.

a wealth of activity. Publication was within the inevitably limited circle of the Welsh market and the Welsh diaspora in populous places like London and Liverpool. But it was not unknown for Welsh composers to have their work published by London houses. Novello published the solo setting by D. Pughe Evans (1866–97) of John Henry Newman's 'Lead, Kindly Light' in 1894, persuaded perhaps by the popularity of Newman's text, though the song became better known in Wales in the translation by Elfed, 'Tyr'd, Oleu Mwyn'.

Questions of copyright and piracy exercised the minds of the musical community in Wales as elsewhere, though cases of undercutting by selling cheap editions appear to have been few and far between; this was largely because of the restricted market and the comparative cheapness of Welsh sheet music, which made piracy unattractive and unprofitable. Copyright disputes were played out in the more limited circles of eisteddfodau and cymanfaoedd canu. Nevertheless, music journals frequently drew attention to cases in the English courts as a lesson to those who reprinted music without leave, a habit most evident in the activities of compilers of local cymanfa ganu programmes who were notorious for reprinting tunes without obtaining the appropriate permission. In a discussion of copyright law in the pages of *Y Cerddor* in 1905, D. Emlyn Evans issued a salutary warning to Welsh musicians to respect 'meum' and 'tuum'.[37] Though cymanfa ganu programmes might appear to be something of a niche market, they represented big business in nineteenth-century Wales because of the scale of activity: hundreds of copies of each programme, containing up to forty hymns and tunes, were printed, and the ubiquity of cymanfaoedd meant that the music they contained was reproduced on a considerable scale. It was rare, however, for disputes to reach the courts, and the one cause célèbre which hit the Welsh headlines was the action brought by Afan Thomas (1881–1928) against a fellow composer, Cyril Jenkins (1885–1978), in 1914 when the latter attempted to pass off Thomas's hymn tune 'Spes' as his own. The judge found for Thomas.[38]

Not all publishers were printers, and those that can be traced in census records are usually described as booksellers and stationers rather than publishers. David Trehearn (1854–1931) was a Rhyl businessman who ran a stationer's shop. He was evidently interested in music and served as chairman of the music committee of the National Eisteddfod held at

---

[37] *Y Cerddor*, 17 (1905), 78–79. A similar warning had been issued in *Y Cerddor*, 14 (1902), 91.
[38] *Y Cerddor*, 26 (1914), 77. Reports of the hearing appeared in the *Cambria Daily Leader*, 10 June 1914, 3; *Carmarthen Weekly Reporter*, 14 August 1914, 5; and several other newspapers.

Rhyl in 1892; but he also published music, including some of the works of the popular songwriter R. S. Hughes (1855–1893), and his shop served as a booking office for local concerts and other attractions. The North Wales Music Company was established in August 1890 to buy out the successful music business of G. Griffith and Co. in Bangor and Caernarfon, and enticed Ellis David Williams (1853–1917) from Liverpool to Bangor to act as its manager. The advertisement inviting people to become shareholders proclaimed the company's intention not only to sell and hire out musical instruments of the best quality, but also to publish 'new and superior music'.[39] After Williams's death, the North Wales Music Co.'s publications and copyrights were acquired by the Swansea music retailer D. J. Snell (1880–1957), who bought up a number of such publishing concerns and so assembled a considerable catalogue of Welsh music which he augmented with his own publications.[40]

The music published by these firms was of variable quality; but until 1914, and beyond, it served an active market dominated by participants in eisteddfodau, concerts and cymanfaoedd canu where the emphasis was on enjoyment as much as on musical standard. One publisher, Stanley Jones of Newport, called his shop 'Eisteddfod Music Warehouse'. The printer-publishers were not, however, best placed to take advantage of the most lucrative tranche of the market in Wales, the printing of hymnals for the major denominations. Hughes and Son published the popular *Llyfr Tonau ac Emynau* (Book of Tunes and Hymns) by Tanymarian and J. D. Jones (1827–70) in 1868, and its successor volume in 1879, which were widely adopted by the nonconformist denomination known as the Welsh Independents (Congregationalists); and the firm of Spurrell in Carmarthen printed the Anglican *Hymnau yr Eglwys* (Hymns of the Church) in numerous editions from 1893 onwards. Generally, however, the best-selling hymnals of the nonconformist denominations, which accounted for the majority of places of worship in Wales in the late nineteenth and early twentieth centuries, were printed by London firms. While such hymnals enjoyed significant sales – the Congregationalists' *Y Caniedydd Cynulleidfaol* (The Congregational Singer) of 1895, printed by Novello, sold 117,460 copies in five years[41] – most Welsh music was produced and sold in comparatively small numbers. Hughes and Son experienced one legendary success with *Swn y Juwbili* (Sound of the

---

[39] *Y Genedl Gymreig*, 3 Medi 1890, 1; *Y Werin*, 6 Medi 1890, 4.
[40] Rhidian Griffiths, 'Swansea's "Mr. Music": The Career of D. J. Snell, Music Publisher', *Y Llyfr yng Nghymru/Welsh Book Studies*, 1 (1998), 59–90.
[41] *Y Cerddor*, 12 (1900), 88.

Jubilee), Ieuan Gwyllt's adaptation of hymns and tunes from Ira D. Sankey's *Sacred Songs and Solos*, published in six parts between 1874 and 1876, which sold 425,000 copies over a period of sixty years; but such successes were rare, and most sales were numbered in hundreds rather than thousands. No Welsh publisher could dream of matching the output of the London publisher of popular songs, Francis, Day and Hunter, who issued at least 25,000 copies of the first printing of each title they published in the years 1906 to 1914.[42] The market for Welsh songs was far more limited, and the typical print run was 500 or 1,000. A few major successes subsidised the large bulk of items published. Welsh publishers acquired copyrights outright, and appear to have varied their payments according to the status of a composer: William Davies (1859–1907), a native of Rhosllannerchrugog, who was a professional singer in the choir of Magdalen College, Oxford and later at St Paul's Cathedral, was paid five pounds by Hughes and Son for his song 'Y Gloch' (The Bell) in 1890 and, the following year, seven guineas for another song, 'Murmur y Nant' (The Rustle of the Brook). In the same period, the composer Wilfrid Jones (1862–1929) received 10s 6d for his song 'Y Bugail' (The Shepherd), and Daniel Protheroe (1866–1934) £1 10s for his male voice chorus 'The Crusaders'.[43] Ironically, Jones's song and Protheroe's chorus enjoyed far greater popularity in Wales than either of Davies's songs. It was concern about the profit that publishers made when no royalties accrued to the composer that impelled many composers to publish their own work, though they found to their cost that housing stock was difficult and distribution cumbersome, and in economically depressed times after World War I, many such composer-publishers sold out to Snell and Hughes and Son.

If copyrights were acquired cheaply, pricing in the market was also low: a booklet of temperance songs, *Y Caniedydd Dirwestol* (The Temperance Singer) by Ieuan Mai of Meifod was criticised by *Y Cerddor* for being priced at 3d rather than 2d, as at the lower price it would have sold better.[44] The same periodical drew attention to the high price of Harry Evans's *Welsh Nursery Rhymes*, published by the Educational Publishing Company (a branch of Hughes and Son) in 1907. Two shillings for a collection of twenty-four songs was expensive:

> Rhaid i ni yn Nghymru gofio fod cyhoeddwyr Seisnig ac Albanaidd ar y maes Cymreig, ac yn fwy-fwy prysur beunydd. Maent hwy yn cofio

---

[42] John Abbott, *The Story of Francis, Day & Hunter* (London: Francis, Day & Hunter, 1952), p. 42.
[43] Hughes and Son, 'Copyrights, Musical', 3 May 1890, 25 June 1891; 23 April 1890, 14 August 1891. (Also see note 28, above.)
[44] *Y Cerddor*, 13 (1901), 133.

moeswers y "chwe cheiniog heini" (*nimble sixpence*), ac yn rhoi i ni rai dwsinau o'n halawon oll hyd yn nôd am geiniog![45]

(We in Wales must remember that English and Scottish publishers are in the field in Wales, and are more active by the day. They remember the moral lesson of the 'nimble sixpence', and give us dozens of our melodies even for a penny!)

Many years before, Ieuan Gwyllt had criticised the pricing by Ashdown and Parry in London of 'Mai' (May), a duet for soprano and contralto by John Owen (Owain Alaw; 1821–83), which at four shillings was 'lawer iawn rhy ddrud i ferched Cymry' (much too expensive for Welsh women).[46] Though in practice the sale price was often less than the cover price, his censure is indicative of different expectations in a country where not only was money less freely available, but much of the practice of music took place among poorer people rather than the so-called leisure class.

Growth in musical activity was also reflected in the development of an active retail trade. Henry Richards (1784–1852), father of the pianist Brinley Richards, ran a music shop in Carmarthen in the early nineteenth century, alongside his work as organist of St Peter's Church and conductor of an instrumental ensemble.[47] Heins & Co. of Brecon went back to 1830, and in 1914 could boast a record of trading over five reigns: they also had outlets in Hereford and Abergavenny.[48] In 1855, R. Waugh of Church Street, Monmouth, who called himself 'Stationer, Music Seller, &c.', advertised 'Pianofortes tuned and let on hire, Harp and Violin Strings, and every other article connected with the Musical Profession'. He also offered 'every description of printing neatly executed'.[49] This not untypical advertisement of its time highlights the growing interest in the piano as both an instrument and a status symbol, but the specific reference to harp and violin strings suggests a level of interest in salon music that had gone beyond the professional. Some years before, in 1841, Londoner John Brader (1819–89) had been encouraged by piano makers Collard and Collard to settle in Swansea, where he established a practice as a piano tuner and sold music and musical instruments. His sons followed him into the business, which fulfilled more than a purely mercantile function: it was

---

[45] *Y Cerddor*, 19 (1907), 42.   [46] *Y Cerddor Cymreig*, 2 (1863–4), 126.
[47] A. J. Heward Rees, 'Henry Brinley Richards (1817–1885): A Nineteenth-Century Propagandist for Welsh Music/Propagandydd dros Gerddoriaeth Gymreig o'r Bedwaredd Ganrif ar Bymtheg', *Welsh Music History/Hanes Cerddoriaeth Cymru*, 2 (1998), 173–192, on pp. 173–174.
[48] See for instance their advertisement in the *Brecon County Times*, 27 May 1914, 7.
[49] His advertisement appears in T. Sherwood Smith, *The Tourist's Guide to the Wye* (London: William Tweedie, 1855). I owe this reference to Eiluned Rees.

Brader and Sons who attracted George Grossmith to perform at the Albert Hall, Swansea in March 1892.[50] Godfrey and Co. was another long-established Swansea business going back to the 1850s, which described itself in 1916 as 'the cheapest house in Wales', selling not only pianos but also soiled sheet music at cut price.[51]

The trade that developed was characterised by diversity. Stationers, such as Isaac Jones in Treherbert, his brother D. L. Jones (Cynalaw; 1841–1916) in Briton Ferry, and Ellis Ylltyr Williams (1835–1911) in Dolgellau, sold music and ancillaries such as pitch pipes, tuning forks and throat lozenges. Isaac Jones was an agent for pianos, which he claimed to be able to 'deliver free, at any Railway Station' from his shop, Stationers Hall,[52] while his brother developed an agency of a different kind, in helping would-be émigrés to book their passage to the United States, Australia or South Africa. The increasing popularity of the home piano offered commercial opportunities. J. E. Jones of the Music Warehouse, 172 High Street, Bangor, was a 'practical pianoforte and harmonium tuner and repairer' who, he claimed, had been tuner to members of the royal family and famous singers. His shop sold 'all kinds of musical instruments at low prices for cash or hire system', and also 'iron pianofortes lent on hire for concerts'.[53] John Jones (1836–1923) of Bethesda in the heartland of the slate-quarrying industry claimed to have the largest stock in Wales of Welsh songs, in a catalogue of over 600 items.[54] Much music retailing was carried out on a small scale and had a certain homespun character. John Evans (1868–1946) of Fishguard was a master butcher whose shop in Vergam Terrace was lined with tiles patterned with depictions of contented sheep and cows. Following an illness which precluded his continuing in his trade, he converted his shop into a music business, and 'Smithfield House' became the 'West End Music Stores', but the tiles and their patterns remained in place.[55]

Towards the end of the period, new inventions brought fresh opportunities. The earliest known commercial recordings of Welsh music were made in 1899: appropriately enough they included Madge Breese singing 'Mae Hen Wlad fy Nhadau' and a male voice choir, the Rhondda Royal Glee Society, singing choruses by Joseph Parry, thus encapsulating what many would see as the key expressions of Welsh music in the century that

---

[50] *Cambrian*, 19 February 1892, 5.   [51] *Cambria Daily Leader*, 27 November 1916, 4.
[52] *Jones's Rhondda Valley Almanack ... 1875.*   [53] *North Wales Chronicle*, 22 October 1887, 1.
[54] His advertisement appears at intervals over a period of more than twenty years, for example *Y Cymro*, 10 Medi 1896, 3; *Baner ac Amserau* Cymru, 11 Hydref 1919, 4.
[55] Information from John Evans's daughter, Mali Evans (1900–95).

followed.[56] Not surprisingly, Welsh retailers branched out to embrace new technologies: in the coastal town of Colwyn Bay in 1909, John Hughes of the exotically named Apollo Music Depot on Abergele Road was advertising not only sheet music and instruments (he was the sole agent for Steck pianos) but also the Columbia Graphophone, with Columbia and Zonophone records in stock.[57] His fellow townsman Arthur James Fleet (1860–1920), a piano tuner who, attracted no doubt by the commercial opportunities offered by a popular and growing seaside resort, had moved from Chester to Colwyn Bay to establish his Music Warehouse on Penrhyn Road, was advertising gramophones in the same year, as was the pioneer film-maker and cinema proprietor Arthur Cheetham (1865–1937) of Queen Street, Rhyl, who was offering the genuine article made by the Gramophone company for £3 10s.[58]

Surveying musical Wales at the beginning of 1899, the editors of *Y Cerddor* were scathing in their criticism:

> Yr hyn sydd hytrach yn ein digaloni yn awr fel erioed, yw y nifer gymhariaethol fychan o'n pobl ieuaingc ydynt yn darllen, ac yn talu sylw i lenyddiaeth gerddorol – o unrhyw fath. Y maent yn barod i *ganu* faint fyd a fynir; ond beth am y deall?[59]
>
> (What tends to dishearten us now as ever, is the comparatively small number of our young people who read, and pay attention to music literature – of any kind. They are willing to *sing* as much as could be wished for; but what about understanding?)

In the same year, Jack Edwards of Aberystwyth criticised a lack of progress in instrumental music and the 'wretchedly limited' repertoire of most of Wales's choirs.[60] When considering the long nineteenth century as a whole, it is reasonable to suggest that Wales's musical energies were dissipated in frenetic activity. The pursuit of music was, by and large, a love of singing, and the country's musical horizons were often circumscribed. Even so, the level of activity could be staggering, with choral concerts and performances of oratorio filling the calendar even in villages and small townships: such liveliness reflects a strong commitment to the pursuit of music as a social activity. Standards varied, and there was undoubtedly plenty of room for criticism; yet for all its

---

[56] See the CD *Y Deryn Pur/Recording Angels* (Aberystwyth: Recordiau'r Gen, 1999), GENCD 8001. Madge Breese was recorded in London on 11 March 1899 and the Rhondda Royal Glee Society in Cardiff on 30 September 1899.
[57] *Welsh Coast Pioneer*, 1 April 1909, 6.
[58] Ibid., 5 August 1909, 2. Arthur Cheetham's career and achievements are discussed by Philip Lloyd, *Silvograph: Arthur Cheetham (1865–1937), Pioneer Film-Maker* (Llanrwst: Gwasg Carreg Gwalch, 2018).
[59] *Y Cerddor*, 11 (1899), 1.
[60] Quoted in *Y Cerddor*, 11 (1899), 76, from a letter addressed to the *Welsh Gazette*.

limitations, it was an age when music became a pursuit for the masses rather than the few, and permeated everyday life and work in a way which a later age would find difficult to understand. The musical culture of nineteenth-century Wales was rich in enthusiasm that tended often to outrun musical refinement: a culture with ragged edges, but a genuinely popular culture nonetheless, which writers, publishers and retailers, as well as practitioners, served with zeal.

Selective List of the Principal Music Publishers in Wales before 1920

Composers who published only their own compositions are not included.

Name of printer / publisher	Location	Years active	Notes
John Daniel (1755?–1823)	Carmarthen	1784–1823	Printed *Cyfaill mewn Llogell* (1797), the first book on music printed in Welsh.
Hughes & Son	Wrexham	1820–1960s	Began publishing music 1860s.
William Rees (1808–73)	Llandovery	1829–73	Printed Maria Jane Williams's *Ancient National Airs of Gwent and Morganwg* (1844).
John Mendus Jones (1814–99)	Llanidloes	1840s–1899	Imprint varies: 'J. M. Jones', 'J. Mendus Jones'. Removed to Bangor 1859.
David Jenkins (1810–72)	Aberystwyth	1840–72	Co-operated with J. Mendus Jones to print the periodical *Blodau Cerdd* (1852).
Isaac Clarke (1824–75)	Ruthin	c.1845–75	Imprint I. Clarke. Stock and copyrights acquired by Hughes & Son.
Robert Jones (1811–77)	Bethesda	c.1850–77	Printed Edward Stephen's oratorio *Ystorm Tiberias* (1855), the first Welsh oratorio published.
John Jones (1836–1923)	Bethesda	c.1855–c.1919	Acquired by Hughes & Son.
Isaac Jones (1835–99)	Treherbert	1872–99	Imprint I. Jones. Music publishing ceased after 1899. Stock and copyrights acquired by Snell 1930.

9 Musical Communications in the Nineteenth Century

(cont.)

Name of printer / publisher	Location	Years active	Notes
D. L. Jones (Cynalaw) (1841–1916)	Briton Ferry; Cardigan	Briton Ferry c.1872–1910; Cardigan 1910–1916	Printing continued at Briton Ferry after 1910; publishing ceased c.1914. Copyrights acquired by Snell 1914, 1927.
Lewis Jones (1841–1877) succeeded by Jane and Elisabeth Jones	Llannerch-y-medd	c.1875–77 1877–1910	Press continued as jobbing printing works. Some titles acquired by Hughes & Son.
Benjamin Parry (1835–1910)	Swansea	1878–1910	Imprint 'B. Parry'. Stock and copyrights acquired by Snell 1910.
D[avid] Jenkins (1848–1915)	Aberystwyth	c.1880?–1915	Acquired by Snell.
David Trehearn (1854–1931)	Rhyl	1880s–1890s	Imprint 'D. Trehearn'. Copyrights acquired by Hughes & Son.
J. R. Lewis (1857–1919)	Carmarthen	1880s–1919	Stock and copyrights acquired by Snell 1924.
W. Gwenlyn Evans (1852–1921)	Caernarfon	1884–c.1970	Firm continued by WGE's daughter and son.
North Wales Music Co. (managed by E. D. Williams (1853–1917))	Bangor	1890–1908	Formed in 1890 to acquire business of G. Griffith & Co., Bangor and Caernarfon. Company liquidated in 1908. Stock and copyrights acquired by Snell 1917.
Cwmni y Cyhoeddwyr Cymreig (Welsh National Publishing Company)	Caernarfon	c.1890–1921	Incorporated publications of D. W. Davies. Stock and copyrights acquired by Snell 1921.
Welsh Church Musical Agency	Carmarthen	?1890–?1910	An imprint of printers W. Spurrell & Co.
Hugh Evans, Gwasg y Brython	Liverpool	1896–1978	Business sold to Gwasg Gomer, Llandysul, 1978. Some music copyrights acquired by Snell, 1935.
D. J. Snell (1880–1957) (later Snell & Sons)	Swansea	1910–c.1963	Retail business closed 1971, reopened as mail order 1982.

CHAPTER 10

Nonconformists and Their Music
Martin V. Clarke

The chapel commands a significant place in the history of musical culture in modern Wales and perceptions about Welsh musicality. Indeed, 'chapel' itself has long been used idiomatically in Wales to describe both nonconformist buildings and affiliation, as well as an associated way of life, typically juxtaposed with 'church', which signifies the Anglican Church. Just as nonconformist chapel buildings themselves are a prominent feature of many Welsh landscapes, actual and in works of art and literature, so too have the musical practices and repertoires associated with them exerted a profound influence on the cultural landscape of Wales. However, the ubiquity of the chapel and its musical culture in popular perceptions of Wales, its people and their music masks a complex social and religious environment. It also highlights the ways in which a relatively short period of concentrated activity in Welsh history has shaped wider notions about the country, and how the legacy of that period has outlived and outgrown the influence of the chapel in day-to-day Welsh life.

The modern religious history of Wales, and with it the place of nonconformist music making in notions of Welsh identity, are inextricably linked to wider demographic, industrial and economic changes that took place from the eighteenth century onwards. Just as these changes radically altered Welsh landscapes and communities, so too did they create an environment in which particular musical repertoires and practices could flourish. Welsh society also displayed a remarkable propensity for religious revivalism from the eighteenth century through to the early years of the twentieth century. While the eighteenth-century Methodist revival in Wales differed significantly in some regards from its counterpart in England, they were roughly contemporaneous, but large-scale revivalism was to play a much more prominent subsequent role in Wales than in England, such as in the nationwide revivals of 1859 and, most famously, 1904–5; but also on a regional level, such as in the Rhondda valleys in 1879. Revivalism and hymnody were closely intertwined; their influence on each other is an important part of the history of nonconformist musical practice and repertoire.

The prominence of chapels in the landscapes of modern Wales highlights one of the principal complicating factors in understanding their influence on Welsh musical life. Much like Protestantism elsewhere in Britain and beyond, Welsh nonconformity has been characterised by considerable institutional fragmentation. While the rapid growth in chapel building owed much to institutional divisions based on theology, doctrine or polity, and attitudes to matters such as models of leadership, evangelistic methods and worshipping practices, language became a further basis for the multiplication of chapels in towns and villages as linguistic trends changed rapidly in the latter part of the nineteenth century; it was common for Welsh- and English-speaking congregations of the same denomination to have separate buildings. The variety of denominations at work in Wales in this period had an obvious effect on nonconformist musical life. For many of them, as their worship was not based on formal liturgical patterns of the type found in the Established Church's Book of Common Prayer, a hymnal was regarded as a significant marker of identity. However, a strictly denominational approach to the history of nonconformist music neglects a significant aspect of revivalism in particular: revival manifested itself in specific places at specific times and typically transcended denominational boundaries. As will be seen later, accounts make clear that when revival meetings were planned in a town or village, practical ecumenism was commonplace, and whichever chapel hosted the principal meetings, it was typical for new converts to be associated with several local congregations.

Despite nonconformity's popular dominance, Welsh religious life was not practised solely in the chapels; Anglicanism in Wales also underwent much change in this period, most notably in the formal separation from the Church of England of the disestablished Church in Wales, granted royal assent in 1914 and enacted in 1920. The musical life of the church as well as the chapel is part of the tapestry of religious music making in Wales.

While the music of nonconformity is commonly held up as a distinctive feature of Welsh culture and is popularly used to express Welsh identity, this examination of its history seeks to evaluate the extent to which its practices and repertoire resemble those of other religious communities, and the degree to which a uniquely Welsh musical tradition can be claimed. While nonconformity and its music in England and elsewhere provide the most obvious and sustained points of comparison, the relationship between church and chapel is also an important consideration.

Musicians, congregations and publications from across Wales feature throughout this chapter, but the village of Senghenydd and the larger geographical and ecclesiastical areas of which it is part, respectively the Aber Valley and the historic parish of Eglwysilan, are used recurrently as a consistent reference point to measure continuity and change. Situated some ten miles north of Cardiff, the village takes its name from the historical cantref, the medieval administrative unit into which Wales was divided, and which covered a significant portion of the county of Morgannwg.

The Parish and the Emergence of Methodism in Wales

Musical sources associated with early modern Welsh Christianity are scarce. However, *Llyfr y Psalmau* (1621), the metrical psalter of Edmwnd Prys (1542/3–1623), Archdeacon of Meirioneth, is of seminal importance in both literary and musical terms. Published in London but the first printed book in the Welsh language to contain musical notation, it ran to 107 editions between 1621 and 1868, although prior to 1770, only three of these contained music (those published in 1621, 1630 and 1638). Prys's education and early clerical career in Cambridge (1570–7), as well as his brief period ministering in the Marches, all influenced the nature and content of his collection. Sally Harper notes that during his time in Cambridge, he may have 'heard little other than metrical psalms', owing to the dominance of Puritanism in the city at that time.[1] St Laurence's parish church in Ludlow, meanwhile, where Prys had been appointed as rector in 1576 and where he resided from 1577 to 1579, had a flourishing musical life, supported by the town corporation. Records testify to the use of both polyphonic choral music and 'hymnes' (metrical psalms) in worship there in this period.[2] Herein lies an obvious but important point of similarity; Prys's training and experience in England had a direct bearing on the musical life of the Welsh Church through his metrical psalter. Moreover, his work in providing text in the vernacular together with music brought the Welsh Church into line with common Protestant practice not only in England, but in Scotland and much of Europe.

By the time Prys engaged in active ministry in Wales from 1579, Welsh-speaking parishes were legally obliged to conduct services in the language

---

[1] Sally Harper, 'Tunes for a Welsh Psalter: Edmwnd Prys's *Llyfr y Psalmau*', *Studia Celtica*, 37 (2003), 221–267, on 241.
[2] Ibid., 241–243.

of the people, and while adherence to this was not absolute, it too was undoubtedly an influential factor in leading Prys to compile his metrical psalter. Prys followed the precedent set by Edward Kyffin and James Rhys Parry in making extensive use of the mesur salm in his versifications; only five of his texts are in other metres. This 8787 metrical pattern, with its consistent pattern of four and three stresses in the longer and shorter lines respectively and its regular rhyme scheme, bears an obvious similarity to the English common metre (8686) that dominated Sternhold and Hopkins's highly influential psalter, although the Welsh pattern is more complex in its rhyme scheme than the English, as well as having longer second and fourth lines. The basic similarity, however, had an obvious impact on the selection of tunes; the first edition of *Llyfr y Psalmau* contained just twelve tunes, eight of which are commonly found in English and Scottish psalters of the period. Naturally, these are common metre tunes and thus do not strictly fit mesur salm. However, the textual underlay shows that a simple solution was adopted, with two syllables appointed to the long final note of the second and fourth lines, indicating that these were to be repeated. The same solution is evident in the four tunes for which no earlier source is known, strongly suggesting that they were not written specifically for Prys's metrical texts.

Musically, then, Prys's psalter sought to align Welsh practice and repertoire closely with those found elsewhere in Britain. This is further underlined in the small number of texts where he departs from mesur salm; these include his version of Psalm 100, which is set to the internationally familiar tune later named 'Old Hundredth'. Harper notes that similarly firm associations exist in English sources between the texts and tunes for two of the other psalms in different metres, 67 and 113, arguing that 'there is good reason to think that these tunes were also being used by those congregations in Wales who sang the Psalms in English before 1621'.[3]

In this period, the parish of Eglwysilan was predominantly rural, with a number of hamlets and the small town of Caerphilly, built around its medieval castle. The mountainside parish church dedicated to St Ilan, situated in a hamlet above Abertridwr, represented the Established Church at this time. Nonconformity in the area can be traced to at least 1662, when a religious society met in members' houses in the Watford area on the southern outskirts of Caerphilly.[4] A chapel was erected at Watford in 1739,

---

[3] Ibid., 254.
[4] 'Welsh Congregationalism: East Glamorgan Quarterly Meeting', *The Western Mail*, 15 October 1891, 6.

with the Independent minister, the Rev. David Williams (1709–84), leading the congregation. The early history of this chapel provides an instructive insight into the religious dynamics that would profoundly shape the development of Welsh nonconformity. Though described as an 'Independent', Williams was heavily influenced by the Methodist revival and closely acquainted with several of its leading figures in both Wales and England. Prior to the opening of the chapel, Williams had invited Howell Harris (1714–73) to the area to lead a meeting. Harris was one of the primary figures in the Methodist revival in Wales; following his religious conversion in 1735, he pursued a vigorous itinerant preaching ministry, which, combined with his organisational flair, was instrumental in the founding of Methodist societies. Two of the other most significant names associated with early Welsh Methodism, Daniel Rowland (1711?–90) and William Williams (Pantycelyn; 1717–91) also visited Watford, where in 1739 they attended the first sasiwn (general meeting) of the Welsh Calvinistic Methodists, which was held at Watford and presided over by George Whitefield, leader of the Calvinistic Methodists in England. Through Whitefield, John Wesley learned of Harris's work, and both John and his brother Charles visited the area in the early 1740s and preached at the Watford chapel. Just three years after the opening of the chapel, however, a secession had taken place; concern over Williams's Arminian theology (as favoured by the Wesley brothers), which brought him into conflict with Harris, and accusations of Arianism, led a faction to leave Watford and form their own society in the nearby hamlet of Groeswen, where they opened a chapel in 1742. While the Wesley brothers' brand of Methodism would gradually dominate in England, Calvinism has characterised Welsh-speaking Methodism. The early eighteenth century also saw the expansion of Caerphilly into a market town, to which the Established Church responded by opening a chapel of ease, Capel Martin, where, in 1741, Whitefield would marry Elizabeth James.

In terms of hymnody, early Methodism exerted considerable influence on religious life in Wales, and while its physical expansion is also significant, its coexistence alongside the Established Church cannot be overlooked. The successive editions of Prys's psalter indicate that psalm singing remained alive in the church, and early Methodist sources provide evidence of musical overlap. John Wesley's first collection of hymn tunes, *A Collection of Tunes, As They Are Commonly Sung at the Foundery* (1742), contained the tune Prys had used for Psalm 2, now labelled 'St Mary' after its designation in multiple editions of Playford's *The Whole Book of Psalms*. Wesley also includes four tunes named after places he had visited in south Wales: Cardiff, Fonmon, Penmark and Wenwo. No earlier Welsh or English sources of these tunes are known.

The most significant figure in early Methodist hymnody in Wales was William Williams (Pantycelyn), commonly known as Williams Pantycelyn, after the Carmarthenshire farmhouse where he lived for much of his life. Having experienced religious conversion under the influence of Howel Harris's preaching, he was ordained deacon in the Established Church in 1740 but left in 1744 following disputes over his Methodist-influenced preaching activity. In the same year, he published his first collection of hymns; over the next 43 years, he would publish almost 1,000 of them, the vast majority in Welsh, but with just over 120 in English. Imbued with scriptural allusion and heavily influenced by his postmillennial religious beliefs, Williams Pantycelyn's hymns made him the 'predominant literary voice of the Methodist Revival in Wales'.[5] While his collections of hymns were published without music, they are nonetheless important sources for understanding the role of hymn singing in eighteenth-century Welsh nonconformity.

In *Caniadau Duwiol* (Devotional Songs; 1757), Williams Pantycelyn gave indications that four texts were to be sung to folk melodies, three of which had English names. Luff notes that while their origins are uncertain, 'they had a wide circulation at that time in Wales and had become naturalized'.[6] Beyond these, it is difficult to pair his texts with specific tunes. However, several aspects of his work cast light on the use of music in early Welsh Methodism. First and foremost, the sheer volume of hymns indicates the prominence given to congregational song by the early Methodist leaders. Though the singing of congregational hymns was neither instigated by nor unique to Methodism, it was the first denomination to embed the practice comprehensively in its activities and to exploit its evangelical potential. Williams Pantycelyn maintained a highly itinerant ministry for half a century, leading religious meetings and services throughout Wales. James notes that his hymns, as with the rest of his considerable literary output, were 'utilitarian, the product of a born, if rather undisciplined, literary genius, spurred on by the need to provide practical literature for the Methodist converts'.[7] His work also broke with

---

[5] E. Wyn James, 'Popular Poetry, Methodism, and the Ascendancy of the Hymn', in *The Cambridge History of Welsh Literature*, ed. by Geraint Evans and Helen Fulton (Cambridge: Cambridge University Press, 2019), pp. 306–334, on p. 317.

[6] Alan Luff, *Welsh Hymns and Their Tunes: Their Background and Place in Welsh History and Culture* (London: Stainer & Bell, 1990), p. 137.

[7] E. Wyn James, 'The Evolution of the Welsh Hymn', in *Dissenting Praise: Religious Dissent and the Hymn in England and Wales*, ed. by Isabel Rivers and David L. Wykes (Oxford: Oxford University Press, 2011), pp. 229–268, on p. 244.

older patterns of Welsh poetry. Noting his English-language education, Luff observes that 'Above all he had not been schooled in the strict Welsh poetic tradition, and although he has been criticized in Wales for this, he was thus free to develop something new and become Wales' first romantic poet.'[8] Among the wide range of metres he used were many that were characteristic of English-language hymnody; English-speaking Methodism's own pre-eminent hymn writer, Charles Wesley, was noted for the vast metrical range of his verse. Williams's hymns would also influence later Welsh writers, including Ann Griffiths (1776–1805). Her work, widely admired for its rich imagery and sense of wonder, has made her one of the most widely known of all Welsh-language hymn writers. Only seventy-six stanzas of her writing exist, many in the 8787D metre used by Williams and Wesley, though with a degree of flexibility that renders some of her verses difficult to set to regular hymn tunes. Many of her texts appear to have been intended for private devotion rather than public worship, pointing to the widespread use of verse in Welsh religious life.[9]

Three salient points emerge from Williams Pantycelyn's hymnody in terms of the musical life and repertoire of eighteenth-century Welsh nonconformity. Each is important in understanding the development of congregational singing in Wales, but there are also close parallels with early English Methodism. First, the existing music of the Established Church, in the form of metrical psalm tunes, exerted an influence and continued to be a feasible source of repertoire. Among Williams's hymns are texts written in the metres of earlier psalters, which could readily have been sung to tunes such as those selected by Edmwnd Prys. The *Foundery Collection* provides direct evidence that John Wesley considered such reuse as profitable for his followers in England. While much Methodist historiography has sought to portray the vitality of the early days of the movement in Wales and England in opposition to an apparently moribund Established Church, it is clear that the two were intertwined. Early leaders, such as Williams Pantycelyn himself and the Wesley brothers, grew up in the Church and would have had their earliest experiences of sacred music in that context. It is therefore unsurprising that, in part, they wrote for musical repertoire they knew and which some of those to

---

[8] Alan Luff, 'William Williams', *The Canterbury Dictionary of Hymnology*, www.hymnology.co.uk/w/william-williams (accessed 25 February 2021).

[9] See A. M. Allchin, *Ann Griffiths: The Furnace and the Fountain* (Cardiff: University of Wales Press, 1976).

whom they ministered would also have recognised through its religious associations.

Second, metrical expansion meant that the psalters could not meet all the musical needs of the Methodist hymn writers. Musical repertoire thus needed to be found from elsewhere, and boundaries between sacred and secular seemed to matter little. While Pantycelyn was content to refer his followers to folk melodies, John Wesley drew on diverse sources including adaptations of contemporary art music and melodies borrowed from the Moravians, some of which had their origins in Germanic folk songs. Methodism was not concerned to cultivate an original musical repertoire; singing was for Pantycelyn, like the Wesleys, a practical matter in service of a greater purpose: to initiate, affirm and embed the Christian faith in the minds and hearts of those who sang or heard the hymns. This is borne out most obviously in some of the most characteristic textual attributes of Pantycelyn's hymns, especially his interweaving of biblical allusion with personalised language, and a strong sense of Christian pilgrimage towards heaven.

Finally, claims for the role music played in the Methodist revival rest primarily on the sheer volume of hymns produced by its leading figures and their integration in all aspects of its activity, rather than any specific musical repertoire that can be definitively labelled as Methodist. If anything was distinctive about Methodist musical repertoire in this period, it was its variety. Musical practice is rather more significant than repertoire. The seiadau (society meetings) of the early Methodists began with singing, and participants would sometimes continue to sing hymns and pray together long after the meeting had officially closed. Herein lie points of both similarity and difference with English Methodism of the same period. There too, hymns played a crucial role in meetings of different types within the connexional network devised by John Wesley. Methodist musical engagement in Wales was based on voracious consumption rather than creation; while this was true in much of England, the flourishing of the movement in large urban centres brought its leaders into contact with fashionable art music composers and performers, some of whom wrote new music for Charles Wesley's hymns. John Wesley attempted to control Methodist musical repertoire on a national level by issuing three collections of hymn tunes; the influence of his familiarity with contemporary art music, principally through his work in London, can be traced in each. The absence of large urban centres in Wales, by contrast, offered no comparable opportunities for a particular style of music to shape its leaders' attitudes. Furthermore, while figures such as Pantycelyn, Harris and Rowland were widely recognised as leading figures in the Welsh Methodist revival, none pursued quite such a centralising programme of organisation and publication as John Wesley. Musical repertoire was one area in which Pantycelyn and other Welsh leaders appear to have been content to trust local judgement.

The Groeswen chapel within the parish of Eglwysilan illustrates the somewhat disorderly spread of eighteenth-century nonconformity in Wales. The secession from the earlier chapel at Watford on theological grounds identified those who left for Groeswen as Calvinistic Methodists, followers of Howell Harris, and it has been claimed that the chapel they erected was the first newly built Calvinistic Methodist place of worship in Wales. However, it is unclear whether the society that met there considered itself Methodist or Independent (denoting an older tradition of Dissent, predating Methodism). As noted earlier, the minister at Watford was an Independent, despite his Methodist sympathies, and the later history of the Groeswen chapel is firmly Independent. However, John Morgan Jones claimed in his history of early Welsh Methodists, *Y Tadau Methodistaidd* (The Methodist Fathers; 1895) that it had been founded as a Methodist chapel. This claim was disputed by the then minister of the chapel, the Rev. C. Tawelfryn Thomas, and a protracted debate played out in the pages of the *Western Mail* newspaper.[10] Boundaries were seemingly rather fluid, and while this may seem to be a point of contrast with England, where John Wesley's complex organisational structure is well documented, the reality was rather more varied, as Jonathan Rodell explores in his account of early Methodism in Bedfordshire.[11] Among the ways in which Rodell notes that local expressions of Methodism diverged from the centralised model is the use of hymns, many of which were drawn from local sources or other widely used collections in addition to those authorised by Wesley. It is likely that a similar situation existed in Wales; Pantycelyn's six collections titled *Aleluia* were published in close proximity between 1744 and 1747, and while his *Caniadau y Rhai Sydd ar y Môr o Wydr* (The Songs of Those Upon the Sea of Glass; 1762) represents a landmark in his own poetic maturity, it did not attempt to position itself as an institutional standard, in the way that Wesley's *Collection of Hymns for the Use of the People Called Methodists* (1780) was to do.

A letter of 19 November 1772 from the Rev. Edmund Jones, an Independent minister from Pontypool, to Howell Harris provides an

---

[10] For a summary see *South Wales Daily News*, 6 November 1897, 4.
[11] Jonathan Rodell, *The Rise of Methodism: A Study of Bedfordshire, 1736–1851* (Woodbridge: Boydell, 2014), pp. 76–77.

example of the integration of music in the life of eighteenth-century Welsh Methodism. In this letter and another sent to Harris two months earlier, he cites the important influence of the Groeswen chapel in a local revival being experienced throughout the Rhymney valley, and draws particular attention to the impact of the singing of several leading figures from that chapel in a revival meeting:

> Dear Sir, I have the pleasure to inform you that having heard of some strong men in prayer belonging to Croes Wen I invited them to come to our meeting; accordingly they came, last Lord's was sevenight, and 6 of the 8 that came to pray, singing Salm or Hymn between each two, except the two first. Mr. Wm. Edwards son being one that prayed one after another, no singing between: and they prayed excellently well; very humbly, judiciously, and spiritual before a great congregation. The 3rd and 5th were also extraordinarily powerful. I was greatly affected, and nearly amazed to hear them, as were very many; most of the people I never heard the like in one place. . . . Our people sang between the two first and the 3rd: between the 3rd and 4th and between the 4th and 5th and sang well: and after that the praying brethren sung their own tunes, with excellent voices, two or three times, and sung better than our people, tho I think ours sung well also. I sha'nt forget how one after another came to kneel and pray upon a raised step between the table and the pulpit with their faces towards the pulpit (in the sight of the congregation) which reflected their voices better through the service.[12]

Jones's letter illustrates the way in which song and prayer were tightly interwoven, and how, in combination, they were integral to the success of the meeting. His description of the men's conduct also shows the spontaneous nature of such meetings. Also significant is the distinction he draws between the singing of his own congregation and the men singing 'their own tunes'. Although the letter does not identify the precise location of this event, the wider context Jones provides make clear that it was in a chapel somewhere in the Rhymney valley. This, therefore, was a meeting that took place within a few miles of Groeswen, yet the two congregations appear to have had different musical repertoires.

Welsh nonconformity grew considerably during the eighteenth century; a substantial body of Welsh-language hymnody emerged with it, while the practice of hymn singing became embedded in the culture of Welsh religious life. Such growth, however, needs to be understood in the context of a still predominantly rural society and the continued presence of older Dissenting congregations. While leading figures such as Pantycelyn and

---

[12] GB-AB MS CMA Trevecka 2724, Edmund Jones to Howel Harris, 19 November 1772.

Harris gained national prominence, as the case of Groeswen shows, the revival was experienced locally and piecemeal over a protracted period. This is reflected in the musical repertoire of the period; while hymn singing was widely adopted, encouraged and celebrated for its powerful effects, it was manifested in ways that were rooted in local contexts.

Nineteenth-Century Expansion

The industrialisation and associated urbanisation of significant areas of Wales in the nineteenth century had a profound effect on the organisation, culture and experience of religion throughout the country. Both the vast south Wales coalfield, where mines and ironworks proliferated, and the north-east of the country, where mining, metalwork, pottery and cotton-milling grew, saw a burgeoning of nonconformist activity, though rural areas also experienced similar growth. Particularly in the new urban areas, religious life was also influenced by the interrelation of patterns of migration, changes in education and publishing developments. The rapid transformation from a rural economy to one dominated by coal and iron established new urban settlements and necessitated significant developments in transport networks. The requirement not only to extract minerals but to transport them made it strategically imperative for landowners and industrialists to ensure that the new communities that grew up around the pits and ironworks were connected to commercial centres; for the south Wales valleys, this increasingly meant to Cardiff, where the opening of the West Bute dock in 1839 was instrumental in the town's growth over the ensuing decades.

The emergence of new population centres and their relative accessibility compared to rural areas presented both opportunities and challenges to religious institutions. Here, an important distinction between the Established Church and the nonconformist denominations, or, colloquially, church and chapel, emerges. The parochial system of the Established Church was defined by geography; every part of the country, no matter how remote from a church building, was part of a parish. The parish system did evolve in response to population changes, as evidenced by the opening of Capel Martin as a chapel of ease within the parish of Eglwysilan as the population of the town of Caerphilly expanded in the eighteenth century. Structural administrative change within the Established Church did not happen quickly, however; despite the town's ancient heritage, the parish of Caerphilly was not formally created until 1850, well after Caerphilly had become a substantial market town, when it was carved out from areas of the older parishes of Eglwysilan and Bedwas. The nonconformist denominations, in contrast, were not bound by the same geographical considerations and were thus able to expand in more flexible, if sometimes idiosyncratic, ways. As noted in the secession from Watford to Groeswen, theological disputes were sometimes the trigger for establishing a new congregation. Institutional differences on theological grounds, such as between General and Particular Baptists, or Wesleyan and Calvinistic Methodists, and on matters of polity and governance, such as Methodist connexionalism and Congregationalism, contributed to a patchwork of religious organisations. The evangelical intent of those particularly associated with revivalism also prioritised setting up new societies on a very localised level to support and embed signs of growth. Meeting houses and chapels therefore sprang up in a somewhat haphazard fashion in the new villages and towns, as local or institutional leaders were eager to capitalise on the opportunities presented by large influxes of people and new patterns of social and cultural life.

The musical repertoire and practices of Welsh chapels in the nineteenth century reflects the growth and nature of Welsh nonconformity. Composers and editors were very active in compiling and publishing collections of tunes; such activity encompassed church as well as chapel, however, as musicians associated with the Established Church made important contributions, especially in the earlier part of the century. Owen Williams (1774–1839) published a two-volume collection, *Brenhinol Ganiadau Seion* (The Royal Songs of Zion) in 1819, which included new tunes and arrangements by Samuel Wesley and Vincent Novello. The two volumes reflect the different repertoires of congregational song that had prevailed in Wales to that time; the first volume provides repertoire in the metres of the metrical psalms, while the second covers a more expansive range in line with Williams Pantycelyn's hymns. The Rev. J. D. Edwards's *Original Sacred Music* (1836) sought to serve the Established Church, and included many of his own compositions.[13] Richard Mills, part of an influential musical family from Llanidloes, published his substantial *Caniadau Seion* (The Songs of Zion; 1840), in which he brought older Welsh tunes, and those by emerging Welsh composers such as R. H. Prichard and J. Ambrose Lloyd, alongside tunes borrowed from English collections and arrangements of melodies by art music composers such as Handel and Haydn. These collections mirror developments in England in two important ways. Most obviously, Mills

---

[13] A second volume was published in 1843.

drew on tunes that had gained considerable popularity in English non-conformist circles, such as 'Lyngham' and 'Lydia'. Luff expresses surprise at the inclusion of these 'rather weak and superficial tunes', but they indicate the necessary balance of musical discernment and popularity that compilers had to manage.[14] Beyond instances of shared repertoire, similarly to many collections produced in the same period by English musicians, these volumes were often locally focused, containing the work of a small number of composers, and were relatively modest in size. They were often intended to be compatible with a range of existing collections of hymn texts.

In addition to indicating some of the repertoire in use in this period, these collections also offer insights into musical practice. The relationship between the musical materials as published and the way in which the tunes were sung in chapels and churches is not straightforward, in part owing to the musical backgrounds of many of the composers and compilers. Luff argues that these musicians were 'working ... under great disadvantages. None of them were professional musicians and this led, particularly in the early part of this period, to their work being important only in a small area of influence. Their tunes were often full of mistakes in the harmony, and have needed the hand of later editors to make them usable today.'[15] His assertion is accurate when the tunes are considered in relation to the conventions of harmony and voice leading that have long characterised the formal teaching of music. The tune 'Claddedigaeth' ('Burial') by John Ellis (see Example 10.1) illustrates Luff's argument; he considers that Ellis's compositions 'show a gift for writing melodies but they are full of weaknesses and mistakes when he comes to composing harmony'.[16]

Sung literally as printed, Ellis's tune would indeed sound ungainly in places, and would also pose awkwardness for the singers: for example, the augmented fifth interval in the bass line in bars 3–4. In a musical culture where the printed notation is accorded the highest authority, as was to become the case in hymnody later in the nineteenth century, and as large-scale collections sought to establish fixed relationships between texts and tunes as well as to print definitive versions of both, considerable editorial intervention would indeed have been required to make Ellis's tune conform to the expected standard. This was not, however, the musical culture that prevailed in Wales when his tunes were first published. Luff himself notes that 'Many of the travelling Psalm teachers were ignorant of music [notation] and simply taught by rote.'[17] The construction of Ellis's tunes,

[14] Luff, *Welsh Hymns*, p. 175. [15] Ibid., p. 162. [16] Ibid., p. 164. [17] Ibid., p. 162.

Example 10.1 John Ellis, 'Claddedigaeth', *Mawl yr Arglwydd* (Trefriw: I. Davies, 1816), bars 1–13

however, make clear that some sort of part-singing was customary; later in the same tune, the melodic material is shared between the treble and bass staves in a brief dialogue. The notation, therefore, is best understood as an imperfect transcription of Ellis's intentions; the occasional presence of chords in the bass part suggests that the score does not represent the totality of what might be sung in performance. Such part-singing would have been markedly different from the tightly constructed four-part harmony that was later to be regarded as a central feature of Welsh musical practice and musicality. However, separate parts for women and men are clearly documented in eighteenth-century nonconformist repertoire in England, and several of the early-nineteenth-century English tunes later borrowed by Richard Mills in *Caniadau Seion* made a particular virtue of having separate parts for them. Both imported and locally composed tunes indicate that the reported unison singing of the eighteenth-century revivalists had given way to some form of part-singing. That it was not firmly based on printed sources is unsurprising, given that the musical education even of those leading congregations was severely limited, let alone that of the congregants themselves. It is possible that in such practices the germ of the Welsh predilection for singing in harmony, so closely associated with hymnody, may be found. While developments in print and music education, most notably the tonic sol-fa system, played a central role in ingraining harmony singing in generations of Welsh chapel goers, the practice of harmony singing without reliance on printed notation may actually be traced back rather further.

By the middle of the century, hymnals containing tunes printed in four parts were becoming increasingly common. The work of Edward Stephen (Tanymarian; 1822–85) was influential in this regard; having assumed the editorship of *Cerddor y Cysegr* (The Sanctuary Musician) in 1859, he set about reharmonising the tunes, drawing on his musical education from the Congregational college in Bala, which indicates that the published version of hymn tunes was by now more highly prized. Even more significant than Tanymarian's work was that of John Roberts (Ieuan Gwyllt; 1822–77), whose *Llyfr Tonau Cynulleidfaol* (Congregational Tune Book; 1859) quickly gained national prominence. While a later tonic sol-fa edition would sell in massive quantities, the sale of some 17,000 copies of the original staff notation edition within three years of its publication is striking. This was not merely a book that sought to document current practice, but one that was central to Ieuan Gwyllt's conviction that Welsh hymn singing was in desperate need of musical reform. Musical education both of ministers and congregation members was central to his vision and his collection was crucial in the establishment of Unions of Congregational Singing in the years following its publication.

Llyfr Tonau Cynulleidfaol is remarkable for its prolific use of Germanic tunes. James describes the book as 'a prescriptive one, aimed at setting new high standards', and notes the use of German melodies in this context.[18] The selection of tunes reflects Ieuan Gwyllt's musical education and background; after spending much of his early life near Aberystwyth, he moved to Liverpool in 1852 to pursue a career in journalism. The time he spent there broadened his musical experience considerably; Luff notes that 'Liverpool was part of a much wider world in every kind of way, not least in the realm of music.'[19] He became a keen concertgoer, frequently reviewing performances for *Yr Amserau* (*The Times*), the newspaper of which he was assistant editor. His particular interest in Germanic sacred music is illustrated by an 1857 article on Felix Mendelssohn, and he also became well acquainted with the music of J. S. Bach. His hymnal, published shortly after his return to Wales and his entry into the Calvinistic Methodist

---

[18] James, 'Evolution of the Welsh Hymn', p. 262.   [19] Luff, *Welsh Hymns*, p. 197.

ministry, draws heavily on Lutheran sources of the seventeenth and early eighteenth centuries. In this regard, it is remarkably similar to *The Chorale Book for England*, which it predates by four years. The musical editors of the latter, William Sterndale Bennett and Otto Goldschmidt, had been personally acquainted with Mendelssohn and his advocacy of Bach's music; Jeremy Dibble notes that 'It was no coincidence that the Chorale Book appeared at a time when the revival of interest in the music of J. S. Bach was gaining momentum.'[20] While Ieuan Gwyllt presented his tunes in open score, Sterndale Bennett and Goldschmidt opted for short score; in each case, there was a clear emphasis on controlling the musical performance, including the part-singing of the congregation. Ieuan Gwyllt's cosmopolitan selection of tunes, drawn from English, Welsh and American sources in addition to German, places *Llyfr Tonau Cynulleidfaol* among several significant British hymnals produced in a similar period that reflect an increasingly professionalised and directive approach to congregational hymnody. The borrowing of German tunes was one facet of a wider interest in reviving older repertoires, of which the renewed advocacy of plainsong by John Mason Neale, Thomas Helmore and others was especially influential. Ieuan Gwyllt's work was typical in its provision not only of an extensive musical repertoire but in its explicit aim of improving musical taste and practice in congregational singing, which he addresses at length in the preface.

The spread of nonconformity within the Aber Valley exemplifies the extent to which religious growth was shaped by industrialisation and associated population patterns. Although Caerphilly, the principal town in the parish of Eglwysilan, had grown considerably in the eighteenth century, by the middle of the nineteenth century, the Aber Valley itself was still sparsely populated. Abertridwr was a small village centred on a mill, while Senghenydd, at the upper end of the valley, consisted only of adjoining farms. An Independent chapel, Adulam, was established in Abertridwr; its unusual name was a Welsh adaptation of Adullam, the biblical cave or fortress where David sought refuge from King Saul. The chapel was originally founded as an outpost from Groeswen and was initially served by the same minister. Coal mining did not begin in the valley until the final decade of the century, with the sinking of the Universal Colliery in Senghenydd in 1891 and the Windsor Colliery in Abertridwr in 1895. These led to a significant population influx, and

---

[20] Jeremy Dibble, 'The Chorale Book for England', *The Canterbury Dictionary of Hymnology*, www.hymnology.co.uk/t/the-chorale-book-for-england (accessed 25 February 2021).

numerous chapels were erected in both villages; their participation in the Welsh Revival of 1904–5 is considered below. In the town of Caerphilly, meanwhile, the parish church of St Martin was built in 1877–9 on the site where the chapel of ease from Eglwysilan had been established. Shortly after its completion, a pipe organ was installed in the church by the renowned organ builder 'Father' Henry Willis.[21] This indicates the influence of the choral revival in the Established Church, which, alongside the building's neo-gothic style, is evidence of the lasting impact of the Oxford Movement. While pipe organs were also installed in some nonconformist chapels, many more acquired harmoniums or other types of reed organ, which were more economical in terms of both space and cost and amply served the need to provide accompaniment for congregational singing.

Hymns and the Welsh Revival of 1904–1905

The period around the turn of the twentieth century has been especially influential in shaping perceptions of Welsh Christianity and its hymnody. Though Wales had experienced religious revivals frequently since the eighteenth century, the revival of 1904–5, aided by the socio-economic impacts of industrialisation, has been the most celebrated. Similarly, while hymn-tune composition in Wales can be traced further back than this period, as discussed in the previous section, a body of repertoire emerged in the latter decades of the nineteenth century and the early part of the twentieth that has come to be regarded as representing the archetypal Welsh hymn tune.

Musically, the roots of this period of extensive compositional activity can be observed in the mid-nineteenth-century publications of Richard Mills, Ieuan Gwyllt and others, as well as in later reactions against the musical aims set out by Ieuan Gwyllt in *Llyfr Tonau Cynulleidfaol*. Tunes such as 'Hyfrydol' by Rowland Huw Prichard (1811–87) and 'Groeswen' by John Ambrose Lloyd (1815–74) began to appear. These tunes display strong and distinctive melodic profiles, often with a clear sense of climax, as well as greater levels of musical security in harmonisation compared with the efforts of earlier figures such as John Ellis. Tunes by a later generation of Welsh composers embedded and heightened such characteristics, but they were also influenced by musical developments from well beyond Wales.

---

[21] *The National Pipe Organ Register*, www.npor.org.uk/NPORView.html?RI=N11896 (accessed 25 February 2021).

The extensive British ministry of the American duo Ira D. Sankey and Dwight L. Moody was consolidated by the publication of many volumes of gospel songs by Sankey and others that were used to great effect in their meetings. Six volumes were published in Welsh translations as *Swn y Juwbili: neu Ganiadau y Diwygiad* (Sound of the Jubilee: or Songs of Revival; 1874–8). Despite the rather austere musical taste exhibited in *Llyfr Tonau Cynulleidfaol*, Ieaun Gwyllt was the translator of these hymns. James suggests two significant factors to explain this apparently radical change of opinion: first, that the success of the cymanfa ganu model and tonic sol-fa in enabling congregations to learn new hymn tunes led Ieuan Gwyllt to be concerned that musical matters had taken precedence over the spiritual dimension of hymnody, and second, that there had been a change in public taste by this time: 'by the 1870s congregations had become tired of the austere style of hymn-tune and hymn-singing Ieuan Gwyllt had been promoting during the previous decade, and were only too ready to adopt gospel songs like Sankey's'.[22]

A rather contorted example of the influence of North American hymnody involves a hymn text by William Rees ('Gwilym Hiraethog', 1802–83), 'Dyma Gariad Fel y Moroedd' ('Here is Love, Vast as the Ocean'). Rees's original Welsh text was set to a variety of tunes by Welsh composers but is particularly associated with Thomas Williams's 'Ebenezer'. The musical history of the English translations made by William Edwards and Howell Elvet Lewis is rather different. These have become tightly wedded to a tune by the prolific American revivalist composer Robert Lowry (1826–99). Lowry's tune was originally titled 'Jesus Only', which has been translated as 'Dim Ond Iesu' in many Welsh hymnals. The Welsh text, most likely sung to 'Ebenezer', was widely used in the 1904–5 revival, after which several American publications title Lowry's tune 'Cymraeg' ('Welsh'), despite the fact that it was composed almost a quarter of a century before the first English translation of Rees's hymn was published in 1900. One of the most emblematic tunes to emerge from the 1904–5 revival, 'Calon Lân' ('A Pure Heart'), composed by John Hughes (1872–1914), bears a striking resemblance to Lowry's tune. Both are in the same metre and exhibit a great deal of melodic and harmonic commonality. While no direct influence can be proved, the similarities mean that it is not possible to attribute any musically unique characteristics to the Welsh tunes of this type that gained great popularity in Wales around the time of the revival and more widely thereafter.

---

[22] James, 'Evolution of the Welsh Hymn', p. 265.

The differences in the associations of words and music between original Welsh hymn texts and their English translations is further illustrated by arguably the most famous of all Welsh hymn tunes, 'Cwm Rhondda' ('Rhondda Valley'), composed by John Hughes of Pontypridd (1873–1932). Hughes's memorable tune rises to a stirring climax in the penultimate musical phrase, extending the characteristic observed in earlier examples by Prichard and Lloyd through its use of a long-held dominant-seventh chord and an element of independence between different voice parts. This has become ubiquitous at Welsh rugby matches in its association with Peter Williams's translation of Williams Pantycelyn's hymn 'Arglwydd, Arwain Trwy'r Anialwch' ('Guide Me, O Thou Great Jehovah'), popularly known as 'Bread of Heaven'. Its association with this text in print has been traced to a 1920 volume of *The Musical Salvationist* that featured several Welsh tunes, reflecting the Salvation Army's presence in Wales since 1874, but Luff notes that the original Welsh text is typically sung to different tunes.[23] 'Cwm Rhondda' also provides further evidence of the variable nature of musical practice in Welsh nonconformity. While most modern hymnals print the fifth phrase of the tune ending with high repeated notes in the treble part, above tenor and bass parts descending in parallel thirds, some versions of the tune have the treble and bass lines descending in parallel tenths, while the tenor part has the repeated high notes. Investigative work by hymnologist Joseph Herl concluded that the former was the original, which is borne out by the manuscript in the composer's hand shown in Figure 10.1.[24] Such interchangeability reflects the legacy of the older practice of placing the melody in the tenor part; the strength of part-singing in Wales in this period, stemming from the cymanfa ganu movement, meant that hymn-tune composers often wrote highly melodic lines for each voice part. In this regard, the tunes bear some similarity to a type of English tune sometimes described as 'Old Methodist'. While often published in the early decades of the nineteenth century, there was a revival of interest in these tunes around the turn of the twentieth century, partly through events to commemorate significant anniversaries such as the centenaries of John Wesley's death and of the birth of Primitive Methodism.

Language has played an important role in the development of Welsh nonconformist repertoire and practice and is closely connected to the

---

[23] Alan Luff, 'John Hughes', *The Canterbury Dictionary of Hymnology*, www.hymnology.co.uk/j/john-hughes (accessed 25 February 2021).

[24] Joseph Herl, 'Earliest Source of "Cwm Rhondda" Found', *The Hymn Society Bulletin*, 21/3 (2015), 98–102.

10 *Nonconformists and Their Music* 237

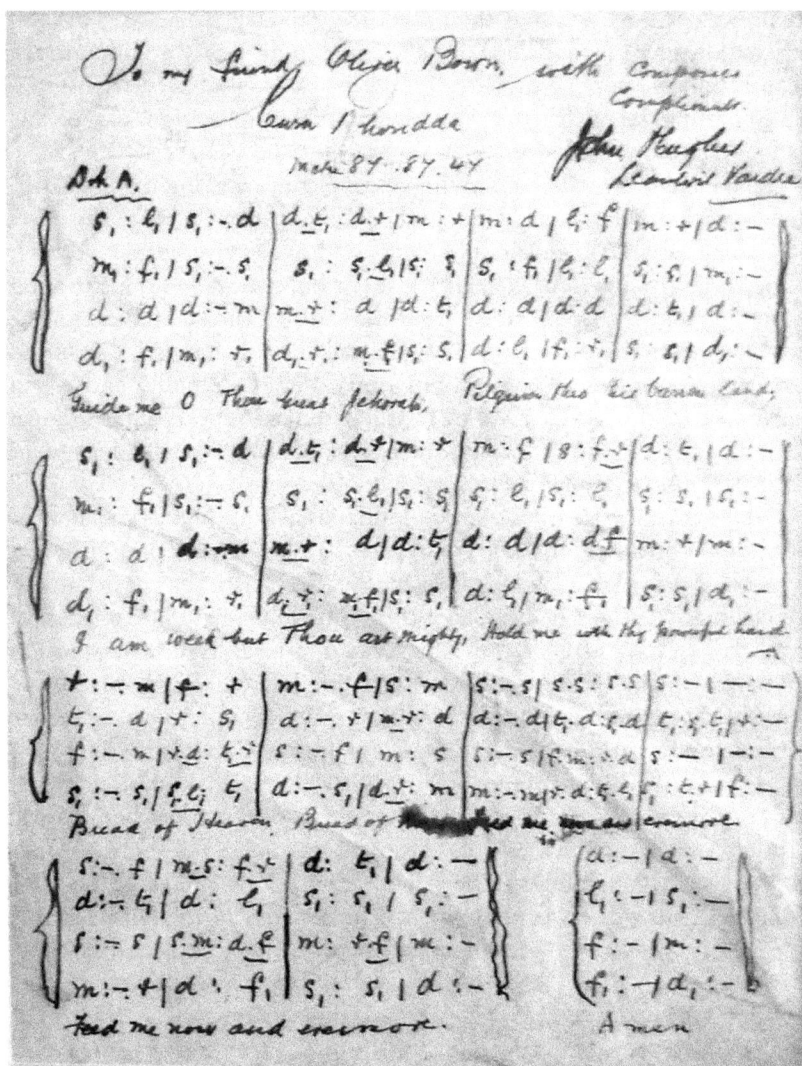

Figure 10.1 Tonic sol-fa score of the hymn 'Cwm Rhondda' (1907) in the hand of, and signed by, the composer John Hughes. By kind permission of the descendants of the composer's friend Mr Oliver Bown

population changes that happened as a result of industrialisation in the latter part of the nineteenth century. The new urban areas saw an influx of workers not only from across Wales but also from England and Ireland which, in many parts of the south Wales coalfield in particular, led to

English displacing Welsh as the most widely spoken language. This also affected the physical landscape of these communities, as in addition to the chapels built by nonconformists of different theological persuasions, separate buildings for Welsh- and English-speaking congregations of the same denomination were also erected in some towns and villages.

Senghenydd provides a striking example of the intensive chapel-building activity that quickly followed population growth and of the effect of theological and linguistic differences. Within twelve years of the pit being sunk in 1891, eight chapels had been built, along with a Salvation Army hall and a chapel of ease from the parish church, St Peter's. The nonconformist chapels included Welsh and English Baptist, Welsh and English Independent, Welsh and English Wesleyan Methodist and Welsh Calvinistic Methodist. Three were rebuilt within a few years of the original construction and many were large buildings; Noddfa Welsh Independent Chapel, for instance, had a capacity of 700.

Despite the apparently clear denominational and linguistic demarcations, the spread of the 1904–5 revival to the Aber Valley provides evidence that, at least sometimes, the chapels coexisted in a collaborative way. The origins of the nationwide revival are imprecise; there were several early centres of activity and leading preachers associated with them. However, the ministry of Evan Roberts (1878–1951) became central to its spread throughout Wales and to its influence being felt internationally. Though he was from a Calvinistic Methodist background, and was training for ministry in that denomination, the revival Roberts led was experienced across denominational boundaries. Music was to play a pivotal role in revival meetings; Brynmor P. Jones notes that: 'Although Evan Roberts had encouraged members of the West Wales team to witness in song, he had no set plan to use music. It was during one of the Gorseinon meetings that five young ladies came forward to offer their talents to the Lord.'[25] These women were to play an important part in the revival meetings, travelling with Roberts around south Wales, and their contributions inspired other singers, male and female, to make their own contributions. Most famous of these was Annie Davies, one of several professionally trained singers who became involved in the revival. She would come to be particularly associated with the hymn 'Dyma Gariad Fel y Moroedd', which was dubbed 'the great

---

[25] Brynmor P. Jones, *Voices from the Welsh Revival 1904–1905* (Bridgend: Evangelical Press of Wales, 1995), p. 52.

hymn of the revival' by D. M. Phillips, himself a noted preacher in the revival and later biographer of Evan Roberts.

Reports of the revival were carried in the Welsh press and did much to aid its spread by raising public awareness. They describe the widespread use of both congregational and solo singing, often apparently in spontaneous response to what was said in sermons, testimonies and prayers. Reporting a meeting led by Evan Roberts in Dowlais, Merthyr Tydfil, the principal journalistic chronicler of the revival, Thomas Davies (who published under the name Awstin), described how 'when the "test" for converts was made, and people rose to signify their surrender, the singing of "Diolch iddo" ("Thanks be to him") became literally triumphant, and when the enthusiasm grew, the singers, hundreds of them, actually clapped their hands with joy, keeping time with the music by the handclapping'.[26] Summarising accounts of Annie Davies's solo singing, meanwhile, Jones describes the prominent role she frequently took in revival meetings: 'Not only would she break across Evan Roberts, but other team members also. When Mary Davies was speaking, for example, or Annie Rees testifying, she would break in, sing her favourite lines and then break down, and the crowd with her.'[27] Though Welsh hymns feature prominently in reports, there are also many accounts of English-language hymns being sung, including revivalist repertoire from the United States by writers such as Sankey and Fanny Crosby. Indeed, the prominent role given to vocal soloists and the reputation some of them – such as Annie Davies – gained owes much to the legacy of Sankey and Moody's partnership, where the latter's preaching and the former's musical contributions were tightly integrated.

Awstin's account of Evan Roberts's visit to Senghenydd on 7 December 1904 provides further evidence of the powerful hymn singing that characterised revival meetings, as well as indicating how local customs and contexts shaped events. Roberts, accompanied by three of his regular team, led three meetings throughout the day: two at the Welsh Calvinistic Methodist chapel interspersed with an afternoon meeting in the Welsh Baptist chapel. Hymn singing is mentioned in relation to all three meetings; Awstin comments on the use of a hymn previously unfamiliar to him at both meetings in the Calvinistic Methodist chapel, describing how 'Cof am y Cyfiawn Iesu' ('Remembering the Righteous Jesus') was sung 'to the

---

[26] *The Religious Revival in Wales, 1904. By Awstin and Other Special Correspondents of the Western Mail*, Vol. 3 (Cardiff: Western Mail, 1905), p. 26.
[27] Jones, *Voices from the Welsh Revival*, p. 54.

old tune "Penry", and repeated with emphatic heartiness' at the early afternoon meeting, and after it was reused at the evening meeting, suggesting that 'is likely to become a favourite with the congregations'. In the mid-afternoon meeting, meanwhile, he notes that after the spiritual temperature was raised by Roberts, '"Throw Out the Life-line" was sung with great earnestness'.[28] In his account of the morning meeting he describes how the conversion of one man was followed by great shouts of 'Songs of Praise I Will Ever Give to Thee', seemingly a reference to Peter Williams's 'Guide Me, O Thou Great Jehovah'. Awstin draws attention to the repetition of a hymn in the morning meeting; such practice was seemingly commonplace; hymns with refrains or tunes with a particularly intense musical climax, such as 'Cwm Rhondda', lent themselves to this practice, which has remained influential. Though Senghenydd experienced the effects of the 1904–5 revival in similar ways to many other towns and villages throughout Wales, its history is dominated by two large-scale mining disasters in a similar period; in 1901, 81 men and boys had been killed by an explosion in the Universal Colliery, and nearly a decade after the revival, 439 men and boys were killed at the same site in Britain's largest mining disaster. Inevitably, some of those killed were members of the local chapels; among the dead in 1901 was John T. Evans, precentor at Noddfa Welsh Independent Chapel.

Decline and Remembrance

In much the same way that the development of the coal-mining industry and the rapid expansion of Welsh nonconformity were interrelated, both experienced significant decline broadly in parallel during the twentieth century. The Universal Colliery in Senghenydd resumed production after the 1913 disaster, but closed in 1928, although the Windsor Colliery in Abertridwr remained open until 1986. Throughout the century, almost all of the various chapels closed so that by the turn of the twenty-first century, only the former English Independent chapel, now a United Reformed Church, remained; many of the others had been demolished and others converted to private dwellings. St Peter's, the daughter church from Eglwysilan, also closed in the early part of the twenty-first century. In keeping with the general decline in religious observance throughout Britain, a similar pattern of closures took place in many towns and villages throughout Wales.

---

[28] Awstin, 'Senghenydd and the Revival', *Western Mail*, 8 December 1904, 5.

In the face of such decline, ecumenical cooperation between the denominations became increasingly necessary, not least in the area of hymnody. The Welsh Calvinistic and Wesleyan Methodists had co-published *Llyfr Emynau a Thonau y Methodistiaid Calfinaidd a Wesleaidd* (The Calvinistic and Wesleyan Methodist Hymn and Tune Book) as early as 1929. Towards the end of the century, a joint venture undertaken by Independents, Baptists, Methodists, Presbyterians (the Calvinistic Methodist Church in Wales adopted the name Eglwys Bresbyteraidd Cymru – The Presbyterian Church of Wales – in 1928) and Anglicans resulted in the publication of *Caneuon Ffydd* (Songs of Faith) in 2001. This substantial volume of over 900 texts included many historic Welsh hymns alongside translations of English hymns from many different periods and traditions, including well-known examples of the worship-song genre by authors and composers such as Graham Kendrick and David Evans.

In common with patterns of religious attendance in other parts of the United Kingdom, there have also been areas of growth. Larger towns and cities have seen growth in evangelical and charismatic congregations, some newly established, but others, such as Cardiff's City Church (formerly City Temple), founded in 1929, have longer histories. As transportation has made such venues accessible to worshippers from a far broader geographical base, so too has technology played a significant role in establishing international repertoires of music, referred to by a variety of names including worship songs and praise and worship. The music of prominent musicians from the UK such as Tim Hughes, Matt Redman and others commonly feature alongside repertoire from the United States, Australia and elsewhere. Little of this repertoire has been produced within Wales, though one of its leading British proponents, Noel Richards (b. 1955), was born in Llantrisant and had his early experience of Christianity through a local Pentecostal church before serving several churches in different parts of England alongside a performing career.[29]

Despite the widespread decline of church and chapel attendance in Wales, the music of Welsh nonconformity maintains a place in the cultural memory and practices of the twenty-first century. The custom of singing hymns such as 'Cwm Rhondda' and 'Calon Lân' at rugby and football matches remains strong, and is explored in Chapter 15. Meanwhile, among the many local events to commemorate the centenary of the 1913 Universal Colliery disaster in Senghenydd was a cymanfa ganu held in the sole remaining nonconformist chapel in the village, with congregational

---

[29] 'Worship Leader Profiles: Noel Richards', *Watton on the Web*, www.watton.org/worship/profiles/noelrichards.shtml (accessed 25 February 2021).

singing led by the Aber Valley Male Voice Choir. Acclaimed Welsh solo singers such as Katherine Jenkins and Charlotte Church and popular ensembles such as Only Men Aloud and Only Boys Aloud also frequently perform and record arrangements of Welsh hymns. Poets and composers have created a substantial body of Welsh hymnody, and while their legacy is significant, the different periods of Welsh nonconformist history discussed here and the legacy of that repertoire in twenty-first-century Wales point to the primary importance of hymnody as a cultural practice that has shaped Welsh society in many different ways.

CHAPTER 11

Professionalisation in the Twentieth Century

Lyn Davies

From the early twentieth century, and especially after 1945, music in Wales benefited from a steady increase in public funding for a professional infrastructure for the arts. This period must be seen in the context of the seismic events that punctuated the period – particularly world wars and the periods of economic stagnation and high unemployment that followed. Even after World War II, the overall economic picture was uncertain, and this uncertainty impacted on the arts and education.

The Victorian Legacy

Composer and educator Joseph Parry (1841–1903) and many of his contemporaries left a potent cultural legacy that lasted well into the twentieth century. Essentially amateur in nature and bound by the attendant nonconformist and eisteddfod milieu and mores, music making both in practical and compositional terms was reflective of those times – hymn tunes, anthems, glee songs, oratorios, cantatas, parlour songs, ballads and folk-song arrangements offering proof of high productivity but varying quality – though many of the hymn tunes of this period are among the finest written. Dramatic vocal *scenas* and parlour songs emerged that have remained favourites in the Welsh music repertoire, among them, for example, R. S. Hughes's 'Arafa Don' ('Be Still, Wave'), which became one of the most performed solo songs in the first half of the twentieth century. Parry's 'Myfanwy', a part-song for male voice choir, is a typical example of the type of British composition identified by Benedict Taylor as raising challenging questions about emotional depth and sentimentality, yet it has remained part of the staple repertoire of Welsh choirs and solo artists alike (see Figure 11.1).[1]

---

[1] Benedict Taylor, 'The Lost Chord: Sentimentality, Sincerity, and the Search for "Emotional Depth" in 19th-Century Music', *International Review of the Aesthetics and Sociology of Music*, 40/2 (2009), 207–233.

Figure 11.1 First page of Joseph Parry's 'Myfanwy' (1875). This version, published by Snell of Swansea in 1931, used the plates of the original printing of 1875 by Isaac Jones of Treherbert

The composers who followed in Parry's wake maintained much of this musical patterning, but gradually moved towards greater discrimination in choosing texts for musical settings and greater awareness of British and continental trends. As Dulais Rhys, Gareth Williams and others have emphasised,[2] Parry lacked true compositional ambition. His songs rarely rise above the mundane Victorian parlour song; he could be derivative and lacked stylistic consistency. Much of his music was saturated with Handelian or Mendelssohnian undertones, with both Verdi and Wagner appearing as influences later in his career. Like many of his contemporaries, he never developed a distinctive voice as a composer. Nonetheless, he was highly revered in Wales and took the bardic title Pencerdd America at the National Eisteddfod in 1865. While his compositions were popular during his lifetime, his role as an educator was vital and his sense of mission drew admiration. His mantle passed to his student at Aberystwyth, David Jenkins, who developed his own role as an educator.

The Next Wave of Composers

The composers who followed in Parry's wake faced a difficult task, but their role was crucial in moving Welsh music away from the Victorian past towards new and more distinctive compositional styles. The *fin-de-siècle* composers emerged in an environment of music practice that was largely amateur. They were aware of the impact of Parry on a nation that had idolised him beyond any other musician in living memory. By the end of his life, Parry was one of a very small number of Welshmen, which included the politician David Lloyd George, whose names were known around the world.

Of the composers active in the first three decades of the twentieth century, none could be said to belong to a school of Welsh composers, but two, David Vaughan Thomas (1873–1934)[3] and David de Lloyd (1883–1948),[4] used their

---

[2] Dulais Rhys, *Joseph Parry: Bachgen Bach o Ferthyr* (Caerdydd: Gwasg Prifysgol Cymru, 1998); Dulais Rhys and Frank Bott, *To Philadelphia and Back: The Life and Music of Joseph Parry* (Llanrwst: Gwasg Carreg Gwalch, 2010); Gareth Williams, *Valleys of Song: Music and Society in Wales, 1840–1914* (Cardiff: University of Wales Press, 1998).

[3] See Lyn Davies, *David Vaughan Thomas*, Composers of Wales Monographs (Cardiff: Welsh Music Information Centre, 2004); Lyn Davies, 'Towards an Authentic Celtic Voice in Music: The Life and Work of David Vaughan Thomas (1873–1934)', *Welsh Music History/Hanes Cerddoriaeth Cymru*, 2 (1997), 213–235. Memories of Vaughan Thomas are published in a special issue of *Tir Newydd*, rhif 16 (Mehefin 1939).

[4] See John Glynne Evans, 'David de Lloyd: Scholar Musician', *Welsh Music/Cerddoriaeth Cymru*, 3/10 (Autumn/Hydref 1971), 4–10.

music to engage deeply with older Welsh poetry and myth in ways that might have led to a nationalistic approach comparable to that of Vaughan Williams in England; few, if any, followed their lead. This generation moved Welsh music forward in a dynamic manner, though few possessed the ability to compose on a large scale or with stylistic consistency. Some, such as E. T. Davies, W. Hubert Davies and Richard Maldwyn Price, were influenced by the work of the Welsh Folk-Song Society, but while their work was technically proficient and often attractive, they did not integrate traditional song into their music as did Vaughan Williams and Gustav Holst. Many were able performers – most were fine pianists, organists (several were Fellows of the Royal College of Organists), conductors, string players (such as W. Hubert Davies and Kenneth Harding) and singers. They made efforts to raise standards in community music making, education, criticism and performance. Their work was also actively promoted by major publishers. Whereas in England the works of modern composers such as Skryabin, Schoenberg, Stravinsky, Richard Strauss and Debussy were frequently heard, in Wales there was a rejection of more radical and 'Teutonic' tendencies, and Vaughan Thomas warned of the dangerous and even pernicious nature of 'foreign' influences.[5]

Vaughan Thomas was as sophisticated a musician as Wales had produced in this period. His work patterns took him away from composing for prolonged periods (he was an overseas examiner for Trinity College London), but he managed to produce an impressive body of work. An Oxford graduate in mathematics, he was a fine keyboard player as well as a poet, a perceptive diarist and a scholar of early Welsh poetry and was widely read in several languages. Until 1914 he produced mainly vocal and choral works. His song 'Angladd y Marchog' ('The Knight's Burial') is a dramatic *scena* for baritone and piano; if not fully consistent stylistically it had consistent popularity. 'Ysbryd y Mynydd' ('The Mountain Spirit') is a more musically thought-through song and stylistically more aligned with the English song tradition of his era. His early anthems and part-songs marked the beginning of a move away from the Victoriana of Welsh music. Several of the early works were large-scale, such as *A Song for St Cecilia's Day* (1909) and *The Bard* (1910). *The Bard* is well crafted with nothing insular in its continental outlook: it heralded a new voice in Welsh music with its declamatory style and Straussian overtones. Disappointed at not being awarded the Chair of Music at Aberystwyth in 1919, when Henry Walford Davies was appointed

---

[5] Davies, 'Towards an Authentic Celtic Voice', p. 216.

Director of Music for the University of Wales, Vaughan Thomas withdrew from fields of musical activity he might have helped shape, but pragmatism appears not to have been his forte. His agnosticism did not stop him from writing very fine hymn tunes. His notion of 'Welshness' in music was manifested in settings of the work of the fourteenth-century poet Dafydd ap Gwilym and others in his *Saith o Ganeuon ar Gywyddau Dafydd ap Gwilym ac Eraill* (Seven Songs on Cywyddau by Dafydd ap Gwilym and Others; 1922). The songs 'Berwyn' and 'O Fair Wen' ('O Mary Fair') are among the most original settings of Welsh poetry and compare favourably with later settings by (for example) Mansel Thomas, Meirion Williams and Dilys Elwyn Edwards. Vaughan Thomas's output includes a fine string quintet in which lyrical musical gestures are tellingly utilised and the style is admirably concise and concentrated. His vision was that of a new kind of Welsh music, embracing early Welsh poetic metres and what he termed 'a deeper understanding of traditional Welsh music and the development of our finest poetry'.[6] This new kind of music is infused with grace notes, more complex harmonies (there are Ravelian touches in *Saith o Ganeuon*) and a feeling for improvisation reminiscent of cerdd dant. His main achievement was to fuse complex poetic metre with musical simplicity.

Just as Vaughan Thomas found solace in the complex poetry of the past, so too did David de Lloyd, one of the most gifted Welsh musicians of his generation. Like Vaughan Thomas, his awareness of continental models was coupled with an indebtedness to his Welsh roots. He was also expert in tonic sol-fa. Indeed, he was to conduct orchestras in later life with scores by the great classical composers transcribed by him into sol-fa. He was born in Skewen and educated at Aberystwyth and Leipzig, before returning to Aberystwyth, where he became a lecturer and finally Gregynog Professor of Music in succession to Walford Davies in 1926. Only an occasional composer because of his heavy academic workload, he nonetheless produced two operas, *Gwenllian* (1924) and *Tir na n-Óg* (The Land of Youth; 1930), both of which contain fine dramatic moments and well-crafted music in a style similar to that of Rutland Boughton. De Lloyd followed the lead of Vaughan Thomas with his *Chwech o Englynion ar Gân* (Six Englynion in Song) in which impressionistic tinges can be heard to good effect. Composed in 1932, the work was probably the first setting of the englyn metre in modern art music. Both Vaughan Thomas and de Lloyd influenced younger composers such as Arwel Hughes (1909–88), Mansel

---

[6] *Tir Newydd*, Rhif 16, 26, quoted in Davies, 'Towards an Authentic Celtic Voice', p. 218.

Thomas (1909–86) and Grace Williams (1906–77). De Lloyd's lecture notes display his industry and sense of detail across the many academic fields he taught at Aberystwyth. His finest work is arguably *Tu Draw i'r Llen* (Beyond the Veil; 1924), a choral and orchestral work that manifests Elgarian traits and a gift for orchestration.

Daniel Protheroe (1866–1934) was born in Breconshire but emigrated to the United States in 1885.[7] He made his reputation as a composer, conductor and adjudicator there, returning to Wales for the National Eisteddfod each summer. At various times he lived in Scranton, Milwaukee and Chicago, where his many choral works such as *Y Mae Afon* (There Is a River) became popular with audiences for their immediacy and tunefulness. Protheroe's male voice works such as *Invictus* and *Nidaros*, and arrangements of hymn tunes for male voices, had enduring popularity in the twentieth century. *Invictus* and *Nidaros* owe something to François Anatole Laurent de Rillé's *The Martyrs of the Arena* and its stirring narrative style. David Jenkins, D. C. Williams and T. Maldwyn Price also followed this fashion, as did T. Osborne Roberts[8] in his *Battle of the Baltic*. Roberts's religious *oeuvre* might be described as a synthesis of 'high chapel and low church', a measured nonconformity with distinctive harmonic progressions, both sturdy and memorable.

E. T. Davies (1878–1969),[9] like so many of his generation, was a fine organist and conductor as well as a folk-tune arranger of considerable ingenuity. He made a considerable impact on Welsh music through his position as Director of Music at the University College of North Wales, Bangor. Having been trained locally and qualified as a Fellow of the Royal College of Organists at a young age, he was thoroughly acquainted with the amateur environment and conducted widely in his locality (from the light operettas of Gilbert and Sullivan to the standard choral repertoire and opera with the Merthyr Operatic Society). He was appointed to Bangor in 1920 and swiftly made his presence felt throughout Wales. His many folk-song arrangements, songs and choral music, and his well-crafted salon chamber music, are the work of a miniaturist with fastidious craftsmanship and polish. Songs such as 'Ynys y Plant' ('The Children's Isle') with its wistful lyricism and the declamatory and dramatic 'A Ballad of Glyndwr's

---

[7] Rhidian Griffiths, 'Daniel Protheroe (1866–1934)', in *Cydymaith i Gerddoriaeth Cymru*, goln. Pwyll ap Siôn a Wyn Thomas (Talybont: Y Lolfa, 2018), tt. 35–36.

[8] See Huw Williams, *Thomas Osborne Roberts 1879–1948* ([Caernarfon]: Cyngor Gwlad Gwynedd, 1980).

[9] A. Tudno Williams, *E. T. Davies: Arloeswr Cerdd* (Dinbych: Gwasg Gee, 1981).

Rising 1400' are fine examples of his craft. If in 'Ynys y Plant' the structural joins are somewhat obvious, 'A Ballad of Glyndwr's Rising' has a more cogent whole and shares superficial similarities with Carl Loewe's 'Edward'. Davies was a fine keyboard player, and his piano writing was always idiomatic. His hymn tunes, such as *'Via Crucis'*, 'Hermon' and 'Pontmorlais', show a sophisticated and considered harmonic idiom. He also achieved much in his work codifying Welsh folk music, but he remained Director of Music at Bangor, never the Professor, to the chagrin of many.

Other composers of this generation included J. Morgan Lloyd, John Morgan Nicholas, D. Afan Thomas and W. Bradwen Jones.[10] A sophisticated song composer, Jones wrote some of the most advanced Welsh songs of the period: 'Mab y Môr' ('Son of the Sea') is a lyrical and meditative work with a typically idiomatic and testing piano part which is well integrated into the whole. Morgan Nicholas's 'Y Dieithryn' ('The Stranger') is one of the finest postwar songs and deserves more critical appraisal outside Wales.

Some composers showed an awareness of continental idioms and an ability to produce orchestral works of an advanced and ambitious nature. They include Morfydd Llwyn Owen, John Rippiner Heath, Cyril Jenkins, Richard Maldwyn Price, W. Hubert Davies, Kenneth Harding and Haydn Morris. John Rippiner Heath (1887–1950)[11] was not born in Wales but spent most of his life as a doctor in Barmouth. After graduating in medicine at Cambridge, he was encouraged by Walford Davies who arranged performances of his work at Aberystwyth. He forged a musical idiom based on late romanticism and impressionism, and his many large-scale works include the literary-inspired *Cupid's Alley* and *Five Pictures of the Night*, which show some indebtedness to Debussy's *Voiles*. He was widely published and some of his work was disseminated abroad. He was also a conductor, active with orchestras such as the London Symphony Orchestra, the Liverpool Philharmonic and Henry Wood's Queen's Hall Orchestra.

---

[10] For J. Morgan Lloyd and John Morgan Nicholas, see *Dictionary of Welsh Biography*, https://biogr aphy.wales/article/s2-LLOY-MOR-1880 and https://biography.wales/article/s12-NICH-MOR-1895 (both accessed 21 July 2021). For D. Afan Thomas, see Lyn Davies, 'D. Afan Thomas, "Cerddor o'r Cwm" (1881–1928)', in *Llynfi ac Afan, Garw ac Ogwr*, Cyfres y Cymoedd, gol. Hywel Teifi Edwards (Llandysul: Gomer, 1988), tt. 163–177. For William Bradwen Jones, see G. I. Jones, *Meistr Cerdd: Bywyd a Gwaith William Bradwen Jones, Cerddor* (Llangefni: Yr Awdur, 1983).

[11] David R. A. Evans, 'J. R. Heath (1887–1950), Medical Practitioner and Composer/J. R. Heath (1887–1950: Meddyg Teulu a Chyfansoddwr', *Welsh Music History/Hanes Cerddoriaeth Cymru*, 1 (1996), 42–76.

Of the composers of this era, the most enigmatic and engaging figure was Morfydd Llwyn Owen (1891–1918).[12] She was one of the most talented musicians produced in Wales and the tragedy of her early death reverberated beyond her own country. She deserves to be widely known as a composer of standing, and her colourful life added to her charisma. Few post-Victorian musicians captured the public imagination as she did. Her creative talent, the dualism (and later tension) of her Welsh roots and religiosity coupled with her exotic friendships, including her marriage to the Freud biographer and psychoanalyst Ernest Jones, all contributed to the attention she attracted in her lifetime. She died young with her creative promise largely unrealised. She was born in Treforest and educated at University College, Cardiff and the Royal Academy of Music, where she excelled as a pianist, singer and composer, winning an impressive series of prizes. The greater part of her output is vocal and choral, but she also produced some orchestral and instrumental music. Her song 'To Our Lady of Sorrows' is highly charged emotionally and manifests a lyrical intensity and a fusion of text and musical utterance. The neo-Slavic tinge of the harmonic progressions strikes a concentrated mood of melancholic contemplation. Her 'Lullaby at Sunset' is another finely crafted early song, along with 'Slumber Song of the Madonna', while 'Gweddi y Pechadur' ('The Sinner's Prayer') became much loved. Her *Nocturne for Orchestra* (1913) is superficially similar to Debussy's *Prélude à l'Après-midi d'un Faune*, and the delicate orchestration marks it out in early twentieth-century Welsh music. Her chamber music, especially for piano, is appealing and wholly idiomatic.

Cyril Jenkins (1885–1978)[13] was equally colourful but also dogmatic and difficult. His talents were real and his music, especially for brass band, remained in the repertoire for much of the twentieth century: his *Coriolanus* and *Love Divine* were among the first original test pieces for the standard brass band formulation to be used in the National Championship. He was musical director of the London County Council before moving to Australia and then the United States, where he conducted the Mormon Tabernacle Choir at Salt Lake City. Jenkins claimed to have studied with Ravel and the clear-cut, impressionistic qualities of

---

[12] Rhian Davies, *Yr Eneth Ddisglair Annwyl: Morfydd Owen (1891–1918): Ei Bywyd Mewn Lluniau/ Never So Pure a Sight: Morfydd Owen (1891–1918): Her Life in Pictures* (Llandysul: Gomer, 1994) and Rhian Davies, 'Mighty Atom: The Life and Music of Morfydd Owen (1891–1918)', *British Music*, 13 (1991), 38–58.

[13] His obituary, written by A. J. Heward Rees and David Wynne, appeared in *Welsh Music/ Cerddoriaeth Cymru*, 5/9 (Summer 1978), 80.

many of his works seem to bear this out. He was also the first to commit to print trenchantly critical views about Welsh music of the past, especially the music of Joseph Parry.[14] Several of Jenkins's own works were performed at the National Eisteddfod. Until his departure to Australia he was considered by some to be the leading 'modernist' in Welsh music. He was not without his detractors, however, and his vicious attacks on Parry made him many enemies. Of Jenkins's other works, a symphony, an oboe concerto, the *Welsh Fantasia for Strings* and the setting of *Young Lochinvar* for chorus and orchestra were regularly performed. Shorter works such as the part-songs 'Deep Jordan's Banks', 'Faery Song', 'A Shepherd's Lullaby' and his arrangements of Welsh folk songs show fastidious craftsmanship if not stylistic consistency.

Equally enamoured of Welsh folk songs was W. Hubert Davies (1893–1965),[15] who used them freely in his compositions. Kenneth Harding (1903–92),[16] also a string player, wrote several large-scale works such as the *Double Concerto for Violin, Cello and Orchestra*, along with colourful orchestral canvasses not far removed in style from Gerald Finzi and Howard Ferguson. The BBC commissioned his oboe concerto, and his *Concertante Quintet* for five violas (1972) was composed for Lionel Tertis, the greatest viola player of his time. Haydn Morris (1891–1965) was as much at home in cerdd dant as in orchestral and chamber music, and large-scale choral composition. His Sunday School cantata *Meseia y Plant* (The Children's Messiah) was written for a world long gone but remains a melodious contribution to a vanished genre. As was the case with many composers of his generation, Morris's compositions quickly became unfashionable.

Jazz was frowned upon by the great majority of these musicians, though it was one of the things that might have tied them more closely to the contemporary world, a more cosmopolitan style and a broader frame of reference. However, some composers worked in more popular styles, including Idris Lewis (1889–1952).[17] After studies at the Royal College of

---

[14] See chapter 27 of E. Keri Evans gyda chynorthwy Cyril Jenkins, *Cofiant Dr. Joseph Parry Mus. Doc. (1841–1903)* (Cardiff: Educational Publishing Company, 1921), tt. 239–244.
[15] J. G. Francis, 'Hubert Davies (1893–1965)', *Welsh Music/Cerddoriaeth Cymru*, 11/1 (Summer/Haf 2009), 5–8; 'William Hubert Davies', *Dictionary of Welsh Biography*, https://biography.wales/article/s2-DAVI-HUB-1893 (accessed 25 June 2021).
[16] The Kenneth Harding Music Manuscripts are held at the National Library of Wales. See also Tom Tatton, 'Kenneth Harding: A Passion for the Viola', *Journal of the American Viola Society* (27 November 2009), http://violaspace.com/avs/javs/2009/11/27/5/ (accessed 25 June 2021).
[17] 'Idris Lewis', *Dictionary of Welsh Biography*, https://biography.wales/article/s2-LEWI-IDR-1889 (accessed 20 July 2021). Rhidian Griffiths, 'Idris Lewis (1889–1952)', *Welsh Music*, 9/1 (Autumn 1989), 27–29.

Music he quickly established himself as a pianist, and from 1933 as Musical Director at the Elstree Studios, which had become the home of British International Pictures. He wrote stylish and attractive music for films such as *Maid of the Mountains*, *Royal Cavalcade* and *The Old Curiosity Shop*. From 1936 he was Music Director of the BBC Welsh Region, where he did much to encourage a future generation of Welsh composers. He also wrote some evergreen favourites such as 'Cân yr Arad Goch' ('The Song of the Red Plough'), 'Bugail Aberdyfi' ('The Shepherd of Aberdovey') and 'Mab y Mynydd' ('Son of the Mountain') which became components of the standard repertoire of several Welsh singers.

Both Alec Templeton (1909–63) and Harry Parr-Davies (1914–55) were hugely popular in their day.[18] Templeton, who was blind from birth, appeared as a pianist with Jack Hylton's Jazz Band, later moving to the United States and signing a recording contract with RCA in 1939. Some of his satirical 'takes', such as 'Mendelssohn Mows 'em Down', made his name and reputation secure. 'Mozart Matriculates' was released by Columbia and further consolidated his name. Throughout the 1950s he appeared with the Cincinnati Symphony Orchestra playing both classical and jazz works. Harry Parr-Davies was famous for being the accompanist of the singer Gracie Fields and for composing songs such as 'Crash, Bang! I Want to Go Home' and 'Wish Me Luck as You Wave Me Goodbye'. The most successful popular Welsh musician of this era, and one who was to play a vitally important role on the stages of the West End and beyond, was Ivor Novello (1893–1951).[19] Novello's mantra, 'I am not a highbrow. I am an entertainer. Empty seats ... mean nothing to me',[20] was a lesson some of his fellow Welsh composers might have done well to learn.

Agencies and Institutions

The infrastructure for music making in Wales during the interwar years was sparse and not professionalised. There was no national opera house, no purpose-built orchestral concert hall or national conservatoire. There were, however, churches, cathedrals and nonconformist chapels, many of which

---

[18] For Alec Templeton, see Laura Kuhn, ed., *Baker's Biographical Dictionary of Twentieth-Century Classical Musicians* (New York: Schirmer Books, 1997), p. 1390. For Harry Parr-Davies see *Dictionary of Welsh Biography* https://biography.wales/article/s2-PARR-HAR-1914 (accessed 25 June 2021), and *Oxford Dictionary of National Biography* (Oxford: Oxford University Press, 2004).
[19] James Harding, *Ivor Novello: A Biography* (Bridgend: Welsh Academic Press, 1997).
[20] Quoted in Paul Webb, *Ivor Novello: A Portrait of a Star* (London: Stage Directions, 1999), p. 110.

were venues for annual oratorio or cantata performances. There were large venues such as the halls in workmen's institutes that could be utilised effectively, even if not designed for musical purposes, and smaller buildings where chamber music could be performed. There were also music festivals and music clubs in several cities and towns. The Cardiff Triennial Festival held first performances of works by Harry Evans, David Evans and David Vaughan Thomas, alongside music by Verdi, Berlioz, Stanford and Elgar. The National Eisteddfod continued its annual events promoting large-scale choral works in its nightly concerts during eisteddfod week.[21] The touring pavilion could, and often did, hold audiences of up to 20,000, as was the case for the first performance in Wales of the Mass in B Minor by J. S. Bach, at the Ammanford National Eisteddfod in 1922 with a choir of over 600 and the London Symphony Orchestra conducted by local musician Gwilym R. Jones.

One of the most enterprising centres for music making was the town of Aberystwyth. David Jenkins carried forward the activities he inherited from Joseph Parry (who had instituted concerts of music devoted to works by a single composer), with performances in various venues including the Pier Pavilion.[22] He was challenged by the arrival in Aberystwyth of Lucie Barbier in 1909. Barbier was the wife of the Professor of French at the university and a trained singer and pianist who had studied at the Paris Conservatoire. She established a College Musical Club and gave recitals and talks on music in neighbouring schools. She knew most of the leading French composers of the day and their music was performed in her concerts alongside English madrigals, French trouvère songs, German lied, Schumann's piano music, and compositions by Somervell, Elgar and Stanford. The Spanish pianist Ricardo Viñes gave recitals of the music of Albéniz, Granados and de Falla. A vocal quartet assembled by her travelled to Paris in 1911 to perform Welsh folk songs (see Chapter 6). There is cause to wonder whether the people of Aberystwyth had more opportunity to hear contemporary French music than did the rest of Britain. Hers was an exotic presence, and her sojourn in the town, though short, was important.[23]

---

[21] Lyn Davies, 'Golwg ar Ddiwylliant Cerddorol Dyffryn Aman, 1910–1922', in *Cwm Aman*, Cyfres y Cymoedd, gol. Hywel Teifi Edwards (Llandysul: Gomer, 1996), tt. 173–212; see also Meredydd Evans, 'Cyngherddau'r Ganrif Ddiwethaf', *Eisteddfota* 2, gol. Gwynn ap Gwilym (Llandybie: Gwasg Christopher Davies, 1979), tt. 80–98.
[22] The papers (some confidential) referring to Joseph Parry are in the Registry archives of Aberystwyth University, as are several concert programmes from his time as Professor.
[23] Ian Parrott, *The Spiritual Pilgrims* (Aberystwyth: Christopher Davies, 1964).

The Walford Davies Effect

Following the Haldane Royal Commission on the condition of the University of Wales in 1916, a new chapter opened with the appointment of one of the leading British musicians, Henry Walford Davies (1869–1941), as Professor of Music at Aberystwyth, Director of Music for the University of Wales and Chair of the National Council of Music in Wales.[24] These roles were to be pivotal in developing music in Wales away from what many perceived to have been a state of inertia and reliance on its Victorian past, and towards raising musical standards and enriching tastes. In 1921 Davies set out his mission for Wales in a paper entitled *Our Mother-Tongue: a Musical Policy for Wales*, in which he suggested that every school in the land should have a gramophone and library of records, and should enjoy a minimum of ten minutes' singing every day as well as weekly concerts. During his tenure at Aberystwyth (he remained Chair of the Council until his death) the weekly concerts included mixed musical fare of classics from the German tradition. The university music ensembles also travelled periodically throughout Wales giving chamber concerts. In November 1919 Walford Davies also introduced an annual orchestral festival in Aberystwyth, held for many years at the Parish Hall, where many leading British conductors and composers appeared. The London Symphony Orchestra was conducted by Davies in a programme which included Ravel's *Pavane pour une Infante Défunte*. The following year, the festival included the first performance of a *Reverie and Allegro* by David de Lloyd. The London Symphony Orchestra was again contracted in 1922, with a programme including the *Pastoral Symphony* by Vaughan Williams. In 1923 conductors included Elgar and Adrian Boult. Cellist Arthur Williams (one of the finest chamber music players of his generation) was the soloist in Elgar's Cello Concerto, conducted by the composer. A notable visitor to the weekly concert series was Béla Bartók, who played in the seventy-seventh college concert series on 16 March 1922, his first public performance in Britain. As well as Beethoven's Trio in E flat major, op. 70, he played a wide selection of his own work including the *Suite*, *Romanian Folk Dances*, *Allegro Barbaro* and the *Bear Dance*. The experience of listening to this music left Walford Davies 'baffled'.[25]

---

[24] See David Ian Allsobrook, *Music for Wales: Walford Davies and the National Council of Music, 1918–41* (Cardiff: University of Wales Press, 1992).

[25] Parrott, *Spiritual Pilgrims*, p. 77. Also Rhian Davies, 'Béla Bartók yn Aberystwyth', *Barn*, 410 (Mawrth 1997), 22–23.

The work of the Council was also the main driving factor in the music departments of the two other University Colleges at Bangor and Cardiff. As Director of Music at Bangor, E. T. Davies established a lively centre for music making, organising weekly chamber concerts and a college orchestra and choral society. During his tenure more than 3,000 chamber concerts were organised. His twenty years as Director of Music at Bangor secured the future of music at the university after the war. The College Trio took their evangelising to the surrounding area and the players also helped to form local orchestras. Professor David Evans (1874–1948)[26] played a similar role at Cardiff and was able to call on the services of many professional players from local theatres as well as encouraging the Arthur Angle Orchestra and the Cardiff University Trio, which played in many venues in nearby communities. The National Council of Music under Walford Davies's guidance had set in motion profound and lasting changes in Welsh musical life.

Although University College, Swansea, which was founded in 1920, had no department of music, the musical life of the town thrived. In 1911 the Beecham Symphony Orchestra was conducted by Hamish McCunn in a concert consisting of music by Vaughan Thomas and *The Desert* by Félicien David. Regular performances by the Swansea and District Male Choir attracted a large following and included what was probably the only performance in Wales of Mendelssohn's *Antigone* with full orchestra. Following on from the establishment of a BBC studio in the town, a trio and small chorus were recruited to broadcast on Friday evenings.[27] In 1926, Vaughan Thomas compiled a programme of chamber music by thirteen Welsh composers and was responsible for music at the National Eisteddfod held that year in the town. He also conducted the Eisteddfod Choir and the London Symphony Orchestra in Bantock's *The Sea Wanderers* and Beethoven's Ninth Symphony. Orchestral performance in the town was revived and given an added spur in 1934 by the completion of the Brangwyn Hall, built as part of the Swansea Guildhall. The BBC Symphony Orchestra appeared there in 1935 under Adrian Boult and the London Philharmonic Orchestra also became regular visitors. Even during the war years some 130 concerts were held at the Brangwyn Hall. A Swansea Festival Orchestra was also formed during this period conducted by Irwyn

---

[26] David Evans's papers are preserved in the National Library of Wales, GB-AB MS DAVANS – David Evans (Musician) Papers. See also *Dictionary of Welsh Biography*, https://biography.wales/article/s2-EVAN-DAV-1874 (accessed 26 June 2021).

[27] John Hugh Thomas, 'The Cultural Tradition: Music', in *The City of Swansea: Challenges and Change*, ed. by Ralph A. Griffiths (Gloucester: Sutton, 1990), pp. 218–228.

Walters, which attracted many international soloists to the town. This gave the impetus for the foundation of the Swansea Festival in 1948. Touring opera companies and later the Welsh National Opera strengthened the tradition of opera production in the town which had begun in the 1880s under the influence of the celebrated tenor Ben Davies.

By the time of Walford Davies's death in 1941 the National Council of Music in Wales had encouraged the improvement of choral singing and choral conducting, and the widespread availability of radio broadcasts in schools, set up a network of communication and raised awareness of classical music. Walford Davies had become a much-loved figure in Wales and his example was emulated in the postwar years through a new infrastructure of County Music Organisers, which was to become a vital feature of local government support for the arts.

The Postwar Period

The immediate post-1945 period heralded important changes to the way the arts were organised and supported in Britain.[28] A Royal Charter granted to the Arts Council of Great Britain in 1946 was to shape the cultural life of Britain for more than seven decades. The Labour government shouldered financial responsibility for the performing arts, museums and galleries through the further development of wartime agencies such as the Council for the Encouragement of Music and the Arts (CEMA). This marked a seismic change in government policy. The Royal Charter stated that the objective of the Arts Council was to 'develop and improve knowledge, understanding and practice of the arts ... [and] increase the accessibility of the arts to the public'.[29] It represented a symbol of hope and regeneration at a time of despair and austerity. In Wales, the immediate actions took time to gain effect but gradual changes to the infrastructure started to take shape, then accelerate in the 1950s through the impetus given by the Festival of Britain in 1951. The Festival, which was

---

[28] A great deal of literature concerning the formation of the Arts Council of Great Britain exists – for example: Richard Hoggart, *The Way We Live Now* (London: Chatto & Windus, 1995), pp. 55–64; Arthur Marwick, *Culture in Britain since 1945* (Oxford: Basil Blackwell, 1991); Andrew Sinclair, *Arts and Cultures: History of the First 50 Years of the Arts Council of Great Britain* (London: Sinclair-Stevenson, 1995); Anna Rosser Upchurch, 'The Arts Council of Great Britain: Keynes's Legacy', in *The Origins of the Arts Council Movement*, ed. by Anna Rosser Upchurch (London: Palgrave Macmillan, 2016), pp. 103–130.

[29] Consolidated Royal Charter (Incorporates 2008, 2011 and 2013 Amendments), p. 2, www.artscouncil.org.uk/sites/default/files/download-file/Consolidated_Royal_Charter_2013.pdf (accessed 20 July 2021).

a multifaceted event, was ostensibly organised to celebrate the centenary of the Great Exhibition of 1851, but its primary purpose was to emphasise Britain's postwar recovery and the country's talents and achievements. The Labour Party politician Herbert Morrison, who led the Festival, declared that he wanted 'to hear the people sing',[30] a wish granted in Swansea, where the Festival's celebrations included a lavish programme with a 'Welcome Ode' by Vernon Watkins, religious services and a commission from Arwel Hughes – his oratorio *Dewi Sant* (St David), which was performed by the Pontarddulais Choral Society and the London Philharmonic Orchestra.

During the 1950s, many distinguished performers visited local music clubs in Wales. By 1962 there were thirty-two such clubs, rising to forty-one a year later. The number of chamber music concerts grew during the same period, from 99 in 1961–2 to 132 the following year.[31] The Welsh Committee of the Arts Council sponsored visits to these clubs by international performers and ensembles. The concerts were attended by children as well as adults and venues were sometimes improvised – the Amadeus String Quartet performed in the Salad Bar of Tenby's Civic Centre.

The general inadequacy of venues and particular needs for a national theatre, new buildings for the National Eisteddfod and International Eisteddfod and a purpose-built concert hall in Cardiff were widely felt, and the dominance of London became a constant irritation in Scotland, Wales and the English regions. During the 1960s the government and the Arts Council published numerous reports calling for an expansion of venues for the arts, but progress was slow. By the mid to late 1960s the potential synergies between the different arts and their commonality of purpose, financial position and artistic aspirations were becoming clarified. The structure of the Arts Council of Great Britain was changed at this time and separate arrangements were made for England, Wales and Scotland. The Chapter Arts Centre in Cardiff opened in 1971, but because of the financial constraints of the 1970s it would be 1983 before St David's Hall was officially opened in Cardiff, one of the first concert halls to be built outside London since 1951, and the Wales Millennium Centre, Cardiff, the largest and most expensive arts facility in Wales, did not open until 2005, though the case for it had been conclusively argued in the preceding decades.[32]

---

[30] Barry Turner, *Beacon for Change: How the 1951 Festival of Britain Shaped the Modern Age* (London: Aurum Press, 2011), p. 7.
[31] The Council for Wales and Monmouthshire, *Report on the Arts in Wales* (London: HMSO, 1965), pp. 44–47.
[32] See, for example, Arts Council of Great Britain, *Housing the Arts in Great Britain* (London: Arts Council of Great Britain, 1959).

Music festivals were founded widely across Wales after the Second World War. The Arts Council also made financial provision for the International Eisteddfod at Llangollen, commissioned new works by Welsh composers and developed relationships with many distinguished orchestras from outside Wales. In 1961–2 five major orchestral concerts were sponsored in Wales but by 1964–5 there were thirty-five, utilising expedient concert venues such as the Cardiff Cathays Pavilion, the Brangwyn Hall in Swansea, the King's Hall in Aberystwyth, Barry Memorial Hall, the Pavilion in Rhyl and what was to become the William Aston Hall in Wrexham. The Arts Council also sponsored the Young Welsh Singer of the Year Competition which commenced in 1962.

The amateur and professional music sectors were sponsored in parallel. The Welsh Region of the National Federation of Music Societies, later called the Welsh Amateur Music Federation, was the focus for amateurism. The Director of the Arts Council's Music Department in Wales was Roy Bohana;[33] he was responsible for setting in motion a series of professional recordings of music by Welsh composers which were of enormous benefit to the careers of many composers including Alun Hoddinott, William Mathias, Grace Williams and Daniel Jones. Bohana was also Director of Music at the Llangollen International Eisteddfod, which applied the eisteddfod idea in the context of a wide international music culture and did much to raise awareness of international choral standards and repertoire, especially from eastern Europe.

In the immediate aftermath of World War II, Wales needed musical leadership. At the BBC the key staff responsible for music were Idris Lewis, Mansel Thomas and Arwel Hughes. Idloes Owen was the central figure in the foundation of Welsh National Opera (WNO), which had it first iteration in Cardiff in 1943 when Owen assembled others of like mind with a view to establishing a national opera company in Wales. During 1944 the company performed operatic excerpts at the Empire Theatre, Cardiff and a year later at the city's Capitol Theatre. The commercial part of this venture was run by Bill Smith, a local businessman, who emulated what he had seen in Italy after World War I. Smith also talked with the various London-based experts regarding new singers. Smith famously owned a car dealership, and it was there the company started, with the cars moved to one side of the showroom to create rehearsal space. One of

---

[33] Roy Bohana, 'Roy Bohana', in *Artists in Wales 2*, ed. by Meic Stephens (Llandysul: Gomer, 1973), pp. 145–154; Bohana, 'Music', in *The Arts in Wales 1950–75*, ed. by Meic Stephens (Cardiff: Welsh Arts Council, 1979), pp. 5–26.

the first musicians to work with the company was the young and gifted conductor Charles Mackerras.

The first full operatic performance was a double bill of *Cavalleria Rusticana* and *Pagliacci* (with the great Welsh tenor Tudor Davies as Canio) with an amateur chorus. *Carmen* was introduced to Cardiff and Porthcawl in 1947, and by 1950 the company had added *Madam Butterfly*, *The Tales of Hoffman*, *The Bartered Bride* and *Die Fledermaus* to its repertoire. Over time, professional singers were contracted. During the 1950s the seasons were extended to six weeks with appearances at Aberystwyth, Cardiff, Swansea and Llandudno. Performances in provincial venues in Wales benefited from the Local Government Act of 1948, which allowed local authorities in Wales to supplement the company's grant from the Arts Council. Operas by Verdi were performed to acclaim – *Nabucco* in 1952 (the first time the opera had been heard in Britain in over a century), *I Lombardi* in 1956 and *La Battaglia di Legnano* in 1960. Chorus members were amateur and available only during their annual holiday leave – hardly the perfect situation for a company with international aspirations. Establishing the chorus on a professional basis became a priority. It was not until 1965 that operas with fewer chorus passages were actively considered to enable the season to expand.[34]

From the mid-1960s the company established a training school for young singers. Throughout the early years, opportunities were given to many singers who went on to establish international careers. The company travelled abroad for the first time to give three performances of *Billy Budd* in Switzerland in 1973. The chorus was professionalised in 1968 and became a full-time professional ensemble in 1973, the same year in which the company formed its own permanent orchestra.

A new era was ushered in from 1976 when Brian McMaster became the General Administrator. McMaster brought in a series of directors for productions such as Kupfer's *Elektra* (1978), Järvefelt's *The Magic Flute*, Stein's *Otello* and Hertz's *Madam Butterfly*. In 1979 the great Wagnerian conductor Reginald Goodall worked with the company on *Tristan und Isolde* and other ambitious inroads were made into new repertoire with works such as Berg's *Lulu*, Martinů's *The Greek Passion* and Handel's *Rodelinda*. One of the outstanding aspects of this era was the performances of Janáček in co-productions with Scottish Opera. Richard Armstrong also

---

[34] Studies of WNO include Richard Fawkes, *Welsh National Opera* (London: McRae, 1986), and Caroline Leech, *Welsh National Opera: Celebrating the First Sixty Years* (Cardiff: Graffeg, 2006). The eventual building of the Wales Millennium Centre is covered in Nicholas Edwards, *Opera House Lottery: Zaha Hadid and the Cardiff Bay Project* (Cardiff: University of Wales Press, 1997).

directed a complete production of Wagner's *Ring* cycle – the first such project by a British provincial opera company. The 1988 production of Verdi's *Falstaff* with Donald Maxwell in the title role and a young Bryn Terfel as Ford was an important landmark, and the company would cement its long association with the works of Verdi with productions of *Rigoletto* (2002) and *Don Carlos* (2005). One of the many highlights was the 1992 production of Debussy's *Pelléas et Mélisande* with Pierre Boulez conducting and Peter Stein directing. The production won an International Classical Music Award and was taken to the Théâtre du Châtelet in Paris. As the General Director said, 'Can you imagine La Scala bringing *Peter Grimes* to London?'[35] Numerous awards were given to the company from 1997 as it consolidated its position on the British and international scene. By 2007 WNO had a permanent company of 250 producing around 9 full-scale operas in 3 seasons each year. Roy Bohana's long tenure at the Welsh Arts Council also helped to make WNO the largest provider of touring opera in Britain and its work with audiences developed apace with WNO Max, which supported a programme of projects, performances and education outreach work offering opportunities for professional and community endeavour. By 2006/7 WNO Max had reached an impressive 31,000 people.

Complementing the work of WNO, Mid Wales Opera was formed in 1989 to take popular opera to parts of Wales where access to professional opera was difficult. The mid-Wales theatre circuit was suited to its pattern of small-scale but high-quality touring productions. By the end of its season in 2003 it had presented operas in eighty venues in Wales and England. National Lottery 'Arts for All' funding (drawn from the UK state-franchised lottery system established in 1994) added further support for opera and music making more generally in Wales.

Music Theatre Wales was formed to fill a different niche from both WNO and Mid Wales Opera. From its foundation in 1988 the company was devoted to contemporary music and performed works by composers including Peter Maxwell Davies and Harrison Birtwistle, and commissioned new works from composers including Lynne Plowman, John Hardy and Guto Puw. The first phase of its development was led by Michael McCarthy and music director Michael Rafferty. From a precarious financial base Music Theatre Wales developed an international reputation from its home at Cardiff's Chapter Arts Centre. Touring regularly in Wales, it consistently produced contemporary opera of the highest quality and took

---

[35] Leech, *Welsh National Opera*, p. 60.

productions to several European centres. Music Theatre Wales was quick to realise that sustaining this highly specialist activity required partnerships and sponsorships, leading to an associate company relationship with the Royal Opera as well as sponsorship from the Hamlyn Foundation, Garfield Weston Foundation and National Lottery funding.

Irwyn Walters, His Majesty's Inspector of Schools for music in Wales, was pivotal in founding the National Youth Orchestra of Wales (NYOW) in 1945, the first national youth orchestra in the world. Among members of the first residential course were several who went on to distinguished careers, including Alun Hoddinott and harpist Osian Ellis. The orchestra was encouraged to travel to concert venues in Britain and abroad, including a visit to the Edinburgh Festival in 1955 where Grace Williams's commissioned *Penillion* was given its premiere. The NYOW has been a vitally important institution in the musical development of Wales's best young talent and formed the apex of a wider scope of activity at county level throughout Wales. Leading Welsh composers have composed for the orchestra and recordings of its performances have frequently been made. The NYOW could justifiably be regarded as the first genuine orchestral success story in Wales, and it has enriched the lives of thousands of young people irrespective of whether they have developed musical careers of their own.[36] A significant role in supporting young people was also played by the Welsh Amateur Music Federation, later Tŷ Cerdd. All the musical groups now represented by National Youth Arts Wales were originated by the Federation.

The BBC has been central to virtually all the major developments in Welsh music through orchestral broadcasts on radio and television, commissions of new music, composer in residence schemes, community and outreach work. The original Cardiff Station Orchestra was formed in 1924, folded in 1931 due to financial constraints, but was re-formed in 1935 as the BBC Welsh Orchestra with twenty players, increasing to thirty-one after World War II under Mansel Thomas. In 1947 a chorus was formed with Arwel Hughes conducting, and during the 1950s the orchestra was further expanded under Rae Jenkins. Concerts were given in many parts of Wales, with programmes including numerous performances of the work of Welsh composers. In 1960 the orchestra expanded to forty-four players, and in 1966 moved to a new studio in Broadcasting House, Cardiff. The chorus was recast as the BBC Welsh Choral Society during the 1970s, but financial

---

[36] Beryl Bowen James and David Allsobrook, *First in the World: The Story of the National Youth Orchestra of Wales* (Cardiff: University of Wales Press, 1995).

constraints again proved problematic. The future of all the BBC's orchestras was placed in doubt, but the Welsh Arts Council enabled the orchestra to expand further and from 1974, when it was renamed the BBC Welsh Symphony Orchestra, there were sixty players. During the 1980s and 1990s the orchestra toured internationally with visits to Canada, Japan and Europe, as well as being one of the most televised orchestras in Britain. From 1993 the orchestra was renamed the BBC National Orchestra of Wales, and the chorus the BBC National Chorus of Wales, the latter remaining an amateur choir. Numerous recordings attest to the high international standards achieved by the orchestra: these include the symphonies of Edmund Rubbra and works by Hoddinott, Mathias, John Metcalf, Frank Bridge, Lennox Berkeley and Michael Berkeley.[37]

One of the major forces for change in Welsh music after World War II was the Guild for the Promotion of Welsh Music (later the Welsh Music Guild). Formed in 1955,[38] the Guild was especially active from the outset in promoting Welsh music through its acknowledgement that Wales was producing a stream of composers of greater standing than in the past. The first Congress of the Guild was held in Gregynog in 1955 and subsequent Congresses benefited from close involvement with the BBC and introduced new music by a range of Welsh composers, including the Second Symphony of David Wynne in 1956 and most notably his *Owain ab Urien* in 1968. The Guild sponsored a piano competition in 1959 and a competition for violinists in 1966, in which the competitors played the specially commissioned Concerto by David Harries.

The University of Wales has made a substantial contribution to the country's music. Under Ian Parrott at Aberystwyth the weekly chamber concerts continued as they did at Bangor and Cardiff, and Parrott did much to encourage young musicians. At Cardiff, Alun Hoddinott was Professor of the largest department of its kind in Europe.[39] Similarly at Bangor, William Mathias helped to place his department at the forefront of music in education. These institutions form the main strand of continuity in the provision of an infrastructure for professional music in Wales and

---

[37] Peter Reynolds, *BBC National Orchestra and Chorus of Wales* (Swansea: BBC Cymru Wales, 2009).

[38] Ian Parrott, *Hanes yr Urdd er Hyrwyddo Cerddoriaeth Cymru, 1955–1980/The Story of the Guild for the Promotion of Welsh Music, 1955–1980* (Swansea: Guild for the Promotion of Welsh Music, 1980).

[39] On Hoddinott as head of department, see John H. Lewis, Christopher Painter, Huw Tregelles Williams, Elinor Bennett, Robin Stowell, Mervyn Burtch, Alun Francis, Tony Small, Andrew Matthews-Owen, Jeremy Huw Williams, Denis Wick and Richard Elfyn Jones, 'Tributes to Alun Hoddinott', *Welsh Music/Cerddoriaeth Cymru*, 11/1 (Summer/Haf 2009), 14–34.

were joined in 1949 by the Cardiff College of Music, later the Royal Welsh College of Music and Drama, which has also done much to promote the music of Wales from its inception.[40] But the developments that shaped the musical life of the country in the modern world most emphatically can be traced only from the second half of the twentieth century.

---

[40] The Cardiff College of Music was founded in 1949; it became the Welsh College of Music and Drama in 1970 and was awarded its Royal title in 2002. On its history, see Royal Welsh College of Music and Drama, *Celebrations: 50th Anniversary 1949–1999* (Cardiff: Royal Welsh College of Music and Drama, 1999).

CHAPTER 12

Composing Cymru
Art Music since 1940

Nicholas Jones

Cymru, Ein Gwlad

> I have certainly used Welsh material from time to time as the basis of certain works, but always in the first instance because of the inherent musical possibilities of this material .... The Welshness is indeed a very satisfying by-product, but it would become dangerous to the purposes of art if this elusive quality were posited as the first priority. If there is a quality of Welshness shared by composers working in Wales today (and it is frankly too early to say), it will be based on something much older and more basic than eighteenth or nineteenth century folk tunes, and it will be present at a much deeper level of consciousness. We should have to look back to those qualities in earlier Celtic art which are clearly to be seen in the great Welsh literary tradition of the Middle Ages. It is an art of paradoxical contrasts – brightly jewelled colours contrasting with dark introspection, declamation with tenderness, and intellectual tautness with an almost improvisatory lyricism.[1]

These words by William Mathias (1934–92), taken from an essay published in 1971, offer an intriguing insight into the contested and problematic notion of 'Welshness' and the ways in which this 'elusive quality' can influence the composition of art music. That Mathias should cite several contrasting qualities inherent in Celtic art to support his argument is highly revealing: it tells us something significant not only about his approach to composition, but also about his conception of what it was to be a composer working in Wales in the early 1970s. Although Mathias's argument is persuasive, one is compelled to question the extent to which it can be considered as the definitive viewpoint. Consequently, this chapter takes a broad approach: while acknowledging Mathias's thought-provoking comments, it also considers other equally important, interconnecting factors: these include an awareness and pride in

---

[1] William Mathias, untitled essay, in *Artists in Wales*, ed. by Meic Stephens (Llandysul: J. D. Lewis & Sons Ltd, 1971), p. 107.

Wales's history, mythology and ancient traditions; a love for the Welsh landscape; and a deep affection for the native homeland, including a sense of place, belonging and rootedness. Indeed, the title of this opening section is a direct reference to the name of a 2002 choral work by Hilary Tann (b. 1947): *Wales, Our Land*. Tann explains that the work was composed in response to a commission from the Welsh Heritage Program at Green Mountain College, Vermont, and sets a poem by an unknown Welsh-American slate quarryman. The text 'speaks of the poet's love of his country of origin, perhaps, even, his longing to return. It is this sense of longing for the homeland (in Welsh, hiraeth) which infuses the composition.'[2]

For the Welsh, hiraeth is a very special word, and one that holds a particular significance and cultural meaning; however, it is a word that is notoriously difficult to translate adequately into English. Tann highlights two basic definitions: a love of, and sense of longing for, the Welsh homeland. But hiraeth embraces much more than this, and involves a complex combination of the notions of homesickness, nostalgia and melancholy, and a profound sense of loss or grief for a person or a landscape, or of a time or place that can never be recovered.[3] Being born in Llwynypia in the Rhondda Valley, but living in Upstate New York since 1980, these meanings clearly carry a powerful, poignant resonance for Tann and manifest themselves in some of her music principally through the intense impact of, and memories associated with, the landscapes and places in and around the area in which she was born. This can be witnessed, for instance, in the choral work *The Moor* (1997); *The Walls of Morlais Castle*, for string orchestra (1998) and chamber trio (2001); and *With the Heather and Small Birds* for chamber orchestra, commissioned by the 1994 Cardiff Festival. The latter work is a homage to the landscape of Tann's childhood – 'a place of freedom, ancientness, and song (songs of the valley, and song of the skylark)' – and takes its title from a translation of a poem, 'Nant y Mynydd' (The Mountain Stream), by Welsh poet and folk song collector, John Ceiriog Hughes (1832–87), in which he wistfully reflects that, far from home, his heart will always be in the mountain with the heather and small birds.[4]

---

[2] Hilary Tann, programme note, *Wales, Our Land*, https://global.oup.com/academic/product/wales-our-land-cymru-ein-gwlad-9780193867451?cc=gb&lang=en&# (accessed 4 April 2021).

[3] The Welsh writer Roland Mathias has described the latter emotion as Gwlad-yr-Haf (the land of the summer), 'the happy past from which we have come and to which we can never return'; untitled essay, in *Artists in Wales*, p. 168.

[4] Tann, programme note, *With the Heather and Small Birds*, https://hilarytann.com/compositions/?series=Chamber%20Orchestra (accessed 4 April 2021).

Example 12.1 Grace Williams, *Hiraeth* (1951), opening bars. © Cwmni Cyhoeddi Gwynn, reproduced with permission

Composed four decades earlier for Welsh harpist Ann Griffiths (1934–2020), *Hiraeth* (1951) by Grace Williams (1906–77) manages to stir similar emotions in the listener, but in this instance the composer is arguably more concerned with foregrounding melancholy and loss. As can be seen in Example 12.1, Williams unfolds a hauntingly beautiful melody, accompanied in the opening bars by the gentle oscillation of bittersweet G minor–major harmonies (*dolente* means painful, sorrowful); as the piece proceeds, the listener is taken to distantly related keys before being brought back to the familiarity and security of the tonic. The harp itself has a very specific relationship to Welsh cultural history and is emblematic of Welsh folk music in particular, and the composer clearly taps into this association. Williams effectively exploits the distinctive characteristic of the harp's evocative string resonance, and in performance the music sounds almost otherworldly, with the fingers of the harpist metaphorically tugging at the listeners' heart strings, eliciting a deep sense of longing and nostalgia. Such a piece could easily descend into cloying sentimentality and stereotype, but Williams carefully avoids this pitfall, presenting the listener instead with a brief but eloquent work, distinguished by its aching tenderness and unassuming sophistication.

There is something profoundly national about this music; its 'Welshness' is deeply inscribed. But this characteristic is not unique to this composer. This chapter argues that the art music written by Welsh composers during the period under discussion cannot reasonably be considered without reference to these composers' relationship to their own cultural identity and environment. Indeed, Wales *in toto* – its culture, its history, its traditions, its legends, its language, its literature, its landscapes – exerted, and continues to exert, a strong gravitational pull on these composers – even for those who have consciously looked beyond Wales for stylistic inspiration and models on which to base their own compositional technique. While it is not possible or practicable to be comprehensive, this chapter – which is broadly chronological – focuses primarily on the repertoires of the composers who have flourished most prominently since 1940.

A Creative Renewal

The emergence in the 1940s of Grace Williams and Daniel Jones (1912–93) as composers of substance and distinction was a watershed in the history of Welsh art music. Not only were they the first Welsh composers to bring to their craft an unequivocal professionalism; they were the first to secure noteworthy profiles in a UK-wide context. Born in the southern coastal town of Barry, Williams was encouraged by her parents to learn the piano and violin from an early age. At school, she demonstrated a talent for composition and was consequently awarded the Morfydd Owen scholarship in 1923 to study at University College, Cardiff. In 1926, she was accepted at the Royal College of Music, where she studied composition with Ralph Vaughan Williams, and four years later, she was awarded a scholarship to study with Egon Wellesz in Vienna. Several of her works from the early to mid-1930s display an awareness of, and willingness to engage with, European modernism – the *Sonatina for Flute and Piano* (1931) and *Suite for Nine Instruments* (1934), for instance, both betray a familiarity with the music of Bartók, Poulenc and Hindemith. But this engagement was short-lived and Williams's compositions during the 1930s and 1940s demonstrate, more typically, the twin influence of a cluster of composers from the romantic era – Wagner, Elgar, Richard Strauss and Mahler – and some of those who rose to prominence in the first half of the twentieth century – Shostakovich, Walton and Britten. But it was Vaughan Williams, above all, who exerted the most profound influence on her compositional voice.

Grace Williams's musical language is fundamentally tonal, characterised by modally inflected harmonies and melodies and enriched by a temperate chromaticism. In a number of different ways, her music also displays a deep and conscious connection to Wales. Naturally, this is most obvious when traditional Welsh melodies are incorporated into original works. For instance, her first purely orchestral work, *Hen Walia* (1930, rev. 1936), uses 'Synnwyr Solomon' and the familiar lullaby, 'Huna Blentyn'.[5] This overture was initially very popular and was broadcast by the BBC on several occasions,[6] but its success was eclipsed by Williams's *Fantasia on Welsh Nursery Tunes* (1940). Like *Hen Walia*, the *Fantasia* includes traditional Welsh melodies.[7] With its colourful orchestration and instantly warm and engaging musical style, it became something of a calling card for the composer. Although unambitious in scope and unrepresentative of her output, the *Fantasia* did possess the crucial advantage of introducing Williams to an audience outside of Wales, and remains even today as one of the most famous and beloved pieces of Welsh music written for the concert hall.

Other compositions from this period that demonstrate Williams's engagement with her Welsh background include *Gogonedawg Arglwydd* (Hymn of Praise, 1939) for chorus and orchestra, which sets a Welsh text drawn from the mid-thirteenth-century Llyfr Du Caerfyrddin (The Black Book of Carmarthen); *Four Illustrations for the Legend of Rhiannon* (1939, rev. 1940) for orchestra, based on episodes from the *Mabinogion*; Symphony No. 1 (1943, rev. 1952; usually known by the title *Symphonic Impressions*), a four-movement musical portrait of Owain Glyndŵr, as depicted by Shakespeare in *Henry IV, Part 1*; and *Sea Sketches* (1944) for string orchestra. The latter effectively evokes the changing moods of the sea of her native Barry, and musically depicts the impact of the weather, in all its vicissitudes, on that seascape. The work rivals the *Fantasia on Welsh Nursery Tunes* in popularity, but according to Malcolm Boyd, 'It is a much better work than the *Fantasia*, and unquestionably the finest thing she had written up to that time.'[8]

Williams is also credited as being the first British woman to compose a score for a full-length feature film.[9] *Blue Scar* (released in 1949) portrays

---

[5] 'Hen Walia' translates into English as 'Old Wales', but Williams herself suggested 'Welsh Overture' as a possible alternative title; see Graeme Cotterill, 'Music in the Blood and Poetry in the Soul? National Identity in the Life and Music of Grace Williams' (PhD thesis, University of Wales, Bangor, 2012), p. 44.

[6] Ibid., pp. 39–40.

[7] There are eight in total: 'Jim Cro', 'Deryn y Bwn', 'Migildi, Magildi', 'Si Hei Lwli 'Mabi', 'Gee, Geffyl Bach', 'Cysga di fy Mhlentyn Tlws', 'Yr Eneth Ffein Ddu' and 'Cadi Ha!'.

[8] Malcolm Boyd, *Grace Williams* (Cardiff: University of Wales Press, 1980), p. 26.

[9] Jan G. Swynnoe, *The Best Years of British Film Music, 1936–58* (Woodbridge: The Boydell Press, 2002), p. 110.

a Welsh mining community and essentially is a critical commentary on the working conditions of coal miners – the title being a reference to the discoloration of skin when coal dust penetrates an open wound. The music is mostly in a pastoral, modal mode of expression, and owes much to the influence of Vaughan Williams, especially for the depiction of the Welsh landscape and for the romantic subplot; it also uses several Welsh folk tunes, such as the opening theme, which is based on 'Mae Nghariad I'n Fenws'.[10] But the orchestration and harmonic and rhythmic language are more hard-edged – spiky, syncopated, mechanical – for the scenes set in London, with Williams using the famous Westminster Chimes melody as inspiration. She also composed the music for three further films: *David* (1951), another film portraying a Welsh mining community; *A Story of Achievement* (1951); and *A Letter for Wales* (1960) – the latter being notable for its symbolic use of monochrome for the scenes set in London's Paddington Station, and colour for the scenes set in Wales. With the Welsh folk song 'Ar Lan y Môr' featuring prominently, the film is thoroughly immersed in hiraeth: now living in London, the central character, The Welshman (played by Welsh actor Donald Houston), wistfully reminisces about the homeland of his birth, recalling trips to Snowdon, Anglesey, Tenby and Dinorwic slate quarry.

In 1947, following a sustained period of ill-health, Williams herself returned to her homeland, moving into her parents' home in Barry, where she was to live for the rest of her life. To support herself financially, she initially worked on educational programmes for the BBC, writing scripts and arranging international folk songs and carols; she also composed incidental music for radio plays and, as already noted, music for film. At the same time, she attempted to pursue a career as a freelance composer – a difficult and highly precarious profession, especially outside of London. However, in contrast to the 1920s, when Williams was a student in Cardiff, the postwar musical landscape in Wales was somewhat more auspicious: in addition to those institutions already established, such as the BBC and the National Eisteddfod, this period witnessed the formation of Welsh National Opera (1943) and the National Youth Orchestra of Wales (1945); the creation of the Welsh Arts Council (established embryonically in 1950); the founding of the Guild for the Promotion of Welsh Music (1955); and the inauguration of music festivals in Swansea (1948), Llandaff (1958), Cardiff (1967), Vale of Glamorgan (1969), Fishguard (1969), St Asaph (1972), Gower (1976) and St Davids (1979).

[10] Ibid., p. 111.

A good number of Welsh composers benefited from the support offered by these institutions, organisations and festivals, including Williams. In the 1950s, one such commission was received from the National Youth Orchestra of Wales; the resulting work, *Penillion* (1955), proved to be a pivotal work for the composer and marked something of a defining moment in her own stylistic development. As Williams states:

> I had a thorough grounding in Welsh airs and Welsh folk songs when I was a child and teenager, and they found their way into some very early works, now withdrawn, and of course the *Fantasia*. Then later on in the fifties there was the influence of the rhythms, intonations and cadences of Welsh oratory, and the atmosphere of the *Mabinogion*, which can be felt in my *Penillion* for orchestra. Later still, I've done some settings of medieval Welsh poetry [*Four Medieval Welsh Poems* (1962)] which I think are very Welsh. Indeed I've always considered myself very fortunate to have been born Welsh.[11]

The title *Penillion* refers to the ancient Welsh form of improvised song with harp accompaniment.[12] Reimagining the vocal form for orchestra, with an important part for harp, Williams retains two vital ingredients of the tradition: a strict stanzaic structure and quasi-improvisatory melodic lines.[13] Moreover, it is noteworthy that the work does not employ a single Welsh folk tune – in fact, none of her original works after 1954 use traditional melodies.[14] *Penillion* was therefore important because it helped point Williams towards a new way of musically engaging with her Welsh heritage, and with this came a renewed sense of confidence. Several orchestral works followed, each one imprinted with a strong individuality and maturity: *Processional* (1962, rev. 1968), Trumpet Concerto (1963), *Carillons* (1965, rev. 1973), *Ballads* (1968) and *Castell Caernarfon* (1969) – the latter written for the Investiture of Charles, Prince of Wales. All of these works foreground a lyrical, declamatory style. Unsurprisingly, then, this period also witnessed a flowering of vocal and choral works, including her first song cycle, *Six Poems by Gerard Manley Hopkins* (1958), for contralto and string sextet; *Carmina Avium* (1967), for chorus, viola and

---

[11] Williams, in conversation with A. J. Heward Rees, 'Views and Revisions: The Composer Grace Williams Talks to A. J. Heward Rees', *Welsh Music/Cerddoriaeth Cymru*, 5/4 (Winter/Gaeaf 1976–7), 18.

[12] Penillion is a word for the form that is more properly called cerdd dant. See also 'Penillion', *Grove Music Online*, www.oxfordmusiconline.com/subscriber/article/grove/music/21250 (accessed 11 May 2021).

[13] Boyd, *Grace Williams*, p. 38; see also Rhiannon Mathias, *Lutyens, Maconchy, Williams and Twentieth-Century British Music: A Blest Trio of Sirens* (Farnham: Ashgate, 2012), pp. 250–256.

[14] Boyd, *Grace Williams*, p. 36.

harp; *Fairest of Stars* (1973), for soprano and orchestra; and *Ave Maris Stella* (1973), for unaccompanied chorus. The latter is a particularly fine work: distanced, mystical, starkly beautiful. But perhaps the two most ambitious vocal projects in this final period were her one-act opera, *The Parlour* (1961), first staged by Welsh National Opera in 1966, and the *Missa Cambrensis* (1968–71), a setting of the mass in Latin and Welsh for soloists, chorus, boys' choir, narrator and orchestra, the premiere of which took place at the Llandaff Festival in 1971.[15]

Another composer who was fully supported by the commissioning system then in operation in Wales was Daniel Jones. Like Williams, Jones's works remain within the bounds of tonality; however, they are extended and expanded by dissonance to a more significant degree, and as a result his music is characterised by a greater sense of harmonic ambiguity. This trait also extended to his treatment of metre and rhythm. During the mid-1930s he devised his own compositional system called 'complex metres', a method of metrical organisation that found its maturity in the Sonata for Three Unaccompanied Kettle Drums (1947) – a work that has remained central to the repertoire of timpanists throughout the world since its publication in 1953. The system is governed by a metrical cycle, comprising alternating time signatures, which remains fixed throughout each individual movement; even though the pattern itself is asymmetrical, this component is intended to provide a unifying element. Against this repeating fixed cycle, diversity is achieved by the development of rhythmic units, providing the opportunity for much variety and invention.[16] Although Jones would go on to use his system in a number of subsequent works, he certainly was not a slave to the method.

Jones was born in Pembroke and grew up in Swansea. After studying English Literature at Swansea University, he went on to study composition with Harry Farjeon and conducting with Henry Wood at the Royal Academy of Music (1934–9). In 1935, he was awarded the Mendelssohn Scholarship which enabled him to visit the Continent and crucially attend numerous concerts and opera performances.[17] Around this time, he was also attached to a Swansea-based artistic circle, which included poet Dylan Thomas, with whom he had been friends since their time at Swansea Grammar School.[18] During the Second World War, Jones used his prodigious linguistic skills as a cryptographer and decoder at the Bletchley Park Allied code-breaking centre and after the war he moved back to Swansea,

---

[15] Cambria is the Latin name for Wales; Cambrensis denotes of or from Wales.
[16] For further explication of the system, see Daniel Jones, 'Some Metrical Experiments', *The Score*, 3 (1950), 32–48.
[17] Daniel Jones, untitled essay, in *Artists in Wales*, p. 113.   [18] Now known as Bishop Gore School.

living there for the remainder of his life. Jones produced works in many genres, including orchestral music, chamber music (most notably eight string quartets), solo instrumental music, vocal music, two operas (*The Knife* (1962) and *Orestes* (1967)), and concertos for violin (1966), oboe (1982) and cello (1986). The foundation of his output, however, rests on a series of thirteen symphonies, composed over five decades, which distinguish Jones not only as the first Welsh symphonist of any significance, but also as one of the key British symphonists of the twentieth century. His is an intensely serious-minded engagement with the genre, with each symphony typified by an expressive, emotional core and dramatic symphonic narrative. Of particular note is the unusual fact that the first twelve are each based on a different note of the chromatic scale.

Markedly aligned with a European symphonic mainstream and wearing a late romantic soundworld clearly on its sleeve, the consciously ambitious and expansive Symphony No. 1 (1945) is the longest essay in the cycle, taking over fifty minutes to perform. The concert premiere took place on 27 October 1949 at the Swansea Festival with the London Philharmonic Orchestra and the composer conducting. As Wales had, up to that point, produced no symphonist of repute, the work made quite an impact at the time and served to stimulate a regeneration of the symphonic genre in Wales.[19] Completed a year later, the Second Symphony shares its predecessor's boldness of scale, but the musical language is decidedly more abrasive. With its proliferation of musical ideas, vibrant orchestration and luminous textures (with an arresting part for celesta), the work is evidence of a fecund, creative imagination. According to Arnold Whittall and Lyn Davies, the notable features of symphonies 5 to 9 are a 'contained lyrical intensity, a readiness to adopt and develop traditional sonata structures and (in the scherzos) sheer spirit',[20] but these works also demonstrate a gradual paring down in scale. The Tenth Symphony (1981), for instance, is twenty minutes in duration and possesses an atmosphere of 'late' style, the opening bell toll lending the music a distinctively sombre disposition. It is a quality that is also explored in his next symphony (1983), the third movement of which is an elegy of a remarkably powerful, Mahlerian intensity. The earlier Symphony No. 4 (1954; Figure 12.1) displays a similar expressive

---

[19] There are two surviving, undated symphonies by Joseph Parry (1841–1903), probably the first by a Welsh composer, and a symphony composed in 1919 by Cyril Jenkins (1885–1978); see Cotterill, *Music in the Blood and Poetry in the Soul*, p. 50, n. 63. Grace Williams's *Symphonic Impressions* (Symphony No. 1) was not publicly performed until March 1950; her Symphony No. 2 followed in 1956 (rev. 1975).

[20] Arnold Whittall and Lyn Davies, 'Jones, Daniel (Jenkyn)', *Grove Music Online*, www.oxfordmusiconline.com/subscriber/article/grove/music/14445 (accessed 10 May 2021).

Figure 12.1 Daniel Jones, Fourth Symphony, first movement, bars 127–131, in the composer's hand. By kind permission of the composer's daughter Cathrin Roberts

elegiac force: arguably Jones's most notable work, it was written in memory of his close friend Dylan Thomas, who died tragically in November 1953.[21] Jones also composed the incidental music for Thomas's celebrated radio play, *Under Milk Wood* (1954), and went on to edit Thomas's poems and write a memoir of their friendship.[22]

National Idiosyncrasies

Speaking in 1984, Daniel Jones argued that 'whereas in literary terms you can say that the writing of Dylan Thomas is distinctly Welsh, that is not true of music. Even though I am something of a loner, there is no national idiosyncrasy.'[23] However, according to Whittall and Davies, 'Jones realized that his Welshness was somehow inexplicably present in his works but that it was subconsciously so rather than deliberate';[24] and Geraint Lewis has argued that: 'The Welsh sense of rhetoric is never far away from Jones's music and his most frequently performed orchestral piece – the popular *Dance Fantasy* (1976) – is imbued with a stirringly Celtic sense of heraldic display.'[25] It will be instructive, then, to pause briefly to reflect further on the notion of Welshness in art music with specific reference to the two composers discussed in the previous section, and to the two that will be discussed in the next.

In 1973, in an article provocatively titled 'How Welsh Is Welsh Music?', Grace Williams made the following rather quirky observation: 'When I am asked for my views on national influences in Welsh music I am reminded of the story of the centipede who, when asked which foot he put down first, got so confused he couldn't walk at all.'[26] She goes on to argue that:

> I have only to consider the ways of life of my fellow-composers to realize that no two are alike. The obvious thing we have in common is a desire to go on living and working in Wales[.] ... As a composer, inspiration has always been free to come from any source. Every now and again ideas have sprung from Welsh sources, giving the music Welsh characteristics of rhythm and melody.[27]

---

[21] Jones's Symphony No. 11 is 'In Memoriam George Froom Tyler', Chairman of the Swansea Festival; his final, unnumbered symphony (1992) is 'In Memoriam John Fussell', Artistic Director of the Gower Festival.
[22] Jones, ed., *The Poems of Dylan Thomas* (New York: New Directions, 1971) and Jones, *My Friend Dylan Thomas* (London: J. M. Dent & Sons, 1977).
[23] Jones, in *Classical Music* (20 October 1984) quoted in Paul Conway, CD liner notes, *Daniel Jones: Symphonies 1 and 10* (Lyrita, SRCD.358, 2017), p. 8.
[24] Whittall and Davies, 'Jones, Daniel (Jenkyn)'.
[25] Geraint Lewis, 'Obituary: Daniel Jones', *The Independent*, 27 April 1993.
[26] Williams, 'How Welsh Is Welsh Music?', *Welsh Music/Cerddoriaeth Cymru*, 4/4 (Summer/Haf 1973), 7.
[27] Ibid., p. 10.

In an interview given twenty-one years later, Alun Hoddinott (1929–2008) responded as follows to the question, 'Is there anything particularly Welsh about your music?':

> This is something that somebody else has to answer because I just write the music that I feel I want to write. I don't write any consciously Welsh music in the same way as Bartók consciously wrote Hungarian music. So, I don't know; there haven't been that number of Welsh composers in the past, so there's not really much of a tradition. The only tradition we really have of art music, composed music, is from the beginning of the twentieth century. And because there are quite a number of Welsh composers now, it's only now that there's beginning to be seen a kind of a common link. It takes a long time to feel these things.[28]

But perhaps the most thorough interrogation of the topic comes from Daniel Jones – unexpectedly, perhaps, given his somewhat forthright viewpoint quoted at the head of this section. In an essay dating from 1971, he raises the intriguing question as to whether a Welsh 'school' of composition has emerged. For him, the straightforward answer is 'no'. Like Williams, he argues that all Welsh composers 'are travelling along paths of their own individual choice'. For him, 'A "school" implies the close contact of artists with one another, if not actual consultation or collaboration, the agreement of aims, and the sharing of characteristics of technique and manner. This is quite different from the appearance of similarities that have come about independently, unintentionally, naturally.' He divides these similarities into two groups: those that appear on the surface of the music, and therefore are only tenuously connected – such as the use of Welsh folk music, words and subject matter, or 'fortuitous coincidences occurring here and there between the movement of the thematic material and Welsh speech rhythms'; and those that exist more concretely at a deeper level – those that are present because the composers 'share a common psychological pattern': 'They are Welsh in personality, upbringing and environment.' In this latter category, he offers three examples: 'a love of structural intricacy and complicated patterns'; 'a tendency to clothe the underlying pattern in a disguise of improvisatory effect, an apparently free flow of sound, sometimes approaching the rhetorical'; and finally, 'lyricism, not necessarily vocal lyricism, but present in the melodic line as a lyrical feeling, however "advanced" the idiom'.[29]

---

[28] Alun Hoddinott, in conversation with Bruce Duffie, June 1994, www.bruceduffie.com/hoddinott.html (accessed 12 May 2021).
[29] Jones, untitled essay, in *Artists in Wales*, pp. 115–116.

Celtic Contrasts

It appears, then, that Daniel Jones shared views broadly similar to those of William Mathias. It will be remembered, though, that Mathias's understanding of Welsh characteristics was centred on the 'paradoxical contrasts' inherent in Celtic art and literature. In the programme note for his orchestral work *Celtic Dances* (1972), he states that 'the music is intended to evoke an area of feeling largely associated with the mythological past, even though such an idea is here expressed in terms of our own time', and that 'Rite and magic, jewelled colours, the spirit of play, wistfulness, lyrical warmth, and (above all) rhythmic vitality' prompted the composition of the work.[30] On a more fundamental level, all of his works from this decade explore what Mathias would later describe as 'typically Celtic contrasts between light and darkness'.[31] Both of these attributes are very much in evidence in the Harp Concerto of 1970, composed for the Welsh harpist Osian Ellis (1928–2021), the first movement of which, while not strictly programmatic, is clearly referential to the landscapes and seascapes of south-west Wales, where the work was written and where the composer was born.[32] The musical language of this first movement is one of Welsh 'impressionism', so to speak, coloured by flute arabesques and expressive trills, and the silvery textures and chiming sonorities of the percussion instruments and celesta (Example 12.2).

There is a lyrical, folk-like quality to the first movement, while the third-movement finale provides an injection of rhythmic verve and quotes, towards the end, the Welsh folk song 'Dadl Dau' – the first of Mathias's orchestral works to quote a traditional Welsh melody.[33] In contrast, the central movement expresses the 'heroic rhetoric and elegiac feeling' of early Welsh poetry,[34] and is prefaced with lines from the poem 'Welsh Landscape' by R. S. Thomas (1913–2000):

> To live in Wales is to be conscious
> At dusk of the spilled blood
> That went into the making of the wild sky,
> Dyeing the immaculate rivers
> In all their courses.[35]

---

[30] Mathias, programme note, *Celtic Dances* (London: Oxford University Press, 1974).
[31] Mathias, 'William Mathias at 50: The Composer Talks to Malcolm Boyd', *The Musical Times*, 125 (November 1984), 627.
[32] Mathias, programme note, Harp Concerto (London: Oxford University Press, 1973).
[33] Boyd, *William Mathias* (Cardiff: University of Wales Press, 1978), pp. 41–43.
[34] Mathias, programme note, Harp Concerto.
[35] R. S. Thomas, *Selected Poems 1946–1968* (Newcastle upon Tyne: Bloodaxe Books, 1986).

Example 12.2 William Mathias, Harp Concerto (1970), first movement, opening. © Oxford University Press, reproduced with permission of Oxford Publishing Limited (Music) through PLSclear

Example 12.2 (cont.)

According to James F. Knapp, 'the poetic world which emerges from the verse of R. S. Thomas is a world of lonely Welsh farms and of the farmers who endure the harshness of their hill country. The vision is realistic and merciless.'[36] Mathias manages to capture this vision in musical terms. In this work one could argue that, on one level, Mathias is engaging with the concept of hiraeth; but here, in the second movement, inspired by Thomas's verse, the musical language is not wistful, but is instead tough and weathered, like Thomas's words and the landscape with which both verse and music are so deeply connected.

A very different geographical area forms the backdrop for Hoddinott's 1975 orchestral work, *Landscapes*. Inspired by the poem 'Eryri' (Snowdonia) by T. H. Parry-Williams (1887–1975), the work, in terms of musical language and temperament, is in stark contrast to Mathias's Harp Concerto. Indeed, Mathias's works from this period exhibit the

---

[36] James F. Knapp, 'The Poetry of R. S. Thomas', *Twentieth Century Literature*, 17/1 (January 1971), 1.

fingerprints that we have come to associate with his eminently communicative style: a punchy and syncopated rhythmic drive, an inventive manipulation of thematic material, a liking for contrasting musical ideas, a penchant for vivacious contrapuntal textures, and an ostensibly tonal but modally enriched harmonic language – all of which is characteristically crowned by an emphatic optimism.[37] Conversely, Hoddinott's style tends to be inherently dark, brooding and uncompromising in character; it is rooted in a world inhabited by chromaticism and dissonance, where moments of stillness are routinely violently punctuated by fiery, often volcanic outbursts. There are, however, points of contact between the two composers, such as their predilection for tuned percussion instruments; but whereas both composers exhibit clear and unmistakable traits of Celtic rhetoric and contrasts of light and darkness in their music, the way in which they realise these qualities is quite different. Example 12.3, for instance, shows the end of the second movement of *Landscapes*, a movement that represents the frosty and snow-covered hills and mountains of Snowdonia. These concluding bars foreground stasis (high, sustained dissonant string chords), atmosphere and colour to articulate stillness, 'whiteness' and light.

Widely regarded as two of the most significant Welsh composers of the twentieth century, Mathias and Hoddinott are often considered in tandem.[38] Both were certainly eager in their early careers to establish a professional status by consciously distancing themselves from the predominantly amateur vocal culture in Wales.[39] But there are several other evident similarities: they were the first Welsh composers to gain international reputations; both were extremely prolific and contributed to almost every genre; both wrote mainly to commission; and both established major music festivals in Wales.[40] The two composers also shared parallel career trajectories: they studied initially in Wales (Mathias at University College, Aberystwyth; Hoddinott at University College, Cardiff) and London (Mathias at the Royal Academy of Music with

---

[37] Nicholas Jones, 'Mathias's String Quartet No. 1: Something to Shout About', *The Musical Times*, 141/1872 (Autumn 2000), 24.
[38] See, for instance, Michael Oliver, 'Two Welsh Composers: Alun Hoddinott and William Mathias', in *British Music Now*, ed. by Lewis Foreman (London: Elek Books, 1975), pp. 86–96 and Jim Samson, 'Instrumental Music II', in *The Blackwell History of Music in Britain – The Twentieth Century*, ed. by Stephen Banfield (Oxford: Blackwell, 1995), pp. 290–291.
[39] See, for instance, Mathias, in conversation with A. J. Heward Rees, 'Servants and Masters', *Welsh Music/Cerddoriaeth Cymru*, 6/5 (Summer/Haf 1980), 17.
[40] Hoddinott founded the Cardiff Festival of Twentieth-Century Music in 1967, and Mathias launched the North Wales Music Festival at St Asaph Cathedral five years later.

Example 12.3 Alun Hoddinott, *Landscapes* (1975), second movement, conclusion. © Oxford University Press, reproduced with permission of Oxford Publishing Limited (Music) through PLSclear

Lennox Berkeley (composition) and Peter Katin (piano); Hoddinott privately with Arthur Benjamin), and later became lecturers – and eventually professors of music and heads of department – at Welsh universities: Mathias at Bangor (1959–68; 1970–87) and Hoddinott at Cardiff (1959–87). However, as Michael Oliver has pointed out, 'the description "academic composer" fits neither and their musical styles are as different as their birthplaces: Hoddinott [came] from Bargoed,

Example 12.3 (cont.)

close to the blighted landscapes of the South Wales coalfield; Mathias from Whitland in rural Carmarthenshire'.[41]

Mathias's works from the early to mid-1950s demonstrate an influence of Hindemith and Bartók, and are characterised by a conscious use of chromaticism and a preoccupation with various aspects of compositional technique. Quasi-serial methods are employed, for instance, in the *Seven Poems of R. S. Thomas* (for tenor, harp and chamber orchestra; 1957) and

[41] Oliver, 'Two Welsh Composers', p. 86.

the *Sextet* (for clarinet, string quartet and piano; 1958), and the use of palindromic structural schemes can also be seen in the later work, as well as in the earlier orchestral *Berceuse* (1956). Such techniques, however, were subsequently rejected, and his next work, the *Divertimento for Strings* (1958), heralded a soundworld that proved to be more widely representative of his style moving forward; it was also his first work to attract widespread critical attention. Cast in three movements, the first and last are rhythmically urgent and contrapuntally rich, and frame an introspective and harmonically pungent slow movement. There followed a number of works – notably the Piano Concerto No. 2 (1960), *Invocation and Dance* for orchestra (1961), *St Teilo* (a masque based on episodes from the life of the saint as recorded in the twelfth-century Book of Llandaff;[42] 1962), and the Concerto for Orchestra (1964) – that led to the compelling and invigorating First Symphony (1965–6), a work that confirmed Mathias's reputation as one of the most promising young British composers of his generation.

The Symphony also proved to be transitional, leading from this 'first' period to the new tonal and structural direction of the ritualistic orchestral work *Litanies* (1967) and String Quartet No. 1 (1967), both of which are constructed from a juxtaposition of non-developmental contrasting ideas and thematic blocks. The historical precedent for this technique is Stravinsky's *Symphonies of Wind Instruments*, but the more obvious inspiration for Mathias would have been Michael Tippett's Piano Sonata No. 2 (1962) and Concerto for Orchestra (1963) – a composer who also deeply affected the musical language of Mathias's Symphony No. 1.[43] Mathias's next work, the virtuosic Piano Concerto No. 3 – premiered at the 1968 Swansea Festival by Mathias himself with the BBC Symphony Orchestra, conducted by Moshe Atzmon – also displayed a new stylistic ingredient: the influence of Latin American music. This can be heard in the syncopated, rumba-like main theme of the first movement,[44] and the employment of a large and colourful percussion section, which includes bongos, timbales and tom-tom; it is a soundworld that is also taken up in the *Holiday Overture* (1971).[45] In the Harpsichord Concerto (1972), Mathias creates a very different soundworld, combining a 'neo-classical framework' with 'melodic, intervallic and rhythmic elements which introduce a neo-medieval flavour into the language'.[46]

---

[42] Digitised by the National Library of Wales, http://hdl.handle.net/10107/4388358.
[43] Jones, 'Something to Shout About', pp. 28–30.   [44] Boyd, *William Mathias*, pp. 36–37.
[45] Ibid., p. 32.
[46] Geraint Lewis, 'Mathias, William (James)', *Grove Music Online*, www.oxfordmusiconline.com/subscriber/article/grove/music/18063 (accessed 17 May 2021).

Mathias has often been described as an 'eclectic', and his works as a whole reflect a musical language that is a marriage of a diversity of styles and influences. And even though he effectively managed to retain his own, highly individual voice, his refusal to engage with contemporary stylistic and technical developments left him open to negative criticism from some quarters.[47] His *Elegy for a Prince* (1972) – a setting for baritone and orchestra of a thirteenth-century Welsh marwnad (elegy), written by Gruffudd ab yr Ynad Coch, and translated by Anthony Conran – is a highly dramatic work which, together with the cantata *This Worlde's Joie* (1974), led naturally to Mathias's only opera, *The Servants*; with a libretto by Iris Murdoch, the work was staged by Welsh National Opera in September 1980. For Mathias, composing the opera provided him with 'an opportunity to draw all the stylistic threads together, in one sense, and in another to use a wide musical language to the full':

> Opera always provides a variety of characters and situations, and a range of stylistic means is therefore essential. This is one reason why I do not find the term 'eclectic' a derogatory one when applied to certain music.[48]

The Servants also reflected a 'strong tendency' in his work at the time 'to move towards the connexion of music and words'.[49] In 1981, he was commissioned to compose the anthem *Let the People Praise Thee, O God*, a setting of Psalm 67 for chorus and organ, for the royal wedding of the Prince of Wales and Lady Diana Spencer. This performance, watched by several hundred million people worldwide, led to numerous choral commissions, including those from choirs in the United States, such as *Rejoice in the Lord* (1986), commissioned by the American Guild of Organists, Springfield, Massachusetts, and *O Lord, our Lord* (1987), written for the Westminster Choir College, Princeton. Mathias, however, had already written a large quantity of liturgical and non-liturgical choral works before the 1980s, most notably *Make a Joyful Noise* (1964), *Festival Te Deum* (1964), *Three Medieval Lyrics* (1966), Magnificat and Nunc Dimittis (1970) and Missa Brevis (1973). But arguably his best-known works for choir are his carols, especially 'The Wassail Carol' (1964), 'Sir Christèmas' (part of the sequence *Ave Rex*; 1969) and 'A Babe is Born' (1971), all of which have found a firm place in the repertoire of countless choirs worldwide, as well as the annual Festival of Nine Lessons and Carols

---

[47] See Nicholas Jones, '"Disparagement and Invidious Comparisons"? Assessing Critical Reactions to Mathias's Symphony No. 1', *Tempo*, 60/238 (October 2006), 8–14.
[48] Mathias, in conversation with A. J. Heward Rees, 'Servants and Masters', pp. 26–27.
[49] Ibid., p. 17.

service at King's College, Cambridge. In his final decade, Mathias would complete two large-scale works for vocal soloists, chorus and orchestra: the requiem *Lux aeterna* (1982) and *World's Fire* (1989); he would also compose a further two symphonies (1983 and 1991), a third string quartet (1985–6) and concertos for organ (1983–4), horn (1984), oboe (1990), violin (1990–1) and flute (1992).

Like Mathias, Hoddinott's music is constructed with great skill and facility. Hoddinott was phenomenally productive; his voluminous worklist includes, for instance, six operas (1970–99), ten symphonies (1954–99), over twenty concertos (1948–2004), much choral and solo vocal music, and numerous works for various chamber combinations (including five string quartets, thirteen piano sonatas and six violin sonatas). In 2009, a new, specially built 350-seat concert hall within the Wales Millennium Centre in Cardiff Bay – home to the BBC National Orchestra of Wales – was named BBC Hoddinott Hall as a tribute to his pre-eminent contribution to musical life in Wales.

Hoddinott's early works – assured, confident, fluent – owe a debt to Walton, Alan Rawsthorne and Hindemith.[50] His breakthrough piece, the Clarinet Concerto No. 1 (1950), was performed to critical acclaim at the 1954 Cheltenham Festival by Gervase de Peyer and the Hallé Orchestra under John Barbirolli, and two years later at the Proms, conducted by Malcolm Sargent. The orchestral *Nocturne* (1952) signalled a change in stylistic direction: this work, and especially the First Symphony, display a more representative musical language and clearly reflect those stylistic traits already highlighted above – music of 'strong contrast, often violent or strident, and of powerful energy and drama', and of 'disturbing upheavals and of strenuous emotional crises'.[51] Like Mathias at this time, Hoddinott's works demonstrate the influence of Bartók, and this is especially evident in the chromaticism of his melodic lines and also in his interest in arch-like structures, such as those used in the first movements of both the First and Second symphonies (1955 and 1962).[52] Another formal influence is the palindrome: in the Piano Concerto No. 1 (1960), for instance, this structural device shapes the entire first movement.[53] In the early 1960s, Hoddinott started to use note sets that were serial in organisation. However, as Lewis has pointed out, his approach was individual and

---

[50] Geraint Lewis, 'Hoddinott, Alun', *Grove Music Online*, www.oxfordmusiconline.com/subscriber/article/grove/music/13118 (accessed 21 May 2021).
[51] Oliver, 'Two Welsh Composers', p. 87.
[52] Basil Deane, *Alun Hoddinott* (Cardiff: University of Wales Press, 1978), pp. 21–22.
[53] Ibid., p. 12.

'never involved the Schoenbergian abandonment of tonality'; indeed, tonality remained a 'cohesive force' throughout Hoddinott's output.[54]

The orchestral *Night Music* (1966) is a further example, among many, of the composer's liking for nocturnal landscapes. Here, the melodic material is kept to a minimum, and in its place harmonic stasis (sustained chords), temporal suspension (sustained passages of inactivity) and orchestral colour are given heightened prominence. His interest in colour naturally led to the augmentation of the percussion section, as witnessed in the orchestral works *Fioriture* (1968) and *The Sun, The Great Luminary of the Universe* (1970). The title of the former – Italian for 'flowering' – motivated the composer to foreground the decorative aspects of his intricate musical textures; the work also highlights his intense interest in Italian culture and baroque musical forms – features also apparent in the earlier orchestral *Variants* (1966).[55] The title of *The Sun* was inspired by a passage in James Joyce's *A Portrait of the Artist as a Young Man*, which vividly describes the vision of the end of time. Characterised by 'whirling, frenzied strings', 'apocalyptic fanfares' and 'grinding dissonance',[56] Hoddinott towards the end of the piece (bar 107), quietly quotes the opening line of Bach's chorale, 'Es ist genug' ('It is enough') on low brass; its inclusion appears to be symbolic, signalling an association with death. In other orchestral works, Hoddinott achieves a parallel connection through the frequent use of a sonorous, tolling bell, such as that encountered in *Night Music*, the Sixth Symphony (1984) and the Second Clarinet Concerto (1987): it is a timbre that lends the music a distinctive funereal air. The Sixth Symphony, according to Lewis, is a culmination of 'a distinctly romantic streak in Hoddinott's expression'.[57] This can be heard in various subsequent works, not least in the Second Violin Concerto (1995), a piece which possesses a warm, darkly glowing, lyrical quality. But on the whole, Hoddinott's music retained a modernist edge to the end. His final orchestral work, *Taliesin* (2007), written for the BBC National Orchestra of Wales, with whom Hoddinott enjoyed a sixty-year association, is a highly evocative tone-poem inspired by the life and work of the sixth-century Welsh bard, and is imbued with the hallmarks typically associated with the

---

[54] Lewis, 'Hoddinott, Alun'.
[55] In interview with Nicola Heywood Thomas in 2004, Hoddinott explained that his first violin teacher, from the age of five, brought him up essentially on Italian baroque violin music and that this exposure turned his own music towards the baroque traditions in preference to the sonata tradition of the Austro-German composers; *Hoddinott: the Composer at 75*, BBC Radio Wales, https://youtu.be/NpL9zW2Ft-g (accessed 24 May 2021).
[56] Oliver, 'Two Welsh Composers', p. 90.   [57] Lewis, 'Hoddinott, Alun'.

composer's orchestral music: dark, ominous sonorities; sensuous, iridescent textures; astringent harmonies; and quick passages, volatile in temperament.

Like choral music, Wales has a long, established tradition of art music for solo voice. Certain Welsh composers, most notably Meirion Williams (1901–76), Mansel Thomas (1909–86) and Dilys Elwyn Edwards (1918–2012), all made important contributions in this area.[58] One of Hoddinott's most effective song cycles, *Landscapes (Ynys Môn)* (1975) for tenor and piano, composed at the same time as he was planning his orchestral *Landscapes*, sets five English-language poems by Welsh writer Emyr Humphreys (1919–2020). Ynys Môn (Anglesey) is the island off the northwest coast of Wales, and each poem explores different places on the island: Mynydd Bodafon (a series of mountain peaks); Din Lligwy (a limestone hut circle close to the village of Moelfre); Llys Dulas (a derelict Victorian mansion); Traeth Bychan (a beach, also close to Moelfre); and Hen Gapel (a ruined chapel). In Hoddinott's setting, Humphreys' words take centre stage and the piano accompaniment is spare and luminous and sympathetic to the vocal line. *Landscapes* (to appropriate Denise Von Glahn's cogent phrase) is a 'place piece':[59] the titles and text strongly anchor the songs to Wales, and the musical response, at some level, manages to evoke these places and capture the rugged beauty and ancient landscapes and seascapes of Ynys Môn.

Dawnsiau'r Nant: A Confluence of Voices

Rhian Samuel (b. 1944) is another Welsh composer who has written several place pieces. For instance, *Nantcol Songs* (2003), for medium/high voice and piano, is inspired by the Snowdonian landscape of Cwm Nantcol; the third and fourth movements of *Tirluniau/Landscapes* – an orchestral piece premiered at the BBC Proms in 2000 – vividly invoke the landscape around Castell y Bere, Snowdonia, and the seascape of Cardigan Bay, west Wales, respectively; and the orchestral work *Dawnsiau'r Nant* (Dances of the Stream, 1999) colourfully depicts the play of light and rain on Nant y Wenallt, a stream close to the composer's birthplace of Aberdare. According to Joyce Andrews, 'Samuel cannot escape the strong influences of nature and of landscapes in her writing, indicative of her

---

[58] See Rachel Schutz, 'An Introduction to Welsh Solo Vocal Repertoire', *Journal of Singing*, 77/1 (September/October 2020), 73–80.
[59] Denise Von Glahn, *The Sounds of Place: Music and the American Cultural Landscape* (Boston, MA: Northwestern University Press, 2003), p. 2.

Welsh heritage'; she also states: 'Samuel readily admits [in a 2002 interview] that her experiences as a child growing up in Wales, especially her recollections of the sights and sounds of her native land, have become an integral part of her composing consciousness.'[60]

Samuel was educated at the University of Reading and in the United States at Washington University, St Louis. In 1984, she returned to the UK and subsequently taught at several English universities, including City University, London. Throughout her career, Samuel has actively engaged with the composition of vocal music in all its forms. One of her first important works, for example, is *The Hare in the Moon* (1978), a setting for soprano and piano of a translated Japanese poem by the Sōtō Zen Buddhist monk, Ryōkan. Compelling and tightly constructed, the work has a fine sense of dramatic pacing and uses both spoken and sung passages to express the text. The composer is particularly renowned for her sensitive and painstaking settings of poetry by women,[61] including Emily Dickinson in *Lovesongs and Observations* (1989), May Sarton in *The White Amaryllis* (1991) and Nesta Wyn Jones in *Pan Ddaw Ust y Nos/When the Calm of Night* (2005) and *Tair Alaw/Three Songs* (2017). Since the mid-1990s, Samuel has been particularly drawn to the work of British-American poet Anne Stevenson (1933–2020), with whom she became close friends and collaborated on a number of important works, the earliest being *Path* (1995) and *Daughters' Letters* (1996), and more recently *A Wildflower Songbook* (2014), *The Listening Eye* (2017) and *The Shape of Trees* (2020).[62]

One of Samuel's most successful and critically acclaimed vocal works, however, is *Clytemnestra* for soprano and orchestra (1994). Based on Aeschylus's account of the death of Agamemnon at the hand of Clytemnestra, Samuel's own adaptation of the translated text focuses poignantly on Clytemnestra's 'deep, personal anguish at the death of her daughter', whom Agamemnon sacrificed on his way to Troy.[63] According to Samuel, 'The work is not offered as a vindication of Clytemnestra's violent act, but as an exploration of her conflicting emotions.'[64] The result is a powerful, disturbing, visceral work, distinguished by its unflinching

---

[60] Joyce Andrews, 'Composer Rhian Samuel: The Female Viewpoint and Welsh Influences in Her Vocal Music', *Women and Music*, 8 (2004), 68, 61.

[61] Stephen Banfield, 'Samuel, Rhian', *The New Grove Dictionary of Women Composers*, ed. by Julie Anne Sadie and Rhian Samuel (London: Macmillan, 1994), p. 403.

[62] See Rhian Samuel, 'Anne Stevenson, 1933–2020: Dear Friend, RIP', www.rhiansamuel.com/p/anne-stevenson-1933-2020-dear-friend-rip.html (accessed 25 May 2021).

[63] Rhian Samuel, CD liner note, *Clytemnestra* (BIS Records, BIS-2408, 2019), 6.

[64] Rhian Samuel, programme note, *Clytemnestra*, https://stainer.co.uk/shop/hl328/ (accessed 25 May 2021).

portrayal of the dramatic narrative, the brilliance of its kaleidoscopic orchestration, and its bold modernist style. However, Samuel is a composer with an agile musical language: while maintaining a consistent, distinctive voice, she possesses the ability to modify her means of musical expression and communication to suit a variety of different contexts and commissions, including the incorporation of tonal elements. Her substantial output reveals a composer of endless inventiveness and of elegantly crafted compositions, where intricate textures, filigree attention to detail and idiomatic writing for instruments and voices are characteristics abundantly in evidence.

Guy Rickards has rightly argued that Samuel's works 'are sometimes tricky to pigeonhole'.[65] Born in the same year as Samuel, Karl Jenkins is also a composer whose music has proved difficult to categorise. Jenkins was born in Neath and brought up in the coastal village of Penclawdd on the Gower Peninsula. He learnt the piano and oboe as a child, and at the age of sixteen he took up the saxophone as a result of his discovery of jazz.[66] After academic study at the University of Wales, Cardiff (1963–6) and the Royal Academy of Music (1966–7), Jenkins toured extensively with various jazz-rock and jazz-fusion groups, most notably Nucleus (1969–72) and Soft Machine (1972–81).[67] From 1981 he worked with keyboardist Mike Ratledge on creating music for commercials. These 'advertising years', as he would later describe them, were 'enormous fun and an education, writing and recording music that spanned the spectrum from the blues to Elgar's Cello Concerto', and involved 'creating a pithy, concise musical statement' and using a 'diversity of musical styles'.[68] Developing out of one particular advertisement, for Delta Airlines, came a series of nine, tonally based compositions for voice and orchestra: released in 1995, *Adiemus: Songs of Sanctuary* enjoyed extraordinary worldwide success.[69] According to Jenkins, *Adiemus* 'is an extended choral-type work based on the European classical tradition'; however, the solo vocal parts 'are intoned in a sometimes ecclesiastical, sometimes Celtic manner', and the choruses are 'ethnic' and 'tribal' in soundworld and draw upon African and Māori choral traditions.[70] Consolidating his achievement with a further four *Adiemus* albums (1997–2003), Jenkins quickly became the best-known,

---

[65] Guy Rickards, 'Hampstead: Rhian Samuel's *Light and Water*', *Tempo*, 58/230 (October 2004), 58.
[66] Karl Jenkins, *Still with the Music* (London: Elliott and Thompson Ltd, 2015), pp. 1–27.
[67] Simon Adams, 'Jenkins, Karl', *Grove Music Online*, www.oxfordmusiconline.com/subscriber/article/grove/music/J228500 (accessed 26 May 2021).
[68] Jenkins, *Still with the Music*, p. 91.   [69] Adams, 'Jenkins, Karl'.
[70] Jenkins, CD liner note, *Adiemus: Songs of Sanctuary* (Virgin Records Ltd, 1995).

best-selling and most-performed living British composer. This status and level of success has inevitably attracted a certain amount of adverse criticism; his music, for instance, has been described as 'trite' and 'bland'.[71] However, one senses that much of the criticism levelled against Jenkins is a haughty disdain that emanates not only from his background in commercial music, especially advertisements, but also from the fact that his music, though based on western art music traditions and forms (such as rondo and ternary), often freely employs and adapts styles and practices from a range of different cultures.

Certainly, the composer's interests and musical influences are diverse and cosmopolitan. In his *Requiem* (2005), for instance, the usual Latin mass movements are interleaved and juxtaposed with settings of five Japanese *haiku* 'death' poems; the orchestration includes the *shakuhachi* (an ancient Japanese flute), the Arabic *darabuca* drum, and Japanese *daiko* and frame drums; and the Dies Irae employs a hip-hop rhythm.[72] Arguably his most popular work is *The Armed Man: A Mass for Peace* (2000), for vocal soloists, chorus and orchestra. 'People tell me I write good tunes', explains Jenkins: 'When *The Armed Man* is performed you get people crying in the aisles. The "Benedictus" is one of the most requested pieces at funerals and one of the most requested pieces on the radio channel Classic FM.'[73]

The strong emotional and often spiritual connection that Jenkins forges with his audiences in these and other choral works is something that can be traced back ultimately to his own experience of Welsh congregational hymn singing in Penclawdd: 'That kind of sound became core to one's life in the sense that every Sunday one was exposed to it. It was very emotional and it was, to an extent, tribal singing because it wasn't controlled or trained in any way.'[74] A relationship to his Welsh heritage is demonstrated more directly in other works, including *Dewi Sant* (1999), for chorus and orchestra; *Over the Stone/Tros y Garreg* (2002), for two

---

[71] See, for instance, Jenkins, in conversation with Michael Roddy, 'Top Composer Jenkins Defends "Accessible" Music', *Reuters*, 3 March 2010, www.reuters.com/article/us-music-jenkins-idUKTRE6221R120100303 (accessed 26 May 2021), and Jenkins, in conversation with Sue Lawley, *Desert Island Discs*, 10 December 2006, www.bbc.co.uk/programmes/p0093tt1 (accessed 27 May 2021).

[72] Jenkins, C D liner note, *Karl Jenkins: Requiem* (EMI Records Ltd, 2005).

[73] Jenkins, in conversation with Roddy, 'Top Composer Jenkins Defends "Accessible" Music'. According to the composer's website, by April 2020 *The Armed Man* had received close to 3,000 performances worldwide, averaging over 2 performances per week since its premiere in 2000; 'Celebrations for the 20th Anniversary of *The Armed Man: A Mass for Peace*', 1 May 2020, www.karljenkins.com/news/news-view/celebrations-for-the-20th-anniversary-of-the-armed-man-a-mass-for-peace (accessed 28 May 2021).

[74] Ibid.

harps, strings and percussion; *In These Stones Horizons Sing* (2004), a setting of Welsh and English texts for vocal and instrumental soloists, choirs and orchestra; and *Cantata Memoria: Er Mwyn y Plant/For the Children* (2016), for soloists, chorus and orchestra – a deeply moving commemoration of the Aberfan disaster of 1966, setting a text by Welsh poet Mererid Hopwood (b. 1964).

This enduring fascination with his native homeland is a characteristic common to all the composers discussed in this chapter, and as a theme has threaded itself throughout the whole of the narrative. Clearly, though, the extent to which a composer's Welsh identity impacts on his or her own music and aesthetic is different in each case. It seems likely, therefore, that the nexus between Welsh identity and art music will remain a complex issue for some time to come. Indeed, one only has to take a cursory glance at the current Tŷ Cerdd Welsh composer database to get a sense of the rich diversity of styles, techniques and approaches.[75] However, as we have seen, Welshness finds many ways to articulate itself, and a musical expression of nationhood often tends to be intrinsic and not always external. Additionally, a great part of all these composers' practice is a shared need to communicate clearly and directly, and to make a powerful connection with their audiences – and this is especially evident in the composers featured in this chapter. It would be more helpful, then, to think not of Welsh composers travelling along individual paths, but rather of a confluence of compositional voices, a flowing together, as it were, of many different tributaries – of many vibrant dancing streams.

---

[75] Tŷ Cerdd, 'Composer Database/Cronfa Cyfansoddwr', www.tycerdd.org/composer-database (accessed 28 May 2021). See also Pwyll ap Siôn, 'Cenedligrwydd a'r Cyfansoddwr Cymreig/ Nationhood and the Welsh Composer', *Welsh Music History/Hanes Cerddoriaeth Cymru*, 7 (2007), 300–303.

CHAPTER 13

Traditions and Interventions
Popular Music 1840–1940

Trevor Herbert

The second half of the nineteenth century has been referred to as the period of a 'Welsh musical renaissance',[1] but in truth it was not a renaissance at all because the developments to which it gave issue had no precedent. The Celtic revivalists accurately identified a strong and enduring tradition of Welsh music, but in the mid-nineteenth century the musical life of the nation changed, and it is from those changes that vaunted notions of the Welsh as a musical nation originate. My period is defined at both ends by a loose set of circumstances that were suggesting the start of a new era. In the 1840s Wales was on the brink of its most dramatic demographic change, when new communities and their attendant cultural predilections were in formation, and by the end of the 1930s new forms of mass media and American popular music culture were transforming popular culture in Wales as emphatically as they were elsewhere.

Demographics

The expansion and redistribution of the population of Wales in the mid-nineteenth century was a consequence of its becoming one of the world's most dynamic industrial economies through the exploitation of coal mining in the south of the country. The demographics do not just provide a context for the development of the popular music culture of Wales: they were causal. The 1851 census showed Wales to have a population of 1,163,139 persons; by 1901 it had risen to 2,012,876; and in 1921 it had risen again to 2,656,474.[2] This can be partly explained by natural growth, but the headlines obscure essential details. External and internal migration impacted disproportionately on the south to create a distinctive type of

---

[1] For example, David Morgans, *Music and Musicians of Merthyr and District: Together with a List of Eisteddfodau to the Year 1901* (Merthyr Tydfil: H. W. Southey, 1922), p. 10.
[2] L. J. Williams, *Digest of Welsh Historical Statistics*, Vol. 1 (Cardiff: The Welsh Office, 1998), p. 7.

urbanisation in the southern valleys, in which chains of dense population were clustered around coal mines. Even by 1851, the first wave of industrialisation had caused the two most populous southern counties – Monmouthshire and Glamorganshire – to account for more than a third of the entire population of Wales; by 1881 it was more than half. There was immigration from other parts of Britain, but a good proportion came from migration to the industrial areas from Welsh rural counties. The pace of change was so rapid that for decades the south Wales valleys must have resembled a massive construction site. The inhabited housing stock of Glamorganshire rose from 32,718 in 1841 to 92,083 in 1881.[3] In the same period the country's operational railway lines increased exponentially and most of this increase too was in the south.

All this had cultural impact. It affected the use and status of the Welsh language and, in consequence, the musical repertoires and practices to which it was intimately connected. Language preferences were not collected in the decennial census until 1891, but at that time, when the total population was a little under 1.7 million, over half a million declared themselves 'Welsh speakers', and a further 400,000 (910,289 in all) spoke both languages. In 1931, with a population of a little less than 2.5 million, the number of Welsh speakers was 909,261, of which about 11 per cent used only Welsh.[4] But here, too, there is a story within a story. In 1891 English was probably the main language of the majority, but in rural areas in particular, Welsh remained the language of choice. This explains why, as late as 1884 when the English-born organist of Bangor Cathedral, Dr Roland Rogers, conducted the Penrhyn Choral Union, he had to communicate through an interpreter because the choir was almost entirely monoglot Welsh.[5]

There were trends, events, agencies and individuals that contributed to reconfigurations in Welsh popular music and the intricate blend of continuities and changes that prevailed. Two agencies had a special impact: religion, which was a conduit for congregational singing and by extension vocal music more generally, and eisteddfodau, which shifted their emphasis in the period from being primarily poetic events to massively popular competitive music festivals with a high level of participation; in

---

[3] Williams, *Digest*, vol. 2, p. 70.
[4] Ibid., Vol. 1, p. 78. The actual number of Welsh speakers is shown to rise until the 1911 census, even though the percentage had declined.
[5] Gareth Williams, *Valleys of Song: Music and Society in Wales, 1840–1914* (Cardiff: University of Wales Press, 1998), p. 154.

this same process eisteddfodau also had an important influence on the curation of Wales's oldest musical traditions.

Popular Music?

It is not unusual for discourses on the 'popular' to carry cautionary provisos, and here it is essential. I use 'popular' to signify the music of the mass of the people: the music with which the greatest number engaged either as practitioners or listeners. 'Popular', even when used in this sense, has often, implicitly, been a marker that distinguishes lower from higher classes of repertoire and practice, often with commensurate inferences of inferiority. This crude classification does not fit here; indeed, it provides a vivid illustration of the vulnerability of such easy categorisations. It was common in most developed countries in the nineteenth century for classical music to be adapted for popular use, but in Wales all repertoires were freely shared. Art music, sacred music and the various types and interpretations of traditional music coalesced along with the dances, marches and the other forms of musical entertainment that the German musicologist Carl Dahlhaus classified with undue indiscrimination as *Trivialmusik*.[6] Music was a feature of everyday life in Wales and shaped by characteristics that were unique in Britain. In Wales, there were no agencies or institutions analogous to the Royal Academy of Music, the Royal Philharmonic Society and the Royal Italian Opera in England, or to equivalent organisations in the long-established centres of cultural production in Edinburgh and Dublin that served to arbitrate aesthetic taste and, by inference, enforce the distinction between high and low culture. It followed that for much of the nineteenth century, the process that the US cultural historian Lawrence Levine termed 'the sacralisation of culture' was largely absent.[7] With these points in mind, in this chapter 'the popular' can be understood in utilitarian terms: it was the music that engaged and provided greatest pleasure to the greatest number, in whatever form it was delivered, and from whatever source it was drawn.

Even in the first half of the century, imported popular music was in circulation. An example can be found in the handwritten musical commonplace book held at the National Library of Wales known as Evan James MS 1.[8] It is famous because it contains 'Glan Rhondda' (The Banks

---

[6] Carl Dahlhaus, *Nineteenth-Century Music*, trans. by J. Bradford Robinson (Berkeley; London: University of California Press, 1989), p. 311.
[7] Lawrence W. Levine, *Highbrow/Lowbrow: The Emergence of Cultural Hierarchy in America* (Cambridge, MA: Harvard University Press, 1990).
[8] Digitised by the National Library of Wales, http://hdl.handle.net/10107/4655569.

of the [River] Rhondda), better known by its opening words 'Mae Hen Wlad fy Nhadau' (Old Land of my Fathers): it is the original autograph source for the Welsh national anthem.[9] 'Glan Rhondda' is given as an unharmonised melody, the Welsh words written beneath the notes, but with no attempt at precise underlay – a sure sign that it was an aide-memoire for a song to be performed by the person who wrote it. It was composed in Pontypridd in 1856 by James James (1833–1902) (the melody) and his father, Evan James (1809–78) (the words). The harmonisation, the removal of the original title and other adjustments were the work of others.

Father and son were artisans, tavern harpists, singers and poets. Both had adopted bardic names – respectively, Ieuan ap Iago and Iago ap Ieuan – and were keen supporters of eisteddfodau. The book, which is mostly in the hand of James James, is interesting because it provides a glimpse into his musical world. It contains songs of the type father and son would have performed publicly or in private, as well as extracts from composers such as Bach, Handel, Mozart and Beethoven, but also a selection of popular instrumental tunes of the time, including polkas and other modern dances. Indeed, the page containing 'Glan Rhondda' is otherwise occupied by the melody of 'The Duke of York's March', a standard in the repertoire of militia bands that was sometimes adapted as a duple-metre dance.

Evan and James James were not major Welsh musicians of their time. If 'Glan Rhondda' had not gained its famous status, 'Evan James MS 1' would probably be regarded as no more than the tune book of a relatively obscure mid-century rural musician. But even if such were the case, it would evidence how repertoire was circulating at a time when south Wales was still on the brink of its major phase of industrialisation; furthermore, it is a far from isolated case. For example, a much larger collection of harp pieces at the National Library, also from the 1850s, contains the repertoire of Thomas David Llewelyn (Llewelyn Alaw; 1828–79) who was a more celebrated figure.[10] From 1851, after briefly working as a coalminer,

---

[9] The manuscript and the origin of the song are described in several sources including Percy A. Scholes, 'Hen Wlad fy Nhadau', *National Library of Wales Journal*, 3/1 & 2 (1943), 1–10, and Rhidian Griffiths, 'Hen Wlad fy Nhadau in Its Musical Context', *Morgannwg: Transactions of the Glamorgan History Society*, 51 (2007), 6–18. Meredydd Evans has identified a further autograph source for the song which James submitted to the 1858 Llangollen Eisteddfod using the alias 'Orpheus'; see 'Pwy Oedd "Orpheus" Eisteddfod Llangollen 1858?/Who Was "Orpheus" of the 1858 Llangollen Eisteddfod?', *Welsh Music History/Hanes Cerddoriaeth Cymru*, 5 (2002), 59–71.

[10] GB-AB MS 337D. Llewelyn Alaw's repertoire seems to have been vast and eclectic. A book of manuscripts, described as his winning entry for a collection of unpublished Welsh airs for the 1858 Llangollen Eisteddfod (GB-AB MS 331D), is greatly extended to include hornpipes and other modern tunes, and a further collection (GB-AB MS 336D) has tunes filling 321 pages and is marked Vol. IX on its title page.

Llewelyn made his living as a professional poet and musician. The collection contains 261 tunes: some are Welsh, but most are waltzes, polkas and quadrilles, accompaniments to songs including 'The Dashing White Sergeant' and faddish local dance tunes such as the 'Aberdare Railway Polka' and the 'Aberaman Hornpipe'. Llewelyn Alaw, like the Jameses, was a journeyman harpist at a time when taverns were venues for entertainments including eisteddfodau, but he was also household harpist to the Williams family of Aberpergwm and to Lord Aberdare, for whom exposure to, as well as a knowledge of, a wide range of repertoire must have been a routine requirement.

Instrumental Ensemble Music

A major and generally under-acknowledged agency for modern instrumental music in rural Britain from the late eighteenth century was military bands, especially those attached to the militia units that were a mandatory requirement for every county. The species originated as the private bands of London military officers, all of whom were drawn from the aristocracy or gentry. They were responsible for the funding of bands of music which were usually directed and mentored by foreigners, typically German bandmasters recruited through specialist London agencies who supplied military clients (often ignorant of such matters) with instruments and other necessary accoutrements for the speedy assembly of a 'band of music'.[11] County militia units were assembled and maintained by the rural gentry, who supported them financially; initially for social reasons in imitation of London behaviour, but later by necessity because military drill regulations changed to take such bands into account.

These bands were distributed throughout Wales. The Denbighshire Militia Band was led for ten years from 1795 by John Parry (Bardd Alaw; 1776–1851) and maintained at least ten players. Like many others, it accommodated the prevailing taste for the exotic by enlisting a black man to play Turkish janissary instruments. Repertoire was purchased from London publishers; it included popular dances and operatic derivatives – there was no standard instrumentation, so the common practice was for printed copies (often keyboard copies) to be adapted for the instruments at hand. The band account books also mention a payment 'for binding Jones's Welch Musick in morocco leather', and another for the purchase in 1795 of 'a pedal harp',

---

[11] Trevor Herbert and Helen Barlow, *Music and the British Military in the Long Nineteenth Century* (New York: Oxford University Press, 2013), chapter 5.

which indicates that, as was commonly the case, irrespective of their military deployments, militia bands were also extensions of the house music of the landed class.[12] The Royal Glamorgan Regiment also employed a harper for indoor entertainments and let out its band for various popular assemblies such as races.[13]

In the first half of the nineteenth century the network of militia bands was an important part of the infrastructure of popular music in Wales. They were well organised, properly funded, efficient and an important and attractive link to sources of popular music production outside the country. There is even evidence of their influence on traditional song, with tunes such as 'The Duke of Gloucester's March' having more than one setting of Welsh words.[14] While a large part of the role of militia bands was to play at private events, especially dances, they also performed in public spaces for the population at large.[15]

Among the many beneficiaries of this legacy was the Cyfarthfa Band of Merthyr Tydfil. It merits attention here because it was probably the most sophisticated and virtuoso instrumental ensemble in Wales before the mid-twentieth century. It is famous for the sources that survive from the relatively short period when it flourished. They include photographs, documents, most of the original instruments and more than a hundred handwritten partbooks, which have enabled part of the repertoire to be performed and recorded on instruments of the period, imitating original performance conventions.[16]

In May 1850, an article in the magazine *Household Words* headed 'Music in Humble Life' told of boys at the Cyfarthfa iron works 'whistling airs rarely heard except in the fashionable ballrooms, opera houses or drawing rooms'.[17] This may well have been true, but to credit this to the enlightened benevolence of Robert Thompson Crawshay, the owner of the ironworks (which is what the article did), was wide of the mark. The band was formed in the mid-1840s as part of Crawshay's idiosyncratic scheme to establish his ostentatious home, Cyfarthfa Castle, as a cultural oasis. None of the features that applied to the much wider working-class amateur brass band movement (which started decades later anyway)

---

[12] GB-AB Chirk Castle Estate Records (1), Group B, No 117.   [13] GB-AB Bute Estate (2) L80/14.
[14] Phyllis Kinney, *Welsh Traditional Music* (Cardiff: University of Wales Press in association with Cymdeithas Alawon Gwerin Cymru, 2011), pp.151–153.
[15] Trevor Herbert, 'Public Military Music and the Promotion of Patriotism in the Provinces, c.1780–c.1850', *Nineteenth-Century Music Review*, 17/3 (2020), 427–444.
[16] Period instrument performances of the repertoire were recorded by The Wallace Collection for *The Origin of the Species*. Nimbus Records WC2013 (1996).
[17] 'Music in Humble Life', *Household Words*, 11 May 1850, 161.

prevailed. The players were not amateur workmen; most were professional players, from itinerant show bands. Others were recruited directly from militia bands. The most famous was Samuel Hughes, the ophicleide player, who had been a member of the Shropshire Militia Band. He left Merthyr in the mid-1850s to become the most celebrated player of that instrument in London. The band's first conductor, John Gratian, was previously at London's Vauxhall Gardens. He was succeeded by Ralph Livesey, then his son George Livesey, both from Wombwell's Menagerie band. Good local jobs and accommodation were secured for the players: an attractive package for Victorian musicians. The band's instruments were supplied by Charles Pace of London, who held the royal warrant. When modern valve instruments were introduced, they were imported from élite Viennese manufacturers. The repertoire was created by the conductor and George D'Artney, a German immigrant, reputedly a brilliant and knowledgeable musician, retained by Crawshay solely to arrange and copy music for the band.

Because the repertoire is handwritten (rather than printed), bespoke and often annotated by the individual players, it evidences their technical and musical competence and reveals them to have had remarkable lyrical and virtuosic skills. The repertoire can be divided unequally into three categories; a small group of functional pieces such as hymns and marches; a large quantity of fashionable dance music that was performed at the elaborate balls that were a feature of life at Cyfarthfa; and a yet larger number of transcriptions of operatic and classical works, including complete symphonies by Haydn and Beethoven. As well as its strictly private role, the band performed in public spaces with Crawshay's permission or as part of his travelling entourage. In September 1869 the 'Mayor, Aldermen and Burgess of the ancient town of Aberystwyth' expressed gratitude to Crawshay, who was ensconced for a week at 8 Marine Terrace with his band performing outside, for:

> your famous band, whose skilled and artistic performances have been the sources of pleasure to the hundreds of persons who have had the privilege of listening to them, and afforded a musical treat to many, amusing the hearers possessing a cultivated knowledge of that delightful science, which they could not otherwise have had.[18]

The band lasted longer than Crawshay, who died in 1879, but by the turn of the century it was in terminal decline. For four decades it had been a major musical institution and a source of superb performances of a rich

---

[18] *Aberystwyth Observer*, 11 September 1869, 4.

and varied repertoire. In this period Cyfarthfa Castle had become something of a destination for the London élite. In 1869 Charlotte Sainton-Dolby, who had been the contralto soloist in the first performance of Mendelssohn's *Elijah*, was a visitor. She wrote a 'Triumphal March' for the band, perhaps the first composition for this genre by a woman composer. It is significantly more idiomatic than is Joseph Parry's 'Tydfil Overture', which was also a commission for the band.

Choralism, Y Côr Mawr and Popular Music as Cultural Nationalism

In the summers of 1872 and 1873, the South Wales Choral Union, a conglomerate of 456 choristers from 11 locations in south Wales, was assembled to compete at a national choral contest at the Crystal Palace in Sydenham. The event was one of the 'National Music Meetings', a scheme organised by the impresario Willert Beale for the Crystal Palace company with the intention of raising standards of music making among amateurs across Britain; at the time it was said to be inspired by the success of Welsh eisteddfodau in meeting such ends. Under its conductor Griffith Rhys Jones (Caradog; 1834–97), the Welsh choir won in both years. It was popularly known as Y Côr Mawr (The Great Choir) and was 'composed of young men and young women of the working classes'.[19]

It gained sponsorship by appealing to grandees such as Lord and Lady Bute (who donated £20) and supplemented its costs further by performing concerts and open rehearsals for the general public, who attended in unprecedented numbers. This had the effect of creating an intense popular interest: so much so that Y Côr Mawr took on a representative mantle, initially of the valleys from which it was raised, and then, by popular momentum, most of Wales. The departures and homecomings of the triumphant choir were accompanied by rituals and ceremonials in their local communities (see Figure 13.1). Caradog, a talented musician, but otherwise a Treorchy publican, became a hero, and memorabilia such as decorative cravats carrying his image were produced. Graphic commemorative posters were circulated with images of 'the conductor and other officers' above the motto 'they led them to victory'. 'Caradog's Army' and 'Cambria's Five Hundred' were among other epithets acquired. Some

[19] *The Cardiff and Merthyr Guardian Glamorgan Monmouth and Brecon Gazette*, 29 June 1872, 5.

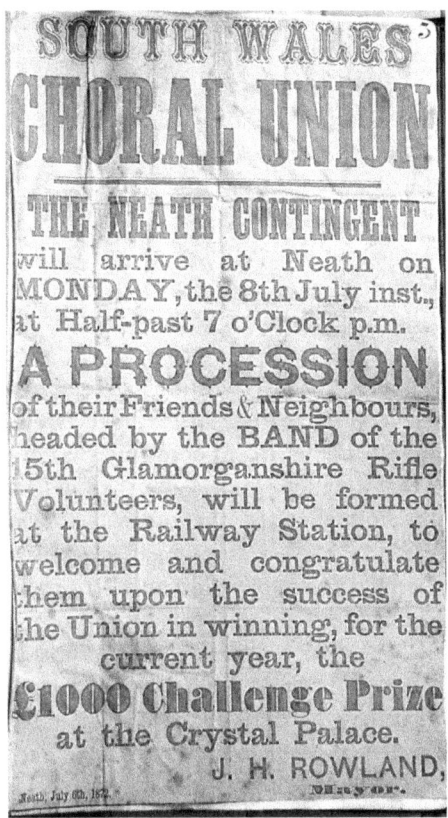

Figure 13.1 A poster widely circulated in Neath by the local council following the success of Y Côr Mawr, which included some of the townspeople. By kind permission of Peter Stevens

newspapers even carried poetic tributes such as 'Waged they the war of song/Aye, the whole world among'.[20]

Welsh expatriates abroad donated to the cause and rejoiced at the outcome. Caradog was the recipient of a *bâton d'or* presented by the Welsh gold-diggers of Australia, and at a rehearsal in Pontypridd in 1873, a visiting deputation of Welsh Americans paid homage to Caradog, the choir and the country they still regarded as home. They described it using a term that was gathering popular use, 'Gwlad y Gân'

---

[20] *Western Mail*, 11 July 1873, 3.

(Land of Song).[21] The events of those two summers became the stuff of legend. Twenty years later at the Chicago World's Fair Eisteddfod, where male choirs from Penrhyn and the Rhondda along with Clara Novello Davies's Welsh Ladies Choir were present, a remarkable scene was stirred when, amid an adjudication, a member of the audience rose to his feet, pointed to a man in an adjacent row and shouted 'Dacw Caradog!' (There's Caradog!), causing the entire massive assembly to rise in tremendous and sustained applause.[22]

It would be easy to dismiss all this as a brief, overblown incident that ignited a bout of collective self-indulgence. In fact, it was one of the most culturally significant episodes in Welsh music history and it impacted indirectly on the whole of Wales.[23] Though the choir was initiated and led by men of influence, it was in all other respects a popular phenomenon: the participants came from communities and families over a geographic area that included recent immigrants from Welsh rural counties. Eisteddfodau had made the musical contest an important feature of Welsh life that provoked anticipation, tensions and thrills in equal proportions: communal emotions for which there were few alternative stimuli.

The performances of Y Côr Mawr also had an impact on audiences in London, and this further increased the currency of the episode in Wales. *The Times* mentioned that the choir's 'attack was as sure as the stroke of a hammer... their precision was never ever at fault', and there was praise for 'the freshness and pungent quality of the voices'.[24] The 1872 adjudication mentioned that one voice from the Welsh choir was equal to three from any in London. The Welsh-language periodical *Y Cerddor Cymreig* (The Welsh Musician) despatched a writer to cover the event who felt he had identified the main reason for the success:

> Mae yn amlwg fod astudiaeth fanwl wedi bod ar y cyfansoddiad hwn, nid yn unig gyda golwg ar gael y seiniau yn gywir, ond gyda golwg ar amser, ansawdd llais, a holl fynegiant ac ysbryd y cyfansoddiad ... Mae y canu yna yn rhywbeth newydd i'r Palas Gwydr. Mae yn amheus a all neb ond

---

[21] The phrase 'Gwlad y gân' gained popular momentum from this time; its origin is not definitely known, but it is often traced back to an englyn by Thomas Jones (Taliesin o Eifion; 1830–76), 'Cymru lân, Cymru lonydd', in which the term appears.

[22] William D. Jones, *Wales in America: Scranton and the Welsh, 1860–1920* (Cardiff: University of Wales Press, 1993), p. 161.

[23] This point is argued in greater detail in Trevor Herbert, 'Popular Nationalism: Griffith Rhys Jones ('Caradog') and the Welsh Choral Tradition', in *Music and British Culture 1785–1914*, ed. by Christina Bashford and Leanne Langley (Oxford: Oxford University Press, 2000), pp. 255–275.

[24] *The Times*, 15 July 1873, 4.

Cymru, a'r rhai hynny wedi ei magu yn nghanol dylanwad yr efengyl, a all ganu fel yna.[25]

(It is clear that a careful study has been made of this composition, not only with a view to getting the notes right, but also with a view to time, quality of voice, and the whole expression of the spirit of the composition ... Such singing is something new to the Crystal Palace. It is unlikely that any but the Welsh, and those of them brought up amid the influence of the gospel, could sing like that.)

It mattered that this was published in the Welsh language and referenced religious nonconformity (for that is what 'the influence of the gospel' was), because it communicated with a constituency that may have otherwise felt less embraced by the collective mood. There had previously been no external competitive event on this scale, in any field of endeavour, at which Wales had been popularly represented, and there was a shared sense that the 'land of song' idea had been both exhibited and verified. In fact, in 1873 no other choir had competed against Y Côr Mawr in the category of choirs exceeding 300 voices and it is likely that its sheer magnitude contributed to the impression it made. Nevertheless, the London-based Cymmrodorion quickly grasped the popular enthusiasm the choir had engendered and offered it up in support of their inclination to regard Welsh musicality as innate and link it with the country's ancient and bardic past.

Songs in Transition

There followed a new, often fanciful and voguish popularity for Welsh music outside the country – especially in London. A flurry of 'Welsh music festivals' at London concert venues were organised at which singers such as Ben Davies and Mary Davies, the harpist John Thomas (Pencerdd Gwalia; 1826–1913) and the pianist Brinley Richards were prominent. These festivals, the propagation of eisteddfodau to venues beyond Wales and the proliferation of Welsh song publications established the idea of Welsh music as a marketable commodity. The most important early impresario was Jules Rivière (1819–1900), who is discussed below in a different context. Rivière had been associated with Louis Jullien, the extravagant French conductor who has been properly credited with transforming the public concert by combining classical and popular repertoire with spectacular modes of presentation: in so doing he created entirely new audiences.

---

[25] *Y Cerddor Cymreig*, 138, 1 Awst 1872, 58.

Rivière, also a conductor, had similar entrepreneurial gifts. In 1874 he instigated a 'Welsh festival' at Covent Garden in which 'nothing but Welsh music and Welsh artists appeared in the programme ... [and] by way of extra sensation ... had the newspaper advertisements translated into Welsh'.[26] It was a tremendous hit, and similar events were soon filling the Royal Albert Hall. This was part of the Côr Mawr effect, as indeed was a new interest in Welsh song.

Before the end of 1873, Boosey & Co. released the first edition of *The Songs of Wales* edited by Carmarthen-born Brinley Richards (1817–85), whose brief prefatory essay to the collection, based on his imperfect understanding of the ancient lineage of Welsh music, offered a manifesto for the future of Welsh music and the eisteddfod, which was being 'felt throughout the civilized world'. The success of Y Côr Mawr, he suggested, assured that the National Music Meetings would always be associated with Wales, and *The Songs of Wales* was 'the best proof of the musical genius of my country'.[27] By 1879 it had four editions and been expanded to seventy-one songs, with settings of Welsh airs with both English and Welsh words. Some were adapted from earlier collections such as those of Edward Jones (Bardd y Brenin; 1752–1824), and Maria Jane Williams's *Ancient National Airs of Gwent and Morganwg* (1844). It also carried modern popular Welsh songs, among them Richards's own setting of Ceiriog Hughes's sycophantic text 'God Bless the Prince of Wales' (1863). 'Mae Hen Wlad fy Nhadau', set as a solo with four-part chorus, was also included and placed as the final item in the collection, perhaps in imitation of the developing habit of its being rendered by standing audiences at the conclusion of just about any secular public gathering that provided a reason. Even by this time the song, which had been written for a much more modest purpose, was gaining favour as a national anthem. The *South Wales Daily News* reported its ritualistic singing at Cardiff's University College on St David's Day 1884, and Hywel Teifi Edwards has suggested that its status was effectively confirmed at the Albert Hall on 12 August 1887 when the Prince of Wales himself stood for its singing.[28]

In 1874 a different collection, but also carrying the title *The Songs of Wales*, was published by J. B. Cramer & Co. edited by John Thomas (Pencerdd Gwalia). With 172 items including solos and part-songs, it claimed to be 'A complete collection of the vocal melodies of the Principality'. The long introductory essay, written not by Thomas but by

---

[26] Jules Rivière, *My Musical Life and Recollections* (London: Sampson Low, Marston and Company, 1893), p. 169.
[27] Brinley Richards, ed., *The Songs of Wales* (London: Boosey & Co., Ltd, 1873), p. ii.
[28] Hywel Teifi Edwards, 'Victorian Wales Seeks Reinstatement', *Planet*, 52 (1985), 12–24.

the Englishman Charles H. Purday, also cited the ancient origins of Welsh music and stated that eisteddfodau were 'no longer allowed to slumber [as] the enthusiasm of the *Cymru* is not confined to the music of their own country: for their competency in choralism has been tested most successfully in the work of the masters … by their carrying off the prize at the Crystal Palace'. In a prefatory note Cramer claimed that his *Songs of Wales* contained 'a larger amount of the National Music of the Principality than any other work'.[29]

Also published in 1873 was *Gems of Welsh Melody*, a selection of songs and 'specimens of *penillion*' with accompaniments for harp or piano by John Owen (Owain Alaw, 1821–83).[30] This was a compilation of collections he had put out from 1860. Its content, the provision of a harp part and the frequency with which it was advertised in Welsh newspapers show that unlike the two London versions of *The Songs of Wales*, it was aimed primarily at the Welsh eisteddfod market.

Hyperbole and superlatives came easily to Victorian publishers, but these publications, and events such as the 'Welsh festivals', signalled an important adjustment in the production of Welsh music culture. Printed collections were published from the eighteenth century onwards, and even from that time the modal tonalities and other characteristics sustained by instinct in an oral culture were, of necessity, compromised by the grammar of musical notation. Such rationalisations are, of course, routine in such transitions and it does not mean that orality ceased: in Welsh-speaking rural areas, traditional song flourished, retained its character and form and was performed privately as well as publicly at local events such as the eisteddfodau and nosweithiau llawen (merry evenings).[31] The effect of the new popular collections was not neutral, however, because they were deliberately intended to facilitate performance among a new *popular* constituency of purchasers who were musically literate but had never heard these songs sung. They were put out by major publishers, and irrespective of the acknowledgements to the tradition from which they

---

[29] John Thomas, ed., with an introduction by Charles Purday, *The Songs of Wales: A Complete Collection of the Vocal Melodies of the Principality* (London: J. B. Cramer & Co., 1874), p. xvi. Digitised in Google Books, https://play.google.com/books/reader?id=N0iPIJ77sVoC.
[30] Digitised by the National Library of Wales, http://hdl.handle.net/10107/4796728.
[31] The noson lawen has been an important part of informal popular communal entertainment in rural areas of Wales. It typically includes impromptu storytelling, instrumental solos, dancing and singing. It has similarities with the Irish and Scottish *ceilidh*. In the age of broadcasting there have been long-running radio and television versions of noson lawen. According to the *Welsh Academy Encyclopedia of Wales*, the term 'noson lawen' was not attested until 1856, but the type of event it represents has a more ancient origin.

were drawn, their shape and format was contrived with an English amateur market in mind. For example, each was given a simple piano accompaniment; just a few items in Thomas's collection were also labelled nominally and alternatively for harp. Publishers were mindful of both the growing domestic piano market that had developed beyond the élite classes and the massification of the educational infrastructure that underpinned it, which included a formidable private sector.

The economic historian Cyril Ehrlich has drawn attention to what he called 'the flood' of musical production that occurred from the 1870s: a new level of music consumerism involving sales of instruments, sheet music, private teaching and the emergence of a generally sharper sense of calculation in the music business.[32] No reliable data is available concerning the ownership of pianos in Wales in this period, but the 1881 census provides an impression, albeit opaque, of information about the growth in private music tuition in the country. The *Report of the 1881 Census of Great Britain* noted a 38-per-cent growth of the music profession in England and Wales from 1871, and this was in addition to a 24-per-cent expansion in the previous decennial period. This accurately reflected the significant rise in the number of people making their living from music. The data is problematic because the categories of occupation used by enumerators were so ill-defined. For example, many who were professional performers described themselves as 'professors of music', a term adopted with equal liberty by, for example, piano and singing teachers. The 1881 census report shows that in 'Monmouthshire and Wales', 617 persons declared themselves to be a 'musician or music master'; a loose attention to gender hides the fact that almost a third of these were women. There were a further 836 in the category of 'teacher or professor' ('schoolmaster/teacher' was a yet-different category), of whom 625 were women. If these categories overlapped in practice, and there was a high and increasing proportion of women in the various branches of the music profession, it would be consistent with the pattern across Britain more generally, as would the assumption that most were teachers of the piano.[33]

Places of Leisure and Entertainment

In this period, chapels became edifices of musical pleasure as well as worship. A good indicator of the growth of congregational singing and

---

[32] Cyril Ehrlich, *The Music Profession in Britain since the Eighteenth Century: A Social History* (Oxford: Clarendon Press, 1985), chapter 5.
[33] *Census of England and Wales, 1881*, Vol. III (London: Printed by Eyre and Spottiswoode, 1883), passim.

the commensurate growth of choralism more generally in Wales is the sale and purchase of hymn books published in Wales. The most significant and extensive was the 1859 collection assembled by John Roberts (Ieuan Gwyllt), *Llyfr Tonau Cynulleidfaol (The Congregational Tune Book)*.[34] It contained 220 four-part settings of hymn tunes with a further set of 21 variants in an appendix. The first edition, in open staff and stave score, sold 17,000 copies in three years; the tonic sol-fa version, published in 1863, sold more than 25,000. It was used in the communal singing classes known as ysgolion cân (singing schools) and in the Unions of Congregational Singing which Ieuan Gwyllt and others pioneered from 1859. These evenings of congregational part-singing became a recreational activity, and because so much of the classical choral repertoire is devoted to settings of sacred texts (such as oratorios), derivatives were quickly assimilated into congregational singing repertoire. The first performance of a complete oratorio in Wales is claimed to have been conducted by Rosser Beynon in Monmouthshire around 1850.[35] This may be true, but confirmatory details are not evident in contemporary newspapers. However, in January 1859 the *North Wales Chronicle* reported a three-hour performance of Handel's *Messiah* (accompanied on a harmonium) at Bethesda before an audience of 2,000 and claimed it to be the first performance of the full work in Wales.[36] The review congratulated the choir on a performance that was rendered 'not only with ease, but to the satisfaction of the thinking part of the audience'. Local dignitaries provided the usual ritual of speeches, mentioning that music 'tended to exalt human nature' and that 'without [it] enjoyments of a degrading kind would be resorted to'. The latter remark may have been inspired by observation of new and worrying forms of musical diversion that were becoming increasingly available.

Small peripatetic entertainment groups performing in set-up theatres or on wagons, along with larger well-organised professional touring shows, such as Wombwell's Menagerie and Cooke's Circus, visited Wales for most

---

[34] Digitised by the National Library of Wales, http://hdl.handle.net/10107/4814268.
[35] T. J. Morgan, *Peasant Culture* (Swansea: University College Swansea, 1962). Morgan may have been referring to performances of *Ystorm Tiberias* (The Storm of Tiberias; 1852) by Edward Stephen (Tanymarian; 1822–85), with which the conductor Rosser Beynon was associated. It is believed to have been the first oratorio written by a Welsh person.
[36] *The North Wales Chronicle and Advertiser for the Principality*, 29 January 1859, 8. The announcement (review) of the event carried an editorial note: 'It is to be regretted that the publication of the announcements to these meetings partake so much of a party character'. Doubt must be cast on the audience's numbering 2,000. As it took place in January, the event must have been held indoors. The largest chapel in Bethesda at that time was Jerusalem with a capacity of just under 1,000; this performance took place in the smaller Bethesda chapel.

of the century. Itinerant musicians also provided an important source of popular musical entertainment,[37] but as the century progressed there was a marked increase in the provision of performance spaces for both local and visiting performers. Venues capable of hosting most forms of music were built in the larger towns; some as speculative commercial ventures, others at the behest of ambitious local authorities. They provided alternatives to the popular music practices of the eisteddfodau, the home, the tavern, the noson lawen and other events generated in places of worship. Some of the new intrusions were perceived as dangerously secular and evidence of creeping anglicisation, but they contributed critically to the infrastructure necessary for the development of popular music in Wales and increased access to repertoire from outside the country.

Some venues built in nineteenth-century Wales were labelled 'music halls' because they were intended primarily for that purpose, and later in the century multipurpose performance spaces, often called music halls, were a routine feature of the workmen's institutes founded across the country. But English 'music hall' as a genre had both a more exact meaning and a somewhat inconsistent reputation. This is why, in 1901, the commissioners of the Mostyn estate confirmed support for Llandudno's new Grand Theatre only on condition 'that under no circumstances was the building to be used for the presentation of Music Hall'.[38]

From the 1850s, music halls gained prominence because of their number, the cleverness of their programming, their commercial potential and the elaborate grandeur of their edifices. Late in the century many became syndicated. Such was the case in south Wales, where the English impresario Oswald Stoll simultaneously ran three Empire theatres, in Newport, Cardiff and Swansea.[39] This business model provided artists with more substantial and predictable contracts, and, combined with the rapidly extending railway networks, allowed audiences to hear performers and repertoires popular throughout Britain.

The English music-hall model was successfully replicated in parts of Wales, but not all Welsh music halls had the same artistic purpose or business model. Cardiff's Theatre Royal opened its doors in 1826, with

---

[37] Romani musicians were important in this regard. Some were itinerant musicians but there were excellent and influential instrumentalists, especially the harpists John Roberts (Telynor Cymru; 1816–94). See Chapter 7 of this book, and Eldra Jarman and A. O. H. Jarman, *The Welsh Gypsies: Children of Abram Wood* (Cardiff: University of Wales Press, 1991).

[38] www.arthurlloyd.co.uk/LlandudnoTheatres.htm (accessed 15 December 2020). The information contained in this site provides data for much of this section of the chapter.

[39] Stoll was one of the most successful entertainment magnates of the century. In 1898 he merged his business with that of Edward Moss to form Moss Empires.

a capacity of 1,000 at a time when the population of the town hovered around just 5,000. It was destroyed by fire in 1877 (a fate of many theatres before the provision of electric lighting). Yet earlier was Swansea's Theatre Royal, which opened in July 1807 with a grand concert. Like most theatres in the period, it was a venue for occasional events and may have stood empty for months at a time, but from the mid-century several had much fuller schedules.

A major centre of development in light music was on the north Wales coast. In the third quarter of the century, the seaside began to be understood as a resort for pleasure rather than a place of rest and recuperation and began to attract a new and much larger clientele. Railways made the north Wales coastal resorts accessible from the industrial districts of northwest England, and though Welsh seaside resorts were generally smaller than those in England, their numbers grew in greater proportion. In 1901 *Seaside Watering Places*, a well-established trade gazette, reported that 57 of the 249 listed coastal resorts in England and Wales were in Wales: thus, Wales, which accounted for just 5 per cent of the population of the two countries, had 24 per cent of the recognised coastal resorts.[40] As with the seaside industry elsewhere, resorts generated a need for entertainment and musicians to provide it.

Five theatres opened in Llandudno between 1863 and 1901. The St George's Hall (renamed Prince's Theatre in 1899) could accommodate 1,000. It opened as a concert hall, but gradually transformed to host a more diverse range of entertainments. The first purpose-built theatre in the town was the Grand Theatre. Its lease was held by Milton Boade, who ran theatres across the UK. It offered Restoration plays as well as popular musicals such as *The Geisha*. Llandudno, Rhyl and Colwyn Bay were to be the main centres for light-music entertainment in north Wales. The most influential musician was Jules Rivière. He had succeeded the great musical showman Louis Jullien as director of the Covent Garden Promenade Concerts in 1871 and imitated his predecessor's extravagant style. In 1887 he was appointed musical director of the Pavilion Theatre at Llandudno and in 1890 was lured to Colwyn Bay's Victoria Pier and Pavilion. His thirteen years in north Wales were influential; he was an expert in light music and had commercial flair. He knew the pragmatisms of the music business and demonstrated that the concept of the 'summer season' could work both artistically and in business terms. Also,

---

[40] Peter Borsay, 'Welsh Seaside Resorts: Historiography, Sources and Themes', *Welsh History Review*, 24/2 (2008), 92–119. See also Nigel Yates, *The Welsh Seaside Resorts: Growth, Decline and Survival*, Trivium Publications Occasional Papers 1 (Lampeter: University of Wales, Lampeter, 2006).

probably mindful of his 'Welsh festivals' at Covent Garden earlier in his career, he promoted Welsh popular music in his seaside schedules, including male choirs from south Wales, on the premise that for English audiences they provided an element of local exoticism.

The Wrexham Hippodrome was a public rather than a commercial hall, opened in 1909 by Sir Watkin Williams Wynn (1860–1944) to accommodate audiences of up to 1,200. The Coliseum Theatre, Aberystwyth (named in imitation of the London Coliseum, which had a reputation for elevated and rational entertainment), opened in 1891, was destroyed by fire in 1902, but was quickly rebuilt in grander style. The reopening concert in 1905 featured Mr and Mrs Tomas Tomas, Mr Bertie Ollerhead (violinist), Madam Juanita Jones and Miss Maggie Davies. The following Sunday there was a 'sacred concert' and the week after that, three consecutive nights were given over to 'John H. Morton's Popular Company of Talented Artistes', including Madam Constance Bellemy (late Prima Donna of Turner's Opera Company) and a Burlesque and Pantomime entitled 'The Rajah of Ranjapore'. Swansea's Grand Theatre was similarly aimed at refinement. Opened in an exaggerated ceremonial style in 1897 by Adelina Patti, it was a venue for respectable concerts and had a permanent musical director. On the other hand, the town's Palace Theatre (known as the Empire from 1892) had no such pretensions. It opened with a variety starring Ida René, a famous songstress of the day; Jerry Hart and Beatrice Leo, American burlesque artists; 'Chester', a vocal comedian; 'La Tosca', an expert mandolin soloist; someone called 'La Belle Maie' who performed a wire act; and a sketch by Jules and Ella Garrison called 'A Bit of Nonsense'.

The largest commercial music halls were in Cardiff, which had five for most of the second half of the century, and Newport, where at one point there were six. Cardiff's new Theatre Royal (later called the Prince of Wales) could accommodate 2,000, including a gallery of 800. It opened in 1878 with a production of W. S. Gilbert's *Pygmalion and Galatea*. The Philharmonic music hall, which opened in 1877, was an especially well-designed concert room. The Grand Theatre opened a decade later under the ownership of Harry Day, one of the leading London impresarios. Oswald Stoll's Empire Theatre opened in 1889, when the communal singing of 'God Bless the Prince of Wales' was followed by 'Dusoni's trained dogs and monkeys', an act called 'The Human Farmyard' and 'a Bicycle Troup', all accompanied by music.[41] The music hall as a species was

---

[41] For details of the development of music hall and music theatres in Wales see www.arthurlloyd.co.uk/AboutMusicHall.htm (accessed 4 December 2020).

a time-limited and more specifically Victorian and Edwardian phenomenon, but it was important to the music industry in Wales because of the links it provided to wider developments in professional popular music entertainment and the extent to which it stood in contrast to most other forms of popular music in Wales at that time.

Exports and Imports

Eisteddfodau and chapels continued to be key elements of the infrastructure of popular participatory music in Wales in the first half of the twentieth century. T. J. Morgan described the popular preoccupation with competitive eisteddfodau and its links with local church and chapel music culture as an 'epidemic and a contagion' – an epidemic because of its geographical scope, and a contagion because it was driven by a chain of local rivalries.[42] Choir trainers and conductors were celebrities defined by their success in contests. David Morgans, writing of 'Terrible Dan' Davies, the hot-tempered but talented south Wales choral conductor, paid him the highest compliment by calling him 'a dangerous competitor'.[43] Male voice choirs became popular from the 1870s, and the shared conventions of eisteddfodau meant that repertoires and performance styles became standardised to the point where an idiom was created that was sufficiently distinctive for it to be regarded internationally as characteristically 'Welsh'. The best male choirs attained celebrity, and some led peripatetic lives. The Welsh Eisteddfod arranged as part of the 1893 Chicago World's Fair saw victories for Clara Novello Davies's Welsh Ladies Choir and The Rhondda Gleemen under the Treherbert publican Tom Stephens, but for the latter group it was not their first visit. They had toured the United States in 1889–90, performing 140 concerts in 6 months.[44] Excursions from Wales to the United States continued in the twentieth century and there was no shortage of audiences. The flow was not entirely in one direction. Choirs from Scranton, Pennsylvania (where the largest contingent of US/Welsh immigrants were situated), travelled to Wales and Liverpool to compete at eisteddfodau in the early part of the century as did the Cleveland Orpheus Choir from Ohio.[45]

At least one group exploited the transatlantic link at a professional level. The Welsh Imperial Singers toured Britain, Canada and the United States

---

[42] Morgan, *A Peasant Culture*, p. 18. [43] Morgans, *Music and Musicians of Merthyr*, p. 155.
[44] Williams, *Valleys of Song*, p. 124.
[45] Gareth Williams, '"This Valley of Coal and Song": Musical Aspects of the Rhondda's Last National Eisteddfod, 1928'. *Morgannwg*, 65 (2021), 74–92.

almost continuously between 1926 and 1939. They were led by Festyn Davies, a Welsh-born, London-educated musician who had emigrated to the United States, established a modest reputation, then returned to form the choir, which was managed simultaneously from Trawsfynydd, Gwynedd and Chicago.[46] Even in the third decade of the new century its programmes were essentially Victorian, with arrangements of works by Arthur Sullivan, dramatic narrative pieces and a liberal sprinkling of sentimentally arranged Welsh folk songs. Its twenty-one members ('each member a noted soloist') appeared in a historically confusing garb of bright red tailcoats, while Festyn Davies was especially striking in black knee-breeches and a golden waist-length jacket. They may have been good, but their product was an anachronistic perpetuation of the Victorian 'land of song' idea that probably seemed weary to even a modestly enlightened observer. On the other hand, in an exaggerated way they captured one of the key continuities in Welsh popular music in the first half of the twentieth century.

This continuity was nurtured most systematically and authentically in cymanfaoedd canu and local eisteddfodau, where the link between music and the Welsh language was fundamental. The important English musician E. H. Fellowes, adjudicating at the 1930 Llanelli National Eisteddfod, was suitably impressed that he did so before an audience of 20,000.[47] The resolute popular loyalty to such agencies could be understood simply as inertia, but it was more than that. Statistically, the use of the Welsh language in Wales was declining.[48] It was also a time of increasing secularisation which found expression not just in falling church and chapel attendance, but in the influx of British and American popular-culture products in new and exciting media such as film, gramophone recordings and broadcasting. Welsh popular music culture had never been truly isolated. After all, Welsh traditional song had embraced tunes from sources as diverse as music hall, military bands and the works of Stephen Foster,[49] but the pace of events in the first half of the twentieth century presented new challenges. Many started to see

---

[46] Alun Trevor, *Cofio Cantorion: Eu Teithiau ym Mhrydain, Canada a'r Unol Daleithiau 1926–1939/The Welsh Imperial Singers: Their Tours of Britain, Canada and the United States 1926–1939* (Llanrwst: Gwasg Carreg Gwalch, 1991), p. 6.

[47] Edmund H. Fellowes, *Memoirs of an Amateur Musician* (London: Methuen & Co. Ltd, 1946), p. 196. Fellowes also mentioned that he felt resentment that an Englishman had been invited to adjudicate the event.

[48] Williams, *Digest*, Vol. 1, p. 86. The proportion of Welsh speakers in Wales (monoglot and bilingual) was 54.4 per cent in 1891, but by 1931 it had dropped to 36.8 per cent.

[49] Kinney, *Welsh Traditional Music*, p. 199.

the incursions as uncommonly swift and powerful, and an unwelcome disturbance to the lives they led and the language they regarded as integral to their being. It is no accident that the movement that led to the national eisteddfod becoming an exclusively Welsh-language event originated at this time. Similar popular phenomena occurred in other parts of the world, as cultures experienced the forced adjustments of modernism. The American historian Neil Harris observed that the music of John Philip Sousa, with its repertoire of patriotic marches and faultless precision of delivery, retained a following among sectors of US society long after the period when it had flourished. It would be easy to see this as little more than nostalgia – for music is good at stimulating that sentiment – but Harris suggested that the reason why loyalty to such agencies endured was that that they provided 'a culture of reassurance' in which musical rituals tempered the onslaught of change. The popular music that first found expression in Wales in the second half of the nineteenth century offered such reassurance, not just through its repertoires, but also in the communal performance practices with which people could personally engage.

It was in the lighter vein that Wales produced its first truly global superstar. Ivor Novello was born in Cardiff in 1893, the son of the exuberant and talented Clara Novello Davies (see Figure 13.2). To claim Ivor Novello as a Welsh talent is justified, but only in the literal sense. Much of his success was engineered by his ambitious and talented mother, but by the time he was ten he had been deposited in a public school in Oxford, and apart from a brief period accompanying his mother's choir in Cardiff in his late teenage years, there is little evidence of his presence in the country. His mother had a more direct influence on Welsh musical life than did her son, for she was one of the first Welsh musicians to make her reputation in the future Welsh capital. Her outlook was always international, but she was self-consciously Welsh, with a pride in her nonconformist lineage. She was an influential teacher and a conductor and (she claimed) the first musician to conduct a live broadcast by a choir.

Clara Novello Davies spent much of her early life in a middle-class neighbourhood near Cardiff's seaport. Within a few decades that neighbourhood had been transformed into the spectacularly cosmopolitan district known as Tiger Bay, one of the first large immigrant communities in Britain, believed to have been host to more than forty nationalities. A major study of black British jazz has concluded that by the 1930s the area had provided the largest group of British-born jazz musicians working

Figure 13.2 Clara Novello Davies with her ten-year-old son Ivor. Taken in 1903 by an unidentified photographer

in London from any place outside that city.[50] The most important influence came from the Deniz family: Frank (1912–2005), Joe (1913–94) and Laurie (1924–96), all children of Antoni Deniz, an African sailor. All three played guitar. Frank, who also became a seaman, met Louis Armstrong when he played at Cardiff's Empire Theatre in 1934. This seems to have

---

[50] See the Open University's Black British Jazz Project, led by Jason Toynbee https://fass.open.ac.uk/research/projects/blackbritishjazz, funded by the UK's Arts and Humanities Research Council; also see relevant entries in the *Oxford Dictionary of National Biography* for information on the Deniz family.

been the impetus for him to move to London with his future wife Clara Wason, a jazz pianist.[51] His brothers soon followed, as did several other Tiger Bay musicians. Oral histories suggest that the integration of the communities in Cardiff had not matured, and the district had the reputation of one to be avoided, but there is evidence that it ignited a change in the popular music of the country even if its manifestation was fully realised in London.

The most important new agency for Welsh popular music in the first half of the twentieth century was BBC radio, which before World War II was the sole broadcaster in Wales. The Cardiff station opened in 1923, with responsibility for Wales and the west of England. Welsh-language programmes were not broadcast until 1935, when a new north Wales transmitter and studio were opened in Bangor. Since that time, the BBC in Wales has broadcast in both languages. The musical offerings were a replication of the existing live music culture. For example, the most popular Welsh-language programme was *Noson Lawen*. *Welsh Rarebit*, the BBC's weekly variety music programme, was one of the most successful programmes of the time and it launched the careers of many performers who were to gain global fame. Its guiding light and producer from the early 1940s was (Gladys May) Mai Jones (1899–1960). She had been an outstanding student at Cardiff University and the Royal Academy of Music and had started her career playing in London dance bands. Her song 'We'll Keep a Welcome' (1949) is her most famous composition. It immediately gained a national status that was to endure, almost certainly because it captured the nostalgic sentiment known in Welsh as 'hiraeth' with which many were eager to associate, not least in its chorus: 'This land of song will still be singing, when you come home again to Wales'.

It was the popular musical life of Wales in the period of this chapter that endowed the country with its lasting reputation as a land of song, even though part of that idea comes from a heavily ornamented version of a not-fully-understood distant heritage. Irrespective of whether the reputation is justified, it is difficult to deny certain characteristics that emerged in the period. Perhaps the most important and lasting is the massification of musical practice that occurred across the entire country among communities that were often culturally mixed. The cyclic occurrences of eisteddfodau provided an informal but systemic structure that supported these practices, literally, on an annual basis. Music making was embedded into

---

[51] Laurence and Frank Deniz can be heard playing the soundtrack to the 1959 Carol Reed movie *Our Man in Havana*, for which they also wrote the score.

Welsh life to an extent that it became utterly normal. Less obvious, but just as important, was the multiplicity of styles that captured the affections of the people. The period started with the apparently contradictory idea that singing as an act of sacred devotion was also, implicitly, a popular leisure activity; it ended in the age of jazz, burlesque and the crooner, but the hymn singing never really abated.

CHAPTER 14

New Traditions
Welsh Popular Music into the Twenty-First Century
Sarah Hill

In Wales, as in every other country around the world, the term 'popular music' is somewhat loaded. A music 'of the people', a music 'liked by many people', a 'pop' product as distinct from an 'art' product; 'popular music' is defined according to distinct and culturally specific criteria, which are never unburdened of value judgements. In Wales, 'the people', y gwerin, are categorised yet further according to linguistic identity: Anglophone or Welsh-speaking. In a country the size of Wales, these delineations might seem excessive, but as I will show here, language is at the very heart of the development of Welsh popular music in the postwar years. In this chapter I will follow an indirect route through the history of popular music in Wales, following themes rather than marking eras, from the end of World War II into the twenty-first century. Although I will note the distinct cultural impulses that drove the development of popular musics in Welsh and in English, my intention here is simply to highlight the tensions and resolutions between the two languages. In this way it will become clear that the relationship between those languages is also a metaphor for the relationship between Wales and the rest of the United Kingdom: the political and linguistic peculiarities of Wales are reflected in her music.[1]

It is important first to summarise the cultural emergence of popular music more generally. The term 'popular music' in postwar Anglo-America might mean big-band swing, or close-harmony singing, or crooning; it might mean a light music flavoured with rhythms and instrumental textures from Latin America, the Caribbean or Africa; it might mean a novelty song or a movie theme tune; it might mean a familiar 'light classical' piece, lightly swung; it might mean stand-alone songs extracted

---

[1] For a more comprehensive survey of the history and meaning of popular music in Wales from the end of World War II to the start of the twenty-first century, see my *'Blerwytirhwng?' The Place of Welsh Pop Music* (Aldershot: Ashgate, 2007).

from famous Broadway musicals, or songs from Broadway musicals based on familiar 'light classical' pieces. Between the end of World War II and the 'dawn of rock 'n' roll', the term 'popular music' in North America and Great Britain embraced many different styles and genres, each one aimed at a different corner of the commercial market. But let it be noted here that the 'commercial market', with its 'mainstream audience', was primarily white, while the musical traditions that underpinned many of those commercial genres were African American in origin. When the blues – a long-standing African American form – reached the ears of the mainstream audience, it was sung by Bill Haley or by Elvis: the history of Anglo-American popular music is therefore also a history of musical appropriation. I mention this here because the history of Welsh popular music is itself a history of adaptation and assimilation. The linguistic and racial demographics of the country, from the end of World War II through to the twenty-first century, shaped the development of popular music in Wales and the role of Welsh popular music in the wider world.

To find a root of 'popular music' in Wales is to look not to the North American model, but to the model of Anglophone 'light entertainment' in Britain, and to the particularly Welsh tradition of the noson lawen (merry evening). Although these two models were not unrelated, they represent distinct musical and cultural formations. A key Welsh figure in Anglophone light entertainment in the 1940s and 1950s was Dorothy Squires (1915–98), whose career maps onto those of many other popular female singers of the time: personal and professional relationship with a popular bandleader, hit recordings, international fame, then sharp decline. In the Welsh-language side of the equation, a nascent 'popular' culture was developing at the same time in village halls and chapel vestries; and at University College of North Wales, Bangor in the 1940s, three students – Robin Williams, Cledwyn Jones and Meredydd Evans – began performing as Triawd y Coleg (the College Trio). Appearing on radio programmes throughout the 1940s singing arrangements of traditional tunes and other original 'light' songs, Triawd y Coleg were perhaps the first Welsh-language 'pop group'. The pop groups that followed in the subsequent twenty years largely adhered to that model: close-harmony arrangements of traditional or comic songs, often presented as part of a programme of skits and comic routines. In the 1950s these groups – generally all-male – adopted signifiers of 'skiffle', thus showing an alignment with broader popular British musical taste; across the next half-century, in the form of Hogia Llandegai and Hogia'r

Wyddfa, this was the enduring mainstream 'light entertainment' in Wales.[2]

In Anglophone Britain, skiffle was overtaken in popularity by the Merseybeat sounds of the Beatles and the pop boom that ensued; but in Welsh-speaking Wales, 'beat' music was late in arriving and quick to depart. The Aberystwyth-based five-piece Y Blew (Hair) made a brief splash at the Bala Eisteddfod in 1967, and released one single, 'Maes B' ('B Field'),[3] but they were alone in attempting to replicate something like contemporary pop sounds – music to dance to – in Welsh. As I will explain, the development of popular music in Welsh was aligned with the language movement, and the gradual establishment of a music industry in Wales reflected the fact that the pop community – performers, producers, audiences – could only grow organically from a fraction of the population of a very small country. Fleeting though it was, Y Blew's performance at the Bala Eisteddfod was a signal event in the growth of the Welsh pop community, the first 'electric' pop performance in Welsh and the first indication of 'pop' music's (grudging) acceptance into mainstream Welsh culture. The next time an electric rock band emerged from this pop community, it was in the context of a large-scale concert to benefit the activities of the Welsh-language movement.

One of the more important details about this brief history is the relationship between the development of popular music in Wales and the emergence of Welsh-language media. In Triawd y Coleg's appearance in the film *Noson Lawen* (dir. Marc Lloyd, 1949), they established an unbreakable connection between traditional Welsh musical culture and the notion of 'the popular'. Furthermore, the popularity of Meredydd Evans and Triawd y Coleg as radio performers, and the critical mass of close-harmony groups that performed at village halls around the country across the second half of the twentieth century, established the centrality of Welsh-language media to the development of what we now hear as 'popular music', and a definition of what 'popular' meant in Welsh culture.

Language

In order to understand the relationship of postwar 'light entertainment' to contemporary 'pop', we must turn to the issue of language politics in the

---

[2] The northern light-entertainment Hogia ('boys') had southern equivalents in the many bands known as 'Bois' (Bois y Blacbord, Bois y Frenni): a subtle and playful linguistic distinction in an otherwise common musical style.

[3] At the time, Maes B was the 'alternative' youth field at the National Eisteddfod. It has become Wales's largest Welsh-language rock and pop festival.

1960s. Although primarily an issue affecting the Welsh-speaking population of Wales, it is fundamental to both the development of Welsh popular music and the establishment of Welsh-language media.

The Welsh language went through a period of steep and sharp decline in the twentieth century. From 1931 to 1961, the percentage of Welsh people able to speak Welsh fell from 36.8 per cent of the population to 26 per cent; in the same period, the percentage of monoglot Welsh speakers fell from 4 to 1 per cent.[4] In the 1971 census the number of Welsh speakers had fallen again, to just over 20 per cent.[5] This crisis was the subject of a radio lecture delivered in February 1962 by Saunders Lewis, *Tynged yr Iaith* (The Fate of the Language), which sparked an extended period of activism around the survival of the Welsh language and its official acceptance in all areas of public life. The foundation of Cymdeithas yr Iaith Gymraeg (The Welsh Language Society) in 1963 was one of the most important actions in the development of Welsh-language popular music: not only was the membership and management of the Cymdeithas largely composed of young people but the Cymdeithas was an early and constant promoter of Welsh-language popular music.

The 'official' institutions of Welsh-language culture – the National Eisteddfod, the Urdd Eisteddfod, the chapel – were slow to encourage and support the development of Welsh popular music beyond its initial acoustic iterations. The appearance of Y Blew at the Pabell Lên (Literature Tent) at the Bala Eisteddfod in 1967 was an unexpected blip; prior to that moment, even skiffle was seen as disruptive of the natural cultural order. With the clear and obvious relationship strengthening between young Welsh speakers and Cymdeithas yr Iaith, and the enthusiasm with which Cymdeithas yr Iaith promoted Welsh pop, it was inevitable that the 'new tradition' of electric music would eventually find a stage on the eisteddfod maes (eisteddfod field).[6]

---

[4] See Emrys Jones and Ieuan L. Griffiths, 'A Linguistic Map of Wales: 1961', *The Geographical Journal*, 129/2 (June 1963), 192–196, and Janet Davies, *The Welsh Language* (Cardiff: University of Wales Press, 1993).

[5] See E. G. Bowen and H. Carter, 'Preliminary Observations on the Distribution of the Welsh Language at the 1971 Census', *The Geographical Journal*, 140/3 (October 1974), 432–440.

[6] It should be stressed that electric music was by no means a 'new tradition' anywhere else in the world. Edward H. Dafis 'plugged in' nearly twenty years *after* Elvis Presley had appeared on the *Ed Sullivan Show* in the United States. By the end of the 1960s, 'electric' popular music had grown and morphed in every single direction, from psychedelia to hard rock. The idea that the pastiche 1950s rock 'n' roll of Edward H. Dafis should have been heard as revolutionary in 1973 speaks to a number of fundamental facts about popular music in the Welsh language: it developed according to its own pace, not the pace that was set by Anglo-American precedents; the audience for Welsh pop did not discriminate against bands that might have sounded atavistic to Anglophone ears; and the

14 Welsh Popular Music into the Twenty-First Century 319

Before popular music was officially sanctioned by the mainstream institutions of Welsh culture, Welsh-language popular culture was a mainstay of Welsh broadcast media. The fact that a radio lecture sparked an increasingly urgent period of language activism is important in itself. Between the 1920s and the date of Saunders Lewis's lecture, there was a gradual increase in the number of radio broadcast hours in Welsh, from roughly 1.5 hours weekly in the 1930s to slightly more by the end of the 1950s; but there was no dedicated Welsh-language channel until the foundation of Radio Cymru in 1977. The foundation of Welsh-language media strengthened the status of the language in Wales and provided a national platform for the expression of political sentiment, via the musical forms that we hear as contemporary 'popular music'. That national platform was a unifying force for the Welsh communities scattered around the country, and for young people in the audience: it was a significant means of representation. Welsh could be the language of youth; Welsh music could speak to contemporary taste; listening to music could be a political act.

Popular Music and the Media

The British pop audience was not well served by the BBC in the 1960s. Although the 'British Invasion', with the Beatles leading the charge, had changed the landscape of Anglophone popular music and prompted the formation of local 'beat' music scenes around the world, in Britain, those new pop sounds were primarily heard on the pirate radio stations anchored offshore, not on the BBC.[7] Radio 1 was established in 1967 as a dedicated 'pop' station, and with it began the career of DJ John Peel, who became a key figure in the promotion of Welsh-language popular music in the ensuing decades. But over in Wales, the key Welsh 'pop' moments were televised.

While still a student at the University of Wales, Cardiff, Dafydd Iwan (b. 1943) was invited onto the Television Wales and the West programme *Y Dydd* (The Day) to sing original songs about current topics. Given that Dafydd Iwan was an outspoken activist for Cymdeithas yr Iaith, this was an unusually progressive programming decision. The songs that Dafydd Iwan performed on *Y Dydd* were generally based on familiar pre-existing tunes – Welsh folk songs, or American tunes made popular by Pete Seeger or Burl

---

combination of youthful optimism and political protest was more important than a more direct stylistic alignment with whatever was popular in the larger Anglo-American culture.

[7] For an analysis of the impact of 'needle time' restrictions to the development of the youth market during this period, see Richard Witts, 'Needle Time: The BBC, the Musicians' Union, Popular Music, and the Reform of Radio in the 1960s', *Popular Music History*, 7/3 (2012), 241–262.

Ives – and reflected a burgeoning sense of Welsh political momentum.[8] In songs such as 'Mae'n Wlad i Mi' ('This Land Is Mine'), 'Bryniau Bro Afallon' ('The Hills of Avalon Vale'), 'Carlo' and 'Croeso '69' ('Welcome '69'), through satire and folk memory, Dafydd Iwan was able to beseech his audience to imagine a future for the Welsh language, and to skewer the British establishment while doing so. This balance of humour and politics was familiar to the Anglo-American audience most notably in the music of Bob Dylan; while Dafydd Iwan was stylistically quite distinct, he nonetheless pushed Welsh popular music into a contemporary musical frame by speaking to the world around him, by serving as the mouthpiece for increasingly urgent language activism and ultimately by founding Sain, the first successful record label for Welsh-language music.

From *Y Dydd* onwards, Welsh-language popular music and the media had a symbiotic, if not always harmonious, relationship. The flowering of musical styles through the 1970s and the ensuing growth of the Welsh pop industry was met with increasingly popular and influential pop programming. By the 1980s, the development of Welsh pop was fairly well aligned with popular taste in the broader Anglo-American market, particularly with the advent of music video and the youth-oriented show *Fideo 9* (1988–92) on S4C, the Welsh-language television channel. It is important to note here that the programme's producer, Geraint Jarman (b. 1950), was himself a significant figure in Welsh-language popular music, having begun his career in the late-1960s as a member of the satirical trio Y Bara Menyn (Bread and Butter) alongside Heather Jones and Meic Stevens, themselves established musicians (and in Stevens's case, notably also established in Anglophone Britain). As a solo artist in the 1970s and 1980s, Geraint Jarman and his band, Y Cynganeddwyr,[9] brought the sound of reggae to Welsh pop, and advanced the idea that a Welsh pop band could be inclusive of non-Welsh-speakers and represent the urban environment of the capital city. Jarman's influence on the younger generation of Welsh artists was undeniable, not only because of his 'freeing-up' of Welsh pop and the political sentiments in his music, but because of his work promoting and encouraging new musical expression via *Fideo 9* and other platforms.[10]

---

[8] This is covered in further depth in E. Wyn James, 'Painting the World Green: Dafydd Iwan and the Welsh Protest Ballad', *Folk Music Journal*, 8/5 (2005), 594–618 and Hill, *'Blerwytirhwng?'*

[9] Broadly, 'cynganneddwyr' translates as 'poets', but specifically it means practitioners of the alliterative, strict-metre form cynghanedd, which has no equivalent outside Welsh poetry.

[10] I discuss Geraint Jarman's work at great length in *'Blerwytirhwng?'* He has remained active as a musician, headlining the Pavilion Gig in the Wales Millennium Centre at the 2018 National Eisteddfod in Cardiff (and being admitted to the Gorsedd), and continuing to record and perform into his seventies.

14 Welsh Popular Music into the Twenty-First Century

The disruptive force during this period was driven by the younger generation of Welsh musicians and music fans, who felt that Welsh popular music had been stagnating on the Sain label. The generational and cultural shift that saw the explosion of punk in Anglo-America was matched in Wales by a new crop of bands with different cultural needs and a renewed sense of political urgency. Along with the new anti-establishment ethos came 'independent' labels aimed at the new youth market; and with the punk/post-punk 'DIY' aesthetic came a belief in the potential for this new Welsh pop to reach a wider audience outside of Wales, in Anglo-America. The tensions that this created between the 'old guard' – the language activist-musicians from the 1960s and early 1970s, many of whom were now involved in programming and planning for the nascent Welsh media – and the younger generation were linguistic as well as musical.

Underlying this tension was the fear that a flirtation with Anglo-America would necessitate a shift to the English language, and that a shift to the English language would lead younger Welsh speakers away from the Welsh pop community and into the arms of the Anglophone beast. This is to assume, wrongly, that young Welsh people in the 1970s and 1980s were not already listening to Anglophone popular music. While it is true that tensions around linguistic 'crossovers' were a constant presence well into the twenty-first century, it is also true that an awareness of the larger musical culture is what injected Welsh popular music with a new life, and an increasing – and increasingly natural – presence in mainstream British media. Spearheading this motion outwards was Rhys Mwyn, member of the band Anhrefn (Chaos) and head of the eponymous independent record label, who adopted a guerrilla-marketing approach to his recordings: delivering demo tapes of young Welsh-language bands in person to record labels and media executives in England. In so doing, Recordiau Anhrefn met the interest of the influential John Peel, who gave them more airtime on Radio 1 than they received from Radio Cymru and Radio Wales put together. Why should a Welsh-language band, however talented, restrict itself solely to a Welsh-language audience, when it was possible to sing in Welsh on a worldwide stage?

Crossovers

The idea of 'crossover' success in the Anglo-American market was not restricted to Welsh speakers. Because London was the centre of the British music industry, and because there were few studio facilities or large venues in Wales to establish or sustain an international career, an attempt at 'making it' necessitated 'breaking in' through one of the main English channels: the stage, the television or the movies. It was through those channels that some of Wales's biggest stars found their fame.

As I have already noted, Dorothy Squires enjoyed an international career as a singer of popular songs in the postwar era, thus establishing a precedent for Welsh women to succeed in mainstream light entertainment. Into this culture came Shirley Bassey (b. 1937). The daughter of a Nigerian father and English mother, Bassey represented a distinct kind of Welshness: Anglophone, mixed-race and from the Cardiff docks. With her uncompromising presence and uniquely powerful alto voice, in 1958 Bassey was the first Welsh singer to reach the top of the British pop charts. She had begun singing in clubs while still a teenager, moving to London in 1955 to sing in the West End, where she discovered her métier: the big show tunes, the songs from popular Hollywood movies, anything that would allow her voice to soar over big-band or orchestral accompaniment. Her recording of the theme song to the James Bond movie, *Goldfinger* (1964) is a perfect example: melodramatic, exacting, fearless. Her hits ran through each subsequent decade – 'Big Spender' (1966); 'Something' (1970), which remained in the album charts for five months; 'The Rhythm Divine' (1987), recorded with Swiss synth-pop band Yello; 'History Repeating' (1997), recorded with English duo Propellerheads – and her appearances at events showcasing Cardiff and celebrating Welsh devolution were reminders of the force that she has held over popular culture for more than sixty years.

At the same time that Shirley Bassey was breaking through to international fame, Tom Jones (b. 1940) was charting a similar course, from Pontypridd to London and beyond. Unlike that of Shirley Bassey, Tom Jones's musical style was influenced by early American rhythm and blues and early-1960s British beat music. His first single, 'It's Not Unusual' (1965) was a top-ten hit in the UK and the United States, and over the next three years he had a string of hits on both sides of the Atlantic, including 'What's New Pussycat' (1965); the theme song to the James Bond film *Thunderball* (1965); 'Green, Green Grass of Home' (1966); and 'Delilah' (1968). From 1969 to 1971 Tom Jones hosted his own television show in the United States, *This Is Tom Jones*, and he was a regular performer at Las Vegas for over forty years. Like Shirley Bassey, Tom Jones had an extraordinarily powerful voice matched with an ease of delivery that enabled him to cultivate a career spanning six decades. And like Shirley Bassey, Tom Jones has been a regular presence on the pop charts in collaborations with younger acts: his cover version of Prince's 'Kiss', recorded with the Art of Noise, was a top-ten hit in 1988; his album of duets, *Reload* (1999) reached the top of the charts during the 'Cool Cymru' era, discussed below. Now in his ninth decade, he is still a forceful presence in popular culture, notably as a judge on the televised talent show, *The Voice*.

Shirley Bassey and Tom Jones represent a very particular British musical tradition wherein 'light entertainment' combines with contemporary 'pop' sounds, cultivated through hard work and sheer raw talent. They are 'crossover' artists, in that they were truly the first singers to represent Wales – Anglophone, urban Wales – in the international market. Their ubiquity in the 1960s pop charts would be notable regardless of their origins, but their popularity also enabled Welsh-speaking artists to break through to the British market – to cross over from the Welsh market to the Anglophone market. The first such crossover was Mary Hopkin (b. 1950), who began her career in Pontardawe, singing in folk groups and as a solo artist for the Cambrian label. In 1968 she recorded a Welsh translation of the Pete Seeger song, 'Turn, Turn, Turn' ('Tro, Tro, Tro'), which brought her to the attention of the producers of the ITV talent show, *Opportunity Knocks*. She appeared on the show for ten weeks, and ultimately won the contest; but perhaps the bigger prize was being offered a recording contract with the Beatles' new label, Apple Records. With Paul McCartney producing, Hopkin's first single, 'Those Were the Days' (1968), reached the top of the charts across Anglo-America and Europe.[11] The subsequent album, *Post Card* (1969), featured songs in a range of styles and genres, and despite its musical incoherence was a top-five hit on the British charts. Her chart success led to her participation in the 1970 Eurovision Song Contest, representing Britain with the song 'Knock, Knock, Who's There?' For the next year, Hopkin struggled with her fame, and after the release of her second album, *Earth Song/Ocean Song* (Apple, 1971), she abandoned her solo career to focus on raising a family. Mary Hopkin's voice and performance style could not have been more different to those of her contemporaries, Shirley Bassey and Tom Jones; but like Bassey and Jones, Mary Hopkin lent her voice to other artists' recordings – David Bowie's *Low* (RCA, 1977), Thin Lizzy's *Bad Reputation* (Vertigo, 1977), The Crocketts' *The Great Brain Robbery* (Blue Dog, 2000) and others.

By surveying these three popular careers, I do not mean to suggest that every Welsh musician who 'crossed over' into Anglo-America sought, or

---

[11] Mary Hopkin's career, from Welsh folk singer to international Anglophone star, is the subject of my article, 'Beyond Borders: The Female Welsh Pop Voice', *Radical Musicology*, 1 (2006), 35 paragraphs, www.radical-musicology.org.uk/2006/Hill.htm (accessed 5 July 2021).

desired, mainstream recognition. In fact, the Welsh musician who has exerted perhaps the most enduring influence over the development of popular music in Anglo-America began his career in the experimental music circles of the east coast of the United States. John Cale (b. 1942) was trained as a pianist and violist, and under the guidance of American composer Aaron Copland, left Britain for the Tanglewood Music Centre in western Massachusetts. Moving soon thereafter to New York, Cale took part in signal events of the avant-garde, contributing to the first performance of Erik Satie's *Vexations* (1963) and joining La Monte Young's Theatre of Eternal Music. In 1964 he began playing music with singer-guitarist Lou Reed, ultimately formalising their band under the name the Velvet Underground. Cale's time with the band was fairly short – they recorded just two albums together – but in that brief period, thanks in part to the band's relationship with then-manager Andy Warhol, the Velvet Underground created an aura of untouchable depth that remains a catalyst for rock music worldwide.[12] Cale then entered into a long and successful career as solo performer, composer and collaborator, and produced many of the canonic albums of the pre-punk era: *The Stooges* (1969), *The Modern Lovers* (1973) and Patti Smith's *Horses* (1975).[13] In a fascinating 'return to roots', or reverse crossover, John Cale collaborated with many of the most popular Welsh and Anglo-Welsh bands of the 'Cool Cymru' era for the film *Beautiful Mistake/Camgymeriad Gwych* (2000). And it was that idea of 'Cool Cymru' that brought the problematic notion of 'Welshness' and Welsh crossovers to the mainstream Anglo-American audience.

'Cool Cymru'

Although my focus to this point has largely been the development of Welsh-language popular music, that descriptor 'Welsh-language' always suggests the presence of another, more culturally powerful, cultural tradition. Anglophone popular music in Wales developed alongside, and in relation to, popular musical styles in Britain and north America. But as I noted above, the centre of the British music industry was London; until the latter part of the twentieth century there were few professional music

---

[12] There is an aphorism, often ascribed to musician and producer Brian Eno, that the Velvet Underground never sold many records, but that everyone who bought one went out and started a band. Apocryphal though it is, it does underline the fact that the most *influential* musician is often not the most *popular*.

[13] For more detail on his extraordinary career see John Cale and Victor Bockris, *What's Welsh for Zen? The Autobiography of John Cale* (London: Bloomsbury, 1999), and Dai Griffiths, '"Home Is Living Like a Man on the Run": John Cale's Welsh Atlantic', *Welsh Music History/Hanes Cerddoriaeth Cymru*, 4 (2000), 159–185.

studios in Wales, and although there were many small venues dotted around the country to promote live performances, the consumer market necessary to sustain a livelihood performing popular music was located in the rest of Britain and further beyond.[14]

Many of the more popular Anglophone Welsh musicians of the 1960s and 1970s maintained proud links with Wales – Spencer Davis, Deke Leonard, Andy Fairweather Low, Dave Edmunds – even as their careers were built elsewhere.[15] The marker 'Welsh' was not always positive, however: because of the institutionalised London-centricity of the music industry, 'provincial' music scenes such as that in Wales were not uniformly celebrated or supported in the mainstream media. As the younger generation of Welsh-speaking musicians sought ways to build their careers on the other side of the Welsh border, 'crossing over' to the English language was perceived as the obvious option. As I noted above, through the marketing strategy of Rhys Mwyn and Anhrefn Records, Radio 1 DJ John Peel introduced his night-time audience to the existence of 'underground' Welsh-language music. With the precedent therefore established, the next wave of young musicians in Wales could attempt the same, if not a greater, level of attention in the British media. It was with this new-found sense of cultural self-confidence that Welsh popular music entered a phase of unprecedented experimentation and, ultimately, international acclaim.

It is difficult to justify the use of the terms 'establishment' and 'underground' in a musical culture as small as Wales, but it is the simplest way to delineate musical styles and cultural growth in the 1980s and 1990s. Key to this distinction is the band Datblygu (Developing), which formed in Cardigan in 1982 (Figure 14.1). With a barbed wit and an uncompromising delivery, lyricist and singer David R. Edwards gave voice to the disillusioned and marginalised youth of Margaret Thatcher's Britain, in a musical style more aligned with contemporary English post-punk and synth-pop than anything previously heard in the history of Welsh-language pop. Their antiestablishment rhetoric – not unlike much contemporary Anglo-American popular music, but unprecedented in Welsh terms – was not embraced by Radio Cymru, though they were fixtures on S4C's influential video

---

[14] See Craig Owen Jones, 'Mapping Live Provisions in Welsh-Language Rock, 1978–80', *Popular Music History*, 7/1 (2012), 53–81.

[15] Deke Leonard, of Anglo-Welsh band Man (initial lifespan 1968–76), wrote a series of autobiographical books charting his life in rock music, which provide great and colourful detail about Welsh culture in the 1960s and 1970s, and the place of Man in Anglo-American popular music more broadly. See in particular *Rhinos, Winos & Lunatics* (Bordon: Northdown Publishing, 1996) and *Maybe I Should've Stayed in Bed? The Flip Side of the Rock 'n' Roll Dream* (Bordon: Northdown Publishing, 2000).

Figure 14.1 Datblygu performing at the Pesda Roc music festival in Bethesda, north Wales (1985). A young Gruff Rhys (later of the Super Furry Animals) is seated in the front row. The decidedly sparse audience is photographic proof of the disconnect between 'popular' and 'influential': fifteen years later, Super Furry Animals' version of the Datblygu song 'Y Teimlad' was included on their critically acclaimed album *Mwng* (2001). Unknown photographer. Creative Commons Licence CCBY 2.0
https://creativecommons.org/licenses/by/2.0/legalcode

programme *Fideo 9*, and further afield, on John Peel's programme. In this sense, the Welsh pop 'establishment' was Radio Cymru and the Sain (Sound) record label, and 'underground' was everything that arose in its wake, most notably the Ankst record label, established in Aberystwyth in 1988.

The smaller Welsh labels that emerged in the 1980s – Fflach (Flash), Anhrefn, Ankst – catered to the broad musical interests and tastes that developed out of the post-punk moment.[16] The first run of recordings released on the Ankst label stretched beyond the safe 'pop' sounds of Sain, embracing everything from the direct social commentary of Datblygu, to the experimental electronic proto-hip-hop of Llwybr Llaethog (Milky

---

[16] Recordiau Fflach deserves more than a footnote. Founded by brothers Richard and Wyn Jones of the new-wave band Ail Symudiad (Second Movement), Fflach grew organically out of their home base in Cardigan into a full-time operation, offering professional studio and production facilities for everything from traditional Welsh folk to new Welsh rock musics. Their contributions to the 'crossover' dialogue are covered in greater depth in Hill, *'Blerwytirhwng?'*

Way), to the nascent club music of Tŷ Gwydr (Glasshouse). These recordings connected Welsh pop to the contemporary sounds of popular music in Anglo-America and around the world, and this expressive freedom resulted in an explosion of creativity that soon captured the attention of the music industry outside of Wales.

It is important to contextualise the early recordings on the Ankst label with the larger underground Anglophone music scene in Wales. As I have already suggested, an 'urban' Welsh identity was some degree removed from the Welshness expressed in the early folk-rock songs of musicians such as Dafydd Iwan.[17] Anglophone Wales was well represented in the 1980s US and UK charts by Bonnie Tyler and The Alarm,[18] but it was not until the 1990s that the underground scenes of Wales moved into the spotlight. Critical interest in Welsh popular music was directly related to the history of 'scenes' in England and the United States. For example, the emergence of 'grunge' in the Seattle area in the early 1990s, and the enormous success of local band Nirvana, was a paradigm shift in mainstream US and UK charts. Hoping to capitalise on the popularity of underground music and discover 'the next Seattle', US journalists turned their focus to the south Wales town of Newport, and a dingy little club there called TJ's.

Less than thirty miles outside Newport is Rockfield Studios. Opened in 1965 as the first such residential facility, Rockfield hosted some of the biggest bands of the rock era,[19] and generated a buzz among young English bands, particularly following an extended residency there by 'Madchester' band the Stone Roses. The Welsh borderland was therefore at the epicentre of the British pop renaissance of the early 1990s, and the surrounding area

---

[17] The traditional strongholds of the Welsh language were located in the west and north of the country; the larger urban centres of Wales are in the south and south-east. While much of Dafydd Iwan's rhetoric in those early songs concerned the preservation of the Welsh language and reflected the pressure campaigns of Cymdeithas yr Iaith, there was a splintering-off of Welsh-language activism in the 1970s, headed by Adfer, which promoted a 'return' to those Welsh-language heartlands in order to develop business and industry there, and to encourage Welsh speakers not to seek work outside of Wales. This explains, in part, Dafydd Iwan's decision at the same time to move the Sain studios to Llandwrog, outside of Caernarfon, and the attendant association of much early Welsh pop with a rural Welsh identity, both social and musical.

[18] Bonnie Tyler's biggest international hits were 'It's a Heartache' (1978), the evergreen 'Total Eclipse of the Heart' (1982) and 'Holding Out for a Hero' (1984). The Alarm were formed in Rhyl in 1981 and broke into the international market at a time when the popular sound of 'Celtic rock' was represented by U2 (Ireland) and Big Country (Scotland). Although The Alarm did not have the same longevity or success as U2, some of their singles – '68 Guns' (1983) and 'Sold Me Down the River' (1989) most notably – broke into both the US and UK charts.

[19] Albums recorded at Rockfield include Black Sabbath's *Paranoid* (1970), Queen's *Night at the Opera* (1975), Adam and the Ants' *Kings of the Wild Frontier* (1980) and the Stone Roses' eponymous debut (1989).

a matter of interest for music journalists. The local bands that played at TJ's around this time – 60 Ft. Dolls and Dub War, most notably – therefore became part of a larger musical network that included international acts like Sonic Youth, but also the collection of bands that were ultimately categorised together under the labels 'Britpop' and 'Cool Cymru'. It is worth noting that none of these bands were associated with 'grunge', but rather signified the next 'big thing'.[20] More importantly, English bands associated with 'Britpop' and Welsh bands associated with 'Cool Cymru' denied the existence of any kinship between them, other than through accidents of geography, temporality and language.

In many ways Britpop was a reaction against grunge, and represented a return to a 'traditional', specifically English, style of melodic songwriting popularised by the bands of the initial 1960s British Invasion. As a marketing slogan, 'Cool Cymru' is a bit more difficult to define, because it embraces bands from both the Anglophone and Welsh-language traditions.[21] The Anglophone Welsh bands Manic Street Preachers and Stereophonics had been actively performing around south Wales long before 'Cool Cymru' entered the public consciousness;[22] in the case of the other bands often included in this category, Catatonia and Super Furry Animals were formed from the remains of various popular Welsh-language bands, and Gorky's Zygotic Mynci had already earned mainstream notice for their experimental, bilingual, postmodern confections. 'Cool Cymru' was simply a means of recognising that 'popular music' in Wales could mean more than the predictable stereotypes of male voice choirs and the 'light entertainment' of Shirley Bassey and Tom Jones, and of containing Welsh pop in one vague marketing category.

This returns us to the idea of an 'underground' Welsh-language music scene and the notion of linguistic 'crossovers'. As I have already noted, Radio 1 DJ John Peel had developed an interest in Welsh-language bands such as Datblygu, and regularly attended gigs at TJ's and at clubs further west. The Welsh bands that emerged during that time had a sense of self-confidence that sparked a resurgence of cultural production in the 1990s.

---

[20] It is usually the case that a genre such as grunge loses its cultural power when it moves from the underground to the mainstream. TJ's may have attracted musicians that fell within that genre – it was famously the place where Nirvana frontman Kurt Cobain proposed to Courtney Love – but it did not restrict its programming to a single genre or musical community.

[21] This is an issue that Rebecca Edwards pursues at length in her unpublished PhD dissertation, '"To Show from Where I Came": Cool Cymru, Pop and National Identity in Wales During the 1990s' (Swansea University, 2008).

[22] Blackwood-based Manic Street Preachers formed in 1986, and released their debut album, *Generation Terrorists*, in 1992; Cwmaman-based Stereophonics were formed in 1992, and released their debut album, *Word Gets Around*, in 1997.

Working against the long-held belief that a turn to the English language would threaten the survival of Welsh-language youth culture, young Welsh musicians sought to establish their careers in the wider market by recording in both Welsh and English, or by turning entirely to English. Two of the more popular Ankst bands of the time, Y Cyrff (The Bodies) and Ffa Coffi Pawb (Everyone's Coffee Beans, or, homophonically, Fuck Off Everybody), are testament to this: the membership of those bands eventually reconfigured into Catatonia and Super Furry Animals, with a view towards making a living in the music industry. Because both Catatonia and Super Furry Animals, and eventually Gorky's Zygotic Mynci, were signed to major (international) labels, they turned to recording in English, thus reaching the ears of audiences in America and further afield. But this engendered a deep conflict between the young, internationally successful bands and the Welsh-language 'establishment'. Nowhere was this more pronounced than at the field of the National Eisteddfod at the height of the 'Cool Cymru' era.

Because the National Eisteddfod had a strict Welsh-only language policy, Super Furry Animals and Gorky's Zygotic Mynci were prohibited from singing their English-language material for their home audience. It seems extraordinary in retrospect that the unprecedented international success of these young Welsh bands was not celebrated at the country's foremost cultural institution.[23] The irony of this intergenerational conflict is that it occurred in an era of youthful optimism: the Labour Party, under Tony Blair, was elected at the 1997 general election, with a promise to hold referenda on Welsh and Scottish devolution. Tony Blair enjoyed unusual access to, and fellowship with, Britpop bands such as Oasis; in Wales, the 'Cool Cymru' bands, Anglophone, Welsh-language and bilingual, supported the 'Yes' campaign which ensured, by the smallest of margins, a new Wales for the twenty-first century.

Pop and Post-devolution Wales

As Wales ended the millennium with new, relative political strength, 'Cool Cymru' became the descriptor for more than just home-grown pop music. The first elections for the newly devolved Welsh Assembly were held on 6 May 1999. Four days later, the Queen attended a gala celebration concert in Cardiff Bay, featuring Tom Jones, Shirley Bassey and then-teenage star, Charlotte Church; Manic Street Preachers, riding a wave of popularity yet

---

[23] On the maes at the 1996 Llandeilo Eisteddfod, for example, Super Furry Animals resorted to whistling the passages that had been recorded in English; in a concert off the maes that same week, Gorky's Zygotic Mynci expressed their anger in no uncertain terms about what they perceived was a form of censorship.

remaining true to their political roots, refused an invitation to perform for royalty. Cardiff was also preparing to host the Rugby World Cup in its newly built (but unfinished) Millennium Stadium, thus bringing the newly devolved nation to a global television audience of 3 billion people. And finally, Manic Street Preachers rang in the new millennium in the new stadium to a sold-out crowd of 60,000 people and a nationwide television audience. Wales had entered a new era of self-confidence as a nation, proclaiming itself on a global stage, proudly joining the international chorus.

With 'Cool Cymru' now firmly entrenched in the public imagination, how did Welsh pop match the momentum of post-devolution Wales? As with any scene suddenly thrust into the spotlight, fractures soon appeared: Catatonia, a mainstay on festival stages and gossip columns, broke up in 2001; Gorky's Zygotic Mynci left Ankst, releasing six albums on mainstream labels before breaking up in 2003. In the new millennium Stereophonics released an additional nine albums, while continuing to perform at larger outdoor events in Wales and further afield;[24] Manic Street Preachers managed to venture furthest afield of all 'Cool Cymru' bands when they became the first western band to play in Cuba, entertaining Fidel Castro himself in 2001.[25]

A clearer signal that Welsh popular music had entered a new era of sophistication and cultural importance was the release of Super Furry Animals' album, *Mwng* ('Mane'; Placid Casual, 2000).[26] Because Super Furry Animals had cultivated a clear balance between their cultural-linguistic roots in Wales and their bona fide independent credentials in the rest of the world, their performances, whether live or recorded, were generally positively received. *Mwng*, however, was a collection of songs sung entirely in the Welsh language, with no obvious gesture in the packaging or marketing materials towards translation or ease of access for non-Welsh speakers. This was not 'foreign' music intended for fans of 'world music'; this was pop music by a familiar band who simply decided to record some songs in their native language. *Mwng* was rapturously received by the mainstream music press, reached number eleven on the

---

[24] Stereophonics have always foregrounded their Welsh identity, before and after the 'Cool Cymru' bubble burst. Dai Griffiths has noted how visible expressions of Welsh pride did not always seem confident, stating that at rock concerts in the 1990s, 'Welsh flags flew like question marks', and that some expressions of Welsh belonging were interpreted by English observers as unnecessarily hostile. See Sarah Hill and Dai Griffiths, 'Postcolonial Music in Contemporary Wales: Hybrids and Weird Geographies', in *Postcolonial Wales*, ed. by Jane Aaron and Chris Williams (Cardiff: University of Wales Press, 2005), pp. 215–233.

[25] A film of this performance, *Louder Than War*, was released on DVD in 2001.

[26] Super Furry Animals' record label, Creation, had recently gone bust, so the band released *Mwng* on their own label.

UK album charts, and was named one of the albums of the year in both *Melody Maker* and *New Musical Express*. The distance that Welsh-language popular music had travelled, from the founding of Cymdeithas yr Iaith Gymraeg to devolution, was magnified by the release of *Mwng*.

With the Senedd's new political powers came a commitment to cultural enrichment. The Welsh Music Foundation was established in 2000 to promote Welsh music overseas, and to offer training in music promotion at home. In its fourteen years of existence, it oversaw the establishment of music festivals in Wales, notably the Green Man Festival, established in 2003 near Crickhowell in the Brecon Beacons, and the Sŵn (Noise) Festival, a weekend-long, multisite festival in a network of small venues in Cardiff city centre. One of the operators behind the Sŵn Festival was Huw Stephens, who had joined Radio 1 as a teenager in 1999. In the decades since, he has faithfully promoted Welsh music on the national airwaves, in television specials and films related to pop history and the contemporary music scene, and through the establishment of Dydd Miwsig Cymru, the government-sponsored Welsh Music Day, aimed at promoting Welsh-language music in schools across the country.[27]

A more organic type of success is exemplified by Welsh-language artists such as 9Bach,[28] whose album *Tincian* ('Tinkle'; Real World, 2015) won the prize for best album at the BBC Radio 2 Folk Awards; and Gwenno, whose concept album, *Y Dydd Olaf* ('The Last Day'; Peski, 2014; Heavenly, 2015), won the Welsh Music Prize and widespread praise, and whose subsequent album, *Le Kov* ('Place of Memory'; Heavenly, 2018), set a standard for popular music in the Cornish language. The mainstream acclaim that Welsh music has garnered would have been unthinkable in the early days of Welsh pop history. But as more Welsh bands are finding their way onto regular rotation on BBC Radio 1 and BBC 6 Music,[29] and onto festival stages across the UK and around the world, Welsh pop has achieved a security and a breadth of expression that could only have come from the struggles and successes of the second half of the twentieth century.

---

[27] See, for example Stephens's 'musical pilgrimage', *Anorac* (Boom Cymru, 2019). On Dydd Miwsig Cymru see https://gov.wales/welsh-language-music-day (accessed 5 July 2021).

[28] 9Bach is a play on words: Nain (pronounced like the English 'nine') is the north Wales word for grandmother, and bach (little) is used as a term of endearment.

[29] It is notable that BBC 6 Music night-time disc jockey Gideon Coe is a firm champion of Welsh-language music, and that eclectic bands such as Colorama, led by endlessly productive frontman Carwyn Ellis, are frequently featured on other programmes as well. Former Catatonia lead singer Cerys Matthews hosts a popular Sunday-morning programme, and while it is not necessarily focused on Welsh music, she does represent a clear echo from the Cool Cymru/Britpop moment. Back in Wales, Rhys Mwyn continues to support and showcase young Welsh talent while also uncovering 'lost' moments in Welsh musical history on his Monday night Radio Cymru programme, *Recordiau Rhys Mwyn*.

CHAPTER 15

Singing Welshness
Sport, Music and the Crowd

Helen Barlow and Martin V. Clarke

With a minute to go I knew we were going to win the Grand Slam and I knew I had made the right decision to retire. We had been down on our knees and it was spirit that pulled us through. The crowd were singing us home for the final 20 minutes and it was inspirational. It made the hairs on your neck stand up.[1]

To the reader familiar with Welsh or indeed British sport, the inclusion in this book of a chapter that focuses on rugby union and football will come as no surprise – though others may require an explanation. The chapter begins in the early twentieth century and the first 'golden era' of Welsh rugby, with a discussion of when and why Welsh sporting supporters acquired their reputation for the powerful, emotional singing that made the crowd the proverbial 'extra man' in national teams, and goes on to consider how Welsh rugby and football have subsequently capitalised on the musical legacy of that period, both perpetuating and reimagining the singing of the crowd in the twenty-first century.

Rugby and football became part of Welsh sporting culture in the late nineteenth century. To begin with they were interchangeably referred to as 'football'. The games came to be differentiated as their organisation became more formally institutionalised: the Football Association (FA) was founded in London in 1863 and its rules came to define association football. Some clubs who wished to retain elements of the rules defined at Rugby School in 1845 broke away, establishing the Rugby Football Union (RFU) in 1871. A further separation occurred in 1895, as some rugby clubs, predominantly from the north of England, broke away to form the Northern Rugby Football Union, playing a different code of the game, known as rugby league. Institutional organisation in Wales quickly

---

[1] Phil Bennett quoted in David Tossell, *Nobody Beats Us: The Inside Story of the Welsh Rugby Team*, Kindle ed. (Edinburgh: Mainstream Publishing, 2009), location 4593.

followed the patterns established in England; the Football Association of Wales (FAW) was founded in 1876 and several organisations overseeing rugby union emerged in the same period, though the present title, the Welsh Rugby Union (WRU) was not adopted until 1934. Throughout this chapter, in keeping with common usage in Wales, we use rugby to denote rugby union and football to denote association football, or 'soccer', as it is known in some countries.

Rugby union, which insisted obstinately on its amateur status until 1995, became the dominant code in Wales, and that in which national success has been most significant, although association football has also had a strong following, especially at club level; rugby league, by contrast, has struggled to establish a foothold in Wales. Rugby union dominated in south and west Wales, imported by colleges and public and grammar schools in towns including Monmouth, Brecon, Llandovery and Lampeter, and encouraged by the rugby union culture of the neighbouring south-west of England, which offered both local competition and the enthusiastic support of large numbers of migrants from south-west England who came to work in the booming coal industry. These influences carried less weight in north Wales, and partly as a consequence, but also because of its proximity to the strong football culture of north-west England, football has historically tended to have a stronger hold there, though it was not until the twenty-first century that the national team began to command as much sustained attention both within and outside Wales as the rugby union team. Both sports were essentially regarded as male pursuits until the late twentieth century. Despite the popularity of women's football in the late nineteenth and early twentieth centuries (Newport, Cardiff, Swansea and Llanelli all fielded women's teams[2]), at international level Wales was represented only by men's teams for much of the period covered in this chapter; the women's national football team was founded in 1973 and its rugby union counterpart in 1987. While awareness of and popular support for both have grown in the twenty-first century, the men's teams continue to dominate public attention and are the focus of this chapter, as it is in the crowds attending their matches that the links between sport, music and notions of Welshness have primarily been expressed.[3]

---

[2] See Jean Williams, *A Game for Rough Girls? A History of Women's Football in Britain* (London: Routledge, 2003), chapter 1, especially pp. 31–33. Many teams were formed by workers in World War I munitions factories, but women's football was effectively banned by the FA in 1921 on the basis that football was an unsuitably vigorous game for women.
[3] See Martin Johnes, *A History of Sport in Wales* (Cardiff: University of Wales Press, 2005), chapters 1 and 2; and Gareth Williams, *1905 and All That: Essays on Rugby Football, Sport and Welsh Society* (Llandysul: Gomer, 1991), chapters 2 and 3.

Rugby and Revivalism: The Secular Turn in Welsh Congregational Singing

With the encouragement of those higher up the social ladder, many of them educated in the schools and colleges through which the game had been introduced into Wales, rugby union quickly gained popularity in working-class communities across the south of the country, and especially its heavily industrialised and densely populated valleys. The Established Church played an important part, not only in public schools and colleges but also at parish level, where it 'helped to found many junior teams such as Dowlais St Illtyd's and Penydarren Church Juniors in Merthyr Tydfil'.[4] While not exactly what Victorian and Edwardian society recognised as a 'rational recreation' (violence on and off the field was the stuff of legend), the sport nonetheless 'offered a useful way of binding the new urban communities that were made up of an agglomeration of people from different classes, localities and nations'.[5] Welsh rugby's first golden era (1900–11) was part of the broader flourishing of Edwardian Wales, when the production of coal was at its height and seemed to many to give Wales an unprecedented status and purpose within the United Kingdom and the British Empire. The year 1905 was particularly auspicious: following its massive expansion as a coal-exporting port, Cardiff was granted city status, becoming Wales's first modern city; and at Westminster, David Lloyd George was appointed President of the Board of Trade, making him the first Welshman to attain high office in the British government since the seventeenth century. It was a time of 'political self-confidence, cultural creativity, national self-awareness and material prosperity, all to a greater or lesser degree generated by the produce of a coalfield which was approaching its zenith, diffusing its wealth into all areas of Welsh life'.[6]

The crowning achievement of this golden era of rugby came towards the end of that year, on 16 December 1905 at Cardiff Arms Park, when the New Zealand All Blacks,[7] having crushed all other opposition including England, Scotland, Ireland, France and numerous club and county sides, were beaten 3–0 by Wales. As a result, rugby 'became indissolubly wedded

---

[4] Gareth Morgan, 'Rugby and Revivalism: Sport and Religion in Edwardian Wales', *The International Journal of the History of Sport*, 22/3 (May 2005), 434–435.
[5] Johnes, *History of Sport*, p. 24.   [6] Williams, *1905 and All That*, p. 72.
[7] They appear to have first been named the 'All Blacks' (the colour of the team's kit) by the British press on this 1905 tour. See Caroline Daley, 'The Invention of 1905', in *Tackling Rugby Myths: Rugby and New Zealand Society 1854–2004*, ed. by Greg Ryan (Dunedin: University of Otago Press, 2005), p. 67.

15 *Singing Welshness: Sport, Music and the Crowd*

to ideas of Welsh nationality',[8] but the reason for this was not only – arguably, it was not even primarily – to do with rugby prowess. In fact, it was if anything largely musical, and the event could be said to mark a secular turn in Welsh congregational singing and the moment when the support of the Welsh for their sporting heroes became synonymous with mass singing.

Music played an important role at matches, particularly internationals. Brass and military bands were hired to entertain the crowd and create atmosphere, and newspaper reports show that the Welsh were already noted for their singing in the build-up to kick-off, and in celebration of a win or simply of points scored – to the extent that a report of the 1901 Scotland–Wales match in Edinburgh lamented the lack of the musical character that Welsh home games had taught people to expect, with 'no singing of national airs to pass away the waiting time such as takes place at the big international games in Wales'.[9] Before the 1905 Wales–Ireland game in Swansea, by contrast:

> the crowd whiled away the time ... singing patriotic songs ... [T]he Aberaman Brass Band was in attendance and rendered several selections, consisting of Irish and Welsh patriotic airs . . . . At 2.40 the brass band struck up the Llanelly football song, 'Sospan Fach', which was immediately taken up by the Welsh spectators.[10]

At neither of these matches, however, did the teams line up before kick-off for the ritual singing of national anthems. It has been suggested that this tradition dates precisely from the 1905 Wales–All Blacks match,[11] although if this is the case, it was not a practice that took root immediately and consistently, and 'Mae Hen Wlad fy Nhadau', though widely accepted as the Welsh national anthem, did not have that official status.

An impressive novelty of the 1905 All Blacks' tour was their performance at the start of matches of a *haka*, a ceremonial challenge belonging to Māori culture. This was new to most British spectators; this being the All Blacks' first tour of the rugby-playing nations of the northern hemisphere, it was the first time most of them would have seen it (although a previous, largely Māori team called the New Zealand Natives had toured in 1888–9 and they too had performed a *haka*).[12] Ahead of the Wales–All Blacks match, one of

---

[8] Williams, *1905 and All That*, p. 20. [9] *Evening Express*, 9 February 1901, 3.
[10] *The Cambrian*, 17 March 1905, 7.
[11] See, for example, Greg Ryan, *The Contest for Rugby Supremacy: Accounting for the 1905 All Blacks* (Christchurch: Canterbury University Press), p. 129.
[12] Greg Ryan, *Forerunners of the All Blacks: The 1888–89 New Zealand Native Football Team in Britain, Australia and New Zealand* (Christchurch: Canterbury University Press, 1993), p. 52. The All Blacks' adoption of the *haka* has not been without controversy; see, for example, Malcolm MacLean, 'Of

the Welsh team selectors suggested that the Welsh team should meet the challenge of the *haka* by singing 'Mae Hen Wlad fy Nhadau' in response, with the expectation that the Welsh spectators would then take up the chorus. They duly did so with great enthusiasm: it was 'the biggest choir... ['Mae Hen Wlad fy Nhadau'] had yet had in its slow ascent to the status of anthem'.[13] The impact was widely described in the press in both the northern and southern hemispheres. The *Manchester Guardian* was struck by three significant features that seemed to mark the 'Welshness' of the singing – the sheer volume of the massed voices, the fact that they were singing in parts, and the religious character of what they sang (despite the fact that 'Mae Hen Wlad fy Nhadau' is not, of course, a hymn): 'a mightly [*sic*] uprolling volume of harmonious sounds, tens of thousands of voices joining in the refrain of a beautiful Welsh hymn which expresses in perfect form the Welshman's love of his inheritance'.[14] The New Zealand newspaper *The Lyttelton Times* reported that:

> The scene at the ground was unique in the New Zealanders' experience. They realise now what Celtic fire and enthusiasm mean. What a contrast between this frenzied throng at Cardiff and that other great gathering [England against the All Blacks] at the Crystal Palace a fortnight previously! The English crowd was quiet, orderly and undemonstrative, only mildly partisan ... The Welsh ... were there to sing and cheer their champions to victory ... It is a peculiarity of Welsh crowds that they always sing while waiting. The love of music is in their blood, and their voices are melodious and well-trained. Their songs are always native airs and hymns, instinct with patriotism and pride of race, and because their singing comes from the heart – for your Welshman is intensely patriotic – the effect is inspiriting and most impressive .... The war cry [*haka*] went well, and the crowd listened and watched in pleased silence, and thundered their approval at its close. But for dramatic effect it was far surpassed by what followed .... Imagine some forty thousand people singing their National Anthem with all the fervour of which the Celtic heart is capable. It was the most impressive incident I have ever witnessed on a football field. It gave a semi-religious solemnity to their memorable contest ... [It] was intensely thrilling, even awe-inspiring[.][15]

Warriors and Blokes: The Problem of Maori Rugby for Pakeha Masculinity in New Zealand', in *Making the Rugby World: Race, Gender, Commerce*, ed. by Timothy J. L. Chandler and John Naught (London and Portland OR: Frank Cass, 1999), p. 17.

[13] David Smith and Gareth Williams, *Fields of Praise: The Official History of the Welsh Rugby Union 1881–1981* (Cardiff: University of Wales Press on behalf of the Welsh Rugby Union, 1980), p. 154.

[14] *Manchester Guardian*, 18 December 1905, 8.   [15] *Lyttelton Times*, 26 January 1906, 2.

The British newspaper the *Daily Mail* used the same word, 'semi-religious', to describe the Welsh singing:

> [T]he 'All Blacks' on Saturday seemed to be labouring under some strange, hypnotic influence from the moment they stepped on to the field. Even the usually awe-inspiring Maori war chant fell a little flat, and its remembrance was speedily engulfed in the crowd's inspiring, soulful response to the Welsh team's lead of 'Land of Our Fathers'. There was a semi-religious, almost fanatical invocation in the fervour with which the vast assembly took up the strain: -
> The land of my fathers! The land of the free!
> The 'All Blacks' listened spell-bound to the weirdly beautiful incantation. They never seemed quite able to shake off its effects while the game lasted.[16]

Some pursued the religious analogy yet more specifically. The Melbourne newspaper *The Australasian* made the connection between the match and the 1904–5 'Welsh' religious revival, which had come to an end earlier in the year. In a report entitled 'Rugby or Revivalism', it noted not only that the Welsh overawed the All Blacks with 'Mae Hen Wlad fy Nhadau' but that in the build-up to the match the crowd were singing 'Throw Out the Lifeline',[17] one of the most popular revival hymns, which had first appeared in one of Ira D. Sankey's hymnals in the 1890s. Revival hymns had quickly become a staple of Welsh rugby crowds – in February of 1905, the *Evening Express*, reporting on the singing before the Scotland–Wales match in Edinburgh, noted that, 'The inevitable "Ton y Botel" ["The Bottle Tune"] and other Revival hymns gave a temporary shock to the staidness of the great Princes-street in Edinburgh, and dour Scots, as they passed along, opened their eyes and marvelled'.[18] ('Ton y Botel', otherwise 'Ebenezer', was the tune to which the hymn text 'Dyma Gariad fel y Moroedd' was widely sung.)

It is hardly surprising that Welsh sporting crowds should have adopted this form of collective expression. The place of chapels in the spiritual, social and musical life of Welsh people remained significant in the early years of the twentieth century, and in a report of the revival, a journalist writing for an Australian newspaper described Sunday night in 1905 in the south Wales valleys in terms which owed something to the myth of the 'land of song', but which also captured a reality: 'The Welsh are pre eminently [*sic*] a musical race. A walk through a town on a Sunday night when all the people are in churches or chapels, would give one the impression that a number of Philharmonic Societies were practising, so whole-hearted and general is the

---

[16] *Daily Mail*, 18 December 1905, 7. [17] *The Australasian*, 3 February 1906, 15.
[18] *Evening Express*, 6 February 1905, 2. 'The Bottle Tune' was so called because of a legend that it was found in a bottle on a Welsh beach.

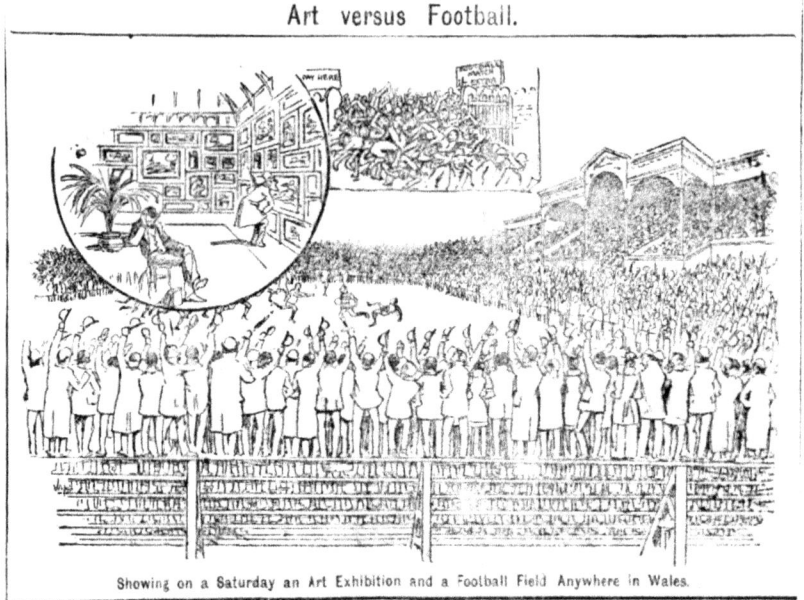

Figure 15.1 A cartoon from a Cardiff newspaper satirising the enthusiasm of the Welsh for rugby (at a time when the term 'football' was used interchangeably for the different codes of the game). *Evening Express*, 11 November 1893

singing'.[19] The cymanfa ganu, hugely popular in the second half of the nineteenth century, was still enthusiastically supported – though some had suggested that it was beginning to lose its appeal in the face of an expanding choice of cultural and leisure activities: as one chapel deacon is said to have remarked to another at an international rugby match in 1900, 'What is the use in preaching against football? We couldn't draw such a crowd as this to a gymanfa' (see Figure 15.1).[20] Nonetheless, mass congregational singing was so tightly woven into Welsh life that it had also come to carry a powerful sense of communal identity. As Simon Frith has said, mass participation in music is one of the cultural activities through which 'social groups ... get to know themselves *as groups*',[21] and while hymn singing undoubtedly still carried spiritual meaning for many participants, for others it was increasingly

---

[19] *Port Macquarrie News and Hastings River Advocate*, 25 March 1905, 3.
[20] *South Wales Daily News*, 7 January 1901, quoted in Williams, *1905 and All That*, p. 77.
[21] Simon Frith, 'Music and Identity', in *Questions of Cultural Identity*, ed. by Stuart Hall and Paul du Gay (London: Sage, 1996), p. 111.

'the performance ..., the process'²² that was meaningful – hence the easy transfer to a secular context of a fundamentally religious musical practice.

It has been said that an emphasis on direct personal experience of God's forgiveness 'tended to make [Welsh nonconformist] religion an emotional thing',²³ and the 1904–5 revival in particular was characterised by heightened emotion based on a joyful emphasis on the loving nature of God. Hymn singing (often taking place spontaneously in the midst of a revival meeting) was perhaps the revival's most characteristic form of expression – it was also widely referred to as the 'singing revival'.²⁴ Along with the practice of mass hymn singing, this expressive quality too was readily transferred to the secular context of sport: Welsh supporters expressed their emotions at sporting events through mass hymn singing because emotional fervour expressed through congregational singing came naturally to them through their upbringing in the chapels, and especially through the musical fervour that many had experienced at first hand in the revival.

At the time, the relationship between the revival and Welsh sport was often cast in negative terms, with numerous instances of rugby and football teams ritually burning their kit and abandoning the evils of sport in favour of religion (if only temporarily). There was also considerable disapproval at the appropriation of hymns: Tom Richards, MP for West Monmouthshire and a lay preacher, delivered a sermon that was widely reported in the Welsh press, in which he denounced what he called 'the football curse' for the rowdy behaviour of supporters and '[the] objectionable ... singing [of] filthy doggerel songs, alternately with the sacred hymns that were associated with some of the most blessed experiences of their parents and friends'.²⁵ But what this type of reaction missed was the extent to which not simply particular hymns, but the practice of congregational singing itself, had come to evoke for the Welsh a sense of 'nation-ness'.²⁶ Mass singing had become a demonstration or performance of Welshness – a way of expressing a collective identity. At the close of a series of revival meetings in Dowlais in January 1905:

> The hymn, 'Marchog Iesu yn llwyddianus' ['Jesus ride in triumph'], was sung, and when this crowning gathering of the Dowlais series was

---

²² Frith, 'Music and Identity', p. 112.
²³ C. R. Williams, 'The Welsh Religious Revival', *The British Journal of Sociology*, 3/3 (Sept. 1952), 243.
²⁴ See, for example, 'Awstin' and Western Mail Special Correspondents, *The Religious Revival in Wales: Contemporaneous Newspaper Accounts of the Welsh Revival of 1904–05 Published by the Western Mail* (Oswestry: Quinta Press, 2004), p. 66.
²⁵ *Cymro a'r Celt Llundain (The London Welshman and Kelt)*, 12 January 1907, 2.
²⁶ A term used by Benedict Anderson as an alternative to the more politically loaded 'nationalism'. See *Imagined Communities: Reflections on the Origin and Spread of Nationalism* (London and New York: Verso, 1983), p. 4.

dispersing, the people sang in the open air, and sang in the street, and sang in the trains that victorious Welsh march, 'Marchog Iesu' [.][27]

The parallels with a victorious Welsh rugby crowd spilling out of Cardiff Arms Park and boarding their trains home to west Wales and the south Wales valleys are impossible to resist.

There was considerable suspicion of the revival at the time, not least among the various nonconformist denominations: it was widely criticised for theological naivety, for too much emphasis on singing and for the superficiality of the new revival hymns, which were unfavourably compared by some with the older Welsh hymns such as 'Marchog Iesu' (by Williams Pantycelyn). Subsequently, the denominations themselves have come in for criticism, with the suggestion that chapel leaders were unable to cope with the raw outpouring of emotion that characterised the revival, and that their reaction revealed 'an inability in Welsh Christianity to deal properly and theologically with the role of emotion in public life'.[28] But by the early twentieth century, there were other forms of mass cultural activity that had no such difficulty. As Robert Pope suggests, if the chapel could not find a way to channel that emotion, the rugby stadium could: 'The mass expression of emotion [in the revival] ... demonstrated that it met a personal and communal need, as have the experiences of those at, say, the Arms Park and the Millennium Stadium since.'[29]

Hymns, Arias and National Anthems: The Singing Crowd in the 1960s and 1970s

Despite the varying fortunes of the national rugby team over the decades that followed, the reputation of Welsh supporters for their awe-inspiring mass singing only increased during the twentieth century, and the connection with religion remained vivid in the minds of listeners. The sports journalist Bernard Darwin wrote of the rugby internationals of the 1920s and 1930s:

> I have been told by those who have played in international matches in Wales that the first moment of stepping on to the ground is paralysing. Rugby

---

[27] 'Awstin', *The Religious Revival*, p. 209.
[28] Robert Pope, 'Evan Roberts in Theological Context', *Transactions of the Honourable Society of Cymmrodorion*, 11 (2004), 169.
[29] Ibid., 169. The Millennium Stadium, built to host the 1999 Rugby World Cup, stands on the same site as the earlier stadium, Cardiff Arms Park. For sponsorship reasons, its name changed again in 2016 to the Principality Stadium.

15 Singing Welshness: Sport, Music and the Crowd

football in South Wales produces an almost religious enthusiasm, and the Welshman has a wonderful power of giving vent to his religion in song. Certainly I have never witnessed anything comparable in emotional excitement to the scene before an international match at Cardiff, and having Welsh blood in my veins I become wholly Welsh on these occasions and so can enjoy them the more intensely. For some time before the match begins the crowd has been singing, and singing as only a Welsh crowd can, but the supreme moment arrives when the band that has been parading round the field marches into the middle of it. Everybody knows what is going to happen, takes off his hat and rises to his feet for "Land of Our Fathers". That famous song is full of such pent-up fervour that it is hard to bear with any attempt at outward decorum. It is not so much a challenge to the enemy as a universal and tremendous prayer for their overthrow. At last it is over and is succeeded by wild and continuous shouting, but always there is that feeling of united prayer behind the tumult.[30]

However, as the century continued, the secular nature of the turn in the mass singing of Welsh sports crowds became more pronounced. As Smith and Williams have pointed out, 'The rugby crowds of the 1950s ... were the last of the harmonious generations brought up on choir practice and the Band of Hope'.[31] Thus, while specific hymns – notably Williams Pantycelyn's 'Arglwydd, Arwain Trwy'r Anialwch' ('Guide Me, O Thou Great Jehovah', better known to rugby supporters as 'Bread of Heaven'), and 'Calon Lân' ('A Pure Heart'), popularised during the Welsh revival – have remained touchstones of the repertoire, secular songs have embedded themselves just as firmly. Tom Jones's 1968 hit 'Delilah' quickly became a staple (though more recently it has been the subject of controversy[32]), while 'Hymns and Arias' (1971), written and performed by the Welsh comedian and entertainer Max Boyce, is notable as a self-referential rugby song about rugby singing. The verses carry a comic narrative in which Welsh rugby supporters go on an 'away' trip to London, to face England at Twickenham, and refer throughout to the standards of Welsh rugby repertoire including 'Delilah', 'Cwm Rhondda' and 'Calon Lân'. Its

---

[30] Bernard Darwin, *British Sports and Games* (London: The British Council, 1940), p. 25.
[31] The Band of Hope was the strand of the temperance movement that addressed itself specifically to children, providing wholesome activities such as hymn singing. Smith and Williams, *Fields of Praise*, p. 340.
[32] Calls for it to be banned for trivialising violence against women were first voiced by the folk singer Dafydd Iwan. See, for example, 'Stop Fans Singing Delilah Before Wales Games? No Chance, Says WRU After Song's Violent Lyrics Are Questioned', *Wales Online*, 10 December 2014, www.walesonline.co.uk/news/wales-news/stop-fans-singing-delilah-before-8264297 (accessed 3 March 2021); and Carolyn Hitt, 'Wales Needs to Talk About Ditching Delilah', *Wales Online*, 20 June 2020, www.walesonline.co.uk/sport/rugby/rugby-news/welsh-rugby-needs-talk-ditching-18455444 (accessed 3 March 2021).

enduring appeal for the crowd lies in the simple, participatory chorus, which sums up the musical nature of Welsh rugby support:

> And we were singing hymns and arias,
> 'Land of My Fathers', 'Ar hyd y nos'.

At the opening ceremony of the 1999 Rugby World Cup, held in Cardiff at the new Millennium Stadium (purpose-built for the tournament), Max Boyce sang a reworked version. The first verse refers to the stadium's innovation of a retractable roof – and it does so in terms that invoke the old association of Welsh rugby and religion:

> They'll slide it back when Wales attack
> So God can watch us play.[33]

The 1960s and 1970s were a period in which the singing of the national anthem before international matches became a particularly sensitive and politicised issue. Like the first, the second golden era of Welsh rugby (1969–79) coincided with a broader sense of national consciousness. There were highly visible manifestations of nationalist sentiment, and while nationalism was not a creed which the majority of Welsh people were ready to endorse, it undoubtedly fostered a renewed national conversation about Welsh identity and Wales's place in the UK. One of the ways in which this found popular expression was in contention over the national anthem. Through much of the twentieth century, 'Mae Hen Wlad fy Nhadau' had co-existed, often uneasily, alongside 'God Save the King/Queen' at international rugby and football matches. Phil Stead notes that during the 1958 (Football) World Cup, 'God Save the Queen' was played before each of Wales's matches.[34] The argument was that 'God Save the Queen' was the *British* national anthem, and so should be sung by all four home nations. The Welsh, however, were increasingly inclined to perceive 'God Save the Queen' as the *English* national anthem, and to resort to booing and jeering while it was played. The cries of protest at its precedence over 'Mae Hen Wlad fy Nhadau' are well documented in the sports and letters pages of even the most conservative British newspapers throughout the 1960s and 1970s. As one Welsh reader of the *Sunday Telegraph* put it, 'Wales has its own National Anthem, an inspiring song called "Hen

---

[33] The performance is captured on YouTube: 'Rugby World Cup 1999, Max Boyce, Hymns and Arias, Opening Ceremony', www.youtube.com/watch?v=O-EKY7z_jeE (accessed 29 April 2021).
[34] Phil Stead, *Red Dragons: The Story of Welsh Football*, revised ed. (Talybont: Y Lolfa, 2015), p. 167.

Wlad fy Nhadau", and we do not need to hear the song of the English to remind us of our subjection.'³⁵

While the English regularly omitted 'Mae Hen Wlad fy Nhadau', the Welsh retaliated by omitting 'God Save the Queen'. Stead highlights a football match against Austria in 1975 as particularly significant:

> For once, there would be no 'God Save the Queen' before the game and only the Welsh anthem was sung by the 29,000 fans packed into Wrexham's Racecourse. There were diplomatic plans that 'The Queen' be played after the match, though it is difficult to imagine anybody took much notice as Wales celebrated a famous win.³⁶

The British anthem was omitted entirely for a match against Czechoslovakia in 1977, while its sole use at the expense of 'Mae Hen Wlad fy Nhadau' in the game against England at Wembley that year provoked a protest from the Welsh players:

> After the military band had played 'God Save the Queen', the English team broke away to begin the game, but, in a display of defiance, the Welsh players remained in line. Ted Croker and the English officials panicked and tried to usher the Welsh team away as the English crowd booed. But [Welsh captain Terry] Yorath's side only moved once their point was made. Incensed, the FAW proposed dispensing with all anthems.³⁷

A similar situation existed on the rugby field. The omission of 'Mae Hen Wlad fy Nhadau' at the England–Wales match at Twickenham in 1974 led to protests by the Welsh to the (English) RFU; many newspaper column inches, including a lengthy article of complaint in the *Daily Express* by Wales's star player Barry John;³⁸ and a stout declaration by Air Commodore Bob Weighill, Secretary of the RFU, that 'My committee are firmly of the opinion that when all the countries of the four home unions play at Twickenham, we play only "The Queen"'.³⁹ Two years later, however, at the next England–Wales match at Twickenham, the Welsh scored an especially important victory: they beat England by twenty-one points to nine, but even more significantly, the RFU gave way and as the teams lined up at the start of the match, the band of the Royal Marines played 'Mae Hen Wlad fy Nhadau'.⁴⁰

---

³⁵ *Sunday Telegraph*, 14 October 1973, 12.   ³⁶ Stead, *Red Dragons*, p. 216.   ³⁷ Ibid., p. 226.
³⁸ *Daily Express*, 22 March 1974, 23.   ³⁹ *Daily Mail*, 18 April 1974, 33.
⁴⁰ *Daily Mail*, 29 April 1977, 33.

#TogetherStronger: The Singing Crowd in Twenty-First-Century Wales

The 1980s and 1990s were periods in which there was little success for Welsh supporters to celebrate; the national rugby team won the European Five Nations Championship[41] only once in each decade, sharing the title with France in 1988 and winning it outright in 1994, while the national football team's repeated failure to qualify for major tournaments resulted in small crowds and a subdued atmosphere not especially conducive to passionate singing for many home fixtures. The twenty-first century saw something of a revival in fortunes, however, with the rugby team securing grand slams (winning all of their matches in the tournament) in 2005, 2008, 2012 and 2019, and the football team reaching the semi-finals of the UEFA European Championships in 2016 (Euro 2016). The team's qualification for the finals of a major international tournament for the first time since 1958 was itself a cause for significant celebration, which was further heightened as the squad exceeded expectations in progressing to be one of the last four teams in the competition, garnering significant public support along the way. While the increased levels of public support were obviously chiefly motivated by the sporting success of the team, they also owed much to a strategic campaign by the FAW that captured the public's imagination, and in which song would come to play an important part.

Ahead of the team's participation in the qualification stage of Euro 2016, the FAW, realising that it had a crop of players of rare talent, made significant efforts to galvanise public support. The success of these efforts naturally rested on the team's success on the pitch, which was, for once, consistently forthcoming. Off the pitch, the FAW's efforts focused on creating a strong brand to bind the team and its supporters together. Harnessing the power of social media, the brand was promoted using the hashtag #TogetherStronger, which was taken up by players and supporters alike, while the supporters were described collectively as the 'Red Wall'. The hashtag drew on the national team's motto, used since 1951: 'Gorau Chwarae Cyd Chwarae', understood in translation as 'Team Play is the Best Play'. Home qualifying matches were played at the Cardiff City Stadium, with all but one attracting crowds in excess of 30,000. While social media played an important role in the branding success, the live

---

[41] The Five Nations Tournament has been played annually between the four British nations and France since 1910. In 2000 it was expanded to include Italy, thus becoming the Six Nations Championship.

context of the matches themselves was obviously central, not least in allowing the collective voice of the crowd to be heard in song.

The singing of 'Mae Hen Wlad fy Nhadau' assumed a crucial role in translating a media-driven campaign into a live experience. The Welsh anthem had long been sung at football internationals, but the degree to which its powerful effect was deliberately exploited by the FAW was new and marked a recognition of the value of communal singing in promoting and sustaining the collective identity of the team's supporters. For each of the home qualifying games, the FAW continued the practice that had been used in both football and rugby internationals for several years of employing a professional singer to lead the team and crowd in the singing of 'Mae Hen Wlad fy Nhadau' before the kick-off. Drawing on the availability of sophisticated sound systems in modern stadia, the soloist's voice is amplified as they sing over an instrumental accompaniment provided either by live musicians, or, in the case of the Euro 2016 qualifiers, a backing track. Live accompaniment by brass or military bands has been customary at rugby matches, while the backing track used by the FAW for the Euro 2016 qualifiers featured a brass band, acknowledging the prominent place of such bands in Welsh musical culture.

Soloists and Cultural Learning

The use of vocal soloists highlights two somewhat contradictory aspects of the place of music in mass expressions of Welsh identity. In one respect, the use of solo singers emphasises the high regard in which both well-known musicians and sportspeople are often held in Welsh culture. Acclaimed Welsh singers associated with a wide variety of musical genres have long been eager to lend their musical talent in support of the nation's sports teams, most commonly in rugby union. Musicians of international fame such as Bryn Terfel and Katherine Jenkins have frequently fulfilled this role at home rugby internationals in Cardiff, sometimes with assembled male voice choirs providing backing in addition to military bands of Welsh regiments. The reputations of the soloists employed by the FAW for the Euro 2016 qualifiers were not of the same order as Terfel or Jenkins; nonetheless, their presence affirmed the close bond between Welsh musicality and sporting pride. The two singers who featured, Lucie Jones and Sophie Evans, had come to national attention, initially through their success in reality television: Jones had been a contestant in *The X Factor* (UK) in 2009, reaching the last eight of the competition, while Evans was runner-up in the 2010 BBC talent contest *Over the Rainbow*; both subsequently forged careers in West End productions.

The presence of high-profile singers such as Terfel and Jenkins added to the already impressive spectacle of home rugby internationals, their amplified voices crowning the musical contributions of crowds of over 70,000 and military bands and male voice choirs. The smaller scale of the qualifying games held at the Cardiff City Stadium suggests that the FAW's decision to make use of vocal soloists in this way can therefore be regarded as a concern to create or ensure a lively, patriotic atmosphere rather than to supplement it. The previous qualifying campaign, for the 2014 FIFA World Cup, had seen average home crowds of under 16,000, as several early defeats all but guaranteed that Wales would not qualify for the finals. Launched against this rather unpromising backdrop, the FAW's #TogetherStronger campaign demanded a firmly proactive approach to mitigate the risk of a half-full stadium engendering a lacklustre environment. The use of lead singers, therefore, must be regarded as part of a plan to translate #TogetherStronger into a positive, live experience by encouraging and ultimately ensuring an impressive rendition of 'Mae Hen Wlad fy Nhadau', even if the stadium was not full. This use of amplified solo singers is one of several ways in which Welsh sporting institutions, along with those of many other nations, have embraced technological opportunities to actively promote and perpetuate the tradition of strong communal singing by sports crowds at home international fixtures.

Early results in the Euro 2016 qualifying campaign were promising, which led to capacity crowds for the final three home games as the team ultimately secured qualification for the finals. Huge numbers of Welsh supporters travelled to France for the tournament, and, as Wales progressed through the opening group stage, the exuberant singing of 'Mae Hen Wlad fy Nhadau' before each game attracted considerable attention from the media. Following Wales's opening game against Slovakia, the French sports daily *L'Équipe* began its report by paying tribute to the passion of the Welsh singing: 'A hymn to give you goosebumps, never-ending singing and the impression all you can see is red'.[42] Further on in the tournament, BBC Wales's Dafydd Pritchard described how, prior to the quarter-final match against Belgium, despite Welsh supporters being heavily outnumbered by Belgians, 'The Welsh national anthem, "Mae

---

[42] Cited in John Doel, 'French Media Blown Away By 'Magnificent' Wales Fans as Shocking Stadium Violence Mars Euro 2016' *Wales Online*, 12 June 2016, www.walesonline.co.uk/sport/football/football-news/french-media-blown-away-magnificent-11460513 (accessed 29 April 2021).

Hen Wlad fy Nhadau", still reverberated around Stade Pierre Mauroy at a spine-tingling volume'.[43] Welsh football commentator Bryn Law's travelogue presents a supporter's view of the tournament and makes frequent reference to the singing of the Welsh fans, for example in relation to the match against Belgium:

> The players emerge from the tunnel, far away on the opposite side of the stadium. They head to their line-up positions and the Belgian anthem's announced first. The majority of the crowd join in, of course, but they can't compete with what comes next. From our corner, from every Welsh voice dotted around the stadium, the sound of something incredible, an ancient language, a song of defiance, '*Gwlad! Gwlad!*' Then the words rise to the crescendo, '*O bydded i'r hen iaith barhau!*' – 'Let the old language endure!' – and, in this moment, it does, on the lips of every man, woman and child supporting the little country to the west of England.[44]

Aside from capturing the fervour of the singing, Law provides a colourful gloss that seeks to record his perception of a large-scale shared experience of Welsh identity and pride, for which song was the ultimate form of expression. While his reflection on the precise meaning of the words was undoubtedly made in hindsight, it highlights a significant point about the visceral conclusion of the anthem in the manner of performance that had become customary. Earlier, recounting the opening game against Slovakia, Law describes this musical phenomenon in more detail:

> The fans' rendition starts a little behind the PA, so it's incredibly loud but the whole thing really takes off when we catch up. '*Gwlad! Gwlad!*' is that meeting point and it's glorious. I've never been sure about the anthem going up at the end, on '*i'r hen iaith barhau*' – it never used to – but it works so well here to create a massively emotive climax. Needless to say, by the time it's over, I have tears rolling down my cheeks.[45]

In this description, Law draws attention to two specific musical features of the Welsh anthem. Consideration of its melodic characteristics, both in composition and performance, help to explain the fervour with which it is customarily performed by sporting crowds. In common with many melodies written for texts with a verse-refrain structure, the opening of the refrain, set to the repeated word 'Gwlad', has an emphatic melodic pattern

---

[43] Dafydd Pritchard, 'Euro 2016: Wales Win Over Belgium Dwarfs Other Achievements', www.bbc.co.uk/sport/football/36692107 (accessed 29 April 2021).
[44] Bryn Law, *Don't Take Me Home: On Tour with The Red Wall at Euro 2016* (Cardiff: St David's Press, 2016), p. 202.
[45] Ibid., pp. 43–44.

Example 15.1 'Mae Hen Wlad fy Nhadau', standard and modified endings

that stands out from the surrounding phrases. The melodic contour across the four phrases of the verse is evenly balanced: the first and third phrases rise gradually, with complementary descents in the second and fourth phrases; the verse begins and ends on a low tonic. The refrain, however, begins with two utterances of 'Gwlad', the first on the dominant note above the original tonic, and the second rising to the tonic at the octave. While the first and third phrases of the verse also ascend to the tonic at the octave, they do so more gradually, arriving there in the third bar of the phrase following much stepwise melodic movement. The clean melodic leap at the beginning of the refrain therefore stands out and is further differentiated rhythmically; its two notes each last for a whole bar, whereas the melody of the verse has been dominated by notes of shorter duration. In combination with the open-mouthed 'a' vowel in 'Gwlad', the effect is dramatically arresting. This corresponds effectively with the lyrical content; 'Gwlad', while literally translated as 'country', carries far stronger resonances of homeland, belonging and national identity. In performance, the crowd's singing typically intensifies at this point, rising in volume as the words are semi-sung, semi-shouted. Thereafter, the original melody follows a pattern very similar to the third and fourth phrases of the verse, ultimately descending to conclude on the tonic with which it began. However, as Law indicates, a melodic modification has become commonplace in more recent years, whereby much of the final phrase is sung an octave higher than in the original version, as shown in Example 15.1.

The exact origin of this modification is difficult to identify, and different versions exist, but it likely has its roots in the performances of solo singers alongside massed crowds such as those mentioned above. Bryn Terfel's album *We'll Keep a Welcome* (2000) includes this modification in the final refrain of the anthem. While the lavish arrangement by Chris Hazell, and performed by Terfel, the Orchestra of Welsh National Opera and the Black Mountain Chorus, is in some ways far removed from the visceral experience of the football or rugby crowd's singing, it nonetheless aims to capture a similar sense of exuberant patriotism. The change of register in the final phrase of the refrain showcases Terfel's vocal prowess while also intimating that his singing is a vehicle for expressing pride in his Welshness. It has become widespread in concert arrangements and performances of the anthem, typified by Jeffrey Howard's arrangement, performed at the National Eisteddfod in 2015.[46]

The modification has also become standard practice at national sporting events, sung by both professional vocal soloists and, increasingly, by Welsh players and supporters. Examples from around the turn of the twenty-first century indicate that while solo singers performed the jump into the higher octave, this was by no means widely taken up by the players or supporters. A video recording of the anthems sung before Wales's rugby union match against England in the 1999 Five Nations tournament captures Max Boyce exuberantly singing the final phrase at the higher octave.[47] Boyce's distinctive voice is clearly heard, and his facial expression confirms the sudden upwards melodic leap. A crowd shot seems to capture at least one supporter joining him, but the predominant aural impression is of the vast majority of singers following the downward contour of the original melody. Similarly, prior to Wales's home fixture against Italy in the 2004 Six Nations tournament, Katherine Jenkins and New Zealander Hayley Westenra make the leap up, though only for the final five notes, while the male voice choir and brass band alongside whom they performed can be clearly heard following the original melody.

Video footage of the anthems sung during the Euro 2016 qualifying campaign testifies to the growing trend towards the change in register, although even in the intense atmosphere ahead of the home fixture against Belgium in June 2015, divergence can clearly be heard; while many of the crowd join soloist Sophie Evans in the upper octave, the original lower-pitched melody remains clearly audible.[48] By the time of the finals themselves in 2016, however, the modified version appears to have become standard, perhaps driven by the team's remarkable success. Amateur footage of the anthem before the quarter-final match against Belgium zooms in

---

[46] 'Mae Hen Wlad fy Nhadau (Welsh National Anthem)', www.youtube.com/watch?v=9wcuwDXFS5Y (accessed 29 April 2021).
[47] 'Five Nations 1999: Wales vs England at Wembley. National Anthems', www.youtube.com/watch?v=aSFQrlG5imc (accessed 29 April 2021).
[48] 'Wales v Belgium – 12.06.2015 (EURO 2016 Qualifying Round Full Re-Run)', www.youtube.com/watch?v=mXZqmfckciw (accessed 29 April 2021).

on the Welsh fans towards the end of the anthem, and the ubiquity of the higher register is apparent both aurally and visually.

Significantly, although recordings of the anthems were played in the stadia throughout Euro 2016, live solo singers did not feature. The Welsh supporters' response was, therefore, of their own volition, without the aural encouragement of a vocal soloist, as had been the case in the home qualification matches. This draws attention to the ways in which the crowd learns the musical practices and repertoire that they use to express their Welsh identity and passionate support for the national team. The influence of solo singers in this cannot be underestimated. Their growing presence at national sports fixtures in the twenty-first century reflects an increasingly institutionalised drive to perpetuate the notion of the Welsh crowd's musicality and passion. However, this in turn needs to be understood against a longer-term national context in which several of the opportunities for massed singing traditionally associated with Wales have been in decline. In common with the United Kingdom at large, religious observance in Wales dropped steadily but significantly over many decades of the twentieth century and on into the twenty-first. The focus of music education in state schools also changed substantially in the latter decades of the twentieth century. Continuing trends begun earlier in the century, emphasis shifted away from massed singing and the teaching by rote of religious hymns or national songs towards a more holistic provision that included activities such as composition and improvisation.[49] While Paul Chambers's claim that 'The male voice choirs of Wales are ageing and increasingly moribund, superseded by the sounds of rock music and "Cool Cymru"'[50] is a rather sweeping generalisation, it nonetheless illustrates one facet of overall decline in the popularity and vitality of several forms of participative music making traditionally associated with Wales.

Perpetuating and Recreating the Tradition

Against this changing backdrop, the persistence of vigorous singing by Welsh football and rugby crowds is a striking phenomenon. The

[49] Gordon Cox, 'Britain: Towards a "Long Overdue Renaissance"?, in *The Origins and Foundations of Music Education: Cross-Cultural Historical Studies of Music in Compulsory Schooling* (London: Continuum 2010), pp. 15–29, esp. pp. 23–26; Janet Mills, 'Secondary Singing Inspected', *British Journal of Music Education*, 17/1 (Mar. 2000), 61–66, doi:10.1017/S0265051700000152 (accessed 29 April 2021).

[50] Paul Chambers, 'Sacred Landscapes, Redundant Chapels and Carpet Warehouses: The Religious Heritage of South West Wales', in *Materialising Religion: Expression, Performance and Ritual*, ed. by Elisabeth Arweck and William Keenan (Aldershot: Ashgate, 2006) p. 21.

proportion of supporters likely to have musical parallels to the patriotic singing in the stadia in other areas of their lives is almost certainly much lower than in earlier generations. While some will lament and others will welcome the decline of the institutions and structures that enabled traditional patterns of music making in Wales, the decreases in religious observance and in membership of organisations such as male voice choirs owe much to a growing indifference towards forms of formalised, membership-based communal activity.[51] The singing of the crowd cannot thus be regarded as an inevitable manifestation of a widespread cultural practice.

Its continued prevalence seems closely bound up with conspicuous displays of national identity and pride on the part of players and supporters, displays that have been encouraged by Welsh sporting authorities and media organisations alike. Two notable examples connected with the Welsh rugby union team centre on the use of the hymn 'Calon Lân', one of the best-known hymns in the Welsh language and one of those most frequently sung at international matches. Ahead of the 2014 Six Nations tournament, BBC Wales launched a campaign to teach Welsh people to sing the hymn to express their support for the team during the competition. Spearheaded by opera singer and BBC Wales presenter Wynne Evans, the campaign comprised a variety of approaches targeting different demographics. A large number of familiar presenters from BBC Radio Wales took part in a video compilation, each performing one or more lines of the hymn, while schools were encouraged to teach the hymn to pupils, and Evans presented a series of online video tutorials aimed at the general public.[52] A lavishly orchestrated arrangement of the hymn performed by the BBC National Orchestra and Chorus of Wales alongside massed choirs from across south Wales was broadcast ahead of Wales's final match against Scotland.[53] Similarly, ahead of the 2019 Rugby World Cup in Japan, the Welsh Rugby Union released a video of Bryn Terfel coaching the squad to

---

[51] For example, membership of political parties in the UK fell by 68.42 per cent between 1980 and 2008. Ingrid Van Biezen, Peter Mair and Thomas Poguntke, 'Going, Going, . . . Gone? The Decline of Party Membership in Contemporary Europe', *European Journal of Political Research*, 51/1 (Jan. 2012), pp. 24–56, doi:10.1111/j.1475-6765.2011.01995.x (accessed 29 April 2021). It is also estimated that church attendance in Wales declined from 14.1 per cent of the population in 1980 to 4.8 per cent in 2015. 'Peter Brierley Estimates of Church Attendance in Britain, 1980–2015', https://faithsurvey.co.uk/download/gb-church-attendance-1980-2015.pdf (accessed 29 April 2021).

[52] 'BBC Radio Wales Presenters sing Calon Lân', www.youtube.com/watch?v=LA4lofoeY7g (accessed 29 April 2021); 'School Report: Learning Welsh Hymn Calon Lan', www.bbc.co.uk/news/av/uk-wales-26734726 (accessed 29 April 2021); 'Calon Lân Final Guide', www.bbc.co.uk/programmes/p01sshn2 (accessed 29 April 2021).

[53] 'Wales v Scotland: Calon Lân – 6 Nations 2014 – BBC Cymru Wales', www.youtube.com/watch?v=yYOxBncgmLQ (accessed 29 April 2021).

sing the hymn, among several other traditional Welsh songs.[54] Schoolchildren in Japan, meanwhile, had learned the hymn in order to welcome the visiting players.[55]

Aside from their obvious function in galvanising support for the national rugby team, both campaigns offer several insights into the ways in which the singing of the Welsh crowd has been simultaneously perpetuated and reimagined in a twenty-first-century context. The perceived need to teach the hymn, whether to the nation at large or the players representing it, reflects the decline in communal singing noted above and the concomitant shrinking of the collectively known corpus of repertoire. That such a need should be identified, however, indicates a desire on the parts of the institutions behind these initiatives to maintain the tradition of vigorous singing by Welsh crowds. Set against the weakening of the cultural infrastructure through which the tradition was originally cultivated, such efforts point to the enduring strength of the association of singing and the crowd within Wales. Participation in the sporting crowd, as Dilwyn Porter argues, can be the type of shared experience that is 'important in shaping the *habitus* out of which an individual's sense of national identity grows'.[56] The prominence of mass musical participation in widely held notions of Welsh identity thus makes it unsurprising that organisations such as the FAW and WRU have been anxious to perpetuate the tradition of passionate singing by Welsh supporters. Though formal religious observance is an increasingly minority activity in Wales, the continued singing of Christian hymns by the crowd indicates that awareness of the nation's religious heritage, and especially the prominence of hymnody in nonconformist worship, is significant. The act of singing together and, moreover, singing particular repertoire, remains central to notions of what it means for a Welsh crowd to express its identity, pride and commitment. Anderson describes how the singing of national anthems creates 'an experience of simultaneity. At precisely such moments, people wholly unknown to each other utter the same verses to the same melody. The image: unisonance'.[57]

The importance of specific repertoire highlights the role of the Welsh language in the construction of the crowd's identity. Although spoken by

---

[54] Twitter @WelshRugbyUnion, https://twitter.com/WelshRugbyUnion/status/1171331167485927425 (accessed 29 April 2021).
[55] 'Rugby World Cup: Japanese Children Sing Calon Lan to Wales Players', www.bbc.co.uk/news/av/uk-wales-49714999 (accessed 29 April 2021).
[56] Dilwyn Porter, 'Sport and National Identity', *The Oxford Handbook of Sports History*, ed. by Robert Edelman and Wayne Wilson (Oxford: Oxford University Press, 2017), p. 479.
[57] Anderson, *Imagined Communities*, p. 145.

a minority of the population in Wales, ranging between 25.2 per cent in 2010 and 29.6 per cent in 2019, the Welsh language appears to have a symbolic significance in terms of the singing of the crowd.[58] Wynne Evans's instructional videos as part of BBC Wales's campaign to teach the nation to sing 'Calon Lân' were squarely aimed at an audience with, at most, a limited knowledge of the language and its pronunciation. By providing phonetic guidance and advice on vocal production of sounds such as 'll' that have no English equivalent, the emphasis was very much on performance rather than understanding. This suggests that the language itself matters more than the precise meaning of the words being sung. The desire that the 'hen iaith' ('old language') of the Welsh anthem should continue to be on the lips of the singing crowd emphasises difference and uniqueness. While English may be the first or indeed only language of most Welsh football or rugby supporters, singing in Welsh stands as an aural marker separating them from their opposing counterparts, most especially in the context of annual Six Nations rugby fixtures against England, Scotland and Ireland.

These examples also demonstrate the significant role played by the media in perpetuating notions of Welsh musicality in relation to national identity. Singing is presented to listeners and viewers as a quintessential feature of a Welsh crowd's efforts to support its national team and that enthusiastic participation. The BBC Wales 'Calon Lân' campaign in particular sought to encourage individual supporters to make a public display of their commitment to the collective whole. The participation of familiar presenters as well as the professional musicians of the BBC National Orchestra of Wales and choristers of all ages was an effort to cultivate a mutual sense of belonging, a sense that the general Welsh public, publicly recognised figures and national institutions shared a common pride in their national identity and desire to encourage the national rugby team. The FAW's #TogetherStronger campaign and the WRU's engagement of Bryn Terfel to provide vocal coaching for the national rugby team in 2019 followed a similar pattern, while placing a particular emphasis on encouraging affinity between players and supporters. The football team's players, including its highest-profile stars, were heavily involved in promoting #TogetherStronger, and the enthusiasm of the supporters' renditions of 'Mae Hen Wlad fy Nhadau' were matched by the visibly impassioned singing of the team members themselves. Their

---

[58] 'Welsh Language Data from the Annual Population Survey: July 2019 to June 2020', https://gov.wales/welsh-language-data-annual-population-survey-july-2019-june-2020 (accessed 29 April 2021).

singing was in marked contrast to that of some of their counterparts of earlier generations, many of whom had stood in solemn silence during the singing of the anthem.

Singing remains a central element in the expression of the Welsh crowd's national identity and pride, but in a manner that has become conspicuously performative. Media coverage, and the influence of social media in particular, have shaped this trend. While replica football and rugby jerseys along with team scarves and hats have long been widely worn by supporters on match days, the display of national emblems in the orchestral and choral performance of 'Calon Lân' for BBC Wales's 2014 campaign extended far beyond such customs. From children dressed in daffodil and leek costumes to adult singers holding Welsh-themed inflatables and orchestral players wearing waistcoats and bowties emblazoned with the Welsh dragon and adorning their instruments with daffodils, the patriotic nature of the performance is overtly expressed visually and audibly. Though the orchestral musicians are in formal concert wear, albeit it with national accoutrements, the singers' uniform is both far less strictly defined and deliberately casual. The visual effect seems designed to evoke the crowd in the stadium, yet it is part of a professionally produced and thoroughly planned performance. In this regard, the costumes of the singers are a visual counterpart to Jeffrey Howard's lavish musical arrangement. Both have their roots in the traditions of the crowd but present them in an idealised fashion that relies on the professionalism of Howard and the orchestral musicians and a carefully choreographed display of apparent visual spontaneity and exuberance to achieve its effect.

Taken together, the use of specific repertoire, the symbolic importance of the Welsh language and the conspicuous performance of national identity and pride combine to perpetuate the rich musical heritage of the Welsh crowd, reinterpreting and reimagining that heritage for a twenty-first-century context. No longer able to rely on the institutional cultures that nurtured and sustained the tradition over many decades, a media-rich culture has found new means of educating, encouraging and connecting supporters to ensure the continued vitality of the crowd's song.

CHAPTER 16

Postscript
Contemporary Wales, Devolution and Digitisation

Trevor Herbert, Sally Harper and Sarah Hill

The historical legacy of Welsh music in modern times has been mentioned in several chapters in this book. Music making continues to be one of the favourite forms of leisure activity in the country. Choralism and various forms of instrumental music (such as brass bands) are especially popular, eisteddfodau continue to thrive and the historic importance of the harp in Wales is easily evidenced by its common presence in schools and homes and the steady supply of performers that Wales provides to the music profession. Also, at the time of writing (2022), the country's two major performance institutions, Welsh National Opera and the BBC National Orchestra of Wales, have achieved sustained international success. The pop music industry continues to be buoyant and there is a thriving intellectual life in the country. All this must be seen in the context of major infrastructural changes that have taken place since the end of the second millennium.

Writing of the present and future in a book that is devoted to history is a perilous and uncomfortable business, not least because both lack the certainty and permanence of the past; but with these points in mind, and mindful too that this book is intended for a global audience, many of whom may never visit Wales, this Postscript provides an overview of the most recent stages of Welsh music history and the relationship of the country to the modern world. As has always been the case, the musical life of Wales in the twenty-first century is a product both of its past and of extramusical interventions, but in this phase the interventions have been technological and political as well as sociocultural.

The *Government of Wales Acts* of 1998 and 2006, which legislated for the devolution of administrative powers from the British Parliament to a Welsh National Assembly in Cardiff (from 2020 called Senedd Cymru (the Welsh Parliament)), initiated a chain of consequences. For example, the new status of Wales as a devolved nation obliged public and private agencies operating in the country to consider the implications of this for their future operation. Furthermore, it quickly became obvious that new national administrations were keen to use devolved powers to project the distinctiveness of Wales as a cultural as well as a political and socio-economic entity.

These events occurred coincidentally but almost simultaneously with wide-scale digitisation and the ubiquitous use of the internet. The age of computing had commenced a decade or two earlier, but it was at the turn of the millennium that its place in the routines of normal life was consolidated. This, of course, was not a Welsh phenomenon – it happened in all developed countries; but thoughts about any nation's cultural path in this period are bound to take it into account. Digital technology introduced profound and transformative effects in the way lives were led. Some aspects were mundane, but fundamentally, the new age (for that is how it should be seen) can be realistically compared to the impact of the introduction of print in Europe in the fifteenth century.[1] There were direct implications for music. At a technical level new models and methods of cultural production and distribution for the music industry were introduced. This affected the entire music business, particularly, but not exclusively, the popular music industry. But the most important prospect was the promise of increasingly powerful and democratic modes of local and global communication in which easier and faster distribution systems for musical products could be deployed. For historians and other researchers, it revolutionised the way knowledge, including knowledge of the musical past and present, could be investigated, curated and displayed to global audiences.

The combined effects of Welsh devolution and digitisation quickly became apparent. In the two decades following 2000, the BBC became increasingly decentralised; Wales became a major production centre for projects destined for the Corporation's UK and global audiences, prompting a growth in the infrastructure of the Welsh media industry more generally. In 2020 'Creative Wales' was initiated as an agency within the Welsh government to encourage growth across the creative sector and nurture new talent and skills. In that year the creative industries contributed £2.2 billion to the Welsh economy and provided employment for 56,000 people in Wales: an increase of 40 per cent over the previous ten-year period.[2]

From early in the millennium, the National Library of Wales, based at Aberystwyth from the time of its foundation in 1907 – a location central to

---

[1] For example, see John Naughton, *From Gutenberg to Zuckerberg: What You Really Need to Know About the Internet* (London: Quercus, 2014).

[2] www.wales.com/creative-wales (accessed 14 July 2021).

the geography of the country, but distant from its main centres of population – embarked on major digitisation projects aimed at providing remote access to swathes of its collections. Perhaps the most important effect of digitisation (combined with the requirements of Welsh-language legislation), was the provision of universal access to bilingual internet sites and simultaneous translation services, which made Welsh-language cultural products accessible to those who could not speak or understand the language.

The Welsh Language and Its Cultural Agencies

In the post-globalisation age, the musical genres, practices and agencies that have been defined by the Welsh language retain an important place. Devolution did not introduce the primary measures that protected the language: the Welsh Language Acts (1967 and 1993), which ensured equality for the Welsh and English languages in Wales,[3] preceded devolution, as did the establishment of the Welsh-language national radio station BBC Radio Cymru in 1977 and the Welsh-language television channel Sianel Pedwar Cymru (S4C) in 1982. The measures had a positive effect. The 2011 UK Census showed that 19 per cent of the Welsh population could 'understand, speak, read or write, in Welsh', and the Welsh Government's Annual Population Survey for the year ending December 2021[4] showed that, of the population over three years old, 892,200 persons (about 29.5 per cent) were able to 'speak Welsh'.[5] An interesting and encouraging feature revealed in the 2011 Census is that the greatest increase in Welsh-language competence is among teenagers, undoubtedly a consequence of the increased availability of schools that teach through the medium of the Welsh language.

Eisteddfodau have continued to play an important part in musical life. The National Eisteddfod of Wales (Eisteddfod Genedlaethol Cymru), held

---

[3] Public bodies in Wales are required to create and deploy a Welsh Language Scheme, which must be approved by a Welsh government agency. See www.gov.uk/government/organisations/valuation-office-agency/about/welsh-language-scheme#introduction (accessed 14 July 2021).

[4] https://gov.wales/welsh-language-data-annual-population-survey-2021, Welsh language data from the Annual Population Survey: 2021 | GOV.WALES (accessed 12 April 2022). The URL for this information changes as new survey data is published. The latest data is easily accessed by searching the GOV.WALES internet site. The Welsh government's 'Cymraeg 2050 Strategy' aims for a million speakers by 2050 https://gov.wales/sites/default/files/publications/2018–12/cymraeg-2050-welsh-language-strategy.pdf (accessed 22 July 2021).

[5] This data was drawn only from those resident in Wales – it did not take account of others living outside the country who could speak and understand the language, so the overall number of Welsh speakers is higher.

in the first week of August each year, attracts about 6,000 competitors annually and total attendances of about 160,000. It is advertised as a 'showcase for music, dance, the visual arts and literature, original performances and much more'.[6] The Festival itself operates solely though the medium of Welsh, but a translation service is provided. Despite the Welsh-only policy, many entrants in musical performance contests may not be Welsh-speaking. The National Eisteddfod's online presence is bilingual and includes an archive of previous events. There are permanent eisteddfod offices in Cardiff and Wrexham, but local committees play an essential part in the organisation of the annual festivals, which are held alternately in north and south Wales. There also continue to be local eisteddfodau; many schools hold eisteddfodau each St David's Day (1 March: the patronal festival). The main national event for children and young people, also through the medium of Welsh, is the annual Urdd Eisteddfod (Eisteddfod yr Urdd). It too is itinerant and attracts more than 90,000 visitors each year. The National and the Urdd eisteddfodau maintain an important focus for amateur music across Wales at local levels. Most of Wales's leading musicians, amateur and professional, are alumni of the eisteddfod system.

S4C transmits the proceedings of National and Urdd eisteddfodau. With the Welsh-language radio station BBC Radio Cymru, it is also the default broadcaster for most music that is embedded in Welsh-language traditions. Among S4C's most enduring programmes are *Dechrau Canu, Dechrau Canmol* (Start Singing, Start Praising) which is centred on communal hymn singing, and *Noson Lawen* (Merry Evening), a modern version of the community entertainments held in rural areas from at least the nineteenth century. While S4C is a Welsh-language broadcaster, it too uses digital technology for simultaneous translation and offers alternative English-language commentary options for many of its most popular programmes, including sports fixtures.

A major new agency Coleg Cymraeg Cenedlaethol (Welsh National College)[7] was established in 2011 to support the Welsh language in higher education and, from 2016, the entire post-16-year-old education sector. Coleg Cymraeg's purpose is essentially strategic, but musical activity has benefited from its work. It sponsored the reference book *Cydymaith i Gerddoriaeth Cymru* (*Handbook of Welsh Music*; 2018) and its transfer to digital form,[8] and sponsors the online journal *Gwerddon* which has

---

[6] https://eisteddfod.wales/about-us (accessed 9 August 2021).
[7] www.colegcymraeg.ac.uk/en/ (accessed 14 July 2021).
[8] https://wici.porth.ac.uk/index.php/Categori:Cerddoriaeth (accessed 14 July 2021).

16 Postscript: Contemporary Wales

devoted a special issue to music.[9] Coleg Cymraeg's purpose is to develop easy and effective use of the Welsh language. It makes a positive impression: it is well organised, has government backing and shows signs of becoming a leading intellectual force in the country.

Institutions and Agencies

The Arts Council of Wales was founded in 1994 to promote the arts in Wales.[10] Among its major clients for public funding are the BBC National Orchestra of Wales (otherwise funded by the BBC) and Welsh National Opera. Both organisations are based at the Wales Millennium Centre in Cardiff which includes the first and only modern purpose-built opera house in Wales (see Figure 16.1). The BBC Hoddinott Hall, also at the Wales Millennium Centre, is a state-of-the-art recording and broadcasting studio that also functions as a small concert auditorium. The main concert hall in Wales is the St David's Hall in Cardiff. Both Welsh National Opera

Figure 16.1 The Wales Millennium Centre, Cardiff Bay; completed 2009. By kind permission of the Wales Millennium Centre, Cardiff

---

[9] www.gwerddon.cymru/en/virtualspecialeditions/music/ (accessed 9 August 2021).
[10] This is the date of the award of a Royal Charter. A previous body with the name the Welsh Arts Council was established in 1967, when a precedent set by Scotland led to the establishment of discrete national bodies for the administration of the arts. Previously (from 1950) there was a Welsh Committee of the Arts Council of Great Britain. The Arts Council Wales website gives access to its 'Research and Evaluation' surveys, https://arts.wales/ (accessed 31 December 2020).

and the BBC National Orchestra of Wales spend part of their time touring. They attract many of the greatest soloists and conductors and are counted as leading performance organisations on the global stage. The St David's Hall hosts the biennial BBC Cardiff Singer of the World competition, one of the most important international events for lieder and opera singing.[11] Since 1947 the small, picturesque northern town of Llangollen has hosted the International Music Eisteddfod, which is a major multicultural music festival. By 2020 more than 300,000 competitors from over 100 nationalities had taken part.[12] Many other annual music festivals take place in towns throughout Wales;[13] among these is the Brecon Jazz Festival which annually attracts a large international attendance of jazz enthusiasts.[14]

Tŷ Cerdd (Music House), based at the Wales Millennium Centre, is a major agency charged with the curation and promotion of Welsh music. It also distributes funding for music projects on behalf of the Arts Council of Wales and the UK's National Lottery Fund. The organisation and funding of the National Youth Orchestra, Brass Band and Choir of Wales, as well the equivalent ensembles for Dance and Theatre are organised by National Youth Arts Wales (Celfyddydau Cenedlaethol Ieuenctid Cymru).[15]

Education and Training

Most western music cultures utilise education and training systems based on overlapping formal and informal processes, and this has been the case in Wales. Amateur and community music making in choirs, bands and orchestras runs parallel with institutional processes such as school curricula, higher education systems and private tuition. Informal participatory local groups play a vital part in the supply to formal training and thence, for some, to the music profession. Informal systems are difficult to quantify, but a 2020 study of the provision of music education for children in Wales showed significant levels of inconsistency in the publicly funded sector.[16] This is a consequence of changes, regarded by many as unwelcome, to funding models for music education in the later

---

[11] BBC Cardiff Singer of the World, www.bbc.co.uk/programmes/articles/11xGqjdDnrX5FzR2y9M Zz8r/about-cardiff-singer (accessed 14 January 2021).
[12] Llangollen International Musical Eisteddfod, https://international-eisteddfod.co.uk/ (accessed 13 January 2021).
[13] BBC Wales Music www.bbc.co.uk/wales/music/sites/festivals-events/ (accessed 14 January 2021).
[14] Brecon Jazz Festival, https://breconjazz.org/ (accessed 14 January 2021).
[15] www.nyaw.org.uk/ (accessed 17 June 2021).
[16] *Music Services Feasibility Study*, Welsh Government, Education Wales (2020) https://gov.wales/sites/def ault/files/publications/2020-01/music-services-feasibility-study-final-report.pdf (accessed 31 December 2020).

decades of the twentieth century. From the late 1950s Welsh local authorities provided an important layer of funding for free music education which impacted significantly on opportunities for talented young musicians to learn and perform, irrespective of their financial means. This infrastructure embraced schools, county youth orchestras, bands and choirs and ultimately national bodies such as the National Youth Orchestra of Wales, which at the time of its foundation in 1945 was the first such ensemble of its kind. The rich and widely distributed network of opportunities of that time has been compared to *El Sistema*, the much-celebrated Venezuelan music education project founded in 1975 by Jose Antonio Abreu which, with remarkable success, simultaneously developed musical talent and, so it is claimed, contributed to wider positive social developments in the country.[17] The Welsh version of *El Sistema* was implemented significantly earlier but obtained the same effect with emphatic success: it was widely regretted that public funding for music education in Wales became more restricted in the later decades of the twentieth century.[18]

Higher education institutions in Wales attract an international studentship and many Welsh students study music in universities and conservatoires outside Wales. Cardiff University and Bangor University provide undergraduate and postgraduate programmes in music, while the Royal Welsh College of Music and Drama, part of the University of South Wales, provides conservatoire education at undergraduate and postgraduate level. The University of South Wales is also the specialist centre for undergraduate and postgraduate programmes in music business, technology and media. The Open University, the UK-wide distance-learning institution, also has a headquarters in Wales and offers undergraduate and postgraduate programmes in music throughout Wales; this book is edited by members of its music department. Some of the main initiatives in Welsh music research have emerged from Bangor University, which hosts the Centre for Advanced Welsh Music Studies. Among its major achievements has been the issue of the seven-volume academic journal *Welsh Music History/Hanes Cerddoriaeth Cymru*.

Scholarship and Its Sources

The National Library of Wales at Aberystwyth is the sole copyright deposit library in Wales and the main repository for its archives, including the

---

[17] See, however, Geoffrey Baker, *El Sistema: Orchestrating Venezuela's Youth* (Oxford: Oxford University Press, 2014) for a detailed critique of this programme.

[18] The oboist John Anderson made this point in a presentation to former members of the Glamorgan Youth Orchestra on 9 June 2021. In May 2022 the Welsh Government announced a National Plan for Music Education.

Screen and Sound Archive of audiovisual material relating to Wales.[19] In 2017 it launched its Welsh Music Archive, which claims to have the most extensive collection of Welsh music in the form of printed and manuscript materials, audio and video recordings and the archives of relevant individuals and institutions.[20] The Library also has an extensive open-access digitisation programme which, as this book is being written, has made available more than half a million items. Some are accessible through permalinks in this book and a list of some of the most valuable digitised items is also given in Appendix 3. The Library also provides free access to a large quantity of digitised periodical publications. They include searchable copies of most newspapers published in Wales (in English or Welsh) before 1919 and more than 450 journals relating to Wales published between 1735 and 2007. In the latter category are most Wales-specific music journals.[21] The St Fagans National Museum of History near Cardiff holds materials relating to traditional music, as well as a collection of musical instruments and oral history recordings of interviewees discussing and performing traditional music, some of which are online.[22] Smaller Welsh museums sometimes hold limited but important collections; for example, the Cyfarthfa Castle Museum at Merthyr Tydfil holds the instruments and original partbooks of the Cyfarthfa Band which is discussed in Chapter 13 of this book. Tŷ Cerdd, Cardiff, has an important multimedia archive of music by Welsh composers as well as other archive sources relevant to Welsh music, including material from the former Welsh Music Information Centre. Much of this material is available online.[23]

Interdisciplinarity and Data Storage

Online resources make an important contribution to the dissemination of knowledge, but the fundamental detection and interrogation of sources about Welsh music history continues to depend on skills developed in the analogue age. This includes research into the Welsh musical past and Welsh studies more generally. The national academy for arts and sciences

---

[19] www.library.wales/collections/learn-more/screen-sound-archive (accessed 22 July 2021).
[20] www.library.wales/collections/learn-more/archives/the-welsh-music-archive (accessed 13 January 2021).
[21] Each of these resources can be accessed through the Library's homepage www.library.wales/ (accessed 22 July 2021).
[22] https://museum.wales/stfagans/ (accessed 13 January 2021).
[23] https://www.tycerdd.org/ (accessed 13 January 2021).

in Wales is the Learned Society of Wales (Cymdeithas Ddysgedig Cymru), which was established in 2010. It exists to champion research, promote learning and debate and contribute expertise. It does this through its elected Fellows, of whom there are more than 500. The Society lists the development of the profile of Wales studies across academic disciplines as one of its strategic priorities.[24] *The Cambridge History of Welsh Literature* (2019)[25] evidences such endeavour, as do other publications that have indirect relevance to music history, such as the *Chronicles of Medieval Wales and the March* (2020),[26] a volume which complements the more extensive three-volume *Repertory of Welsh Manuscripts and their Scribes c.800 – c.1800* (2022) by Daniel Huws, which in turn brings to light a mass of evidence of the contexts of other primary sources in early Welsh cultural history.[27] The latter work is published by the University of Wales Centre for Advanced Welsh and Celtic Studies, which is an important agency for detailed and prolonged research of major topics in Welsh cultural history. Among its major projects have been 'Iolo Morganwg and the Romantic Tradition in Wales 1740–1918', and 'The Celtic Languages and Cultural Identity'.[28]

Digitisation does more than transfer data from one form into another: it holds the promise of revolutionary approaches to the ways history is studied and understood. It makes research questions tenable that were previously impractical to ask, and equally important, it allows old and apparently well-settled questions to be revisited with entirely new techniques. The challenge of preserving large data sets for posterity is formidable, and this is as true in Wales as elsewhere. Major institutions such as the National Library of Wales have robust systems in this regard, but the stability and permanence of important data sets is not yet fully embraced by central processes analogous to those that operate for print products through copyright deposit libraries.[29] It is an issue that is especially

---

[24] www.learnedsociety.wales/ (accessed 14 July 2021).
[25] Geraint Evans and Helen Fulton, eds., *The Cambridge History of Welsh Literature* (Cambridge: Cambridge University Press, 2019).
[26] Ben Guy, Georgia Henley, Owain Wyn Jones and Rebecca Thomas, eds., *The Chronicles of Medieval Wales and the March: New Contexts, Studies and Texts* (Turnhout: Brepols, 2020).
[27] Daniel Huws, *A Repertory of Welsh Manuscripts and Scribes c.800–c.1800* (Aberystwyth: University of Wales Centre for Advanced Welsh and Celtic Studies and the National Library of Wales, 2022).
[28] www.wales.ac.uk/en/CentreforAdvancedWelshCelticStudies/IntroductiontotheCentre.aspx (accessed 22 July 2021).
[29] This provision appears to be in hand, but adherence to it is not common practice among those who create important open-access data sets. See www.bl.uk/help/how-to-deposit-your-digital-publications (accessed 20 September 2021).

important as this book goes to press, with signs in some countries of a shift from 'cold storage', in which data sets are acknowledged to have a maximum life at which time they are expired, and 'warm storage', which offers the prospect of preservation in perpetuity.

Welsh Pop and New Media

One of the most interesting aspects of musical life in the twenty-first century is found in the development of the music industry, particularly popular music. The business models that operate in the pop music industry have always struck a balance between live performances and the sale of audio recordings and other products. The most recent species of delivery for commercial recordings, and probably the most likely to achieve permanence, is streaming. In December 2018, the internet streaming service Spotify announced that the first Welsh band to pass a million plays on the platform was a teenaged duo called Alffa. Their song 'Gwenwyn' ('Poison') had been included in a number of Spotify-curated playlists, which gave them unprecedented exposure across the southern hemisphere. Their career arc is notable: they formed while still at school in Llanrug and were soon named as participants in the Horizons/Gorwelion scheme, a partnership between BBC Cymru Wales and the Arts Council of Wales created in 2014 to promote contemporary Welsh music at home and abroad. Alffa benefited not only from institutionally supported showcase events in Wales but from a global platform where all musics are theoretically treated equally. A song in Welsh could sit easily on a playlist alongside a song in Spanish or Portuguese; in the new media landscape, inclusion on a corporate-curated playlist is enough to build an audience anywhere in the world.[30]

One of the running themes of the brief history of Welsh popular music has been the inevitability of generational change: when 'the system' stops working, a new system takes its place. This is true of genre shifts (from acoustic to electric, from folk to rock, from rock to punk), industry mechanisms (mainstream vs. underground, professional vs. amateur),

---

[30] The financial reward for international Spotify success is less clear, however, and is unlikely to be enough to sustain a career. The issue of artists' royalties on platforms such as Spotify and iTunes has generated a great deal of chatter in the industry and in popular music and media studies; but as with any new technological developments, analyses often seem outdated by the time they are published. A recent summary of the royalties system from the perspective of a mainstream French industry executive offers a fair snapshot of the first half of 2021: www.musicbusinessworldwide.com/the-streaming-music-industry-must-switch-to-a-fair-and-logical-payout-model-there-is-no-time-to-lose/ (accessed 29 June 2021).

and linguistic choice (Anglophone, Welsh or bilingual). In the case of the digital revolution, the historically dominant music industry structure was subverted: it was no longer necessary for a band to have major-label support, or to record in a studio or to sing in English. Though schemes such as Horizons/Gorwelion may not last indefinitely, they do provide the training and support necessary for any young person looking to build a career on this new terrain.[31] It is impossible to know what the Welsh music industry will face in future; but if the development of Welsh 'popular music' over the past century has proven anything, it is that Welsh culture can adapt to challenge and build new traditions.

---

[31] It is important to note the role played here by Alun Llwyd, founder of Recordiau Ankst and manager of Super Furry Animals and others, whose company, PYST, is the first Welsh distribution service established to support independent artists. Because of his long engagement with Welsh-language activism (he is a former chair of Cymdeithas yr Iaith) and his experience of the Welsh music industry at the dawn of 'Cool Cymru', he is an obvious steward of the new generation of Welsh bands through the digital thickets.

APPENDIX I

Selective, Chronological List of Traditional Music Published up to 1920

The table includes selected publications of Welsh traditional music up to 1920, a date which encompasses the early publications of the Welsh Folk-Song Society and its pioneering members J. Lloyd Williams, Ruth Herbert Lewis and Grace Gwyneddon Davies. A much fuller bibliography, which includes the main printed collections up to 2004 and covers research publications about Welsh traditional music, is found in Wyn Thomas's *Cerddoriaeth Draddodiadol yng Nghymru: Llyfryddiaeth/Traditional Music in Wales: Bibliography*, 3rd ed. (Llanrwst: Gwasg Carreg Gwalch, 2006).

Date	Author/editor/compiler	Title	Publication	Comments	Link to digitised source
c.1726	Urquahart, Alex, Dermot O'Connar, Hugh Edwards	*Aria di Camera: being A Choice Collection of Scotch, Irish & Welsh Air's*	London: Printed for Dan. Wright and Dan. Wright Junr.	Digitised by the National Library of Wales.	http://hdl.handle.net/10107/4796728
1742	Parry, John (Ruabon), Evan Williams	*Antient British Music*	London: Printed for and sold by the Compilers	Digitised by the National Library of Wales. Intended as Part 1. Part 2 remained unpublished; the MS, dated 1745, was found in the library of the Royal College of Music, London in the 1970s (GB-Lcm MS4861).	http://hdl.handle.net/10107/4675582
1752 or 1761	Parry, John (Ruabon)	*A Collection of Welsh, English and Scotch Airs*	London: Printed for and sold by the Author	Digitised by the National Library of Wales. Some uncertainty about the publication date; both 1752 and 1761	http://hdl.handle.net/10107/4675850

(cont.)

Date	Author/editor/compiler	Title	Publication	Comments	Link to digitised source
				have been given, but evidence for 1752 is thin. Digitised copy is 1761.	
1781	Parry, John (Ruabon)	*British Harmony*	Ruabon and London: Printed for and Sold by John Parry, Ruabon, Denbighshire & P. Hodgson, London	Digitised by the National Library of Wales.	Two copies, http://hdl.handle.net/10107/558633 and http://hdl.handle.net/10107/4675640
1784	Jones, Edward	*Musical and Poetical Relicks of the Welsh Bards*	London: Printed for the Author	Digitised by the National Library of Wales. The 2nd edition of 1794 was significantly expanded; 4th ed., 1825	1784 ed. – http://hdl.handle.net/10107/4675108 ; 1794 ed. – http://hdl.handle.net/10107/4674868 ; 4th ed., 1825 – http://hdl.handle.net/10107/4675201
c.1796	Biggs, Edward Smith	*Six Welch Airs*	London: Robert Birchall	Digitised by the National Library of Wales. Digitised edition tentatively dated 1795.	http://hdl.handle.net/10107/4842449

1800	Biggs, Edward Smith	*A Second Sett of Welch Airs*	London: Robert Birchall	Digitised by the National Library of Wales.	http://hdl.handle.net/10107/4828573
1800	Hulse, Henry	*The Beauties of Cambrian Melodies*	Caernarvon: H. Humphreys		
1801–187	Jones, Owen (Owain Myfyr) Edward Williams (Iolo Morganwg), William Owen Pughe (Idrison)	*The Myvyrian Archaiology of Wales*	London: S. Rousseau	3 vols, digitised by the National Library of Wales. Vol. 3 contains a copy by Iolo Morganwg of the Robert ap Huw MS. 1870: 2nd ed., with explanatory chapter by John Thomas (Pencerdd Gwalia).	http://hdl.handle.net/10107/4805623
1802	Jones, Edward	*The Bardic Museum*	London: A. Strahan	Digitised by the National Library of Wales.	http://hdl.handle.net/10107/4675439
1803	Bingley, William	*Sixty of the most admired Welsh airs*	London: E. Williams		
1804	Bingley, William	*North Wales; Including its Scenery, Antiquities, Customs and Some Sketches of*	London: T. N. Longman and O. Rees	2 vols. Vol. 2 includes 'A Sketch of the History of the Welsh Bards and Music' and 'Sixteen admired Welsh	https://archive.org/details/northwalesdelinoobinggoog

(cont.)

Date	Author/editor/compiler	Title	Publication	Comments	Link to digitised source
1804	Parry, John (Bardd Alaw)	its Natural History The Ancient Britons' Martial Music	London	Airs'. Available in Internet Archive.	
1806–7	Crotch, William	Specimens of Various Styles of Music	London: Robert Birchall	Includes forty-two Welsh tunes. An edition of 1808 is available in Internet Archive.	https://archive.org/details/specimensofvariooocrot
1809	Parry, John (Bardd Alaw)	A Selection of Welsh Melodies	London: Bland & Wellers		
1809, 1811, 1817	Thomson, George	A Select Collection of Original Welsh Airs	London: Edinburgh: T. Preston, G. Thomson	3 vols, 1809, 1811, 1817. Arrangements by Haydn, Beethoven and Kozeluch.	
1810	Parry, John (Bardd Alaw)	A Collection of Welsh Airs	London: Goulding & Company		
1810	Parry, John (Bardd Alaw)	National Melodies	London		

1810	Parry, John (Ruabon)	Cambrian Harmony	London		2 vols.
1811	Hart, W. Burton	Annual Cambrian Trifles or South Wales Polite Repertory of Country Dances for 1812	London		Reprinted by the Welsh Folk Dance Society/ Cymdeithas Ddawns Werin Cymru, 1994, ed./ gol. Robin Huw Bowen.
1813–14	Jansen, Louis	Twelve favourite Welch airs, or melodies	London		
1817	Dovaston, J. F. M.	A Selection of British Melodies	Dublin and London: W. Power's Music House		2 vols, 1817, 1820
1820, 1825	Jones, Edward	Hên Ganiadau Cymru	London	http://hdl.handle.net/10107/4675268	Published in two parts, 1820 and 1825. NLW has digitised a composite volume tentatively dated 1825.
1822	Parry, John (Bardd Alaw)	A Selection of Welsh Melodies	London		
1825	Leathart, William	Welsh Pennillion	London: W. T. Moncrieff		
1828?	Parry, John (Bardd Alaw)	Pen Rhaw: Welsh Melody with Variation for the Harp	London: J. Power		

(cont.)

Date	Author/editor/compiler	Title	Publication	Comments	Link to digitised source
1829	Roberts, Richard	*Cambrian Harmony*	Dublin: Published for the author		
c.1835	Hayden, H. S.	*A Collection of the Most Popular Welsh Airs*	London: Zenas T. Purday		
1839	Parry, John (Bardd Alaw)	*The Welsh Harper*	London and Chester: D'Almaine and Co. and E. Parry	Second volume published 1848 (see separate entry). Digitised by the National Library of Wales.	http://hdl.handle.net/10107/4675974
1841	Parry, John (Bardd Alaw)	*Two Thousand Melodies*	London: D'Almaine and Co.	Includes a number of previously unpublished Welsh airs.	
1844	Williams, Maria Jane	*Ancient National Airs of Gwent and Morganwg*	Llandovery: William Rees	1988, Cymdeithas Alawon Gwerin Cymru: Aberystwyth, a facsimile of the 1844 edition; with Introduction and notes by Daniel Huws. 1844 ed. digitised by the National Library of Wales.	http://hdl.handle.net/10107/5726885

Date	Author	Title	Publisher	Notes	URL
1845	Thomas, John (Ieuan Ddu)	*Y Caniedydd Cymreig/The Cambrian Minstrel*	Merthyr Tydvil: David Jones	Digitised by the National Library of Wales.	http://hdl.handle.net/10107/5727212
1848	Parry, John (Bardd Alaw)	*The Welsh Harper ... Volume II*	London: D'Almaine and Co.	The MS collections included those of Owen Jones (Owain Myfyr) and John Jenkins (Ifor Ceri). Some airs reprinted by permission from Maria Jane Williams's 1844 collection. Digitised by the National Library of Wales as a single item with Volume 1.	http://hdl.handle.net/10107/4675974
1849?	Owen, William	*Seren Bethlehem*	Caernarfon: William Owen		
c.1850	Pryse, John	*The Cambrian Melodist*	Llanidloes: J. Pryse		
c.1850–5	Jones, Edward	*A Choice Collection of Welsh Airs*	Caernarvon: H. Humphreys		
1850?	Iolen, Pugh	*Y Carolydd*	Llanrwst: argraphwyd dros y cyhoeddwr gan John Jones	Five carol arrangements.	

(*cont.*)

Date	Author/editor/compiler	Title	Publication	Comments	Link to digitised source
1854	Williams, Maria Jane	*Ancient Welsh Music*	Tenby: R. Mason	Twenty melodies from the MS collection of John Jenkins (Ifor Ceri), reprinted from *The Cambrian Journal*. Appears to have been published again (Tenby, 1859) with John Jenkins's name in place of Maria Jane Williams.	
1857	Jones, J. D.	*Caniadau Bethlehem*	Rhuthyn: Isaac Clarke	Christmas carols set to traditional melodies.	
1857	Morris, T. D.	*A Selection of the Most Popular Welsh Airs*	Chester; London: Catherall & Prichard; D'Almaine and Co.		
1859?	Davidson, G. H.	*Davidson's Musical Miracles: Two hundred and fifty Welsh airs for a shilling*	London: Davidson	Facsimile reprint Felinfach: Llanerch, 1999?	

Date	Author	Title	Publisher	Notes	URL
1860? 1865?	Jones, J.D.	*Carolau Nadolig gyda Chymdeithranau*	Wrexham: Hughes	Includes twelve carols set to traditional melodies.	http://hdl.handle.net/10107/4796728
1860–4	Owen, John (Owain Alaw)	*Gems of Welsh Melody*	Ruthin: Isaac Clarke	Further publication dates: 1861, 1862, 1864, c.1870, 1873, c.1880. 2nd ed., London; Simpkin, Marshall & Co., and Wrexham; Hughes & Son. Digitised by the National Library of Wales.	
c.1860	William, E. Ylltyr	*Alawon y Bobl*	Llanerchymedd: Argraffwyd dros y cyhoeddwr gan Lewis Jones	Includes a number of traditional melodies. Sol-fa notation only.	
1861	Linley, George	*Selections of Welsh Melodies*	London		
1862, 1870, 1874	Thomas, John (Pencerdd Gwalia)	*Welsh Melodies*	London: Addison, Hollier and Lucas; Lamborn Cock & Co.; J. B. Cramer & Co.	4 vols. Vols 1 & 2 published 1862; Vol. 3, 1870; Vol. 4, 1874.	
1864–73	Roberts, John (Ieuan Gwyllt; gol.)	*Y Cerddor Cymreig*	By John Roberts to 1865; taken over by Hughes & Son, Wrexham, 1865	Between 1864 and 1873 the magazine included folk songs and national airs in a section entitled 'Ystafell yr Hen Alawon'.	

(cont.)

Date	Author/editor/compiler	Title	Publication	Comments	Link to digitised source
1865?	Williams, R. O.	*Newyddion Da am Enedigaeth Ceidwad*	Bethesda: R. Jones	Includes carols set to traditional melodies.	
1869	Davies, Owen Humphrey (Eos Llechid)	*Y Gyff Nadolig*	Wrexham: R. Hughes a'i Fab	Includes carols set to traditional melodies.	
1871	Mills, Richard	*Llyfr Carolau yn nodiant y solfa*	Wrexham: R. Hughes a'i Fab	Includes some traditional melodies. Sol-fa notation only. Also a two-volume publication called *Llyfr Carolau*, 1880 and 1885.	
1872	Miles, Alfred H.	*Our National Songs*	London	180 songs from England, Ireland, Scotland and Wales.	
1873, 1879	Richards, Brinley	*The Songs of Wales/Caneuon Cymru*	London: Boosey & Co.	4th, enlarged ed., 1879.	
1874	Jones, J. Eiddon	*Cerddor y Deml*	Wrecasm: Hughes a'i Fab	Selection of melodies from Richards, *Songs of Wales*.	

1874	Metzler & Co's Popular Music Library	Welsh Songs – No. 11	London: Metzler & Co.	
1874	Purday, Charles H., and John Thomas	The Songs of Wales: A Complete Collection of the Vocal Melodies of the Principality	London: J. B. Cramer & Co.	Digitised in Google Books. https://play.google.com/books/reader?id=NoiPIJ77sVoC
1884?	Peters, James (Afan Alaw)	James Peters' Selection of Welsh Airs for Drum and Fife Bands	Swansea: B. Parry	
1885	Jones, John (Idris Vychan)	An Essay on Pennillion Singing / Hanes a Henafiaeth Canu Gyda'r Tannau	London: Honourable Society of Cymmrodorion	Contains six penillion settings. Available online at Hathi Trust. https://babel.hathitrust.org/cgi/pt?id=uc1.b4440032&view=1up&seq=7&skin=2021
c.1886	Parry, John (Bardd Alaw)	A Select Collection of Welch Airs	London	
c.1889	Evans, D. Emlyn	Alawon Cymru / Melodies of Wales	Aberystwyth: D. Jenkins	Two parts. Further publications with the title Melodies of Wales and/or Alawon Cymru: Aberystwyth, 1900, 1905.
1891?	Smith, W. Gwynne	Selection of Welsh Airs for Drum and Fife Bands	Swansea: B. Parry	Sol-fa notation only.

(cont.)

Date	Author/editor/compiler	Title	Publication	Comments	Link to digitised source
1892	Boulton, Harold; Somervell, Arthur	*Songs of the Four Nations*	London: Cramer	Of fifty songs, twelve are Welsh.	
c.1893	Jenkins, David	*Cerddi Cymru i'r Plant/Welsh Airs for use in Day Schools*	Wrexham: Hughes & Son	Sol-fa notation only. Three vols.	
1893	Parry, Joseph; Rowlands, David	*Cambrian Minstrelsie (Alawon Gwalia)*	Edinburgh: T. C. & E. C. Jack	6 vols.	
1896	Bennett, Nicholas	*Alawon Fy Ngwlad – The Lays of My Land*	Newtown: Phillips & Son	2 vols, digitised as a single item by the National Library of Wales.	http://hdl.handle.net/10107/4676271
1898	Edwards, O. M. (gol.)	*Diliau'r Delyn: Alawon i Gyfarfodydd Urdd ac i Gartrefi Cymry ymbob man*	Gwrecsam: Hughes a'i Fab	Collection from the magazine *Cymru'r Plant*. Sol-fa notation only.	
1903?	Rhuddenfab (Lewis Jones)	*Y Delyn Aur*	Wrecsam	Sacred songs for Sunday School and Band of Hope, set to traditional melodies. Sol-fa only.	

1903	Roberts, Ellis (Eos Meirion)	Manual or Method of Instruction for Playing the Welsh Harp	London; Boston, MA: Vincent Music Co.; Oliver Ditson	The original MS won the prize at the Llangollen Eisteddfod of 1858.
1904, 1905	Bryan, Robert	Alawon y Celt	Caernarfon: W. Gwenlyn Evans	Two parts – Rhan 1, 1904; Rhan 2, 1905.
1904, 1907?		The People's Welsh Songs	London: J. Leng	Vol. 1, 1904; Vol. 2, 1907? Staff and sol-fa notation.
1905	Edwards, Thomas (gol.)	Carolau Nadolig Novello	London and New York: Novello and Company	Staff and sol-fa editions.
c.1905	Lewis, D. W., and L. D. Jones (Llew Tegid)	Caneuon y Plant/ The Children's Songbook	Cardiff: Educational Publishing Co.	3 vols (pamphlets)
1906	Moffat, Alfred	The Minstrelsy of Wales	London: Augener	
1906	Evans, Thomas Christopher (Cadrawd), and Harry Evans	Welsh Nursery Rhymes	Merthyr Tydfil: Educational Publishing Co.	
1907, 1909	Williams, J. Lloyd, and Arthur Somervell	Sixteen Welsh Melodies	London: Boosey & Co.	Part 1, 1907; Part 2, 1909.

(*cont.*)

Date	Author/editor/compiler	Title	Publication	Comments	Link to digitised source
1909–	Cymdeithas Alawon Gwerin Cymru/ Welsh Folk-Song Society	*Cylchgrawn Cymdeithas Alawon Cymru/ Journal of the Welsh Folk-Song Society*, renamed *Canu Gwerin/ Folk Song* from 1978		Includes many songs from oral, manuscript and published sources. 1909–77 issues digitised.	www.canugwerin.com/
1909	Evans, D. Emlyn	*Treasury of Welsh Songs*	Wrexham; Cardiff: Hughes & Son; Educational Publishing Co.	Published in various editions: piano, vocal, English and Welsh words, Welsh only, staff and sol-fa, sol-fa only.	
*c.*1909	Williams, J. Lloyd	*Ceinion y Canorion: Alawon Cymreig wedi eu trefnu i S.A.T.B.*	Bangor: Evan Thomas	Sol-fa.	
1910	Tomlyn, A.W., and D. Emlyn Evans	*Gem Selection: Songs of Wales*	Edinburgh: Andersons		

1911	Roberts, David (Telynor Mawddwy)	*Y Tant Aur; sef gwers-lyfr ar ganu gyda'r Delyn*	Abermaw: W. Jones	Penillion settings; the airs and vocal counterpoint in sol-fa only.
c.1912		*Eighteen Welsh Songs with Welsh and English Words: The Cavendish Music Books (Vol. 83)*	London: Boosey & Co.	
1913	Dewi Mai o Feirion	*Diliau'r Plant: Llawlyfr ar ganu gyda'r tannau*	Blaenau Ffestiniog: J. D. Davies & Co.	Sol-fa.
1913	Griffith, Robert	*Llyfr Cerdd Dannau, ymchwiliad i hanes hen gerddoriaeth a'r dulliau hynaf o ganu*	Caernarfon: Cwmni y Cyhoeddwyr Cymreig	Contains penillion settings.
1913	Griffith, Robert	*Y Delyn Gymreig*	Caernarfon: Cwmni y Cyhoeddwyr Cymreig	Arrangements for harp.
1913	Kidson, Frank	*Songs of Britain*	London: Boosey & Co.	
1914	Davies, Grace Gwyneddon	*Alawon Gwerin Môn*	Caernarvon: The Welsh Publishing Company	Two vols. All songs from oral sources.

(*cont.*)

Date	Author/editor/compiler	Title	Publication	Comments	Link to digitised source
1914	Lewis, Ruth Herbert	*Folk-Songs Collected in Flintshire and The Vale of Clwyd*	Wrexham: Hughes & Son	All songs from oral sources.	
1915	Lewis, P. H., and David Roberts (Telynor Mawddwy)	*Cainc y Delyn*	Abermaw: Telynor Mawddwy	Penillion settings.	
1919	Davies, W. Hubert	*Welsh Folk-Songs /Caneuon Gwerin Cymru*	Wrexham: Hughes & Son		
1920	Evans, T. Hopkin	*School Song Book*	Cardiff: Educational Publishing Co.	Staff and sofa editions.	
1920; 1923; 1924	Williams, J. Lloyd, and L. D. Jones (Llew Tegid)	*Alawon Gwerin Cymru/Welsh Folk Songs, Arranged for Schools*	Wrexham: Hughes & Son	3 vols. Piano edition and vocal edition in sol-fa.	

APPENDIX 2

Selective, Chronological List of Hymn Collections Published in Wales or for Use by Welsh Congregations from 1621 to 1900

Links to open-access digitised sources are given where they are known to exist, but some may be of later editions.

Date	Author/editor/compiler	Title	Publication	Comments	Link to Digitised Source
1621	Prys, Edmwnd	Llyfr y Psalmau	Llundain	Psalms and canticles; contains twelve tunes	http://hdl.handle.net/10107/5191521
1703	Baddy, Thomas	Hymnau Sacramentaidd Scrythurol	Unknown	Appended to *Pasc y Christion*, Baddy's translation of Thomas Dolittle's *The Christian Passover*; texts only	http://hdl.handle.net/10107/5421257
1705	Owen, James	Hymnau Scrythurol	Llundain	Texts only	http://hdl.handle.net/10107/5427228
1744	Williams (Pantycelyn), William	Aleluia	Caerfyrddin: Samuel Lewis	Texts only; six parts, 1744–17; including original hymns by Williams and other Welsh writers, and translations from English; reissued in a single volume in 1749 and later with *Hosanna i Fab Dafydd*	http://hdl.handle.net/10107/4772239; http://hdl.handle.net/10107/4772100; http://hdl.handle.net/10107/4772033; http://hdl.handle.net/10107/5393330; http://hdl.handle.net/10107/4769315
1751	Williams (Pantycelyn), William	Hosanna i Fab Dafydd	Bristol: Felix Farley	Texts only; three parts, 1751–4; later published complete with all six volumes of *Aleluia*	http://hdl.handle.net/10107/4769244; http://hdl.handle.net/10107/4772566

1757	Williams (Pantycelyn), William	*Rhai Hymnau a Chaniadau Duwiol ar Amryw Ystryiaethau*	Caerfyrddin: Evan Powel	Texts only	http://hdl.handle.net/10107/4769665
1758	Thomas, John	*Caniadau Sion*	Trefecca	Texts only; 6 volumes, 1758–88	http://hdl.handle.net/10107/5238050
1759	Williams (Pantycelyn), William	*Hosannah to the Son of David*	Bristol: John Grabham	Texts only; includes new English texts and translations from *Hosanna i Fab Dafydd*	http://hdl.handle.net/10107/4772892
1762	Williams (Pantycelyn), William	*Caniadau y rhai sydd ar y Môr o Wydr*	Caerfyrddin: E & D Powell	Texts only; expanded editions 1764, 1773	http://hdl.handle.net/10107/4770313
1763	Williams (Pantycelyn), William	*Ffarwel Weledig, Groesaw Anweledig Bethau*	Caerfyrddin: J. Ross	Texts only; three parts, 1763–9; reissued in a single volume as *Haleluia Drachefn*, 1791	http://hdl.handle.net/10107/4771887; http://hdl.handle.net/10107/4773483; http://hdl.handle.net/10107/4770500
1764	Rhys, Morgan	*Golwg o Ben Nebo ar Wlad yr Addewid*	Caerfyrddin: Rhys Thomas	Texts; earlier smaller edition, Bristol, 1755	http://hdl.handle.net/10107/5342013
1766	Rowland, Daniel	*Rhai hymnau duwjol*	Caerfyrddin: Samuel Lewis	Texts only	http://hdl.handle.net/10107/5326207
1770	William, Ifan	*Llyfr gweddi gyffredin*	Cambridge: [Cambridge University Press]	The Book of Common Prayer, with twenty-four tunes appended	http://hdl.handle.net/10107/5310034

(*cont.*)

Date	Author/editor/compiler	Title	Publication	Comments	Link to Digitised Source
1771	Jones, Dafydd	*Caniadau Duwjol*	Caerfyrddin: Ioan Ross	Texts only; translation of Isaac Watts, Divine Songs	https://books.google.co.uk/books?id=SdYCAAAAQAAJ
1771	Williams, Peter	*Hymns on various subjects Together with the novice instructed*	Carmarthen: J. Ross	Texts only	http://hdl.handle.net/10107/4801970
1771	Williams (Pantycelyn), William	*Gloria in Excelsis: neu Hymnau o Faul i Dduw a'r Oen*	Llanymddyfri: Rees Thomas	Texts only; two parts, 1771–2; English version 1772	http://hdl.handle.net/10107/4770210; http://hdl.handle.net/10107/4769822; http://hdl.handle.net/10107/4774514
1774	Williams (Pantycelyn), William	*Ychydig hymnau*	Carmarthen: John Ross?	Texts only	http://hdl.handle.net/10107/4774631
1775	Jones, Dafydd	*Hymnau a Chaniadau Ysprydol*	Caerfyrddin: Ioan Ross	Texts only; translation of Isaac Watts, *Hymns and Spiritual Songs*	https://books.google.co.in/books?id=M1RVAAAAcAAJ
1781	Williams (Pantycelyn), William	*Rhai hymnau newyddion*	Aberhonddu: Evan Evans	Texts only; three parts, 1781–7	http://hdl.handle.net/10107/4773177; http://hdl.handle.net/10107/4773578
1795	Jones, Robert	*Grawn-syppiau Canaan*	Liverpool: Daniel Jones	Texts only; Calvinistic Methodist	http://hdl.handle.net/10107/5215633

Year	Author	Title	Publisher	Notes	URL
1797	Williams, John	*Cyfaill mewn llogell*	Caerfyrddin: I. Daniel	Includes an introduction to the rudiments of music, with hand-drawn staff notation, followed by hymn texts	http://hdl.handle.net/10107/5212315
1802	Hughes, John	*Diferion y Cysegr*	Chester: W. C. Jones	Texts only; Wesleyan Methodist, including translations of hymns by Charles Wesley; also printed in London	
1802	Lewis, Titus	*Mawl i'r Oen a Ladduyd*	Carmarthen: John Evans	Texts only; Baptist	
1805	Jones, J. R.	*Emynau, neu Ganiadau Cristianogol*	Dolgellau: Thomas Williams	Texts only	
1806	Griffiths, Ann	*Casgliad o Hymnau*	Bala: R. Saunderson	Texts only	http://hdl.handle.net/10107/4789494
1810	Jones, David	*Casgliad o Bum Cant o Hymnau*	Holywell: E. Carnes	Texts only; Congregationalist; expanded edition, 1821	https://books.google.co.uk/books?id=wGw9AAAAYAAJ
1811	James, John	*Pigion o Hymnau*	Aberystwyth: James and Williams	Texts only; Baptist	http://hdl.handle.net/10107/5334572
1811	Williams, John	*Gwaith Prydyddawl y Diweddar Barchedig William Williams, o Bant-y-celyn*	Caerfyrddin: Jonathan Harris	Texts only; Calvinistic Methodist	

(*cont.*)

Date	Author/editor/compiler	Title	Publication	Comments	Link to Digitised Source
1816	Ellis, John	*Mawl yr Arglwydd*	Llanrwst: I. Davies	Texts and tunes; includes a musical grammar	
1817	Rogers, David, Williams, John, and Jones, William	*Casgliad o Hymnau, Athrawiaethol, Profiadol, Ymarferol, ac Achlysurol, i'w Harferyd gan y Bobl a Elwir Methodistiaid Wesleyaidd*	Llundain: Thomas Cordeux	Texts only; Wesleyan Methodist	
1819	Williams, Owen	*Brenhinol Ganiadau Seion*	Llundain: W. Mitchell	Two volumes of tunes: vol. 1 tunes in metres used in Prys, 1621; vol. 2 tunes in metres used by Williams, Pantycelyn	
1821	Harris, Joseph	*Casgliad o Hymnau*	Abertawe: Seren Gomer	Texts only; Baptist	https://books.google.co.uk/books?id=kqJhAAAAcAAJ
1822	Jones, J. R.	*Aleluia*	Caernarfon: Peter Evans	Texts only	
1824	William, Thomas	*Dyfroedd Bethesda*	Caerdydd: R. Lloyd	Texts only	

1828	Owen, William	*Y Caniedydd Crefyddol*	Caerlleon: J. Parry	Tunes and musical instructions	
1832	Davies, Morris	*Casgliad o Salmau a Hymnau*	Bala: Robert Saunderson	Texts only; Calvinistic Methodist	https://books.google.co.uk/books?vid=BL:A0017244534
1836	Edwards, John David	*Original Sacred Music*	Carnarvon:	H. Humphreys	Second volumes c.1843; tunes; Anglican
1837	Parry, John	*Peroriaeth Hyfryd*	Caerlleon: J. & J. Parry	Mostly tunes from English sources with some older Welsh tunes, harm. John Roberts (Henllan)	
1838	Evans, Evan (Ieuan Glan Geirionydd)	*Y Seraph*	Caerlleon: J. Seacome	Tunes	
1839	Roberts, John (Henllan)	*Caniadau y Cyssegr*	Dinbych: Thomas Gee	Mostly Welsh tunes, harmonised for four voices	
1840	Edwards, Roger	*Y Salmydd Cymreig*	Dinbych: T. Gee	Texts only; Calvinistic Methodist	
1840	Mills, Richard	*Caniadau Seion*	Llanidloes: John M. Jones	Tunes and anthems	
1840	Williams, Richard; Williams, Joseph	*Hymnau a Salmau*	Liverpool: R. Ll. Morris	Texts only; Calvinistic Methodist	https://books.google.li/books?id=q9gDAAAAQAAJ

(cont.)

Date	Author/editor/compiler	Title	Publication	Comments	Link to Digitised Source
1841	Roberts, Samuel	Casgliad o dros Ddwy Fil o Hymnau	Llanelli: D. Rees	Texts only; Congregationalist	https://archive.org/details/casgliadodrosddwoorobe
1841	Welsh Calvinistic Methodist Association in the South	Casgliad o Hymnau, at Wasanaeth y Trefnyddion Calfinaidd	Newcastle Emlyn: W. Jones	Texts only; Calvinistic Methodist	https://books.google.co.uk/books?id=dKIvAAAAYAAJ
1842	Mills, Richard	Attodiad i'r Caniadau Seion	Llanidloes: J. M. Jones	Tunes	
1843	Lloyd, John Ambrose	Casgliad o Donau	Liverpool: J. Jones	Tunes	
1844	Jacob, William	Eos Cymru	Llanidloes: J. M. Jones	Tunes, chants and anthems	
1844	Prichard, Rowland Huw	Cyfaill i'r Cantorion	Llanidloes: John M. Jones	Tunes; for Sunday Schools	
1845	Evans, David	Casgliad o Hymnau at Wasanaeth y Methodistiaid Wesleyaidd	Llanidloes: David Davies	Texts; Wesleyan Methodist	https://books.google.co.uk/books?id=OA5hAAAAcAAJ
1845	Jones, Daniel	Crynhodeb o Hymnau Cristnogol	Caerdydd: Owen & Roberts	Texts only; Baptist	https://books.google.co.uk/books?vid=BL:A0019925346

Year	Author	Title	Publisher	Notes	URL
1846	Jones, Joseph David	*Y Perganiedydd*		Tunes	
1846	Mills, John and Richard (Jr)	*Cerddor Eglwysig*	Llanidloes: Richard Mills	Tunes; supplement 1847	
1846	Prichard, Rowland Huw	*Y Fasged Gerddorol*	Bala: Griffith Jones	Tunes	
1846	Williams, Thomas	*Y Salmydd Cenedlaethol*	Llanidloes: Thomas Williams	Tunes and anthems; Anglican	
1847	Jones, Daniel	*Caniedydd Israel*	Llanelli: Rees & Williams	Texts only	
1848	Beynon, Rosser	*Telyn Seion*	Llanidloes: J. M. Jones	Tunes and anthems	
1849	Harris, Griffith	*Halelwiah*	Caerfyrddin: M. Jones	Texts and tunes	
1851	Jones, Robert	*Casgliad o Hymnau*	Llangollen: W. Williams	Texts; Baptist	https://books.google.co.uk/books?id=oOxUAAAAcAAJ
1851		*Zion's Melodies*	Carmarthen: M. Jones	Tunes	
1852		*Emynau Catholig, &c wedi eu troi o'r Lladin, er llês i ffyddloniaid Cymru*	Treffynnon: James Davies	Texts only; Catholic, including Welsh translations of Latin hymns	http://hdl.handle.net/10107/5195590

(*cont.*)

Date	Author/editor/compiler	Title	Publication	Comments	Link to Digitised Source
1852	Owen, William (Prysgol)	*Y Perl Cerddorol*	Caernarfon: William Owen	Tunes and anthems	
1852	Williams, Robert	*Cydymaith yr Addolydd*	Llanidloes: J. M. Jones	Texts and tunes; Wesleyan Methodist	
1852	Williams, Thomas	*Ceinion Cerddoriaeth*	Llanidloes: Thomas Williams	Two volumes; tunes, anthems, choruses	
1853	Roberts, John (Aberystwyth)	*Perorydd y Cysegr*	London: J. Hart	Tunes	
1854	Davies, Thomas	*Y Blwch Cerddorol*	Merthyr Tydfil: P. Williams	Tunes by Welsh composers	
1855	Griffiths, Evan	*Casgliad o Hymnau*	Swansea: E. Griffiths	Texts; Congregationalist	
1855	Harris, Griffith	*Haleluiah Drachefn*	Caerfyrddin: M. Jones	Texts and tunes	
1858		*Y Tonau Gregoraidd a chaniadau yr Eglwys*	Treffynnon: William Morris	Chants	
1859	Jones, Thomas	*Welsh Church Tune and Chant Book*	London: Wertheim, MacIntosh, & Hunt	Texts, tunes and chants; Anglican; several subsequent enlarged editions in staff notation and tonic sol-fa	

Year	Author	Title	Publisher	Notes	URL
1859	Roberts, John (Ieuan Gwyllt)	*Llyfr Tonau Cynulleidfaol*	Llundain: J. Haddon	Tunes; sol-fa edition 1863	http://hdl.handle.net/10107/4814268
1859	Stephen, Edward (Tanymarian)	*Cerddor y Cysegr*	Bethesda: R. Jones	Texts and tunes	
1860	Davies, Morris	*Jeduthun*	Bethesda: R. Jones	Tunes	
1861	Roberts, Eleazer	*Hymnau a Thonau yr Ysgol Sabbothol*	Wrexham: Hughes a'i Fab	Texts and tunes for Sunday schools	
1862	Richards, David	*Sŵn Addoli*	Llanidloes: Owen Mills	Tunes	
1865	Evans, Daniel	*Hymnau a Thonau, er gwasanaeth yr Eglwys yn Nghymru*	Llundain: Novello	Texts and tunes; Anglican; supplement published in 1875	
1867	Jones, Lewis	*Casgliad o Ddeuddeg Cant ac Un o Hymnau*	Blaenau: William Roberts	Texts only; Baptist	https://books.google.co.uk/books?id=G-I-AAAAYAAJ
1868	Stephen, Edward (Tanymarian)	*Llyfr Tonau ac Emynau*	Wrexham: Hughes a'i Fab	Texts and tunes; Congregationalist	
1868	Jones, Owen and Shadrach Price	*Hymnau ben a newydd: ynghyd a thonau i'w harfer yngwasanaeth yr eglwys*	Llundain: John Haddon	Texts and tunes	
1869	Diocese of Bangor	*Caniadau ac Emynau yr Eglwys*	Bangor: Nixon and Jarvis	Text and tunes; Anglican	

(*cont.*)

Date	Author/editor/compiler	Title	Publication	Comments	Link to Digitised Source
1869	General Assembly of the Welsh Calvinistic Methodist Connexion	*Llyfr Hymnau y Methodistiaid Calfinaidd*	Dinbych: Thomas Gee	Texts only; Calvinistic Methodist	https://books.google.co.uk/books?vid=BL:A0019777100
1872	Williams, W.A.	*Lluybrau Moliant*	Wrexham: Hughes a'i Fab	Tunes	https://books.google.co.uk/books?id=ZnOA-4kwZS8C
1873	Lloyd, John Ambrose; Rees, William	*Aberth Moliant*	Llundain: J. Haddon	Tunes; Congregationalist	
1874	Roberts, John (Ieuan Gwyllt)	*Sum y Juwbili [Jiwbili]*	Wrexham: Hughes a'i Fab	Texts and tunes; translations from Sankey and Moody	
1879	Stephen, Edward (Tanymarian)	*Ail Llyfr Tonau ac Emynau*	Wrexham: Hughes a'i Fab	Texts and tunes; Congregationalist	
1880	Roberts, J. H.	*Llawlyfr Moliant*	Bangor: Samuel Hughes	Texts and tunes; staff notation and sol-fa editions; Baptist	https://imslp.org/wiki/Llawlyfr_Moliant_(Roberts%2C_John_Henry)
1883	Wyn, Watcyn and W. T. Samuel	*Odlau'r Efengyl*	Swansea: B. Parry	Translations and arrangements of hymns by Ira D. Sankey	

1883	Williams, John Cledan	*Moliant Seion*	Treherbert: I. Jones	Texts and tunes
1883	Jenkins, David	*Tunes, Chants & Anthems*	Aberystwyth: D. Jenkins	Supplement 1894
1887	Parry, Joseph	*Llyfr Tonau Cynulleidfaol Cenedlaethol Cymru*	Swansea: J. Parry & Son	Tunes
1892	Jones, W. Emlyn	*Y Salmydd*	Llandeilo: G. Jones & Sons	Texts, tunes and anthems; Congregationalist
1892	Roberts, Ellis (Elis Wyn o Wyrfai)	*Hymnau yr Eglwys*		Texts only; edition with tunes in 1893
1893	J. Trehern Jones and Ben Jones	*Y Moliannydd: Casgliad o Emynau a Thonau at Wasanaeth y Christadelphiaid*	Treforis: J. Jones	Texts and tunes; Christadelphian
1895	Adams, David [et al.]	*Y Caniedydd Cynulleidfaol*	London: Undeb yr Annibynwyr Cymraeg	Texts and tunes; Congregationalist
1895	Lloyd, D. Lewis, and Roland Rogers	*Emyniadur yr Eglwys yng Nghymru*	Bangor: Jarvis & Foster	Texts and tunes; Anglican
1896	General Assembly of the Welsh Calvinistic Methodist Connexion	*Llyfr Hymnau y Methodistiaid Calfinaidd*	Caernarfon: Llyfrfa y Cyfundeb	Texts only; Calvinistic Methodist; tune book published in 1897

(*cont.*)

Date	Author/editor/compiler	Title	Publication	Comments	Link to Digitised Source
1896	Jones, D. Eiddil, William Harries, and J. Hathren Davies	*Perlau Moliant: (Pearls of Praise) sef Casgliad o Emynau, Tonau, a Salm- Donau, at Wasanaeth Egluysi Undodaidd Cymru*	Merthyr Tydfil	Texts and tunes; Unitarian	
1897	Roberts, J. H. and W. T. Samuel	*Llawlyfr Moliant yr Ysgol Sabbothol*	Caernarfon: W. Gwenlyn Evans	Texts and tunes; for Sunday schools	
1899	Adams, D. [et al.]	*Caniedydd yr Ysgol Sul*	Llundain: Undeb yr Annibynwyr Cymreig	Texts and tunes; for Sunday schools	
1900	Hughes, John	*Llyfr Emynau y Methodistiaid Wesleyaidd*	Bangor: Pwyllgor y Llyfrfa Wesleyaidd	Texts only; Wesleyan Methodist	

APPENDIX 3

Selective List of Major Published and Manuscript Sources Available in Open-Access Digitised Form

The sources listed below are also to be found elsewhere in the book – in the chapters or Appendices 1 and 2, which give more information about them. They are gathered together here as an indication of the open-access resources for the study of Welsh music history. This list is based on, and largely made up of, material digitised by the National Library of Wales. Most links are 'permalinks' and are unlikely to change or become unavailable. Digitisation is ongoing at the National Library as at other major libraries and archives, so library catalogues will always be the best sources for investigation.

Some key web resources

Cylchgrawn Cymdeithas Alawon Gwerin Cymru/Journal of the Welsh Folk-Song Society, the journal of Cymdeithas Alawon Gwerin Cymru/the Welsh Folk-Song Society (digitised up to 1977), www.canugwerin.com/

Dictionary of Welsh Biography, biographies of people who have made a significant contribution to Welsh life, https://biography.wales/

Geiriadur Prifysgol Cymru/A Dictionary of the Welsh Language, the standard historical Welsh dictionary, www.welsh-dictionary.ac.uk/

Welsh Journals, many periodicals relating to Wales published between 1735 and 2007, https://journals.library.wales/

Welsh Newspapers, most newspapers published in Wales, in English or Welsh, before 1919, https://newspapers.library.wales/

Rhyddiaith Gymraeg/Welsh Prose 1300–1425, transcriptions of many medieval Welsh texts, www.rhyddiaithganoloesol.caerdydd.ac.uk/

Manuscripts

In alphabetical order by title or author surname.

The Bardic Grammars in GB-AB MS Peniarth 20	14th c.	http://hdl.handle.net/10107/4754463
The Book of Llandaff, Liber Landavensis, GB-AB MS 17110i-iiiE	c.1120–1134	http://hdl.handle.net/10107/4388358
Brut y Tywysogion (Chronicle of the Princes) in GB-AB MS Peniarth 20 (c.1330)	c.1330	http://hdl.handle.net/10107/4754463
Robert Bulkeley, an Anglesey diary, GB-AB NLW MS 3150B	1630–6	http://hdl.handle.net/10107/4703116.
Evan James, Llyfr Tonau Iago ap Ieuan (1849–63) GB-AB Evan James MS 1	Mid-19thc.	http://hdl.handle.net/10107/4655569
John Jenkins (Ifor Ceri), Melus-geingciau Deheubarth Cymru, GB-AB J. Lloyd Williams AH1/34	c.1815	http://hdl.handle.net/10107/4655492
John Jenkins (Ifor Ceri), Melus-seiniau Cymru, GB-AB MS 1940iA	1817–25	http://hdl.handle.net/10107/4655107
John Jenkins (Ifor Ceri), Per-seiniau Cymru, GB-AB MS 1940iiA	1824–5	http://hdl.handle.net/10107/4654909
Rhygyfarch's *Life* of St David, GB-Lbl Cotton MS Vespasian A XIV, ff. 61 r–70 v.	11th c.	www.bl.uk/manuscripts/FullDisplay.aspx?ref=Cotton_MS_Vespasian_A_XIV
John Thomas's fiddle manuscript, GB-AB MS J. Lloyd Williams AH1/36 (formerly J. Lloyd Wiliams 39)	c.1752	http://hdl.handle.net/10107/5130424
The Welsh Laws/Laws of Hywel Dda, as copied in GB-AB Peniarth MS 28	10th c.	http://hdl.handle.net/10107/4400109

Publications

In alphabetical order by author surname.

Anon.	1852	*Emynau Catholig, &c wedi eu troi o'r Lladin, er llês i ffyddloniaid Cymru*	http://hdl.handle.net/10107/5195590
Thomas Baddy	1703	*Hymnau Sacramentaidd Scrythurol*	http://hdl.handle.net/10107/5421257
Nicholas Bennett	1896	*Alawon fy Ngwlad/The Lays of My Land*	http://hdl.handle.net/10107/4676271
Edward Smith Biggs	1796	*Six Welch Airs*	http://hdl.handle.net/10107/4842449

Appendix 3
(cont.)

Edward Smith Biggs	1800	*A Second Sett of Welch Airs*	http://hdl.handle.net/1010 7/4828573
William Bingley	1804	*North Wales; Including Its Scenery, Antiquities, Customs and Some Sketches of Its Natural History, Vol. 2*	https://archive.org/details/ northwalesdelin00 binggoog
William Crotch	1806–7	*Specimens of Various Styles of Music*	https://archive.org/details/ specimensofvario00crot
Morris Davies	1832	*Casgliad o Salmau a Hymnau*	https://books.google.co.uk /books?vid=BL: A0017244534
David Evans	1845	*Casgliad o Hymnau at Wasanaeth y Methodistiaid Wesleyaidd*	https://books.google.co.uk/ books? id=OA5hAAAAcAAJ
Theophilus Evans	1794 edition	*Drych y Prif Oesoedd*	http://hdl.handle.net/1010 7/5218245
General Assembly of the Welsh Calvinistic Methodist Connexion	1869	*Llyfr Hymnau y Methodistiaid Calfinaidd*	https://books.google.co.uk /books?vid=BL: A0019777100
Ann Griffiths	1806	*Casgliad o Hymnau: gan mwyaf heb erioed eu hargraffu o'r blaen*	http://hdl.handle.net/1010 7/4789494
Joseph Harris	1821	*Casgliad o Hymnau*	https://books.google.co.uk /books? id=kqJhAAAAcAAJ
John James	1811	*Pigion o Hymnau*	http://hdl.handle.net/1010 7/5334572
Dafydd Jones	1771	*Caniadau Duwiol*	https://books.google.co.uk/ books?id=SdY CAAAA QAAJ
	1775	*Hymnau a Chaniadau Ysprydol*	https://books.google.co.in/ books? id=M1RVAAAAcAAJ
Daniel Jones	1845	*Crynhodeb o Hymnau Cristnogol*	https://books.google.co.uk /books?vid=BL: A0019925346
Davd Jones	1810	*Casgliad o Bum Cant o Hymnau*	https://books.google.co.uk /books? id=wGw9AAAAYAAJ
Edward Jones (Bardd y Brenin)	1784	*Musical and Poetical Relicks of the Welsh Bards*	http://hdl.handle.net/1010 7/4675108
	1794	*Musical and Poetical Relicks of the Welsh Bards*	http://hdl.handle.net/1010 7/4674868

	1802	*The Bardic Museum, of primitive British literature*	http://hdl.handle.net/10107/4675439
	1825	*Musical and Poetical Relicks of the Welsh Bards*, 4th ed.	http://hdl.handle.net/10107/4675201
	1825?	*Hên Ganiadau Cymru. Cambro-British melodies*	http://hdl.handle.net/10107/4675268
John Jones (Idris Vychan)	1885	*An Essay on Pennillion Singing/ Hanes a Henafiaeth Canu Gyda'r Tannau*	https://babel.hathitrust.org/cgi/pt?id=uc1.b4440032&view=1up&seq=7&skin=2021
Lewis Jones	1867	*Casgliad o Ddeuddeg Cant ac Un o Hymnau*	https://books.google.co.uk/books?id=G-I-AAAAYAAJ
Owen Jones (Owain Myfyr), William Owen Pughe, Edward Williams (Iolo Morganwg),	1801–7	*The Myvyrian Archaiology of Wales*, 3 vols – music material is in Vol. 3:	Vol 1: http://hdl.handle.net/10107/4791917 Vol 2: http://hdl.handle.net/10107/4797084 Vol 3: http://hdl.handle.net/10107/4805623
Robert Jones	1795	*Grawn-syppiau Canaan*	http://hdl.handle.net/10107/5215633
Robert Jones	1851	*Casgliad o Hymnau*	https://books.google.co.uk/books?id=0OxUAAAAcAAJ
Theophilus Jones	1805	*A History of the County of Brecknock*, Vol. 2	http://hdl.handle.net/10107/4806924.
Richard Mills	[1853] 3rd ed.	*Yr Arweinydd Cerddorol*	http://hdl.handle.net/10107/5565456
Richard Mills, N. Cynhafal Jones	1881	*Buchdraeth y Parch. John Mills*	http://hdl.handle.net/10107/5578818
William Morgan	1588	*Y Beibl Cyssegr-lan*	http://hdl.handle.net/10107/4701320
James Owen	1705	*Hymnau Scrythurol*	http://hdl.handle.net/10107/5427228
John Owen (Owain Alaw)	1860–4	*Gems of Welsh Melody*	http://hdl.handle.net/10107/4796728
John Parry (Bardd Alaw)	1839	*The Welsh Harper* (Vol. 1)	http://hdl.handle.net/10107/4675974
John Parry (Ruabon) and Evan Williams	1742	*Antient British Music*	http://hdl.handle.net/10107/4675582

John Parry (Ruabon)	1761	*A Collection of Welsh, English & Scotch Airs*	http://hdl.handle.net/10107/4675850
	1781	*British Harmony*	http://hdl.handle.net/10107/4675640
Thomas Pennant	1784 edition	*A Tour in Wales*	http://hdl.handle.net/10107/4692237
David Powel	1584	*The Historie of Cambria*	http://hdl.handle.net/10107/4787807
Edmwnd Prys	1621	*Llyfr y Psalmau*	http://hdl.handle.net/10107/5191521
Morgan Rhys	1764	*Golwg o Ben Nebo ar Wlad yr Addewid*	http://hdl.handle.net/10107/5342013
J.H. Roberts	1880	*Llawlyfr Moliant*	https://imslp.org/wiki/Llawlyfr_Moliant_(Roberts%2C_John_Henry)
John Roberts (Ieuan Gwyllt)	1859	*Llyfr Tonau Cynulleidfaol*	http://hdl.handle.net/10107/4814268
Samuel Roberts	1841	*Casgliad o dros Ddwy Fil o Hymnau*	https://archive.org/details/casgliadodrosddwoorobe
Daniel Rowland	1766	*Rhai hymnau duwjol*	http://hdl.handle.net/10107/5326207
William Salesbury	1551	*Kynniver llith a Ban*	http://hdl.handle.net/10107/5413188
	1567	*Lliver gweddi Gyffredin*	http://hdl.handle.net/10107/4856515
	1567	*Testament Newydd ein Arglwydd Iesv Christ*	http://hdl.handle.net/10107/4755114
John Stradling	1607	*Epigrammatum Libri Qvatvor*	http://hdl.handle.net/10107/5346980
Alexander Urquahart, Dermot O'Connar and Hugh Edwards	1726	*Aria di Camera: being A Choice Collection of Scotch, Irish & Welsh Air's*	http://hdl.handle.net/10107/5470148
Welsh Calvinistic Methodist Association in the South	1841	*Casgliad o Hymnau, at Wasanaeth y Trefnyddion Calfinaidd*	https://books.google.co.uk/books?id=dKIvAAAAYAAJ
Ifan Wiliam	1770	*Llyfr gweddi gyffredin*	http://hdl.handle.net/10107/5310034
Jane Williams (Ysgafell)	1845 and 1855	*The Literary Remains of the Rev. Thomas Price, Carnhuanawc*	Vol. 1 http://hdl.handle.net/10107/5533058 Vol. 2 http://hdl.handle.net/10107/5560162

John Williams (Ioan Wiliam; Siôn Singer)	1797	*Cyfaill mewn llogell*	http://hdl.handle.net/10107/5212315
Williams, Peter	1771	*Hymns on Various Subjects Together with the novice instructed*	http://hdl.handle.net/10107/4801970
Richard Williams, Joseph Williams	1840	*Hymnau a Salmau*	https://books.google.li/books?id=q9gDAAAAQAAJ
W. A. Williams	1872	*Llwybrau Moliant*	https://books.google.co.uk/books?id=ZnOA-4kwZS8C
William Williams Pantycelyn	1744–7	*Aleluia* (six parts)	http://hdl.handle.net/10107/4772239; http://hdl.handle.net/10107/4772100; http://hdl.handle.net/10107/4772033; http://hdl.handle.net/10107/5393330; http://hdl.handle.net/10107/4769315
	1749	*Aleluia* (single volume)	http://hdl.handle.net/10107/4769315
	1751–4	*Hosanna i Fab Dafydd*	http://hdl.handle.net/10107/4769244; http://hdl.handle.net/10107/4772566
	1757	*Rhai Hymnau a Chaniadau Duwiol ar Amryw Ystyriaethau*	http://hdl.handle.net/10107/4769665
	1759	*Hosannah to the Son of David*	http://hdl.handle.net/10107/4772892
	1762	*Caniadau y rhai sydd ar y Môr o Wydr*	http://hdl.handle.net/10107/4770313
	1763–9	*Ffarwel Weledig, Groesaw Anweledig Bethau* (3 parts)	http://hdl.handle.net/10107/4771887; http://hdl.handle.net/10107/4773483
	1771–2	*Gloria in Excelsis* (two parts)	http://hdl.handle.net/10107/4770210; http://hdl.handle.net/10107/4769822
	1772	*Gloria in Excelsis* (in English)	http://hdl.handle.net/10107/4774514

(cont.)

1774	*Ychydig Hymnau*	http://hdl.handle.net/10107/4774631
1781–7	*Rhai Hymnau Newyddion*	http://hdl.handle.net/10107/4773177; http://hdl.handle.net/10107/4773578
1791	*Haleluia Drachefn* (*Ffarwel Weledig* in one volume)	http://hdl.handle.net/10107/4770500

Bibliography

The bibliography is restricted to published works cited in the chapters and other published material relevant to topics covered in the book. However, newspaper articles are excluded, as are online sources such as websites and social media platforms; these are fully referenced in footnotes. Unpublished material cited in the book is referenced in footnotes, usually using RISM sigla. A key to the RISM sigla used in the book is given at the conclusion of the Preface.

Selective List of Welsh Periodical Publications Devoted to Music

This list includes only print publications that were intended to cover musical matters. Many important articles have been carried by other periodical publications such as those primarily devoted to Welsh history, county histories and other specialist fields. At least some issues of almost all the following publications are available online in *Welsh Journals*. *Cylchgrawn Cymdeithas Alawon Gwerin Cymru/ Journal of the Welsh Folk-Song Society* has been digitised from 1909 to 1977, and these issues are available online at www.canugwerin.com.

Allwedd y Tannau (journal of Cymdeithas Cerdd Dant Cymru)	1936–	n.p.
Yr Athraw Cerddorol	1854	Llanidloes
Blodau Cerdd	1852–3	Aberystwyth
Y Cerbyd Cerddorol	1860–1	Holywell
Y Cerddor	1889–1921	Wrexham
Y Cerddor (third series)	1930–9	Wrexham
Y Cerddor Cymreig	1861–73	Merthyr Tydfil and Wrexham
Cerddor y Cymry	1883–94	Llanelli
Y Cerddor Newydd	1922–9	Wrexham
Cerddor y Tonic Sol-ffa	1869–74	Wrexham
Cronicl y Cerddor	1880–3	Treherbert

Cylchgrawn Cymdeithas Alawon Gwerin Cymru/ Journal of the Welsh Folk-Song Society, renamed *Canu Gwerin/Folk Song from 1978*	1909–	n.p.
Y Delyn: The Welsh Music Review	1947	Llangollen
Y Gerddorfa	1872–81	Pontypridd
Greal y Corau	1861–63	Denbigh
Music Wales	1997–9	Cardiff
Perl Cerddorol	1880	Merthyr Tydfil
Y Solffaydd	1891–2	Pontarddulais
South Wales Musical Review	1897	Cardiff
Welsh Music/Cerddoriaeth Cymru	1959–2009	n.p.
Welsh Music History/Hanes Cerddoriaeth Cymru	1996–2007	Cardiff
Yr Ysgol Gerddorol	1878–80	Llanelli

Selective List of Welsh Journals

Many, probably the majority, of scholarly periodicals dedicated to Welsh history are publications of local and county historical and antiquarian societies. For obvious reasons, writings dedicated to music history in such publications concern topics that are within the geographical orbits of each society, but their value to Welsh music history should not be underestimated. Several periodicals are devoted to themes such as the history of religion in Wales. There are also a significant number of popular periodicals of mixed historical, cultural and literary content, as well as some that were published in the Welsh diasporas. Periodicals of all types can be located by using the browsing facility at the National Library of Wales online *Welsh Journals* site: https://journals.library.wales/home.

The brief list that follows is selective and restricted to two categories: periodicals published in or about Wales, many of which are now defunct, and journals dedicated to the academic study of the history of Wales, or which are relevant to that endeavour. At least some issues of each of these are available online in *Welsh Journals* unless otherwise stated.

Archaeologica Cambrensis	1846–	n.p.	English-language journal of the Cambrian Archaeological Society, which includes articles on history, manuscripts, literature and folklore.
Bye-gones	1871–1939	Oswestry	Quarterly English-language antiquarian periodical relating to Wales and the Welsh Marches.

Cambrian Journal	1854–64	London	English-language quarterly journal of the Cambrian Institute, with articles on a wide range of subjects including music.
Cymru	1891–1927	Caernarfon, subsequently Wrexham	Popular Welsh-language monthly magazine important in promoting cultural patriotism, containing articles on the arts.
Journal of the Welsh Bibliographical Society	1910–84	n.p.	Published annually up to the end of the 1950s and intermittently thereafter; containing articles, some in English, some Welsh, on Welsh writers and bibliographical research.
Llafur: The Journal of the Society for the Study of Welsh Labour History	1972–	n.p.	English-language journal published annually. 2004 is the last available issue in *Welsh Journals*. Subsequently renamed *Llafur: The Journal of Welsh People's History*.
National Library of Wales Journal/ Cylchgrawn Llyfrgell Genedlaethol Cymru	1939–	n.p.	Scholarly articles (some in English, some in Welsh) on historical topics relating to the Library's collections. 2007 was the last print issue; the journal continued online from 2008.
North American Journal of Welsh Studies	2001–	n.p.	A multidisciplinary journal. Not in *Welsh Journals*.
Y Traethodydd	1845–	Dinbych; Holywell; Caernarfon; Llandysul	Quarterly Welsh-language cultural magazine.
Transactions of the Honourable Society of Cymmrodorion	1893–	[London]	Annual English-language periodical containing historical and literary essays and reviews. 1902 is the first available issue in *Welsh Journals* and 2004 the last.

(cont.)

Welsh History Review/ Cylchgrawn Hanes Cymru	1960–	[Cardiff]	Important English-language Welsh history journal. 2000 is the last available issue in *Welsh Journals*.
Welsh Outlook: A Monthly Journal of National Social Progress	1915–33	Cardiff	English-language popular magazine with a broadly liberal agenda, containing news and articles on the arts and education.
Young Wales	1895–1903	Aberystwyth	Monthly English-language magazine of the Young Wales movement, containing articles on politics, current affairs, Welsh history and literature.

Published Primary and Secondary Sources

Abbott, John. *The Story of Francis, Day & Hunter* (London: Francis, Day & Hunter, 1952).

Allchin, A. M. *Ann Griffiths: The Furnace and the Fountain* (Cardiff: University of Wales Press, 1976).

Allsobrook, David. 'Music Education in Wales: The Case for Biography/Addysg Cerddoriaeth yng Nghymru: Yr Achos o Blaid Bywgraffiad'. *Welsh Music History/Hanes Cerddoriaeth Cymru*, 4 (2000), 1–20.

Music for Wales (Cardiff: University of Wales Press, 1992).

Anderson, Benedict. *Imagined Communities: Reflections on the Origin and Spread of Nationalism* (London and New York: Verso, 1983).

Andrews, C. Bruyn, ed. *The Torrington Diaries: Containing the Tours through England and Wales of the Hon. John Byng*. Vol. 1 (London: Eyre and Spottiswoode, 1934).

Andrews, Joyce. 'Composer Rhian Samuel: The Female Viewpoint and Welsh Influences in Her Vocal Music'. *Women and Music*, 8 (2004), 61–72.

Andrews, Rhian M., ed. *Welsh Court Poems* (Cardiff: University of Wales Press, 2007).

ap Gwilym, Dafydd. 'Y Gainc'. In *Gwaith Dafydd ap Gwilym*, no. 91, ed. by Dafydd Johnston (www.dafyddapgwilym.net, accessed 25 June 2021).

ap Gwilym, Ifor. 'Argraffu cerddoriaeth yn Llanidloes'. In Gwynn ap Gwilym and Richard H. Lewis (goln), *Maldwyn a'i Chyffiniau* (Abertawe: Christopher Davies, 1981), tt. 169–186.
ap Huw, Robert. *Musica: Llawysgrif Robert ap Huw/Musica: The Robert ap Huw Manuscript*, facsimile ed. (Godstone: Scolar Press, 1982).
  Musica neu Beroriaeth: B. M. Additional Ms 14905, facsimile ed. (Cardiff: University of Wales Press, 1936).
ap Siôn, Pwyll. 'Cenedligrwydd a'r Cyfansoddwr Cymreig/Nationhood and the Welsh Composer'. *Welsh Music History/Hanes Cerddoriaeth Cymru*, 7 (2007), 265–303.
  '"Yn y Fro": Mudiad Adfer a'r Canu Pop Cymraeg yn ystod y 1970au/"Yn y Fro": Mudiad Adfer and Welsh Popular Song During the 1970s'. *Welsh Music History/Hanes Cerddoriaeth Cymru*, 5 (2002), 162–216.
ap Siôn, Pwyll, a Wyn Thomas, goln. *Cydymaith i Gerddoriaeth Cymru* (Talybont: Y Lolfa, 2018).
Arts Council of Great Britain. *Housing the Arts in Britain* (London: Arts Council of Great Britain, 1959).
'Awstin' and *Western Mail* Special Correspondents. *The Religious Revival in Wales: Contemporaneous Newspapers Accounts of the Welsh Revival of 1904–05 Published by the Western Mail* (Oswestry: Quinta Press, 2004).
Baker, Geoffrey. *El Sistema: Orchestrating Venezuela's Youth* (Oxford: Oxford University Press, 2014).
Balfour, Henry. 'The Old British "Pibcorn" or "Hornpipe" and Its Affinities'. *Journal of the Anthropological Institute of Great Britain and Ireland*, 20 (1891), 142–154.
Ballinger, John, ed. *Calendar of Wynn (of Gwydir) Papers, 1515–1690, in the National Library of Wales and Elsewhere* (Aberystwyth: National Library of Wales, 1926).
Barlow, Helen, '"Praise the Lord! We Are a Musical Nation": The Welsh Working Classes and Religious Singing'. *Nineteenth-Century Music Review*, 17/3 (2020), 445–472.
  'Progress and Tradition: Listening to the Singing of the Welsh *c*. 1870 to *c*. 1920', in *The Experience of Listening to Music: Methodologies, Identities, Histories*, ed. by Helen Barlow and David Rowland (Milton Keynes: The Open University, 2019) https://ledbooks.org/proceedings2019/ (accessed 27 May 2022).
Barlow, Rachelle, '"Land of Song": Gender and Identity in Welsh Choral Music, 1872–1918' (Ph.D. thesis, Cardiff University, 2015).
Barrington, Daines. 'Some Account of Two Musical Instruments Used in Wales'. *Archaeologia*, III (1775), 30–34.
Bashford, Christina, and Leanne Langley, eds. *Music and British Culture, 1785–1914: Essays in Honour of Cyril Ehrlich* (Oxford: Oxford University Press, 2000).
Bassett, Thomas. *Braslun o Hanes Hughes a'i Fab, Cyhoeddwyr, Wrecsam* (Croesoswallt: dros Gymdeithas Lyfryddol Cymru, 1946).

Belcham, Elizabeth F. *About Aberpergwm: The Home of the Williams Family in the Vale of Neath, Glamorgan* (Glynneath: Heritage Ventures, 1992).

Beresford, Maurice. *The New Towns of the Middle Ages: Town Plantation in England, Wales and Gascony* (London: Phillimore, 1966).

Biezen, Ingrid van, Peter Mair and Thomas Poguntke, 'Going, Going, . . . Gone? The Decline of Party Membership in Contemporary Europe'. *European Journal of Political Research*, 51/1 (2012), 24–56.

Boden, Anthony, ed. *Thomas Tomkins, the Last Elizabethan* (Aldershot: Ashgate, 2005).

Bohana, Roy. 'Music', in *The Arts in Wales 1950–75*, ed. by Meic Stephens (Cardiff: Welsh Arts Council, 1979), pp. 5–26.

'Roy Bohana', in *Artists in Wales 2*, ed. by Meic Stephens (Llandysul: Gomer, 1973), pp. 145–154.

Boorde, Andrew. *The Fyrst Bok of the Introduction of Knowledge*, ed. by Frederick James Furnivall (London: Published for the Early English Text Society, Extra Series, 10, by N.T. Trübner & Co, 1870).

Borsay, Peter. 'Welsh Seaside Resorts: Historiography, Sources and Themes'. *Welsh History Review*, 24/2 (2008), 92–119.

Bowen, E. G. *Seaways and Settlements in the Celtic Lands* (Cardiff: University of Wales Press, 1969).

The Settlements of the Celtic Saints in Wales, 2nd ed. (Cardiff: University of Wales Press, 1956).

'Yr Eglwys Geltaidd – Oes y Seintiau', in *Atlas Môn*, gol. Meville Richards (Llangefni: Cyngor Gwlad Môn, 1972), tt. 24–27.

Bowen, E. G., and H. Carter. 'Preliminary Observations on the Distribution of the Welsh Language at the 1971 Census'. *The Geographical Journal*, 140/3 (1974), 432–440.

Bowen, Lloyd, ed. *Family and Society in Early Stuart Glamorgan: The Household Accounts of Sir Thomas Aubrey of Llantrithyd, c.1565–1641* (Cardiff: South Wales Record Society, 2006).

Bowett, Adam, 'The Cotehele Cupboard Revisited: One Cupboard or Two?'*Journal of the Regional Furniture Society*, 28 (2014), https://regionalfurnituresociety.files.wordpress.com/2013/02/02-bowett-cotehele.pdf (accessed 22 September 2021).

Boyd, Malcolm. *Grace Williams* (Cardiff: University of Wales Press, 1980).

William Mathias (Cardiff: University of Wales Press, 1978).

Bramley, Kathleen Anne and Morfydd E. Owen, goln. *Gwaith Llywelyn Fardd I ac Eraill o Feirdd y Ddeuddegfed Ganrif* (Caerdydd: Gwasg Prifysgol Cymru, 1994).

Bromwich, Rachel and D. Simon Evans, eds. *Culhwch ac Olwen: An Edition and Study of the Oldest Arthurian Tale.* (Cardiff: University of Wales Press, 1992).

Brown, Carleton, ed. *Poems by Sir John Salusbury and Robert Chester*, EETS, Extra Series, 113 (London: Kegan Paul Trench Truebner, 1914).

Brown, Cedric. 'The Chirk Castle Entertainment of 1634'. *Milton Quarterly*, 11 (1977), 76–86.

Brown, Michelle P. 'The Lichfield/Llandeilo Gospels Reinterpreted', in *Authority and Subjugation in Writing of Medieval Wales*, ed. by Ruth Kennedy and Simon Meecham-Jones, New Middle Ages Series, ed. Bonnie Wheeler (New York: Palgrave Macmillan, 2008), pp. 57–70.

Brown, Roger L. 'The Age of Saints to the Victorian Church', in *A New History of the Church in Wales: Governance and Ministry, Theology and Society*, ed. by Norman Doe (Cambridge: Cambridge University Press, 2020), pp. 9–26.

Buckley, A. 'What Was the Timpán? A Problem in Ethnohistorical Organology: Evidence in Irish Literature', *Jahrbuch für musikalische Volks- und Volkerkunde*, 9 (1978), 53–88.

Buisman, Frans. 'A Parallel between Scottish Pibroch and Early Welsh Harp Music/ Cyffelybiaeth rhwng Cerddoriaeth Pibroch Albanaidd a Cherddoriaeth Gynnar Gymreig i'r Delyn'. *Welsh Music History/Hanes Cerddoriaeth Cymru*, 6 (2004), 1–46.

Bullard, Beth, ed. *Musica Getutscht: A Treatise on Musical Instruments by Sebastian Virdung* (Cambridge: Cambridge University Press, 1993).

Caldwell, John, ed. *Early Tudor Organ Music I: Music for the Office*. Vol. 6, *Early English Church Music* (London: Stainer and Bell for The British Academy, 1966).

Cale, John, and Victor Bockris. *What's Welsh for Zen? The Autobiography of John Cale* (London: Bloomsbury, 1999).

Valor Ecclesiasticus Temp. Henr. VIII, ed. by John Caley and Joseph Hunter, 6 vols (London: Record Commission, 1810–34).

Carr, Glenda. *William Owen Pughe* (Caerdydd: Gwasg Prifysgol Cymru, 1983).

—— 'William Owen Pughe and the London Societies', in *A Guide to Welsh Literature c. 1700–1800*, ed. by Branwen Jarvis (Cardiff: University of Wales Press, 2000), pp. 168–186.

Chadwick, Owen, 'The Evidence of Welsh Dedications in the Early History of the Welsh Church', in *Studies in Early British History*, ed. by Nora K. Chadwick (Cambridge: Cambridge University Press, 1959), pp. 173–188.

Chambers, Paul. 'Sacred Landscapes, Redundant Chapels and Carpet Warehouses: The Religious Heritage of South West Wales', in *Materialising Religion: Expression, Performance and Ritual*, ed. by Elisabeth Arweck and William Keenan (Aldershot: Ashgate, 2006), pp. 21–31.

Charles-Edwards, T. M. *The Welsh Laws* (Cardiff: University of Wales Press, 1989).

Charnell-White, Cathryn. *Welsh Poetry of the French Revolution, 1789–1805* (Cardiff: University of Wales Press, 2012).

Clancy, Joseph P. *Medieval Welsh Poems* (Dublin: Four Courts Press, 2003).

Cockman, Irwen. 'Robert Peilin (*c.*1575–*c.*1638) a "Josseffüs", Ei Draethawd ar Gerddoriaeth/Robert Peilin (*c.*1575–*c.*1638) and His Essay on Music, "Josseffüs"'. *Welsh Music History/Hanes Cerddoriaeth Cymru*, 4 (2000), 39–87.

—— 'Traethawd ar Gerddoriaeth gan y Telynor Robert Peilin (*c.*1613)' (MPhil thesis, University of Wales, Aberystwyth, 1999).

Collier, J. P., ed. *Memoirs of Edward Alleyn, Founder of Dulwich College* (London: Shakespeare Society, 1841).
Connerton, David. *How Societies Remember* (Cambridge: Cambridge University Press, 1989).
Conran, Tony. *Welsh Verse* (Bridgend: Seren, 1992).
Cooke, James Francis. 'A Momentous Musical Meeting: Thomas A. Edison and Lt. Comm. John Philip Sousa Meet for the First Time and Talk Upon Music'. *The Etude*, 41/10 (1923), 663–664.
Cooper, Barry. 'The Welsh Folk-Song Melodies Set by Beethoven: A Preliminary Investigation/Yr Alawon Gwerin Cymreig a Osodwyd gan Beethoven: Ymchwiliad Rhagarweiniol'. *Welsh Music History/Hanes Cerddoriaeth Cymru*, 1 (1996), 5–41.
Cotterill, Graeme. 'Music in the Blood and Poetry in the Soul? National Identity in the Life and Music of Grace Williams' (PhD thesis, Bangor University, 2012).
The Council for Wales and Monmouthshire. *Report on the Arts in Wales* (London: HMSO, 1965).
Cox, Gordon. *The Origins and Foundations of Music Education: Cross-Cultural Historical Studies of Music in Compulsory Schooling* (London: Continuum, 2010).
Crossley-Holland, Peter. 'The Robert ap Huw Composers/Cyfansoddwyr Robert ap Huw'. *Welsh Music History/Hanes Cerddoriaeth Cymru*, 3 (1999), 183–216.
  'The Tonal Limits of Welsh Folk Song'. *Journal of the Welsh Folk-Song Society/ Cylchgrawn Cymdeithas Alawon Gwerin Cymru*, 5 (1964), 46–73.
Crotch, William. *Specimens of Various Styles of Music, Referred to in a Course of Lectures Read at Oxford and London, and Adapted to Keyed Instruments* (London: Robert Birchall, 1806–7).
Cusworth, Andrew. 'Towards a Digital Land of Song: A Digital Approach to the Archival Record of Welsh Traditional Music, Its Performance and Its Reception' (Ph.D. thesis, Open University, 2016).
Dafydd, Mair. 'Argraffu, Cyhoeddi a Llyfrwerthu yng Nghaerfyrddin, 1840–1890'. *Y Llyfr yng Nghymru/Welsh Book Studies*, 8 (2007), 54–76.
Dahlhaus, Carl. *Nineteenth-Century Music*, trans. by J. Bradford Robinson (Berkeley and London: University of California Press, 1989).
Daley, Caroline. 'The Invention of 1905', in *Tackling Rugby Myths: Rugby and New Zealand Society 1854–2004*, ed. by Greg Ryan (Dunedin: University of Otago Press, 2005), pp. 67–87.
Daniel, R. Iestyn, 'Iorwerth Beli', in *Gwaith Gruffudd ap Dafydd ap Tudur, Gwilym Ddu o Arfon, Trahaearn Brydydd Mawr ac Iorwerth Beli*, goln. N. G. Costigan, R. Iestyn Daniel and Dafydd Johnston (Aberystwyth: Canolfan Uwchefrydiau Cymreig a Cheltaidd Prifysgol Cymru, 1995).
Darwin, Bernard. *British Sports and Games* (London: The British Council, 1940).
Davies, Damian Walford. '"Ailysgrifennwn y Llyfraith": Barddoniaeth y Canu Pop/ "Rewriting the Law Books": The Poetry of Welsh Pop Music'. *Welsh Music History/Hanes Cerddoriaeth Cymru*, 1 (1996), 180–240.

Davies, Damian Walford, and Lynda Pratt. *Wales and the Romantic Imagination* (Cardiff: University of Wales Press, 2007).
Davies, Grace Gwyneddon. *Ail Gasgliad o Alawon Gwerin Môn* (Caerdydd: Hughes a'i Fab, [1924]).
Alawon Gwerin Môn/Folk Songs from Anglesey (Caernarfon: The Welsh Publishing Company, 1914).
Chwech o Alawon Gwerin Cymreig/Six Welsh Folk Songs (Wrexham: Hughes & Son, 1933).
Davies, Janet. *The Welsh Language* (Cardiff: University of Wales Press, 1993).
Davies, John. *Hanes Cymru: A History of Wales in Welsh* (London: Allen Lane, 1990).
A History of Wales, revised ed. (London: Penguin, 2007).
Davies, John, Nigel Jenkins, Menna Baines and Peredur I. Lynch, eds. *The Welsh Academy Encyclopaedia of Wales* (Cardiff: University of Wales Press, 2008). (Also published in Welsh: *Gwyddoniadur Cymru yr Academi Gymreig*.)
Davies, John H., ed. *The Letters of Lewis, Richard, William and John Morris, of Anglesey (Morrisiaid Mon) 1728–1765*, 2 vols (Aberystwyth: Published privately by the Editor, 1907–9).
Davies, John Iorwerth. *Argraffwyr Sir Drefaldwyn o 1789 Ymlaen* (Machynlleth: Eisteddfod Genedlaethol Maldwyn a'i Chyffiniau, 1981).
Davies, Lyn. 'D. Afan Thomas, "Cerddor o'r Cwm" (1881–1928)', in *Llynfi ac Afan, Garw ac Ogwr*, gol. Hywel Teifi Edwards (Llandysul: Gomer, 1998), tt. 163–177.
David Vaughan Thomas, Composers of Wales Monographs (Cardiff: Welsh Music Information Centre, 2004).
'Golwg ar Ddiwylliant Cerddorol Dyffryn Aman, 1910–1922', in *Cwm Aman*, Cyfres y Cymoedd, gol. Hywel Teifi Edwards (Llandysul: Gomer, 1996), tt. 173–212.
'Towards an Authentic Celtic Voice in Music: The Life and Work of David Vaughan Thomas (1873–1934)'. *Welsh Music History/Hanes Cerddoriaeth Cymru*, 2 (1997), 213–235.
Davies, Oliver. *Celtic Christianity in Early Medieval Wales* (Cardiff: University of Wales Press, 1996).
Davies, Rhian. 'Béla Bartók yn Aberystwyth'. *Barn*, 410 (1997), 22–23.
'Mighty Atom: The Life and Music of Morfydd Owen (1891–1918)'. *British Music*, 13 (1991), 38–58.
Yr Eneth Ddisglair Annwyl: Morfydd Owen (1891–1918): Ei Bywyd Mewn Lluniau/Never So Pure a Sight: Morfydd Owen (1891–1918): Her Life in Pictures (Llandysul: Gomer, 1994).
Davies, Robert Gwyneddon. 'The Collecting of Anglesey Folk Songs'. *Anglesey Antiquarian and Field Club Transactions*, 23 (1923), 94–96.
Davies, R. R. *The Age of Conquest: Wales 1063–1415* (Oxford: Oxford University Press, 2000).
'The Peoples of Britain'. *Transactions of the Royal Historical Society*, 4 (December 1994), 1–20.

Davies, Sioned, ed. and trans. *The Mabinogion* (Oxford: Oxford University Press, 2007).
Davies, Wendy. *Wales in the Early Middle Ages* (Leicester: Leicester University Press, 1982).
Deane, Basil. *Alun Hoddinott* (Cardiff: University of Wales Press, 1978).
Doctor, Jenny and Sophie Fuller, ed. *Music, Life and Changing Times: Selected Correspondence between British Composers Elizabeth Maconchy and Grace Williams, 1927–77: Volume 1* (London and New York: Routledge, 2019).
Doe, Norman, ed. *A New History of the Church in Wales: Governance and Ministry, Theology and Society* (Cambridge: Cambridge University Press, 2020).
Dowland, John. *Andreas Ornithoparcus His Micrologus, or Introduction, Containing the Art of Singing, 1609*, facsimile ed., The English Experience (Amsterdam: Theatrum Orbis Terrarum, 1969).
Duffett, Mark. *Understanding Fandom: An Introduction to the Study of Media Fan Culture* (London: Bloomsbury, 2013).
Dugdale, William. *Monasticon Anglicanum*, ed. by John Caley, Henry Ellis and Bulkeley Bandinel, 6 vols in 8 books (London: T. G. March, 1849).
Ebenezer, Lyn. *Ar Log ers Ugain Mlynedd* (Llanrwst: Gwasg Carreg Gwalch, 1996).
Edwards, Elizabeth. 'Romantic Wales and the Eisteddfod', in *The Cambridge History of Welsh Literature*, ed. by Geraint Evans and Helen Fulton (Cambridge: Cambridge University Press, 2019), pp. 285–305.
Edwards, Hywel Teifi. *The Eisteddfod* (Cardiff: University of Wales Press, 1990).
Eisteddfod Ffair y Byd Chicago, 1893 (Llandysul: Gomer, 1990).
Gŵyl Gwalia: Yr Eisteddfod Genedlaethol yn Oes Aur Victoria 1858–1868 (Llandysul: Gomer, 1980).
'Victorian Wales Seeks Reinstatement', *Planet*, 52 (1985), 12–24.
Yr Eisteddfod: Cyfrol Ddathlu Wythganmlwyddiant yr Eisteddfod, 1176–1976 (Llandysul: Gwasg Gomer [ar ran] Llys yr Eisteddfod Genedlaethol, 1976).
Edwards, Nicholas, *Opera House Lottery: Zaha Hadid and the Cardiff Bay Project* (Cardiff: University of Wales Press, 1997).
Edwards, Owain Tudor. *Matins, Lauds and Vespers for St David's Day: The Medieval Office of the Welsh Patron Saint in National Library of Wales MA 20541E* (Cambridge: D. S. Brewer, 1990).
'Music in Wales', in *Anatomy of Wales*, ed. by R. Brinley Jones (Peterston-super-Ely: Gwerin Publications, 1972).
National Library of Wales Ms 20541E: The Penpont Antiphonal, facsimile ed. (Ottawa: The Institute of Mediaeval Music, 1997).
Edwards, Rebecca. '"To Show from Where I Came": Cool Cymru, Pop and National Identity in Wales During the 1990s' (Ph.D. thesis, Swansea University, 2008).
Ehrlich, Cyril. *The Music Profession in Britain since the Eighteenth Century: A Social History* (Oxford: Clarendon Press, 1985).
Ellis, Osian. *The Story of the Harp in Wales* (Cardiff: University of Wales Press, 1991).

Ellis, Tecwyn. *Edward Jones, Bardd y Brenin 1752–1824* (Caerdydd: Gwasg Prifysgol Cymru, 1957).
— 'Welsh Music in Georgian Times'. *Welsh Music/Cerddoriaeth Cymru*, 3/10 (Autumn/Hydref 1971), 11–19.
Ellis, Thomas E. *Speeches and Addresses by the Late T. E. Ellis* (Wrexham: Hughes & Son, 1912).
Evans, David R. A. 'J. R. Heath (1887–1950), Medical Practitioner and Composer/ J.R. Heath (1887–1950), Meddyg Teulu a Chyfansoddwr'. *Welsh Music History/Hanes Cerddoriaeth Cymru*, 1 (1996), 42–76.
Evans, Dylan Foster, gol. *Gwaith Rhys Goch Eryri* (Aberystwyth: Canolfan Uwchefrydiau Cymreig a Cheltaidd Prifsgol Cymru, 2007).
Evans, E. Keri gyda chynorthwy Cyril Jenkins. *Cofiant Dr. Joseph Parry Mus. Doc. (1841–1903)* (Cardiff: Educational Publishing Company, 1921).
Evans, Geraint and Helen Fulton, eds. *The Cambridge History of Welsh Literature* (Cambridge: Cambridge University Press, 2019).
Evans, J. Wyn and Jonathan M. Wooding, eds. *St David of Wales: Cult, Church and Nation* (Woodbridge: The Boydell Press, 2007).
Evans, John Glynne. 'David De Lloyd: Scholar Musician'. *Welsh Music/ Cerddoriaeth Cymru*, 3/10 (Autumn/Hydref 1971), 4–10.
Evans, Meredydd. 'Canu Gorchest/Contest Singing'. *Welsh Music History/Hanes Cerddoriaeth Cymru*, 1 (1996), 77–91.
— 'Cipdrem ar Rai o Alawon Richard Morris'. *Welsh Music/Cerddoriaeth Cymru*, 4/6 (Spring/Gwanwyn 1974), 20–6.
— 'Cyngherddau'r Ganrif Ddiwethaf', in *Eisteddfota 2*, gol. Gwynn ap Gwilym (Llandybie: Gwasg Christopher Davies, 1979), tt. 80–98.
— *Hela'r Hen Ganeuon* (Talybont: Y Lolfa, 2009).
— 'Pwy Oedd "Orpheus" Eisteddfod Llangollen 1858?/Who Was "Orpheus" of the 1858 Llangollen Eisteddfod?' *Welsh Music History/Hanes Cerddoriaeth Cymru*, 5 (2002), 59–71.
— *Serch a'i Helyntion* (Talybont: Y Lolfa, 2019).
Evans, Meredydd, and Phyllis Kinney. 'Hanes a Datblygiad Canu Gyda'r Tannau/ The History and Development of *Canu Gyda'r Tannau*'. *Welsh Music History/Hanes Cerddoriaeth Cymru*, 6 (2006), 155–192.
Evans, Nia Gwyn. *Bywyd a Gwaith Dr Nansi Richards Jones 'Telynores Maldwyn' (1888–1979)* (Llanrwst: Gwasg Carreg Gwalch, 2015).
Fawkes, Richard. *Welsh National Opera* (London: McRae, 1986).
Fellowes, Edmund H. *Memoirs of an Amateur Musician* (London: Methuen & Co. Ltd, 1946).
Fenn, R. W. D., and J. B. Sinclair. 'Old Radnor Church'. *The Radnorshire Society Transactions*, 58 (1988), 78–91.
Ffrancon, Ann and Geraint H. Jenkins, goln. *Merêd: Detholiad o Ysgrifau Dr. Meredydd Evans* (Llandysul: Gomer, 1994).
Final Report of the Royal Commission on University Education in Wales (London: HMSO, 1918).

Ford, Patrick K. 'Performance and Literacy in Medieval Welsh Poetry'. *Modern Language Review*, 100 (2005), xxx–xlviii.
Forder, Helen. *High Hats and Harps: The Life and Times of Lord and Lady Llanover* (n.p.: TallyBerry Publishing, 2012).
Francis, J. G. 'Hubert Davies (1893–1965)'. *Welsh Music/Cerddoriaeth Cymru*, 11/1 (Summer/Haf 2009), 5–8.
Fraser, Maxwell. 'Sir Benjamin and Lady Hall in the 1840's: Part I: 1840–1845'. *The National Library of Wales Journal/Cylchgrawn Llyfrgell Genedlaethol Cymru*, 14/1 (1965), 35–52.
Frere, W. H., ed. *Visitation Articles and Injunctions of the Period of the Reformation*, 3 vols, Alcuin Club Collections, 14–16 (London: Longmans, Green, 1910).
Frith, Simon. 'Music and Identity', in *Questions of Cultural Identity*, ed. by Stuart Hall and Paul du Gay (London: Sage, 1996), pp. 108–127.
Frost, Maurice. *English and Scottish Psalm and Hymn Tunes c. 1543–1677* (London: SPCK and Oxford University Press, 1953).
Gainer, Jeffrey. 'The Road to Disestablishment', in *A New History of the Church in Wales: Governance and Ministry, Theology and Society*, ed. by Norman Doe (Cambridge: Cambridge University Press, 2020), pp. 27–44.
Galpin, Francis. *Old English Instruments of Music* (London: Methuen, 1910).
Gelbart, Matthew. *The Invention of 'Folk Music' and 'Art Music': Emerging Categories from Ossian to Wagner* (Cambridge: Cambridge University Press, 2011).
Giraldus Cambrensis. *Descriptio Kambriae, Giraldi Cambrensis Opera*, ed. J. F. Dimock (London: Rolls Series, 1868).
— *The Description of Wales*, trans. L. Thorpe (London: Penguin, 1978).
— *The History and Topography of Ireland*, trans. John J. O'Meara, revised ed. (Portlaoise: North America Humanities Press; Dolmen Press, 1982).
— *Topographia Hibernica, Giraldi Cambrensis Opera*, ed. by J. V. Dimock, V (London: Rolls Series, 1867).
Gosden, David. 'The Origin and Survival of Tunes for the Hymns of William Williams, "Pantycelyn"/Tarddiad a Pharhad y Tonau i Emynau William Williams, "Pantycelyn"'. *Welsh Music History/Hanes Cerddoriaeth Cymru*, 5 (2002), 72–104.
Graham, John. *A Century of Welsh Music* (London: Kegan Paul, Trench, Trubner, 1923).
Gramich, Katie, ed. and trans. *The Works of Gwerful Mechain* (Peterborough, Canada: Broadview Press, 2018).
Gray, J., trans. and J. Richards (arr. and transcr.). *Eight Operatic Songs from the Bohemian Girl by M. W. Balfe and Maritana by W. V. Wallace* (Swansea: B. Parry, [1889]).
Greenhill, Peter. 'Melodic Formulas in the Robert ap Huw Manuscript/ Fformiwlâu Melodig yn Llawysgrif Robert ap Huw'. *Welsh Music History/ Hanes Cerddoriaeth Cymru*, 3 (1999), 217–251.

'The Robert ap Huw Manuscript: An Exploration of Its Possible Solutions' (private dissertation, 1995–). www.cl.cam.ac.uk/~rja14/musicfiles/manuscripts/aphuw/ (accessed 25 June 2021).
Griffith, R. D. *Hanes Canu Cynulleidfaol Cymru* (Caerdydd: Gwasg Prifysgol Cymru, 1948).
Griffith, Robert. *Llyfr Cerdd Dannau* (Caernarfon: Cwmni y Cyhoeddwyr Cymreig, [1913]).
Griffith, W. P. 'Tudor Prelude', in *The Welsh in London 1500–2000*, ed. by Emrys Jones (Cardiff: University of Wales Press on behalf of the Honourable Society of Cymmrodorion, 2001), pp. 8–34.
Griffith, Wyn. *The Welsh* (Harmondsworth: Penguin, 1950).
Griffiths, Dai. '"Home Is Living Like a Man on the Run": John Cale's Welsh Atlantic/"Home Is Living Like a Man on the Run": Iwerydd Cymreig John Cale'. *Welsh Music History/Hanes Cerddoriaeth Cymru*, 4 (2000), 159–185.
Griffiths, Ralph A. *Sir Rhys ap Thomas and His Family: A Study in the Wars of the Roses and Early Tudor Politics* (Cardiff: University of Wales Press, 1993).
Griffiths, Rhidian. 'Benjamin Parry, Cyhoeddwr Cerddoriaeth/Benjamin Parry, Music Publisher'. *Welsh Music History/Hanes Cerddoriaeth Cymru*, 6 (2004), 193–216.
'Daniel Protheroe (1866–1934)', in *Cydymaith i Gerddoriaeth Cymru*, goln. Pwyll ap Siôn a Wyn Thomas (Talybont: Y Lolfa, 2018), tt. 35–36.
'Folk Roots of Welsh Hymn Tunes'. *Bulletin (Hymn Society of Great Britain and Ireland)*, 22/1 (2018), 11–24.
'"Gwlad y Gân": Y Traddodiad Cerddorol yn Oes Victoria', in *Cof Cenedl VIII: Ysgrifau ar Hanes Cymru*, gol. Geraint H. Jenkins (Llandysul: Gwasg Gomer, 1993), tt. 103–132.
'*Hen Wlad fy Nhadau* in Its Musical Context'. *Morgannwg*, 51 (2007), 6–18.
'Isaac Jones, Music Printer and Publisher'. *Y Llyfr yng Nghymru / Welsh Book Studies*, 5 (2003), 44–53.
'Music and Popular Culture'. *Cardiganshire County History*, 3 (1998), 588–601.
'Musical Life in the Nineteenth Century'. *Glamorgan County History*, 6 (1988), 367–379.
'Swansea's "Mr. Music": The Career of D. J. Snell, Music Publisher'. *Y Llyfr yng Nghymru/Welsh Book Studies*, 1 (1998), 59–90.
'Welsh Chapel Music: The Making of a Tradition'. *Journal of Welsh Ecclesiastical History*, 6 (1989), 35–43.
'"Y Cyfansoddwr Gorau": Ieuan Gwyllt a'r Alaw Gymreig/"The Best Composer": Ieuan Gwyllt and the Welsh Melody', in *Cynheiliaid y Gân: Ysgrifau i Anrhydeddu Phyllis Kinney a Meredydd Evans / Bearers of Song: Essays in Honour of Phyllis Kinney and Meredydd Evans* (Cardiff: University of Wales Press, 2007), pp. 93–116.
'Y Methodistiaid Laddodd Gerddoriaeth Werin yng Nghymru'. *Canu Gwerin/Folk Song*, 37 (2014), 9–21.
'"Yn y Dechreuad …": A. P. Graves a J. Lloyd Williams'. *Canu Gwerin/Folk Song*, 43 (2020), 27–43.

Guy, Ben, Georgia Henley, Owain Wyn Jones and Rebecca Thomas, eds. *The Chronicles of Medieval Wales and the March: New Contexts, Studies and Texts* (Turnhout: Brepols, 2019).
Gwenynen Gwent (Mrs Hall of Llanover). *Gwent and Dyfed Royal Eisteddfod 1834. The Prize Essay on the Advantages Resulting from the Preservation of the Welsh Language and National Costumes of Wales* (London and Cardiff: Longman, Rees, Orme, Brown, Green and Longman/William Bird, 1836).
Harding, James. *Ivor Novello: A Biography* (Bridgend: Welsh Academic Press, 1997).
Harker, Dave. *Fakesong: The Manufacture of British Folk Song, 1700 to the Present Day* (Milton Keynes: Open University Press, 1985).
Harper, John. 'Contexts for the Late Medieval Pontifical of Anian, Bishop of Bangor: Issues of the "Local" and the "More-Than-Local"', in *Music and Liturgy in Medieval Britain and Ireland*, ed. by Ann Buckley and Lisa Colton (Cambridge: Cambridge University Press, 2022), pp. 17–49.
'An Organ for St Teilo: A Welsh Instrument in the Pre-Reformation Tradition'. *Journal of the British Institute of Organ Studies*, 35 (2011), 134–153.
'Peter Crossley-Holland and Early Welsh Music Studies/Peter Crossley-Holland ac Efrydiaethau Cerddoriaeth Gynnar Cymru'. *Welsh Music History/Hanes Cerddoriaeth Cymru*, 5 (2002), 1–21.
'Philip ap Rhys and His Liturgical Organ Music Revisited/Ailolwg ar Philip ap Rhys a'i Gerddoriaeth Organ Litwrgïaidd'. *Welsh Music History/Hanes Cerddoriaeth Cymru*, 2 (1997), 126–172.
Harper, Sally. 'The Bangor Pontifical: A Pontifical of the Use of Salisbury/Esgoblyfr Bangor: Esgoblyfr Arfer Caersallog'. *Welsh Music History/Hanes Cerddoriaeth Cymru*, 2 (1997), 65–100.
'Dafydd ap Gwilym, Poet and Musician', in *Gwaith Dafydd ap Gwilym*, ed. by Dafydd Johnston, www.dafyddapgwilym.net/essays/sally_harper/index_eng.php (accessed 25 June 2021).
'An Elizabethan Tune List from Lleweni Hall, North Wales'. *Royal Musical Association Research Chronicle*, 39 (2005), 45–98.
'Instrumental Music in Medieval Wales'. *North American Journal of Welsh Studies*, 4 (2004), 20–42.
'Issues in Dating the Repertory of *Cerdd Dant*'. *Studia Celtica*, 35 (2001), 325–340.
Music in Welsh Culture before 1650: A Study of the Principal Sources (Aldershot: Ashgate, 2007).
'The Robert ap Huw Manuscript and the Canon of Sixteenth-Century Harp Music/Llawysgrif Robert ap Huw a Chanon Cerddoriaeth Gymreig i'r Delyn yn yr Unfed Ganrif ar Bymtheg'. *Welsh Music History/Hanes Cerddoriaeth Cymru*, 3 (1999), 130–161.
'So How Many Irishmen Went to Glyn Achlach? Early Accounts of the Formation of Cerdd Dant'. *Cambrian Medieval Celtic Studies*, 42 (2001), 1–25.

'"Songes of the Doeinges of Their Auncestors": Aspects of Welsh and English Musical Traditions', in *Authority and Subjugation in Writing of Medieval Wales*, ed. by Ruth Kennedy and Simon Meecham-Jones, New Middle Ages series, ed. by Bonnie Wheeler (London: Palgrave Macmillan, 2008), pp. 231–250.

'Tunes for a Welsh Psalter: Edmwnd Prys's *Llyfr y Psalmau*'. *Studia Celtica*, 37 (2003), 221–267.

Harper, Sally, and Wyn Thomas. *Cynheiliaid y Gân: Ysgrifau i Anrhydeddu Phyllis Kinney a Meredydd Evans/Bearers of Song: Essays in Honour of Phyllis Kinney and Meredydd Evans* (Cardiff: University of Wales Press, 2007).

Harvey, John. 'Nicholas Evans: Paintings by a Mad Pianist/Nicholas Evans: Darluniau gan Bianydd Gwallgof'. *Welsh Music History/Hanes Cerddoriaeth Cymru*, 2 (1997), 236–252.

Hawkins, John. *A General History of the Science and Practice of Music* (London: T. Payne and Son, 1776).

Hensel, Sebastian. *Die Familie Mendelssohn 1729–1847: Nach Briefen und Tagebüchern*, Vol. 1 (Berlin: B. Behr's Verlag, 1904).

Herbert, Trevor. 'A Lament for Sam Hughes: The Last Ophicleidist'. *Planet: the Welsh Internationalist*, 87 (1991), 66–75.

'Late Welsh Victorian Bands: Taste, Virtuosity and Cymmrodorion Attitudes/ Bandiau Cymreig y Cyfnod Fictoraidd Diweddar: Chwaeth, Pencampwriaeth ac Agweddau'r Cymmrodorion'. *Welsh Music History/ Hanes Cerddoriaeth Cymru*, 1 (1996), 92–113.

'Popular Nationalism: Griffith Rhys Jones ('Caradog') and the Welsh Choral Tradition', in *Music and British Culture 1785–1914*, ed. by Christina Bashford and Leanne Langley (Oxford: Oxford University Press, 2000), pp. 255–275.

'Public Military Music and the Promotion of Patriotism in the Provinces, c.1780–c.1850', *Nineteenth-Century Music Review*, 17/3 (2020), 427–444.

'The Practice and Context of a Private Victorian Brass Band', in *Nineteenth-Century British Music Studies*, ed. by Bennett Zon (Aldershot: Ashgate, 1999), pp. 105–18.

'Reconstruction of Nineteenth-Century Band Repertory: Towards a Protocol', in *Perspectives in Brass Scholarship: Proceedings of the International Historic Brass Society Symposium, Amherst, 1995*, ed. by Stewart Carter (Stuyvesant, NY: Pendragon Press, 1997), pp. 185–213.

'The Repertory of a Victorian Provincial Brass Band'. *Popular Music*, 9/1 (1990), 117–132.

'A Softening Influence: R. T. Crawshay and the Cyfarthfa Band'. *The Merthyr Historian*, 5 (1992), 35–42.

'The Virtuosi of Merthyr'. *Llafur: The Journal of the Society for the Study of Welsh Labour History*, 5/1 (1988), 60–69.

Herbert, Trevor, ed. *The British Brass Band: A Musical and Social History* (Oxford: Oxford University Press, 2000).

Herbert, Trevor, and Helen Barlow. *Music and the British Military in the Long Nineteenth Century* (New York: Oxford University Press, 2013).

Herbert, Trevor, and Gareth Elwyn Jones, ed. *Edward I and Wales* (Cardiff: University of Wales Press, 1988).
People and Protest: Wales 1815–1880 (Cardiff: University of Wales Press, 1988).
Post-War Wales (Cardiff: University of Wales Press, 1995).
The Remaking of Wales in the Eighteenth Century (Cardiff: University of Wales Press, 1988).
Tudor Wales (Cardiff: University of Wales Press, 1988).
Wales 1880–1914 (Cardiff: University of Wales Press, 1988).
Wales between the Wars (Cardiff: University of Wales Press, 1988).
Herbert, Trevor, and Arnold Myers. *Catalogue of the European Wind and Percussion Instruments in the Cyfarthfa Castle Museum Collection* (Merthyr Tydfil: Cyfarthfa Castle Museum and Art Gallery, 1990).
'Instruments of the Cyfarthfa Band'. *Galpin Society Journal*, 41 (1988), 2–10.
Herbert, Trevor, Arnold Myers and John Wallace, ed. *The Cambridge Encyclopedia of Brass Instruments* (Cambridge: Cambridge University Press, 2019).
Herbert, Trevor, and Peter Stead. *Hymns and Arias: Great Welsh Voices* (Cardiff: University of Wales Press, 2001).
Herl, Joseph. 'Earliest Source of "Cwm Rhondda" Found'. *The Hymn Society Bulletin*, 21/3 (2015), 98–102.
Hill, Sarah. 'Beyond Borders: The Female Welsh Pop Voice'. *Radical Musicology*, 1 (2006), 35 paras, www.radical-musicology.org.uk/2006/Hill.htm (accessed 5 July 2021).
'Blerwytirhwng?' The Place of Welsh Pop Music (Aldershot: Ashgate, 2007).
'Families of Resemblance: Welsh Popular Music and Other Marginalia/ Teuluoedd Tebygrwydd: Cerddoriaeth Boblogaidd Gymreig ac Ymylnodau Eraill'. *Welsh Music History/Hanes Cerddoriaeth Cymru*, 4 (2000), 138–158.
Hill, Sarah and Dai Griffiths. 'Postcolonial Music in Contemporary Wales: Hybrids and Weird Geographies', in *Postcolonial Wales*, ed. by Jane Aaron and Chris Williams (Cardiff: University of Wales Press, 2005), pp. 215–233.
Hobsbawm, Eric and Terence Ranger, eds. *The Invention of Tradition* (Cambridge: Cambridge University Press, 1983).
Hoggart, Richard. *The Way We Live Now* (London: Chatto & Windus, 1995).
Holt, Richard. *Sport and the British: A Modern History* (Oxford: Clarendon, 1989).
Hopwood, C. H., ed. *A Calendar of the Middle Temple Records* (London: Masters of the Bench, 1903).
Hughes, Ian, ed. *Math Uab Mathonwy: The Fourth Branch of the Mabinogi* (Dublin: Dublin Institute for Advanced Studies, 2013).
Hurd, Michael. *Vincent Novello – and Company* (St Albans: Granada, 1981).
Huws, Bleddyn Owen. *Y Canu Gofyn a Diolch, c.1350–c.1630* (Caerdydd: Gwasg Prifysgol Cymru, 1998).

Huws, Daniel. 'Gwisgo Merched a Mesurau/Dressing Women in Tunes', in *Cynheiliaid y Gân: Ysgrifau i Anrhydeddu Phyllis Kinney a Meredydd Evans/ Bearers of Song: Essays in Honour of Phyllis Kinney and Meredydd Evans*, ed. by Sally Harper and Wyn Thomas (Cardiff: University of Wales Press, 2007), pp. 145–188.

'Iolo Morganwg and Traditional Music', in *A Rattleskull Genius: The Many Faces of Iolo Morganwg*, ed. by Geraint H. Jenkins (Cardiff: University of Wales Press, 2009), pp. 333–356.

'Melus-Seiniau Cymru', *Canu Gwerin/Folk Song*, 8 (1985), 32–50.

'Melus-Seiniau Cymru: Atodiadau', *Canu Gwerin/Folk Song*, 9 (1986), 47–57.

'Notes on the Robert ap Huw Manuscript/Nodiadau ar Lawysgrif Robert ap Huw', *Welsh Music History/Hanes Cerddoriaeth Cymru*, 6 (2006), 47–62.

A Repertory of Welsh Manuscripts and Scribes c.800–c.1800 (Aberystwyth: University of Wales Centre for Advanced Welsh and Celtic Studies and the National Library of Wales, 2022).

'Rhagymadrodd/Introduction', in Maria Jane Williams, *Ancient National Airs of Gwent and Morganwg*, facsimile edn (Cymdeithas Alawon Gwerin Cymru/ The Welsh Folk-Song Society, 1988), pp. xi–xxxviii.

'St David in the Liturgy', in *St David of Wales: Cult, Church and Nation*, ed. by J. Wyn Evans and Jonathan M. Wooding (Woodbridge: The Boydell Press, 2007), pp. 220–232.

Ifans, Rhiannon. *Red Hearts and Roses? Welsh Valentine Songs and Poems* (Cardiff: University of Wales Press, 2019).

James, Beryl Bowen and David Allsobrook. *First in the World: The Story of the National Youth Orchestra of Wales* (Cardiff: University of Wales Press, 1995).

James, E. Wyn. 'An "English" Lady among Welsh Folk: Ruth Herbert Lewis and the Welsh Folk-Song Society', in Ian Russell and David Atkinson, eds., *Folk Song: Tradition, Revival and Re-creation* (Aberdeen: The Elphinstone Institute, University of Aberdeen, 2004), pp. 266–283. Also available at www.cardiff.ac.uk/cy/special-collections/subject-guides/welsh-ballads/ruth-herbert-lewis (accessed 22 September 2021).

'The Evolution of the Welsh Hymn', in *Dissenting Praise: Religious Dissent and the Hymn in England and Wales*, ed. by Isabel Rivers and David L. Wykes (Oxford: Oxford University Press, 2011), pp. 229–268.

'Painting the World Green: Dafydd Iwan and the Welsh Protest Ballad'. *Folk Music Journal*, 8/5 (2005), 594–618.

'Popular Poetry, Methodism, and the Ascendancy of the Hymn', in *The Cambridge History of Welsh Literature*, ed. by Geraint Evans and Helen Fulton (Cambridge: Cambridge University Press, 2019), pp. 306–234.

James, E. Wyn, and Tecwyn Vaughan Jones. *Gwerin Gwlad: Ysgrifau ar Ddiwylliant Gwerin Cymru Cyfrol 1* (Llanrwst: Carreg Gwalch, 2008).

Jarman, A. O. H. 'Telyn a Chrwth'. *Llên Cymru*, 6 (1960–61), 154–175.

Jarman, Eldra and A. O. H. Jarman. *The Welsh Gypsies: Children of Abram Wood* (Cardiff: University of Wales Press, 1991).

Jarvis, Branwen. *A Guide to Welsh Literature c.1700–1800* (Cardiff: University of Wales Press, 2000).
Jenkins, Bethan M. *Between Wales and England: Anglophone Welsh Writing of the Eighteenth Century* (Cardiff: University of Wales Press, 2017).
Jenkins, D. *Sut i Ddysgu yr Hen Nodiant drwy y Sol-Ffa* (Wrexham: Hughes & Son, 1898).
Jenkins, Dafydd. 'Bardd Teulu and *Pencerdd*', in *The Welsh King and His Court*, ed. by T. M. Charles-Edwards, Morfydd E. Owen and Paul Russell (Cardiff: University of Wales Press, 2000).
    ed., *Damweiniau Colan: Llyfr y Damweiniau yn ôl Llawysgrif Peniarth 30* (Aberystwyth: Cymdeithas Lyfrau Ceredigion, 1973).
    ed., *The Law of Hywel Dda: Law Texts from Medieval Wales*. trans. Dafydd Jenkins, The Welsh Classics 2 (Llandysul: Gomer Press, 1986).
Jenkins, Geraint H. *The Foundations of Modern Wales: Wales 1642–1780* (Oxford: Oxford University Press, 1993; originally published 1987).
    'Historical Writing in the Eighteenth Century', in *A Guide to Welsh Literature c. 1700–1800*, ed. by Branwen Jarvis (Cardiff: University of Wales Press, 2000), pp. 23–44.
    'On the Trail of a "Rattleskull Genius": Introduction', in *A Rattleskull Genius: The Many Faces of Iolo Morganwg*, ed. by Geraint H. Jenkins (Cardiff: University of Wales Press, 2009), pp. 1–28.
    ed., *A Rattleskull Genius: The Many Faces of Iolo Morganwg* (Cardiff: University of Wales Press, 2009).
Jenkins, Karl. *Still with the Music* (London: Elliott and Thompson Ltd, 2015).
Jenkins, Philip. *The Making of a Ruling Class: The Glamorgan Gentry 1640–1790* (Cambridge: Cambridge University Press, 1983).
Jenkins, R. T., and Helen M. Ramage. *A History of the Honourable Society of Cymmrodorion and of the Gwyneddigion and Cymreigyddion Societies (1751–1951)* (London: The Honourable Society of Cymmrodorion, 1951).
John, Angela V., ed. *Our Mothers' Land: Chapters in Welsh Women's History 1830–1939* (Cardiff: University of Wales Press, 1991).
Johnes, Martin. *A History of Sport in Wales* (Cardiff: University of Wales Press, 2005).
Johnston, Dafydd, ed. *Gwaith Iolo Goch* (Caerdydd: Gwasg Prifysgol Cymru, 1988).
    ed., *Iolo Goch: Poems* (Llandysul: Gomer, 1993).
    et al., goln. *Cerddi Dafydd ap Gwilym* (Caerdydd: Gwasg Prifysgol Cymru, 2010).
Jones, Bill. 'Welsh Identities in Ballarat, Australia, During the Late Nineteenth Century'. *Welsh History Review*, 20 (2000–1), 283–307.
Jones, Brynmor P. *Voices from the Welsh Revival 1904–1905* (Bridgend: Evangelical Press of Wales, 1995).
Jones, Craig Owen. '"Beatbox Taffia": Welsh Underground Music in the 1990s/"Beatbox Taffia": Cerddoriaeth Danddaearol Gymraeg yn y 1990au'. *Welsh Music History/Hanes Cerddoriaeth Cymru*, 6 (2006), 217–259.

"'Beatbox Taffia" II: Prevailing Trends in Welsh-Language Hip-Hop and Underground Music/"Beatbox Taffia" II: Y Tueddiadau Amlycaf mewn Cerddoriaeth Hip-Hop a Thanddaearol Cymraeg'. *Welsh Music History/ Hanes Cerddoriaeth Cymru*, 7 (2007), 225–264.

'Mapping Live Provisions in Welsh-Language Rock, 1978–80'. *Popular Music History*, 7/1 (2012), 53–81.

Jones, Daniel. 'Daniel Jones', in *Artists in Wales*, ed. by Meic Stephens (Llandysul: J. D. Lewis & Sons Ltd, 1971), pp. 109–118.

My Friend Dylan Thomas (London: J. M. Dent & Sons, 1977).

'Some Metrical Experiments'. *The Score*, 3 (1950), 32–48.

ed., *The Poems of Dylan Thomas* (New York: New Directions, 1971).

Jones, David R. 'Nationalism, Folk Song and Welsh Art Music: One Man's Vision/Cenedlaetholdeb, Canu Gwerin a Cherddoriaeth Gelfyddydol Gymreig: Gweledigaeth Un Dyn'. *Welsh Music History/Hanes Cerddoriaeth Cymru*, 7 (2007), 161–224.

Jones, Edward. *The Bardic Museum* (London: A Strahan, 1802).

Hen Ganiadau Cymru: Cambro-British Melodies (London: 1820).

Musical and Poetical Relicks of the Welsh Bards (London: Printed for the Author, 1784).

Musical and Poetical Relicks of the Welsh Bards, 2nd ed. (London: Printed for the Author, 1794).

Jones, Emrys, ed. *The Welsh in London 1500–2000* (Cardiff: University of Wales on behalf of the Honourable Society of Cymmrodorion, 2001).

Jones, Emrys, and Ieuan L. Griffiths. 'A Linguistic Map of Wales: 1961'. *The Geographical Journal*, 129/2 (1963), 192–196.

Jones, Elin M., gol., gyda chymorth Nerys Ann Jones. *Gwaith Llywarch ap Llywelyn 'Prydydd y Moch'* (Caerdydd: Gwasg Prifysgol Cymru, 1991).

Jones, Ffion Mair. '"To Know Him Is to Esteem Him": John Jenkins, Ifor Ceri 1770–1829'. *Montgomeryshire Collections*, 99 (2011), 53–82.

Jones, G. I. *Meistr Cerdd: Bywyd a Gwaith William Bradwen Jones, Cerddor* (Llangefni: Yr Awdur, 1983).

Jones, John Gwynfor. 'Cerdd a Bonedd Yng Nghymru 1540–1640: Rhai Argraffiadau'. *Welsh Music/Cerddoriaeth Cymru*, 6/9 (Winter/Gaeaf 1981–2), 22–33; 7/1 (Summer/Haf 1982), 25–40; 7/3 (Spring/Gwanwyn 1983), 30–47.

The Wynn Family of Gwydir: Origins, Growth and Development c.1490–1674 (Aberystwyth: Centre for Educational Studies, 1995).

Jones, Kitty Idwal. 'Adventures in Folk-Song Collecting'. *Welsh Music/ Cerddoriaeth Cymru*, 5/5 (Spring/Gwanwyn 1977), 33–52.

Jones, Nerys Ann. *Hywel ab Owain Gwynedd: Bardd-Dywysog* (Caerdydd:Gwasg Prifysgol Cymru, 2009).

Jones, Nicholas. '"Disparagement and Invidious Comparisons"? Assessing Critical Reactions to Mathias's Symphony No. 1'. *Tempo*, 60/238 (October 2006), 8–14.

'Mathias's String Quartet No. 1: Something to Shout About'. *The Musical Times*, 141/1872 (Autumn 2000), 24–32.

Jones, Owen, Edward Williams and William Owen Pughe. *The Myvyrian Archaiology of Wales: Collected out of Ancient Manuscripts* (London: S. Rousseau, 1801/1807).

Jones, Philip Henry. 'A Golden Age Reappraised: Welsh-Language Publishing in the Nineteenth Century', in *Images and Texts: Their Production and Distribution in the 18th and 19th Centuries*, ed. by Peter Isaac and Barry McKay (Winchester: St Paul's Bibliographies; Delaware: Oak Knoll Press, 1997), pp. 121–141.

Jones, Philip Henry and Eiluned Rees, ed. *A Nation and Its Books: A History of the Book in Wales* (Aberystwyth: National Library of Wales, 1998).

Jones, R. Tudur. *Faith and the Crisis of a Nation: Wales 1890–1914*, ed. by Robert Pope and trans. by Sylvia Prys Jones (Cardiff: University of Wales Press, 2004).

Jones, Theophilus. *A History of the County of Brecknock*, 2 vols (Brecon: George North, 1805–9).

Jones, Thomas, trans. *Brut y Tywysogyon or the Chronicle of the Princes: Peniarth Ms. 20 Version* (Cardiff: University of Wales Press, 1952).

Jones, W. D. *Wales in America: Scranton and the Welsh, 1860–1920* (Cardiff: University of Wales Press, 1993).

Jones-Baker, Doris. 'Mediaeval and Tudor Music and Musicians in Hertfordshire: The Graffiti Evidence', in *Hertfordshire in History: Essays Presented to Lionel Munby*, ed. by Doris Jones-Baker (Hatfield: Hertfordshire Publications, 2004), pp. 22–46.

Keegan-Phipps, Simon. 'Déjà Vu? Folk Music, Education, and Institutionalization in Contemporary England'. *Yearbook for Traditional Music*, 39 (2007), 84–107.

Keen, Elen Wyn. 'Camp Cerddor a Gallu Gwyddonydd: J. Lloyd Williams a'i Gylchgrawn/A Musician's Art and Scientific Prowess: J. Lloyd Williams and his Journal'. *Welsh Music History/Hanes Cerddoriaeth Cymru*, 5 (2002), 135–161.

Kinney, Phyllis. 'Hunting the Wren/Hela'r Dryw'. *Welsh Music History/Hanes Cerddoriaeth Cymru*, 6 (2006), 104–128.

'An Irish/Welsh Tune Family/Teulu o Alawon Gwyddelig/Cymreig'. *Welsh Music History/Hanes Cerddoriaeth Cymru*, 1 (1996), 114–127.

'John Thomas's Fiddle Manuscript'. *Canu Gwerin/Folk Song*, 22 (1999), 43–51.

'The Tunes of the Welsh Christmas Carols'. *Canu Gwerin*, 11 (1988), 28–57; *Canu Gwerin*, 12 (1989), 5–29.

Welsh Traditional Music (Cardiff: University of Wales Press in association with Cymdeithas Alawon Gwerin Cymru, 2011).

Kinney, Phyllis and Meredydd Evans. *Hen Alawon (Carolau a Cherddi): Casgliad John Owen, Dwyran* (Cymdeithas Alawon Gwerin Cymru mewn cydweithrediad ag Amgueddfa Genedlaethol Cymru, 1993).

Klausner, David. 'Family Entertainments among the Salusburys of Lleweni and Their Circle, 1595–1641/Diddanwch Teuluaidd ymysg Salsbriaid Lleweni a'u Cylch, 1595–1641'. *Welsh Music History/Hanes Cerddoriaeth Cymru*, 6 (2006), 129–154.
—— 'Statud Gruffudd ap Cynan/The Statute of Gruffudd ap Cynan'. *Welsh Music History/Hanes Cerddoriaeth Cymru*, 3 (1999), 282–298.
Klausner, David N., ed. *Records of Early Drama: Wales*, Records of Early English Drama (Toronto: University of Toronto Press, 2005).
Knapp, James F. 'The Poetry of R. S. Thomas'. *Twentieth Century Literature*, 17/1 (1971), 1–9.
Lambert, W. R. *Drink and Sobriety in Victorian Wales c.1820–c.1895* (Cardiff: University of Wales Press, 1983).
Law, Bryn. *Don't Take Me Home: On Tour with the Red Wall at Euro 2016* (Cardiff: St David's Press, 2016).
Le Huray, Peter. 'The Chirk Castle Partbooks'. *Early Music History*, 2 (1982), 17–42.
Leathart, William. *The Origin and Progress of the Gwyneddigion Society of London, Instituted 1770* (London: Hugh Pierce Hughes, 1831).
—— *Welsh Pennillion; with Translations into English, Adapted for Singing to the Harp* (London: W. T. Moncrieff, 1825).
Leech, Caroline. *Welsh National Opera: Celebrating the First Sixty Years* (Cardiff: Graffeg, 2006).
Leonard, Deke. *Maybe I Should've Stayed in Bed? The Flip Side of the Rock'n'roll Dream* (Bordon: Northdown Publishing, 2000).
—— *Rhinos, Winos & Lunatics: The Legend of Man, a Rock'n'Roll Band* (Bordon: Northdown Publishing, 1996).
Levine, Lawrence W. *Highbrow/Lowbrow: The Emergence of Cultural Hierarchy in America* (Cambridge, MA; London: Harvard University Press, 1990).
Lewis, Geraint. 'Hoddinott and the Symphony'. *The Musical Times*, 130/1758 (August 1989), 455–459.
—— '"Welsh" Music'. *Welsh Music/Cerddoriaeth Cymru*, 7/2 (Winter/Gaeaf 1982–3), 6–19.
Lewis, John H., Christopher Painter, Huw Tregelles Williams, Elinor Bennett, Robin Stowell, Mervyn Burtch, Alun Francis, Tony Small, Andrew Matthews-Owen, Jeremy Huw Williams, Denis Wick and Richard Elfyn Jones. 'Tributes to Alun Hoddinott'. *Welsh Music/Cerddoriaeth Cymru*, 11/1 (Summer/Haf 2009), 14–34.
Lewis, Richard and David Wood. 'Culture, Politics and Assimilation: The Welsh on Teesside, c. 1850–1940'. *Welsh History Review*, 17 (1994–5), 550–570.
Lewis, Ruth Herbert. *Folk Songs Collected in Flintshire and the Vale of Clwyd* (Wrexham: Hughes & Son, 1914).
—— *Second Collection of Welsh Folk-Songs* (Wrexham: Hughes & Son; Cardiff: Educational Publishing Co., 1934).
Lewis, Timothy. 'The Paris Hexameron', *The Dragon*, XXXVI (1910–11), 219–222.

Ley, Rachel. 'Arglwyddes Llanofer a'r Delyn Deires/Lady Llanover and the Triple Harp'. *Welsh Music History/Hanes Cerddoriaeth Cymru* (1996), 128–143.

Arglwyddes Llanofer, Gwenynen Gwent (Caernarfon Gwasg Gwynedd, 2001).

Lhuyd, Edward. *Archaeologia Britannica, Giving Some Account Additional to what has been hitherto Publish'd, of the Languages, Histories and Customs of the Original Inhabitants of Great Britain: From Collections and Observations in Travels through Wales, Cornwal, Bas-Bretagne, Ireland and Scotland* (Oxford: Printed at the Theater for the Author, 1707).

Livingston, Tamara. 'Music Revivals: Towards a General Theory'. *Ethnomusicology*, 43 (1999), 66–85.

Lloyd, Philip. *Silvograph: Arthur Cheetham (1865–1937), Pioneer Film-Maker* (Llanrwst: Gwasg Carreg Gwalch, 2018).

Llwyd, Alan. *Blynyddoedd y Locustiaid: Hanes Eisteddfod Genedlaethol Cymru 1919–1936* (Felindre: Cyhoeddiadau Barddas, 2007)

Prifysgol y Werin: Hanes Eisteddfod Genedlaethol Cymru, 1900–1918 (Felindre: Cyhoeddiadau Barddas, 2008).

Y Gaer Fechan Olaf: Hanes Eisteddfod Genedlaethol Cymru 1937–1950 (Felindre: Cyhoeddiadau Barddas, 2006).

Luff, Alan. *Welsh Hymns and Their Tunes: Their Background and Place in Welsh History and Culture* (London: Stainer & Bell, 1990).

MacLean, Malcolm. 'Of Warriors and Blokes: The Problem of Maori Rugby for Pakeha Masculinity in New Zealand', in *Making the Rugby World: Race, Gender, Commerce*, ed. by Timothy J. Chandler and John Naught (London and Portland OR: Frank Cass, 1999), pp. 1–26.

Mangan, J. A., ed. *Pleasure, Profit, Proselytism: British Culture and Sport at Home and Abroad 1700–1914* (Frank Cass, 1988).

Marwick, Arthur. *Culture in Britain since 1945* (Oxford: Basil Blackwell, 1991).

Mathias, Rhiannon. *Lutyens, Maconchy, Williams and Twentieth-Century British Music: A Blest Trio of Sirens* (Farnham: Ashgate, 2012).

Mathias, Roland. 'Roland Mathias', in *Artists in Wales*, ed. by Meic Stephens (Llandysul: J.D. Lewis & Sons Ltd, 1971).

Matthias, William, 'William Matthias', in *Artists in Wales*, ed. by Meic Stephens (Llandysul: J. D. Lewis & Sons Ltd, 1971).

Mathias, William, and Malcolm Boyd. 'William Mathias at 50: The Composer Talks to Malcolm Boyd'. *The Musical Times*, 125/1701 (November 1984), 626–627.

Mathias, William, in conversation with A. J. Heward Rees. 'Perspectives and Prospects'. *Welsh Music/Cerddoriaeth Cymru*, 4/10 (Summer/Haf 1975), 11–22.

Mathias, William, in conversation with A. J. Heward Rees. 'Servants and Masters'. *Welsh Music/Cerddoriaeth Cymru*, 6/5 (Summer/Haf 1980), 17–27.

McAulay, Karen. *Our Ancient National Airs: Scottish Song Collecting from the Enlightenment to the Romantic Era* (Farnham: Ashgate, 2013).

McKerrell, Simon. 'Traditional Arts and the State: The Scottish Case'. *Cultural Trends*, 23 (2014), 159–168.
McKibbin, Ross. *Classes and Cultures, England 1918–51* (Oxford: Oxford University Press, 1998).
McVeigh, Simon. *Concert Life in London from Mozart to Haydn* (Cambridge: Cambridge University Press, 1993).
Meurig, Cass. 'Composing Traditional Music', in *Cynheiliaid y Gân: Ysgrifau i Anrhydeddu Phyllis Kinney a Meredydd Evans/Bearers of Song: Essays in Honour of Phyllis Kinney and Meredydd Evans*, ed. by Sally Harper and Wyn Thomas (Cardiff: University of Wales Press, 2007), pp. 240–250.
'Dance in Wales in the Seventeenth and Eighteenth Centuries/Dawns yng Nghymru yn yr Ail Ganrif ar Bymtheg a'r Ddeunawfed Ganrif'. *Welsh Music History/Hanes Cerddoriaeth Cymru*, 7 (2007), 55–91.
'The Fiddler in Eighteenth-Century Wales/Y Ffidler yng Nghymru'r Ddeunawfed Ganrif'. *Welsh Music History/Hanes Cerddoriaeth Cymru*, 5 (2002), 22–58.
ed., *Alawon John Thomas: A Fiddler's Tune Book from Eighteenth-Century Wales* (Aberystwyth: Llyfrgell Genedlaethol Cymru/The National Library of Wales, 2004).
Miles, Bethan. 'Crwth'. In *Cydymaith i Gerddoriaeth Cymru*, goln. Pwyll ap Siôn a Wyn Thomas (Talybont: Y Lolfa, 2018), tt. 107–109.
'Crythorion'. In *Cydymaith i Gerddoriaeth Cymru*, goln. Pwyll ap Siôn a Wyn Thomas (Talybont: Y Lolfa, 2018), tt. 109–112.
Mills, Janet. 'Secondary Singing Inspected'. *British Journal of Music Education*, 17/1 (March 2000), 61–66, doi:10.1017/S0265051700000152 (accessed 29 April 2021).
Mills, Richard. *Yr Arweinydd Cerddorol*, y rhan gyntaf (Llanidloes: John Mendus Jones, ail. arg 1844).
Mills, Richard, and N. Cynhafal Jones. *Buchdraeth y Parch. John Mills* (Aberdar: Mills a Lynch, 1844).
Morgan, Gareth. 'Rugby and Revivalism: Sport and Religion in Edwardian Wales'. *The International Journal of the History of Sport*, 22/3 (May 2005), 434–456.
Morgan, Kenneth O. *Rebirth of a Nation: Wales 1880–1980*, History of Wales Series (Oxford: Clarendon Press, 1981).
Morgan, Prys. *The Eighteenth Century Renaissance*, A New History of Wales (Llandybie: Christopher Davies, 1981).
'From a Death to a View: The Hunt for the Welsh Past in the Romantic Period', in *The Invention of Tradition*, ed. by Eric Hobsbawm and Terence Ranger (Cambridge: Cambridge University Press, 1983), pp. 43–100.
Morgan, T. J. *Peasant Culture* (Swansea: University College of Swansea, 1962).
Morgans, David. *Music and Musicians of Merthyr and District: Together with a List of Eisteddfodau to the Year 1901* (Merthyr Tydfil: H. W. Southey, 1922).

Morgans, Delyth. *Cydymaith Caneuon Ffydd*, arg. newydd ([Aberystwyth]: Pwyllgor y Llyfr Emynau Cydenwadol, 2008).
'*Y Cerddor*: Cyfnodolyn y Werin/*Y Cerddor*: Periodical of the People', *Welsh Music History/Hanes Cerddoriaeth Cymru*, 5 (2002), 105–134.
Morris, W. Meredith. *Famous Fiddlers* ([Cardiff]: Welsh Folk Museum, 1983).
Munrow, David. *Instruments of the Middle Ages and Renaissance* (Oxford: Oxford University Press, 1976).
Myddelton, W. M. *Chirk Castle Accounts, AD 1605–66* (St Albans: Privately printed, 1908).
Naughton, John. *From Gutenberg to Zuckerberg: What You Really Need to Know About the Internet* (London: Quercus, 2014).
Nettel, Reginald. *North Staffordshire Music: A Social Experiment* (Rickmansworth: Triad, 1977).
O'Connor, Tina. 'The Cotehele Cupboard: An Elegy in Oak'. *Journal of the Regional Furniture Society*, 28 (2014), https://regionalfurnituresociety.files.wordpress.com/2013/02/01-oconnor.pdf (accessed 22 Sept. 2021).
O'Leary, Paul. 'Revolution, Culture, and Industry, *c*. 1700–1850', in *The Cambridge History of Welsh Literature*, ed. by Geraint Evans and Helen Fulton (Cambridge: Cambridge University Press, 2019), pp. 253–263.
Oliver, Michael. 'Two Welsh Composers: Alun Hoddinott and William Mathias', in *British Music Now*, ed. by Lewis Foreman (London: Elek Books, 1975), pp. 86–96.
Owen, Hugh. 'The Diary of Bulkeley of Dronwy, Anglesey, 1630–1636'. *Transactions of the Anglesey Antiquarian Society and Field Club* (1937), 26–172.
——— ed., *Additional Letters of the Morrises of Anglesey (1735–1786)*, 2 vols (London: The Honourable Society of Cymmrodorion, 1947–9).
Owen, John (Owain Alaw). *Gems of Welsh Melody* (Ruthin and Wrexham: Isaac Clarke/ Hughes and Son, 1860–4).
Parrott, Ian. *Hanes Yr Urdd er Hyrwyddo Cerddoriaeth Cymru, 1955–1980/The Story of the Guild for the Promotion of Welsh Music, 1955–1980* (Swansea: Guild for the Promotion of Welsh Music, 1980).
——— *The Spiritual Pilgrims* (Aberystwyth: Christopher Davies, 1964).
Parry, John (Bardd Alaw). *The Welsh Harper* (London and Chester: D'Almaine and Co., and E. Parry, 1839).
——— *The Welsh Harper ... Volume II* (London: D'Almaine, 1848).
Parry, John (Ruabon). *British Harmony* (Ruabon and London: Printed for and Sold by John Parry, Ruabon, Denbighshire & P. Hodgson, London, 1781).
——— *Cambrian Harmony* (London: n.p., 1810).
Parry, John (Ruabon) and Evan Williams. *Antient British Music* (London: Printed for and sold by the Compilers, 1742).
Parry, Thomas, gol. *Gwaith Dafydd ap Gwilym* (Caerdydd: Gwasg Prifysgol Cymru, 1952).
Parry-Williams, T. H., gol. *Llawysgrif Richard Morris o Gerddi, [B.M. Add. Ms. 14, 992]* (Caerdydd: Gwasg Prifysgol Cymru, 1931).

Phillips, Geraint. *'Dyn Heb ei Gyffelyb yn y Byd': Owain Myfyr a'i Gysylltiadau Llenyddol* (Caerdydd: Gwasg Prifysgol Cymru, 2010).
Pope, Robert. 'Evan Roberts in Theological Context'. *Transactions of the Honourable Society of Cymmrodorion*, 11 (2004), 144–169.
Porter, Dilwyn. 'Sport and National Identity', in *The Oxford Handbook of Sports History*, ed. by Robert Edelman and Wayne Wilson (Oxford: Oxford University Press, 2017).
Powel, David. *The Historie of Cambria*, facsimile ed. (Amsterdam and New York: Theatrum Orbis Terrarum and Da Capo Press, 1969).
Powell, Nia. 'Robert ap Huw: A Wanton Minstrel of Anglesey/Robert ap Huw: Clerwr Gwyllt o Fôn'. *Welsh Music History/Hanes Cerddoriaeth Cymru*, 3 (1999), 5–53.
Prescott, Sarah. *Eighteenth-Century Writing from Wales: Bards and Britons* (Cardiff: University of Wales Press, 2008).
Pritchard, T. W. *The Wynns at Wynnstay* (Caerwys: Old Court Press, 1982).
Pryse, John. *The Cambrian Melodist* (Llanidloes: [*c*.1850]).
Quitsland, Beth. *The Reformation in Rhyme: Sternhold, Hopkins and the English Metrical Psalter, 1547–1603* (Aldershot: Ashgate, 2008).
Rees, A. J. Heward. 'Henry Brinley Richards (1817–1885): A Nineteenth-Century Propagandist for Welsh Music/Henry Brinley Richards (1817–1885): Propagandydd dros Gerddoriaeth Gymreig o'r Bedwaredd Ganrif ar Bymtheg'. *Welsh Music History/Hanes Cerddoriaeth Cymru*, 2 (1998), 173–212.
'Views and Revisions: The Composer Grace Williams Talks to A.J. Heward Rees'. *Welsh Music/Cerddoriaeth Cymru*, 5/4 (Winter/Gaeaf 1976–7), 7–18.
Rees, A. J. Heward, and David Wynne. 'Cyril Jenkins'. *Welsh Music/Cerddoriaeth Cymru*, 5/9 (Summer/Haf 1978), 80.
Rees, Eiluned. *Libri Walliae* (Aberystwyth: Llyfrgell Genedlaethol Cymru/ National Library of Wales, 1987).
Rees, Ronald. *A Nation of Singing Birds: Sermon and Song in Wales and among the Welsh in North America* (Talybont: Y Lolfa, 2021).
Rees, Stephen P. 'Adnewyddiad Creadigol yn y Traddodiad Offerynnol yng Nghymru'. *Canu Gwerin/Folk Song*, 42 (2019), 27–46.
'English Descant and a Source of Vernacular Music Theory from Medieval Wales/Degant Seisnig a Ffynhonnell Theori Cerddoriaeth Frodorol o Gymru'r Oesoedd Canol'. *Welsh Music History/Hanes Cerddoriaeth Cymru*, 1 (1996), 144–163.
'A New Celtic Tradition? Group Instrumental Performance in the Welsh Folk Revival, *c*.1975–*c*.1989/Traddodiad Celtaidd Newydd? Perfformiad Offerynnol gan Grwpiau yn yr Adfywiad Gwerin yng Nghymru, *c*. 1975– *c*.1989'. *Welsh Music History/Hanes Cerddoriaeth Cymru*, 7 (2007), 304–343.
Rees, Stephen P., and Sally Harper. 'Aspects of the Palaeography and History of the Robert ap Huw Manuscript/Agweddau ar Balaeograffeg a Hanes Llawysgrif Robert ap Huw'. *Welsh Music History/Hanes Cerddoriaeth Cymru*, 3 (1999), 54–67.

The Religious Revival in Wales, 1904. By Awstin and Other Special Correspondents of the Western Mail, Vol. 3 (Cardiff: Western Mail, 1905).

Reynolds, Peter. *BBC National Orchestra and Chorus of Wales* (Swansea: BBC Cymru Wales, 2009).

Reynolds, Thomas William. 'A Study of Music and Liturgy: Choirs and Organs in Monastic and Secular Foundations in Wales and the Borderlands, 1485–1645' (PhD thesis, Bangor University, 2002). https://research.bangor.ac.uk/portal/en/theses/a-study-of-music-and-liturgy–choirs-and-organs-in-monastic-and-secular-foundations-in-wales-and-the-borderlands-14851645(7d84e8de-005e-49e2-a6a4-2d64b028c137).html (accessed 30 June 2021).

Reynolds, William. 'Chirk Castle Organ and Organbook: An Insight into Performance Practice Involving a Seventeenth-Century "Transposing" Organ'. *Journal of the British Institute of Organ Studies*, 21 (1997), 28–55.

—— 'Middleton's Household Chapel: Church Music on the Welsh Border in the Seventeenth Century/Capel Teuluol Middleton: Cerddoriaeth Eglwysig ar y Gororau yn yr Ail Ganrif ar Bymtheg'. *Welsh Music History/Hanes Cerddoriaeth Cymru*, 4 (2000), 111–137.

Rhys, Dulais. *Joseph Parry: Bachgen Bach o Ferthyr* (Caerdydd: Gwasg Prifysgol Cymru, 1998).

Rhys, Dulais and Frank Bott. *To Philadelphia and Back: The Life and Music of Joseph Parry* (Llanrwst: Gwasg Carreg Gwalch, 2010).

Riall, Nicholas. 'A Tudor Cupboard at Cotehele and Associated Carpentry Work from the Welsh Marches'. *Journal of the Regional Furniture Society*, 26 (2012), https://regionalfurnituresociety.files.wordpress.com/2013/02/a02-riall.pdf (accessed 22 September 2021).

Richards, Brinley, ed. *The Songs of Wales* (London: Boosey & Co., Ltd, 1873).

Rickards, Guy. 'Hampstead: Rhian Samuel's "Light and Water"'. *Tempo*, 58/230 (October 2004), 58–60.

Rimmer, Joan. 'Edward Jones's *Musical and Poetical Relicks of the Welsh Bards*, 1784: A Re-assessment'. *The Galpin Society Journal*, 39 (1986), 77–96.

—— 'Telynores Maldwyn: Nansi Richards, a Welsh Harpist, 1888–1979'. *Studia Instrumentorum Musicae Popularis*, 7 (1981), 127–133.

Rivière, Jules. *My Musical Life and Recollections* (London: Sampson Low, Marston and Company, 1893).

Roberts, Brynley F., ed. *Breudwyt Maxen Wledic* (Dublin: Dublin Institute for Advanced Studies, 2005).

Roberts, Carys Ann. 'Agwedd Gosmopolitanaidd John Thomas, "Pencerdd Gwalia" (1826–1913)'/'The Cosmopolitan Aspect of John Thomas, "Pencerdd Gwalia" (1826–1913)'. *Welsh Music History/Hanes Cerddoriaeth Cymru*, 4 (2000), 88–110.

Roberts, David. *Gramadeg Cerddorol* (Bala: G. Jones, 1848).

Roberts, E. Ernest. *John Roberts, Telynor Cymru* (Dinbych: Gwasg Gee, 1978).

Roberts, Gwyneth Tyson. *The Language of the Blue Books: Wales and Colonial Prejudice* (Cardiff: University of Wales Press, 2011).

Roberts, Huw and Llio Rhydderch. *Telynorion Llannerch-y-medd: Teulu'r Britannia ac Eraill/The Harpers of Llannerch-y-medd: The Britannia Family and Others* (Cyngor Sir Ynys Môn, 2000).

Roberts, Thomas, gol. *Gwaith Dafydd ab Edmwnd* (Bangor: Bangor Manuscripts Society, 1914).

gol., *Gwaith Tudur Penllyn ac Ieuan ap Tudur Penllyn* (Caerdydd: Gwasg Prifysgol Cymru, 1958).

Robertson, Dora H. *Sarum Close*, 2nd ed. (Bath: Firecrest Publishing 1969).

Rodell, Jonathan *The Rise of Methodism: A Study of Bedfordshire, 1736–1851* (Woodbridge: Boydell, 2014).

Rosselli, John. *Music and Musicians in Nineteenth-Century Italy* (Portland, OR: Amadeus Press, 1991).

The Opera Industry in Italy from Cimarosa to Verdi: The Role of the Impresario (Cambridge: Cambridge University Press, 1984).

Rosser, Ann. *Telyn a Thelynor: Hanes y Delyn yng Nghymru 1700–1900* ([Caerdydd]: Amgueddfa Werin Cymru, 1981).

Rowlands, William ('Gwilym Lleyn'). *Llyfryddiaeth y Cymry/Cambrian Bibliography* (Llanidloes: John Pryse, 1869).

Royal Commission on Historical Manuscripts. *Report on Manuscripts in the Welsh Language*, 2 vols (London: HMSO, 1898–1910).

Royal Welsh College of Music and Drama. *Celebrations: 50th Anniversary 1949–1999* (Cardiff: Royal Welsh College of Music and Drama, 1999).

Ryan, Greg. *The Contest for Rugby Supremacy: Accounting for the 1905 All Blacks* (Christchurch: Canterbury University Press, 2005).

Forerunners of the All Blacks: The 1888–89 New Zealand Native Football Team in Britain, Australia and New Zealand (Christchurch: Canterbury University Press, 1993).

Rycroft, Marjorie E. 'Haydn's Welsh Songs: George Thomson's Musical and Literary Sources/Caneuon Cymreig Haydn: Ffynonellau Cerddorol a Llenyddol George Thomson'. *Welsh Music History/Hanes Cerddoriaeth Cymru*, 7 (2007), 92–160.

Saer, D. Roy. *Cymdeithas Alawon Gwerin Cymru: Canrif Gron/The Welsh Folk-Song Society: a Whole Century* (Cymdeithas Alawon Gwerin Cymru, 2006).

Y Delyn yng Nghymru Mewn Lluniau/The Harp in Wales in Pictures (Llandysul and Caerdydd: Gwasg Gomer/Amgueddfa Genedlaethol Cymru, 1991).

Saer, Roy. *'Canu at Iws' ac Ysgrifau Eraill/'Song for Use' and Other Articles* (Talybont: Cymdeithas Alawon Gwerin Cymru, 2013).

'Eos Dâr: "Y Canwr Penillion Digyffelyb"', in *'Canu at Iws' ac Ysgrifau Eraill* (Talybont: Cymdeithas Alawon Gwerin Cymru, 2013), pp. 123–137.

'Traditional Dance in Wales during the Eighteenth Century', in *'Canu at Iws' ac Ysgrifau Eraill* (Talybont: Cymdeithas Alawon Gwerin Cymru, 2013), pp. 287–304.

'Welsh Gipsies and the Triple Harp', in *'Canu at Iws' ac Ysgrifau Eraill* (Talybont: Cymdeithas Alawon Gwerin Cymru, 2013), pp. 251–267.

Samson, Jim. 'Instrumental Music II', in *The Blackwell History of Music in Britain – the Twentieth Century*, ed. by Stephen Banfield (Oxford: Blackwell, 1995), pp. 290–291.

Scholes, Percy A. 'Hen Wlad Fy Nhadau'. *National Library of Wales Journal*, 3/1 & 2 (1943), 1–10.

The Mirror of Music 1844–1944, 2 vols (London: Novello & Co. with Oxford University Press, 1947).

Schutz, Rachel. 'An Introduction to Welsh Solo Vocal Repertoire'. *Journal of Singing*, 77/1 (2020), 73–80.

Sharpe, Richard and John Reuben Davies, ed. and trans. 'Rhygyfarch's *Life of St David*', in *St David of Wales: Cult, Church and Nation*, ed. by J. Wyn Evans and Jonathan M. Wooding (Woodbridge: The Boydell Press, 2007), pp. 107–155.

Simon, Herbert. *Song and Words: A History of the Curwen Press* (London: George Allen & Unwin, 1973).

Sinclair, Andrew. *Arts and Cultures: History of the First 50 Years of the Arts Council of Great Britain* (London: Sinclair-Stevenson, 1995).

Slocum, Kay B. *Liturgies in Honour of Thomas Becket* (Toronto: Toronto University Press, 2004).

Small, Christopher. *Musicking: The Meanings of Performing and Listening* (Hanover, NH and London: Wesleyan University Press, 1998).

Smith, Alan. 'Elizabethan Church Music at Ludlow'. *Music and Letters*, 49 (1968), 108–121.

Smith, David, and Gareth Williams. *Fields of Praise: The Official History of the Welsh Rugby Union 1881–1981* (Cardiff: University of Wales Press on behalf of the Welsh Rugby Union, 1980).

Smith, Lucy Toulmin, ed. *The Itinerary of John Leland in Wales in or About the Years 1536–1539* (London: George Bell & Sons, 1906).

Smith, W. J., ed. *Calendar of Salusbury Correspondence 1553–c.1700* (Cardiff: University of Wales Press, 1954).

Stead, Phil. *Red Dragons: The Story of Welsh Football*, revised ed. (Talybont: Y Lolfa, 2015).

Stephens, Meic. *Artists in Wales 1* (Llandysul: Gwasg Gomer, 1971).

Artists in Wales 2 (Llandysul: Gomer Press, 1973).

The Arts in Wales, 1950–75 ([Cardiff]: Welsh Arts Council, 1979).

Stevens, Denis, ed. *Early Tudor Organ Music II: Music for the Mass*, Vol. 10, *Early English Church Music* (London: Stainer and Bell for the British Academy, 1969).

Stevens, John. *The History of the Antient Abbeys, Monasteries, Hospitals, Cathedrals and Collegiate Churches. Being Two Additional Volumes to Sir W. Dugdale's Monasticon Anglicanum*, 2 vols (London: Printed for Tho. Taylor et al., 1722–3).

Stradling, John. *Ioannis Stradlingi Epigrammatum Libri Quatuor* (London: Impensis Georgii Bishop & Ioannis Norton, 1607).

Sweet, Rosemary. *Antiquaries: The Discovery of the Past in Eighteenth-Century Britain* (London and New York: Hambledon and London, 2004).

Swynnoe, Jan G. *The Best Years of British Film Music, 1936–58* (Woodbridge: The Boydell Press, 2002).

Tamboer, Annemies and Raino Ritta. 'A Singing Bone from the Convent Quarter of Medieval Turku, Finland: Swedish or German Import, Baltic Influence or Variation on a Finnish Theme?' *Publications of the ICTM Study Group for Musicology*, 2 (2020), 109–131.

Tatton, Tom. 'Kenneth Harding: A Passion for the Viola'. *Journal of the American Viola Society* (2009). http://violaspace.com/avs/javs/2009/11/27/5/ (accessed 25 June 2021).

Taylor, Benedict. 'The Lost Chord: Sentimentality, Sincerity, and the Search for "Emotional Depth" in 19th-Century Music'. *International Review of the Aesthetics and Sociology of Music*, 40/2 (2009), 207–233.

Taylor, William. 'Robert ap Huw's Harp Technique/Techneg Telyn Robert ap Huw'. *Welsh Music History/Hanes Cerddoriaeth Cymru*, 3 (1999), 82–96.

Thomas, Gwyn. *Eisteddfodau Caerwys: The Caerwys Eisteddfodau* (Caerdydd: Gwasg Prifysgol Cymru, 1968).

— 'Two Prose Writers: Ellis Wynne and Theophilus Evans', in *A Guide to Welsh Literature c. 1700–1800*, ed. by Branwen Jarvis (Cardiff: University of Wales Press, 2000), pp. 45–63.

Thomas, John, ed., with an Introduction by Charles Purday. *The Songs of Wales: A Complete Collection of the Vocal Melodies of the Principality* (London: J. B. Cramer & Co., 1874).

Thomas, John (Ieuan Ddu). *Y Caniedydd Cymreig; The Cambrian Minstrel* (Merthyr Tudful: 1845).

Thomas, John Hugh. 'The Cultural Tradition: Music', in *The City of Swansea: Challenges and Change*, ed. by Ralph A. Griffiths (Gloucester: Sutton, 1990), pp. 218–228.

Thomas, Mair Elvet. *Afiaith yng Ngwent: Hanes Cymdeithas Cymreigyddion Y Fenni 1833–1854* (Caerdydd: Gwasg Prifysgol Cymru, 1978).

Thomas, Owen. *Cofiant y Parchedig John Jones, Talsarn* (Wrexham: Hughes a'i Fab, [1874]).

Thomas, Peter D. G. *Politics in Eighteenth-Century Wales* (Cardiff: University of Wales Press, 1998).

Thomas, R. S. *Selected Poems 1946–1968* (Newcastle upon Tyne: Bloodaxe Books, 1986).

Thomas, Wyn. 'Annie "Cwrt Mawr" a Chanorion Aberystwyth'. *Canu Gwerin*, 30 (2007), 3–44.

— *Cerddoriaeth Draddodiadol yng Nghymru: Llyfryddiaeth/Traditional Music in Wales: A Bibliography*, 3rd ed. (Llanrwst: Gwasg Carreg Gwalch, 2006).

— 'Ffarwel i Aberystwyth ... Golwg ar Gyfraniad Jennie Williams (1885–1971) i Fyd yr Alaw Werin yng Nghymru'. *Ceredigion*, 15/2 (2006), 27–72.

— 'Grace Gwyneddon Davies, Llanwnda a Cherddoriaeth Frodorol Cymru'. *Transactions of the Caernarfonshire Historical Society*, 71 (2010), 114–131.

'John Roberts, 'Telynor Cymru' (1816–1894)'. *Welsh Music History/Hanes Cerddoriaeth Cymru*, 1 (1996), 163–179.

'Mary Davies, *grande dame* of Welsh Music'. *Transactions of the Honourable Society of Cymmrodorion*, N.S. 4 (1998), 111–123.

'Mary Davies: *grande dame* yr Alaw Werin yng Nghymru'. *Canu Gwerin*, 20 (1997), 28–42.

Meistres 'Graianfryn' a Cherddoriaeth Frodorol yng Nghymru, Darlith Goffa Amy Parry-Williams 1999 ([Aberystwyth]: Cymdeithas Alawon Gwerin Cymru, 1999).

'Y Ffonograff a Byd Cerddoriaeth Draddodiadol yng Nghymru'. *Canu Gwerin*, 29 (2006), 40–64.

gol. *Cerdd a Chân: Golwg ar Gerddoriaeth Draddodiadol Yng Nghymru* ([Dinbych]: Gwasg Gee, 1982).

Thomson, Derick S., ed. *Branwen Uerch Lyr* (Dublin: Dublin Institute for Advanced Studies, 1976).

Thomson, George. *A Select Collection of Original Welsh Airs* (London and Edinburgh: 1809, 1811, 1817).

Thomson, Robert L., ed. *Ystorya Gereint uab Erbin* (Dublin: Dublin Institute for Advanced Studies, 1997).

Tir Newydd, Rhifyn Arbennig: David Vaughan Thomas, 16 (Mehefin, 1939).

Toivanen, Pekka. 'The Robert ap Huw Manuscript and the Dilemma of Transcription/Llawysgrif Robert ap Huw a Phenbleth Trawsgrifio'. *Welsh Music History/Hanes Cerddoriaeth Cymru*, 3 (1999), 97–129.

Tossell, David. *Nobody Beats Us: The Inside Story of the 1970s Wales Rugby Team* (Edinburgh: Mainstream Publishing, 2009).

Traherne, J. M., ed. *Stradling Correspondence: A Series of Letters Written in the Reign of Queen Elizabeth* (London: Longmans, 1840).

Trevor, Alun. *Cofio Cantorion: Eu Teithiau ym Mhrydain, Canada a'r Unol Daleithiau 1926–1939/The Welsh Imperial Singers: Their Tours of Britain, Canada and the United States 1926–1939* (Llanrwst: Gwasg Carreg Gwalch, 1991).

Turner, Barry. *Beacon for Change: How the 1951 Festival of Britain Shaped the Modern Age* (London: Aurum Press, 2011).

Upchurch, Anna Rosser. 'The Arts Council of Great Britain: Keynes's Legacy', in *The Origins of the Arts Council Movement*, ed. by Anna Rosser Upchurch (London: Palgrave Macmillan, 2016), pp. 103–130.

ed., *The Origins of the Arts Council Movement* (London: Palgrave Macmillan, 2016).

Urquahart, Alex, Dermot O'Connar and Hugh Edwards. *Aria Di Camera* (London: Printed for Dan. Wright and Dan. Wright Junr., [c.1726]).

Valor Ecclesiasticus Temp. Henr. VIII, ed. by John Caley and Joseph Hunter, 6 vols (London: Record Commission, 1810–34).

Von Glahn, Denise. *The Sounds of Place: Music and the American Cultural Landscape* (Boston, MA: Northwestern University Press, 2003).

Watkin, Thomas Glyn. *The Legal History of Wales*, 2nd ed. (Cardiff University of Wales Press, 2012).

Webb, Paul. *Ivor Novello: A Portrait of a Star* (London: Stage Directions, 1999).

Weller, Philip. 'Gerald of Wales's View of Music/Golwg Gerallt Gymro ar Gerddoriaeth'. *Welsh Music History/Hanes Cerddoriaeth Cymru*, 2 (1997), 1–32.

Welsh Folk-Song Society. *Third Annual Report* (Bangor: Jarvis & Foster, 1911).

Whitelaw, James. *An Essay on the Population of Dublin* (Dublin: Graisberry and Campbell, 1805).

Whittaker, Paul D. 'British Museum Additional Ms 14905: An Interpretation and Re-examination of the Music and Text' (MA dissertation, University of Wales, 1974), www.bangor.ac.uk/music-and-media/CAWMS/robertaphuw.php.en (accessed 25 August 2021).

— 'Harmonic Forms in the Robert ap Huw Manuscript/Ffurfiau Harmonig yn Llawysgrif Robert ap Huw'. *Welsh Music History/Hanes Cerddoriaeth Cymru*, 7 (2007), 1–54.

— 'The Role of Robert ap Huw in the Creation of *Lbl* Ms Add. 14905/Swyddogaeth Robert ap Huw yng Nghreadigaeth *Lbl* Ms Add. 14905'. *Welsh Music History/Hanes Cerddoriaeth Cymru*, 6 (2004), 62–103.

— 'The Tablature of the Iolo Morganwg Manuscript (British Library, Ms Add. 14970)/Tabluniau Llawysgrif Iolo Morganwg (Y Llyfrgell Brydeinig, Ms Add. 14970)'. *Welsh Music History/Hanes Cerddoriaeth Cymru*, 3 (1999), 252–281.

Whittall, Arnold. 'Grace Williams 1906–1977'. *Soundings*, 7 (1978), 19–37.

Wiliam, Aled Rhys, ed. *Llyfr Iorwerth: A Critical Text of the Venedotian Code of Medieval Welsh Law; Mainly from BM. Cotton Ms Titus Dii* (Cardiff: University of Wales Press, 1960).

Wiliam, Dafydd Wyn. *Cofiant Richard Morris (1702/3–79)* ([Bodedern]: D. W. Wiliam, 1999).

— *Cofiant William Morris (1705–63)* ([Bodedern]: D. W. Wiliam, 1995).

— 'Ffarwel i Inc Llannerch--y-medd'. *Y Casglwr*, 21 (1983), 13.

— 'Ifan ab y Gof, Llywelyn ab Ifan ab y Gof, a Dafydd ab y Gof (Dafydd Athro): Tri Chyfansoddwr Cerddoriaeth o Fôn?/Ifan ab y Gof, Llywelyn ab Ifan ab y Gof, a Dafydd ab y Gof (Dafydd Athro): Three Anglesey Composers?' *Welsh Music History/Hanes Cerddoriaeth Cymru*, 4 (2000), 21–28.

— 'Mwy am Inc Llannerch--y-medd'. *Y Casglwr*, 23 (1984), 15.

Williams, A. Tudno. *E. T. Davies: Arloeswr Cerd* (Dinbych: Gwasg Gee, 1981).

Williams, C. R. 'The Welsh Religious Revival'. *The British Journal of Sociology*, 3/3 (Sept. 1952), 242–259.

Williams, G. J. and E. J. Jones, goln. *Gramadegau'r Penceirddiaid* (Caerdydd: Gwasg Prifysgol Cymru, 1934).

Williams, Gareth. *1905 and All That: Essays on Rugby Football, Sport and Welsh Society* (Llandysul: Gomer, 1991).

— *Do You Hear the People Sing? The Male Voice Choirs of Wales* (Llandysul: Gomer, 2015).

'"How's the Tenors in Dowlais?": The Choral Culture of the South Wales Coalfield c. 1880–1930'. *Transactions of the Honourable Society of Cymmrodorion 2004*, New Series 11 (2005), 170–188.

'"This Valley of Coal and Song": Musical Aspects of the Rhondda's Last National Eisteddfod, 1928'. *Morgannwg* 65 (2021), 74–92

Valleys of Song: Music and Society in Wales, 1840–1914 (Cardiff: University of Wales Press, 1998).

Williams, Glanmor. 'The Collegiate Church of Llanddewibrefi'. *Ceredigion: Journal of the Cardiganshire Antiquarian Society*, 4 (1960–3), 336–352.

Wales and the Reformation (Cardiff: University of Wales Press, 1997).

The Welsh Church from Conquest to Reformation. 2nd ed. (Cardiff: University of Wales Press, 1976).

Williams, Grace. 'Grace Williams: A Self Portrait'. *Welsh Music/Cerddoriaeth Cymru*, 8/5 (Spring/Gwanwyn 1987), 7–16.

'How Welsh Is Welsh Music?' *Welsh Music/Cerddoriaeth Cymru*, 4/4 (Summer/Haf 1973), 7–12.

Williams, Gwyn, trans. *Welsh Poems: Sixth Century to 1600* (London: Faber, 1973).

Williams, Hugh, ed. and trans. *Gildas: De Excidio Britanniae, or the Ruin of Britain* (Gloucester: Dodo Press, 2010) (Originally published in London by The Honourable Society of Cymmrodorion, 1899), p. 28.

Williams, Huw. *Taro Tant: Detholiad o Ysgrifau ac Erthyglau* (Dinbych: Gwasg Gee, 1994).

Thomas Osborne Roberts 1879–1948 ([Caernarfon]: Cyngor Gwlad Gwynedd, 1980).

Williams, Ifor, ed. *The Poems of Taliesin* (Dublin: Dublin Institute for Advanced Studies, 1968).

Williams, J. Lloyd. *Ceinion y Canorion* (Bangor: Evan Thomas, c.1909).

'The History of the Welsh Folk-Song Society'. *Journal of the Welsh Folk-Song Society/Cylchgrawn Cymdeithas Alawon Gwerin Cymru*, III/2 (1934), 46–57, 89–102.

'Welsh National Melodies and Folk-Song'. *Transactions of the Honourable Society of Cymmrodorion*, Session 1907–08 (1909), 1–46.

Y Tri Thelynor: Arloeswyr Cerddodrol Cymru yn y Ddeunawfed Ganrif (Llundain: Cwmni Cymraeg Foyle, [1945]).

Williams, J. Lloyd, and L. D. Jones. *Aelwyd Angharad* (Bangor: Evan Thomas, 1910).

Williams, Jane (Ysgafell). *The Literary Remains of the Rev. Thomas Price, Carnhuanawc*, 2 vols. (Llandovery and London: William Rees/Longman & Co., 1855).

Williams, Jean. *A Game for Rough Girls? A History of Women's Football in Britain* (London: Routledge, 2003).

Williams, John (Ioan Wiliam). *Cyfaill mewn Llogell* (Caerfyrddin: I. Daniel, 1797).

Williams, L. J. *Digest of Welsh Historical Statistics*, 2 vols. (Cardiff: The Welsh Office, 1998).

Williams, Maria Jane. *Ancient National Airs of Gwent and Morganwg* (Llandovery; London: William Rees; D'Almaine and MacKinlay, 1844).

Ancient National Airs of Gwent and Morganwg: Ffacsimile O Argraffiad 1844/a Facsimile of the 1844 Edition (Aberystwyth: Cymdeithas Alawon Gwerin Cymru, 1988).

Williams, R. M. *Seiri Cerdd Nanconwy* (Llanrwst: Gwasg Carreg Gwalch, 1982).

Williams, W. S. Gwynn. *Welsh National Music and Dance*, 4th ed. (Llangollen: Gwynn Publishing Co. 1971).

Wilson, Jen. *Freedom Music: Wales, Emancipation and Jazz 1850–1950* (Cardiff: University of Wales Press, 2019).

Witts, Richard. 'Needle Time: The BBC, the Musicians' Union, Popular Music, and the Reform of Radio in the 1960s'. *Popular Music History*, 7/3 (2012), 241–262.

Yardley, Edward. *Menevia Sacra*, ed. Francis Green (London: Bedford Press, 1927).

Yates, Nigel. *The Welsh Seaside Resorts: Growth, Decline, and Survival*, Trivium Publications Occasional Papers 1 (Lampeter: University of Wales, Lampeter, 2006).

Index

The index includes both English and Welsh words. Mindful that the book will be used by an international readership, we have ordered it in the sequence of the English alphabet rather than the Welsh, where forms such as 'll' and 'ch' are letters of the alphabet in their own right.

9Bach, 331
60 Ft. Dolls, 328

Aberdare, 109, 159, 209
Aberdare, Lord, 295
Abergavenny, 11, 189, 191, 193
Abergwili, 57, 58, 67
Aberjaber, 166, 167
Abertridwr, 221, 233, 240
Aberystwyth, 253, 297, 356, 361
Acts of Union, 4, 93, 171
Alarm, The, 327
Alaw Ddu, 199
Alawydd, 198
Alffa, 364
Amner, John, 71
Angharad Choir, 138
Anhrefn, 321
Anhrefn (record label), 321, 325, 326
Anian I, Bishop of Bangor, 59
Anian II, Bishop of Bangor, 59
Ankst (record label), 326, 327, 329
anterliwt, 155, 157
Anthony, Griffith, 204
ap Rhys, Philip, 66
Apollo Music Depot, 215
Ar Log (group), 164
Aria di Camera, 99, 178
Arts Council of Great Britain, 256, 257
Arts Council of Wales, 269, 359, 364
Arthur, King, 25, 49
Augustine, 55
awdl, 37, 38, 81
Awstin, 239

bagpipe, 32, 48, 80, 81, 160, 165, 166
Bala, 177, 317, 318

Bangor, 55, 60, 81, 248, 255, 313, 361
Bantock, Granville, 111
Bara Menyn, Y, 320
Barbier, Lucie, 134–137, 253
Bardd Alaw *see* Parry, John (1776–1851)
bardd teulu, 30, 82
Bardd y Brenin, *see* Jones, Edward
Bardic Grammar, the, 30–32, 36, 46
Bartók, Béla, 254
Bassey, Shirley, 2, 23, 322
BBC, the, 252, 255, 258, 261, 262, 313, 319, 356, 364
BBC Cardiff Singer of the World, 360
BBC National Chorus of Wales, 262
BBC National Orchestra of Wales, 23, 355, 359, 360
BBC Welsh Choral Society, 261
BBC Welsh Orchestra, 23, 261
BBC Welsh Symphony Orchestra, 262
Beaumaris, 110, 187
Beibl Cyssegr-lan, Y, 73
Bek, Thomas, 57–58
Bendigeidfran, 49, 51
Bernard (Bishop of Wales), 6
Bethesda, 207, 305
Beynon, Rosser, 207, 305
Black Book of Carmarthen *see* Llyfr Du Caerfyrddin
Black Mountain Chorus, 348
Blayney, Thomas, 188
Blew, Y, 317, 318
Blodeuwedd, 50
'Blue Books' (1847 Commission on Education), 12, 105
Bodorgan, 154, 179
Bowen, Robin Huw, 165
Boyce, Max, 341, 342, 349
Brader, John, 213

Branwen, 49, 51
Brecon, 58, 64, 67, 189
Brecon Jazz Festival, 360
Breese, Madge, 214
Breuddwyd Maxen Wledic, 50
Britpop, 328
Broadwood, Lucy, 123
bugle horn, 159
Bulkeley (family), 72, 95, 154
Bull, John, 66
Burgess, Thomas, 185
Burney, Charles, 101
Burrows, Stuart, 115
Burward, John, 69
Butt, G. M. 209

cadi-ha, 128
Caerfallwch *see* Edwards, Thomas
Caernarfon, 4, 148, 165
Caerphilly, 221, 222, 228, 233, 234
Caerwys, 32, 87, 89, 91, 96, 101, 145
cainc, 42
Cale, John, 324
Cambrian (record label), 323
Cambrian Music Office, 207
Cambrian Society of Dyfed, 185
Cantorion Teifi, 116
Capel Martin, 222, 228
Caradog, xxii, 298–300
Cardiff, 4, 255, 257, 284, 308, 313, 330, 334, 361
Cardiff College of Music, 263
Cardiff Triennial Festival, 205, 253
Cardigan, 86, 100
Carmarthen, 32, 86, 101, 110, 185, 207, 213
Carnhuanawc, 145, 187–188, 189
Catatonia, 23, 328, 330
Ceiriog, 265, 302
Celfyddydau Cenedlaethol Ieuenctid Cymru *see* National Youth Arts Wales
Celtic revival, 10, 17, 164, 166, 171–194
CEMA *see* Council for the Encouragement of Music and the Arts
Centre for Advanced Welsh Music Studies, Bangor, 361
cerdd dafod, 3, 29, 32, 33, 45, 80, 86
cerdd dant, 2, 3, 22, 29, 32, 33, 45, 80, 87, 88–90, 93, 151–152
Cerddor Towy *see* Richards, Brinley
CF1 (choir), 116
chantries, 63, 65
Chapter Arts Centre, Cardiff, 257
Cheetham, Arthur, 215
Chicago, 18, 116, 300, 309
Chirk, 68–72, 98–99

Christ College, Brecon, 67
Church, Charlotte, 242
Clare (Suffolk), 59–60
Clarke, Isaac, 206–207
clas, 56, 57
Clee, W. D. 113
clerwr, *pl.* clêr, 30, 46
Coleg Cymraeg Cenedlaethol, 358–359
Coleridge-Taylor, Samuel, 111–112
'Cool Cymru', 324–329, 330
Côr Eifionydd, 116
Côr Mawr, Y, 298–301, 302
Côrdydd, 116
corn buelin, 159
Council for the Encouragement of Music and the Arts, 256
Council of Music in Wales *see* National Council of Music in Wales
Council of Wales and the Marches, 4, 54
Cowen, Frederic Hymen, 10
Cramer, J. B. & Co. 302–303
Crawshay, Robert Thompson, 296–298
Creative Wales, 356
Cromlech (group), 166
crowd *see* crwth
crwth, 28, 32, 51, 80, 81, 85, 86, 88, 152–154
Crystal Palace, 16, 110, 206, 298
Culhwch ac Olwen, 25, 29, 49, 51
Curtis, William, 68
Curwen, John, 201
Curwen, John Spencer, 205
Curwen Press, 203
'Cŵl Cymru' *see* 'Cool Cymru'
Cyfarthfa Band, 160, 296
Cyfarthfa Castle, 296, 298
cymanfa ganu (*pl.* cymanfaoedd canu), 20, 204, 235, 236, 241, 310, 338
Cymdeithas Alawon Gwerin Cymru, 11, 21, 121
Cymdeithas Cerdd Dant Cymru, 151, 152
Cymdeithas Ddysgedig Cymru *see* Learned Society of Wales
Cymdeithas yr Iaith Gymraeg, 318, 331
Cymmrodorion Dirwestol, Merthyr Tydfil, 104–105
Cymmrodorion *see* Honourable Society of Cymmrodorion
Cymreigyddion a Phrydyddion Merthyr, 103
Cymreigyddion y Fenni, 104, 105, 150, 187–189, 190–191
Cynalaw, 214
Cynddelw 'Brydydd Mawr', 36
Cynganeddwyr, Y, 320
cynghanedd, 38, 84
Cyrff, Y, 329
cywydd, *pl.* cywyddau, 38, 43, 48, 84, 86, 89, 95

Index

Dafydd ab Edmwnd, 34, 86
Dafydd ab Hywel, 86
Dafydd ab Owain, 37
Dafydd ap Gwilym, 10, 38–43, 47, 84, 93, 185, 247
Dafydd Iwan, 319–320, 327
Dafydd Nantglyn, 101
Daniel, John, 195
D'Artney, George, 297
Datblygu, 325–326, 328
David, St (office), 61
Davies, Annie, 238, 239
Davies, Ben, 256, 301
Davies, Clara Novello, 17, 18, 121, 300, 309, 311
Davies, Dan, 106
Davies, David *see* Dewi Alaw
Davies, E. T., 246, 248–249
Davies, Festyn, 310
Davies, Grace Gwyneddon, 17, 130–133
Davies, Harry Parr *see* Parr-Davies, Harry
Davies, Henry Walford, xx, 21–22, 113, 246, 254–256
Davies, Hugh *see* Pencerdd Maelor
Davies, John, 73
Davies, Mary, 17, 122–127, 301
Davies, Richard, 73
Davies, Robert Gwyneddon, 131
Davies, Thomas *see* Awstin
Davies, W. Hubert, 246, 251
Davies, William, 212
Davies, William Cadwaladr, 123
de Lloyd, David, 205, 245, 247
Deane, William, 69, 70, 71
Dechrau Canu, Dechrau Canmol (TV programme), 358
Deniz, *family*, 312–313
Dewi Alaw, 199
Dic Dywyll, 149
Dolgellau, 107, 148
Dowlais, 16, 111, 239, 339
Dub War, 328
Duhamel, Maurice, 141
Dydd Miwsig Cymru, 331
Dydd, Y (TV programme), 319
Dyffryn Tawe Temperance Choral Society, 116

Early Welsh Music Society, 133
Ednam, Richard, 60
Educational Publishing Company, 212
Edward I, King, 25, 47, 58, 59, 69, 81
Edwards, David R. 325
Edwards, Dilys Elwyn, 247, 286
Edwards, J. D. 229
Edward(s), Morris, 157
Edwards, Thomas *see* Twm o'r Nant
Edwards, Thomas (Caerfallwch), 106

Eglwysilan, 220, 221, 228, 233, 234, 240
eisteddfod, 2, 9–11, 100–120, 357–358
 provincial eisteddfodau, 184–191
Ellis, Annie, 138–140
Ellis, John, 197, 230
Ellis, Osian, 17, 151, 261, 276
Ellis, T. E. 13
Elwyn-Edwards, Dilys *see* Edwards, Dilys Elwyn
Eos Cymru *see* Wynne, Sarah Edith
Eos Dâr, 151
Eos Twrog *see* Roberts, Lewis
Evans, D. Emlyn, 103, 200, 210
Evans, D. Pughe, 210
Evans, Daniel *see* Eos Dâr
Evans, David, 201, 204, 255
Evans, Harry, 111
Evans, Hugh, 197
Evans, John, 214
Evans, John T., 240
Evans, Meredydd, xx, xxi
Evans, Silas, 202
Evans, Theophilus, 174, 175
Evans, Wynne, 351, 353

Fellowes, Edmund H., 112, 310
Festival of Britain, 256–257
Ffa Coffi Pawb, 329
Fflach (record label), 165, 326
Fideo 9 (TV programme), 320, 326
fiddle (*see also* violin), 144, 154–159, 169
Fleet, Arthur James, 215
Flint, north Wales, 47–48
folk songs *see* traditional songs
Football Association of Wales, 333

George, David Lloyd *see* Lloyd George, David
Gerald of Wales *see* Giraldus Cambrensis
Gibbons, Orlando, 75
Gilchrist, Anne, 123
Gildas, 33
Giraldus Cambrensis, 80, 83
'Glan Rhondda', 293–294
Glover, Sarah, 201
Godfrey and Co. 214
gogynfeirdd, 35, 36, 38, 43, 48, 51
Gorky's Zygotic Mynci, 24, 328, 329, 330
gorsedd, xxii, 10, 102, 117, 174, 185
Government of Wales Acts, 355–356
Green Man Festival, 331
Greenly, Elizabeth, 189, 191, 193
Gregynog, 262
Griffith, Robert, 146
Griffith, Thomas, 150
Griffiths, Ann (1776–1805), 16, 224
Griffiths, Ann (1934–2020), 266

Griffiths, William *see* Ivander
Groeswen, 222, 226, 227, 228, 233
Gruffudd, Huw, 152
Gruffudd ap Cynan, 36, 88, 89
  Statute, 32, 33, 87, 88, 91
Gruffudd ap Nicolas, 101
Guest, Charlotte, 121, 188
Guest, Josiah John, 189
Guild for the Promotion of Welsh Music, 262, 269
Gwenno, 331
Gwilym Ddu Glan Hafren *see* Owen, William
'Gwlad y Gân', 299
Gwydion, 51
gwylmabsant, 145, 155
gwylnos, 145
Gwyneddigion Society, 102, 176–178, 185
Gwynneth, John, 54

Hadow, William Henry, 19
Haldane Commission, 19–21, 201, 254
Hall, Augusta *see* Llanover, Lady
Hall, Benjamin, 189
Harding, Kenneth, 251
harmonium, 144, 234
harp, 28, 29–30, 32, 40–42, 51, 78, 80, 81, 82–83, 145–151
Harris, Griffith, 208
Harris, Howell, 222
Heath, John Rippiner, 249
Heins & Co., 213
Herbert, Augusta, 150
Hoddinott, Alun, 261, 262, 275, 278–281, 284–286
Hoddinott Hall, 284, 359
Hogia Llandegai, 316
Hogia'r Wyddfa, 316
Honourable and Loyal Society of Antient Britons, 175
Honourable Society of Cymmrodorion, 9, 175–176
Hopkin, Mary, 323
Horizons/Gorwelion, 364
Howard, Jeffrey, 349, 354
Huet, Thomas, 73
Hughes, Arwel, 247, 258, 261
Hughes, John (Colwyn Bay), 215
Hughes, John (Dolhiryd), 155
Hughes, John (1872–1914), 235
Hughes, John (1873–1932), 236
Hughes, John Ceiriog *see* Ceiriog
Hughes, Mary, 139
Hughes, Megan Watts, 16, 108
Hughes, R. S. 211
Hughes and Son, 206–207

Humphreys, Hugh, 209
Hwntws, Yr, 167
hymns and hymn tunes
  'Arglwydd, Arwain Trwy'r Anialwch', 236, 341
  'Bread of Heaven', 236, 341
  'Calon Lân', 235, 241, 341, 351, 353, 354
  'Cof am y Cyfiawn Iesu', 239
  'Cwm Rhondda', 236, 240, 241
  'Cymraeg', 235
  'Dim ond Iesu', 235
  'Dyma Gariad fel y moroedd', 235, 238, 337
  'Ebenezer', 235, 337
  'Groeswen', 234
  'Guide Me, O Thou Great Jehovah', 236, 240, 341
  'Hermon', 249
  'Hyfrydol', 234
  'Jesus Only', 235
  'Marchog Iesu', 340
  'Penry', 240
  'Pontmorlais', 249
  'St Mary', 77, 222
  'Song 67', 75
  'Throw Out the Life-Line', 240
  'Via Crucis', 249

Iago ap Ieuan *see* James, James
Ieuan ap Iago *see* James, Evan
Ieuan Ddu *see* Thomas, John (Ieuan Ddu)
Ieuan Gwyllt, 107, 202, 204, 212, 213, 232–233, 235, 305
Ifan Wiliam *see* Williams, Evan
Ifor Ceri, 102, 184–185, 186, 192–193
Ioan Rhagfyr *see* Williams, John (Ioan Rhagfyr)
Ioan Tegid *see* Jones, John (Ioan Tegid)
Iolo Goch, 43, 84
Iolo Morganwg, xxi, 9, 102, 145, 154, 174, 177, 185, 187, 189, 192
Ivander, 116
Iwan, Dafydd *see* Dafydd Iwan

James, Evan, 294
James, James, 294
Jarman, Eldra, 165
Jarman, Geraint, 320
jazz, 251, 311
Jenkins, Cyril, 18, 210, 250–251
Jenkins, David, 107, 200, 204, 205, 206, 245, 248, 253
Jenkins, John *see* Ifor Ceri
Jenkins, Karl, 288–290
Jenkins, Katherine, 242, 345, 349
Jenkins, Rae, 261
Jones, Bassett, 150, 167
Jones, D. L. *see* Cynalaw

Jones, Daniel, 267, 271–274, 275, 276
Jones, Dora Herbert, 17, 135
Jones, Edmund, 226–227
Jones, Edward (Bardd y Brenin), xix, xxii, 9, 14, 101, 145, 147–148, 149, 152, 159, 160, 163, 181–183, 184, 302
   The Bardic Museum, 147, 182, 183
   Hên Ganiadau Cymru, 147, 183
   Musical and Poetical Relicks of the Welsh Bards, xix, 9, 101, 147, 152, 159, 181
Jones, Elisabeth, 208
Jones, Griffith, 14
Jones, Griffith Rhys *see* Caradog
Jones, Gwilym R., 253
Jones, Heather, 320
Jones, Isaac, 208, 214
Jones, Jane, 208
Jones, John (Ioan Tegid), 188
Jones, John (of Tal-y-sarn), 157
Jones, John (1836–1923), 214
Jones, John Mendus, 197, 207
Jones, Lewis, 208
Jones, Mai, 23, 313
Jones, Mary, 207
Jones, Owen *see* Owain Myfyr
Jones, Robert, 207, 208
Jones, Stanley, 211
Jones, Tom, 2, 23, 322–323, 341
Jones, Thomas, 102
Jones, W. Bradwen, 249
Jones, Wilfrid, 212

Kinney, Phyllis, xx
Kyffin, Edward, 74, 221

'Land of my Fathers' *see* 'Mae Hen Wlad fy Nhadau'
Land of Song *see* Gwlad y Gân
Learned Society of Wales, 363
Lewis, D. W. 207
Lewis, David, 109
Lewis, Idris, 251–252, 258
Lewis, Lewis William *see* Llew Llwyfo
Lewis, Ruth Herbert, 17, 123, 127–130, 140
Lewis, Saunders, 318, 319
Lewis, Thomas, 154
Lewys, Dyfed, 112, 115
Lhuyd, Edward, 173–174
Llandaff, 55
Llandudno, 307
Llanfairpwllgwyngyll, 133
Llangollen, 155, 258, 360
Llanidloes, 197, 207
Llannerch-y-medd, 150, 165, 208
Llanover, Lady, 17, 104, 150, 189

Llew Llwyfo, 109
Llewelyn Alaw, 149, 159, 163, 165, 294–295
Llewelyn Ddu o Fôn *see* Morris, Lewis
Llewelyn, Thomas David *see* Llewelyn Alaw
Llinos, *see* Williams, Maria Jane
Lloyd, David, 115
Lloyd, J. Morgan, 249
Lloyd, John, 54
Lloyd, John Ambrose, 109, 199, 229, 234
Lloyd, Tom (Telynor Ceiriog), 164
Lloyd George, David, 19, 123, 245, 334
Llwybr Llaethog, 326
Llwyd, Angharad, 121
Llyfr Coch Hergest, 48
Llyfr Du Caerfyrddin, 268
Llyfr Gwyn Rhydderch, 48
Llyfrgell Genedlaethol Cymru *see* National Library of Wales
Llywarch ap Llywelyn, 'Prydydd y Moch', 36
Llywelyn ap Gruffudd, 4, 25, 38, 83
Llywelyn ap Iorwerth, 'Llywelyn Fawr', 25, 36, 81
Llywelyn Goch ap Meurig Hen, 45
London Welsh Choral Union, 151
Ludlow, 4, 54, 72, 220

Mabinogion, 25, 28, 48–51, 121, 188, 268
'Mae Hen Wlad fy Nhadau', 214, 294, 335, 336, 337, 342, 343, 345, 346, 353
Maelgwn Gwynedd, 33
Mair Mynorydd *see* Davies, Mary
Manic Street Preachers, The, 2, 23, 328, 330
Mari Lwyd, 156
Math uab Mathonwy, 50
Mathias, William, 262, 264, 276–278, 281–284
Matholwch, 49
Merthyr Tydfil, 4, 103, 104, 105, 106, 108, 160, 172, 296
mesur salm, 74–75, 221
Meyrick (family), 154
Mid Wales Opera, 260
military bands, 295–296
Millennium Stadium, 330, 342
Mills, John, 197, 198
Mills, Richard, 197, 229, 231
Morgan, Dafydd Siencyn, 198
Morris, Haydn, 251
Morris, Lewis, 152, 175, 179–180
Morris, Richard, 154, 156, 175, 176, 179, 181
Morris, William, 178
Morriston Orpheus Choir, 116
Music Theatre Wales, 260
Mwyn, Rhys *see* Rhys Mwyn
Myddelton, Thomas (1550–1631), 69
Myddelton, Thomas (1586–1666), 69, 71, 72

National Assembly for Wales, 355
National Council of Music in Wales, xx, 21, 22, 114, 130, 133, 254, 255, 256
National Eisteddfod Association, 21, 110, 117
National Library of Wales, xviii, xxi, 189, 293, 356–357, 361, 363
National Screen and Sound Archive of Wales, xxi, 362
National Youth Arts Wales, 261, 360
National Youth Brass Band of Wales, 360
National Youth Choir of Wales, 360
National Youth Orchestra of Wales, 269, 270, 360, 361
New Zealand All Blacks, 334, 335–337
Newport, 110, 190, 308, 327
Nicholas, John Morgan, 249
North Wales Music Company, 211
noson lawen, *pl.* nosweithiau llawen, 303, 316
Noson Lawen (film), 317
Noson Lawen (radio programme), 313
Noson Lawen (TV programme), 358
Novello, Ivor, 23, 252, 311

Old Radnor, 65–66, 67, 70
Only Boys Aloud, 242
Only Men Aloud, 242
Open University, 361
organ(s), 63, 64–67, 68, 81
Owain Alaw, xxii, 213, 303
    Gems of Welsh Melody, 206, 303
Owain Gwynedd, 25, 36
Owain Myfyr, 176, 177
Owen, Daniel, 207
Owen, George, 160
Owen, Idloes, 258
Owen, John *see* Owain Alaw
Owen, Morfydd Llwyn, 17, 250
Owen, William, 197

Parr-Davies, Harry, 252
Parrott, Ian, 262
Parry, Benjamin, 208–209
Parry, James Rhys, 221
Parry, John (*c.* 1710–82), xix, 99, 147, 151, 172, 173, 175, 176, 178, 184
    Antient British Music, xix, 99, 147, 151, 172, 176, 178, 179, 180
    A Collection of Welsh, English and Scotch Airs, 180
Parry, John (1776–1851), 103, 150, 159, 183–184, 186, 295
    The Welsh Harper, 184, 188, 193
Parry, John Orlando, 150
Parry, Joseph, 108, 204, 208, 243, 251, 253, 298
    'Myfanwy', 208, 243

Parry, Owen, 131
Patagonia, 18, 100
Patey-Whytock, Janet, 109
Patti, Adelina, 308
Peel, John, 319, 321, 325
pencerdd, 30, 46, 80, 82, 83, 88, 161
Pencerdd America *see* Parry, Joseph
Pencerdd Gwalia *see* Thomas, John (Pencerdd Gwalia)
Pencerdd Maelor, 209
Pencerddes Morgannwg *see* Davies, Clara Novello
Penpont antiphonal, 61–62, 63, 64
Penrhyn Choral Union, 292
pibgorn, 160–163
pipes, 28, 32, 80, 81, 83, 160
Pontarddulais Choral Society, 257
Preece, Amy, 134
Preece, William, 123
Price, Richard Maldwyn, 246, 249
Price, T. Maldwyn, 248
Price, Thomas *see* Carnhuanawc
Prichard, Rowland Huw, 229, 234
Protheroe, Daniel, 212, 248
Prys, Edmwnd, 74–77, 220–221
psaltery, 42
Pughe, William Owen, 172, 177
punk, 321, 324, 325, 326
Purday, Charles H. 303

Red Book of Hergest *see* Llyfr Coch Hergest
Rees, J. T. 109
Rees, William Thomas *see* Alaw Ddu
reggae, 320
Report of the Commissioners of Inquiry . . . (1847) *see* 'Blue Books'
Rhondda Royal Glee Society (Rhondda Gleemen), 214, 309
Rhydderch, Llio, 165
Rhygyfarch, 54, 56, 62
Rhys Goch Eryri, 45
Rhys Mwyn, 321, 325
Richard, John, 147, 150
Richards, Brinley, 9, 104, 109, 123, 301, 302
    'God Bless the Prince of Wales', 302, 308
    The Songs of Wales, 302
Richards, Henry, 213
Richards, Nansi, 17, 164, 165
Richards, Noel, 241
Richards, Susan Barrington Griffith, 150
Richards, Tom, 339
Rivière, Jules, 301, 307
Robert ap Huw, 3, 84, 91–93, 167, 177, 179
Roberts, Dafydd (Telynor Mawddwy), 152
Roberts, David *see* Alawydd

Roberts, Eleazar, 201
Roberts, Evan, 238–240
Roberts, J. L. 150
Roberts, John (Telynor Cymru), 150
Roberts, John (1822–77) *see* Ieuan Gwyllt
Roberts, Lewis (Eos Twrog), 102
Roberts, T. Osborne, 117, 248
Roberts, W. Jarrett, 209
Roberts, William Morgan, 200
Rockfield Studios, 327
Rogers, Roland, 292
Rowland, Daniel, 222
Rowland, David, 185
Rowlands, Dora *see* Jones, Dora Herbert
Rowlands, Evan, 142
Rowlands, Henry, 174
Royal Commission on University Education in Wales *see* Haldane Commission
Royal Glamorgan Regiment, 296
Royal Welsh College of Music and Drama, 263, 361
Royal Welsh Ladies' Choir, 121, 300, 309

S4C (TV channel), 320, 325, 357, 358
Saer, Roy, xx
Sain (record label), 165, 320, 321
St Asaph, 44, 55
St Davids, 55, 58, 62, 63, 81
St Thomas of Canterbury, 61, 63
Salesbury, William, 73
Samuel, Rhian, 286–288
Samuel, W. T. 202
sawtring, 42
Scotch Cattle (society), 189
Senedd, 355
Senghenydd, 220, 233, 238, 240, 241
Sianel Pedwar Cymru *see* S4C (TV channel)
siffan, 42
sinffan, 42
Siôn Eos, 34
Siôn Singer *see* Williams, John (Siôn Singer)
skiffle, 316, 317
Snell, D. J. 114, 211
'Sospan Fach', 335
South Wales Choral Union *see* Côr Mawr
Spurrell (publisher), 211
Squires, Dorothy, 316, 322
Stephen, Edward *see* Tanymarian
Stephens, Huw, 331
Stephens, Tom, 309
Stereophonics, 23, 328, 330
Stevens, Meic, 320
Super Furry Animals, 23–24, 328, 329, 330
Swansea, xxiii, 68, 208
Sŵn (festival), 331

TJ's (club), 327
tabwrdd, 28
Taliesin, 34, 82
Taliesin ab Iolo, 187, 194
Tann, Hilary, 265
Tanymarian, 204, 232
telyn *see* harp
telyn deires *see* triple harp
Telynor Ceiriog *see* Lloyd, Tom
Telynor Cymru *see* Roberts, John (Telynor Cymru)
Telynor Mawddwy *see* Roberts, Dafydd
Telynores Maldwyn *see* Richards, Nansi
Templeton, Alec, 252
Terfel, Bryn, 115, 119, 345, 348, 351, 353
Thomas, D. Afan, 210, 249
Thomas, David Vaughan, 245, 246–247, 255
Thomas, Dylan, 115, 271, 274
Thomas, John (Ieuan Ddu), 104, 191
Thomas, John (Pencerdd Gwalia), 113, 123, 150–151, 301, 302
Thomas, John (*fl.* 1752), 155, 157
Thomas, John (1839–1921), 109, 199
Thomas, John Weston, 167
Thomas, Mansel, 247–248, 258, 261, 286
Thomson, George, 183
Tiger Bay, 311–313
timpán, 28, 32
Tlws y Cerddor, 109
Tomkins, Thomas (*c.* 1545–1627), 54–55
Tomkins, Thomas (1572–1656), 55
'Tôn y Botel' *see* hymns and hymn tunes, 'Ebenezer'
tonic sol-fa, 201–206, 232, 235
traditional songs
  'Ar Lan y Môr', 269
  'Cân Dei Cantwr', 140
  'Cân yr Asyn', 140
  'Cariad Cywir', 142
  'Cob Malltraeth', 131
  'Cŵn Hela', 140
  'Cwyn Mam-yng-Nghyfraith', 131
  'Dacw 'Nghariad i Lawr yn y Berllan', 126
  'Dadl Dau', 276
  'Doli', 139
  'Ffarwel i Dre Caernarfon Lon', 129
  'Gwcw Fach', 136, 139
  'Huna Blentyn', 268
  'Lliw Gwyn Rhosyn yr Haf', 129
  'Lliw'r Heulwen', 142
  'Mae 'Nghariad i'n Fenwys', 269
  'Mentra Gwen', 136
  'Merch o Bedlam', 140
  'Mwynen Mai', 157
  'Mynwent Eglwys', 129

traditional songs (cont.)
  'Roedd yn y Wlad honno', 129
  'Synnwyr Solomon', 268
  'Titrwm, Tatrwm', 131
  'Tra bo Dau', 136
  'Wrth Fynd efo Deio i Dywyn', 126
  'Y Cyntaf Dydd o'r Gwyliau', 132
  'Y Ddau Farch', 132
  'Y Folantein', 142
  'Y Gelynen', 131
  'Y Gog Lwydlas', 132
  'Yr Hen Erddygan', 136
Trehearn, David, 210–211
Treorchy Male Voice Choir, 116
Triawd y Coleg, 316, 317
triple harp, 99, 104, 146–151, 164, 165, 167, 188, 189
Tudor, Siôn, 74
Tudur Aled, 87
Tudur Penllyn, 47, 52
Twm o'r Nant, 155
Tŷ Cerdd, 261, 290, 360, 362
Tŷ Gwydr, 327
Tyler, Bonnie, 327

uchelwyr, 28, 38, 43, 83
University of South Wales, 361
University of Wales, 17, 19–20, 254, 262
University of Wales Centre for Advanced Welsh and Celtic Studies, xxi, 363

Velvet Underground, the, 324
violin, 154

Wales Millennium Centre, 359
Walters, Irwyn, 261
Wason, Clara, 313
Watkins, David, 188
Waugh, R. 213
'We'll Keep a Welcome', 23, 313
Welsh Amateur Music Federation, 258, 261
Welsh Assembly *see* National Assembly for Wales
Welsh Church Act (1914), 12
Welsh Folk-Song Society *see* Cymdeithas Alawon Gwerin Cymru
Welsh folk songs, *see* traditional songs
Welsh Imperial Singers, 309–310
Welsh Language Acts, 357
Welsh Manuscripts Society, 187

Welsh Music Archive, 362
Welsh Music Day *see* Dydd Miwsig Cymru
Welsh Music Foundation, 331
Welsh Music Guild *see* Guild for the Promotion of Welsh Music
Welsh Music Information Centre *see* Tŷ Cerdd
Welsh National Opera, 23, 256, 258, 269, 355, 359
Welsh Quartet, the, 135–137
Welsh Rarebit (radio programme), 23, 313
Welsh Rugby Union, 333
Wesley, Charles, 224, 225
Wesley, John, 222, 225, 226
White Book of Rhydderch *see* Llyfr Gwyn Rhydderch
Williams, Benjamin Morris, 208
Williams, D. C., 248
Williams, Edward *see* Iolo Morganwg
Williams, Ellis David, 211
Williams, Ellis Ylltyr, 214
Williams, Evan, 147, 176, 178
Williams, Grace, 17, 119, 248, 261, 267–271, 274
Williams, J. Lloyd, 121, 122, 131, 136, 138, 140
Williams, Jane, 129
Williams, Jane (Ysgafell), 188, 189
Williams, Jennie, 140–143
Williams, John (Ioan Rhagfyr), 198
Williams, John (Siôn Singer), 195
Williams, Maria Jane, xxi, xxii, 11, 17, 104, 121, 172, 173, 191, 193, 302
  Ancient National Airs of Gwent and Morganwg, 11, 172, 302
Williams, Meirion, 247, 286
Williams, Owen, 229
Williams, Richard *see* Dic Dywyll
Williams, Robert, 197
Williams, Taliesin *see* Taliesin ab Iolo
Williams, W. Albert, 114
Williams, William, 189
Williams, William (Pantycelyn), 222, 223–226
Williams Wynn, Watkin, 147, 175
World's Fair Eisteddfod (1893), 18, 116, 300, 309
W. Towyn Roberts scholarship, 115
Wylyam, John, 64
Wynne, David, 262
Wynne, (Sarah) Edith, 16, 109, 115

Young Welsh Singer of the Year, 258
Ysgafell *see* Williams, Jane (Ysgafell)

For EU product safety concerns, contact us at Calle de José Abascal, 56–1°, 28003 Madrid, Spain or eugpsr@cambridge.org.

www.ingramcontent.com/pod-product-compliance
Ingram Content Group UK Ltd.
Pitfield, Milton Keynes, MK11 3LW, UK
UKHW022237230426
12048UKWH00018BA/1321